Berlin

"All you've got to do is decide to go
and the hardest part is over.

So go!"

TONY WHEELER, COFOUNDER – LONELY PLANET

Andrea Schulte-Peevers

Contents

(left) **Neue Synagoge p141** A symbol of Berlin's revitalised Jewish community.

(above) **Berlin Wall segments p122** Outside Potsdamer Platz train station.

(right) **Pfannkuchen p53** Donut-like pastries.

Prenzlauer Berg p193

Scheunenviertel p138

City West & Charlottenburg p209

Potsdamer Platz & Tiergarten p120

Historic Mitte p80

Museumsinsel & Alexanderplatz p99

Friedrichshain p180

Kreuzberg & Neukölln p155

Welcome to Berlin

Berlin's combo of glamour and grit is bound to mesmerise all those keen to explore its vibrant culture, cutting-edge architecture, fabulous food, intense parties and tangible history.

High on History

Bismarck and Marx, Einstein and Hitler, JFK and Bowie, they've all shaped – and been shaped by – Berlin, whose richly textured history confronts you at every turn. This is a city that staged a revolution, became the headquarters of the Nazis, was bombed to bits, divided in two and finally reunited – and that was just in the 20th century! Walk along remnants of the Berlin Wall, marvel at the splendour of a Prussian palace, visit Checkpoint Charlie or stand in the very room where the Holocaust was planned. Berlin is like an endlessly fascinating 3D textbook where the past is very much present wherever you go.

Party Paradise

Forget about New York – Berlin is the city that truly never sleeps. Sometimes it seems as though Berliners are the lotus-eaters of Germany, people who love nothing more than a good time. The city's vast party spectrum caters for every taste, budget and age group. From tiny basement clubs to industrial techno temples, chestnut-canopied beer gardens to fancy cocktail caverns, saucy cabarets to ear-pleasing symphonies – Berlin delivers hot-stepping odysseys, and not just after dark and on weekends but pretty much 24/7. Pack your stamina!

Cultural Trendsetter

When it comes to creativity, the sky's the limit in Berlin, which is one of Europe's big start-up capitals. In the last 20 years, the city has become a lab of cultural experimentation thanks to a spirit that nurtures and encourages new ideas as well as to space and cheap rent once abundant, although the last two of these are definitely a thing of the past. Top international performers still grace Berlin's theatre, concert and opera stages; international art-world stars like Olafur Eliasson and Jonathan Meese make their home here; and Clooney and Hanks shoot blockbusters in the German capital. Highbrow, lowbrow and everything in between – there's plenty of room for the full gamut of cultural expression.

Laid-back Lifestyle

Berlin is a big multicultural metropolis but deep down it maintains the unpretentious charm of an international village. Locals follow the credo 'live and let live' and put greater emphasis on personal freedom and a creative lifestyle than on material wealth and status symbols. Cafes are jammed at all hours, drinking is a religious rite and clubs keep going through the weekend into Monday. Size-wise, Berlin is pretty big but its key areas are wonderfully compact and easily navigated on foot, by bike or with public transport.

MATTHIAS MAKARINUS/GETTY IMAGES ©

Why I Love Berlin

By Andrea Schulte-Peevers, Writer

Berlin is a bon vivant, passionately feasting on the smorgasbord of life, never taking things – or itself – too seriously. To me, this city is nothing short of addictive. It embraces me, inspires me, accepts me and makes me feel good about myself, the world and other people. I enjoy its iconic sights, its vast swathes of green, its sky bars and chic restaurants, but I love its gritty sides more. There's nothing static about Berlin: it's unpredictable, unpretentious and irresistible. And it loves you back – if you let it in.

For more about our writers, see p352

Top: Berlin skyline

Berlin's
Top 10

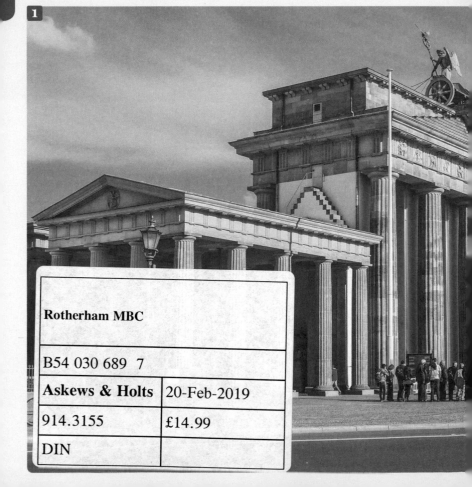

1

Rotherham MBC	
B54 030 689 7	
Askews & Holts	20-Feb-2019
914.3155	£14.99
DIN	

Brandenburger Tor (p84)

1 Prussian kings, Napoleon and Hitler have marched through this neoclassical royal city gate that was once trapped east of the Berlin Wall. Since 1989 it has gone from a symbol of division and oppression to the symbol of a united Germany. The landmark, which overlooks the stately Pariser Platz with its embassies and banks, is at its most atmospheric – and photogenic – at night when light bathes its stately columns and proud Goddess of Victory sculpture in a mesmerising golden glow.

⊙ *Historic Mitte*

Reichstag (p82)

2 This famous Berlin landmark has been set on fire, bombed, left to crumble, and wrapped in fabric before emerging as the home of the German parliament (the Bundestag) and focal point of the reunited country's government quarter. A free lift whisks visitors to the rooftop for lovely views of the Brandenburg Gate, Tiergarten park and other landmarks as well as a chance to saunter up the spiralling ramp of the glass dome, the building's dazzling beacon designed by British architect Norman Foster.

⊙ *Historic Mitte*

CLAUDIO DIVIZIA/SHUTTERSTOCK ©

MIBIRDY/GETTY IMAGES ©

3

4

Museumsinsel

(p101)

3 Berlin's 'Louvre on the Spree', this imposing ensemble of five treasure houses is the undisputed highlight of the city's museum landscape. Declared a Unesco World Heritage Site, Museum Island represents 6000 years of art and cultural history, from the Stone Age to the 19th century. Feast your eyes on majestic antiquities at the Pergamonmuseum and Altes Museum, report for an audience with Egyptian queen Nefertiti at the Neues Museum, take in 19th-century art at the Alte Nationalgalerie and marvel at medieval sculptures at the Bode-Museum. TOP LEFT: LION FROM THE PROCESSIONAL WAY AT PERGAMONMUSEUM (P105)

⊙ *Historic Mitte*

Nightlife *(p188)*

4 Berlin's techno temple Berghain may be one of the world's most famous clubs, but when it comes to nightlife, the entire city is your oyster. Gothic raves to hip-hop hoedowns, craft-beer pubs to riverside bars, beer gardens to underground dives – finding a party to match your mood is a snap. Not into hobnobbing with hipsters at hot-stepping bars or clubs? Why not relive the roaring twenties in a high-kicking cabaret, enjoy symphonic ear candy in iconic concert halls or point your highbrow compass towards one of three opera houses? BOTTOM LEFT: STRANDBAR MITTE (P150)

🍷 *Drinking & Nightlife*

Berlin Wall *(p35)*

5 Few events in history have the power to move the entire world. The Kennedy assassination. The moon landing. The events of 9/11. And, of course, the fall of the Berlin Wall in 1989. If you were old enough back then, you may remember the crowds of euphoric revellers cheering and dancing at the Brandenburg Gate. Although little is left of the physical barrier, its legacy lives on in the imagination, and in such places as Checkpoint Charlie (pictured above), the Gedenkstätte Berliner Mauer and the East Side Gallery.

⊙ *Prenzlauer Berg*

Street Art & Alternative Living *(p161)*

6 Berlin has world-class art, cultural events galore and increasingly sophisticated dining – but so do most other capital cities. What makes this metropolis different is the unbridled climate of openness and tolerance that fosters experimentation, a DIY ethos and a thriving subculture. Hip and funky Kreuzberg, Friedrichshain and Neukölln are all trendsetting laboratories of diversity and creativity. No surprise, then, that some of the city's finest street art is brightening up the streetscapes around here and elsewhere, such as the house-sized Astronaut Mural by Victor Ash.

⊙ *The Berlin Art Scene*

Schloss Charlottenburg *(p211)*

7 We can pretty much guarantee that your camera will have a love affair with Berlin's largest and loveliest remaining royal palace. A late-baroque jewel inspired by Versailles, it backs up against an idyllic park, complete with carp pond, rhododendron-lined paths, two smaller palaces and a mausoleum. The palace itself is clad in a subtle yellow favoured by the royal Hohenzollern family and adorned with slender columns and geometrically arranged windows. A copper-domed tower overlooks the forecourt and the equestrian statue of the Great Elector Friedrich Wilhelm.

⊙ *Charlottenburg*

6

CAROL ANNE/SHUTTERSTOCK ©

Holocaust Memorial *(p85)*

8 Listen to the sound of your footsteps and feel the presence of uncounted souls as you make your way through the massive warped labyrinth that is Germany's central memorial to the Jewish victims of the Nazi-orchestrated genocide. New York architect Peter Eisenman poignantly captures this unspeakable horror with a maze of 2711 tomblike concrete plinths of varying heights that rise from an unsettlingly wavy ground. The memorial's abstract narrative contrasts with the graphic and emotional exhibits in the subterranean information centre.

⊙ Historic Mitte

Potsdamer Platz (p122)

9 No other area around town better reflects the 'New Berlin' than this quarter forged from the death-strip that separated East and West Berlin for 28 years. The world's biggest construction site through much of the 1990s, Potsdamer Platz 2.0 is a postmodern take on the historic area that until WWII was Berlin's equivalent of Times Square. A cluster of plazas, offices, museums, cinemas, theatres, hotels and flats, it shows off the talents of seminal architects of our times, including Helmut Jahn and Renzo Piano.

◉ *Potsdamer Platz & Tiergarten*

Kulturforum (p125)

10 Conceived in the 1950s, the Kulturforum was West Berlin's answer to Museumsinsel and is a similarly enthralling cluster of cultural venues, albeit in modern buildings. One of the city's most important art museums, the Gemäldegalerie, wows fans with Old Masters from Rembrandt to Vermeer. Other museums zero in on prints and drawings, arts and crafts, and musical instruments. Next door, the Berliner Philharmoniker (pictured above), one of the world's finest orchestras, has its home base in a honey-coloured free-form concert hall designed by Hans Scharoun.

◉ *Potsdamer Platz & Tiergarten*

What's New

Museum Closures

The Neue Nationalgalerie (p131) will remain closed for renovation until at least 2020. The north wing and the Pergamon Altar at the Pergamonmuseum (p104) and the Bauhaus Archiv are also closed for extensive facelifts until at least 2023.

Pergamon Panorama

Until the real Pergamon Altar inside the eponymous museum reopens in 2023, the majesty of this massive antique relic can be enjoyed in a custom-built rotunda that pairs a grand panorama with original sculptures from the site. (p106)

James Simon Galerie

Construction of the central Museum Island entrance building is well under way and may open some time in 2019.

Humboldt Forum

The reconstruction of the Prussian royal city palace opposite Museumsinsel is officially on schedule to be finished in 2019 and set to open as the Humboldt Forum museum and cultural centre by the end of 2019 or early 2020. (p114)

Schloss Charlottenburg

Now that restoration is complete on the palace's Alter Flügel (Old Wing), all major sections of Schloss Charlottenburg are open. (p211)

Urban Nation

Given Berlin's street-art pedigree, it's only natural that the world's first urban art museum should open in the German capital. And best of all: it's free! (p47)

Pierre Boulez Saal

When it comes to high-brow musical venues, Berliners are already spoiled for choice but the addition of this intimate Frank Gehry–designed concert hall adds yet another jewel in the crown. (p97)

Staatsoper Unter den Linden

Berlin's most prestigious opera house, commissioned by King Frederick the Great, has finally emerged from a top-to-bottom renovation and again delights aficionados with its top-notch repertory. (p92)

Spreepark Tours

While it's being morphed into a public park, the spooky relics of this GDR-era amusement park can be explored on guided tours (book way ahead). (p162)

Museum Barberini

This private art museum in a rebuilt 18th-century mansion is a new Potsdam crowd-magnet and stages an eclectic potpourri of three first-class exhibits per year. (p228)

Neues Palais

After years of renovation, the stunning Grottensaal (Grotto Hall) and Marmorsaal (Marble Hall) at the Neues Palais in Sanssouci Park in Potsdam have reopened in sparkling splendour. (p227)

Stadtbad Oderberger Strasse

After decades of disuse, Prenzlauer Berg's historic public baths have been renovated and reopened. (p177)

For more recommendations and reviews, see **lonelyplanet. com/germany/berlin**

Need to Know

For more information, see Survival Guide (p295)

Currency
Euro (€)

Language
German

Visas
Generally not required for tourist stays of up to 90 days (or at all for EU nationals); some nationalities need a Schengen visa.

Money
ATMs widespread. Cash is king; credit card acceptance is growing, but don't count on it.

Mobile Phones
➡ Mobile phones operate on GSM900/1800.

➡ Local SIM cards can be used in unlocked European and Australian phones.

➡ US multiband phones also work in Germany.

Time
Central European Time (GMT/UTC plus one hour)

Tourist Information
Visit Berlin (www.visitberlin.de) has branches at the airports, the main train station, the Brandenburg Gate, Alexanderplatz, the Central Bus Station (ZOB) and on Kurfürstendamm, plus a call centre (☑030-2500 2333; ☺9am-6pm Mon-Fri) for information and bookings.

Daily Costs
Budget:
Less than €100
➡ Dorm bed or peer-to-peer rental: €18–35

➡ Doner kebab: €3–4

➡ Club cover: €5–15

➡ Public transport day pass: €7

Midrange:
€100–200
➡ Private apartment or double room: €80–120

➡ Two-course dinner with wine: €40–60

➡ Guided tour: €10–20

➡ Museum admission: €8–20

Top end:
More than €200
➡ Upmarket apartment or double in top-end hotel: from €180

➡ Gourmet two-course dinner with wine: €80

➡ Cabaret ticket: €50–80

➡ Taxi ride: €25

Advance Planning
Two to three months before Book tickets for the Berliner Philharmonie, the Staatsoper, Sammlung Boros and top-flight events.

One month before Reserve a table at trendy or Michelin-starred restaurants, especially for Friday and Saturday dinners.

Two weeks before Book online tickets for the Reichstag dome, the Neues Museum and the Pergamonmuseum.

Useful Websites
Lonely Planet (www.lonely planet.com/germany/berlin) Destination information, hotel bookings, traveller forum and more.

Visit Berlin (www.visitberlin.de) Official tourist authority info.

Museumsportal (www. museumsportal-berlin.de) Gateway to the city's museums.

BVG (www.bvg.de) Public transport authority site with handy journey planner.

Resident Advisor (www. residentadvisor.net) Guide to parties and clubbing.

Exberliner (www.exberliner. com) Expat-geared monthly English-language Berlin culture magazine.

WHEN TO GO

July and August are warm but often rainy. May, June, September and October offer plenty of festivals and cooler weather. Winters are cold and quiet.

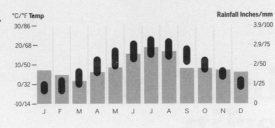

Arriving in Berlin

Tegel Airport TXL express bus to Alexanderplatz (40 minutes) and bus X9 for CityWest (eg Zoo station, 20 minutes), €2.80; taxi €25.

Schönefeld Airport Airport-Express trains (RB14 or RE7) to central Berlin twice hourly (30 minutes), and S9 trains every 20 minutes for Friedrichshain and Prenzlauer Berg, €3.40; taxi to city centre €45 to €50.

Hauptbahnhof Main train station in the city centre; served by S-Bahn, U-Bahn, tram, bus and taxi.

Zentraler Omnibusbahnhof (ZOB) The central bus station is on the western city edge. U-Bahn U2 to city centre (eg Bahnhof Zoo, eight minutes; Alexanderplatz, 28 minutes), €2.80; taxi to CityWest €14, to Alexanderplatz €24.

For much more on **arrival** see p296

Getting Around

U-Bahn Most efficient way to travel; operates 4am to 12.30am and all night Friday, Saturday and public holidays. From Sunday to Thursday, half-hourly night buses take over in the interim.

S-Bahn Less frequent than U-Bahn trains but with fewer stops, and thus useful for longer distances. Same operating hours as the U-Bahn.

Bus Slow but useful for sightseeing on the cheap. Run frequently 4.30am to 12.30am; half-hourly night buses in the interim. MetroBuses (designated eg M1, M19) operate 24/7.

Tram Only in the eastern districts; MetroTrams (designated eg M1, M2) run 24/7.

Bicycle Bike lanes and rental stations abound; bikes allowed in specially marked U-Bahn and S-Bahn carriages.

Taxi Can be hailed, ordered by phone or picked up at ranks.

For much more on **getting around** see p298

Sleeping

Berlin has over 142,000 hotel rooms but the most desirable book up quickly, especially in summer and around holidays, festivals and trade shows; prices soar and reservations are essential during these periods. Otherwise, rates are mercifully low by Western capital standards. Options range from luxurious ports of call to ho-hum international chains, trendy designer boutique hotels to Old Berlin–style B&Bs, happening hostels to handy self-catering apartments.

Useful Websites

Lonely Planet (lonelyplanet.com/germany/hotels) Lonely Planet's online booking service with insider low-down on the best places to stay.

Visit Berlin (www.visitberlin.de) Official Berlin tourist office; books rooms at partner hotels with a best-price guarantee.

Boutique Hotels Berlin (www.boutiquehotels-berlin.com) Booking service for about 20 hand-picked boutique hotels.

Berlin30 (www.berlin30.com) Online low-cost booking agency for hotels, hostels, apartments and B&Bs in Berlin.

For much more on **sleeping** see p238

First Time Berlin

For more information, see Survival Guide (p295)

Checklist

➡ Ensure your passport is valid for at least four months past your arrival date

➡ Check airline baggage restrictions

➡ Inform your debit-/ credit-card company of your upcoming trip

➡ Organise travel insurance

➡ Check if your mobile (cell) phone will work in Germany and the cost of roaming

➡ If taking prescription medicine, bring enough for your entire trip and put it in your carry-on luggage

➡ No vaccinations are needed to visit Germany

What to Pack

➡ Good walking shoes – Berlin is best appreciated on foot

➡ Umbrella or rain jacket – rain is possible any time of year

➡ Small daypack

➡ Travel adaptor plug

➡ Sun hat and sunglasses

➡ Curiosity and a sense of humour

Top Tips for Your Trip

➡ Plan on doing most of your sightseeing on foot. Only by walking will you truly experience Berlin. To cover larger areas quickly, rent a bicycle. Otherwise, public transport is the best way to get around.

➡ Go local – Berlin's spirit reveals itself to those walking around a neighbourhood, people-watching in a park or simply being curious about local food and drink.

➡ There is no curfew, so pace your alcohol intake on bar-hops and in clubs to keep your stamina up.

➡ When picking a place to stay, consider which type of experience you're most keen on – shopping, clubbing, museums, the outdoors, urban cool, partying, history – then choose a neighbourhood to match.

What to Wear

The short answer is: whatever you want. Berlin is an extremely casual city when it comes to fashion. Basically anything goes, including jeans at the opera or a little black dress in a beer garden. Individuality trumps conformity and expensive labels at any time. In fact, flaunting your own style – any style – is often the ticket to making it past a picky club bouncer. Venues or restaurants with official dress codes are extremely rare.

Berlin weather is immensely changeable, even in summer, so make sure you bring layers of clothing. A waterproof coat and sturdy shoes are a good idea for all-weather sightseeing. Winters can get fiercely cold, so be sure you bring your favourite gloves, hat, boots and heavy coat.

Be Forewarned

Berlin is one of the safest capital cities in the world, but that doesn't mean you should let your guard down.

➡ Pickpocketing has dramatically increased, so watch your belongings, especially in tourist-heavy areas, in crowds and at events.

➡ Crime levels have risen notably around Kottbusser Tor in Kreuzberg and the RAW Gelände in Friedrichshain. This includes drug dealing, pickpocketing, assault and sexual assault. Exercise caution.

➡ Carry enough cash for a cab ride back to wherever you're staying.

Money

Germany is still largely a cash-based society, although things are slowly changing. Hotels, department stores, supermarkets and taxis usually accept credit cards, but do enquire first.

ATMs are ubiquitous in all central neighbourhoods. Machines don't recognise pins with more than four digits. Debit cards featuring the MasterCard or Visa logos are fairly widely used. Chip-and-pin is common, but contactless payment systems are increasingly popping up as well.

Taxes & Refunds

Value-added tax (VAT, *Mehrwertsteuer*) is a 19% sales tax levied on most goods. The rate for food, books and services is usually 7%. VAT is always included in the price. If your permanent residence is outside the EU, you may be able to partially claim back the VAT you paid on purchased goods.

Tipping

It's considered rude to leave the tip on the table. Instead, tell the server the total amount you want to pay. If you don't want change back, say 'Stimmt so' (that's fine).

Hotels Room cleaners €1 to €2 per day, porters the same per bag.

Restaurants For good service 10% or more.

Bars & pubs 5% to 10% for table service, rounded to the nearest euro, no tip for self-service.

Taxis 10%, always rounding to a full euro.

Toilet attendants €0.50.

Language

You can easily have a great time in Berlin without speaking a word of German. In fact, some bars and restaurants in expat-heavy Kreuzberg and Neukölln have entirely English- (and sometimes Spanish-) speaking staff. Many restaurant and cafe menus are now available in English and German (and sometimes only in English).

 Do you accept credit cards?
Nehmen Sie Kreditkarten?
nay·men zee kre·deet·kar·ten

Cash is still king in Germany, so don't assume you'll be able to pay by credit card – it's best to enquire first.

 Which beer would you recommend?
Welches Bier empfehlen Sie?
vel·khes beer emp·fay·len zee

Who better to ask for advice on beer than the Germans, whether at a beer garden, hall, cellar or on a brewery tour?

 Can I get this without meat?
Kann ich das ohne Fleisch bekommen?
kan ikh das aw·ne flaish be·ko·men

In the land of *Wurst* and *Schnitzel* it may be difficult to find a variety of vegetarian meals, especially in smaller towns.

 Do you speak English?
Sprechen Sie Englisch?
shpre·khen zee eng·lish

Given Berlin's cosmopolitan tapestry, the answer will most likely be 'yes' but it's still polite not to assume and to ask first.

 Do you run original versions?
Spielen auch Originalversionen?
shpee·len owkh o·ri·gi·nahl·fer·zi·aw·nen

German cinemas usually run movies dubbed into German – look for a cinema that runs subtitled original versions.

Etiquette

Although Berlin is fairly informal, there are a few general rules worth keeping in mind when meeting strangers.

Greetings Shake hands and say *'Guten Morgen'* (before noon), *'Guten Tag'* (between noon and 6pm) or *'Guten Abend'* (after 6pm). Use the formal *'Sie'* (you) with strangers and only switch to the informal *'du'* and first names if invited to do so. With friends and children, use first names and *'du'*.

Asking for help Germans use the same word – *Entschuldigung* – to say 'excuse me' (to attract attention) and 'sorry' (to apologise).

Eating and drinking At the table, say *'Guten Appetit'* before digging in. Germans hold the fork in the left hand and the knife in the right hand. To signal that you have finished eating, lay your knife and fork parallel across your plate. If drinking wine, the proper toast is *'Zum Wohl'*; with beer it's *'Prost'*.

Top Itineraries

Day One

Historic Mitte (p80)

 One day in Berlin? Follow this whirlwind itinerary to take in all the key sights. Book ahead for an early lift ride up to the dome of the **Reichstag**, then snap a picture of the **Brandenburg Gate** before exploring the maze of the **Holocaust Memorial** and admiring the contemporary architecture of **Potsdamer Platz**. View the **Berlin Wall remnants**, then head to **Checkpoint Charlie** to ponder the full extent of the Cold War madness. Saunter up Friedrichstrasse to soak up the glory of **Gendarmenmarkt** before your lunch.

 Lunch Recharge at Augustiner am Gendarmenmarkt (p95).

Museumsinsel & Alexanderplatz (p99)

Follow Unter den Linden east to **Museumsinsel** and spend the afternoon marvelling at the antiquities in the **Pergamonmuseum**. Beer-o'clock! Head over to **Brauhaus Georgbräu**, a brewpub on the Spree River in the Nikolaiviertel.

Dinner Book ahead for dinner at Katz Orange (p147).

Scheunenviertel (p138)

Stroll over to the all-ages **Clärchens Ballhaus** for a spin on the dance floor or process the day's impressions over a prime cocktail at swanky-cool **Buck & Breck**.

Day Two

Prenzlauer Berg (p193)

 Spend a couple of hours coming to grips with what life in Berlin was like when the Wall still stood by exploring the **Gedenkstätte Berliner Mauer**. Take a quick spin around **Mauerpark**, then grab a coffee at **Bonanza Coffee Heroes** and poke around the boutiques on Kastanienallee.

Lunch W-Der Imbiss (p200) is a buzzy pit stop on Kastanienallee.

Museumsinsel & Alexanderplatz (p99)

 Start the afternoon holding court with Queen Nefertiti and other treasures at the stunning **Neues Museum**, then relax while letting the sights drift by on a one-hour **river cruise** around Museumsinsel. Walk over to the **Berliner Dom**, into the crypt and then up the gallery to see how the rebuilt Prussian royal city palace – called **Humboldt Forum** – fits into the cityscape. Enjoy a swanky sundowner at eyelevel with the Fernsehturm (TV Tower) from the **Park Inn Panorama Terrasse**.

Dinner Head to Kreuzberg and for dinner at Orania (p168).

Kreuzberg & Neukölln (p155)

After dinner, go bar-hopping around Kottbusser Tor, pulling up for cocktails at **Würgeengel** or **Ora**, beer at **Möbel Olfe** or wine at **Otto Rink**.

Day Three

City West & Charlottenburg (p209)

 Day three starts at **Schloss Charlottenburg**, where the Neuer Flügel (New Wing) and the palace garden are essential stops. Take the bus to Zoologischer Garten and meditate upon the futility of war at the **Kaiser-Wilhelm-Gedächtniskirche**, then – assuming it's not Sunday – satisfy your shopping cravings along **Kurfürstendamm** and its side streets. Keep your wallet handy and drop by the **Bikini Berlin** shopping mall and **KaDeWe** department store.

 Lunch Enjoy a casual lunch in the KaDeWe (p73) food hall.

Kreuzberg & Neukölln (p155)

Spend an hour or two at the striking Daniel Libeskind–designed **Jüdisches Museum**, then head down to the wide open fields of **Tempelhofer Feld** to see how an old airport can be recycled into a sustainable park and playground. Have a break at the **Luftgarten** beer garden or find a favourite cafe among the many in northern Neukölln.

Dinner Make reservations at eins44 (p169) or Coda (p169).

Kreuzberg & Neukölln (p155)

You're already in party central, so hit the bars on Weserstrasse and its side streets, then move on to the dance floor at **Griessmühle** if you want to extend your evening.

Day Four

Potsdam (p223)

 There's plenty more to do in Berlin proper, but we recommend you spend the better part of the day exploring the parks and royal palaces in Potsdam, a mere 40-minute S-Bahn ride away. Buy online tickets for your favourite time slot to see **Schloss Sanssouci**, a rococo jewel of a palace. Afterwards, explore the surrounding park and its many smaller palaces at leisure. The **Chinesisches Haus** is a must see.

 Lunch Bring a picnic lunch to enjoy in the park.

Potsdam (p223)

If you're done with your park explorations, head to Potsdam's old town for a spin around the **Holländisches Viertel** (Dutch Quarter) or a take a look at the latest art exhibit at the dashing **Museum Barberini** before heading back to Berlin for a well-deserved post-sightseeing drink at **Prater** beer garden.

Dinner Pull up a stool at Prenzlauer Berg's lovely Umami (p200).

Prenzlauer Berg (p193)

After dinner, enjoy a stroll around beautiful Kollwitzplatz. Still got stamina? Turn your evening into a barhop, perhaps stopping at **Bryk Bar** or **Becketts Kopf** for fine cocktails.

If You Like...

Museums

Pergamonmuseum A treasure trove of monumental architecture from ancient civilisations. (p104)

Neues Museum Pay your respects to Queen Nefertiti, star of the Egyptian collection, then explore other priceless artefacts from ancient Troy and elsewhere. (p106)

Jüdisches Museum Comprehensive exhibits going beyond the Holocaust, tracing the rich history of Jews in Germany. (p157)

Museum für Naturkunde Meet giant dinos in Berlin's own 'Jurassic Park', then learn about the universe, evolution and even the anatomy of a housefly. (p142)

Deutsches Technikmuseum Plenty of planes, trains, boats and automobiles, plus the world's first computer and other techno gems. (p159)

Clubbing

Berghain/Panorama Bar Big, bad Berghain is still Berlin's premier dancing den of iniquity. (p188)

://about blank Wild, trashy, unpredictable and with a great garden for daytime partying. (p189)

Ritter Butzke Labyrinthine party house for extended electro-house dance-a-thons. (p172)

Clärchens Ballhaus Salsa, tango, ballroom, disco and swing's the thing in this campy retro ballroom in Scheunenviertel. (p150)

KitKatClub Hedonistic pleasure pit for sexually curious (or adventurous) party animals. (p174)

LUCIANO MORTULA/SHUTTERSTOCK ©

Deutsches Technikmuseum (p159)

Anomalie Art Club Wondrous playground with two art-filled tech-house floors, projection mapping, beer garden, vegan restaurant and arty vibe. (p189)

Markets

Flohmarkt am Mauerpark Gets deluged with visitors in summer but still offers a primo urban archaeology experience. (p208)

Street Food Thursday Global bites, local craft beer and people-watching in a 19th-century market hall. (p167)

Türkischer Markt Berlin meets the Bosphorus at this bustling canal-side farmers market with budget-priced produce. (p178)

Nowkoelln Flowmarkt Hipster flea market with lots of hand-made treasures and impromptu concerts. (p178)

Kollwitzplatzmarkt Discerning gourmets can source the finest morsels for that ultimate picnic. (p208)

Views

Fernsehturm Check off the landmarks from the needle-like Fernsehturm (TV Tower), Germany's tallest building. (p111)

Reichstag Dome Book ahead for the lift to the landmark glass dome atop German's historic parliament building. (p82)

Panoramapunkt Catch Europe's fastest lift at Potsdamer Platz for top views of the city centre. (p123)

Berliner Dom Climb into Berlin's largest church dome for gobsmacking views of Museum Island and the Humboldt Forum construction site. (p113)

Park Inn Panorama Terrasse Eyeball the Fernsehturm on this open-air rooftop lounge atop the Park Inn Hotel. (p118)

Weltballon Berlin Soar above Berlin in this tethered hot-air balloon near Checkpoint Charlie. (p98)

Cold War History

Gedenkstätte Berliner Mauer Find out all you ever wanted to know about the Berlin Wall in a 1.4km long indoor-outdoor exhibit. (p195)

Stasimuseum Learn about the machinations of East Germany's secret police in its historic headquarters. (p187)

Stasi Prison Take a tour for a behind-the-scenes look at East Berlin's most notorious prison. (p187)

East Side Gallery Wander along the longest remaining stretch of the Berlin Wall, now a street-art canvas. (p182)

Tränenpalast Connect with the emotional impact of the Berlin Wall at this 'Palace of Tears' border-crossing pavilion. (p92)

WWII Sites

Topographie des Terrors Peels away the layers of brutality of the Nazi regime on the site of the SS and Gestapo command centres. (p89)

Holocaust Memorial This haunting site is Germany's central memorial to the Nazi-orchestrated genocide of European Jews. (p85)

Sachsenhausen A visit to one of Nazi Germany's first concentration camps, in Oranienburg just north of Berlin, will leave no one untouched. (p229)

Gedenkstätte Deutscher Widerstand Tells the stories of the brave German Nazi resistance, including the White Rose and Stauffenberg's failed 'Operation Valkyrie'. (p129)

For more top Berlin spots, see the following:
→ Eating (p50)
→ Drinking & Nightlife (p56)
→ LGBT+ Berlin (p64)
→ Entertainment (p68)
→ Shopping (p73)

Haus der Wannsee-Konferenz Get shivers while standing in the very room where Nazi leaders discussed the Final Solution. (p234)

Free Stuff

East Side Gallery The longest surviving section of the Berlin Wall, now an open-air mural. (p182)

Gedenkstätte Berliner Mauer Memorial exhibit that offers a primer on the wall and its impact. (p195)

Reichstag Free access to the cupola with online advance reservations. (p82)

Clärchens Ballhaus Great 19th-century dance hall; book a table. (p150)

Tempelhofer Feld Hang out on former runways at one of the world's largest urban parks. (p165)

Bearpit Karaoke Crowds go crazy for this pop-up karaoke phenomenon in the Mauerpark's amphitheatre. (p204)

Modern Architecture

Jüdisches Museum Daniel Libeskind's astonishing zigzag-shaped architectural metaphor for Jewish history in Germany. (p157)

Neues Museum David Chipperfield's reconstructed New

Museum ingeniously blends old and new into something bold and beautiful. (p106)

Sony Center Helmut Jahn's svelte glass-and-steel complex is the most striking piece of architecture on Potsdamer Platz. (p122)

IM Pei Bau Relentlessly geometrical, glass-spiral-fronted museum annexe by the 'Mandarin of Modernism', after whom it is named. (p86)

'Berlin Brain' Reichstag Dome architect Norman Foster also dreamed up the curvaceous, egg-shaped Philology Library of the Free University. (p233)

Music

Berliner Philharmonie Berlin's most iconic classical concert venue and home of the world-famous Berliner Philharmoniker. (p137)

Bearpit Karaoke Feel-good Sunday karaoke event in the Mauerpark drawing wannabe stars from around the world. (p204)

Konzerthaus This jewel designed by Karl Friedrich Schinkel graces Gendarmenmarkt and is a fabulous classical music venue. (p97)

Sonntagskonzerte Intimate concerts amid the faded glamour of a century-old mirror-clad ballroom. (p70)

Astra Kulturhaus This midsize concert hall with commie-era decor draws big rock, pop and electro names. (p191)

Quirky Experiences

Badeschiff Cool off in summer in this river–barge turned swimming pool with attached beach club. (p177)

Silent Green Kulturquartier Take in a concert, movie or have a bite to eat in this crematorium turned culture hub. (p207)

Roses Experience the wildest, wackiest and campiest bar in Kreuzberg (hint: pink fur on the walls). (p171)

Monster Ronson's Ichiban Karaoke Loosen your throat and your inhibitions to hang with the crowd. (p189)

Monsterkabinett Descend into a dark and bizarre underworld inhabited by a small army of endearingly spooky mechanical monsters. (p153)

Art Collections

Gemäldegalerie An Aladdin's cave of Old Masters has heads turning in its expansive Kulturforum space. (p125)

Sammlung Boros World-class private collection of contemporary art in a WWII bunker. (p144)

Hamburger Bahnhof Sweeping survey of post-1950 global art in a spectacularly converted train station. (p140)

Museum Berggruen Priceless Picassos plus works by Klee and Giacometti in a newly expanded building. (p214)

Brücke-Museum Groundbreaking canvases by 'The Bridge', Germany's first modern-artist group (1905–13). (p232)

Sammlung Scharf-Gerstenberg A journey into the psychological depth of surrealism. (p214)

Naughty Berlin

KitKatClub Dive in and be as nice or as nasty as you desire – but do follow the dress code. (p174)

Insomnia Worship at the altar of hedonism at this sassy, sexy dance club with performances and playrooms. (p174)

Schwarzer Reiter Classy purveyor of anything individuals with imagination might need for a fun encounter. (p154)

Lab.oratory *The* place for gays to live out their most frisky and completely uncensored fantasies. (p189)

Other Nature Discover alternative pleasures at this sex shop with a feminist and queer focus. (p179)

Royal Encounters

Schloss Charlottenburg This pretty Prussian power display delivers a glimpse into the sumptuous lifestyles of the rich and royal. (p211)

Schloss Sanssouci The most famous palace in Park Sanssouci drips in opulence and overlooks vine-draped terraces and a big fountain. (p223)

Berliner Dom The royal court church has impressive dimensions, a palatial design and elaborately carved sarcophagi for the remains of kings and queens. (p113)

Pfaueninsel Romantic island with a fanciful palace and strutting peacocks, built by a king for tête-à-têtes with his mistress. (p234)

Schloss Schönhausen Petite palace built for Frederick the Great's wife and which later hosted Castro and Gaddafi. (p202)

Tours

Fat Tire Tours An eclectic roster including English-language tours for foodies, history buffs and urban explorers. (p300)

(Top) Tiergarten (p131) is the perfect spot to take a sightseeing break
(Bottom) Tour Berlin in a GDR-made Trabant car with Trabi Safari (p98)

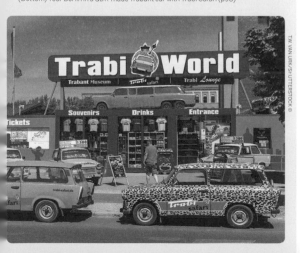

Trabi Safari Turn the clock back while driving yourself around the city in an original East German Trabant car. (p98)

Berliner Unterwelten Get a look at Berlin from below as you explore a dark and dank WWII bunker. (p198)

Berlin Music Tours See where the late, great Bowie lived, recorded and partied while staying in Berlin in the '70s. (p301)

Alternative Berlin Tours Tap deep into Berlin's graffiti scene on artist-led street-art tours followed by your own hands-on session. (p299)

Green Me Berlin Tours Join insider walking tours that take you behind the scenes of Berlin's active and creative eco and sustainability scenes. (p301)

Parks & Gardens

Tiergarten Take pleasure in getting lost amid the lawns, trees and paths of one of the world's largest city parks. (p131)

Schlossgarten Charlottenburg Stake out a picnic spot near the carp pond and ponder royal splendours. (p211)

Park Sanssouci Find your favourite corner away from the crowds for a little time *sans souci* (without cares). (p224)

Volkspark Friedrichshain Explore this rambling 'people's park' offering plenty of diversions and covering two 'mountains' made from WWII debris. (p184)

Viktoriapark Seek out this pint-sized park atop Berlin's highest 'peak', the 66m-high Kreuzberg, with beer garden and playground. (p159)

Month by Month

January

New Year's Eve may be wrapped up, but night-time hot spots aren't slowing down. Cold weather invites extended museum visits and foraging at the Internationale Grüne Woche (Green Week) food fair.

🔒 Berlin Fashion Week

Twice a year, in January and again in July, international fashion folk book up all the trendy hotels (and restaurants) while here to present or assess next season's threads.

✕ Internationale Grüne Woche

Find out more about the latest food trends and gorge on tasty global morsels at this nine-day fair (www.gruenewoche.de) of food, agriculture and gardening.

February

The days are still short but Berlin perks up when glamour comes to town during the famous film festival. A full theatre, opera, concert and party schedule is also on offer to tempt people out of the house.

✨ Transmediale

Digital-media art gets full bandwidth at this edgy festival (www.transmediale.de), which investigates the links between art, culture and technology through exhibitions, conferences, screenings and performances.

☆ Berlinale

Berlin's international film festival (p143) draws stars, starlets, directors, critics and the world's A-to-Z-list celebrities for two weeks of screenings and glamorous parties around the city. The best films get to go home with a Golden or Silver Bear.

March

Could there be spring in the air? This is still a good time to see the sights without the crowds, but hotel rooms fill to capacity during the big ITB tourism fair.

✨ Internationale Tourismus Börse (ITB)

Take a virtual trip around the globe at the world's largest international travel expo (www.itb-berlin.de); it's trade-only during the week but open to the public at the weekend.

☆ MaerzMusik

'Music' or 'soundscapes'? You decide after a day at this contemporary music festival (www.berlinerfestspiele.de), which explores and celebrates a boundary-pushing palette of sounds – from orchestral symphonies through to experimental recitals.

April

Life starts moving outdoors as cafe tables appear on pavements. Hotels get busy over the Easter holidays.

☆ Festtage

Daniel Barenboim, music director of Berlin's internationally renowned Staatsoper (State Opera; www.staatsoper-berlin.de), brings the world's finest conductors, soloists and orchestras together for this 10-day highbrow hoedown of gala concerts and operas.

☆ Achtung Berlin

Flicks about Berlin, and at least partially produced in the city, compete for the New Berlin Film Award at this festival (achtungberlin. de). Screenings are often in the company of writers, directors, producers and actors associated with the movie.

☆ Gallery Weekend

Join collectors, critics and other art aficionados in keeping tabs on the Berlin art scene on a free hop around 40 of the city's best galleries (www.gallery-weekend-berlin.de) over the last weekend in April.

May

Spring has finally arrived, making this a fabulous month to visit Berlin. Time for beer gardens, picnics and walks among blossoming trees. Don't forget your sunglasses! Several public holidays bring in big crowds.

☆ Theatertreffen

The Berlin Theatre Meeting (www.theatertreffen-berlin. de) is a three-week showcase of new productions by emerging and established German-language ensembles from Germany, Austria and Switzerland.

☆ Karneval der Kulturen

Every Whitsuntide (Pentecost; seven weeks after Easter) weekend, the Carnival of Cultures (www.karneval-berlin.de) celebrates Berlin's multicultural tapestry with four days of music, dance, art and culture, culminating in a raucous parade of flamboyantly dressed performers shimmying through the streets of Kreuzberg.

June

Festival season kicks into high gear around the summer solstice with plenty of alfresco events, thanks to a rising temperature gauge.

☆ Berlin Biennale

This biennial curated forum (p143) for contemporary art explores international trends and invites newcomers to showcase their work around town for about eight weeks. The next is in 2020.

☆ Fête de la Musique

Summer starts with good vibrations thanks to hundreds of free concerts during this global music festival

(www.fetedelamusique.de) that started in Paris in 1982. Held each year on 21 June (solstice).

☆ 48 Hours Neukölln

For one long summer weekend Neukölln's multicultural denizens transform shops, courtyards, parks, churches, pavements, galleries, bars and other spaces into an offbeat contemporary art and culture showcase (www.48-stunden-neukoelln.de).

July

Hot summer days send Berliners scurrying to the lakes in town or the surrounding countryside. Gourmets rejoice in the bounty of fresh local produce in the markets. Expect long lines at main sights and attractions.

☆ Classic Open-Air Festival

Five nights, five alfresco concerts – from opera to pop – delight an adoring crowd hunkered on bleachers before the palatial backdrop of the Konzerthaus (www.classicopenair.de) on Gendarmenmarkt.

MAY DAY/MYFEST

May Day demonstrations used to be riotous affairs with heavily armed police and leftist groups facing off in Kreuzberg, complete with flying stones and burning cars. Although an official 'Revolutionary May Day' demonstration still draws as many as 15,000 anticapitalist, antifascist protesters, it's been completely peaceful in recent years. This is due partly to an enormous police presence, and partly to the alternative, largely apolitical Myfest, held in Kreuzberg since 2003. It runs from noon to midnight. The actual Revolutionary May Day demonstration starts at 6pm at Lausitzer Platz.

Berlin Fashion Week

Local and international designers present next year's spring fashions during the summer edition of Berlin's fashion fair with an emphasis on sustainable fashion (www.fashion-week-berlin.com).

Christopher Street Day

No matter what your sexual persuasion, come out and paint the town pink at this huge pride parade (p66) featuring floats often decorated with queer political statements and filled with naked torsos writhing to techno beats.

Wassermusik

The Haus der Kulturen der Welt makes waves with this popular series of water-themed concerts (www.hkw.de/wassermusik) held on its roof terrace and combined with related events like markets and movies.

August

More outdoor fun than you can handle with concerts in parks, daytime clubbing, languid boat rides, beach-bar partying, lake swimming and a huge beer festival.

Berliner Bierfestival

Who needs Oktoberfest when you can have the 'world's longest beer garden' (www.bierfestival -berlin.de)? As the bands play on, pick your poison from some 350 breweries representing 90 countries with over 2400 beers along 2.2km of Karl-Marx-Allee.

(Top) Karneval der Kulturen (p25) celebrates multiculturalism

(Bottom) The Berlinale film festival (p143) draws stars, directors and critics for screenings

CHRISTIAN MUELLER/SHUTTERSTOCK ©

DENIS MAKARENKO/SHUTTERSTOCK ©

✖ Holi Festival of Colours

Since 2012 the Holi Festival tour (www.holifestival. com) has made a stop in Berlin. Join in the custom of throwing colourful powder *(gulal)* into the sky and onto each other while dancing for hours to bands and DJs.

◉ Lange Nacht der Museen

Culture meets entertainment during the Lange Nacht der Museen (Long Night of the Museums; www.lange-nacht-der-museen.de) when around 80 museums welcome visitors between 6pm and 2am.

✖ Zug der Liebe

Nonprofit parade with floats and music to demonstrate in favour of love, community and equality and against populism, gentrification and other hot topics.

September

Kids are back in school but there's still plenty of partying to be done and often fine weather to enjoy. As days get shorter, the new theatre, concert and opera season begins.

☆ Musikfest Berlin

World-renowned orchestras, choirs, conductors and soloists come together for 21 days of concerts (www. berlinerfestspiele.de) at the Philharmonie and other venues.

🏃 Berlin Marathon

Sweat it out with over 40,000 other runners or just cheer 'em on during Germany's biggest street race, which has seen nine world records set since the first race in 1974.

✖ Berlin Art Week

This contemporary art fair (www.berlinartweek.de) combines art exhibits, fairs and awards with talks, film and tours. It also provides a chance to see private collections, project spaces and artist studios.

October

It's getting nippy again and trees start shedding their summer coats, but Berlin keeps a bright disposition, and not only during the Festival of Lights.

✖ Tag der Deutschen Einheit

Raise a toast to reunification on 3 October, the German national holiday celebrated with street parties across town – from the Brandenburg Gate to the Rotes Rathaus (town hall).

✖ Festival of Lights

For 10 days Berlin is all about 'lightseeing' during this shimmering festival (www.festival-of-lights.de) when historic landmarks such as the Fernsehturm (TV Tower), the Berliner Dom and the Brandenburg Gate sparkle with illuminations, projections and fireworks.

✖ Porn Film Festival

Vintage porn, Japanese porn, indie porn, sci-fi porn – the 'Berlinale' of sex (www.pornfilmfestival berlin.de) brings alternative skin flicks out of the smut corner and onto the big screen.

November

A great time to visit if you don't like crowds. Weatherwise it's not the prettiest of months, but don't let that darken your mood.

☆ JazzFest Berlin

This top-rated jazz festival has doo-wopped in Berlin since 1964 and presents fresh and big-time talent in dozens of performances all over town.

December

Days are short and cold but the mood is festive, thanks to illuminated streets and and Christmas markets redolent with the aroma of roast almonds and mulled wine.

🗋 Christmas Markets

Pick up shimmering ornaments or indulge in mulled wine at dozens of Yuletide markets throughout the city.

✖ Nikolaus

On the night before St Nicholas' Day (6 December) children leave their shoes outside their door to receive sweets if they've been nice, or a stone if they've been naughty; eventually this developed into Santa's international rounds. Germans are pretty attached to the original – all kinds of clubs hold Nikolaus parties, complete with costumed St Nicks.

✖ Silvester

New Year's Eve is the time to hug strangers, coo at fireworks, guzzle bubbly and generally misbehave. The biggest public bash is at the Brandenburg Gate.

With Kids

Travelling to Berlin with kids can be child's play, especially if you keep a light schedule and involve them in day-to-day planning. There's plenty to do to keep youngsters occupied, from zoos to kid-oriented museums. Parks and imaginative playgrounds abound in all neighbourhoods, as do public pools.

HANDHIKI/SHUTTERSTOCK©

Deutsches Technikmuseum (p159)

Museums

Museum für Naturkunde

Meet giant dinosaurs, travel through space back to the beginning of time and find out why zebras are striped in the eye-opening Museum of Natural History (p142).

Science Center Spectrum

Toddlers to teens get to play with, experience and learn about such things as balance, weight, water, air and electricity by pushing buttons, pulling levers and otherwise engaging in dozens of hands-on science experiments (p159).

Deutsches Technikmuseum

Next to the Science Center Spectrum, the collection at the German Museum of Technology is so vast, it is best to concentrate time and energy on two or three sections that interest your tech-loving kids the most. The one-hour kid-geared audioguide tour provides a good introduction (p159).

Madame Tussauds

Kids of any age are all smiles when posing with the waxen likeness of their favourite pop star or celluloid celebrity (p91).

Legoland Discovery Centre

The milk-tooth set delights in this Lego wonderland (p123) with rides, entertainment and interactive stations.

Computerspielemuseum

Teens can get their kicks in this universe of computer games (p184) – from Pac-Man to World of Warcraft.

Mauermuseum

Teenagers with an interest in history and a decent attention span may enjoy the ingenious homemade contraptions used to escape from East Germany (p93).

Labyrinth Kindermuseum

Slip into a fantasy world while learning about tolerance, working together and just having fun at this interactive **space** (☎030-8009 31150; www.kindermuseum-labyrinth.de; Osloer Strasse 12; admission €6.50; ⊙1-6pm Thu & Fri, 11am-6pm Sat & Sun, closed Thu May-Sep; Ⓤanstrasse).

Parks, Pools & Playgrounds

Park am Gleisdreieck

This family-friendly park (p159) is packed with fun zones including adventure playgrounds, basketball courts, a huge skate park and a nature garden.

Kollwitzplatz

This square (p197) sports three playgrounds for different age groups, including one with giant wooden toys. All get busy in the afternoon and on weekends. Cafes and ice-cream parlours are just a hop, skip and jump away.

Kinderbad Monbijou

Keep cool on hot days splashing about this family-friendly public **pool** (⏰030-2219 0011; www.berlinerbaeder.de; Oranienburger Strasse 78; adult/child €5.50/3.50; ⏰11am-7pm Jun–early Sep; 🚇M1, ⓈHackescher Markt, Oranienburger Strasse) in the Scheunenviertel.

Volkspark Friedrichshain

Play in the 'Indian Village', gather your pirate mateys on the boat in the 'harbour' or find your favourite fairy-tale characters at the enchanting Märchenbrunnen (fountain of fairy tales) at this park (p184).

Animals

Zoo Berlin

If the 20,000 furry, feathered and finned friends fail to enchant the little ones, there's also the enormous adventure playground (p215).

Tierpark Berlin

Expect plenty of ooh and aah moments when kids watch baby elephants at play or see lions and tigers being fed at this vast animal **park** (⏰030-515 310; www.tierpark-berlin.de; Am Tierpark 125; adult/concession/child 4-15yr €14/9/7; ⏰zoo 9am-6.30pm Apr-Sep, to 6pm Mar & Oct, to 4.30pm Nov-Feb, palace 11am-6pm Tue-Sun Apr-Oct, to 4.30pm Nov-Mar; P 🚻; ⓊTierpark).

Sealife Berlin

At Sealife (p113), little ones get to press their noses against dozens of fish-filled tanks, solve puzzles and admire starfish and sea anemones up close.

Domäne Dahlem

Kids can interact with their favourite barnyard animals, help collect eggs, harvest potatoes or just generally watch daily farm life unfold at this fun working **farm** (⏰030-666 3000; www.domaene-dahlem.de; Königin-Luise-Strasse 49; grounds free, museum adult/concession/under 18 €5/3/free; ⏰grounds 8am-9pm May-Sep, to 7pm Oct-Apr, museum 10am-5pm Wed-Sun; P 🚻; ⓊDahlem-Dorf).

Jugendfarm Moritzhof

A farm playground (p205) for kids complete with barnyard animals and courses in basketweaving, forging, felting and other old-timey crafts.

Eating Out with Kids

It's fine to eat out as a family any time of the day, especially in cafes, bistros and pizzerias. Many offer a limited *Kindermenü* (children's menu) or *Kinderteller* (children's dishes) to meet small appetite requirements. If they don't, most places will be happy to serve half-size portions or prepare a simple meal. Popular dishes include schnitzel, *Pommes mit Ketchup* or *Mayonnaise* (fries with ketchup or mayo), *Nudeln mit Tomatensosse* (noodles with tomato sauce) and *Fischstäbchen* (fish sticks).

Large malls have food courts while larger department stores feature self-service cafeterias. Farmers markets have food stalls selling kid-friendly snacks. Bakeries selling scrumptious cakes and sandwiches are plentiful. The most popular snacks-on-the-run are bratwurst in a bun or *Döner Kebab* (sliced meat tucked into a pitta pocket with salad and sauce).

Baby food, infant formula, soya and cow's milk, disposable nappies (diapers) and the like are widely available in supermarkets and chemists (drugstores).

Like a Local

Local life in Berlin is not as settled upon as in other cities but is defined to some extent by the enormous influx of neo-Berliners from abroad and other parts of Germany. It's comparatively easy to engage with locals and to participate in their daily lives.

Fresh *Brötchen* (rolls) on sale at a bakery

Dining Like a Local

Berliners love to dine out and do so quite frequently, from scarfing down a quick doner at the local kebab joint to indulging in an eight-course tasting menu at a Michelin-starred dining shrine. Eating out is rarely just about getting fed – it is also a social experience. Meeting friends or family over a meal is a great way to catch up, engage in heated discussions or exchange the latest gossip.

Going out for breakfast is a beloved pastime, especially on weekends. Enjoying a meal out at lunchtime is no longer the domain of desk jockeys and business people on expense accounts, as many restaurants (including Michelin-starred ones) now offer daily specials or set menus at a discount. The traditional German afternoon coffee-and-cake ritual is more the realm of more mature generations and not practised widely among Berlin millennials.

The main going-out meal is dinner, with restaurant tables usually filled at 7.30pm or 8pm. Since it's customary to stretch meals to two hours and then linger over cocktails or another glass of wine, restaurants – for now – only count on one seating per table per night. Servers will not present you with the bill until you ask for it.

Partying Like a Local

Most Berliners start the night around 9pm or 10pm in a pub or bar, although among younger people it's common to first meet at someone's home for a few cheap drinks in a ritual called *'Vorglühen'* (literally 'pre-glowing'). Once out on the town, people either stay for a few drinks at the same place or pop into several spots, before moving on to a club around 1am or 2am at the earliest.

In most pubs and bars, it's common practice to place orders with a server rather than pick up your own drinks at the bar. Only do the latter if that's what everyone does or if you see a sign saying *'Selbstbedienung'* (self-service). Among Germans it is not expected (nor customary) to buy entire rounds for everyone at the table.

Once in the club, how long one stays depends on your inclination and alcohol and drug consumption. Hardy types stagger out into the morning sunshine, although the most hardcore may last even longer. Since some clubs don't close at all on weekends, it's becoming increasingly popular to start the party in the daytime and go home at, say 11pm, for a normal night's sleep. But don't feel bad if that's not your thing. Partying in Berlin does require some stamina...

Shopping Like a Local

Berliners pretty much fulfil all their shopping needs in their local *Kiez* (neighbourhood). There will usually be three or four supermarkets, including at least one 'Bio' (ie organic) supermarket, within walking distance. Most people don't get all their grocery shopping done in one fell swoop but rather make several smaller trips spread over the course of the week. Since some supermarkets have started home delivery, ordering online is becoming more popular.

For many locals the farmers markets are the preferred source of fresh produce and speciality products like handmade noodles, artisanal cheese and Turkish cheese spreads. Days start with fresh *Brötchen* (rolls) bought from the bakery around the corner. Nonfood needs such as gifts, flowers, books, hardware and wine are also met locally where possible.

Clothing will come from a mix of places that may include high-street chains, indie boutiques, vintage stores, flea markets and, of course, online shops. When Berliners venture out of their neighbourhoods to shop, it's usually to buy big-ticket items like furniture or vehicles, or speciality items not available locally. There are a few big malls in the city centre, such as LP12 Mall of Berlin (p137) and Alexa (p119), but generally these are more commonly located in the suburbs.

Living Like a Local

The typical Berlin dwelling is a spacious rented two-bedroom flat on at least the 1st floor of a large early-20th-century apartment building (no one wants to live at street level), probably facing on to a *Hinterhof* (back courtyard) full of bicycles

and coloured recycling bins. The apartment itself has very high ceilings, large windows and, as often as not, stripped wooden plank floors. The kitchen will almost invariably be the smallest room in the house and right next to the bathroom. Some kitchens have small pantries and/or storage rooms.

Apartments in new buildings follow a more contemporary layout and usually have an open kitchen facing out to the living/dining room, walk-in closets, guest toilets, lower ceilings and balconies.

Berlin flats are usually nicely turned out with much attention paid to design, though comfort is also considered. At least one item of furniture will come from a certain Swedish furniture chain. Depending on income, the rest may come from the Stilwerk design centre, Polish crafters, a flea market, eBay – or, most likely, any combination thereof.

Relaxing Like a Local

Although they are passionate about their city, Berliners also love to get out of town, especially in summer. If they're not jetting off to Mallorca or Mauritius, they will at least try to make it out to a local lake on a sunny day. There are dozens right in town, including the Plötzensee (p207) in Wedding, the Weissensee near Prenzlauer Berg, the vast Müggelsee (p236) in Köpenick and the Wannsee (p235) in Zehlendorf – all easily reached by public transport. Hundreds more are just a quick car or train ride away in the surrounding countryside of Brandenburg. Everyone's got their favourite body of water and, having staked out the perfect spot, tends to return there time and again.

A cyclist passes St Marienkirche (p112) and the Fernsehturm (p111)

With equally easy access to some fabulous parks, Berliners love heading for the greenery to chill with friends and a cold beer, relax in the shade, play frisbee or catch up on their reading. Some parks have areas where barbecuing is permitted.

Sightseeing Like a Local

Most locals – especially more recent arrivals – are very appreciative of Berlin's cultural offerings and keep tabs on the latest museum and gallery openings, theatre productions and construction projects. It's quite common to discuss the merits of the latest play or exhibit at dinner tables.

Although they love being a tourist in their own city, Berliners stay away from the big-ticket museums and sights in summer when the world comes to town. More likely they will bide their time until the cold and dark winter months or visit on late-opening nights with smaller crowds. The annual Lange Nacht der Museen (Long Night of the Museums, usually in August), when dozens of museums stay open past midnight, brings out culture vultures by the tens of thousands.

Local Obsessions

Soccer

Many Berliners live and die by the fortunes of the local soccer team, Hertha BSC, which has seen its shares of ups and downs in recent years. After a brief stint in *2. Fussball-Bundesliga* (Second Soccer League), the team returned to the top-level Bundesliga in the 2013–14 season – much to the relief of locals. Still, true fans don't quit the team when it's down and, during the season, many will inevitably don their blue-and-white gear to make the trek out to the Olympiastadion (p219) for home games. In 2018, they cheered especially loudly when Hertha player Marvin Plattenhardt was selected for the *Mannschaft* (German national team) playing at the FIFA World Cup in Russia.

Berlin's other major team, 1. FC Union, plays in the second league and has an especially passionate following in the eastern parts of the city.

The Weather

Many locals are hobby meteorologists who will never pass up a chance to express their opinion on tomorrow's weather or on whether it's been a good summer so far, whether the last winter was mild or brutal, what to expect from the next one, and so on... So if you run out of things to say to a local, get the conversation going again by mentioning the weather. Other popular topics are rising rents, the perceived ineptitude of the local government or the much delayed opening of the Berlin Brandenburg Airport.

For Free

It's no secret that you can still get more bang for your euro in Berlin than in many other Western European capitals. Better still, there are plenty of ways to stretch your budget even further by cashing in on some tip-top freebies, including such sights as the Reichstag dome and the Gedenkstätte Berliner Mauer (Berlin Wall Memorial).

CAROL.ANNE/SHUTTERSTOCK ©

Haus der Wannsee-Konferenz (p234)

Free History Exhibits

Given that Germany has played a disproportionate role in 20th-century history, it's only natural that there are plenty of memorial sites and exhibits shedding light on various (mostly grim) milestones. Best of all, they're all free.

WWII

Study up on the SS, Gestapo and other organisations of the Nazi power apparatus at the Topographie des Terrors (p89) exhibit, then see the desk where WWII ended with the signing of Germany's unconditional surrender at the Deutsch-Russisches Museum Berlin-Karlshorst (p237). You can stand in the very room where the Final Solution was planned at the Haus der Wannsee-Konferenz (p234), get shivers while walking around the Sachsenhausen (p229) concentration camp, then pay your respects to Jewish Nazi victims at the Holocaust Memorial (p85). German resistance against the Nazis is the focus of the Gedenkstätte Deutscher Widerstand (p129), the Gedenkstätte Stille Helden (p131) and the Museum Blindenwerkstatt Otto Weidt (p153).

Cold War

The East Side Gallery (p182) may be the longest surviving section of the Berlin Wall, but to get the full picture of the Wall's physical appearance and human impact check out the Gedenkstätte Berliner Mauer (p195) and the Tränenpalast (p92). For an eyeful of what daily life was like behind the Iron Curtain, drop by the new Museum in der Kulturbrauerei (p197). At Checkpoint Charlie (p93), an outdoor exhibit chronicles milestones in Cold War history. For the Cold War years from the point of view of the western Allies, swing by the AlliiertenMuseum (p233).

Free Museums & Galleries
State museums

Admission to the permanent exhibits at Berlin's state museums – including the Pergamonmuseum (p104), Neues Museum (p106), Gemäldegalerie (p125) and Hamburger Bahnhof (p140) – is free for anyone under 18.

Niche museums

Although the blockbuster state museums do charge admission for adults, a few niche museums don't. Learn about the history of German democracy at the Deutscher Dom (p87), life during the Biedermeier at the Knoblauchhaus (p115), and Berlin's equivalent of Oskar Schindler at the Museum Blindenwerkstatt Otto Weidt (p153). The best among the art freebies are Urban Nation (p47), a street art museum, and the Daimler Contemporary Berlin (p128) gallery. There are also free exhibits at the Rotes Rathaus (p112). Military and airplane buffs should head to the city outskirts for the Militärhistorisches Museum – Flugplatz Berlin-Gatow (p231).

Sometimes free

Museums offering free admission at certain times include the Akademie der Künste (p133) from 4pm to 8pm Tuesday; useum für Film und Fernsehen (p123) from 4pm to 8pm Thursday; and the Museum Ephraim-Palais (p115) and Museum Nikolaikirche (p115) on the first Wednesday of the month.

Free Guided Tours

Many museums and galleries include free multilingual audioguides in the admission price; some also offer free guided tours, although these are usually in German.

Alternative Berlin Tours (p299), New Berlin Tours (p300) and Brewer's Berlin Tours (p300) are English-language walking tour companies that advertise 'free'

guided tours, although the guides actually depend on tips.

Free Music

Free gigs and music events take place all the time, in pubs, bars, parks and churches. See the listings magazines for what's on during your stay.

Summer concerts

In summer, many of Berlin's parks and gardens ring out with the free sound of jazz, pop, samba and classical music. Case in point: the lovely Teehaus im Englischen Garten (p135) presents two Sunday concerts (at 4pm and 7pm) in July and August.

Karaoke

The Mauerpark is a zoo-and-a-half on hot summer Sundays, thanks largely to the massively entertaining outdoor Bearpit Karaoke (p204), which sees thousands of spectators cramming in to the stone bleachers to cheer and applaud crooners of various talent levels.

Classical

At 1pm on Tuesday from September to mid-June, the foyer of the Berliner Philharmonie (p137) fills with music lovers for free lunchtime chamber-music concerts. Students of the prestigious Hochschule für Musik Hanns Eisler (p97) also show off their skills at several free recitals weekly. At 12.30pm from Tuesday to Sunday, you can enjoy free organ recitals at the Matthäuskirche (p131) in the Kulturforum. The Französischer Dom (p87) has free organ concerts at the same time from Tuesday to Friday.

Rock & jazz

For one-off free concerts, check the listings magazines. Jazz fans can bop gratis at A-Trane (p221) on Monday and at the late-night jam session after 12.30am on Saturday. On Wednesday, b-Flat (p152) has its own free jam sessions. **Kunstfabrik Schlot** (☏030-448 2160; www.kunstfabrik-schlot.de; Invalidenstrasse 117, Schlegelstrasse 26; varies, often free; ⊙daily; Ⓢ Nordbahnhof, Ⓤ Naturkundemuseum) is the go-to freebie several times a week.

Erich Honecker and Leonid Brezhnev lock lips in Dmitri Vrubel's *My God, Help Me To Survive This Deadly Love*

◉ The Berlin Wall

It's more than a tad ironic that Berlin's most popular tourist attraction is one that no longer exists. For 28 years the Berlin Wall, the most potent symbol of the Cold War, divided not only a city but the world.

The Beginning

Shortly after midnight on 13 August 1961, East German soldiers and police began rolling out miles of barbed wire that would soon be replaced with prefab concrete slabs. Overnight streets were cut in two, transportation between the city halves was halted and East Germans, including commuters, were no longer allowed to travel to West Berlin.

The Berlin Wall was a desperate measure launched by the German Democratic Republic (GDR, East Germany) to stop the sustained brain-and-brawn drain the country had experienced since its 1949 founding. Some 3.6 million people had already headed to western Germany, putting the GDR on the brink of economic and political collapse. The actual construction of the Wall, however,

came as a shock to many: only a couple of months before that fateful August day, GDR head of state Walter Ulbricht had declared at a press conference that there were no plans to build a wall.

The Physical Border

Euphemistically called the 'Anti-Fascist Protection Barrier', the Berlin Wall was an instrument of oppression that turned West Berlin into an island of democracy within a sea of socialism. It consisted of a 43km-long inner-city barrier separating West from East Berlin and a 112km border between West Berlin and East Germany. Each reinforced concrete segment was 3.6m high, 1.2m wide and weighed 2.6 tonnes. In some areas, the border strip included the Spree River or canals.

Continually reinforced and refined over time, the Berlin Wall grew into a complex border-security system consisting of two walls: the main wall abutting the border with West Berlin and the hinterland security wall, with the 'death strip' in between. A would-be escapee who managed to scale the hinterland wall was first confronted with an electrified fence that triggered an alarm. After this, he or she would have to contend with guard dogs, spiked fences, trenches and other obstacles. Other elements included a patrol path with lamp posts that would flood the death strip with glaring light at night. Set up at regular intervals along the entire border were 300 watchtowers staffed by guards with shoot-to-kill orders. Only nine towers remain, including the one at Erna-Berger-Strasse (p128) near Potsdamer Platz.

In West Berlin, the Wall came right up to residential areas. Artists tried to humanise the grey concrete scar by covering it in colourful graffiti. The West Berlin government erected viewing platforms, which people could climb to peek across into East Berlin.

Escapes

There are no exact numbers, but it is believed that of the nearly 100,000 GDR citizens who tried to escape, hundreds died in the process, many by drowning, suffering fatal accidents or committing suicide when caught. More than 100 were shot and killed by border guards – the first only a few days after 13 August 1961. Guards who prevented an escape were rewarded with commendations, promotions and bonuses.

The first person to be shot at the Wall was 24-year-old tailor Günter Litfin. Construction of the fortification had begun only days earlier when a hailstorm of bullets ripped through his body as he tried to swim across a 40m-wide canal (the Humboldt Harbour) on 24 August 1961. Since 2003, Günter's legacy is kept with a **memorial exhibit** (030-2362 6183; http://gedenkstaette-guenter-litfin.de; Kieler Strasse 2; tours adult/concession €5/3; 11am-5pm Sat & Sun May-Sep; TXL, Schwarzkopfstrasse) FREE in a GDR watchtower near where he was killed. It's a bit off the beaten path but well worth visiting.

Another incident illustrating the barbarity of the shoot-to-kill order occurred on 17 August 1962 when Peter Fechter was shot and wounded and then left to bleed to death. There's a memorial (p90) in his honour on Zimmerstrasse, near Checkpoint Charlie. Behind the Reichstag, on the

Cycling Tour
Berlin Wall

START BORNHOLMER BRÜCKE AT S-BAHN STATION BORNHOLMER STRASSE
END EAST SIDE GALLERY
LENGTH 15KM; 2.5 HOURS

This easy ride follows the former course of the Berlin Wall and begins on Bornholmer Brücke. A free outdoor exhibit chronicles the events of 9 November 1989 when the **1 Bornholmer Strasse Border Crossing** became the first to open in the city.

Head east on Bornholmer Strasse, turn right on Malmöer Strasse and right again on Behmstrasse. Near the hilltop, cross the street and take the Schwedter Steg footbridge over the railway tracks. Continuing straight takes you to **2 Mauerpark** (p197), a hugely popular park built atop the former death strip. A roughly 300m-long section of the inner wall runs along the back of the Friedrich-Ludwig-Jahn-Stadion; it was higher here than usual to deter would-be escapees from among the spectators.

Mauerpark adjoins Bernauer Strasse, home to the **3 Gedenkstätte Berliner Mauer** (p195; Berlin Wall Memorial), a 1.4km-long indoor-outdoor exhibit that's the best place in town to understand what the Wall looked liked and how it shaped everyday life. Follow Bernauer Strasse past vestiges of the border installations and escape tunnels, a chapel, a monument and an original section of Wall.

Bernauer Strasse culminates at the **4 S-Bahn station Nordbahnhof**, a so-called 'Ghost Station', for the Wall also divided the city's transportation system. Three lines that originated in West Berlin travelled along tracks beneath the eastern sector before returning back on the western side. An exhibit inside the station explains the situation in detail.

From Nordbahnhof, continue west on Invalidenstrasse, then head south on Chausseestrasse. Just past the Spree River looms a former border crossing pavilion nicknamed **5 Tränenpalast** (p92; Palace of Tears) because of the many tearful goodbyes suffered here. Stop to check out the free exhibit inside before following the Spree via the Reichstagsufer.

Turn right on Luisenstrasse and left on Adele-Schreiber-Krieger-Strasse to the

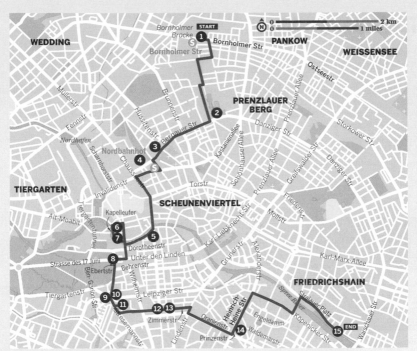

6 **Parlament der Bäume** (p90; Parliament of Trees), a garden-like art installation by Ben Wagin to remember those who died at the Berlin Wall. For another Ben Wagin Wall Installation, carry your bike down the stairs to the Schiffbauerdamm river walk and pedal a short stretch to the **7** **Marie-Elisabeth-Lüders-Haus** (p88). Lined up in the basement is a row of original Wall segments, each painted with a year and the number of people killed at the border in that year.

Continue on Schiffbauerdamm, turn right on Luisenbrücke and right again on Unter den Linden to get to the **8** **Brandenburger Tor** (p84; Brandenburg Gate), where construction of the Wall began on 13 August 1961. Past the Brandenburger Tor, turn left on Ebertstrasse and head south to **9** **Potsdamer Platz** (p122), which used to be a massive no man's land during the city's division. The death strip was several hundred metres wide here. Outside the S-Bahn station entrance are a few **10** **Berlin Wall segments** (p122).

Continue south on Stresemannstrasse, then hook a left on Erna-Berger-Strasse to get to one of the few remaining **11** **GDR watchtowers** (p128). Guards had to climb up a slim round shaft via an iron ladder to reach the octagonal observation perch on top.

Backtrack and continue south on Stresemannstrasse, then turn left on Niederkirchner Strasse to get to a 200m-long section of the original outer border wall. Badly scarred by souvenir hunters, it's now protected by a fence.

Keep going east on Niederkirchner Strasse (which becomes Zimmerstrasse) to arrive at **12** **Checkpoint Charlie** (p93), which took its name from the NATO phonetic alphabet. Continue east on Zimmerstrasse, past a **13** **memorial to Peter Fechter** (p90), a would-be escapee who was shot and left to bleed to death by East German guards. Turn right on Axel-Springer-Strasse and left on Oranienstrasse, then left again (at Moritzplatz) onto Prinzenstrasse. Just past the intersection with Sebastianstrasse was the **14** **Heinrich-Heine-Strasse** border crossing, used primarily for mail and merchandise and by West Germans.

Follow Heinrich-Heine-Strasse north, turn right on Köpenicker Strasse, left on Engeldamm, cross the Spree, turn right on Stralauer Strasse and you'll soon arrive at the **15** **East Side Gallery** (p182), a 1.3km-long stretch of outer wall painted by artists in 1990. The river itself belonged to East Berlin and border guards patrolled the Spree in boats.

The Berlin Wall

The construction of the Berlin Wall was a unique event in human history, not only for physically bisecting a city but by becoming a dividing line between competing ideologies and political systems. It's this global impact and universal legacy that continues to fascinate people decades after its triumphant tear-down. Fortunately, plenty of original Wall segments and other vestiges remain, along with museums and memorials, to help fathom the realities and challenges of daily life in Berlin during the Cold War.

Our illustration points out the top highlights you can visit to learn about different aspects of these often tense decades. The best place to start is the **❶ Gedenkstätte Berliner Mauer**, for an excellent introduction to what the inner-city border really looked liked and what it meant to live in its shadow. Reflect upon what you've learned while relaxing along the former death strip, now the **❷ Mauerpark**, before heading to the emotionally charged exhibit at the **❸ Tränenpalast**, an actual border-crossing pavilion. Relive the euphoria of the

Brandenburger Tor
People around the world cheered as East and West Berliners partied together atop the Berlin Wall in front of the iconic city gate, which today is a photogenic symbol of united Germany.

Potsdamer Platz
Nowhere was the death strip as wide as on the former no-man's-land around Potsdamer Platz from which sprouted a new postmodern city quarter in the 1990s. A tiny section of the Berlin Wall serves as a reminder.

Checkpoint Charlie
Only diplomats and foreigners were allowed to use this border crossing. Weeks after the Wall was built, US and Soviet tanks faced off here in one of the hottest moments of the Cold War.

Tränenpalast
This modernist 1962 glass-and-steel border pavilion was dubbed 'Palace of Tears' because of the many tearful farewells that took place outside the building as East Germans and their western visitors had to say goodbye.

Bernauer Strasse

Chaussestr

Unter den Linden

Leipziger Str

Wall's demise at the **4 Brandenburger Tor**, then marvel at the revival of **5 Potsdamer Platz**, which was nothing but death-strip wasteland until the 1990s. The Wall's geopolitical significance is the focus at **6 Checkpoint Charlie**, which saw some of the tensest moments of the Cold War. Wrap up with finding your favourite mural motif at the **7 East Side Gallery**.

It's possible to explore these sights by using a combination of walking and public transport, but a bike ride is the best method for gaining a sense of the former Wall's erratic flow through the central city.

FAST FACTS

Beginning of construction 13 August 1961

Fall of the Wall 9 November 1989

Total length 155km

Height 3.6m

Weight of each segment 2.6 tonnes

Number of watchtowers 300

Remnants of the Wall →

Mauerpark
Famous for its flea market and karaoke, this popular park actually occupies a converted section of the death strip. A 30m segment of surviving Wall is now an official practice ground for budding graffiti artists.

LINK A OZOM/GETTY IMAGES ©

Alexanderplatz

Alexanderstr

East Side Gallery
Paralleling the Spree for 1.3km, this is the longest Wall vestige. After its collapse, more than a hundred international artists expressed their feelings about this historic moment in a series of colourful murals.

EWAIS/SHUTTERSTOCK ©

southern bank of the Spree River, the seven white crosses of the Gedenkort Weisse Kreuze (p90) commemorate the Wall victims, as does the emotional 'Window of Remembrance' at the Gedenkstätte Berliner Mauer (p195). This memorial features the names and photographs of all the people who were shot or died in an accident while attempting to escape.

The Gedenkstätte Berliner Mauer runs along 1.4km of Bernauer Strasse, which was literally split in two by the Berlin Wall, with one side of apartment buildings on the western side and the other in the east. As the barrier was erected, many residents on the eastern side decided to flee spontaneously by jumping into rescue nets or sliding down ropes, risking severe injury and death. Bernauer Strasse was also where several escape tunnels were dug, most famously Tunnel 29 in 1962, so named because 29 people managed to flee to the West before border guards detected the route.

The fact that there was no limit to the ingenuity of would-be escapees is documented at the Mauermuseum (p93) near Checkpoint Charlie. On display are several original contraptions used to flee East Germany, including a hot-air balloon, a hollow surfboard, a specially rigged car and even a homemade mini-submarine.

The End

The Wall's demise came as unexpectedly as its creation. Once again the GDR was losing its people in droves, this time via Hungary, which had opened its borders with Austria. Thus emboldened, East Germans took to the streets by the hundreds of thousands, demanding improved human rights and an end to the dictatorship of the SED (Sozialistische Einheitspartei Deutschland), the single party in East Germany. A series of demonstrations culminated in a gathering of half a million people on Alexanderplatz on 4 November 1989, vociferously demanding political reform. Something had to give.

It did, on 9 November, when government spokesperson Günter Schabowski announced during a press conference on live TV that all travel restrictions to the West would be lifted. When asked by a reporter when this regulation would come into effect, he nervously shuffled his papers looking for the answer, then responded with the historic words: 'As far as I know, immediately.' In fact, the ruling was not supposed

to take effect until the following day, but no one had informed Schabowski.

The news spread through East Berlin like wildfire, with hundreds of thousands heading towards the Wall. Border guards had no choice but to stand back. Amid scenes of wild partying and mile-long parades of GDR-made Trabant cars, the two Berlins came together again.

Today

The dismantling of the border fortifications began almost immediately and by now the city halves have visually merged so perfectly that it takes a keen eye to tell East from West. Fortunately, there's help in the form of a double row of cobblestones with bronze plaques inscribed 'Berliner Mauer 1961-1989' that guides you along 5.7km of the Wall's course. Also keep an eye out for the **Berlin Wall History Mile** (www.berlin.de/mauer/en/history/history-mile), which consists of 32 information panels set up along the course of the Wall. They draw attention, in four languages, to specific events that took place at each location. Berlin's division, the construction of the Wall, how the Wall fell, and the people who died at the Wall are all addressed.

Only about 2km of the actual concrete barrier still stands today; most famous is the 1.3km stretch that is now the East Side Gallery (p182). But there are plenty of other traces scattered throughout the city, including lamps, patrol paths, fences, perimeter defences, switch boxes etc. Most are so perfectly integrated they're only discernible to the practised eye. A brilliant source for tracking down these fragments is the **Memorial Landscape Berlin Wall** (www.berlin-wall-map.com), an interactive Geographic Information System (GIS) that documents all remaining bits and pieces.

Tours

Fat Tire Bike Tours (p300) and Berlin on Bike (p300) offer guided cycling tours along the course of the Wall. If you're feeling ambitious, rent a bike for a DIY tour of all or part of the 160km-long **Berliner Mauerweg** (Berlin Wall Trail), a signposted walking and cycling path that runs along the former border fortifications, with 40 multilingual information stations posted along the way. For a description and route maps in English, go to www.berlin.de/mauer/en/wall-trail.

DENSART/SHUTTERSTOCK ©

Topographie des Terrors (p89)

⊙ Historical Museums & Memorials

From its humble medieval beginnings, Berlin's history – especially its key role in major events of the 20th century – has created a rich and endlessly fascinating tapestry. It's also extremely well documented in numerous museums, memorial sites and monuments, many of them in original historic locations that are open to the public.

The Evolution of Berlin & Germany

Trace Berlin's evolution from its medieval birth to today's modern metropolis at the Märkisches Museum (p114), or head to the Story of Berlin (p216) for a more experiential and multimedia approach, providing insight into Berlin's various epochs. For history in a nutshell (or in 20 minutes), take in the multimedia show, Brandenburger Tor Museum (p90).

For a comprehensive survey of German history from the early Middle Ages to the present, visit the Deutsches Historisches Museum (p86). Berlin's Jewish history gets the spotlight at the Jüdisches Museum (p157).

The Third Reich

Few periods shaped the fate of Berlin as much as its 12-year stint as capital of Nazi Germany. Numerous museums and memorial sites, almost all of them free, keep the memory alive. For insight into the sinister machinations of the Nazi state, visit the Topographie des Terrors (p89). Nazi leaders decided on the implementation of the so-called Final Solution in a lakeside villa that is now the Haus der Wannsee-Konferenz (p234).

The unfathomable impact of Nazi terror is emotionally documented at the Ort der Information (p85) below the Holocaust Memorial

NEED TO KNOW

Tickets

Admission to many museums and memorial sites is free (p33), including Gedenkstätte Berliner Mauer, Topographie des Terrors, and Gedenkstätte Deutscher Widerstand. Major historical museums that do charge admission include the Jüdisches Museum, Märkisches Museum, Spy Museum, Deutsches Historisches Museum, Mauermuseum, Story of Berlin and Schloss Cecilienhof.

Opening Hours

➡ Core museum hours are 10am to 6pm, with a number of major venues open until 8pm one day a week.

➡ Closed Monday: Märkisches Museum, Ort der Information, Schloss Cecilienhof, Deutsch-Russisches Museum Berlin-Karlshorst, Tränenpalast, AlliiertenMuseum, Urban Nation and Museum in der Kulturbrauerei.

(p85) and at the Sachsenhausen (p229) concentration camp. Brave locals who tried to stand up against the Nazis are commemorated at the Gedenkstätte Deutscher Widerstand (p129), the Gedenkstätte Stille Helden (p131) and the Museum Blindenwerkstatt Otto Weidt (p153).

When WWII finally came to an end, the German surrender was signed at what is now the Deutsch-Russisches Museum Berlin-Karlshorst (p237), whose exhibits chronicle WWII from the point of view of the Soviet Union. Two giant monuments honour the Russian soldiers who died in the Battle of Berlin: the Sowjetisches Ehrenmal Treptow (p162) and the Sowjetisches Ehrenmal Tiergarten (p88). To see where the victorious Allies hammered out Germany's postwar fate, visit **Schloss Cecilienhof** (☎0331-969 4200; www.spsg.de; Im Neuen Garten 11; conference room adult/concession €8/6, royal quarters €6/5; ☺10am-5.30pm Tue-Sun Apr-Oct, to 5pm Nov-Dec, to 4.30pm Tue Jan-Mar; 🚌603) in Potsdam.

The Cold War

After WWII, Berlin was caught in the cross hairs of the Cold War superpowers – the US and the Soviet Union – as epitomised in the city's division and the construction of the Berlin Wall. The longest surviving vestige of this barrier is the East Side Gallery (p182).

To deepen your understanding of the border fortifications and their human toll, the Gedenkstätte Berliner Mauer (p195) and the Tränenpalast (p92) are essential stops.

Daily life behind the Iron Curtain is documented in interactive fashion at the DDR Museum (p113), while the free Museum in der Kulturbrauerei (p197) follows a traditional approach to the subject. Both exhibits also address the role of East Germany's Ministry of State Security (the Stasi) in shoring up the power base of the country's regime. Learn more at the Stasimuseum (p187) and on a guided tour of the Stasi Prison (p187) where regime critics were incarcerated.

Near Checkpoint Charlie (p93), you can learn about the daring attempts by East Germans to escape to the West at the privately run Mauermuseum (p93). For a take on the Cold War in Berlin from the perspective of the occupying Western allies, visit the AlliiertenMuseum (p233). Berlin's legacy as the capital of spies is the subject of the German Spy Museum (p128) on Leipziger Platz.

Historical Museums & Memorials by Neighbourhood

Historic Mitte BlackBox Kalter Krieg, Deutsches Historisches Museum, Mauermuseum, Ort der Information, Sowjetisches Ehrenmal Tiergarten, Brandenburger Tor Museum, Topographie des Terrors, Tränenpalast, asisi Panorama Berlin.

Museumsinsel & Alexanderplatz DDR Museum, Märkisches Museum.

Potsdamer Platz & Tiergarten Berlin Story Museum, Berlin Wall Watchtower Erna-Berger-Strasse, Gedenkstätte Stille Helden, Gedenkstätte Deutscher Widerstand, Spy Museum.

Scheunenviertel Museum Blindenwerkstatt Otto Weidt.

City West & Charlottenburg Kaiser-Wilhelm-Gedächtniskirche, Story of Berlin.

Kreuzberg & Neukölln Jüdisches Museum.

Prenzlauer Berg Gedenkstätte Berliner Mauer, Jüdischer Friedhof Schönhauser Allee, Museum in der Kulturbrauerei.

Outer Berlin Deutsch-Russisches Museum Berlin-Karlshorst, AlliiertenMuseum, Gedenkstätte Plötzensee, Haus der Wannsee-Konferenz, Sachsenhausen, Stasi Prison, Stasimuseum, Sowjetisches Ehrenmal Treptow.

Potsdam Memorial Leistikowstrasse (KGB Prison), Schloss Cecilienhof.

Lonely Planet's Top Choices

Gedenkstätte Berliner Mauer (p195) Indoor-outdoor multimedia exhibit vividly illustrates the history, physical appearance and social impact of the Berlin Wall.

Topographie des Terrors (p89) Gripping examination of the origins of Nazism, its perpetrators and its victims, on the site of the SS and Gestapo headquarters.

Jüdisches Museum (p157) Daniel Libeskind's contorted building is a striking backdrop for this thorough survey of the history and cultural heritage of Jews in Germany.

Gedenkstätte und Museum Sachsenhausen (p229) No book or movie comes close to the emotional impact of actually standing in a concentration camp.

Deutsches Historisches Museum (p86) Charts German history in the European context from the Middle Ages to the present, in a former Prussian armoury.

Best in Historic Locations

Stasi Prison (p187) Tours of this infamous jail, which had a starring role in the Academy Award–winning *The Lives of Others*, are sometimes led by former inmates.

Stasimuseum (p187) The headquarters of East Germany's feared and loathed Ministry of State Security are now a museum.

Tränenpalast (p92) Exhibit explains why tears once flowed in this Friedrichstrasse border

pavilion, as East Germans said farewell to their loved ones.

Gedenkstätte und Museum Sachsenhausen (p229) North of Berlin, this early concentration camp served as a model for many others.

Best for Jewish Remembrance

Jüdisches Museum (p157) Engagingly laid out chronicle and celebration of nearly 2000 years of Jewish life in Germany.

Ort der Information (p85) Chilling exhibit below the Holocaust Memorial examining personal aspects of this unfathomable chapter in human history.

Museum Blindenwerkstatt Otto Weidt (p153) Learn how one heroic man saved many Jewish lives.

Gleis 17 Memorial (p232) Haunting train tracks memorialise the departure point for trains heading to the concentration camps.

Mendelssohn Exhibit (p94) A homage to one of Berlin's most prominent Jewish families.

Best for Kids

DDR Museum (p113) Experiential and hands-on journey into daily life behind the Iron Curtain.

Story of Berlin (p216) Plenty of engaging visuals and a tour of an atomic bunker make this one a winner with teens.

Mauermuseum (p93) Fascinating collection of ingenious, original contraptions used by East Germans to escape their country.

Best for Momentous Moments

Haus der Wannsee-Konferenz (p234) Get the shivers in the very room where Nazi leaders planned the systematic annihilation of European Jews on 20 January 1942.

Deutsch-Russisches Museum Berlin-Karlshorst (p237) With the stroke of a pen WWII ended on 8 May 1945 with the signing of the German surrender at this former seat of the Soviet Military Administration.

Schloss Cecilienhof (p42) The Potsdam Conference brought Stalin, Truman and Attlee to this pretty palace between 17 July and 2 August 1945 to divvy Germany up into four occupation zones.

Gedenkstätte Deutscher Widerstand (p129) Stand in the rooms where army officer Claus von Stauffenberg and his cohorts planned the ill-fated assassination of Hitler.

Best for Architecture

Jüdisches Museum (p157) Daniel Libeskind's structures are never just buildings, they're also evocative metaphors, as beautifully illustrated by Berlin's Jewish Museum.

Märkisches Museum (p114) This imposing red-brick pile is a clever mash-up of actual historic buildings from the surrounding state of Brandenburg.

Deutsches Historisches Museum (p86) Highlights of this ex-armoury are the baroque dying-warrior sculptures in the courtyard and the modern annexe by IM Pei.

Museum Berggruen (p214)

◉ The Berlin Art Scene

Art aficionados will find their compass on perpetual spin in Berlin. With hundreds of galleries, scores of world-class collections and some 33,000 international artists, the city has assumed a pole position on the global artistic circuit. Perpetual energy, restlessness and experimental spirit combined and infused with an undercurrent of grit are what give this 'eternally unfinished' city its art cred.

Major Art Museums

Berlin's most famous art museums are administered by the Staatliche Museen Berlin (Berlin State Museums; www.smb. museum). The main locations:

Gemäldegalerie (p125) Encyclopedic collection of European painting from the 13th to the 18th century – Rembrandt, Caravaggio and Vermeer included; at the Kulturforum.

Alte Nationalgalerie (p110) Neoclassical, Romantic, impressionist and early modernist art, including Caspar David Friedrich, Adolf Menzel and Monet; on Museumsinsel.

Hamburger Bahnhof (p140) International contemporary art – Warhol to Rauschenberg to Beuys; east of the Hauptbahnhof.

Museum Berggruen (p214) Classical modernist art, mostly Picasso and Klee; near Schloss Charlottenburg.

Sammlung Scharf-Gerstenberg (p214) Surrealist art by Goya, Magritte, Jean Dubuffet, Max Ernst and more; near Schloss Charlottenburg.

Neue Nationalgalerie (p131) Early 20th-century art, especially German expressionists. It's part of the Kulturforum but is closed for renovation until at least 2020.

Aside from these heavy hitters, Berlin teems with smaller museums specialising in a particular artist or genre. You can admire the colourful canvases of expressionist artist group Die Brücke in a lovely museum (p232) on the eastern edge of the Grunewald; see the paintings of Max Liebermann while standing in the very studio where he painted them in the Liebermann-Villa am Wannsee (p234); or take a survey of a century of Berlin-made art in the Berlinische Galerie (p159).

The main exhibition spaces without their own collections are the Martin-Gropius-Bau (p128) and the Haus der Kulturen der Welt (p88). Both mount superb temporary and travelling art shows, the latter with a special focus on contemporary arts from non-European cultures and societies.

Two museums train the spotlight on women: the Käthe-Kollwitz-Museum (p216), which is dedicated to one of the finest and most outspoken early-20th-century German artists, and the **Das Verborgene Museum** (Hidden Museum; ☎030-313 3656; www.dasverborgenemuseum.de; Schlüterstrasse 70; adult/concession €3/1.50; ☺3-7pm Thu & Fri,

NEED TO KNOW

Tickets

➡ Generally you can buy tickets at the gallery or museum; prebook for the hottest tickets (p45).

➡ Commercial galleries do not charge admission. Most hold *vernissage* (opening) and *finissage* (closing) parties.

➡ The Berlin Museum Pass (€29, concession €14.50) buys admission to about 30 museums and galleries for a three-day period. Available at participating museums and the tourist offices.

Advance Planning

➡ Blockbuster visiting shows often sell out so it's best to prepurchase tickets online. Same goes for Pergamonmuseum and Neues Museum.

➡ Most private collections require advance registration; reserve months ahead for the Sammlung Boros.

Opening Hours

➡ The big museums and galleries are typically open from 10am to 6pm, with extended viewing one day a week, usually Thursday. Some are closed on Monday.

➡ Commercial galleries tend to be open from noon to 6pm Tuesday to Saturday and by appointment.

➡ The Neue Nationalgalerie, the Bauhaus Archiv and parts of the Pergamonmuseum (including the Pergamon Altar itself) are closed for restoration.

Tours

GoArt! Berlin (www.goart-berlin.de) runs customised tours that demystify Berlin's art scene by opening doors to private collections, artist studios and galleries or by taking you to exciting street-art locations. Also does art consulting.

Websites

Museumsportal (www.museumsportal. de) Gateway to the city's museums and galleries.

Landesverband Berliner Galerien (www. berliner-galerien.de) For a list and links to Berlin's most important galleries

Top: Thierry Noir's *Homage to the Young Generation* mural at the East Side Gallery (p182)

Bottom: Gemäldegalerie (p125)

noon-4pm Sat & Sun; ⑤Savignyplatz, ⑪Ernst-Reuter-Platz), which champions lesser known German female artists from the same period.

There are also corporate collections like the Palais Populaire (p91) or the Daimler Contemporary (p128) and private ones like Me Collectors Room (p143), Sammlung Hoffmann (p144) and the must-see Sammlung Boros (p144).

Commercial Art Galleries

The **Galleries Association of Berlin** (www.berliner-galerien.de) counts some 400 galleries within the city. In addition, there are at least 200 noncommercial showrooms and off-spaces that regularly show new exhibitions. Although the orientation is global, it's well worth keeping an eye out for the latest works by major contemporary artists living and working in Berlin, including Thomas Demand, Jonathan Meese, Via Lewandowsky, Isa Genzken, Tino Sehgal, Esra Ersen, John Bock and the artist duo Ingar Dragset and Michael Elmgreen.

Galleries cluster in four main areas:

Scheunenviertel (Mitte) Auguststrasse and Linienstrasse were the birthplaces of Berlin's post-Wall contemporary art scene. Some pioneers have since moved on to bigger digs but key players like Eigen+Art, neugerriemschneider, Kicken and Galerie Neu remain. Another seminal contender on nearby Museumsinsel is Contemporary Fine Arts. Other galleries to keep an eye on include KOW and Mehdi Chouakri.

Checkpoint Charlie area (northern Kreuzberg) A number of key galleries hold forth on Zimmerstrasse, Charlottenstrasse, Rudi-Dutschke-Strasse and Markgrafenstrasse, including Galerie Thomas Schulte, Galerie Barbara Thumm and Galerie Tammen & Partner. A bit further east, on Lindenstrasse, the Galerienhaus (www.galerienhaus.com) houses 11 contemporary art galleries.

Potsdamer Strasse & Around (Schöneberg) In recent years, the gritty area around Potsdamer Strasse and Kurfürstenstrasse has emerged as one of Berlin's most dynamic art quarters with a great mix of established galleries and newcomers. Heavy hitters include Galerie Isabella Bortolozzi, Loock Galerie, Galerie Thomas Fischer and Jarmuschek + Partner.

Around Savignyplatz (Charlottenburg) In the traditional gallery district in the western city

centre, standouts include Camera Work, Galerie Michael Schultz, Galerie Max Hetzler and Galerie Brockstedt.

Street Art & Where to Find It

Stencils, paste-ups, throw-ups, burners and bombings. These are some of the magic words in street art and graffiti, the edgy art forms that have helped shape the aesthetic of contemporary Berlin. A capital of street art, the city is now home to the world's first urban art museum, the Urban Nation in Schöneberg. Out in the field, Berlin is the canvas of such international heavyweights as Blu, JR, Os Gemeos, Romero, Shepard Fairey and ROA, along with local talent like Alias, El Bocho and XOOOOX. Every night, hundreds of hopeful next-gen artists haunt the streets, staying one step ahead of the police as they aerosol their screaming visions, often within seconds.

There's street art pretty much everywhere, and the area around U-Bahn station Schlesisches Tor in Kreuzberg has some house-wall-size classics, including Pink Man (p161) by Blu and Yellow Man (p161) by the Brazilian twins Os Gemeos. Skalitzer Strasse is also a fertile hunting ground with Victor Ash's Astronaut (p161) and ROA's Nature Morte being highlights (you can even spot them on the northern side of the tracks when riding the above-ground U1). There's a work by street-art superstar Shepard Fairey called **Make Art Not War** on Mehringplatz.

STREET ART ON THE WALL

Creating a museum for street art may be akin to caging a wild animal. Yet, **Urban Nation's** (www.urban-nation.com; Bülowstrasse 7; ◷10am-6pm Tue-Sun; ⑪Nollendorfplatz) showcase of works by top urban artists pulls the genre out from the underpasses and abandoned buildings and makes them accessible to an entirely new audience. From Alias to Zezao, the beautiful bi-level space designed by Graft architects is a handy introduction to the various players and the style they employ – stencils to paste-up to sculpture. Even the facade doubles as an ever-changing canvas.

Across the Spree River in Friedrichshain, the RAW Gelände (p184) is a constantly evolving canvas and even has a dedicated street art gallery, the Urban Spree (p184). Around Boxhagener Platz you'll find works by Boxi, Alias and El Bocho. The facade of the Kino Intimes (p191) is also worth checking out. In Mitte, there's plenty of art underneath the S-Bahn arches, although the undisputed hub is the courtyard of Haus Schwarzenberg (p153). Prenzlauer Berg has the Mauerpark (p197), where budding artists may legally hone their skills along a section of the Berlin Wall. In the entryway of the dilapidated building at Kastanienallee 86 are nice works by Alias and El Bocho. You'll also pass by plenty of graffiti when riding the circle S41/S42.

Several walking tour companies offer street-art tours, including Alternative Berlin Tours (p299) whose four-hour tours are artist-led and end with a hands-on street-art workshop. A good book on the subject is *Street Art in Berlin* by Kai Jakob (2015).

Public Art

Free installations, sculptures and paintings? Absolutely. Public art is big in Berlin, which happens to be home to the world's longest outdoor mural, the 1.3km-long East Side Gallery (p182). No matter which neighbourhood you walk in, you're going to encounter public art on a grand scale. Daimler City (p124), in the Potsdamer Platz area, offers especially rich pickings, including works by Keith Haring, Mark di Suvero and Frank Stella.

Alte Nationalgalerie (p110)

The Berlin Art Scene by Neighbourhood

Historic Mitte Akademie der Künste – Pariser Platz, Contemporary Fine Arts, galleries in and around Checkpoint Charlie, Haus der Kulturen der Welt.

Museumsinsel & Alexanderplatz Alte Nationalgalerie, Altes Museum, Bode-Museum.

Potsdamer Platz & Tiergarten Daimler Contemporary, Gemäldegalerie, Martin-Gropius-Bau, public art in Daimler City.

Scheunenviertel Hamburger Bahnhof, me Collectors Room, Sammlung Boros, Sammlung Hoffmann, street art, top-notch galleries around Auguststrasse.

City West & Charlottenburg C/O Berlin, high-end galleries around Savignyplatz, Käthe-Kollwitz-Museum, Museum Berggruen, Museum für Fotografie, Sammlung Scharf-Gerstenberg.

Kreuzberg & Neukölln Best for street art; also Berlinische Galerie, König Galerie @ St Agnes Kirche

Friedrichshain East Side Gallery, street art at RAW Gelände.

TOP THREE BERLIN ART BLOGS

Berlin Art Link (www.berlinartlink.com) Online magazine delving into the contemporary art scene via studio visits and artist interviews, reviews and event listings.

Street Art Berlin (www.streetartbln.com) Keeps tabs on new works, profiles Berlin artists and posts about events.

Art Berlin (www.artberlin.de) Opens the door to the city's art scene by portraying artists, galleries, collections, exhibits and fairs; in German only.

Lonely Planet's Top Choices

Gemäldegalerie (p125) Sweeping survey of Old Masters from Germany, Italy, France, Spain and the Netherlands from the 13th to the 18th centuries.

Hamburger Bahnhof (p140) Warhol, Beuys and Twombly are among the many legends aboard the contemporary-art express at this former train station.

Sammlung Boros (p144) Book months' ahead for tickets to see this stunning cutting-edge private collection housed in a WWII bunker.

Martin-Gropius-Bau (p128) First-rate travelling exhibits take up residence in this gorgeous Renaissance-style building.

Best Single-Artist Galleries

Käthe-Kollwitz-Museum (p216) Representative collection of works by Germany's greatest female artist, famous for her haunting depictions of war and human loss and suffering.

Liebermann-Villa am Wannsee (p234) Charming exhibit set up in the lakeside summer home of the great German impressionist and leading Berlin Secession founder Max Liebermann.

Dalí – Die Ausstellung (p128) Private collection showcasing lesser-known drawings, illustrated books and sculptures by the famous Catalan surrealist.

Best Artistic Genre Galleries

Museum Berggruen (p214) Picasso, Klee and Giacometti form the heart of this stunning classical-modernist collection sold to the city by the art dealer and collector Heinz Berggruen.

Sammlung Scharf-Gerstenberg (p214) Across from Museum Berggruen, this space delves into the fantastical worlds conjured up by Goya, Max Ernst, Magritte and other giants of the surrealist genre.

Alte Nationalgalerie (p110) This venerable art temple is packed with 19th-century art, including Romantic masterpieces by such genre practitioners as Caspar David Friedrich, Karl Friedrich Schinkel and Carl Blechen.

Brücke-Museum (p232) Forest-framed gem focusing on German expressionism, with works by Karl Schmidt-Rottluff, Ernst Ludwig Kirchner and other members of the Bridge, Germany's first modern-artist group.

Altes Museum (p107) Sculptures by the ancient Greeks, Romans and Etruscans are showcased in this stunning museum by Karl Friedrich Schinkel.

Best Private Collections

Sammlung Boros (p144) The latest works by established and emerging artists displayed in a labyrinthine WWII bunker.

Sammlung Hoffmann (p144) Every Saturday, artficionados can join a tour of long-time collector Erika Hoffmann's private loft.

Me Collectors Room (p143) Thomas Olbricht's 'cabinet of curiosities', plus exhibits drawn from his own collection and from other international collectors.

Best Art Museum Architecture

Hamburger Bahnhof (p140) Flanked by two towers and centred on a cathedral-like hall, this 19th-century train station is home to one of Germany's finest collections of contemporary art.

Neue Nationalgalerie (p131) Ludwig Mies van der Rohe's temple-like final masterpiece is as edgy today as it was at its 1967 opening (closed for renovation until at least late 2020).

Bauhaus Archiv (p133) Walter Gropius himself drew up the blueprints for this complex, distinguished by its curved shed-roof silhouette. It's closed for renovation until 2023.

Sammlung Boros (p144) A sombre WWII bunker has been turned into an exhibition space presenting edgy and often custom-created art.

Best Art Exhibition Halls

Martin-Gropius-Bau (p128) Top of the heap with headline-making travelling art exhibits from all fields of creative endeavour.

Haus der Kulturen der Welt (p88) Mounts shows with a special focus on non-European cultures and societies.

Akademie der Künste (p90) Berlin's oldest arts institution (founded in 1696) presents genre-hopping exhibits drawn from its archives in two locations.

Palais Populaire (p91) Shines the spotlight on the art scene in emerging countries and examines the effects of globalisation on the art world.

Gourmet dining at Weinbar Rutz (p149)

 # Eating

Berlin's food scene is growing in leaps and bounds and maturing as beautifully as a fine Barolo. Sure, you can still get your fill of traditional German comfort staples, from sausage to roast pork knuckle, but it's the influx of experimental chefs from around the globe that makes eating in the capital such a delicious and exciting experience.

Currywurst

PLAN YOUR TRIP EATING

Food Trends

As with art and fashion, Berliners are always onto the next hot thing when it comes to food. You'll find plenty of culinary obsessions in the capital.

MODERN REGIONAL CUISINE

Healthy eating is sexy, which is why the organic, slow-food and seasonal movements have become an obsession in Berlin. Sometimes it seems as though the city's growing clique of cosmopolitan chefs wants to outdo each other with just how locavore they can get. Restaurants like Nobelhart & Schmutzig (p96) and Einsunternull (p149) have pushed the envelope even further by banning any ingredient not grown in the region from their kitchens. The Michelin testers considered this approach so innovative, they awarded both with a coveted star. But even on menus of less highfalutin restaurants, apple-fed pork from the Havelland, fish from the Müritz Lake District or wild boar from the Schorfheide are becoming quite commonplace. This also extends to vegetables which, this being Berlin, means mostly root vegetables like parsnip, parsley root and beetroot. Also still popular are techniques for preserving seasonal ingredients for future use through pickling, brining and fermentation.

VEGAN

A meal featuring meat is so last millennium, which is why vegan restaurants are spreading faster than rabbits on Viagra in Berlin. In 2018, Berlin's finest meat-free temple, Cookies Cream (p95), even entered the constellation of Michelin stars.

NEED TO KNOW

Opening Hours

Cafes open from 8am to 8pm, restaurants 11am to 11pm, and fast-food joints 11am to midnight or later.

Price Ranges

The following price ranges refer to the average cost of a main course.

€ less than €12

€€ €12 to €25

€€€ more than €25

Bills & Tipping

➡ Your bill won't be presented until you ask for it: 'Zahlen, bitte'.

➡ It's customary to add 10% for good service.

➡ Tip as you hand over the money, rather than leaving it on the table (as this is considered rude). For example, if your bill comes to €28 and you want to give a €2 tip, say €30. If you have the exact amount and don't need change, just say 'Stimmt so' (that's fine).

Reservations

Reservations are essential at the top eateries and are recommended for midrange restaurants – especially for dinner and at weekends. Book the trendiest places four or more weeks in advance. Many restaurant websites now offer an online booking function. Berliners tend to linger at the table, so if a place is full at 8pm it's likely that it will stay that way for a couple of hours. Some restaurants are introducing a time limit for seatings (usually two hours) but this is still very rare.

Late-Night & Sunday Shopping

➡ One handy feature of Berlin culture is the Spätkauf (Späti in local vernacular), which are small neighbourhood stores stocked with the basics and open from early evening until 2am or later.

➡ Some supermarkets stay open until midnight; a few are open 24 hours.

➡ Shops and supermarkets in major train stations (Hauptbahnhof, Ostbahnhof, Friedrichstrasse) are open late and on Sunday.

TOP FIVE BERLIN FOOD & LIFESTYLE BLOGS

It's no secret that Berlin is a fast-changing city and so it's only natural that the food scene is also developing at lightning speed. Fortunately there are a number of passionate foodies keeping an eye on new openings and developments and generously sharing them on their (English-language) blogs. If you read German, also check out Mit Vergnügen (www.mitvergnuegen.com), Berlin Ick Liebe Dir (www.berlin-ick-liebe-dir.de) and GastroInferno (www.gastroinferno.com).

Berlin Food Stories (www.berlinfoodstories.com) Excellent up-to-the-minute site by a dedicated food lover who keeps tabs on new restaurants and visits each one several times before writing honest, mouth-watering reviews. Also runs food tours – see the website for dates.

Stil in Berlin (www.stilinberlin.de) One of the longest-running city blogs (since 2006), Mary Sherpe's 'baby' keeps track of developments in food, fashion, style and art.

CeeCee (www.ceecee.cc) Stylish blog on what's hot and what's not across Berlin's culinary and cultural spectrum.

I Heart Berlin (www.iheartberlin.de) Long-running blog spreads the love about cool places and upcoming events.

Eatler (www.eatler.de) Irreverent and opinionated blog on restaurant openings and closings and emerging trends.

And in 'regular' restaurants, vegetables are often the star of the show, such as at BRLO Brwhouse (p164), Orania (p168) or Einsunternull (p149). Berlin spawned the world's first all-vegan supermarket chain, Veganz, in 2011. Detox trends like raw food and cold-press juice cleanses have also made significant inroads; Rawtastic (p203) ranks among the pioneers. For a comprehensive list of vegetarian and vegan restaurants in Berlin, visit www.happycow.net.

NOSE TO TAIL

The antithesis to the vegan avalanche is the nose-to-tail trend where recipes star not just filet cuts but all animal parts, including tongue, sweetbread, heart or bone marrow. This holistic approach provides a logical segue to the farm-to-table and orchard-to-bottle movements that have been spinning the culinary compass lately.

STREET FOOD

Street food and food trucks have been part of Berlin's culinary scene for years now, not just in random locations at markets, parties and events around town but also at regular gatherings.

Still going strong is Street Food Thursday (p167) at Markthalle Neun in Kreuzberg, the year-round event that started the craze back in 2013. In spring and summer, it is joined by a number of alfresco schemes like Bite Club (p167), which sets up on Friday on the Spree next to the Badeschiff and makes for a tasty place to get your stomach in shape for a long weekend of partying. Roughly once a month, it is grill and grind at Burgers & Hip Hop (p167), which has a residency at Prince Charles club on Moritzplatz. In Prenzlauer Berg, Street Food auf Achse (p202) draws scores of streetfood fans to the Kulturbrauerei on Sunday even in winter.

The street-food experience has proven so successful for some chefs that they've taken their concept to a bricks-and-mortar level. Graduates from Markthalle Neun include Bun Bao (p199), **Koshary Lux** (☎030-8140 6190; www.klx-kosharylux.com; Grolmanstrasse 27; mains €4.50-9.20; ☉noon-3pm & 6-9pm Mon-Thu, noon-10pm Fri & Sat; Ⓢ Savignyplatz, Ⓤ Uhlandstrasse) and Chicha (p166).

MIDDLE EASTERN FOOD

Hummus and other Middle Eastern dishes like shakshuka, sabich and tabouli were practically unknown to German palates until just a few years ago. But thanks to a growing influx of enterprising Israelis and refugees from countries such as Syria, Iran and Iraq, the city is now seeing a growing crop of restaurants, including Yafo (p198), Hummus & Friends (p147) and Kanaan (p199). The hunt is also on for the city's best pastrami, with Mogg (p148) probably the most serious contender.

SHARING PLATES & CASUAL FINE DINING

These aren't exactly a new trend in most places around the world, but in Germany ordering a bunch of small dishes and putting them in the middle for everyone to tuck in to and help themselves is actually quite a new thing.

So is the concept of casual fine dining. Stuffy restaurants definitely don't go well with Berlin's idiosyncratic spirit, which is probably why the trend has been embraced with such vengeance. Indeed, even the new crop of Michelin restaurants – Tulus Lotrek (p164), Einsunternull (p149), Nobelhart & Schmutzig (p96), among them – eschews stuffiness in favour of an ambience of dining with friends.

Eating Like a Local

Restaurants are often formal places with full menus, crisp white linen and high prices. Some restaurants are open for lunch and dinner only, but more casual places tend to be open all day. Same goes for cafes, which usually serve both coffee and alcohol, as well as light meals, although ordering food is not obligatory. Many cafes and restaurants offer inexpensive weekday 'business lunches' that usually include a starter, main course and drink for under €10.

English menus are now quite common, and some places (especially those owned by neo-Berliners from the US, UK or around Europe) don't even bother with German menus at all. When it comes to paying, sometimes the person who invites pays, but very often Germans split the bill. This might mean everyone chipping in at the end of a meal or asking the server to pay separately (*getrennte Rechnung*).

Handy speed-feed shops, called *Imbiss*, serve all sorts of savoury fodder, from sausage-in-a-bun to *Döner Kebab* and pizza. Many bakeries serve sandwiches alongside pastries.

Locals love to shop at farmers markets and nearly every *Kiez* (neighbourhood) runs at least one or two during the week.

LOCAL SPECIALITIES YOU SHOULD TRY – AT LEAST ONCE

Pfannkuchen Known as 'Berliner' in other parts of Germany, these donut-like pastries are made from a yeasty dough, stuffed with a dollop of jam, deep fried and tossed in granulated sugar.

Currywurst This classic cult snack, allegedly invented in Berlin in 1949, is a smallish fried or

Pork knuckle with sauerkraut at Zur Letzten Instanz (p118)

Eating by Neighbourhood

Prenzlauer Berg
Lively cafe scene,
comfy neighbourhood
eateries (p198)

Scheunenviertel
Trendy, progressive
eating for all budgets
(p145)

**Potsdamer Platz
& Tiergarten**
Fine dining
in five-star
hotels (p133)

Fernsehturm

Friedrichshain
Mostly cheap eats
with pockets of
sophistication (p185)

**City West &
Charlottenburg**
Excellent Asian, Italian
and other international
fare (p216)

Historic Mitte
Swanky, cosmopolitan,
Michelin-starred
dining (p94)

**Museumsinsel &
Alexanderplatz**
Tourist-geared
fast food and
traditional German
(p117)

Spree River

**Kreuzberg
& Neukölln**
Eclectic ethnic and
creative contemporary
options (p163)

grilled *Wiener* (sausage) sliced into bite-sized ringlets, swimming in a spicy tomato sauce and dusted with curry powder. It's available '*mit*' or '*ohne*' (with or without) its crunchy epidermis and traditionally served on a flimsy plate with a plastic toothpick for stabbing.

Döner Spit-roasted meat may have been around forever, but the idea of serving it in a lightly toasted bread pocket with copious amounts of fresh salad and a healthy drizzle of yoghurt-based *Kräuter* (herb), *scharf* (spicy) or *Knoblauch* (garlic) sauce was allegedly invented by a Turkish immigrant in 1970s West Berlin.

Boulette Called *Frikadelle* in other parts of Germany, this cross between a meatball and a

hamburger is eaten with a little mustard and an optional dry roll. The name is French for 'little ball' and might have originated during Napoleon's occupation of Berlin in the early 19th century.

Eisbein or Grillhaxe Boiled or grilled pork hock typically paired with sauerkraut and boiled potatoes.

Königsberger Klopse This classic dish may have its origin in Königsberg in eastern Prussia (today's Kaliningrad in Russia), but it has of late made a huge comeback on Berlin menus. It's a simple but elegant plate of golf-ball-sized veal meatballs in a caper-laced white sauce served with a side of boiled potatoes and beetroot.

Lonely Planet's Top Choices

Restaurant Tim Raue (p96) Berlin's top toque is famous for his mash-up of Asian and Western flavours.

Einsunternull (p149) Gourmet food deconstructed to the essentials using regional ingredients.

Restaurant Faubourg (p217) Elevated French cuisine, sensitively interpreted and served in an eye-candy setting.

Katz Orange (p147) Cosy country-style farm-to-table lair in gorgeously recycled brewery.

Restaurant am Steinplatz (p218) German classics reinterpreted for the 21st century amid 1920s glamour.

Best By Budget: €

Street Food Thursday (p167) Global treats at a weekly street-food fair in a 19th-century market hall.

Sironi (p164) Some of the best sourdough ciabatta you'll ever have.

Hummus & Friends (p147) Hip Tel Aviv import makes kosher hummus and more next to the New Synagogue.

W-Der Imbiss (p200) Perfect yin and yang of Italian-Indian cooking amid tiki decor.

Burgermeister (p165) Succulent two-handful burgers and fries doused in homemade sauces in a former public latrine.

Best By Budget: €€

BRLO Brwhouse (p164) Super-creative, flawless craft beer and food pairings in shipping containers with beer garden.

Umami (p164) Sharp Indochine nosh for fans of the classics and the innovative amid sensuous lounge decor.

Taverna Ousia (p217) Berlin's best Greek restaurant with traditional flair and sharing plates.

Cafe Jacques (p169) Empty tables are as rare as hen's teeth in this candelit cocoon with top Mediterranean food and wine.

Mrs Robinson's (p200) Casual fine dining in a stylishly stripped down space.

Best By Budget: €€€

Tulus Lotrek (p164) Michelin-standard restaurant serving intensely flavoured fare paired with feel-good flair.

Schwein (p218) Elevated nose-to-tail cuisine with stunning wine and gin selection.

Horvàth (p167) Groundbreaking ode to Austrian cooking has double Michelin pedigree.

Katz Orange (p147) This stylish 'cat' fancies anything that's regional, seasonal and creative amid chic country decor.

Pauly Saal (p148) Time-honoured regional dishes reinterpreted in modern Michelin-decorated fashion.

Best Modern German

Lokal (p148) True to its name, only top notch local products are rendered into feisty flavour bombs.

Restaurant am Steinplatz (p218) Diverse and sometimes surprising array of ingredients find their destination in superb creations.

Orania (p168) Produce-conscious menu is a perfect foil for Berlin's worldly spirit.

eins44 (p169) Neukölln fine-dining pioneer with clever but unfussy French-leaning food in a pimped-up old distillery.

Best Middle Eastern

Damaskus Konditorei (p168) Bites from this baklava king guarantee a (so-worth-it) sugar rush.

Fes Turkish Barbecue (p166) Grill your own meat and veg at this Turkish spin of Korean barbecue.

Kanaan (p199) Feel-good Israeli-Palestinian joint with fabulous hummus and more.

Defne (p166) Turkish delights beyond the doner kebab, on the terrace in summer.

Habba Habba (p199) This hole-in-the-wall stuffs Middle Eastern wraps with unexpected meatless ingredients.

Koshary Lux (p52) Snack place specialising in perky street food from Morocco to Yemen.

Best Vegan & Vegetarian

Cookies Cream (p95) Clandestine meatfree Michelin kitchen tiptoes between hip and haute.

Kanaan (p199) Israeli-Palestinian co-production serves divine hummus, shakshuka and sabich.

Ataya Caffe (p199) Senegal meets Sardinia on the plate and in the decor at this adorable neighbourhood cafe.

Vöner (p185) Delicous vegan doner since long before the animal-free trend went mainstream.

Chay Long (p199) Stylishly simple eatery serving Buddhist monastery-style Vietnamese fare.

MARK READ/LONELY PLANET ©

Clärchens Ballhaus (p150)

Drinking & Nightlife

As one of Europe's primo party playgrounds, Berlin offers a thousand and one scenarios for getting your cocktails and kicks (or wine or beer, for that matter). From cocktail lairs and concept bars, craft beer pubs to rooftop lounge, the next thirst parlour is usually within stumbling distance.

Drinking

Berlin is a notoriously late city: bars stay packed from dusk to dawn, and some clubs don't hit their stride until 4am and stay open nonstop until Monday morning. The lack of a curfew never created a tradition of binge drinking, which is why many party folk prefer to pace their alcohol consumption and thus manage to keep going until the wee hours. Of course there's no denying that illegal drugs also play their part...

Edgier, more underground venues cluster in Kreuzberg, Friedrichshain, Neukölln and, to a certain extent, parts of Lichtenberg (east of Friedrichshain). Places in Charlottenburg, Mitte and Prenzlauer Berg tend to be quieter, close earlier and are more suited for date nights than dedicated drinking. Generally, the emphasis here is on style and atmosphere and some proprietors have gone to extraordinary lengths to come up with creative design concepts.

The line between cafe and bar is often blurred, with many changing stripes as the hands move around the clock. Alcohol, however, is served (and consumed) pretty much all day.

Some bars have happy hours that usually run from 6pm to 9pm but overall the happy hour concept isn't as prevalent in Berlin as in other cities. This is partly because drinks prices (especially for beer) are still lower than in many other major cities. Still, they are creeping up here as well, partly fuelled by a growing demand for quality over quantity, especially when it comes to cocktails, craft beer and wine.

On the flip side, some of Berlin's late-night convenience stores (called *Spätkauf* or *Späti* for short) cater to the cash-strapped by putting out tables on the sidewalks for patrons to gather and consume their store-bought beverages.

BEER

Predictably, beer is big in Berlin and served – and consumed – almost everywhere all day long. Most places pour a variety of local, national and imported brews, including at least one draught beer (*vom Fass*) served in 300mL or 500mL glasses. In summer, drinking your lager as an Alster, Radler or Diesel (mixed with Sprite, Fanta or Coke, respectively) is a popular thirst quencher.

NEED TO KNOW

Opening Hours

➜ Pubs are open from around noon to midnight or 1am (later on weekends).

➜ Trendy places and cocktail bars open around 8pm or 9pm until the last tippler leaves.

➜ Clubs open at 11pm or midnight and start filling up around 1am or 2am

Costs

Big clubs like Berghain/Panorama Bar or Watergate will set you back €15 or more, but there are plenty of others that charge between €5 and €10. Places that open a bit earlier don't charge admission until a certain hour, usually 11pm or midnight. Student discounts are virtually unheard of, as are 'Ladies Nights'.

Dress Code

Berlin's clubs are very relaxed. In general, individual style almost always trumps high heels and Armani. Cocktail bars and some disco-style clubs may prefer a more glam look, but in pubs anything goes.

Etiquette

Table service is common, and you shouldn't order at the bar unless you intend to hang out there or there's a sign saying *Selbstbedienung* (self-service). In traditional German pubs, it's customary to keep a tab instead of paying for each round separately. In bars with DJs €1 or €2 is usually added to the cost of your first drink. Tip bartenders about 5%, servers 10%. Drinking in public is legal and widely practised, especially around party zones. Try to be civilised about it, though. No puking on the U-Bahn, please!

Other German and imported beers are widely available. There's plenty of Beck's and Heineken around but for more flavour look for Jever Pilsener from northern Germany, Rothaus Tannenzäpfle from the Black Forest, Zywiec from Poland, and Krušovice and Budweiser from the Czech Republic. American Budweiser is practically nonexistent here.

Top: BRLO Brwhouse (p164)

Bottom: Mojitos

CLASSIC GERMAN BEERS

The most common classic German brews include the following:

Pils (pilsner) Bottom-fermented beer with a pronounced hop flavour and a creamy head.

Weizenbier/Weissbier (wheat beer) Top-fermented wheat beer that's fruity and refreshing. Comes bottled either as *Hefeweizen,* which has a stronger shot of yeast, or the filtered and fizzier *Kristallweizen.*

Berliner Weisse This cloudy, slightly sour wheat beer is typically sweetened with a *Schuss* (shot) of woodruff or raspberry syrup. It's quite refreshing on a hot day but few locals drink it.

Schwarzbier (black beer, like porter) This full-bodied dark beer is fermented using roasted malt.

Bockbier Strong beer with around 7% alcohol; brewed seasonally. Maibock shows up in May, Weihnachtsbock around Christmas.

CRAFT BEER

Thanks to Germany's famous Reinheitsgebot (Beer Purity Law), which celebrated its 500th anniversary in 2016, the quality of beer has always been high here, which is one of the reasons it took such a long time for the craft beer craze to reach the country. In recent years, though, it has arrived with a vengeance, leading to a virtual explosion of breweries specialising in handmade suds.

In Berlin, local pioneers such as Heidenpeters, Vagabund, Schoppe Bräu, Eschenbräu and Hops & Barley have been joined by dozens more small breweries. International brands like Stone Brewing, BrewDog and Mikkeler have also opened their own tap rooms in the capital.

To tap deeper into the scene, have a look at the online magazine *Hopfenhelden* (www.hopfenhelden.de/en); check out local festivals like Berlin Beer Week, Braufest or Craft Beer Festival; or join an English-language craft beer tour offered by such outfits as Original Berlin Walks (p299) and Alternative Berlin Tours (p299).

WINE

Oenophiles can rejoice as there is finally a respectable crop of wine bars in Berlin. Run by wine enthusiasts, they have an egalitarian rather than elitist mood and pour with a sense of humour and free-spiritedness devoid of snobbery. Since the quality of wine produced in Germany has markedly improved in recent years, you'll now find more Riesling on wine lists

---

NEW FRONTIER: RUMMELSBURG BAY

Displaced by development, rising rents and noise complaints, a growing number of clubs are trading the central districts for locations in suburbs like Lichtenberg, just southeast of Friedrichshain. An area called Rummelsburger Bucht, along the Spree, has emerged as a new frontier, especially for open-air clubs such as **Sisyphos** (☏030-9836 6839; www.sisyphos-berlin.net; Hauptstrasse 15; ⊘hours vary, usually midnight Fri-10am Mon May-Aug; 🚊21, ⑤Ostkreuz). Festival and club-night host **Funkhaus** (☏030-1208 5416; www.funkhaus-berlin.net; Nalepastrasse 18; ⊘hours vary; 🚊21) is also here. The area is served by tram 21 from Ostkreuz.

---

than ever before. Other varietals enjoying huge popularity are sauvignon blanc and Grauburgunder (Pinot gris).

V*in naturel* ('natural wine', ie organically grown and handled with minimal chemical interference), which often looks cloudy and tastes a bit tart at first, also has a devoted following.

In regular pubs and bars the quality of wine ranges from drinkable to abysmal. In these places, wine is usually served in 200mL glasses and costs from €4 to €6. In better establishments, finer vintages are served in mere 100mL glasses and usually start at €5.

In summer, many Germans like to mix (cheap) white wine with fizzy water, which is called a *Weinschorle.*

Sparkling wine comes in 100mL flutes. Depending on where a place sees itself on the trendiness scale, it will offer German *Sekt,* Italian Prosecco or French *cremant.* In clubs it's often served on the rocks (*Sekt auf Eis*). Champagne is popular among the monied set.

In winter, and especially at the Christmas markets, *Glühwein* (mulled wine) is a popular beverage to stave off the chills.

COCKTAILS

Dedicated cocktail bars are booming in Berlin and new arrivals have measurably elevated the 'liquid art' scene. Classic drinking dens tend to be elegant cocoons with mellow lighting and low sound levels

A TASTE OF BERLIN

In recent years a flurry of indie boutique beverage purveyors has cropped up in Berlin. Look for them at kiosks, cool bars, pubs and even supermarkets. Here are our favourites:

Berliner Brandstifter Berliner Vincent Honrodt is the man behind the Brandstifter Korn, a premium schnapps that gets extraordinary smoothness from a seven-stage filtering process. It also makes a mean gin.

Original Berlin Cidre (www.obc-cidre.com) OBC is made from 100% German apples by two Berliners, Urs Breitenstein and Thomas Godel. There are three varieties: the dry OBC Strong, the sweet OBC Classic and the fruity OBC Rose.

Adler Berlin Dry Gin Crafted by the Preussische Spirituosen Manufaktur (p207) that once served Kaiser Wilhelm II, this creamy and balanced gin is aromatised with juniper, lavender, coriander, ginger and lemon peel.

Our/Berlin (www.ourvodka.com) Made with Berlin water and German wheat, this smooth vodka is distilled in small batches at Flutgraben 2 on the Kreuzberg–Treptow border and sold in stylish bottles right there and in select shops.

Berliner Luft Peppermint schnapps has gained cult status despite tasting like mouthwash. Consumed as a shot, it's a popular method to get blasted fast.

Wostok This Kreuzberg-made certified organic lemonade comes in six flavours, the most famous of which is the pine-scented Tannenwald based on an original 1973 Soviet soft drink recipe.

but of late buzzier cocktail bars with less stuffy ambience have also thrown themselves into the mix. All are helmed by mixmeisters keen on applying their training to both classics and boundary-pushing riffs. A good cocktail will set you back between €10 and €15. Most bars and pubs serve cocktails, too, but of the Sex on the Beach and Cosmopolitan variety. Prices are lower (between €8 and €10) and quality can be hit or miss due to mediocre mixing talents and/or inferior spirits.

Clubbing

Since the 1990s, Berlin's club culture has taken on near-mythical status and, to no small degree, contributed to the magnetism of the German capital. It has incubated trends and sounds, launched the careers of such internationally renowned DJs as Paul van Dyk, Ricardo Villalobos, Ellen Allien and Paul Kalkbrenner, and put Berlin firmly on the map of global music fans who turn night into day in the over 200 clubs in this curfew-free city.

What distinguishes the Berlin scene from other party capitals is a focus on independent, non-mainstream niche venues, run by owners or collectives with a creative rather than a corporate background. The shared goal is to promote a diverse, inclusive and progressive club culture rather than to

maximize profit. This is also reflected in a door policy that strives to create a harmonious balance in terms of age, gender and attitude.

Electronic music in its infinite varieties continues to define Berlin's after-dark action but other sounds like hip-hop, dancehall, rock, swing and funk have also made inroads. The edgiest clubs have taken up residence in power plants, transformer stations, abandoned apartment buildings and other repurposed locations. Most are in Kreuzberg, Neukölln, Friedrichshain and parts of Treptow and Lichtenberg.

The scene is in constant flux as experienced club owners look for new challenges and a younger generation of promoters enters the scene with new ideas and impetus. Overall, though, rising rents, development, noise complaints and investors focused on profit maximisation have forced many smaller venues to close, thereby threatening Berlin's cult status as one of Europe's most free-wheeling and biggest party hubs.

WHEN TO GO

Whatever club or party you're heading for, don't bother showing up before 1am unless you want to have a deep conversation with a bored bartender. And don't worry about closing times – Berlin's famously long nights have gotten even later of late and, thanks to a growing number of after parties and daytime clubs, not going home until Monday night is definitely an option at weekends. In fact, savvy clubbers put in a good night's sleep, then hit the dance floor when other people head for Sunday church or afternoon tea.

AT THE DOOR

Doors are notoriously tough at Berlin's best clubs (eg Watergate, Berghain/Panorama Bar and ://aboutblank) as door staff strive to sift out people that would feel uncomfortable with the music, the vibe or the libertine ways beyond the door. Except at some disco-type establishments, flaunting fancy labels and glam cocktail dresses can actually get in the way of your getting in. Wear something black and casual. If your attitude is right, age rarely matters. Be respectful in the queue, don't drink and don't talk too loudly (seriously!). Don't arrive wasted. As elsewhere, large groups (even mixed ones) have a lower chance of getting in, so split up if you can. Stag and hen parties are rarely welcome. If you do get turned away, don't argue.

And don't worry, there's always another party somewhere...

Party Miles
FRIEDRICHSHAIN

RAW Gelände & Revaler Strasse The skinny-jeanster set invades the gritty clubs and bars along the 'techno strip' sprawling out over a former train repair station. Live concerts at Astra Kulturhaus, techno-electro at Suicide Circus, eclectic sounds at Cassiopeia and various off-kilter bars in between.

Ostkreuz Draw a bead on this party zone by staggering through the dark trying to find the entrance to Salon zur Wilden Renate or ://about blank.

Ostbahnhof Hardcore partying at Berghain/Panorama Bar and mellow chilling at Yaam.

Simon-Dach-Strasse If you need a cheap buzz, head to this well-trodden booze strip popular with field-tripping school groups and stag parties.

KREUZBERG & NEUKÖLLN

Weserstrasse & Around The main party drag in the hyped hood of Neukölln is packed with an eclectic mix of pubs and bars, from trashy to stylish.

Club der Visionäre (p172)

Drinking & Nightlife by Neighbourhood

Prenzlauer Berg
Cocktails, beer
gardens, comfy
cafes (p203)

Scheunenviertel
Trendy with chic,
cosmopolitan bars
(p150)

**Potsdamer Platz
& Tiergarten**
Snazzy hotel bars,
tourist haunts
(p136)

Fernsehturm

Friedrichshain
RAW 'party village',
Berghain, student
pubs (p188)

**City West &
Charlottenburg**
Old-school,
grown-up, chic
(p218)

Historic Mitte
Upmarket hotel bars,
gets quiet early
(p96)

**Museumsinsel &
Alexanderplatz**
Old Berlin pubs,
mainstream bars
(p118)

Spree River

**Kreuzberg &
Neukölln**
Gritty-cool clubs
and edgy bars
(p169)

Kottbusser Tor & Oranienstrasse Grunge-tastic area perfect for dedicated drink-a-thons with a punky-funky flair.

Schlesische Strasse Freestyle strip with a potpourri of party stations from beer gardens to concert venues, techno temples to daytime outdoor chill zones.

Skalitzer Strasse Eclectic drag with small clubs and some quality cocktail bars just off it.

SCHEUNENVIERTEL

Torstrasse This strip is where Berlin demonstrates that it, too, can grow up. A globe-spanning roster of monied creatives populates the chic drinking dens with their well-thought-out bar concepts and drinks made with top-shelf spirits.

Oranienburger Strasse Tourist zone where you have to hopscotch around sex workers and pub crawlers to find the few remaining thirst parlours worth your money.

Lonely Planet's Top Choices

Berghain/Panorama Bar (p188) Hyped but still happening Holy Grail of techno clubs with DJ royalty every weekend.

Clärchens Ballhaus (p150) Hipsters mix it up with grannies for tango and jitterbug in a kitsch-glam 1913 ballroom.

Club der Visionäre (p172) Summers wouldn't be the same without chilling and dancing in this historic canal-side boat shed.

Prater Biergarten (p203) Berlin's oldest beer garden has been rocking beneath the chestnuts since 1837.

Würgeengel (p170) Fun crowd keeps the cocktails and conversation flowing in a '50s setting.

Best Clubs

Berghain/Panorama Bar (p188) Big bad Berghain is still the best in town.

Griessmühle (p173) Attitude-free party parlour with canalside outdoor zone.

://about blank (p189) Gritty techno hot spot with enchanting summer garden.

Sisyphos (p59) Summer-only party village in retired dog food factory.

Ritter Butzke (p172) Low-key but high-calibre electro club in ex-factory keeps it real with mostly local DJs and a crowd that appreciates them.

Club der Visionäre (p172) Outdoor spot with willows on an idyllic canal popular for day-to-night partying.

Best Craft Beer Pubs

Hopfenreich (p172) Berlin's first craft beer bar also has tastings, tap takeovers and guest brewers.

BrewDog (p203) Trendy Mitte flagship with 30 taps dispensing its own and guest draughts.

Herman (p206) Specialises in Belgian suds from tap and bottle with over 100 on offer.

Vagabund Brauerei (p207) Craft beer pioneers run by a trio of friends with a taproom in Wedding.

Hops & Barley (p190) Fabulous unfiltered pilsner, dark and wheat beer made in a former butcher's shop.

Heidenpeters (p178) Tiny taproom brewed in the cellar of the Markthalle Neun.

Eschenbräu (p207) Trend free craft brewery with cosy cellar and chestnut-canopied beer garden, also makes fruit brandies.

Best Cocktail Bars

Schwarze Traube (p171) Pint-sized drinking parlour with bespoke cocktails.

Becketts Kopf (p205) Wait for Godot while sipping classics and seasonal inspirations.

Thelonius (p173) Neukölln drinking reaches new heights at this perfect trifecta of soft sounds, lovely light and expert cocktails.

Bar am Steinplatz (p219) Newbies and seasoned imbibers will be impressed by the supreme libations in this classy den.

Buck and Breck (p151) Cocktail classics for grown-ups in a speakeasy-style setting.

Best Wine Bars

Briefmarken Weine (p188) Oenophile den in former stamp shop for Italian wine fanciers.

Vin Aqua Vin (p175) Eliminates wine bar trepidation with casual vibe and wallet-friendly vintages.

Otto Rink (p170) For relaxed but demanding wine fans with a penchant for German wines.

Best Rooftop Bars

Klunkerkranich (p173) Hipster spot with urban garden and great sunset views atop Neukölln shopping centre.

Deck 5 (p206) Beach vibe with a view from the top parking deck of a Prenzlauer Berg shopping mall.

House of Weekend (p119) Club-affiliate delivers cocktails and barbecue at eye level with the Fernsehturm (TV Tower).

Monkey Bar (p220) Trendy West Berlin lair with exotic tiki drinks and a view of the baboons at the Berlin Zoo.

Amano Bar (p150) Bird's-eye views of the Scheunenviertel at the sleek summer edition of the fashionable Amano hotel bar.

Best Cafes

Kuchenladen (p218) Some of the most tantalising cakes in town.

Father Carpenter (p150) Top-notch coffee in a hidden courtyard near Hackesche Höfe.

Café Bravo (p150) Breakfast, cafe and cocktails in an arty glass pavilion designed by US artist Dan Graham.

Tadshikische Teestube (p147) Russian tea and food in an original Tajik tearoom gifted to the East Berlin government in the '70s.

Aunt Benny (p185) Local hangout with delicious homemade American-style cakes.

Christopher Street Day celebrations (p66)

LGBT+ Berlin

Berlin's legendary liberalism has spawned one of the world's biggest, most divine and diverse LGBT+ playgrounds. Anything goes in 'Homopolis' (and we do mean anything!), from the highbrow to the hands-on, the bourgeois to the bizarre, the mainstream to the flamboyant. Except for the most hardcore places, gay spots get their share of opposite-sex and straight patrons.

Gay in Berlin

Generally speaking, Berlin's gayscape runs the entire spectrum from mellow cafes, campy bars and cinemas to saunas, cruising areas, clubs with darkrooms and all-out sex venues. In fact, sex and sexuality are entirely everyday matters to the unshockable city folks and there are very few, if any, itches that can't be quite openly and legally scratched. As elsewhere, gay men have more options for having fun, but grrrrls of all stripes won't feel left out either.

History

Berlin's emergence as a gay capital has roots in 1897 when sexual scientist Magnus Hirschfeld founded the Scientific Humanitarian Committee, the world's first homosexual advocacy group. Gay life thrived in the wild and wacky 1920s, driven by a demimonde that drew and inspired writers like Christopher Isherwood, until the Nazis put an end to the fun in 1933. Postwar recovery came slowly, but by the 1970s the scene was firmly re-established, at least in the western part of the city. From 2001 to 2014, Berlin was governed by an openly gay mayor, Klaus Wowereit. To learn more about Berlin's LGBTIQ history, visit the Schwules Museum (p133).

Parties & Clubbing

Berlin's scene is especially fickle and venues and dates may change at any time, so make sure you always check the websites or the listings magazines for the latest scoop. One important alternative queer party space is **Südblock** (www.suedblock.org) at Kottbusser Tor in Kreuzberg, which is famous for its inclusive programming and diverse clientele.

Long-running gay party places include SchwuZ (p174), Berghain (p188), Lab.oratory (p189) and **Connection** (☏030-218 1432; www.connectionclub.de; Fuggerstrasse 33; ☉11pm-6am Fri & Sat; Ⓤ Wittenbergplatz), but there are also lots of regular parties held in various other locations. A selection follows. Unless noted, all are geared towards men.

B:East Party (http://beastparty.com) Monthly party for gays and friends with techno, house and disco, now at Polygon (p190). Last Saturday of the month.

Cafe Fatal All comers descend on SO36 (p173) for the ultimate rainbow tea dance, which goes from 'strictly ballroom' to 'dirty dancing' in a flash. If you can't tell a waltz from a foxtrot, come at 7pm for free lessons. Sundays.

Chantals House of Shame (www.facebook.com/ChantalsHouseofShame) Trash diva Chantal's louche lair at Suicide Circus (p189) is a beloved institution, not so much for the glam factor as for the over-the-top drag shows and the hotties who love 'em. Thursdays.

CockTail d'Amore (www.facebook.com/cocktaildamoreberlin) Alt-flavoured electro party with indoor and outdoor dancing and partying at Griessmühle (p173). First Saturday of the month.

Gayhane Geared towards gay and lesbian Muslims, but everyone's welcome to rock the kasbah when this 'homoriental' party takes over SO36 (p173) with Middle Eastern beats and belly dancing. Last Saturday of the month.

G day (www.facebook.com/GdayBerlin) Long-running gay party with a residency at Suicide Circus (p189) with uninhibited indoor and outdoor partying.

Gegen (www.gegenberlin.com) Countercultural party at KitKatClub (p174) brings in anti-trendy types for crazy electro and wacky art performances. First Friday, alternate months.

Girls Town (www.girlstown-berlin.de) Suse and Zoe's buzzy girl-fest takes over Gretchen (p175) in Kreuzberg with down-and-dirty pop, electro, indie

PLAN YOUR TRIP LGBT+ BERLIN

NEED TO KNOW

Websites

Gay Berlin4u (www.gayberlin4u.com) Covers all aspects of Berlin's gay scene, in English.

GayCities Berlin (https://berlin.gaycities.com) Berlin edition of the worldwide guide offers a basic overview of the scene, in English.

Patroc Gay Guide (www.patroc.de/berlin) Focuses on events but also has some info on venues; in German.

Magazines

Blu (www.blu.fm) Online and freebie print magazine with searchable, up-to-the-minute location and event listings.

L-Mag (www.l-mag.de) Bimonthly magazine for lesbians.

Siegessäule (www.siegessaeule.de) Free weekly lesbigay 'bible'.

Tours

Queer Berlin (p299) Long-running tour company Original Berlin Walks taps into the city's LGBTIQ legacy on tours through Kreuzberg and Schöneberg.

Berlinagenten (p301) Customised gay-lifestyle tours (nightlife, shopping, luxury, history, culinary).

Lügentour (www.luegentour.de) An interactive and humorous walking tour takes you back to the lesbigay scene in 1920s Schöneberg; alas, in German only.

Schröder Reisen Comedy Bus (www.comedy-im-bus.de) Outrageous comedy bus tours led by trash drag royalty Edith Schröder (aka Ades Zabel) and friends.

Help

Mann-O-Meter (www.mann-o-meter.de) Gay men's information centre.

Maneo (www.maneo.de) Gay victim support centre and gay-attack hotline.

Lesbenberatung (www.lesbenberatung-berlin.de) Lesbian resource centre.

and rock. Second Saturday, alternate months, September to May.

GMF (www.gmf-berlin.de) Berlin's premier techno-house Sunday club, currently at House of Weekend (p119), is known for excessive SM (standing and modelling) with lots of smooth surfaces. Predominantly boyz, but girls are welcome.

Horse Meat Disco (www.horsemeatdiscoberlin) This classic import from the UK does a bi-monthly shout-out to a dance-crazy queer crowd of all stripes. Check website for current location.

Irrenhouse The name means 'insane asylum', and that's no joke. Party hostess with the mostest, trash queen Nina Queer puts on nutty, naughty shows at Kreuzberg's Musik & Frieden (p176), which are not for the faint-of-heart. Expect the best. Fear the worst. Third Saturday of the month.

L-Tunes (www.l-tunes.com) Lesbians get their groove on in the dancing pits of various locations around town, including **Spindler & Klatt** ([☎]030-319 881 860; www.spindlerklatt.com; Köpenicker Strasse 16-17; mains €15.50-19.50; [⏰]restaurant 7-11pm Thu-Sun, club 11pm-late Fri & Sat; [P][📶]; [U]Schlesisches Tor) and **Quasimodo** ([☎]030-3180 4560; www.quasimodo.de; Kantstrasse 12a; admission varies; [⏰]doors 8pm, concerts 10pm; [S]Zoologischer Garten, [U]Zoologischer Garten). Last Saturday of the month.

Members (www.members-berlin.de) Monthly tech-house party has been running strong since 2013 on Hoppetosse moored in the Spree.

Revolver (www.facebook.com/RevolverParty Global) This London export hosted by Oliver and Gary is a sizzling and sexy party at the KitKatClub (p174) with no special dress code required. Second Friday of the month.

Festivals & Events

Easter Berlin (www.easterberlin.de; various locations; [⏰]Easter) One of Europe's biggest fetish fests whips the leather, rubber, skin and military sets out of the dungeons and into the clubs over the long Easter weekend. It culminates with the crowning of the 'German Mr Leather'.

Lesbisch-Schwules Stadtfest (Lesbigay Street Festival; www.stadtfest.berlin; [⏰]Jul; [U]Nollendorfplatz) The Lesbigay City Festival takes over the Schöneberg rainbow village in June, with bands, food, info booths and partying.

Christopher Street Day (www.csd-berlin.de; various locations; [⏰]Jun or Jul) Later in June, hundreds of thousands of people of various sexual persuasions paint the town pink with a huge semi-political parade and more queens than a royal wedding.

Lesbischwules Parkfest (www.parkfest-friedrichshain.de; Volkspark Friedrichshain; [⏰]Aug; [🖥]200) The gay community takes over the Volkspark Friedrichshain for this delightfully noncommercial festival in August.

Folsom Europe (www.folsomeurope.info; [⏰]early Sep; [U]Nollendorfplatz) The leather crowd returns in early September for another weekend of kinky partying.

Hustlaball (www.hustlaball.de; [⏰]Oct) The party year wraps up in October with a weekend of debauched fun in the company of porn stars, go-gos, trash queens, stripping hunks and about 3000 other men who love 'em.

LGBT+ Berlin by Neighbourhood

Museumsinsel & Alexanderplatz GMF, the best gay Sunday party, currently has a residency at House of Weekend.

Scheunenviertel Gets a mixed crowd, but its trendy bars and cafes (especially near Hackescher Markt and on Torstrasse) also draw a sizeable contingent of gay customers.

Kreuzberg & Neukölln Hipster central. Things are comparatively subdued in the bars and cafes along main-strip Mehringdamm. Around Kottbusser Tor and along Oranienstrasse the crowd skews younger, wilder and more alternative, and key venues stay open till sunrise and beyond. For a DIY subcultural vibe, head across the canal to Neukölln.

Friedrichshain This area is thin on gay bars but is still a de rigueur stop on the gay nightlife circuit thanks to clubs like Berghain, the hands-on Lab. oratory, Suicide Circus and ://about blank.

Prenzlauer Berg East Berlin's pink hub before the fall of the Wall has a few surviving bar relics as well as a couple of popular cruising dens and fun stations for the fetish set, mostly around the Schönhauser Allee S-/U-Bahn station.

Schöneberg The area around Nollendorfplatz (Motzstrasse and Fuggerstrasse especially) has been a gay beacon since the 1920s. Institutions like **Heile Welt** (Motzstrasse 5; [⏰]7pm-3am; [U]Nollendorfplatz), **Tom's Bar** (www.tomsbar.de; Motzstrasse 19; [⏰]10pm-6am; [U]Nollendorfplatz) Connection and **Hafen** (www.hafen-berlin.de; Motzstrasse 19; [⏰]from 7pm; [U]Nollendorfplatz) pull in punters night after night, and there's also plenty of nocturnal action for the leather and fetish set.

Lonely Planet's Top Choices

GMF (p119) Glamtastic Sunday party with pretty people in stylish and central location.

Roses (p171) Plush, pink, campy madhouse – an essential late-night stop on a dedicated bar hop.

Möbel Olfe (p170) Old furniture shop recast as busy drinking den; there's standing room only on (unofficial) gay Thursdays.

Chantals House of Shame (p190) Eponymous trash-drag diva's weekly parties run wild and wicked.

SchwuZ (p174) LGBTIQ club with different parties – great for scene newbies.

Best Venues by Day of the Week

Monday
Monster Ronson's Ichiban Karaoke (p189) Loosen those lungs and get louche.

Tom's Bar (p66) Two-for-one drinks.

Kino International (p191) Queer movies during 'Mongay'.

Tuesday
Rauschgold (p171) 'Time Tunnel' retro party.

Möbel Olfe (p170) Comfortably cheerful femme fave.

Wednesday
Himmelreich (p189) Two-for-one drinks.

Thursday
Möbel Olfe (p170) Ma(i)nly men get-together.

Chantals House of Shame (p190) Over-the-top drag queen-hosted party.

Friday
SchwuZ (p174) Weekend warm-up.

Lab.oratory (p189) Two-for-one drinks, no dress code.

Saturday
SchwuZ (p174) Good for newbies.

Berghain (p188) Advanced partying.

Sunday
GMF (p119) Hot-stepping weekend wrap-up.

Cafe Fatal @ SO36 (p173) All-ages tea dance.

Best Gay Bars

Möbel Olfe (p170) Relaxed Kreuzberg joint goes into gay turbodrive on Thursdays; women dominate on Tuesdays.

Heile Welt (p66) Stylish lounge good for chatting and mingling over cocktails.

Himmelreich (p189) This '50s retro lounge is a lesbigay-scene stalwart in Friedrichshain.

Roses (p171) Over-the-top late-night dive with camp factor and strong drinks.

Coven (p151) Stylish Mitte bar with industrial decor and strong drinks.

Best Lesbian Bars & Parties

Himmelreich (p189) Women's Lounge on Tuesday brings cool chicks to this comfy Friedrichshain bar.

Möbel Olfe (p170) Pop, disco and rock music get lesbians and their friends into party mood on Tuesday.

L-Tunes (www.l-tunes.com) Flirting, dancing and making out at legendary SchwuZ (p174) on the last Saturday of the month.

Best Sex Clubs/ Darkrooms

Lab.oratory (p189) Fetish-oriented experimental play zone in industrial setting below Berghain.

Greifbar (p206) Friendly cruising bar in Prenzlauer Berg with video, darkroom and private areas.

Connection Club (p65) Legendary dance club in Schöneberg with Berlin's largest cruising labyrinth.

Best for Camp

Rauschgold (p171) Small glitter-glam bar for all-night fun with pop, karaoke and drag shows.

Roses (p171) This pink-fur-walled kitsch institution is an unmissable late-night fuelling stop.

Zum Schmutzigen Hobby (p191) Fabulously wacky party pen in a former fire station.

WILHELM CHANG/SHUTTERSTOCK ©

Berliner Philharmoniker (p137)

 # Entertainment

Berlin's cultural scene is lively, edgy and the richest and most varied in the German-speaking world. With three state-supported opera houses, five major orchestras – including the world-class Berliner Philharmoniker – scores of theatres, cinemas, cabarets and concert venues, Berlin is replete with entertainment options.

Classical Music

Classical-music fans are truly spoilt in Berlin. Not only is there a phenomenal range of concerts throughout the year, but most of the major concert halls are architectural and acoustic gems of the highest order. Trips to the Philharmonie or the Konzerthaus are a particular treat, and regular concerts are also organised in churches like the Berliner Dom and palaces such as Schloss Charlottenburg.

Top of the pops is, of course, the world-famous Berliner Philharmoniker (p137), which was founded in 1882 and counts Hans Bülow, Wilhelm Furtwängler and Herbert von Karajan among its music directors. Since 2002, Sir Simon Rattle has continued the tradition. He will be succeeded by Russia-born Kirill Petrenko in 2019.

Though not in quite the same lofty league, the other orchestras are certainly no musical slouches either. Treat your ears to concerts by the Berliner Symphoniker, the Deutsches Symphonie-Orchester, the Konzerthausorchester and the Rundfunk-Sinfonieorchester Berlin. Note that most venues take a summer hiatus (usually July and August).

Berlin also has two music academies: the prestigious Hochschule für Musik Hanns Eisler (p97) and the new Barenboim-Said Academy (https://barenboimsaid.de), which supports mainly musicians from North Africa and the Middle East. Students often perform free concerts in various venues, including the new Pierre Boulez Saal (p97) in Mitte.

Opera

Not many cities afford themselves the luxury of three state-funded opera houses, but then opera has been popular in Berlin ever since the first fat lady loosened her lungs. Today fans can catch some of Germany's biggest and best performances here. Leading the pack in the prestige department is the Staatsoper Unter den Linden (p92), the oldest among the three, founded by Frederick the Great in 1743. The hallowed hall hosted many world premieres, including Carl Maria von Weber's *Der Freischütz* and Alban Berg's *Wozzeck*. Giacomo Meyerbeer, Richard Strauss and Herbert von Karajan were among its music directors. Since re-unification, Daniel Barenboim has swung the baton.

The Komische Oper (p97) opened in 1947 with *Die Fledermaus* by Johann Strauss II and still champions light opera, operettas and dance theatre. Across town in Charlottenburg, the Deutsche Oper Berlin (p221) entered the scene in 1912 with Beethoven's *Fidelio*. It was founded by local citizens keen on creating a counterpoint to the royal Staatsoper.

Live Rock, Pop, Jazz & Blues

Berlin's live-music scene is as diverse as the city itself. There's no Berlin sound as such, but many simultaneous trends, from punk rock to hardcore rap and hip-hop, reggae to sugary pop and downtempo jazz. With four clubs – Musik & Frieden, Bii Nuu, Lido and Privatclub – the area around Schlesisches Tor U-Bahn station in Kreuzberg is sound central. Another prime venue, the Astra Kulturhaus, is just across the river in Friedrichshain. Some venues segue smoothly from concert to party on some nights. Scores of pubs and bars also host concerts.

International top artists perform at various venues around town:

Columbiahalle (☏030-6981 2814; http://columbiahalle.berlin; Columbiadamm 13-21; ⓤPlatz der Luftbrücke) Originally a gym for members of the US air force, this hall now packs in up to 3500 people for rock and pop concerts.

Kindl-Bühne Wuhlheide (www.kindl-buehne-wuhlheide.de; An der Wuhlheide 187; ⓢMay-Sep; ⓢWuhlheide) This 17,000-seat outdoor stage in the shape of an amphitheatre was built in the

NEED TO KNOW

Ticket Bookings
➡ Early bookings are always advisable and are essential in the case of the Berliner Philharmoniker, the Staatsoper and big-name concerts.

➡ Some venues let you book tickets online for free or only a small surcharge using a credit card. Pick them up before the show at the box office.

Ticket Agencies
Theaterkasse Ticket outlets commonly found in shopping malls charge hefty fees.

Eventim (www.eventim.de) The main online agency.

Hekticket Half-price tickets for same-day performances online, by phone and in person at its outlets near **Zoo station** (☏030-230 9930; www.hekticket.de; Kulturbox, Hardenbergplatz 1) and **Alexanderplatz** (1st fl, Alexanderstrasse 1).

Koka 36 (☏030-6110 1313; www.koka36.de) For indie concerts and events.

Discount Tickets
➡ Some theatres sell unsold tickets at a discount 30 minutes or an hour before shows commence. Some restrict this to students.

➡ It's fine to buy spare tickets from other theatregoers but show them to the box-office clerk to make sure they're genuine before forking over any cash.

➡ The ClassicCard (www.classiccard.de) offers savings for classical-music aficionados under 30.

Resources
Tip (www.tip-berlin.de) Biweekly listings magazine (in German).

Zitty (www.zitty.de) Biweekly listings magazine (in German).

Ex-Berliner (www.ex-berliner.de) Expat-oriented English-language monthly.

Gratis in Berlin (www.gratis-in-berlin.de) Free events (in German).

Berlin Bühnen (www.berlin-buehnen.de) Browse events by genre.

early 1950s and is a popular venue for German pop and rock concerts.

SUNDAY CONCERTS IN VINTAGE VENUE

From roughly September to June, clued-in classical music fans gather for **Sonntagskonzerte** (☎030-5268 0256; www.sonntagskonzerte.de; Augustrasse 24; adult/concession €12/8; ⊙Sep-Jun; 🚋M1, Ⓢ Oranienburger Strasse, Ⓤ Oranienburger Tor) on Sunday evenings amid the faded elegance of an early-20th-century Spiegelsaal (Mirror Hall) for piano concerts, opera recitals, string quartets and other musical offerings. It's upstairs from Clärchens Ballhaus (p150). Make reservations online or drop by at least an hour before the show for tickets. There are no assigned seats.

With its cracked and blinded mirrors, elaborate chandeliers, stucco ceilings and old-timey wallpaper, the hall recalls the grandeur of a past era when it was the domain of the city's elite, while the common folks hit the planks in the ballroom downstairs.

Mercedez-Benz Arena (p191) Berlin's professional ice hockey and basketball teams play their home games at this state-of-the-art Friedrichshain arena that's also the preferred venue of international entertainment stars.

Olympiastadion (p219) With a seating capacity of nearly 75,000, the storied Olympic Stadium has hosted top music acts, the premier league soccer team Hertha BSC and even the Pope.

Tempodrom (☎tickets 01806 554 111; www.tempodrom.de; Möckernstrasse 10; Ⓢ Anhalter Bahnhof) This midsize hall in an eye-catching tent-shaped building has great acoustics and eclectic programming from concerts to snooker championships.

Waldbühne Berlin (☎tickets 01806 570 070; www.waldbuehne-berlin.de; Glockenturmstrasse 1; ⊙May-Sep; Ⓢ Pichelsberg) Built for the 1936 Olympics, this 22,000-seat open-air amphitheatre in the woods is a magical place for summer concerts.

Film

Berliners keep a wide array of cinemas in business, from indie art houses and tiny neighbourhood screens to stadium-style megaplexes with the latest technology. Mainstream Hollywood movies are dubbed into German, but numerous theatres also show flicks in their original language, denoted in listings by the acronym 'OF' (*Originalfassung*) or 'OV' (*Originalversion*); those with German subtitles are marked 'OmU' (*Original mit Untertiteln*). The Cinestar Original im Sony Center (p137) in Potsdamer Platz only screens films in the original English.

Food and drink may be taken inside the auditoriums, although you are of course expected to purchase your beer and popcorn (usually at inflated prices) at the theatre. Almost all cinemas also add a sneaky *Überlängezuschlag* (overrun supplement) of €0.50 to €1.50 for films longer than 90 minutes. There's also a surcharge for 3D movies plus a €1 rental fee if you don't have your own glasses. Seeing a flick on a *Kinotag* (film day, usually Monday or Tuesday) can save you a couple of euros.

Theatre

With more than 100 stages around town, theatre is a mainstay of Berlin's cultural scene. Add in a particularly active collection of roaming companies and experimental outfits and you'll find there are more than enough offerings to satisfy all possible tastes. Kurfürstendamm in Charlottenburg and the area around Friedrichstrasse in Mitte (the 'East End') are Berlin's main drama drags.

Most plays are performed in German, naturally, but of late several of the major stages – including Schaubühne (p220), **Volksbühne** (☎030-2406 5777; www.volksbuehne-berlin.de; Rosa-Luxemburg-Platz; tickets €10-40; Ⓤ Rosa-Luxemburg-Platz) and Gorki (p97) – have started using English subtitles in some of their productions. There's also the English Theatre Berlin (p175), which has some pretty innovative productions often dealing with socio-political themes, including racism, identity and expat-related issues.

Many theatres are closed on Monday and from mid-July to late August.

The Berliner Theatertreffen (Berlin Theatre Meeting; www.theatertreffen-berlin.de), in May, is a three-week-long celebration of new plays and productions that brings together top ensembles from Germany, Austria and Switzerland.

Live Comedy

Berlin's vast expat community fuels a lively English-language comedy scene with everything from stand-up to sketch and musical comedy being performed around town. Upcoming events are posted on www.comedyinenglish.de. The Kookaburra (p206) comedy club does English-language shows some nights.

Cabaret

The light, lively and lavish variety shows of the Golden Twenties have been undergoing a sweeping revival in Berlin. Get ready for an evening of dancing and singing, jugglers, acrobats and other entertainers. A popular venue is the Bar Jeder Vernunft (p220) and its larger sister Tipi am Kanzleramt (p97) whose occasional reprise of the musical *Cabaret* plays to sell-out audiences. In the heart of the 'East End' theatre district, Friedrichstadtpalast (p152) is Europe's largest revue theatre and the realm of leggy dancers and Vegas-worthy technology. The nearby Chamäleon Varieté (p152) is considerably more intimate. Travelling shows camp out at the lovely **Wintergarten Varieté** (030-588 433; www.wintergarten-variete.de; Potsdamer Strasse 96; ticket prices vary; U Kurfürstenstrasse).

These 'cabarets' should not be confused with *Kabarett,* which are political and satirical shows with monologues and skits.

Dance

With independent choreographers and youthful companies consistently promoting experimental choreography, Berlin's independent dance scene is thriving as never before. The biggest name in choreography is Sasha Waltz, whose company Sasha Waltz

& Guests has a residency at the cutting-edge Radialsystem V (p191). Other indie venues include the **Sophiensaele** (030-283 5266; www.sophiensaele.com; Sophienstrasse 18; tickets €10-15; M1, S Hackescher Markt, U Weinmeisterstrasse), **Dock 11** (030-448 1222; www.dock11-berlin.de; Kastanienallee 79; M1, U Eberswalder Strasse) and Hebbel am Ufer (p175). The last of these, in cooperation with Tanzwerkstatt Berlin, organises Tanz im August (www.tanzimaugust.de), Germany's largest contemporary dance festival, which attracts loose-limbed talent and highly experimental choreography from around the globe.

In the mainstream, the Staatsballett Berlin (Berlin State Ballet) performs both at the Staatsoper and at the Deutsche Oper Berlin.

Entertainment by Neighbourhood

Historic Mitte Tops for classical music and opera.

Potsdamer Platz & Tiergarten State-of-the-art multiplexes, art-house cinema, casino.

Scheunenviertel Cabaret, comedy, cinema and the 'East End' theatre district.

Kreuzberg & Neukölln Live music, off-theatre, art-house cinemas.

Friedrichshain Live music, outdoor cinema.

Prenzlauer Berg Live music.

City West & Charlottenburg Theatre, opera, jazz and indie screens.

OUTDOOR CINEMAS

From May to September, alfresco screenings are a popular tradition, with classic and contemporary flicks spooling off in *Freiluftkinos* (open-air cinemas). Come early to stake out a good spot and bring pillows, blankets and snacks. Films are usually screened in their original language with German subtitles, or in German with English subtitles.

Here's a shortlist of our favourite summertime movie haunts:

Freiluftkino Insel im Cassiopeia (p191) Indie movies next to a beer garden and bunker-turned-climbing wall on the RAW Gelände in Friedrichshain.

Freiluftkino Friedrichshain (p191) Vast amphitheatre-style venue at Volkspark Friedrichshain with drink-and-snack kiosk.

Freiluftkino Kreuzberg (p176) Presents movies in the original language in the courtyard of Kunstquartier Bethanien arts centre.

Open-air Kino Central (p153) Tiny space tucked into the final courtyard of nonprofit arts centre Haus Schwarzenberg in the Scheuenviertel.

Lonely Planet's Top Choices

Berliner Philharmoniker (p137) One of the world's top orchestras within its own 'cathedral of sound'.

Staatsoper Unter den Linden (p92) Top opera house.

Babylon (p151) Diverse and intelligent film programming in a 1920s building.

Lido (p176) Head-bobbing platform for indie bands, big names included.

Best Live Music Venues

Lido (p176) Great for catching future headliners of the rock-indie-electro-pop persuasions.

Privatclub (p176) Small retro joint with an anything-goes booking policy.

Astra Kulturhaus (p191) Clued-in bookers fill this rambling space with everything from big-name artists to electro swing parties.

Waldbühne (p70) Berliner Philharmoniker to the Rolling Stones: they've all rocked this enchanting outdoor amphitheatre near the Olympic Stadium.

Best Classical Music Venues

Berliner Philharmonie (p137) The one and only. Enough said.

Konzerthaus Berlin (p97) Schinkel-designed concert hall festooned with fine sculpture.

Sonntagskonzerte (p70) Intimate concerts amid charmingly faded 1920s grandeur.

Berliner Dom (p113) Former court church host concerts, sometimes played on the famous Sauer organ.

Pierre Boulez Saal (p97) Small-ish venue designed by Frank Gehry hosts mostly chamber music concerts.

Best Rock & Punk

SO36 (p173) This venerable club fixture has been rocking the crowd since the 1970s.

Wild at Heart (p176) Friendly biker-style dive with loud music and cheap beers.

Duncker Club (p206) Off-the-beaten-track Duncker is favoured by a local crowd, especially for the free Thursday concerts.

Best Free Entertainment

Bearpit Karaoke (p204) A huge crowd turns out to sing and cheer on Sunday at the Mauerpark.

Berliner Philharmonie (p137) Free Tuesday lunchtime concerts in the foyer of this famous concert hall.

Hochschule für Musik Hanns Eisler (p97) The gifted students of this conservatory show off their talent.

A-Trane Jazz Jam (p221) Mondays bring down the house in this well-established jazz club.

Französischer Dom Organ Recitals (p87) Lovely lunch break in historic church at 12.30pm Tuesday to Friday.

Teehaus im Englischen Garten (p135) Jazz to hip-hop concerts on summer Sundays at this Tiergarten beer garden.

Best Cabaret

Chamäleon Varieté (p152) Historic variety theatre in the Hackesche Höfe presents mesmerising contemporary spins

on acrobatics, dance, theatre, magic and music.

Bar Jeder Vernunft (p220) An art nouveau mirrored tent provides a suitably glam backdrop for high-quality entertainment.

Tipi am Kanzleramt (p97) There's not a bad seat in the house at this festive dinner theatre in a tent on the edge of the Tiergarten park.

Best Cinemas

Babylon (p151) Art-house cinema in protected 1920s Bauhaus building with restored theatre organ.

Cinestar Original (p137) The best place to see English-language blockbusters in the original language.

Arsenal (p137) Arty fare from around the world in the original language, often with English subtitles.

Freiluftkino Friedrichshain (p191) Classics, indies, documentaries and blockbusters under the stars in the vast Volkspark Friedrichshain.

Kino Central (p153) At the funky Haus Schwarzenberg, this small indie house plays new and classic art-house fare; also outdoors in summer.

Best Theatre

English Theatre Berlin (p175) Innovative and often provocative productions by Berlin's English-language theatre.

Schaubühne (p220) Contemporary plays in repurposed 1920s Streamline Moderne cinema; with English surtitles.

Gorki (p97) 'Postmigrant' theatre with multicultural cast picks up on works that address upheavals and transitions in society; with English surtitles.

SERGEY KOHL/SHUTTERSTOCK ©

LP12 Mall of Berlin (p137)

Shopping

Berlin is a great place to shop, and we're definitely not talking malls and chains. The city's appetite for the individual manifests in small neighbourhood boutiques and buzzing markets that are a pleasure to explore. Shopping here is as much about visual stimulus as it is about actually spending your cash, no matter whether you're ultrafrugal or a power-shopper.

Where to Shop

Berlin's main shopping boulevard is Kurfürstendamm (Ku'damm) in the City West and Charlottenburg, which is largely the purview of mainstream retailers (from H&M to Prada). Its extension, Tauentzienstrasse, is anchored by **KaDeWe** (www.kadewe.de; Tauentzienstrasse 21-24; ☑ 030-212 10; ⊙10am-8pm Mon-Thu, to 9pm Fri, 9.30am-8pm Sat), continental Europe's largest department store. Standouts among the city's dozens of other shopping centres are the concept mall Bikini Berlin and the vast LP12 Mall of Berlin at Leipziger Platz.

Getting the most out of shopping in Berlin, though, means venturing off the high street and into the *Kieze* (neighbourhoods). This is where you'll discover a cosmopolitan cocktail of indie boutiques stirred by the city's zest for life, envelope-pushing energy and entrepreneurial spirit.

Home-Grown Designers

Michael Michalsky may be Berlin's best-known fashion export, but hot on his heels are plenty of other fashion-forward local designers such as C.Neeon, Anna von Griesheim, Firma Berlin, Esther Perbandt, C'est Tout, Claudia Skoda, Kostas Murkudis, Kaviar Gauche, Potipoti and Leyla Piedayesh. In typical Berlin style, they walk the line between

NEED TO KNOW

Opening Hours

➡ Malls, department stores and supermarkets open from 9.30am to 8pm or 9pm; some supermarkets are open 24 hours.

➡ Boutiques and other smaller shops have flexible hours, usually from 11am to 7pm weekdays, and to 4pm or 5pm Saturday.

Taxes & Refunds

If your permanent residence is outside the EU, you may be able to partially claim back the 19% value-added tax (VAT, *Mehrwertsteuer*) you have paid on goods purchased in stores displaying the 'Tax-Free for Tourists' sign.

Clothing Sizes

For women's clothing sizes, a German size 36 equals a size 6 in the US and a size 10 in the UK, then increases in increments of two, making size 38 a US 8 and UK 12, and so on.

Sunday Shopping

Stores are closed on Sunday, except for some bakeries, flower shops, souvenir shops, and supermarkets in major train stations, including Hauptbahnhof, Friedrichstrasse and Ostbahnhof. Shops may also open from 1pm to 8pm on two December Sundays before Christmas and on a further six Sundays throughout the year, the latter being determined by local government.

originality and contemporary trends in a way that more mainstream labels do not.

Names on the watch list include Hien Le, Sadak, Julian Zigerli, Marina Hoermanseder and Jen Gilpin. Trend-pushers also include Umasan's vegan fashion, schmidttakahashi's take on upcycling, and high-end sustainable fashion by Christine Mayer. When it comes to accessories, look for eyewear by ic! Berlin and Mykita, bags by Liebeskind and Tausche, shoes by Trippen, and hats by Fiona Bennett and Rike Feurstein.

Flea Markets

Flea markets are like urban archaeology: you'll need plenty of patience and luck when sifting through other people's cast-offs, but oh, the thrill, when you finally unearth a piece of treasure! Berlin's numerous hunting grounds set up on weekends (usually Sunday) year-round – rain or shine – and are also the purview of fledgling local fashion designers and jewellery makers. The most famous market is the weekly Flohmarkt am Mauerpark (p208) in Prenzlauer Berg, which is easily combined with a visit to nearby Trödelmarkt Arkonaplatz (p208).

Shopping by Neighbourhood

Historic Mitte (p97) Souvenir shops on Unter den Linden; top-flight retailers, concept stores and galleries on and around Friedrichstrasse.

Museumsinsel & Alexanderplatz (p119) Eastern Berlin's mainstream shopping hub, plus a weekend collectables market.

Potsdamer Platz & Tiergarten (p137) Two big malls and little else.

Scheunenviertel (p152) Edgy international labels alongside local designers and accessories in chic boutiques and concept stores.

Kreuzberg & Neukölln (p177) Vintage fashion and streetwear along with music and accessories, all in indie boutiques.

Friedrichshain (p192) Up-and-coming area centred on Boxhagener Platz, site of a Sunday flea market; antiques market at Ostbahnhof.

Prenzlauer Berg (p208) Fashionable boutiques and accessories on Kastanienallee, children's stores around Helmholtzplatz and a fabulous flea market.

City West & Charlottenburg (p221) Mainstream on Kurfürstendamm, indie boutiques in the side streets, concept stores at Bikini Berlin, and homewares on Kantstrasse.

Lonely Planet's Top Choices

KaDeWe (p73) The ultimate consumer temple has seemingly everything every heart desires.

Bikini Berlin (p221) Edgy shopping in a revitalised 1950s landmark building near Zoo Station.

Galeries Lafayette (p98) French *je ne sais quoi* in an uber-stylish building by Jean Nouvel.

Dussmann – Das Kulturkaufhaus (p98) The mother lode of books and music with high-profile author readings and signings.

Rausch Schokoladenhaus (p98) Palace of pralines and chocolate, plus ingenious model-sized replicas of famous Berlin landmarks – made of chocolate, of course.

Hard Wax (p178) Key music stop for electro heads.

Best Berlin Fashion & Accessories

lala Berlin (p154) Big city fashion label that reflects the idiosyncratic Berlin spirit.

IC! Berlin (p119) Unbreakable and stylish eyewear for the fashion-forward.

Trippen (p154) Handmade designer footwear that's sustainable, ergonomic and stylish.

Kauf Dich Glücklich (p153) Indie concept store sells its own chic KDG collection along with Scandinavian designer brands.

Best Bookshops

Another Country (p178) Quirkily run English-language bookstore-library-community living room.

Pro Qm (p154) Floor-to-ceiling shelves crammed with tomes on art, architecture and design.

Hundt Hammer Stein (p152) Expertly curated literary bookshop run by well-read staff.

Dussmann – Das Kulturkaufhaus (p98) Vast literature and music emporium with extended shopping hours.

Best Flea Markets

Flohmarkt am Mauerpark (p208) The mother of all markets is overrun but still a good show.

Nowkoelln Flowmarkt (p178) This internationally flavoured market is also a showcase of local creativity.

Flohmarkt am Boxhagener Platz (p192) Fun finds abound at this charmer on a leafy square.

RAW Flohmarkt (p192) Bargains can still be had at this little market on the grounds of a railway repair station turned party zone.

Best Gastro Delights

KaDeWe Food Hall (p73) Mind-boggling bonanza of gourmet treats from around the world.

Markthalle Neun (p178) Revitalised historic market hall with thrice-weekly farmers market and global bites during Street Food Thursday.

Bonbonmacherei (p152) Willy Wonka would feel right at home in this old-fashioned candy kitchen.

Best Gifts & Souvenirs

Ampelmann Berlin (p154) Berlin's cute 'traffic-light man'

graces everything from bibs to bags.

Bonbonmacherei (p152) Souvenir candy made by hand in an old-fashioned candy kitchen.

Herrlich (p179) Practical, stylish and tasteful gifts for men.

Käthe Wohlfahrt (p221) Huge assortment of Christmas decorations and ornaments year-round.

VEB Orange (p208) Fun and funky knick-knacks from yesteryear.

Best Malls & Department Stores

Bikini Berlin (p221) The city's first concept mall with hip stores and views of the monkeys at Berlin Zoo.

LP12 Mall of Berlin (p137) Huge high-end shopping quarter with around 300 stores alongside apartments, a hotel and offices.

Alexa (p119) Vast all-purpose mall with all the usual high-street chains and an exhibit of Berlin in miniature.

KaDeWe (p73) The largest department store in continental Europe.

Best Quirky Stores

1. Absinth Depot Berlin (p154) Make your acquaintance with the Green Fairy at this quaint Old Berlin–style shop.

Käthe Wohlfahrt (p221) Where it's Christmas 365 days of the year so you can stock up on things that shine and glitter in July.

Ampelmann Berlin (p154) The little traffic-light guy that helps you across the street has his own franchise.

Explore Berlin

BERLIN'S
TOP SIGHTS

Neighbourhoods at a Glance

1 Historic Mitte p80

A cocktail of culture, commerce and history, Mitte packs it in when it comes to blockbuster sights: the Reichstag, the Brandenburg Gate, the Holocaust Memorial and Checkpoint Charlie are all within its confines. Central Berlin is at its poshest along Friedrichstrasse, where there's good shopping and dining, and around the gorgeous Gendarmenmarkt.

2 Museumsinsel & Alexanderplatz p99

This historic area is sightseeing central, especially for museum lovers who hit the jackpot on the little Spree island of Museumsinsel, home to five world-class museums, including the unmissable Pergamonmuseum. The Berliner Dom (Berlin cathedral) watches serenely over it all, including the reconstructed

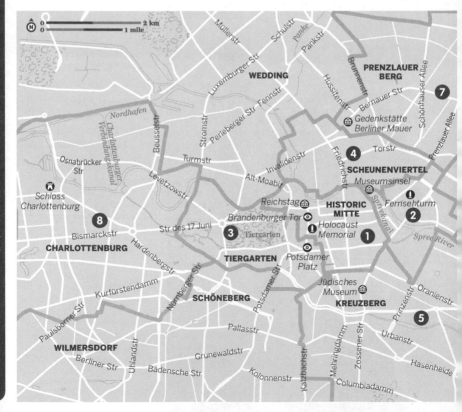

Berlin City Palace (aka Humboldt Forum) across the street.

❸ Potsdamer Platz & Tiergarten p120

This new quarter is a showcase of fabulous contemporary architecture. Culture lovers should not skip the Kulturforum museums, especially the Gemäldegalerie, which sits next to the world-class Berliner Philharmonie. The leafy Tiergarten, with its rambling paths, monuments and hidden beer gardens, makes for a perfect sightseeing break.

❹ Scheunenviertel p138

Scheunenviertel packs a mother lode of charisma into its relatively compact size and is a joy to explore by day and hang out in at night. Its greatest charms reveal themselves in the labyrinth of quiet lanes fanning out from its main drags, Oranienburger Strasse

and Rosenthaler Strasse. A distinctive feature of the quarter is its *Höfe* – interlinked courtyards filled with cafes, shops and drinking temples.

❺ Kreuzberg & Neukölln p155

Kreuzberg and Neukölln across the canal are Berlin's most dynamic and hip neighbourhoods. With the Jewish Museum and the German Museum of Technology, the area offers a couple of blockbuster sights, but its main draw is its global village atmosphere, accompanied by a burgeoning roster of eclectic eateries, bars, nightlife and shopping.

❻ Friedrichshain p180

The eastern district of Friedrichshain is famous for high-profile GDR-era relics such as the longest surviving stretch of the Berlin Wall (the East Side Gallery), the socialist boulevard Karl-Marx-Allee and the former Stasi headquarters. But the area also stakes its reputation on having Berlin's most rambunctious nightlife scene, with a glut of clubs and bars holding forth along Revaler Strasse and around the Ostkreuz train station.

❼ Prenzlauer Berg p193

Splendidly well-groomed Prenzlauer Berg is one of Berlin's most charismatic residential neighbourhoods, filled with cafes, historic buildings and indie boutiques. On Sundays, the world descends on its Mauerpark for flea marketeering. It's easily combined with a visit to the quarter's main sightseeing attraction, the Gedenkstätte Berliner Mauer, an engrossing exhibit that explains how the Berlin Wall shaped the city.

❽ City West & Charlottenburg p209

The glittering heart of West Berlin during the Cold War, Charlottenburg is a big draw for shopaholics, royal groupies and art lovers. Its main sightseeing attraction is Schloss Charlottenburg, with its park and adjacent art museums. About 3.5km southeast of here, the City West area, around Zoologischer Garten (Zoo Station), is characterised by Berlin's biggest shopping boulevard, the Ku'damm.

Historic Mitte

GOVERNMENT QUARTER & NORTHERN TIERGARTEN | BRANDENBURGER TOR & UNTER DEN LINDEN | FRIEDRICH-STRASSE & CHECKPOINT CHARLIE | GENDARMENMARKT

Neighbourhood Top Five

❶ Brandenburger Tor (p84) Snapping a selfie with this famous landmark and symbol of German reunification.

❷ Gendarmenmarkt (p87) Taking in the architectural symmetry of this square before indulging in a gourmet meal at one of the top restaurants in the area.

❸ Holocaust Memorial (p85) Soaking in the stillness and presence of uncounted souls at this haunting site before gaining an insight into the horrors of the Holocaust at the underground exhibit.

❹ Reichstag (p82) Standing in awe of history at Germany's government building, then pinpointing the sights while meandering up its landmark glass dome.

❺ Topographie des Terrors (p89) Understanding the machinations of Nazi Germany at this haunting exhibit standing on the one-time site of the Gestapo and SS headquarters.

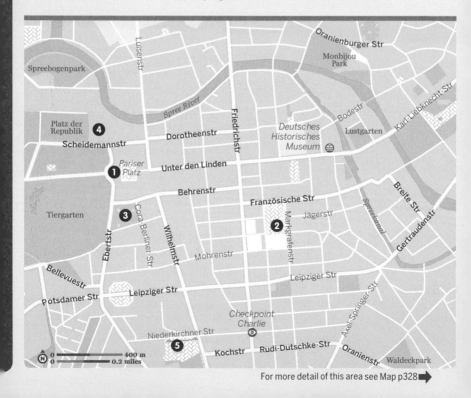

For more detail of this area see Map p328 ➡

Explore Historic Mitte

With a high concentration of sights clustered within a walkable area, the most historic part of Berlin is naturally a prime port of call for most first-time visitors. Book ahead for access to the Reichstag (p82) dome, then snap a picture of the Brandenburger Tor (p84) and commune with lost souls at the Holocaust Memorial (p85) before dipping into Berlin's Prussian past on a stroll along the normally grand boulevard Unter den Linden. These days, though, expect to hopscotch around several major construction sites on account of a new U-Bahn line.

Unaffected by the temporary turmoil is Friedrichstrasse, which bisects Unter den Linden and runs north into the 'East End' theatre district and south to Checkpoint Charlie. Gendarmenmarkt (p87), Berlin's most beautiful square, is just one block east and is surrounded by ritzy restaurants and fancy shops. Its Konzerthaus (p87) provides high-brow after-dark diversion, but aside from a few posh bars, this area is pretty devoid of nightlife. There's more going on going near the theatres north of Friedrichstrasse train station, especially on Schiffbauerdamm.

Local Life

Glamour shopping Brand-name bunnies hop to Friedrichstrasse to give their credit cards a workout. Aside from boutiques, the Friedrichstadtpassagen (p92), led by the Galeries Lafayette, beckons with top-flight Berlin and international designers.

High-brow culture Music fans are drawn to performances at the Staatsoper Berlin (p96), the Konzert-haus Berlin (p97) and the Pierre Boulez Saal (p97), as well as opera at the Komische Oper (p97).

Power of words Open until midnight, Dussmann (p98), the self-titled 'cultural department store', is an eldorado for bookworms and has a huge music selection plus free readings and other events.

Getting There & Away

Bus Buses 100 and 200 run along most of Unter den Linden from Alexanderplatz.

S-Bahn S1 and S2/25 stop at Brandenburger Tor and Friedrichstrasse.

U-Bahn Stadtmitte (U2, U6), Französische Strasse (U6) and Hausvogteiplatz (U2) are all convenient for Gendarmenmarkt. For Unter den Linden, get off at Brandenburger Tor (U55), Friedrichstrasse (U6) or Französische Strasse (U6).

Tram The M1 travels down Friedrichstrasse en route between Museumsinsel and Prenzlauer Berg.

Lonely Planet's Top Tip

There is definitely a mystique to Checkpoint Charlie, so by all means drop by to take a look. However, in order to truly understand what it was like to cross between West and East Berlin, swing by the excellent – and free – exhibit in the Tränenpalast (p92), an actual border pavilion, a bit north on Friedrichstrasse.

✖ Best Places to Eat

➡ India Club (p94)
➡ Augustiner am Gendarmenmarkt (p95)
➡ Cookies Cream (p95)
➡ Restaurant Tim Raue (p96)
➡ Ishin (p95)

For reviews, see p94.➡

☕ Best Places to Drink

➡ Bar Tausend (p96)
➡ Rooftop Terrace (p96)
➡ Crackers (p96)
➡ Berliner Republik (p95)

For reviews, see p96.➡

🔒 Best Places to Shop

➡ Dussmann – Das Kulturkaufhaus (p98)
➡ Rausch Schokoladenhaus (p98)
➡ Frau Tonis Parfum (p98)

For reviews, see p97.

TOP SIGHT
REICHSTAG

It's been burned, bombed, rebuilt, buttressed by the Berlin Wall, wrapped in fabric and finally turned into the modern home of the German parliament by Norman Foster: the Reichstag is one of Berlin's most iconic buildings. Its most eye-catching feature is the glistening glass dome, which draws more than three million visitors each year.

Dome

Resembling a giant glass beehive, the sparkling cupola is open at the top and bottom and sits right above the plenary chamber as a visual metaphor for transparency and openness in politics. A lift whisks you to the rooftop terrace, from where you can easily pinpoint such sights as the curvaceous House of World Cultures and the majestic Berliner Dom (Berlin Cathedral) or marvel at the enormous dimensions of Tiergarten park. To learn more about these and other landmarks, the Reichstag building and the workings of parliament, pick up a free multilingual audioguide as you exit the lift. The commentary starts automatically as you mosey up the dome's 230m-long ramp, which spirals around a mirror-clad cone that deflects daylight down into the plenary chamber.

Main Facade

Stylistically, the monumental west-facing main facade borrows heavily from the Italian Renaissance, with a few neo-baroque elements thrown into the mix. A massive staircase leads up to a portico curtained by six Corinthian columns and topped by the dedication 'Dem Deutschen Volke' (To the German People), which wasn't added until 1916.

DON'T MISS

➡ Views from the rooftop
➡ The facade
➡ Audioguide tour of the dome

PRACTICALITIES

➡ Map p328, C3
➡ www.bundestag.de
➡ Platz der Republik 1, Visitors' Centre, Scheidemannstrasse
➡ admission free
➡ ⊙lift 8am-midnight, last entry 9.45pm, Visitors' Centre 8am-8pm Apr-Oct, to 6pm Nov-Mar
➡ ♿
➡ 🚌100, Ⓢ Brandenburger Tor, Hauptbahnhof, Ⓤ Brandenburger Tor, Bundestag

83

HISTORIC MITTE REICHSTAG

The bronze letters were designed by Peter Behrens, one of the fathers of modern architecture, and cast from two French cannons captured during the Napoleonic Wars of 1813–15. The original dome, made of steel and glass and considered a high-tech marvel at the time, was destroyed during the Reichstag fire in 1933.

Home of the Bundestag

Today, the Reichstag is the historic anchor of the new federal government quarter built after reunification. The Bundestag, Germany's parliament, has hammered out its policies here since moving from the former German capital of Bonn to Berlin in 1999. The parliament's arrival followed a complete architectural revamp masterminded by Lord Norman Foster, who preserved only the building's 19th-century shell and added the landmark glass dome.

Historic Milestones

The grand old structure was designed by Paul Wallot and completed in 1894, when Germany was still a constitutional monarchy known as the Deutsches Reich (German Empire) – hence the building's name. Home of the German parliament from 1894 to 1933 and again from 1999, the hulking building will likely give you more flashbacks to high-school history than any other Berlin landmark. On 9 November 1919, parliament member Philipp Scheidemann proclaimed the German republic from one of its windows. In 1933, the Nazis used a mysterious fire as a pretext to seize dictatorial powers. A dozen years later, victorious Red Army troops raised the Soviet flag on the bombed-out building, which stood damaged and empty on the western side of the Berlin Wall throughout the Cold War. In the late 1980s, megastars including David Bowie, Pink Floyd and Michael Jackson performed concerts on the lawn in front of the building.

The Wall collapsed soon thereafter, paving the way to German reunification, which was enacted here in 1990. Five years later, the Reichstag made headlines once again when the artist couple Christo and Jeanne-Claude wrapped the massive structure in silvery fabric. It had taken an act of the German parliament to approve the project, which was intended to mark the end of the Cold War and the beginning of a new era. For two weeks starting in late June 1995, visitors from around the world flocked to Berlin to admire this unique sight. Shortly after the fabric came down, Lord Norman Foster set to work.

An extensive photographic exhibit at the bottom of the dome captures many of these historic moments.

VISITING THE DOME

Free reservations for visiting the Reichstag dome must be made at www.bundestag.de. Book early, especially in summer, and prepare to show picture ID, pass through a metal detector and have your belongings X-rayed. Guided tours and lectures can also be booked via the website. If you haven't prebooked, enquire at the Visitors' Centre near the Reichstag about remaining tickets for that day or the next two. You can also reach the rooftop by making reservations at the Dachgartenrestaurant Käfer.

It was the night of 27 February 1933: the Reichstag was ablaze. In the aftermath, a Dutch anarchist named Marinus van der Lubbe was arrested for arson without conclusive proof. Historians regard the incident as a pivotal moment in Hitler's power grab. Claiming that the fire was part of a large-scale Communist conspiracy, the Nazis pushed through the 'Reichstag Fire Decree', quashing civil rights and triggering the persecution of political opponents. The true events of that night remain a mystery. Its impact on history does not.

TOP SIGHT
BRANDENBURGER TOR

The Brandenburg Gate is Berlin's most famous – and most photographed – landmark. Trapped right behind the Berlin Wall during the Cold War, it went from symbol of division to epitomising German reunification when the hated barrier fell in 1989. It now serves as a photogenic backdrop for raucous New Years' Eve parties, concerts, festivals and mega-events including FIFA World Cup finals.

Commissioned by Prussian king Friedrich Wilhelm II, the gate was completed in 1791 as a symbol of peace and a suitably impressive entrance to the grand boulevard Unter den Linden. Architect Carl Gotthard Langhans looked to the Acropolis in Athens for inspiration for this elegant triumphal arch, which is the only surviving one of 18 city gates that once ringed historic Berlin.

Crowning the Brandenburg Gate is the *Quadriga,* Johann Gottfried Schadow's famous sculpture of a winged goddess piloting a chariot drawn by four horses. After trouncing Prussia in 1806, Napoleon kidnapped the lady and held her hostage in Paris until she was freed by a gallant Prussian general in 1815. Afterwards, the goddess, who originally represented Eirene (the goddess of peace), was promoted to Victoria (the goddess of victory) and equipped with a new trophy designed by Karl Friedrich Schinkel: an iron cross wrapped into an oak wreath and topped with a Prussian eagle.

DON'T MISS

➡ Quadriga
➡ View from Pariser Platz at sunset

PRACTICALITIES

➡ Brandenburg Gate
➡ Map p328, C3
➡ Pariser Platz
➡ S Brandenburger Tor, U Brandenburger Tor

TOP SIGHT
HOLOCAUST MEMORIAL

The Denkmal für die ermordeten Juden Europas (Memorial to the Murdered Jews of Europe) was officially dedicated in 2005. Colloquially known as the Holocaust Memorial, it's Germany's central memorial to the Nazi-planned genocide during the Third Reich. For the football-field-sized space, New York architect Peter Eisenman created 2711 sarcophagi-like concrete stelae (slabs) of equal size but various heights, rising in sombre silence from undulating ground.

You're free to access this massive concrete maze at any point and make your individual journey through it. At first it may seem austere, even sterile. But take time to feel the coolness of the stone and contemplate the interplay of light and shadow, then stumble aimlessly among the narrow passageways, and you'll soon connect with a metaphorical sense of disorientation, confusion and claustrophobia.

For context, visit the subterranean **Ort der Information** (Information Centre; Map p328; ☑030-7407 2929; www.holocaust-mahnmal.de; Cora-Berliner-Strasse 1; audio guide €3; ⊙10am-8pm Tue-Sun Apr-Sep, to 7pm Oct-Mar, last admission 45min before closing) FREE, which movingly lifts the veil of anonymity from the six million Holocaust victims. A graphic timeline of Jewish persecution during the Third Reich is followed by a series of rooms documenting the fates of individuals and families. The most visceral is the darkened Room of Names, where the names and years of birth and death of Jewish victims are projected onto all four walls while a solemn voice reads their short biographies. Poignant and heart-wrenching, these exhibits leave no one untouched. Not recommended for children under 14.

DON'T MISS

→ Field of stelae
→ Ort der Information
→ Room of Names

PRACTICALITIES

→ Memorial to the Murdered Jews of Europe
→ Map p328, C4
→ ☑030-2639 4336
→ www.stiftung-denkmal.de
→ Cora-Berliner-Strasse 1
→ audio guide €3
→ ⊙24hr
→ Ⓢ Brandenburger Tor, Ⓤ Brandenburger Tor

TOP SIGHT
DEUTSCHES HISTORISCHES MUSEUM

If you're wondering what the Germans have been up to for the past 1500 years, take a spin around this engaging museum in the baroque Zeughaus, formerly the Prussian arsenal. Upstairs, displays concentrate on the period from the 6th century AD to the end of WWI in 1918, while the ground floor tracks the 20th century until the early post-reunification years.

Permanent Exhibit

All the major milestones in German history are dealt with in a European context and examine political history as it was shaped by rulers. The timeline begins with the coronation of Charlemagne, the founding of the Holy Roman Empire and everyday life in the Middle Ages. It then jumps ahead to Martin Luther and the Reformation, the bloody Thirty Years' War and its aftermath, Napoleon and the collapse of the Holy Roman Empire in 1806, and the founding of the German Empire in 1871. WWI, which brought the end of the monarchy and led to the Weimar Republic, is a major theme, as of course are the Nazi era and the Cold War. The exhibit ends in 1994 with the withdrawal of Allied troops from German territory.

Displays are a potpourri of documents, paintings, books, dishes, textiles, weapons, furniture, machines and other objects ranging from the sublime to the trivial. One of the oldest objects is a 3rd-century **Roman milestone**. There's also splendid medieval body armour for horse and rider and a **felt hat** worn by Napoleon I during the Battle of Waterloo. Among the more unusual objects is a **pulpit hourglass**, which was introduced after the Reformation to limit the length of sermons to one hour. A startling highlight is a big **globe** that originally stood in the Nazi Foreign Office, with a bullet hole where Germany should be. Among the newer objects is a 1985 **Robotron PC 1715**, the first PC made in East Germany.

DON'T MISS

→ Schlüter's sculptures in the courtyard
→ IM Pei Exhibition Hall
→ GDR-era Robotron personal computer
→ Painting of Martin Luther by Lucas Cranach the Elder
→ Nazi globe

PRACTICALITIES

→ German Historical Museum
→ Map p328, G3
→ ☎030-203 040
→ www.dhm.de
→ Unter den Linden 2
→ adult/concession/ child under 18 incl IM Pei Bau €8/4/free
→ ⊙10am-6pm
→ 🚌100, 200, Ⓤ Hausvogteiplatz, Ⓢ Hackescher Markt

The Building

The rose-coloured Zeughaus, which was used as a weapons depot until 1876, was a collaboration of four architects: Johann Arnold Nering, Martin Grünberg, Andreas Schlüter and Jean de Bodt. Completed in 1730, it is the oldest building along Unter den Linden and a beautiful example of secular baroque architecture. This is in no small part thanks to Schlüter's magnificent **sculptures**, especially the heads of dying soldiers, their faces contorted in agony, that grace the facades in the glass-covered courtyard. Although intended to represent vanquished Prussian enemies, they actually make more of a pacifist statement for modern viewers.

IM Pei Exhibition Hall

High-calibre temporary exhibits take up a spectacular contemporary **annexe** (Map p328; Hinter dem Giesshaus 3) designed by Chinese-American architect IM Pei. Fronted by a glass spiral, it's an uncompromisingly geometrical space, made entirely from triangles, rectangles and circles, yet imbued with a sense of lightness achieved through an airy atrium and generous use of glass.

TOP SIGHT
GENDARMENMARKT

The graceful Gendarmenmarkt is widely considered Berlin's prettiest public square and – surrounded by luxury hotels, fancy restaurants and bars – shows off the city at its ritziest. It was laid out around 1690 and named after the Gens d'Armes, an 18th-century Prussian regiment of French Huguenots who settled here after being expelled from France in 1685.

The 1705 **Französischer Dom** (French Cathedral; Map p328; www.franzoesischer-dom.de; church free; ⊙church noon-5pm Tue-Sun) was built by Huguenot refugees and consists of two buildings: the soaring domed tower, which was added by Carl von Gontard in 1785, and the attached Französische Kirche (French Church), a copy of the Huguenots' mother church in Charenton. Note that the tower, which normally houses the Huguenot Museum and provides access to a viewing platform, is closed for renovation.

The **Deutscher Dom** (German Cathedral; Map p328; ☑030-2273 0431; www.bundestag.de/deutscherdom; Gendarmenmarkt 1; ⊙10am-7pm Tue-Sun May-Sep, to 6pm Oct-Apr) FREE wasn't much of a looker before being topped by Gontard's dazzling galleried dome in 1785. Built as the Neue Kirche (New Church) between 1702 and 1708 for German-speaking congregants, it is now home to an **exhibit** charting Germany's path to parliamentary democracy. English audioguides and tours are available.

One of Karl Friedrich Schinkel's finest buildings, the 1821 **Konzerthaus** (Map p328; ☑030-203 092 333; www.konzerthaus.de; Gendarmenmarkt 2) rose from the ashes of Carl Gotthard Langhans' Schauspielhaus (National Theatre). Schinkel kept the surviving walls and columns and added a grand staircase leading to a raised columned portico. The building is fronted by an elaborate **sculpture** of 18th-century poet and playwright Friedrich Schiller. For a look inside this beacon of Berlin high-brow culture, catch a concert or take a guided **tour** (offered at 1pm or 3pm on select days).

DON'T MISS

➡ Free organ recital in the Französische Kirche

➡ Concert at the Konzerthaus

PRACTICALITIES

➡ Map p328, F4

➡ Ⓤ Französische Strasse, Stadtmitte

◉ SIGHTS

Berlin's historic centre flanks the boulevard Unter den Linden and handily packs numerous blockbuster sights into a compact area. A visit here is easily combined with a stroll around the Tiergarten to the west, a look at the new Potsdamer Platz city quarter to the south or a spin around the stunners at Museum Island just east of here.

◉ Government Quarter & Northern Tiergarten

REICHSTAG   HISTORIC BUILDING
See p82.

BUNDESKANZLERAMT   NOTABLE BUILDING
Map p328 (Federal Chancellery; Willy-Brandt-Strasse 1; ⊘closed to public; ☐100, ⓤBundestag) The Federal Chancellery, Germany's 'White House', is a sparkling, modern compound designed by Axel Schultes and Charlotte Frank. It consists of two parallel office blocks flanking a central white cube. Eduardo Chillida's rusted-steel *Berlin* sculpture graces the eastern forecourt. The best views of the building are from the Moltkebrücke (bridge) or the northern Spree River promenade.

PAUL-LÖBE-HAUS   NOTABLE BUILDING
Map p328 (www.bundestag.de; Konrad-Adenauer-Strasse; ⊘tours 2pm Sat; ☐100, ⓈHauptbahnhof, ⓤBundestag, Hauptbahnhof) The glass-and-concrete Paul-Löbe-Haus contains offices for the Bundestag's parliamentary committees. It's filled with modern art that can be viewed only during free guided tours (in German) at 2pm on Saturday. Advance online registration is required.

MARIE-ELISABETH-LÜDERS-HAUS   NOTABLE BUILDING
Map p328 (www.bundestag.de; Schiffbauerdamm; ⊘galleries 11am-5pm Tue-Sun; ⓈHauptbahnhof, ⓤBundestag, Hauptbahnhof) FREE Home to the parliamentary library, this recently expanded, extravagant structure has a massive tapered stairway, a flat roofline jutting out like a springboard and giant circular windows. In the basement is an art installation (p90) by Ben Wagin featuring original segments of the Berlin Wall.

Accessible from the Luisenstrasse entrance is the Kunst-Raum, which presents politically infused contemporary art.

STRASSE DES 17 JUNI   STREET
Map p328 (ⓈBrandenburger Tor, ⓤBrandenburger Tor) The broad boulevard bisecting Tiergarten was named Street of 17 June in honour of the victims of the bloodily quashed 1953 workers' uprising in East Berlin. It was originally created in 1697 as a pathway linking two royal palaces, and was paved and expanded into a major thoroughfare in 1799. Hitler converted it to a triumphal road lined with Nazi flags.

SOWJETISCHES EHRENMAL TIERGARTEN   MEMORIAL
Map p328 (Soviet War Memorial; Strasse des 17 Juni; ⊘24hr; ⓈBrandenburger Tor, ⓤBrandenburger Tor) FREE Berlin lay in ruins when this imposing memorial was dedicated in November 1945. It is one of three in the city that honours the 80,000 Soviet soldiers who died in the Battle of Berlin, including the 2000 buried behind its colonnades. The memorial's entrance is flanked by two Russian T-34 tanks, said to have been the first to enter the city.

HAUS DER KULTUREN DER WELT   NOTABLE BUILDING
Map p328 (House of World Cultures; ☎030-3978 7175; www.hkw.de; John-Foster-Dulles-Allee 10; admission varies; ⊘exhibits 11am-7pm Wed-Mon; Ⓟ; ☐100, ⓈHauptbahnhof, ⓤBundestag, Hauptbahnhof) This highly respected cultural centre showcases contemporary non-European art, music, dance, literature, films and theatre, and also serves as a discussion forum on zeitgeist-reflecting issues. The gravity-defying parabolic roof of Hugh Stubbins' extravagant building, designed as the American contribution to a 1957 architectural exhibition, is echoed by Henry Moore's sculpture *Butterfly* in the reflecting pool.

Computerised chime concerts ring out at noon and 6pm daily from the nearby 68-bell carillon, and live concerts take place on Sunday at 3pm from May to September (also at 2pm in December).

DENKMAL FÜR DIE IM NATIONALSOZIALISMUS ERMORDETEN SINTI UND ROMA EUROPAS   MEMORIAL
Map p328 (Memorial to the Sinti & Roma of Europe Murdered under the Nazi Regime; www.stiftung-denkmal.de; Scheidemannstrasse; ⊘24hr; ☐100, ⓈBrandenburger Tor, ⓤBrandenburger Tor) FREE This memorial commemorates the Sinti and Roma victims of the Holocaust

TOP SIGHT
TOPOGRAPHIE DES TERRORS

In the spot where there once stood the most feared institutions of Nazi Germany (including the Gestapo headquarters, the SS leadership and, during the war, the Reich Security Main Office) this compelling exhibit dissects the anatomy of the Nazi state. It discusses the stages of terror and persecution, puts a face on the perpetrators and details the impact these brutal institutions had on all of Europe. From their desks, top Nazi commanders such as Himmler and Heydrich hatched Holocaust plans and organised the systematic persecution of political opponents, many of whom suffered torture and death in the Gestapo prison.

From spring to autumn, another exhibit called 'Berlin 1933–1945: Between Propaganda & Terror' opens in a trench against the glassed-in foundations of the Gestapo prison cells. It looks at how the Nazis were able to turn liberal Berlin into a nexus of their leadership's political power and how life changed for local residents as a result. In addition, a self-guided tour of the historic grounds takes you past 15 information stations with photos, documents and 3D graphics as well as a 200m stretch of the Berlin Wall along Niederkirchner Strasse.

DON'T MISS

➜ Model of the grounds in the foyer
➜ Diagram of the concentration camp system

PRACTICALITIES

➜ Topography of Terror
➜ Map p328, D7
➜ www.topographie.de
➜ Niederkirchner Strasse 8
➜ admission free
➜ ⊙10am-8pm, grounds close at dusk or 8pm at the latest
➜ ▣M41, ⓈPotsdamer Platz, ⓊPotsdamer Platz

HISTORIC MITTE SIGHTS

---

and consists of a circular reflecting pool with a floating stone decorated daily with a fresh flower. On the edge of Tiergarten park, it was designed by Israeli sculptor Dani Karavan and inaugurated in 2012.

DENKMAL FÜR DIE IM NATIONALSOZIALISMUS VERFOLGTEN HOMOSEXUELLEN   MEMORIAL

Map p328 (Memorial to the Homosexuals Persecuted under the Nazi Regime; www.stiftung-denkmal.de; Ebertstrasse; ⊙24hr; ⓈBrandenburger Tor, Potsdamer Platz, ⓊBrandenburger Tor, Potsdamer Platz) FREE Since 2008 this memorial has trained the spotlight on the tremendous suffering of Europe's LGBT community under the Nazis. The freestanding, 4m-high, off-kilter concrete cube was designed by Danish-Norwegian artists Michael Elmgreen and Ingar Dragset. A looped video plays through a warped, narrow window.

⊙ Brandenburger Tor & Unter den Linden

BRANDENBURGER TOR   LANDMARK
See p84.

HOLOCAUST MEMORIAL   MEMORIAL
See p85.

DEUTSCHES HISTORISCHES MUSEUM   MUSEUM
See p86.

PARISER PLATZ   SQUARE
Map p328 (ⓈBrandenburger Tor, ⓊBrandenburger Tor) Lorded over by the landmark Brandenburg Gate (p84), this elegant square was completely flattened in WWII, then spent the Cold War trapped just east of the Berlin Wall. Look around now: the US, French and British embassies, banks and a luxury hotel have returned to their original sites and once again frame the bustling plaza, just as they did during its 19th century heyday.

AKADEMIE DER KÜNSTE – PARISER PLATZ   ARTS CENTRE
Map p328 (Academy of Arts; ☎030-200 571000; www.adk.de; Pariser Platz 4; admission varies; ⊙Bldg 10am-8pm, exhibits vary; ⓈBrandenburger Tor, ⓊBrandenburger Tor) The only building on Pariser Platz with a glass facade, the Academy of Arts was designed by Günter

Behnisch and is the successor of Berlin's oldest cultural institution, the Prussian Academy of Arts, founded in 1696 by Prussian duke Friedrich III (who later became King Friedrich I). It presents a varied program of high-brow readings, lectures, workshops and exhibits, many of them free.

DZ BANK
NOTABLE BUILDING

Map p328 (Pariser Platz 3; ⓢBrandenburger Tor, ⓤBrandenburger Tor) FREE Constrained by rigid building regulations, architect Frank Gehry had to transfer his trademark sculptural approach to the atrium of the Berlin headquarters of the DZ Bank. If the doors are open, pop in to catch a glimpse of the glass-roofed atrium with its expressive free-form sculpture that's actually used as a conference room.

BRANDENBURGER TOR MUSEUM
MUSEUM

Map p328 (⌥030-236 078 436; www.branden burgertor-museum.de; Pariser Platz 4a; admission €5; ⓣhours vary Mon-Fri, 10am-8pm Sat & Sun; ⓢBrandenburger Tor, ⓤBrandenburger Tor) Get the gist of Berlin's history – revolutions,

war, Hitler, Kennedy, the Berlin Wall, reunification – in 20 minutes without opening a book in this whirlwind multimedia show, which features sound effects, historical footage and documents projected onto 87 screens.

ERLEBNIS EUROPA
MUSEUM

Map p328 (Europe Experience; ⌥030-2280 2900; www.erlebnis-europa.de; Unter den Linden 78; ⓣ10am-6pm; ⓢBrandenburger Tor, ⓤBrandenburger Tor) FREE In times when many question the future of the EU, this exhibit works hard to make the case for a united Europe. Funded by the European Commission, you can learn more about each member country, find out how the EU works and what it's like to be a European citizen – in 24 languages. Attend a plenary session of the European Parliament in the 360° cinema or take a selfie and send an electronic postcard from 'Europe'.

SITE OF HITLER'S BUNKER
HISTORIC SITE

Map p328 (cnr In den Ministergärten & Gertrud-Kolmar-Strasse; ⓣ24hr; ⓢBrandenburger Tor,

---

WALL VICTIM MEMORIALS

The Berlin Wall cut right past the Brandenburg Gate and crossed the Spree River behind the Reichstag, which is why there are several memorials here that commemorate those unfortunate souls who died trying to escape across it in search of freedom in the West.

Wall Memorial 'Parlament der Bäume' (Parliament of Trees; Map p328; cnr Schiffbau-erdamm & Adele-Schreiber-Krieger-Strasse; ⓣ24hr; ⓤBundestag) What looks like a post-apocalyptic garden is actually a memorial site created in 1990 by environmental artist Ben Wagin atop a section of the Berlin Wall. The installation centres on 16 trees, each representing a German state (hence the name), which are surrounded by 58 original pieces of the Wall listing the names of 258 people who died trying to escape to the West. It's a poignant and contemplative place, further enhanced by pictures, text and memorial stones.

Mauer Mahnmal im Marie-Elisabeth-Lüders-Haus (Berlin Wall Memorial at the German Bundestag; Map p328; ⌥030-2273 2027; www.mauer-mahnmal.de; Schiffbauerdamm; ⓣ11am-5pm Tue-Sun; ⓠTXL, ⓤBundestag) This memorial installation by artist Ben Wagin runs along the original course of the Berlin Wall and consists of original segments, each painted with a year and the number of people killed at the Wall that year. It's in the basement of the Marie-Elisabeth-Lüders-Haus (p88) and accessible via the Spree Promenade. If doors are closed, you can easily sneak a peak through the window.

Gedenkort Weisse Kreuze (White Crosses Memorial; Map p328; Reichstagufer; ⓠ100, ⓤBundestag) The seven white crosses on the southern Spree bank behind the Reichstag were put there in 1971 by a group of West Germans in memory of the East Germans who died in their attempt to flee to the West.

Peter Fechter Memorial (Map p328; Zimmerstrasse; ⓣ24hr; ⓤKochstrasse) On 17 August 1962, 18-year-old would-be escapee Peter Fechter was shot and wounded by Berlin Wall border guards and then left to bleed to death as the guards looked on. A simple memorial pillar on Zimmerstrasse marks the site where he died.

U Brandenburger Tor) Berlin was burning and Soviet tanks advancing relentlessly when Adolf Hitler killed himself on 30 April 1945, alongside Eva Braun, his long-time female companion, hours after their marriage. Today, a parking lot covers the site, revealing its dark history only via an information panel with a diagram of the vast bunker network, construction data and the site's post-WWII history.

The interior was blown up and sealed off by the Soviets in 1947. The 2004 movie *The Downfall* vividly chronicles Hitler's last days in the Führerbunker.

MADAME TUSSAUDS   MUSEUM
Map p328 (✆01806-545 800; www.madame tussauds.com/berlin; Unter den Linden 74; adult/child €23.50/18.50; ☉10am-6pm Mon-Fri, to 7pm Sat & Sun, last entry 1hr before closing; ☐100, ⑤Brandenburger Tor, UBrandenburger Tor) No celebrity in town to snare your stare? Don't fret: at this legendary wax museum, the world's biggest pop stars, Hollywood legends, sports heroes and historical icons stand still – very still – for you to snap their picture. Sure, it's an expensive haven of kitsch and camp, but where else can you have a candlelit dinner with George Clooney, play piano with Beethoven or time-travel to the '70s with Ziggy Stardust? Avoid queues and save money by buying tickets online.

PALAIS POPULAIRE   GALLERY
Map p328 (www.db-palaispopulaire.de; Unter den Linden 5; ☐100, 200, TXL, UHausvogteiplatz) Contemporary art, culture and sports activities are the focus of this gallery sponsored by Deutsche Bank and set within the updated rooms of a rococo palace built as a residence for Prussian princesses. Readings, workshops, talks and other activities complement the annually changing exhibits. Check the website for hours and admission prices.

HUMBOLDT UNIVERSITÄT ZU BERLIN   NOTABLE BUILDING
Map p328 (✆030-2093 2951; www.hu-berlin.de/en; Unter den Linden 6; ☐100, 200, TXL, UFranzösische Strasse) Marx and Engels studied here, and the Brothers Grimm and Albert Einstein taught here: Humboldt is Berlin's oldest university, founded in 1810 in a palace built by Frederick the Great for his brother Heinrich. Statues of the uni's founder, philosopher Wilhelm von Humboldt, and his

explorer brother Alexander flank the main entrance.

The university had produced 29 Nobel laureates by the 1950s, including Max Planck (physics, 1918) and Albert Einstein (physics, 1921). The last prize went to Werner Forssmann for medicine in 1956. These days, some 32,500 students try to follow this illustrious legacy.

REITERDENKMAL FRIEDRICH DER GROSSE   MONUMENT
Map p328 (Unter den Linden 6; ☐100, 200, TXL, UFranzösische Strasse, Hausvogteiplatz) Seemingly surveying his domain, Frederick the Great cuts a commanding figure on horseback in this famous 1850 monument that kept sculptor Christian Daniel Rauch busy for a dozen years. The plinth is decorated with a parade of German military men, scientists, artists and thinkers.

BEBELPLATZ   SQUARE
Map p328 (☐100, 200, TXL, UHausvogteiplatz) The heart of a cultural centre envisioned by King Frederick the Great, austere Bebelplatz is infamous as the site of the first full-blown public book burning in Nazi Germany. Members of the Nazi German Students' League cheered as works by Brecht, Mann, Marx and others deemed 'subversive' went up in flames on 10 May 1933. Originally called Opernplatz, it was renamed for August Bebel, the co-founder of Germany's Social Democratic Party (SPD), in 1947.

ST HEDWIGS-KATHEDRALE BERLIN   CATHEDRAL
Map p328 (✆030-203 4810; www.hedwigs-kathedrale.de; Hinter der Katholischen Kirche 3; ☉10am-5pm Mon-Wed, Fri & Sat, 11am-5pm Thu, 1-5pm Sun; ☐100, 200, UHausvogteiplatz) FREE This copper-domed church (1773) was commissioned by Frederick the Great, designed by Knobelsdorff, modelled after the Pantheon in Rome and named for the patron saint of Silesia. It was Berlin's first post-Reformation Catholic church and remained the only one until 1854.

Restored after WWII, its circular, modern interior is lidded by a ribbed dome and accented with Gothic sculpture and an altar cross made of gilded and enamel-decorated ivory. In the crypt lie the remains of Bernard Lichtenberg, the parish priest who turned St Hedwig's into a centre of Catholic Nazi resistance. He died en route to the Dachau concentration camp in 1943 and was beatified in 1996.

ALTE BIBLIOTHEK HISTORIC BUILDING

Map p328 (Old Library; Bebelplatz; ☺9am-9.30pm Mon-Fri, to 6pm Sat, 1-6pm Sun; ☐100, 200, TXL, ⓊHausvogteiplatz) Berlin's first library is a baroque beauty commissioned by Frederick the Great to shelter the royal book collection. Completed in 1780, its design mimics the St Michael's Wing of the imperial palace in Vienna. It's commonly known as *Kommode* (chest of drawers) because of its curvaceous facade.

STAATSOPER

UNTER DEN LINDEN HISTORIC BUILDING

Map p328 (✆030-2035 4555; www.staatsoperberlin.de; Bebelplatz; ☐100, 200, TXL, ⓊHausvogteiplatz) Berlin's opulent state opera was commissioned as the royal opera house by Frederick the Great and designed by his friend and master architect Georg Wenzeslaus von Knobelsdorff. It has graced Bebelplatz since 1742 and risen from the ashes three times. After completion of an extensive refurbishment, it's been staging grand operas under the direction of Daniel Barenboim since October 2017.

NEUE WACHE MEMORIAL

Map p328 (New Guardhouse; Unter den Linden 4; ☺10am-6pm; ☐100, 200, TXL) **FREE** This temple-like neoclassical structure (1818) was Karl Friedrich Schinkel's first important Berlin commission. Originally a royal guardhouse and a memorial to the victims of the Napoleonic Wars, Neue Wache is now Germany's central memorial for the victims of war and dictatorship. Its sombre and austere interior is dominated by Käthe Kollwitz' heart-wrenching Pietà-style sculpture of a mother helplessly cradling her dead soldier son.

SCHLOSSBRÜCKE BRIDGE

Map p328 (Palace Bridge; Unter den Linden; ☐100, 200, TXL) Marking the transition from Unter den Linden to Museum Island, the Palace Bridge is considered among Berlin's prettiest. Designed by Karl Friedrich Schinkel in the 1820s, it is decorated with eight marble sculptures depicting the life and death of a warrior. Alas, empty royal coffers kept them from being chiselled until the late 1840s, a few years after the master's death.

◉ Friedrichstrasse & Checkpoint Charlie

TRÄNENPALAST MUSEUM

Map p328 (✆030-4677 77911; www.hdg.de; Reichstagufer 17; ☺9am-7pm Tue-Fri, 10am-6pm Sat & Sun; Ⓢ Friedrichstrasse, ⓊFriedrichstrasse) **FREE** During the Cold War, tears flowed copiously in this glass-and-steel border-crossing pavilion where East Berliners had to bid adieu to family visiting from West Germany – hence its 'Palace of Tears' moniker. The exhibit uses original objects (including the claustrophobic passport control booths and a border auto-firing system), photographs and historical footage to document the division's social impact on the daily lives of Germans on both sides of the border.

FRIEDRICHSTADTPASSAGEN ARCHITECTURE

Map p328 (Friedrichstrasse, btwn Französische Strasse & Mohrenstrasse; ☺10am-8pm Mon-Sat; Ⓟ; ⓊFranzösische Strasse, Stadtmitte) This trio of shopping complexes (called *Quartiere*), built during the post-reunification construction boom years, never really succeeded at triggering the revival of southern Friedrichstrasse into a luxury retail spine and now finds itself partly facing bankruptcy. It's still worth checking out the striking interiors, especially the shimmering glass funnel inside the Jean Nouvel-designed Galeries Lafayette (p98). Next door, Quartier 206 is an art deco–style symphony in coloured marble, while John Chamberlain's crushed-car tower anchors Quartier 205.

ASISI PANORAMA BERLIN GALLERY

Map p328 (✆030-355 5340; www.asisi.de; Friedrichstrasse 205; adult/concession/child €10/8/4; ☺10am-6pm, last entry 5.30pm; ⓊKochstrasse) Artist Yadegar Asisi is famous for creating bafflingly detailed monumental photographic panoramas. In Berlin, the giant 'Die Mauer' next to Checkpoint Charlie transports visitors to the divided city on a random day in the 1980s. Standing on a scaffold in the West, they get to look across the 'death strip' and contemplate what it was like to live in the shadow of barbed wire and guard towers. Sound and light intensify the mood of bleakness and oppression.

BLACKBOX KALTER KRIEG MUSEUM

Map p328 (✆030-216 3571; www.bfgg.de; Friedrichstrasse 47; adult/concession/child under

14 €5/3.50/free; ⊙10am-6pm; Ⓤ Kochstrasse) This small exhibit right by Checkpoint Charlie provides an easily accessible chronicle of the Cold War using photographs, maps, original footage and recordings and various memorabilia. It also explains how the Berlin Wall fitted into the conflict and how proxy wars in Korea and Vietnam fuelled the tension between the US and the Soviet Union.

MAUERMUSEUM MUSEUM

Map p328 (Haus am Checkpoint Charlie; ☑ 030-253 7250; www.mauermuseum.de; Friedrichstrasse 43-45; adult/concession/child €14.50/9.50/7.50, audioguide €5; ⊙9am-10pm; Ⓤ Kochstrasse) The Cold War years, especially the history and horror of the Berlin Wall, are engagingly, if haphazardly, documented in this privately run tourist magnet. Open since 1961, the ageing exhibit is still strong when it comes to telling the stories of escape attempts from East to West. Original devices used in the process, including a hot-air balloon, a one-person submarine and a BMW Isetta, are crowd favourites.

TRABI MUSEUM MUSEUM

Map p328 (☑ 030-3020 1030; www.trabi-museum.com; Zimmerstrasse 14-15; adult/child under 12 €5/free; ⊙10am-6pm; Ⓤ Kochstrasse) If you were lucky enough to own a car in East Germany, it would most likely have been a Trabant (Trabi in short), a tinny two-stroker whose name ('satellite' in English) was inspired by the launch of the Soviet Sputnik in 1956. This small exhibit displays a wide variety of Trabis, including rare wooden and racing versions as well as a campervan model.

MUSEUM FÜR KOMMUNIKATION BERLIN MUSEUM

Map p328 (☑ 030-202 940; www.mfk-berlin.de; Leipziger Strasse 16; adult/concession/child under 17 €5/3/free; ⊙9am-8pm Tue, 9am-5pm Wed-Fri, 10am-6pm Sat & Sun; 🚌200, Ⓤ Mohrenstrasse, Stadtmitte) Three cheeky robots welcome you to this elegant, neo-baroque museum, which takes you on an entertaining romp through the evolution of communication, from smoke signals to smartphones. Admire such rare items as a Blue Mauritius stamp or one of the world's first telephones, test milestones in communication techniques, or ponder the impact of technology on our daily lives.

TOP SIGHT
CHECKPOINT CHARLIE

Checkpoint Charlie was the principal gateway for foreigners and diplomats between the two Berlins from 1961 to 1990. Since it was the third Allied checkpoint to open, it was named 'Charlie' in reference to the third letter in the NATO phonetic alphabet (alfa, bravo, charlie...). The only direct Cold War–era confrontation between the US and the Soviet Union took place at this very spot, when tanks faced off shortly after the Wall went up, nearly triggering a third world war. A simple **plaque** affixed to a pile of sandbags in front of a replica army guardhouse commemorates this tense moment.

Alas, little else indicates Checkpoint Charlie's historical importance, as the site has been allowed to degenerate into a tacky tourist trap. Souvenir shops and fast-food restaurants line Friedrichstrasse and young men dressed as American or Soviet border guards pose with tourists for tips. A rare redeeming aspect is the free **open-air gallery** that uses photos and documents to illustrate milestones in Cold War history, as does the **BlackBox Kalter Krieg**. Although a bit pricey, Yadegar Asisi's **asisi Panorama Berlin** also adds an element of authenticity.

DON'T MISS

➜ Open-air gallery
➜ asisi Panorama Berlin

PRACTICALITIES

➜ Map p328, F6
➜ cnr Zimmerstrasse & Friedrichstrasse
➜ admission free
➜ ⊙24hr
➜ Ⓤ Kochstrasse

DEUTSCHES
CURRYWURST MUSEUM   MUSEUM
Map p328 ([☎]030-8871 8647; www.currywurst museum.com; Schützenstrasse 70; adult/conces-sion/child 6-13yr incl sausage snack €11/8.50/7; [☺]10am-6pm;   [U]Stadtmitte,   Kochstrasse) Bright, fun and interactive, this museum is an ode to Berlin's iconic sausage snack, the *Currywurst*. Sniff out curry secrets in the Spice Chamber, listen to *Currywurst* songs, learn about the wurst's history and watch a movie about one woman's quest for the best *Currywurst*. Tickets include a wurst tast-ing in the snack bar.

MENDELSSOHN AUSSTELLUNG   MUSEUM
Map p328 (Mendelssohn Exhibit; [☎]030-8170 4726; www.jaegerstrasse.de; Jägerstrasse 51; donations welcome; [☺]noon-6pm;   [U]Franzö-sische Strasse, Hausvogteiplatz) [FREE] This exhibit traces the fate and history of the Mendelssohn family, one of Germany's most influential dynasties starting with the *pater familias*, Jewish Enlightenment philosopher Moses Mendelssohn (1729–86). It's located in the counter hall of the private banking house founded by his sons Joseph and Abraham in 1795 on Jägerstrasse, Ber-lin's equivalent of Wall Street. After the Na-zis forced the bank into bankruptcy, many family members fled Germany.

✗̸ EATING

Historic Mitte is awash with swanky restaurants where the decor is fabulous, the crowds cosmopolitan and menus stylish. Sure, some places may be more sizzle than substance, but the see-and-be-seen punters don't seem to mind. The area also has several Michelin-starred restaurants.

✗̸ Government Quarter

DACHGARTENRESTAURANT
KÄFER IM BUNDESTAG   INTERNATIONAL €€€
Map p328 ([☎]030-226 2990; www.feinkost-kaefer. de/berlin; Platz der Republik; mains €24-33; [☺]9am-4.30pm & 6.30pm-midnight; [🚌]100, [U]Bun-destag) While politicians debate treaties and taxes in the plenary hall below, you can enjoy breakfast and hot meals with a regional bent at the restaurant on the Reichstag rooftop. Reservations here also give you direct access

to the landmark glass dome crowning the building; book at least two weeks ahead.

Note that for security reasons, all guests must provide their name and date of birth at least 24 hours in advance.

✗̸ Brandenburger Tor & Unter den Linden

★INDIA CLUB   NORTH INDIAN €€
Map p328 ([☎]030-2062 8610; www.india-club -berlin.com; Behrenstrasse 72; mains €16-27; [☺]6-10.30pm; [✎]; [S]Brandenburger Tor) No need to book a flight to Mumbai or London: au-thentic Indian cuisine has finally landed in Berlin. Thanks to top toque Manish Ba-hukhandi, these curries are like culinary poetry, the chicken tikka perfectly succulent and the stuffed cauliflower an inspiration. The dark mahogany furniture is enlivened by splashes of colour in the plates, the chan-deliers and the servers' uniforms.

EINSTEIN UNTER DEN LINDEN   AUSTRIAN €€
Map p328 ([☎]030-204 3632; www.einstein-udl. com/en; Unter den Linden 42; mains €16-25; [☺]7am-11pm Mon-Fri, from 8am Sat & Sun; [🚌]100, 200, TXL, [S]Brandenburger Tor, Friedichstrasse, [U]Brandenburger Tor, Friedichstrasse) A coffee house with big-city flair, this cosmopolitan spot is great for scanning the power-crowd for famous politicians, artists or actors – discreetly, please – while noshing on Wie-ner Schnitzel, homemade apple strudel and other Austrian fare. Also a good spot for an afternoon break over coffee and divine cakes.

CAFE IM ZEUGHAUS   GERMAN €€
Map p328 ([☎]030-2064 2744; www.kofler kompanie.com; Unter den Linden 2; mains €10-18; [☺]10am-6pm; [🚌]100, 200, TXL, [S]Hackescher Markt, [U]Hausvogteiplatz) Even if history leaves you cold, this cafe inside the Ger-man Historical Museum is a lovely spot for breakfast, cakes, a snack or a full meal, es-pecially in summer when the Spree-facing terrace opens. It's accessible without a mu-seum ticket.

✗̸ Gendarmenmarkt

CHIPPS   VEGETARIAN €
Map p328 ([☎]030-3644 4588; www.chipps.eu; Jägerstrasse 35; mains breakfast €7.50-11.50,

salads €7.50-12.50; ☺9am-11pm Mon-Sat, to 5pm Sun; 🐾📶; Ⓤ Hausvogteiplatz) This crisp corner spot with a show-kitchen and panoramic windows is a great day-time destination, which turns heads with yummy cooked breakfasts (served any time), build-your-own salads and creative hot specials that spin regional, seasonal ingredients into taste-bud magic. Dinners are more elaborate.

AUGUSTINER
AM GENDARMENMARKT   GERMAN €€
Map p328 (📋030-2045 4020; www.augustiner-braeu-berlin.de; Charlottenstrasse 55; mains €7.50-30, lunch special €5.90; ☺10am-2am; Ⓤ Französische Strasse) Tourists, concertgoers and hearty-food lovers rub shoulders at rustic tables in this authentic Bavarian beer hall. Soak up the down-to-earth vibe right along with a mug of full-bodied Augustiner brew straight from Munich. Sausages, roast pork and pretzels provide rib-sticking sustenance with only a token salad offered for non-carnivores. Good-value weekday lunch specials.

GOODTIME   THAI €€
Map p328 (📋030-2007 4870; www.goodtime-berlin.de; Hausvogteiplatz 11; mains €12.50-25; ☺noon-midnight; 📶; Ⓤ Hausvogteiplatz) Sweep on down to this busy dining room with a garden courtyard for fragrant Thai and Indonesian dishes. Creamy curries, succulent shrimp or roast duck all taste flavourful and fresh, if a bit easy on the heat to accommodate German stomachs. If you like it hot, order Api Sapi (aka 'beef in hell').

BORCHARDT   FRENCH €€€
Map p328 (📋030-8188 6262; www.borchardt-restaurant.de; Französische Strasse 47; dinner mains €20-40; ☺11.30am-midnight; Ⓤ Französische Strasse) Jagger, Clooney and Redford are among the celebs who have tucked into dry-aged steaks and plump oysters in the marble-pillared dining hall of this Berlin institution, established in 1853 by a caterer to the Kaiser. No dish, however, moves as fast as the Wiener Schnitzel, a wafer-thin slice of breaded veal fried to crisp perfection.

✖ Friedrichstrasse & Checkpoint Charlie

ISHIN   JAPANESE €
Map p328 (📋030-2067 4829; www.ishin.de; Mittelstrasse 24; sushi platter €8.50-21, bowl €5.60-

12.20; ☺11.30am-9.30pm Mon-Fri, from noon Sat; Ⓢ Friedrichstrasse, Ⓤ Friedrichstrasse) The ambience is a bit ho-hum but who cares when the sushi is super-fresh, the rice bowls generously topped with fish or meat, and a cup of green tea comes free. Prices drop during happy hour (all day Wednesday and Saturday, and until 4pm on other days).

CHA CHĀ   THAI €
Map p328 (📋030-206 259 613; www.eatcha cha.com; Friedrichstrasse 63; mains €8-11; ☺11.30am-10pm Mon-Fri, noon-10pm Sat, 12.30-8.30pm Sun; 🐾📶; Ⓤ Stadtmitte) Feeling worn out from sightseeing or power-shopping? No problem: a helping of massaman beef curry should quickly return you to top form – according to the menu of this Thai nosh spot, the dish has an 'activating' effect. In fact, all menu items are described as having a 'positive eating' benefit, be it vitalising, soothing or stimulating.

BERLINER REPUBLIK   GASTROPUB €€
Map p328 (📋030-3087 2293; www.die-berliner-republik.de; Schiffbauerdamm 8; mains €8-22; ☺10am-5am; 📶; Ⓢ Friedrichstrasse, Ⓤ Friedrichstrasse) Just as in a mini stock exchange, the price of beer (18 varieties on tap!) fluctuates with demand after 5pm at this tourist-geared riverside pub. Everyone goes Pavlovian when a heavy brass bell rings, signalling rock-bottom prices. In summer, seats on the terrace are the most coveted. A full menu of home-style Berlin and German fare provides sustenance.

★ COOKIES CREAM   VEGETARIAN €€€
Map p328 (📋030-2749 2940; www.cookies cream.com; Behrenstrasse 55; mains €25, 3-/4-course menu €49/59; ☺6pm-midnight Tue-Sat; 📶; Ⓤ Französische Strasse) In 2017, this perennial local favourite became Berlin's first flesh-free restaurant to enter the Michelin pantheon, on its 10th anniversary no less. Its industrial look and clandestine location are as unorthodox as the compositions of head chef Stephan Hentschel. The entrance is off the service alley of the Westin Grand Hotel (past the chandelier, ring the bell).

RESTAURANT TIM RAUE   ASIAN €€€
Map p328 (📋030-2593 7930; www.tim-raue.com; Rudi-Dutschke-Strasse 26; 3-/4-course lunch €58/68, 8-course dinner €198, mains €48-66; ☺noon-3pm & 7pm-midnight Wed-Sat; Ⓤ Kochstrasse) Now here's a double-Michelin-starred

restaurant we can get our mind around. Unstuffy ambience and a stylishly reduced design with walnut and Vitra chairs perfectly juxtapose with Berlin-born Tim Raue's brilliant Asian-inspired plates, which each shine the spotlight on a few choice ingredients. His interpretation of Peking duck is a perennial bestseller.

CRACKERS INTERNATIONAL €€€

Map p328 (☑030-680 730 488; www.crackers berlin.com; Friedrichstrasse 158; mains €18-34; ⊘6.30pm-1am; ⓤFranzösische Strasse) With Crackers, Berlin nightlife impresario Heinz 'Cookie' Gindullis transformed his former nightclub, Cookies, into a cosmopolitan gastro-cathedral with a ceiling as lofty as the food. Enter through the kitchen to arrive in a seductively lit space, where head chef Stephan Hentschel regales patrons with the likes of Charolais beef entrecôte and Icelandic cod. On weekends, DJs heat up the vibe.

It's also a good place to pop in for late-night cocktails.

NOBELHART & SCHMUTZIG INTERNATIONAL €€€

Map p328 (☑030-2594 0610; www.nobelhartund schmutzig.com; Friedrichstrasse 218; 10-course menu Tue & Wed €95, Thu-Sat €120; ⊘6.30pm-midnight Tue-Sat; ⓤKochstrasse) 'Brutally local' is the motto at the Michelin-starred restaurant of star sommelier Billy Wagner. All ingredients hail – without exception – from producers in and around Berlin and the nearby Baltic Sea – hence, no pepper or lemons. The seating and service quite literally break down boundaries, as guests are seated along the kitchen counter to observe staff fussing over their 10-course dinner.

🍷 DRINKING & NIGHTLIFE
🍸

Since Historic Mitte isn't a residential area, bars and nightlife cater mostly to visitors and are often confined to the hotels. Notable exceptions are a few riverside haunts along Schiffbauerdamm, off Friedrichstrasse, which are also popular with the local post-theatre crowd.

ROOFTOP TERRACE BAR

Map p328 (☑030-460 6090; www.roccoforte hotels.com; Behrenstrasse 37, Hotel de Rome;

⊘3-11pm Mon-Fri, from noon Sat & Sun May-Sep, weather permitting; ☎; ☐100, 200, TXL, ⓤHausvogteiplatz) A hushed, refined ambience reigns at the rooftop bar of the exclusive Hotel de Rome (p242), where you can keep an eye on the Fernsehturm (TV Tower), historic landmarks and the construction projects along Unter den Linden. It's a chill spot for an afternoon coffee, a glass of homemade ginger lemonade or sunset cocktails with bar snacks.

BRICKS CLUB

Map p328 (☑0174 282 8000; www.bricks-berlin. club; Mohrenstrasse 30; ⊘11pm-6am Thu-Sat; ☎; ⓤStadtmitte) This Hilton-based party boîte holds up the hip-hop and house tradition in techno-centric Berlin. A cosmopolitan vibe lures cashed-up, dressed-up weekend warriors to the glamour-industrial basement space with three dance floors, two bars and a 400-speaker sound ceiling. VIP tables with bottle service may be reserved.

BAR TAUSEND BAR

Map p328 (www.tausendberlin.com; Schiffbauerdamm 11; ⊘7.30pm-late Tue-Sat; ⑤Friedrichstrasse, ⓤFriedrichstrasse) No sign, no light, no bell; just an anonymous steel door tucked under a railway bridge leads to one of Berlin's chicest clandestine bars. The tunnel-shaped space is clad in mirrors and bookended by a dance floor and a giant light fixture resembling an eye. DJs and bands fuel the glam vibe nightly. Selective door.

⭐ ENTERTAINMENT

STAATSOPER BERLIN OPERA

Map p328 (☑030-2035 4554; www.staatsoper-berlin.de; Unter den Linden 7; tickets €12-250; ☐100, 200, TXL, ⓤFranzösische Strasse) After a seven-year exile, Berlin's most famous opera company once again performs at the neoclassical Staatsoper Unter den Linden, which emerged from a massive refurbishment in 2017. Its repertory includes works from four centuries along with concerts and classical and modern ballet, all under the musical leadership of Daniel Barenboim.

KOMISCHE OPER OPERA

Map p328 (Comic Opera; ☑tickets 030-4799 7400; www.komische-oper-berlin.de; Behrenstrasse 55-57; tickets €12-90; ⊘box office 11am-7pm Mon-Sat, 1-4pm Sun; ☐100, 200, TXL, ⓤFranzösische

Strasse) The smallest among Berlin's trio of opera houses is also its least stuffy, even if its flashy neo-baroque auditorium might suggest otherwise. Productions are innovative and unconventional – yet top quality – and often reinterpret classic (and sometimes obscure) pieces in zeitgeist-capturing ways. Seats feature an ingenious subtitling system in English, Turkish and other languages.

KONZERTHAUS BERLIN   CLASSICAL MUSIC

Map p328 (✆tickets 030-203 092 101; www.kon zerthaus.de; Gendarmenmarkt 2; tickets €15-85; Ⓤ Stadtmitte, Französische Strasse) This lovely classical music venue – a Schinkel design from 1821 – counts the top-ranked Konzerthausorchester Berlin as its 'house band', but also hosts visiting soloists and orchestras in three venues. For a sightseeing break, check the schedule for weekly one-hour lunchtime 'Espresso Concerts' costing a mere €8.

PIERRE BOULEZ SAAL   CONCERT VENUE

Map p328 (✆tickets 030-4799 7411; www. boulezsaal.de; Französische Strasse 33d; tickets €10-65; 🚌100, 200, TXL, 147, Ⓤ Hausvogteiplatz, Stadtmitte) Open since 2017, this intimate concert hall was designed by Frank Gehry and conceived by Daniel Barenboim as a venue to promote dialogue between cultures through music. The musical line-up spans the arc from classical to jazz, electronic to Arab music, performed by top international artists, students of the affiliated Barenboim-Said Academy as well as the Boulez Ensemble.

GORKI   THEATRE

Map p328 (✆030-2022 1115; www.gorki.de; Am Festungsgraben 2; tickets €10-34; 🚌100, 200, TXL, 🚋M1, 12, Ⓢ Friedrichstrasse, Ⓤ Friedrichstrasse) Artistic co-directors Shermin Langhoff and Jens Hillje have made the smallest of Berlin's four state-funded theatres the dedicated home of what Langhoff has called 'postmigrant theatre'. The multiracial ensemble cast puts on classic and original productions that examine such issues as integration, identity, transition and discrimination. All performances have English subtitles.

TIPI AM KANZLERAMT   CABARET

Map p328 (✆tickets 030-3906 6550; www. tipi-am-kanzleramt.de; Grosse Querallee; tickets €30-50; 🚌100, Ⓢ Hauptbahnhof, Ⓤ Bundestag) Tipi stages a year-round program of professional cabaret, dance, acrobatics, musical comedy and magic shows starring German and international artists. It's all presented in a festively decorated, cabaret-style tent, set up on the edge of Tiergarten park. Preshow dinner is available.

HOCHSCHULE FÜR
MUSIK HANNS EISLER   CLASSICAL MUSIC

Map p328 (✆tickets 030-203 092 101; www.hfm-berlin.de; Charlottenstrasse 55; Ⓤ Stadtmitte, Französische Strasse) The gifted students at Berlin's top-rated music academy stage as many as 400 performances annually, many of them in the **Neuer Marstall** (New Royal Stables; Map p332; Schlossplatz 7; 🚌100, 200, TXL, Ⓤ Hausvogteiplatz), where the Prussian royals once kept their coaches and horses. Many concerts are free or low cost. See the website for the full schedule.

ADMIRALSPALAST   PERFORMING ARTS

Map p328 (✆tickets 030-2250 7000; www. admiralspalast.de; Friedrichstrasse 101; 🚋M1, Ⓢ Friedrichstrasse, Ⓤ Friedrichstrasse) This beautifully restored 1920s 'palace' stages crowd-pleasing musicals and concerts in its glamorous historic grand hall. More intimate programs like readings or comedy shows are presented at the smaller F101 theatre on the 3rd floor or the Studio on the 4th floor. Many performances are suitable for non-German speakers, but do check ahead. Ticket prices vary.

🛍 SHOPPING

There are some souvenir shops along Unter den Linden and around Checkpoint Charlie, but for fancy fashion and accessories, make a beeline for Friedrichstrasse with its high-end boutiques, the Friedrichstadtpassagen (p92) malls and Galeries Lafayette.

★ DUSSMANN – DAS
KULTURKAUFHAUS   BOOKS

Map p328 (✆030-2025 1111; www.kulturkauf haus.de; Friedrichstrasse 90; ⊙9am-11.30pm Mon-Sat; 🕿; Ⓢ Friedrichstrasse, Ⓤ Friedrichstrasse) It's easy to lose track of time in this cultural playground with wall-to-wall books (including an extensive English section), DVDs and CDs, leaving no genre unaccounted for. Bonus points for the downstairs cafe, the vertical garden, and the performance space used for free concerts, political discussions and high-profile book readings and signings.

★**FRAU TONIS PARFUM** PERFUME
Map p328 (📞030-2021 5310; www.frau-tonis-parfum.com; Zimmerstrasse 13; ⊙10am-6pm Mon-Sat; Ⓤ Kochstrasse) Follow your nose to this scent-sational made-in-Berlin perfume boutique, where a 'scent test' reveals if you're the floral, fruity, woody or oriental type to help you choose a matching fragrance. Bestsellers include the fresh and light 'Berlin Summer'. Individualists can have their own customised blend created in a one-hour session (€125, including 50ml eau de parfum; reservations advised).

RAUSCH SCHOKOLADENHAUS CHOCOLATE
Map p328 (📞030-757 880; www.rausch.de; Charlottenstrasse 60; ⊙10am-8pm Mon-Sat, from 11am Sun; Ⓤ Stadtmitte) If the Aztecs regarded chocolate as the elixir of the gods, then this emporium of truffles and pralines must be heaven. The shop features Instaworthy replicas of Berlin landmarks such as the Brandenburg Gate and Fernsehturm (TV Tower), while the upstairs cafe-restaurant delivers views of Gendarmenmarkt along with sinful drinking chocolates and artsy handmade cakes and *tartes*.

GALERIES LAFAYETTE DEPARTMENT STORE
Map p328 (📞030-209 480; www.galeriesla fayette.de; Friedrichstrasse 76-78; ⊙10am-8pm Mon-Sat; Ⓤ Französische Strasse) Stop by the Berlin branch of the exquisite French fashion emporium if only to check out the show-stealing interior (designed by Jean Nouvel, no less), centred on a huge glass cone shimmering with kaleidoscopic intensity. Around it wrap three circular floors filled with fancy fashions, fragrances and accessories, while glorious gourmet treats await in the basement food hall.

RITTER SPORT
BUNTE SCHOKOWELT CHOCOLATE
Map p328 (📞030-2009 5080; www.ritter-sport. de; Französische Strasse 24; ⊙10am-7pm Mon-Wed, to 8pm Thu-Sat, to 6pm Sun; 👶; Ⓤ Französische Strasse) Fans of Ritter Sport's colourful square chocolate bars can pick up limited edition, organic, vegan and diet varieties in addition to all the classics at this flagship store. Upstairs, a free exhibit explains the journey from cocoa bean to finished product, but kids are more enchanted by the chocolate kitchen, where staff create your own personalised bars.

VIELFACH – DAS
KREATIVKAUFHAUS GIFTS & SOUVENIRS
Map p328 (📞030-9148 4678; www.fachmiete. de; Zimmerstrasse 11; ⊙11am-7pm Mon-Fri, to 4pm Sat; Ⓤ Kochstrasse) Pick up unique gifts or souvenirs handmade in Germany at this store where artists and craftspeople can rent shelf space to display beauty products, stuffed animals, bags, ceramics, photographs and lots of other pretty things. The store occupies a beautifully renovated listed building near Checkpoint Charlie.

ANTIK- UND BUCHMARKT
AM BODEMUSEUM MARKET
Map p328 (www.antik-buchmarkt.de; Am Kupfergraben; ⊙11am-5pm Sat & Sun; 🚌M1, 12, Ⓢ Hackescher Markt, Ⓤ Hackescher Markt) This book and collectibles market has about 60 vendors in a gorgeous setting with Museum Island as a backdrop. Bookworms have plenty of boxes to sift through, alongside a smattering of furniture, toys, coins, bric-a-brac and old photographs.

🏃 SPORTS & ACTIVITIES

TRABI SAFARI DRIVING
Map p328 (📞030-3020 1030; www.trabi-safari. de; Zimmerstrasse 97; adult/child under 17 from €49/free; Ⓤ Kochstrasse) Catch the *Good Bye, Lenin!* vibe on tours of Berlin with you driving or riding as a passenger in a convoy of GDR-made Trabant (Trabi) cars, with live commentary (in English by prior arrangement) in your vehicle. The 'compact' tour lasts 1¼ hours, the 'XXL' tour 2¼ hours; both travel to both eastern and western Berlin.

To experience Berlin from the American perspective, check out the company's Mustang Safaris (www.mustang-safari.de).

WELTBALLON BERLIN BALLOONING
Map p328 (📞030-5321 5321; www.air-service -berlin.de; Zimmerstrasse 95; adult/concession/ child 3-10yr €23/18/10; ⊙10am-10pm Apr-Sep; Ⓤ Kochstrasse) Drift up but not away for about 15 minutes aboard this helium-filled balloon, which remains tethered to the ground as it lifts you noiselessly 150m into the air for panoramas of the historic city centre. Your pilot will help you pinpoint all the key sights. Confirm ahead as flights are cancelled in poor weather conditions. Up to 30 people fit onto the enclosed platform.

Museumsinsel & Alexanderplatz

ALEXANDERPLATZ | HUMBOLDT-FORUM & NIKOLAIVIERTEL

Neighbourhood Top Five

1 Pergamonmuseum (p104) Time-travelling through ancient Greece and Babylon to the Middle East at this glorious museum.

2 Neues Museum (p106) Making a date with Nefertiti and her royal entourage at this stunningly rebuilt repository.

3 Berlin by Boat (p115) Letting the sights drift by while enjoying cold drinks on the deck of a Spree River tour boat.

4 DDR Museum (p113) Dipping behind the Iron Curtain at this interactive exhibit.

5 Fernsehturm (p111) Getting high on the knockout views from the top of Germany's tallest structure.

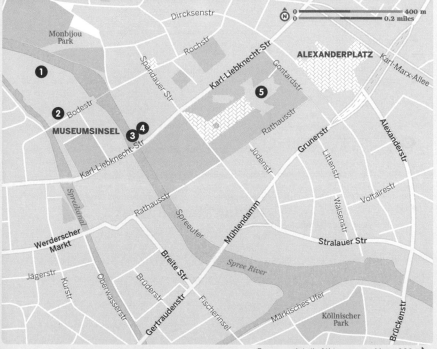

For more detail of this area see Map p332 ➡

Lonely Planet's Top Tip

It would take superhuman stamina to visit all five museums on Museumsinsel in one day, so don't even try; concentrate your energy on those that interest you most. Skip the worst crowds by arriving first thing in the morning, at lunchtime, late in the afternoon or on Thursdays, when all museums stay open until 8pm.

✕ Best Places to Eat

➡ Ishin (p117)

➡ Brauhaus Georgbräu (p118)

➡ Zur Letzten Instanz (p118)

➡ Dolores (p117)

For reviews, see p117.➡

🍷 Best Places to Drink

➡ Braufactum Berlin (p119)

➡ House of Weekend (p119)

➡ Club Avenue (p119)

➡ Golden Gate (p119)

For reviews, see p118.➡

◉ Best Non-Museum Sights

➡ Berliner Dom (p113)

➡ Fernsehturm (p111)

➡ St Marienkirche (p112)

➡ Nikolaiviertel (p114)

For reviews, see p112.➡

Explore Museumsinsel & Alexanderplatz

This historic area packs most of eastern Berlin's trophy sights into a compact frame and is best explored on foot. A good place to start is on vast and amorphous Alexanderplatz, a mainstream shopping hub and home to Germany's most prominent landmark, the 368m-high Fernsehturm (TV Tower; p111). In clear weather, take the lift to the viewing platform to get your bearings.

The open area west of the Fernsehturm links up with the Nikolaiviertel (p114), Berlin's medieval birthplace, which was first torn down, then rebuilt by the East German government. The surrealism of this pseudo-quaint quarter can be a hoot, but don't expect to find too many Berliners patronising the pricey cafes and souvenir shops.

Better save your energy for the stunning treasures of the five museums on Museumsinsel (p101) (Museum Island). If you only have time for one or two, focus on the Pergamonmuseum (p104) with its monumental antiquities or the Egyptian collection at the Neues Museum (p106). For more recent – and local – history, take a spin around the DDR Museum (p113), which playfully captures the contradictions of daily life in East Germany.

If you need a break, relax during a one-hour boat ride (p115) through the historic centre, or hang out on the Lustgarten lawn in front of the Berliner Dom (p113) with a view of the Humboldt Forum (p114), a cultural centre built to look like the historic Prussian city palace.

Local Life

Late-night openings The best time to see the Museumsinsel collections without the crowds is on Thursday evening, when all five museums stay open until 8pm.

Shopping Big shopping centres are scarce in central Berlin, which probably explains the enormous local popularity of the Alexa (p119) megamall.

Drinks with a view There are few better places for summertime sunset cocktails than the rooftop terrace of the House of Weekend (p119) club.

Getting There & Away

Bus M48 and 200 link Alexanderplatz with Potsdamer Platz; bus 247 goes to the Nikolaiviertel.

S-Bahn S5, S7 and S75 all converge at Alexanderplatz.

Tram M4, M5 and M6 connect Alexanderplatz with Marienkirche and Hackescher Markt.

U-Bahn U2, U5 and U8 stop at Alexanderplatz. Other main stops are Klosterstrasse and Märkisches Museum (U2) and Jannowitzbrücke (U8).

TOP SIGHT
MUSEUMSINSEL

Walk through ancient Babylon, meet an Egyptian queen or be mesmerised by Monet's landscapes. Welcome to Museumsinsel, Berlin's famous treasure trove of 6000 years' worth of art, artefacts, sculpture and architecture from Europe and beyond. Spread across five grand museums built between 1830 and 1930, the complex covers the northern half of the Spree Island where Berlin's settlement began in the 13th century.

DON'T MISS

➡ Ishtar Gate
➡ Bust of Nefertiti
➡ Berliner Goldhut
➡ *Praying Boy*
➡ Sculpture by Tilman Riemenschneider
➡ Paintings by Caspar David Friedrich

PRACTICALITIES

➡ Map p332, A3
➡ ☎030-266 424 242
➡ www.smb.museum
➡ day tickets for all 5 museums adult/concession/under 18 €18/9/free
➡ ⊙varies by museum
➡ 🚌100, 200, TXL, ⓢHackescher Markt, Friedrichstrasse, ⓤFriedrichstrasse

Berlin's Louvre

The first repository to open was the **Altes Museum** (Old Museum), completed in 1830 next to the Berlin Cathedral and the Lustgarten park. Today it presents Greek, Etruscan and Roman antiquities. Behind it, the **Neues Museum** (New Museum) showcases the Egyptian collection, most famously the bust of Queen Nefertiti, and also houses the Museum of Pre- and Early History. The temple-like **Alte Nationalgalerie** (Old National Gallery) trains the focus on 19th-century European art. The island's top draw is the **Pergamonmuseum**, with its monumental architecture from ancient worlds, including the namesake Pergamon Altar. The **Bode-Museum**, at the island's northern tip, is famous for its medieval sculptures.

Museumsinsel Masterplan

In 1999 the Museumsinsel repositories collectively became a Unesco World Heritage Site. The distinction was at least partly achieved because of a master plan for the renovation and modernisation of the complex, which is expected to be completed in 2026 under the aegis of British architect David Chipperfield. Except for the Pergamon, whose exhibits are currently being reorganised, the restoration of the museums themselves has been completed. Construction is also under way

Museumsinsel

A HALF-DAY TOUR

Navigating around this five-museum treasure repository can be daunting, so we've created this itinerary to help you find the must-see highlights while maximising your time and energy. You'll need at least four hours and a Museumsinsel ticket for entry to all museums.

Start in the Altes Museum where you can admire the roll call of antique gods guarded by a perky bronze statue called the **1 Praying Boy**, the poster child of a prized collection of antiquities. Next up, head to the Neues Museum for your audience with **2 Queen Nefertiti**, the star of the Egyptian collection atop the grand central staircase.

One more floor up, don't miss the dazzling Bronze Age **3 Berliner Goldhut** (room 305). Leaving the Neues Museum, turn left for the Pergamonmuseum. With the namesake altar off limits until at least 2023, the first major sight you'll see is the **4 Ishtar Gate**. Upstairs, pick your way through the Islamic collection, past carpets, prayer niches and a caliph's palace facade to the intricately painted **5 Aleppo Room**.

Jump ahead to the 19th century at the Alte Nationalgalerie to zero in on paintings by **6 Caspar David Friedrich** on the 3rd floor and precious sculptures such as Schadow's **7 Statue of Two Princesses** on the first floor. Wrap up your explorations at the Bode-Museum, reached in a five-minute walk. Admire the foyer with its equestrian statue of Friedrich Wilhelm, then feast your eyes on European sculpture without missing masterpieces by **8 Tilman Riemenschneider**.

FAST FACTS

Oldest object 700,000-year-old Paleolithic hand axe at Neues Museum

Newest object A piece of barbed wire from the Berlin Wall at Neues Museum

Oldest museum Altes Museum, 1830

Most popular museum on Museumsinsel Neues Museum (777,000 visitors)

Total Museumsinsel visitors (2017) 2.33 million

Sculptures by Tilman Riemenschneider (Bode-Museum)
Dazzling detail and great emotional expressiveness characterise the wooden sculptures by late-Gothic master carver Tilman Riemenschneider, as in his portrayal of *St Anne and Her Three Husbands* from around 1510.

Bust of Queen Nefertiti (Room 210, Neues Museum)
In the north dome, fall in love with Berlin's most beautiful woman – the 3330-year-old Egyptian queen Nefertiti, she of the long graceful neck and timeless good looks – despite the odd wrinkle and a missing eye.

VLADIMIR WRANGEL/SHUTTERSTOCK ©

Aleppo Room (Room 16, Pergamonmuseum)

A highlight of the Museum of Islamic Art, this richly painted, wood-panelled reception room from a Christian merchant's home in 17th-century Aleppo, Syria, combines Islamic floral and geometric motifs with courtly scenes and Christian themes.

Ishtar Gate (Room 9, Pergamonmuseum)

Draw breath as you enter the 2600-year-old city gate to Babylon, which has soaring walls sheathed in radiant blue-glazed bricks and adorned with ochre reliefs of strutting lions, bulls and dragons representing Babylonian gods.

Spree River

Pergamonmuseum

5
4
6

Alte Nationalgalerie

7

Entrance

2

Entrance

Entrance

Neues Museum

3

Bodestrasse

1

Altes Museum

Entrance

Berliner Dom

Lustgarten

Paintings by Caspar David Friedrich (Top Floor, Alte Nationalgalerie)

A key artist of the romantic period, Caspar David Friedrich put his own stamp on landscape painting with his dark, moody and subtly dramatic meditations on the boundaries of human life versus the infinity of nature.

Statue of Two Princesses (1st Floor, Alte Nationalgalerie)

Johann Gottfried Schadow captures Prussian princesses (and sisters) Luise and Friederike in a moment of intimacy and thoughtfulness in this double marble statue created in 1795 at the height of the neoclassical period.

Berliner Goldhut (Room 305, Neues Museum)

Marvel at the Bronze Age artistry of the Berlin Gold Hat, a ceremonial gold cone embossed with ornamental bands believed to have been used in predicting the best times for planting and harvesting.

Praying Boy (Room 5, Altes Museum)

The top draw at the Old Museum is the *Praying Boy*, ancient Greece's 'Next Top Model'. The life-size bronze statue of a young male nude is the epitome of physical perfection and was cast around 300 BC in Rhodes.

TOP TIPS

➡ Avoid culture fatigue by focusing on just two of the five museums in a single day.

➡ If you plan on visiting more than one museum, save money by buying the Museumsinsel ticket (€18, concession €9), good for one-day admission to all five museums.

➡ Admission is free for those under 18.

➡ Arrive early or late on weekdays, or skip the queues by purchasing your ticket online.

➡ Make use of the excellent multilanguage audioguides included in the admission price.

➡ In good weather, the lawns of the Lustgarten, outside the Altes Museum, are an inviting spot to chill.

Pergamon was the capital of the Kingdom of Pergamon, which reigned over vast stretches of the eastern Mediterranean in the 3rd and 2nd centuries BC. Inspired by Athens, its rulers, the Attalids, turned their royal residence into a major cultural and intellectual centre. Draped over a 330m-high ridge were grand palaces, a library, a theatre and glorious temples dedicated to Trajan, Dionysus and Athena.

on the colonnaded **James-Simon-Galerie**, the new entrance building named for an early-20th-century German-Jewish patron and philanthropist. Expected to open in 2019, the building will serve as the central visitors centre with ticket desks, a cafe, a shop and direct access to the Pergamonmuseum and the Neues Museum. It will also lead to the 'Archaeological Promenade', a subterranean walkway set to link the Altes Museum with the Bode-Museum in the north. For details see www.museumsinsel-berlin.de.

Pergamonmuseum

The **Pergamonmuseum** (Map p332; ☎030-266 424 242; www.smb.museum; Bodestrasse 1-3; adult/concession/ under 18yr €12/6/free; ☉10am-6pm Fri-Wed, to 8pm Thu) opens a fascinating window on to the ancient world. Completed in 1930, the palatial three-wing complex presents a rich feast of classical sculpture and monumental architecture from Greece, Rome, Babylon and the Middle East in three collections: the Collection of Classical Antiquities, the Museum of the Ancient Near East and the Museum of Islamic Art. Most of the pieces were excavated and spirited to Berlin by German archaeologists around the turn of the 20th century.

The Pergamonmuseum is the fourth treasure chest on Museumsinsel to undergo extensive, restoration work that will leave some sections closed for years. The north wing and the hall containing the namesake Pergamon Altar will be off limits until 2023. During the second phase, the south wing will be closed and a fourth wing facing the Spree River will be constructed so that in future all parts of the museum can be experienced on a continuous walk.

During the revamp, the museum entrance is off Bodestrasse, behind the Neues Museum.

Antikensammlung

The Antikensammlung (Collection of Classical Antiquities) presents artworks from ancient Greece and Rome here and at the Altes Museum. Since the Pergamon Altar is closed to the public until 2023, the main sight is now the 2nd-century AD **Market Gate of Miletus**. Merchants and customers once flooded through the splendid 17m-high gate into the bustling market square of this wealthy Roman trading town in modern-day Turkey. A strong earthquake levelled much of the town in the early Middle Ages, but German archaeologists dug up the site between 1903 and 1905 and managed to put the puzzle back together. The richly decorated marble gate blends Greek and Roman design features and is the world's single largest monument ever to be reassembled in a museum.

Also from Miletus is a beautifully restored **floor mosaic** starring Orpheus, from ancient Greek mythology, whose lyre-playing charmed even the beasts surrounding him. It originally graced the dining room of a 2nd-century Roman villa.

Vorderasiatisches Museum

Step through the Gate of Miletus and travel back 800 years to yet another culture and civilisation: Babylon during the reign of King Nebuchadnezzar II (604–562 BC). You're now in the Museum of the Ancient Near East, where it's impossible not to be awed by the magnificence of the **Ishtar Gate**, the **Processional Way** leading to it and the facade of the **king's throne hall**. All are sheathed in radiant blue glazed bricks and adorned with ochre reliefs of strutting lions, bulls and dragons representing Babylonian gods. They're so striking, you can almost hear the roaring and fanfare as the procession rolls into town.

Other treasures from the collection include the colossal statue of the weather god Hadad (775 BC, room 2) from Syria and the nearly 5000-year-old cone mosaic temple facade from Uruk (room 5).

Museum fur Islamische Kunst

Top billing in the Museum of Islamic Art upstairs belongs to the facade from the **Caliph's Palace of Mshatta** (8th century, room 9) in today's Jordan, which was a gift to Kaiser Wilhelm II from the Ottoman Sultan Abdul Hamid II. A masterpiece of early Islamic art, it depicts animals and mythical creatures frolicking peacefully amid a riot of floral motifs in an allusion to the Garden of Eden.

Other rooms feature fabulous ceramics, carvings, glasses and other artistic objects as well as the brightly turquoise 11th-century **prayer niche** from a mosque in Konya, Turkey, and an intricately patterned cedar-and-poplar **ceiling dome** from the Alhambra in Spain's Granada.

Capping a tour of the museum is the **Aleppo Room** (room 16). Guests arriving in this richly painted, wood-panelled reception room would have had no doubt as to the wealth and power of its owner, a Christian merchant in 17th-century Aleppo, Syria. The paintings depict both Christian themes and courtly scenes like those portrayed in Persian book illustrations, suggesting a high level of religious tolerance.

....

PERGAMONMUSEUM

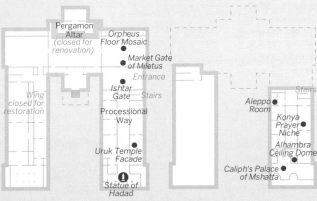

Ground Floor   Upper Floor

TAKE A BREAK

Allegretto (Map p332; ☑030-2804 2307; www.allegretto-neuesmuseum.de; Neues Museum, Bodestrasse 1; dishes €3-10; ☺10am-6pm Fri-Wed, to 8pm Thu; ☑100, 200, TXL, ⑤Hackescher Markt) at the Neues Museum serves salads, Arabic dishes and soups, plus coffee and homemade cakes.

The Pergamonmuseum was purposebuilt between 1910 and 1930 to house the massive volume of ancient art and scientists treasure excavated by German scientists at such sites as Babylon, Assur, Uruk and Miletus. Designed by Alfred Messel, the building was constructed by his close friend Ludwig Hoffmann following Messel's death, and was later badly pummelled in WWII. Lots of objects were whisked to the Soviet Union as war booty but many were returned in 1958.

In summer, head to Strandbar Mitte (p150) for alfresco refreshments and pizza with a view of Museumsinsel across the Spree River.

Neues Museum

Asisi Panorama

While the Pergamon Altar will be closed for restoration until at least 2023, visitors will still be able to grasp its impressive beauty in a temporary exhibit that will present masterpieces excavated at Pergamon with a 360° panorama by Iranian artist and architect Yadegar Asisi. Doors to a purpose-built rotunda opposite the Bode-Museum will be open to the public from summer 2018. The panorama is an updated version of a similar project erected outside the Pergamon Museum in 2011/12 and presents a vision of the city in AD 129. On display will be 80 original sculptures from the site, including a colossal head of Heracles and a big piece from the famous Telephos frieze.

Neues Museum

David Chipperfield's reconstruction of the bombed-out **Neues Museum** (New Museum; Map p332; ☑030-266 424 242; www.smb.museum; Bodestrasse 1-3; adult/concession/under 18yr €12/6/free; ☺10am-6pm Fri-Wed, to 8pm Thu) is the residence of Queen Nefertiti, the showstopper of the **Ägyptisches Museum** (Egyptian Museum) alongside the equally enthralling **Museum für Vor- und Frühgeschichte** (Museum of Pre- and Early History). As if piecing together a giant jigsaw puzzle, the British architect incorporated every original shard, scrap and brick he could find into the new building. This brilliant blend of the historic and modern creates a dynamic space that beautifully juxtaposes massive stairwells and domed rooms with muralled halls and high ceilings.

Museum tickets are only valid for admission during a designated half-hour time slot. Skip the queue by buying advance tickets online.

Ägyptisches Museum

The Egyptian Museum occupies three floors in the northern wing of the Neues Museum. Most visitors come here for an audience with the eternally gorgeous Egyptian queen **Nefertiti**. Her bust was created around 1340 BC by the court sculptor Thutmose. Extremely well preserved, the sculpture was part of the treasure trove unearthed around 1912 by a Berlin expedition of archaeologists who were sifting through the sands of Armana, the royal city built by Nefertiti's husband, King Akhenaten (r 1353–1336 BC).

Another famous work is the so-called **Berlin Green Head** – the bald head of a priest carved from smooth green stone. Created around 400 BC in the Late Egyptian Period, it shows Greek influence and is unusual in that it is not an actual portrait of a specific person but an idealised figure meant to exude universal wisdom and experience.

Museum für Vor- und Frühgeschichte

Highlights within this collection are the **Trojan antiquities** discovered by archaeologist Heinrich Schliemann in 1870 near Hisarlik in modern-day Turkey. However, most of the elaborate jewellery, ornate weapons and gold mugs on display are replicas because the originals became Soviet war booty after WWII and remain in Moscow. Exceptions are the three humble-looking 4500-year-old silver jars proudly displayed in their own glass case.

One floor up the grand staircase, in the Bacchus Hall awaits another head turner: the bronze **Xanten Youth** who, since 2016, has been surrounded by items from the **Barbarian Treasure of Neupotz** buried in the Rhine in the 3rd century. The iron tools, shackles, cauldrons and silverware provide important insight into daily life in the Roman-occupied Rhineland.

The exhibit on the top floor travels back even further to the Stone, Bronze and Iron ages. Highlights include the 45,000-year-old **fossilised skull** of an 11-year-old Neanderthal boy found in 1909 in Le Moustier, as well as a newly added reconstruction of his face. The biggest crowds of all gather around the 3000-year-old **Berliner Goldhut** (Berlin Gold Hat, room 305). Resembling a wizard's hat, it is covered in elaborate bands of astronomical symbols and must indeed have struck the Bronze Age people as something magical. It's one of only four of its kind unearthed worldwide.

Altes Museum

Architect Karl Friedrich Schinkel pulled out all the stops for the grand neoclassical **Altes Museum** (Old Museum; Map p332; ☑030-266 424 242; www.smb.museum; Am Lustgarten; adult/concession/under 18 €10/5/free; ☉10am-6pm Tue, Wed & Fri-Sun, to 8pm Thu), which was the first exhibition space to open on Museumsinsel in 1830. A curtain of fluted columns gives way to a Pantheon-inspired rotunda that's the focal point of a prized antiquities collection. In the downstairs galleries, sculptures, vases, tomb reliefs and jewellery shed light on various facets of life in ancient Greece, while upstairs the focus is on the Etruscans and Romans. Top draws include the *Praying Boy* bronze sculpture, Roman silver vessels and portraits of Caesar and Cleopatra.

Greeks

This chronologically arranged exhibit on the ground floor spans all periods in ancient Greek art from the 10th to the 1st centuries BC. Among the oldest items is a collection of bronze helmets, but it's the monumental statues and elaborate vases that show the greatest artistry.

DANCING UNDER THE STARS

In summer, there's nightly outdoor tango, salsa and swing dancing at riverside Strandbar Mitte (p150), across the River Spree opposite the Bode-Museum.

Looking like a baptismal font for giants, the massive granite basin outside the Altes Museum was designed by Karl Friedrich Schinkel and carved from a single slab by Christian Gottlieb Cantian. It was considered an artistic and technical feat back in the 1820s. The original plan to install it in the museum's rotunda had to be ditched when the bowl ended up being too massive to fit into the site allocated for it. Almost 7m in diameter, it was carved in situ from a massive boulder in Brandenburg and transported via a custom-built wooden railway to the Spree and from there by barge to Berlin.

Among the first eye-catchers is the strapping **Kouros** (room 2), a nude male with a Mona Lisa smile and a great mop of hair. In the next gallery, all eyes are on the **Berlin Goddess**, a beautifully preserved funerary statue of a wealthy young woman in a fancy red dress. The finely carved **Seated Goddess of Tarent** (room 9) is another highlight.

The biggest crowd pleaser is the **Praying Boy** (room 5), an idealised young male nude sculpted in Rhodes around 300 BC and brought to Berlin by Frederick the Great in 1747. Both Napoleon and Stalin took a fancy to the pretty boy and temporarily abducted him as war booty to Paris and Moscow, respectively. Today, his serene smile once again radiates beneath the museum's soaring **rotunda**, which is lidded by a grand coffered and frescoed ceiling. Light filters through a central skylight illuminating 20 large-scale statues representing a who's who of ancient gods, including Nike, Zeus and Fortuna.

Etruscans & Romans

The museum's Etruscan collection is one of the largest outside Italy and contains some stunning pieces. Admire a circular shield from the grave of a warrior alongside amphorae, jewellery, coins and other items from daily life dating back as far as the 8th century BC. Learn about the Etruscan language by studying the **tablet from Capua** and about funerary rites by examining the highly decorated **cinerary urns** and **sarcophagi**.

Adjacent rooms are dedicated to the Romans. There's fantastic sculpture, a superb 70-piece silver table service called the **Hildesheim Treasure** and busts of Roman leaders, including Caesar and Cleopatra. An adults-only **erotic cabinet** (behind a closed door) brims with not-so-subtle depictions of satyrs, hermaphrodites and giant phalli.

Bode-Museum

Mighty and majestic, the **Bode-Museum** (Map p332; ☑030-266 424 242; www.smb.museum; cnr Am Kupfergraben & Monbijoubrücke; adult/concession/under 18 €12/6/free; ☉10am-6pm Tue, Wed & Fri-Sun, to 8pm Thu) has pushed against the northern tip of Museumsinsel like a proud ship's bow since 1904. The gloriously restored neobaroque beauty presents several collections in mostly naturally lit galleries.

The building, designed by Ernst von Ihne, was originally named Kaiser-Friedrich-Museum before being renamed for its first director, Wilhelm von Bode, in 1956. It's a beautifully proportioned architectural composition built around a central axis. Sweeping staircases, interior courtyards, frescoed ceilings and marble floors give the museum the grandeur of a palace.

THE MYSTERY OF PRIAM'S TREASURE

Heinrich Schliemann (1822–90) was not a particularly careful or skilled archaeologist but he was certainly one of the luckiest. Obsessed with the idea of uncovering Homer's Troy, he hit pay dirt in 1873 near Hisarlik in today's Turkey, putting paid to the belief that the town mentioned in the *Iliad* was mere myth. He also famously unearthed a hoard of gold and silver vessels, vases and jewellery, which he believed had once belonged to King Priam. The fact that it later turned out to be a good thousand years older than Homer's Troy doesn't make the find any less spectacular.

Schliemann illegally smuggled the cache to Berlin, had to pay a fine to the Ottoman Empire and eventually donated it to Berlin's ethnological museum. In a strange twist of fate, the treasure was carted off as WWII war booty by the Soviets, who remained mum about its whereabouts until 1993. It remains at the Pushkin Museum in Moscow to this day, leaving only replicas in Berlin.

The tone is set in the grand domed entrance hall where visitors are greeted by Andreas Schlüter's monumental sculpture of Great Elector Friedrich Wilhelm on horseback. From here head straight to the central Italian Renaissance–style basilica, where all eyes are on a colourfully glazed terracotta sculpture by Luca della Robbia. This leads to a smaller domed, rococo-style hall with marble statues of Frederick the Great and his generals. The galleries radiate from both sides of this axis and continue upstairs.

Skulpturensammlung

The majority of rooms showcase the Bode's Sculpture Collection, which former British Museum director Neil MacGregor hailed as 'the most comprehensive display of European sculpture anywhere'. The works span the arc of artistic creativity from the early Middle Ages to the late 18th century, with a special focus on the Italian Renaissance. There are priceless masterpieces like Donatello's **Pazzi Madonna**, Giovanni Pisano's **Man of Sorrows** relief, and the portrait busts of Desiderio da Settignano. Staying on the ground floor, you can cruise from the Italians to the Germans by admiring the 12th-century **Gröninger Empore**, a church gallery from a former monastery that is considered a major work of the Romanesque period.

Most of the German sculptures are upstairs, including a clutch of works by the late-Gothic master carver Tilman Riemenschneider. Highlights include the exquisite **St Anne and Her Three Husbands** as well as the **Four Evangelists**. Compare Riemenschneider's emotiveness to that of his contemporaries Hans Multscher and Nicolaus Gerhaert van Leyden, whose work is also displayed here. The monumental **knight-saints** from the period of the Thirty Years' War (17th century) are another standout on this floor.

Museum für Byzantinische Kunst

Before breaking for coffee at the elegant cafe, pop back down to the ground floor where the Museum of Byzantine Art takes up just a few rooms off the grand domed foyer. It presents late Antique and Byzantine works of art. The elaborate Roman sarcophagi, the ivory carvings and the mosaic icons point to the high level of artistry in these early days of Christianity.

Münzsammlung

Coin collectors will get a kick out of the Numismatic Collection on the 2nd floor. With half a million coins – and counting – it's one of the largest of its kind in the world, even if only a small fraction can be displayed at one time. The oldest farthing is from the 7th century BC and displayed in a special case alongside the smallest, largest, fattest and thinnest coins.

LUSTGARTEN

The Lustgarten (Pleasure Garden), as the patch of green fronting the Altes Museum is called, has seen many makeovers. It started as a royal kitchen garden and became a military exercise ground before being turned into a pleasure garden by Schinkel. The Nazis held mass rallies here, the East Germans ignored it. Restored to its Schinkel-era appearance, it's now a favourite resting spot for foot-weary tourists.

The banker JHW Wagener was an avid collector of art and arts patron who, in 1861, bequeathed his entire collection of 262 paintings to the Prussian state to form the basis of a national gallery. Just one year later, William I commissioned Friedrich August Stüler to design a suitable museum. He came up with the Alte Nationalgalerie, an imposing temple-like structure perched on a pedestal and fronted by a curtain of Corinthian columns. The entrance is reached via a sweeping double staircase crowned by a statue of King Friedrich Wilhelm IV on horseback.

Bode-Museum (p108)

Alte Nationalgalerie

The Greek temple–style **Alte Nationalgalerie** (Old National Gallery; Map p332; ☑030-266 424 242; www.smb. museum; Bodestrasse 1-3; adult/concession €10/5; ⊙10am-6pm Tue, Wed & Fri-Sun, to 8pm Thu), open since 1876, is a showcase of first-rate 19th-century European art. It was a tumultuous century, characterised by revolutions and industrialisation that brought profound changes in society. Artists reacted to the new realities in different ways. While German Romantics like Caspar David Friedrich sought solace in nature and Nazarenes like Anselm Feuerbach turned to religious subjects, the epic canvases of Adolf Menzel and Franz Krüger glorified moments in Prussian history, and the impressionists focused on light and aesthetics.

On the 1st floor, Johann Gottfried Schadow's **Statue of Two Princesses** and a bust of Johann Wolfgang von Goethe are standout sculptures. The painter Adolf Menzel also gets the star treatment – look for his famous **A Flute Concert of Frederick the Great at Sanssouci**.

The 2nd floor shows impressionist paintings by famous French artists including Monet, Degas, Cézanne, Renoir and Manet, the last of whose **In the Conservatory** is considered a masterpiece. Among the Germans, there's Arnold Böcklin's **Isle of Death** and several canvases by Max Liebermann.

Romantics rule the top floor where all eyes are on Caspar David Friedrich's mystical landscapes and the Gothic fantasies of Karl Friedrich Schinkel. Also look for key works by Carl Blechen and portraits by Philipp Otto Runge and Carl Spitzweg.

TOP SIGHT
FERNSEHTURM

No matter where you are in Berlin, look up and chances are you'll see the Fernsehturm. The TV Tower – Germany's tallest structure – is as iconic to the city as the Eiffel Tower is to Paris and has been soaring 368m high (including the antenna) since 1969. Pinpoint city landmarks from the panorama platform at 203m (with bar) or from the upstairs Sphere restaurant (p117) (207m) – views are stunning on clear days.

Ordered by East German government leader Walter Ulbricht in the 1950s, the tower was built not only as a transmitter for radio and TV programs but also as a demonstration of the GDR's strength and technological prowess. However, it ended up becoming a bit of a laughing stock when it turned out that, when struck by the sun, the steel sphere below the antenna produced the reflection of a giant cross. This inspired a popular joke (not appreciated by the GDR leadership) that the phenomenon was the 'Pope's revenge' on the secular socialist state for having removed crucifixes from churches.

The tower's rocketlike shape was inspired by the space race of the 1960s and in particular the launch of the first satellite, the Soviet Sputnik. The tower is made up of the base, a 250m-high shaft, the 4800-ton sphere and the 118m-high antenna. Its original location was supposed to be the Müggelberg hills on the city's southeastern edge. Construction had already begun when the authorities realised that the tower would be in the flight path of the planned airport at nearby Schönefeld. Ulbricht then decided on its current location.

DON'T MISS

➡ Observation Deck
➡ Sunset cocktails, Sphere (p117).

PRACTICALITIES

➡ TV Tower
➡ Map p332, C3
➡ ☏030-247 575 875
➡ www.tv-turm.de
➡ Panoramastrasse 1a
➡ adult/child €15.50/9.50, fast track online ticket €19.50/12
➡ ⊘9am-midnight Mar-Oct, 10am-midnight Nov-Feb, last ascent 11.30pm
➡ ☐100, 200, TXL, Ⓤ Alexanderplatz, Ⓢ Alexanderplatz

◉ SIGHTS

It's practically impossible to visit Berlin without spending time in this area. Explore the city's beginnings in the Nikolaiviertel, then check out the Humboldt Forum in the reconstructed Berlin City Palace, skip around superb museums, take a river cruise and keep an eye on it all from the top of the Fernsehturm.

MUSEUMSINSEL   MUSEUM
See p101.

◉ Alexanderplatz

FERNSEHTURM   LANDMARK
See p111.

ST MARIENKIRCHE   CHURCH
Map p332 (St Mary's Church; www.marienkirche-berlin.de; Karl-Liebknecht-Strasse 8; ⊙10am-6pm Apr-Dec, to 4pm Jan-Mar; ⛻100, 200, TXL, ⑤Hackescher Markt, Alexanderplatz, ⓤAlexanderplatz) This Gothic brick gem has welcomed worshippers since the early 14th century, making it one of Berlin's oldest surviving churches. A 22m-long *Dance of Death* fresco in the vestibule inspired by a 15th-century plague leads to a relatively plain interior enlivened by numerous other art treasures. The oldest is the 1437 bronze baptismal font buttressed by a trio of dragons. The baroque alabaster pulpit by Andreas Schlüter from 1703 is equally eye-catching.

The baroque dome, by the way, was designed by the Brandenburg Gate architect Carl Gotthard Langhans. Check the website for organ concerts and English-language services.

ROTES RATHAUS   HISTORIC BUILDING
Map p332 (Red Town Hall; ⌨030-9026 2032; www.berlin.de/berliner-rathaus; Rathausstrasse 15; ⊙9am-6pm Mon-Fri; ⑤Alexanderplatz, ⓤAlexanderplatz, Klosterstrasse) FREE The Rotes Rathaus is the seat of Berlin's governing mayor and a red-brick neo-Renaissance pile completed in 1869. Outside, note the terracotta frieze that illustrates Berlin milestones until 1871. Except during special events, much of the town hall is open to the public – pick up a brochure with a self-guided tour in the foyer and also check out the free special exhibits.

The moniker 'red', by the way, was inspired by the red brick facade and not (necessarily) the political leanings of its occupants.

NEPTUNBRUNNEN   FOUNTAIN
Map p332 (Rathausplatz; ⛻100, 200, TXL, ⓤKlosterstrasse, Alexanderplatz, ⑤Alexanderplatz) This elaborate fountain was designed by Reinhold Begas in 1891 and depicts Neptune holding court over a quartet of buxom beauties symbolising the rivers Rhine, Elbe, Oder and Vistula. Kids get a kick out of the water-squirting turtle, seal, crocodile and snake.

BLOCK DER FRAUEN   MEMORIAL
Map p332 (Block of Women; Rosenstrasse; ⑤Hackescher Markt, Alexanderplatz, ⓤAlexanderplatz) A reddish sandstone memorial in a small park on Rosenstrasse called *Block der Frauen* by Jewish-German artist Inge Hunzinger (1915–2009) pays tribute to the non-Jewish German women who peacefully but tenaciously protested against the planned

---

THE NEW U5

Almost 120 years after the first U-Bahn train embarked on its maiden journey, Berlin's subway network is getting an extension – of the U5 line from Alexanderplatz to the Brandenburg Gate. There, it will link with the already completed U55 and continue to the Hauptbahnhof (main train station), thus closing a major east–west gap.

The ground-breaking ceremony for the 2.2km-long stretch was held in 2010 but construction had to be halted after archaeological remnants were discovered near the Berliner Rathaus (Berlin Town Hall). It resumed in 2012 and, if all goes according to plan, the line might start operation in late 2020.

Three new stations are being built: Unter den Linden (at the intersection of Unter den Linden and Friedrichstrasse), Museumsinsel and Berliner Rathaus (next to Nikolaiviertel). The tunnel was carved 12m below ground by a custom-built 75m-long steel mole nicknamed Bärlinde at a speed of 8m per day. How this worked is explained in a five-minute film (in German) in the **U5-Infowaggon** (Map p332; cnr Rathausstrasse & Poststrasse; ⊙noon-6pm Tue-Sun; ⛻100, 200, TXL, ⓤKlosterstrasse) near the Nikolaiviertel.

⊙ TOP SIGHT
DDR MUSEUM

How did regular East Germans spend their day-to-day lives? The 'touchy-feely' DDR Museum does an entertaining job of pulling back the iron curtain on an extinct society. In hands-on fashion you'll learn how, under socialism, kids were put through collective potty training, engineers earned little more than farmers, and everyone, it seems, went on nudist holidays. You get to rummage through school bags, open drawers and cupboards or watch TV in a 1970s living room. And it's not only kids who love squeezing behind the wheel of a Trabant (Trabi) car for a virtual drive through an East Berlin *Plattenbauten* (prefab concrete-slab housing) estate.

The more sinister sides of life in the GDR are also addressed, including chronic supply shortages, surveillance by the Stasi (secret police) and the Sozialistische Einheitspartei Deutschlands (SED) party's monopoly on power. You can stand in a recreated prison cell, or imagine what it was like to be in the cross hairs of a Stasi officer's sights by sitting on the victim's chair in a tiny, windowless interrogation room.

DON'T MISS
➡ Trabi ride
➡ Stasi interrogation room

PRACTICALITIES
➡ GDR Museum
➡ Map p332, B4
➡ ☏030-847 123 731
➡ www.ddr-museum.de
➡ Karl-Liebknecht-Strasse 1
➡ adult/concession €9.80/6
➡ ⊙10am-8pm Sun-Fri, to 10pm Sat
➡ ⊒100, 200, TXL, ⑤Hackescher Markt

---

deportation of their Jewish husbands who had been detained near this site in 1943. It was a rare, courageous – and ultimately successful – act of defiance against the Nazi regime.

SEALIFE BERLIN   AQUARIUM
Map p332 (☏0180-666 690 101; www.visitsealife. com; Spandauer Strasse 3; adult/child €18/14.50, cheaper online; ⊙10am-7pm, last admission 6pm; ⊒100, 200, TXL, ⑤Hackescher Markt, Alexanderplatz) Smile-inducing seahorses, ethereal jellyfish, Ophira the octopus and a marine dinosaur skeleton that can be 'reanimated' are some of the crowd favourites among the 5000 denizens of this rambling aquarium, where visits conclude with a slow lift ride through the Aquadom, a 25m-high cylindrical tropical fish tank.

Also popular are the feeding sessions of rays, sharks, catfish and other creatures that take place between 11.30am and 3.30pm.

BERLIN DUNGEON   AMUSEMENT PARK
Map p332 (☏0180-625 5544; www.thedun geons.com/berlin; Spandauer Strasse 2; adult/child 10-14 €21.50/17.50; ⊙10am-6pm Apr-Oct, shorter hours rest of year; ⊒100, 200, TXL, ⑤Hackescher Markt) This is a 70-minute tour through a camped-up chamber of horrors that's brought to life by actors in nine shows with such spine-tingling names as 'Elevator of Doom', 'Torture Chamber' and 'Serial Killer of Berlin'. Lucky ones get to escape the plague on a river raft ride across the Spree. English tours at 2.30pm and 4.45pm. Check the website for ticket discounts.

⊙ Humboldt Forum & Nikolaiviertel

BERLINER DOM   CHURCH
Map p332 (Berlin Cathedral; ☏box office 030-2026 9136; www.berlinerdom.de; Am Lustgarten; adult/concession €7/5; ⊙9am-8pm Apr-Sep, to 7pm Oct-Mar; ⊒100, 200, TXL, ⑤Hackescher Markt) Pompous yet majestic, the Italian Renaissance–style former royal court church (1905) does triple duty as house of worship, museum and concert hall. Inside it's gilt to the hilt and outfitted with a lavish marble-and-onyx altar, a 7269-pipe Sauer organ and elaborate royal sarcophagi. Climb up the 267 steps to the gallery for glorious city views.

For more dead royals, albeit in less extravagant coffins, drop below to the crypt.

HUMBOLDT-FORUM: BERLIN'S NEW CULTURAL QUARTER

In the heart of Berlin, across from the Berlin Dom and the famous museums of Museumsinsel, looms the **Humboldt Forum im Berliner Schloss** (Map p332; www.humboldt forum.com; Schlossplatz; ⎆100, 200, TXL, Ⓤ Klosterstrasse), a cultural hub built to look like an exact replica of the baroque Berlin City Palace, but with a modern interior.

Although barely damaged in WWII, the grand palace where Prussian rulers had made their home since 1443 was blown up by East Germany's government in 1950 to drop the final curtain on Prussian and Nazi rule. To emphasise the point, the new communist rulers built their own modernist parliament – called Palast der Repubilk (Palace of the Republic) – on top of the ruins 26 years later. Riddled with asbestos, it too had a date with the wrecking ball in 2006.

After two decades of debate and bickering, construction of the replica finally kicked off in July 2013. The building itself is said to be on schedule for completion by early 2019. If all then continues to go according to plan, the Humboldt Forum could open to the public – at least partly – by the end of that year.

When it does, it will not only be the new home of the **Museum of Ethnology** and the **Museum of Asian Art** but will also host films and lectures that explore topical issues in science, art, religion, politics and business. The **Berlin Ausstellung** (Berlin Exhibit) will focus on the links between Berlin and the world and examine such issues as migration, war, fashion, revolution, free spaces, borders and entertainment. Also on the 1st floor will be the university-run **Humboldt Laboratory**, an interdisciplinary exhibition and cultural space that unravels the processes that result in the creation of new knowledge and shows how science is relevant to all of us. Admission to all permanent exhibits is expected to be free for the first three years.

The Schloss 2.0 comes with a projected price tag of €590 million for the building alone, with most of the bill having been footed by the federal government. The design by Italian architect Franco Stella has three sides of the facade looking like a baroque blast from the past, thus visually restoring the historic ensemble of Museumsinsel, Berliner Dom and the Neuer Marstall (New Royal Stables). Only the facade facing the Spree River will be without baroque adornments. A cupola graces the western end.

Skip the cathedral museum unless you're interested in the building's construction. The sanctuary has great acoustics and is often used for classical concerts, sometimes played on the famous Sauer organ. Multilanguage audioguides for €3.

NIKOLAIVIERTEL AREA

Map p332 (btwn Rathausstrasse, Breite Strasse, Spandauer Strasse & Mühlendamm; Ⓤ Klosterstrasse) FREE Commissioned by the East German government to celebrate Berlin's 750th birthday, the twee Nicholas Quarter is a half-hearted attempt at recreating the city's medieval birthplace around its oldest surviving building, the 1230 Nikolaikirche. The maze of cobbled lanes is worth a quick stroll, while several olde-worlde-style restaurants provide sustenance.

MÄRKISCHES MUSEUM MUSEUM

Map p332 (✆030-2400 2162; www.stadt museum.de; Am Köllnischen Park 5; adult/concession/under 18 €7/4/free; ⊙10am-6pm Tue-Sun; Ⓤ Märkisches Museum) Compact, engaging and interactive, the permanent exhibit at this local history museum zeroes in on historic milestones and key protagonists that shaped Berlin's evolution from the medieval trading village of Berlin-Cölln into today's European metropolis. Displays tackle questions such as to what gives Berlin its special character and how its residents impact the city and vice versa. Period rooms like the Gothic Hall with its displays of medieval religious art, the Guild Hall and the Weapons Hall provide atmospheric eye candy.

Curators also mount changing exhibits on the ground floor that shine the spotlight on specific themes of Berlin's often turbulent past. The museum itself is housed in an imposing mash-up of parts of historic buildings from the surrounding region, including a bishop's palace tower and the Gothic gables of a church. A copy of the Roland statue, a medieval symbol of civic liberty and freedom, stands guard at the entrance. Note that the museum is set to close for an extended restoration in 2021.

MUSEUM NIKOLAIKIRCHE   MUSEUM

Map p332 (☑030-2400 2162; www.stadt museum.de; Nikolaikirchplatz; adult/concession/under 18 €5/3/free, 1st Wed of month free; ☺10am-6pm; 🚌M48, Ⓤ Klosterstrasse) The late-Gothic Church of St Nicholas (1230) is Berlin's oldest surviving building and is now a museum documenting the architecture and history of the church and the surrounding Nikolai quarter. Grab the free audioguide for the scoop on the octagonal baptismal font and the triumphal cross, or to find out why the building is nicknamed the 'pantheon of prominent Berliners'.

There's a free 30-minute organ recital on Fridays at 5pm. At other times, head up to the gallery for close-ups of the organ, a sweeping view of the interior and a chance to listen to recorded church hymns.

MUSEUM EPHRAIM-PALAIS   MUSEUM

Map p332 (☑030-2400 2162; www.stadtmuseum. de; Poststrasse 16; adult/concession/under 18 €7/5/free, 1st Wed of month free; ☺10am-6pm Tue & Thu-Sun, noon-8pm Wed; 🚌248, M48, Ⓤ Klosterstrasse) Once the home of Veitel Heine Ephraim – court jeweller and coin minter to Frederick the Great – this pretty, pint-size 1766 town palace hosts changing exhibits focusing on aspects of Berlin's artistic and cultural legacy.

The original building was levelled in 1935 during the construction of the Mühlendamm bridge. Only the curved rococo facade with its gilded ironwork balconies and sculptural ornamentation was saved and stored in what later became West Berlin. In 1984 it was returned to East Berlin and incorporated in the Palais' reconstruction. Inside, architectural highlights include the oval staircase and the Schlüterdecke, an ornate ceiling on the 1st floor.

KNOBLAUCHHAUS   MUSEUM

Map p332 (☑030-2400 2162; www.stadtmuseum. de; Poststrasse 23; donation requested; ☺10am-6pm Tue-Sun; Ⓤ Klosterstrasse) This private

late-baroque home features a series of painstakingly restored period rooms that impart a sense of how the well-to-do lived, dressed and spent their days during the Biedermeier period (1815–48). The structure once belonged to the prominent Knoblauch family, which included politicians, architects and patrons of the arts who enjoyed tea and talk with architect Schinkel, sculptor Schadow and other luminaries of the day.

HANF MUSEUM   MUSEUM

Map p332 (Hemp Museum; ☑030-242 4827; www.hanfmuseum.de; Mühlendamm 5; adult/concession €4.50/3; ☺10am-8pm Tue-Fri, noon-8pm Sat & Sun; Ⓤ Klosterstrasse) This eight-room exhibit examines the many uses of hemp as well as its cultural, practical, medicinal and religious significance in various cultures going back thousands of years.

ZILLE MUSEUM   MUSEUM

Map p332 (☑030-2463 2500; www.zillemuseum-berlin.de; Propststrasse 11; adult/concession €7/5; ☺11am-6pm; Ⓤ Klosterstrasse) Like no other artist of his time, Heinrich Zille (1858–1929) managed to capture the hardships of working-class life in the industrial age with empathy and humour. This small private museum in the Nikolaiviertel preserves his legacy with a selection of drawings, photographs and graphic art. There's also an interesting video on his life (in German only).

Afterwards, you can channel Zille's ghost over a beer at the nearby Zum Nussbaum (p118) pub, a rather authentic recreation of his favourite watering hole.

STAATSRATSGEBÄUDE   HISTORIC BUILDING

Map p332 (Schlossplatz 1; 🚌100, 200, TXL, Ⓤ Hausvogteiplatz) The hulking 1960 State Council Building is the only remaining Schlossplatz structure from the GDR era. It integrates the arched portal of the original, demolished Berlin City Palace, from which Karl Liebknecht proclaimed a socialist republic on 9 November 1918.

BERLIN BY BOAT

A lovely way to experience Berlin from April to October – and take a break from museum-hopping – is on the open-air deck of a river cruiser. Several companies run relaxing Spree spins through the city centre from landing docks on the eastern side of Museumsinsel, for example outside the DDR Museum (p113) and from the Nikolaiviertel. Sip refreshments while a guide showers you with anecdotes (in English and German) as you glide past grand old buildings and museums and the government quarter. Expect the one-hour tour to cost between €12 and €14.

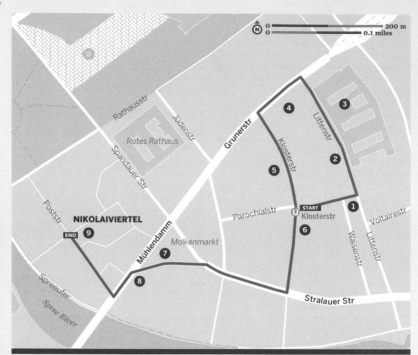

🏃 Neighbourhood Walk
History Ramble

START KLOSTERSTRASSE U-BAHN
FINISH NIKOLAIVIERTEL
LENGTH 1.3KM; ONE HOUR

This walk charts Berlin's history from its medieval beginnings to the 20th century. From U-Bahn station Klosterstrasse, walk east on Parochialstrasse. Note Berlin's oldest restaurant, **1 Zur Letzten Instanz** (p118), which has been serving pork knuckle for nearly 400 years, then turn left on Littenstrasse and stop at a crude 8m-long pile of boulders and bricks. This is what's left of **2 Stadtmauer**, the city wall built around 1250 to protect the first settlers from marauders. Looming above is the monumental **3 Justizgebäude Littenstrasse**, a 1912 courthouse with a grand art nouveau foyer – feel free to pop in and take a look.

On your left, the Gothic **4 Franziskaner Klosterkirche** (Franciscan Monastery Church) was once a prestigious school for luminaries such as Schinkel and Bismarck and is now used for art exhibits and concerts. Follow Littenstrasse north, turn left on Grun-

erstrasse and left again on Klosterstrasse. The big building on your right is **5 Altes Stadthaus** (Old City Hall), whose distinctive 87m-high domed tower is crowned by the goddess Fortuna. Continue on Klosterstrasse to the 17th-century **6 Parochialkirche**, which manages to be at once graceful and monumental. Designed by the same architect as Schloss Charlottenburg, it was burnt out in WWII and, though restored, deliberately still reveals the scars of war.

Turn right on Stralauer Strasse, which leads to **7 Molkenmarkt**, Berlin's oldest square and one-time thriving marketplace. The ornate building at No 2 is the historic **8 Alte Münze**, the old mint (now an event location). Reichsmark, GDR Mark, Deutsche Mark and euro coins were all minted here until 2006. Note the decorative frieze depicting the evolution of metallurgy and coin minting.

Across the street, the **9 Nikolaiviertel** (p114) may look medieval, but it's a product of the 1980s, built by the East German government to celebrate Berlin's 750th birthday. The 1230 Nikolaikirche and a handful of small museums are worth a visit.

The colourful window in the foyer is by the East German socialist realism artist Walter Womacka and depicts scenes from the German workers' movement. Somewhat ironically, the building is now used by a private international business school financed by such blue-chip corporations as Bayer, Deutsche Bank and Siemens.

HISTORISCHER HAFEN BERLIN HARBOUR
Map p332 (Historical Harbour Berlin; ☑030-2147 3257; Märkisches Ufer; adult/concession €2/1.50; ⊘11am-6pm Sat & Sun; Ⓤ Märkisches Museum) Laced by rivers, canals and lakes, it's not surprising that Berlin has a long history of inland navigation and that it had the busiest river port in Germany until WWII. This outdoor museum showcases nearly 20 vessels, barges and tugboats, many still operational. One boat doubles as a cafe in summer while another contains a small exhibit documenting 250 years of river shipping on the Spree and Havel.

✖ EATING

With its abundant fast-food outlets, Alexanderplatz itself isn't a foodie haven, although there's a respectable self-service cafeteria in the Galeria Kaufhof (p119). Otherwise, try the food court in Alexa (p119), the traditional German restaurants in the Nikolaiviertel or head to the Scheunenviertel for better options.

✖ Alexanderplatz

DOLORES CALIFORNIAN €
Map p332 (☑030-2809 9597; www.dolores-online.de; Rosa-Luxemburg-Strasse 7; burritos from €4.50; ⊘11.30am-10pm Mon-Sat, 1-10pm Sun; 🛜🍴; 🚌100, 200, Ⓢ Alexanderplatz, Ⓤ Alexanderplatz) Dolores hasn't lost a step since introducing the California-style burrito to Berlin. Pick your favourites from among the marinated meats (or tofu), rice, beans, veggies, cheeses and homemade salsas, and the cheerful staff will build it on the spot. Goes perfectly with an *agua fresca* (Mexican-style lemonade).

VAPIANO ITALIAN €
Map p332 (☑030-2789 0400; www.vapiano.com; Rathausstrasse 6; mains €6.50-11; ⊘10am-1am Mon-Thu & Sat, to midnight Fri & Sun; 🛜; Ⓢ Alexanderplatz, Ⓤ Alexanderplatz) Mix-and-match pastas, creative salads and crusty pizzas are all

MOBILE WURST

They're all over Alexanderplatz – the Grillwalkers, or what we cheekily call 'Self-Contained Underpaid Bratwurst Apparatus', aka SCUBA. Picture this: guys with a mobile gas grill strapped around their bellies upon which sizzling bratwursts wait for customers. At €1.70 a pop, squished into a roll and slathered with mustard or ketchup, those crunchy wieners are going fast.

prepared right before your eyes at this successful German chain of Italian self-service eateries. Nice touch: fresh basil in the condiment baskets. In summer, sit on the terrace right below the Fernsehturm.

ISHIN JAPANESE €€
Map p332 (☑030-2352 2762; www.ishin.de; Lilfass-Platz 1; sushi platter €8.50-21, bowl €5.60-12.20; ⊘noon-9.30pm Mon-Sat; 🚇M1, Ⓢ Hackescher Markt) The newest outpost of this small local sushi chain dishes up freshly prepared and good-value sushi along with *donburi* rice bowls and dishes prepared in the bamboo steamer. Prices for sushi menus drop during Happy Hour, which runs all day Wednesday and Saturday and until 4pm on other opening days.

HOFBRÄUHAUS BERLIN GERMAN €€
Map p332 (☑030-679 665 520; www.hofbraeu-wirtshaus.de/berlin; Karl-Liebknecht-Strasse 30; sausages €6-9, mains €11-20; ⊘10am-1am Sun-Thu, to 2am Fri & Sat; 🍴; Ⓢ Alexanderplatz, Ⓤ Alexanderplatz) Popular with coach tourists and field-tripping teens, this giant beer hall with 2km of wooden benches does not have the patina of the Munich original but at least it serves the same litre-size mugs of beer and big plates piled high with gut-busting German fare.

SPHERE GERMAN, INTERNATIONAL €€€
Map p332 (☑030-247 575 875; www.tv-turm.de/en/bar-restaurant; Panoramastrasse 1; mains lunch €10.50-18, dinner €12.50-28; ⊘10am-11pm; 🛜; 🚌100, 200, TXL, Ⓤ Alexanderplatz, Ⓢ Alexanderplatz) Berlin's highest restaurant may not take demanding taste buds for a spin but it will take you around in a full circle within one hour. The revolving eatery, 207m up the iconic Fernsehturm (p111), delivers classic Berlin and international cuisine along with sweeping city views. Annoyingly,

LOCAL KNOWLEDGE

EYE-POPPING VIEWS ON A BUDGET

Heading up the Fernsehturm (p111) may give you bragging rights for having been atop Germany's tallest structure, but those wonderful vistas come at a price (and long lines unless you prebook). Here are some nearby alternatives that'll cost less and have the added benefit of featuring the photogenic TV tower itself in your snapshots.

Park Inn Panorama Terrasse (Map p332; ☎030-238 90; www.parkinn-berlin.de/en/panorama-terrace; Alexanderplatz 7; €4; ⊙noon-10pm Apr-Oct, to 6pm Nov-Mar, weather permitting; ⓊAlexanderplatz, ⓈAlexanderplatz) At 150m above the ground, the Panorama Terrasse atop the Park Inn Hotel on Alexanderplatz puts you 53m lower than the viewing platform of the Fernsehturm, but lets you relax with a cold drink while draped over a sunlounger or marvelling at gutsy base-flyers leaping off the edge of the building (Friday to Sunday only). Attached to a special winch rappel system usually used by stunt performers, these daredevils plunge towards the ground in a controlled fall, reaching near free-fall speeds.

House of Weekend (p119) On a hot summer night, the absolute high point for party people is the rooftop garden of this club atop the GDR-era Haus des Reisens (House of Travel). Aside from picture-postcard views, you can look forward to a fun crowd and cool cocktails. After 11pm, the action moves down to the 15th floor for some quality dancing until the wee hours.

eating here requires buying a regular lift ticket, which adds €19.50 for an aisle table or €23.50 for a window table per person to the final tab.

✗ Nikolaiviertel

BRAUHAUS GEORGBRÄU   GERMAN €€

Map p332 (☎030-242 4244; www.brauhaus-georgbraeu.de; Spreeufer 4; mains €6-15; ⊙noon-midnight; ⓊKlosterstrasse) Solidly on the tourist track, this old-style gastropub churns out its own light and dark Georg-Bräu, which can even be ordered by the metre (12 glasses at 0.2L). In winter, the woodsy beer hall is perfect for tucking into hearty Berlin-style fare. In summer tables in the riverside beer garden are golden.

A perennial menu favourite is the boiled pork knuckle (*Eisbein*), served with sauerkraut, mushy peas, potatoes, a small beer and a schnapps for €12.20.

ZUM NUSSBAUM   GERMAN €€

Map p332 (☎030-242 3095; Am Nussbaum 3; mains €8-16; ⊙noon-midnight; ⓊKlosterstrasse) This cute little inn is a faithful replica of the 1507 original, a favourite watering hole of writers and artists, including the caricaturist Heinrich Zille, until it was destroyed in WWII. Today it does a roaring trade with global nomads searching for a slice of Old Berlin and laden with platters of classic local fare.

ZUR LETZTEN INSTANZ   GERMAN €€

Map p332 (☎030-242 5528; www.zurletzteninstanz.de; Waisenstrasse 14-16; mains €13-23; ⊙noon-1am Tue-Sat, noon-10pm Sun; ⓊKlosterstrasse) With its folksy Old Berlin charm, this rustic eatery has been an enduring hit since 1621 and has fed everyone from Napoleon to Beethoven to Angela Merkel. Although the restaurant is now tourist-geared, the food quality is reassuringly high when it comes to such local rib-stickers as grilled pork knuckle or meatballs in caper sauce.

In winter the seats around the green-tiled stove are the cosiest. Note that hot meals are not served between 3pm and 6pm.

🍷 DRINKING & NIGHTLIFE

Aside from a few tourist-oriented bars on Alexanderplatz and inside a clutch of hotels, there are few imbibing stations to be found in this area. For beer and Old Berlin flair, head to the restaurants in the Nikolaiviertel. For better options, stroll over to the Scheunenviertel.

BRAUFACTUM BERLIN   CRAFT BEER

Map p332 (☎030-8471 2959; www.braufactum.de; Memhardstrasse 1; ⊙noon-midnight Sun-Thu, to 2am Fri & Sat; ▣100, ⓊAlexanderplatz, ⓈAlexanderplatz) With its urban-contempo looks and big terrace, this concept-driven craft beer outpost shakes up the gastro wasteland of Alexanderplatz. Aside from the dozen house brews like the subtly sweet-bitter India Pale Ale Progusta and the whisky-barrel matured Barrel 1, the blackboard menu also features suds from other breweries like Mikkeler and Firestone Walker. Elevated pub grub helps keep brains in balance.

CLUB AVENUE   CLUB
(⏱0174 600 3000; www.avenue-berlin.com; Karl-Marx-Allee 34; ☺11pm-6am Fri & Sat; Ⓤ Schillingstrasse) This high-octane club has taken up residency at Café Moskau, a protected East Berlin landmark. Dress to impress the door staff in order to gyrate on the dance floor to hip-hop, house or disco, depending on the night. The sleek retro decor is the work of the decorating team behind Berghain/Panorama Bar.

GMF   GAY
Map p332 (www.gmf-berlin.de; Alexanderstrasse 7; entry €12; ☺11pm Sun; Ⓤ Alexanderplatz, Ⓢ Alexanderplatz) Berlin's premier Sunday club is known for excessive SM (standing and modelling) with lots of smooth surfaces – and that goes for both the crowd and the setting. Predominantly boyz, but girls OK. It currently has a residency at the House of Weekend club but has often changed location, so check the website for the latest.

GOLDEN GATE   CLUB
Map p332 (www.goldengate-berlin.de; Schicklerstrasse 4; ☺hours vary, usually from midnight Thu-Sun; Ⓤ Jannowitzbrücke) If you yearn for the rough sound and aesthetics of '90s Berlin, you'll break into a sweaty flashback at this small club in a derelict building beneath the Jannowitzbrücke train tracks. Dedicated hedonists, dressed down for business, slam the dance floor for extended technofests fuelled by (mostly) local DJs.

The 'Donnerdogge' Thursday parties are legendary.

HOUSE OF WEEKEND   CLUB
Map p332 (⏱reservations 0152 2429 3140; www.houseofweekend.berlin; Am Alexanderplatz 5; ☺11pm-6am Fri & Sat, roof garden from 7pm, weather permitting; Ⓢ Alexanderplatz, Ⓤ Alexanderplatz) This veteran electro club has a high-flying location on the 15th floor of a socialist-era office building and often has big-name local and international DJs helming its decks. In summer, the action expands

to the rooftop terrace for sundowners, private cabanas and 360° views.

ALLEGRETTO GRAN CAFE   CAFE
Map p332 (⏱030-308 777 517; Anna-Louisa-Karsch-Strasse 2; mains €10-13; ☺10am-8pm; 🛜; 🚌100, 200, TXL, Ⓢ Hackescher Markt) Combat sightseeing fatigue with coffee and cake or a full meal at a terrace table at this modern cafe with terrific views of the Berliner Dom.

🛍 SHOPPING

Alexanderplatz is the hub of mainstream shopping in the eastern centre with department stores around the square itself and the massive Alexa mall ensuring that you can pick up a rainbow of goods in one compact area. Souvenir and trinket collectors should check out the little shops in the Nikolaiviertel.

ALEXA   MALL
Map p332 (⏱030-269 3400; www.alexacentre.com; Grunerstrasse 20; ☺10am-9pm Mon-Sat; Ⓢ Alexanderplatz, Ⓤ Alexanderplatz) Power shoppers love this XXL mall, which cuts a rose-hued presence near Alexanderplatz and features the predictable range of high-street retailers. Good food court for a bite on the run.

GALERIA KAUFHOF   DEPARTMENT STORE
Map p332 (⏱030-247 430; www.galeria-kaufhof.de; Alexanderplatz 9; ☺9.30am-8pm Mon-Wed, to 10pm Thu-Sat; Ⓢ Alexanderplatz, Ⓤ Alexanderplatz) A full makeover by the late Josef Paul Kleihues turned this former GDR-era department store into a glitzy retail cube, complete with a glass-domed light court and a sleek travertine skin that glows green at night. There's little you won't find on the five football-field-size floors, including a gourmet supermarket on the ground floor.

IC! BERLIN   FASHION & ACCESSORIES
Map p332 (⏱030-220 666 055; www.ic-berlin.de; Münzstrasse 5; ☺10am-8pm Mon-Sat; 🛜; Ⓤ Weinmeisterstrasse) The flagship store of this Berlin-based but internationally famous eyewear maker stocks more than 500 featherweight frames with their signature klutz-proof, screwless hinges. If needed, there's an optician onsite to assess your prescription, and coffee and a sofa for chilled shopping. Ask about its free factory tours.

Potsdamer Platz & Tiergarten

POTSDAMER PLATZ | KULTURFORUM | TIERGARTEN & DIPLOMATENVIERTEL

Neighbourhood Top Five

❶ **Gemäldegalerie** (p125) Perusing an Aladdin's cave of Old Masters – from Rembrandt to Vermeer.

❷ **Sony Center** (p122) Stopping for a beer and people-watching beneath the magnificent canopy of this svelte glass-and-steel landmark designed by Helmut Jahn.

❸ **Panoramapunkt** (p123) Catching Europe's fastest lift to take in Berlin's impressive cityscape and enjoy refreshments in the sky.

❹ **Tiergarten** (p131) Getting lost amid the trees and leafy paths of this sprawling city park with its monuments and beer gardens.

❺ **Gedenkstätte Deutscher Widerstand** (p129) Admiring the brave people who stood up to the Nazis at this memorial exhibit in the offices where the 20 July 1944 assassination attempt on Hitler was plotted.

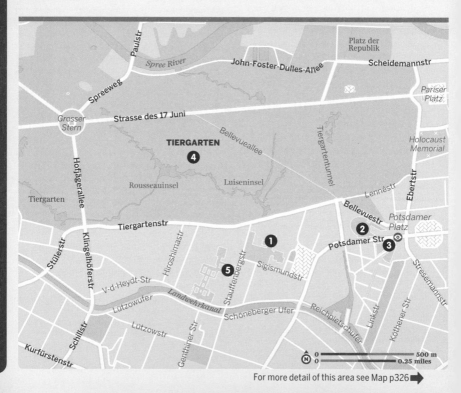

For more detail of this area see Map p326 ➡

Explore Potsdamer Platz & Tiergarten

Despite the name, Potsdamer Platz (p122) is not really a square but Berlin's newest quarter, forged in the '90s from terrain once bisected by the Berlin Wall. A collaborative effort by the world's finest architects, it is a vibrant showcase of urban renewal. The area itself is rather compact and quickly explored – unless you choose to linger in the shopping mall, have a restorative coffee in the Sony Center plaza (p122), see Berlin from above from the Panoramapunkt (p123) or dive into German film history at the Museum für Film und Fernsehen (p123).

A visit to Potsdamer Platz is easily combined with the nearby Kulturforum complex, a cluster of museums that zeroes in on art, music and design. Seeing them all would easily keep you busy for a day, so if time is tight, stick to the Old Masters in the Gemäldegalerie (p125). Architecture aficionados can admire edgy contemporary structures on a stroll around the Diplomatenviertel (Diplomatic Quarter; p133) west of the Kulturforum, perhaps followed by some leafy respite in the vast Tiergarten (p131). East of Potsdamer Platz, the octagonal Leipziger Platz square has the huge and fancy LP12 Mall of Berlin (p137).

Local Life

Tiergarten When the sun is out, Berliners just want to get outdoors to the sweeping lawns, shady paths and romantic corners of the Tiergarten park (p131), followed up with a cold beer and pizza at the beer garden of Café am Neuen See (p137).

Beer garden concerts On Sundays in July and August, the Teehaus im Englischen Garten (p135) turns into a big garden party with free rock, pop and jazz concerts (www.konzertsommer-berlin.de).

Traffic light The clock-tower-shaped replica of Europe's first traffic light, from 1924, at the corner of Potsdamer Platz and Stresemannstrasse is a popular meeting point.

Getting There & Away

Bus No 200 comes through en route from Bahnhof Zoologischer Garten and Alexanderplatz; M41 links the Hauptbahnhof with Kreuzberg and Neukölln via Potsdamer Platz; and the M29 connects with Checkpoint Charlie.

S-Bahn S1 and S2 link Potsdamer Platz with Unter den Linden and the Scheunenviertel.

U-Bahn U2 stops at Potsdamer Platz and Mendelssohn-Bartholdy-Park.

Lonely Planet's Top Tip

From September until June, join hundreds of classical music fans – from students to tourists to desk jockeys – for free one-hour chamber concerts on Tuesdays at 1pm in the foyer of the Berliner Philharmonie.

✕ Best Places to Eat

➡ Ki-Nova (p135)

➡ Mabuhay (p133)

➡ Facil (p136)

➡ Qiu (p135)

For reviews, see p133.➡

◪ Best Places to Drink

➡ Café am Neuen See (p137)

➡ Stue Bar (p137)

➡ Solar Lounge (p137)

➡ Curtain Club (p136)

➡ Fragrances (p136)

For reviews, see p136.➡

◉ Best Architecture

➡ Sony Center (p122)

➡ Berliner Philharmonie (p130)

➡ Martin-Gropius-Bau (p128)

For reviews, see p122.➡

POTSDAMER PLATZ & TIERGARTEN

TOP SIGHT
POTSDAMER PLATZ

The rebirth of the historic Potsdamer Platz was Europe's biggest building project of the 1990s, a showcase of urban renewal masterminded by such top international architects as Renzo Piano and Helmut Jahn. An entire city quarter sprouted on terrain once divided by the Berlin Wall and today houses offices, theatres and cinemas, hotels, apartments and museums.

Until WWII sucked all life out of the area, Potsdamer Platz was Berlin's central traffic, entertainment and commercial hub. Its modern reinterpretation is again divided into three sections, of which the **Sony Center** is the flashiest and most visitor friendly, with a central plaza canopied by a glass roof that erupts in changing colours after dark. Segments from the **Berlin Wall** (Map p326) stand in the corner of Potsdamer Strasse and Ebertstrasse. Across Potsdamer Strasse, **Daimler City** has big hotels, a shopping mall, sprinkles of public art and entertainment venues that host movie premieres and galas during the Berlinale film festival in February. The **Beisheim Center**, with the Ritz-Carlton Hotel, is modelled after classic American skyscrapers.

DON'T MISS
- ➡ Panoramapunkt
- ➡ Museum für Film und Fernsehen
- ➡ Berlin Wall remnants
- ➡ Ice cream at Caffe e Gelato

PRACTICALITIES
- ➡ Map p326, G5
- ➡ Alte Potsdamer Strasse
- ➡ 🚌200, Ⓢ Potsdamer Platz, Ⓤ Potsdamer Platz

Sony Center

Designed by Helmut Jahn, the visually dramatic **Sony Center** (Map p326; www.potsdamer -platz.net; Potsdamer Strasse) is fronted by a 26-floor, glass-and-steel tower that's the highest building on Potsdamer Platz. It integrates rare relics from Potsdamer Platz' prewar era, such as a section of the facade of the **Hotel Esplanade** (visible from Bellevuestrasse) and the opulent **Kaisersaal**, whose 75m move to its current location required some wizardly technology. The heart of the Sony Center is a central plaza canopied by a tentlike glass roof with supporting beams radiating like bicycle spokes. The plaza and its many cafes lend themselves to hanging out and people-watching.

Museum für Film und Fernsehen

From silent movies to sci-fi, Germany's long and il-lustrious film history gets the star treatment at the engaging **Museum für Film und Fernsehen** (Map p326; Museum for Film & Television; ☑030-300 9030; www.deutsche-kinemathek.de; Potsdamer Strasse 2; adult/concession €8/5, free 4-8pm Thu; ⊙10am-6pm Wed & Fri-Mon, to 8pm Thu). The tour kicks off with an appropriate sense of drama as it sends you through a dizzying mirrored walkway that conjures visions of *The Cabinet of Dr Caligari.* Major themes include pioneers and early divas, silent-era classics such as Fritz Lang's *Metropolis,* Leni Riefenstahl's ground-breaking Nazi-era documentary *Olympia,* German exiles in Hollywood and post-WWII movies. Steal-ing the show, as she did in real life, is femme fatale Marlene Dietrich, whose glamour lives on through her original costumes, personal finery, photographs and documents. The **TV exhibit** upstairs has more niche appeal but is still fun if you always wanted to know what *Star Trek* sounds like in German.

Make use of the excellent audioguide (€2) as you work your way through various themed galleries.

The museum is part of the Filmhaus, which also harbours a film school, the Arsenal cinema (p137), a library and a museum shop.

Legoland Discovery Centre

The **Legoland Discovery Centre** (Map p326; ☑01806-6669 0110; www.legolanddiscoverycentre.de/berlin; Potsdamer Strasse 4; €19.50; ⊙10am-7pm, last admission 5pm) is an indoor amusement park made entirely of those little coloured plastic building blocks that many of us grew up with. Cute but low tech, it's best suited for kids aged three to eight. Skip the promotional intro-ductory film and head straight to adventure stations such as Ninjago to battle snakes and brave a laser labyrinth, or Merlin's Magic Library to become a wizard apprentice and 'fly' through a magical potion room. Other thrills include the 4D cinema (with tac-tile special effects), a slow-mo ride through the Drag-on's Castle, and a 'torture-tickle chamber'. Kids also love Space Mission, where they can build their own shuttle, explore galaxies and meet aliens. Grown-ups will have fun marvelling at a Berlin in miniature at Miniland, which uses more than two million Lego bricks to recreate major landmarks.

The website has tickets deals and combination tickets with other attractions.

Panoramapunkt

Europe's fastest lift, **Panoramapunkt** (Map p326; ☑030-2593 7080; www.panoramapunkt.de; Potsdamer Platz 1; adult/concession €7.50/6, without wait €11.50/9;

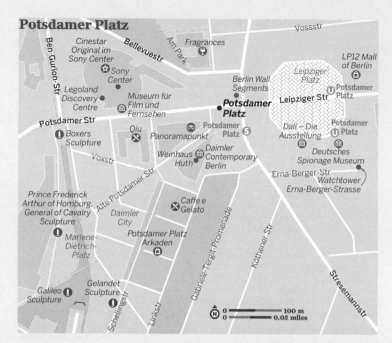

Potsdamer Platz

Map labels:
Vossstr
Ben-Gurion-Str
Cinestar Original im Sony Center
Bellevuestr
Am Park
Fragrances
LP12 Mall of Berlin
Sony Center
Legoland Discovery Centre
Museum für Film und Fernsehen
Berlin Wall Segments
Leipziger Platz
Potsdamer Platz
Potsdamer Platz
Leipziger Str
Potsdamer Str
Boxers Sculpture
Qiu
Panoramapunkt
Potsdamer Platz
Dalí – Die Ausstellung
Potsdamer Platz
Voxstr
Alte Potsdamer Str
Weinhaus Huth
Daimler Contemporary Berlin
Deutsches Spionage Museum
Erna-Berger-Str
Watchtower
Erna-Berger-Strasse
Prince Frederick Arthur of Homburg, General of Cavalry Sculpture
Daimler City
Caffe e Gelato
Marlene-Dietrich-Platz
Potsdamer Platz Arkaden
Gabriele-Tergit-Promenade
Köthener Str
Stresemannstr
Schellingstr
Linkstr
Galileo Sculpture
Gelandet Sculpture
0   100 m
0   0.05 miles

⊙10am-8pm Apr-Oct, to 6pm Nov-Mar) yo-yos up and down the red-brick postmodern Kollhoff Tower in 20 seconds. From the bilevel viewing platform at a lofty 100m, you can pinpoint the sights, make a java stop in the 1930s-style cafe, enjoy sunset from the terrace and check out the exhibit that peels back the layers of the square's history.

Daimler City Public Sculpture Tour

Daimler City is not only a postmodern urban landscape but also an exquisite outdoor gallery. Large-scale abstract sculptures by artists like Keith Haring and Mark di Suvero explore the relationship between art and urban space and inject much-needed visual appeal into what would otherwise be an austere environment. All public art on display is part of the Daimler Art Collection, which also maintains a permanent gallery space, the Daimler Contemporary Berlin (p128), at Potsdamer Platz.

A self-guided tour might start with Haring's **Boxers** (cnr Eichhornstrasse & Potsdamer Strasse), which shows two cut-steel stick figures – one blue, one red – seemingly punching each other out. Or are they embracing each other? You decide, then walk south to Marlene-Dietrich-Platz to ponder Frank Stella's otherworldly **Prince Frederick Arthur of Homburg, General of Cavalry** (Marlene-Dietrich-Platz). Made of white-silver aluminium, carbon and fibreglass, it explores the relationships of space, colour and form in a three-dimensional setting.

Just beyond, in the middle of a pond, is Mark di Suvero's **Galileo** (Eichhornstrasse), an abstract jumble of rusted steel T-beams assembled into a gravity-defying sculpture. A bit harder to detect is Auke de Vries's **Gelandet** (Schellingstrasse), Landed, which looks like a flying object teetering on the roof edge of the Atrium Tower. The tallest building on Potsdamer Platz, it was designed by Renzo Piano and is easily recognised by the square tower topped by a green cube.

TOP SIGHT
GEMÄLDEGALERIE

The Gemäldegalerie ranks among the world's finest and most comprehensive collections of European art from the 13th to the 18th centuries. Expect to feast your eyes on masterpieces by Titian, Goya, Botticelli, Holbein, Gainsborough, Canaletto, Hals, Rubens, Vermeer and many other Old Masters. The gallery also hosts high-profile visiting exhibits featuring works from the great artists of this period.

Collection Overview

The Gemäldegalerie's opening in a purpose-built Kulturforum space in 1998 marked the happy reunion of a collection separated by the Cold War for half a century. Some works had remained at the Bode-Museum in East Berlin, the rest went on display in the West Berlin suburb of Dahlem. Today, about 1500 paintings span the arc of artistic vision over five centuries. Dutch and Flemish painters, including Rembrandt, are especially well represented, as are exponents of the Italian Renaissance. Another focus is on German artists from the late Middle Ages, and there's also a sprinkling of British, French and Spanish masters.

East Wing: German, Dutch & Flemish Masters

The exhibit kicks off with religious paintings from the Middle Ages and moves quickly to the Renaissance and works by two of the era's most famous artists: Albrecht Dürer and Lucas Cranach the Elder. A standout in Room 2 is Dürer's **Portrait of Hieronymus Holzschuher** (1526), a Nuremberg

DON'T MISS

➡ Rembrandt Room (Room X)

➡ *Amor Victorius* (Room XIV)

➡ *Dutch Proverbs* (Room 7)

➡ *Fountain of Youth* (Room III)

PRACTICALITIES

➡ Gallery of Old Masters

➡ Map p326, E5

➡ 030-266 424 242

➡ www.smb.museum/gg

➡ Matthäikirchplatz

➡ adult/concession/ under 18 €10/5/free

➡ ⊙10am–6pm Tue, Wed & Fri, to 8pm Thu, 11am–6pm Sat & Sun

➡ ♿

➡ 🚌M29, M48, M85, 200, ⑤Potsdamer Platz, ⓤPotsdamer Platz

TOP TIPS

➡ Take advantage of the excellent free audioguide to get the low-down on selected works.

➡ Note that the room numbering system is quite confusing as both Latin (I, II, III) and Arabic numbers (1, 2, 3) are used.

➡ A tour of all 72 rooms covers almost 2km, so allow at least a couple of hours for your visit and wear comfortable shoes.

➡ Admission is free to anyone under 18.

The building housing this encyclopedic art collection was designed by the Munich firm Hilmer & Sattler and is essentially a postmodern interpretation of the clear lines and stark symmetry of the Schinkel era. The entrance sits atop a sloping piazza, while the permanent galleries radiate from the football-field-size central hall anchored by a fountain designed by Walter De Maria. Usually deliberately empty, this space has been used for temporary exhibits since 2017.

patrician, career politician and strong supporter of the Reformation. Note how the artist brilliantly lasers in on his friend's features with utmost precision, down to the furrows, wrinkles and thinning hair.

One of Cranach's finest works is **Fountain of Youth** (1546) in Room III, which illustrates humankind's yearning for eternal youth. Old crones plunge into a pool of water and emerge as dashing hotties – no need for plastic surgeons! The transition is also reflected in the landscape, which is stark and craggy on the left and lush and fertile on the right.

A main exponent of the Dutch Renaissance was Pieter Bruegel the Elder who here is represented with the dazzling **Dutch Proverbs** (1559) in Room 7. The moralistic yet humorous painting crams more than 100 proverbs and idioms into a single seaside village scene. While some point up the absurdity of human behaviour, others unmask its imprudence and sinfulness. Some sayings are still in use today, among them 'swimming against the tide' and 'armed to the teeth'.

North Wing: Dutch 17th-Century Paintings

The first galleries in the north wing feature some exceptional portraits, most notably Frans Hals' **Malle Babbe** (1633) in Room 13. Note how Hals ingeniously captures the character and vitality of his subject 'Crazy Barbara' with free-wielding brushstrokes. Hals met the woman with the near-demonic laugh in the workhouse for the mentally ill where his son Pieter was also a resident. The tin mug and owl are symbols of Babbe's fondness for a tipple.

Another eye-catcher is **Woman with a Pearl Necklace** (1662) in Room 18, one of the most famous paintings by Dutch realist Jan Vermeer. It depicts a young woman studying herself in the mirror while fastening a pearl necklace around her neck, an intimate moment beautifully captured with characteristic soft brushstrokes.

The real highlight of the north wing awaits in the octagonal Room X, which is dedicated to Rembrandt and dominated by the large-scale **Mennonite Minister Cornelis Claesz Anslo** (1641), which shows the preacher in conversation with his wife. The huge open Bible and his gesturing hand sticking out in almost 3D-style from the centre of the painting are meant to emphasise the strength of his religious convictions. Also note Rembrandt's small self-portrait next to it.

GEMÄLDEGALERIE

West Wing: Italian Masterpieces

The first galleries in the west wing stay in the 17th and 18th centuries. Crowds often form before Canaletto's **Il Campo di Rialto** (1758–63) in Room XII, which depicts the arcaded main market square of the artist's home town, Venice, with stunning precision and perspective. Note the goldsmith shops on the left, the wig-wearing merchants in the centre and the stores selling paintings and furniture on the right.

Older by 150 years is Caravaggio's delightful **Amor Victorius** (1602/3) in Room XIV. Wearing nothing but a mischievous grin, a pair of black angel wings and a fistful of arrows, this cheeky Amor means business. Note the near-photographic realism achieved by the dramatic use of light and shadow.

The next galleries travel back to the Renaissance when Raphael, Titian and Correggio dominated Italian art. Correggio's **Leda with the Swan** (1532) in Room XV is worth a closer look. Judging by her blissed-out expression, Leda is having a fine time with that swan who, according to Greek mythology, is none other than Zeus himself. The erotically charged nature of this painting apparently so incensed its one-time owner Louis of Orleans that he cut off Leda's head with a knife. It was later restored.

Lest you think that all West Wing paintings have a naughty subtext, let us draw your attention to Sandro Botticelli's **Madonna with Child and Singing Angels** (1477) in Room XVIII. This circular painting (a format called a *tondo*) shows Mary flanked by two sets of four wingless angels. It's an intimate moment that shows the Virgin tenderly embracing – perhaps even about to breastfeed – her child. The white lilies are symbols of her purity.

◉ SIGHTS

Sights in this compact area are handily clustered around Potsdamer Platz itself and in the adjacent Kulturforum museum complex. The Diplomatic Quarter is just west of here, the Tiergarten park to the north. It's all easily explored on foot.

◉ Potsdamer Platz

POTSDAMER PLATZ   AREA
See p122.

MARTIN-GROPIUS-BAU   GALLERY
Map p326 (✆030-254 860; www.gropiusbau.de; Niederkirchner Strasse 7; cost varies, usually €10-12, under 16 free; ◷10am-7pm Wed-Mon; ☒M41, ⓢPotsdamer Platz, ⓤPotsdamer Platz) With its mosaics, terracotta reliefs and airy atrium, this Italian Renaissance–style exhibit space named for its architect (Bauhaus founder Walter Gropius' great-uncle) is a celebrated venue for high-calibre art and cultural exhibits. Whether it's a David Bowie retrospective, the latest works of Ai Weiwei or an ethnological exhibit on the mysteries of Angkor Wat, it's bound to be well curated and utterly fascinating.

The Berlin state parliament convenes in the stately neo-Renaissance structure (the Abgeordnetenhaus) across the street.

WATCHTOWER ERNA-
BERGER-STRASSE   MEMORIAL
Map p326 (www.berlinwallexpo.de; Erna-Berger-Strasse; €3.50; ◷11am-5pm, weather permitting; ☒M41, ⓤPotsdamer Platz, ⓢPotsdamer Platz) Imagine what it was like to be a Berlin Wall border guard when climbing up the iron ladder of one of the few remaining watchtowers. The octagonal observation perch of this 1969 model was particularly cramped and later replaced by larger square towers. After a thorough restoration by a nonprofit group, the tower is now open to the public.

DALÍ – DIE AUSSTELLUNG   GALLERY
Map p326 (www.daliberlin.de; Leipziger Platz 7; adult/concession €12.50/9.50, with tour €19.50/14; ◷10am-8pm Jul & Aug, noon-8pm Sep-Jun; ☒200, M41, M48, M85, ⓢPotsdamer Platz, ⓤPotsdamer Platz) If you only know Salvador Dalí as the painter of melting watches, burning giraffes and other surrealist imagery, this private collection will likely open new perspectives on the man and his work. Here, the focus is on his graphics, illustrations, sculptures, drawings and films, with highlights including etchings on the theme of Tristan and Isolde and epic sculptures like *Surrealist Angel*, as well as the *Don Quixote* lithographs.

If you need a little help understanding this fantasy world, join a guided tour offered throughout the day by Dali Scouts.

DEUTSCHES SPIONAGE MUSEUM   MUSEUM
Map p326 (German Spy Museum; ✆030-398 200 451; www.deutsches-spionagemuseum. de; Leipziger Platz 9; adult/concession €12/8; ◷10am-8pm, last entry 7pm; ☒200, ⓢPotsdamer Platz, ⓤPotsdamer Platz) High-tech and interactive, this private museum not only documents the evolution of spying from ancient Egypt to the 20th century, it also displays hundreds of ingenious tools of the trade, including a lipstick pistol, shoe bugs and an ultra-rare Enigma cipher machine. You learn about famous spies, get to encrypt a message, and discover your digital transparency in the Facebook puzzle. A hit with kids of all ages is the wicked laser labyrinth.

Film buffs, meanwhile, love to linger among the original props from fictional spy hero James Bond. The exhibit also addresses a hot topic issue of our times: big data as well as data security, rights in the surveillance society and issues surrounding social media.

DAIMLER
CONTEMPORARY BERLIN   GALLERY
Map p326 (✆030-2594 1420; www.art.daimler. com; Alte Potsdamer Strasse 5, Weinhaus Huth, 4th fl; ◷11am-6pm; ☒200, ⓢPotsdamer Platz, ⓤPotsdamer Platz) 〔FREE〕 Escape the city bustle at this quiet, loft-style gallery where the Daimler corporation shares selections from its considerable collection of international abstract, conceptual and minimalist art with the public. It's on the top floor of the historic **Weinhaus Huth** (Map p326), a rare surviving building from pre-WWII Potsdamer Platz. Ring the bell to be buzzed in.

◉ Kulturforum

GEMÄLDEGALERIE   GALLERY
See p125.

TOP SIGHT
GEDENKSTÄTTE DEUTSCHER WIDERSTAND

If you've seen the movie *Valkyrie* you know the story of Claus von Stauffenberg, the poster boy of the German resistance against Hitler and the Third Reich. The very rooms where senior army officers led by Stauffenberg plotted their bold but ill-fated assassination attempt on the Führer on 20 July 1944 are now home to the **German Resistance Memorial Centre**. The building itself, the historic Bendlerblock, harboured the Wehrmacht high command from 1935 to 1945 and today is the secondary seat of the German defence ministry (the primary is still in Bonn).

Aside from detailing the Stauffenberg-led coup, the centre also comprehensively documents the efforts of many other Germans who risked their lives opposing the Third Reich for ideological, ethical, religious or military reasons. Most were just regular folks, such as the students Hans and Sophie Scholl of the White Rose, or the craftmaker Georg Elser; others were prominent citizens like the artist Käthe Kollwitz and the theologian Dietrich Bonhoeffer.

In the yard, a sculpture marks the spot where Stauffenberg and three of his co-conspirators were executed right after the failed coup.

DON'T MISS

→ Stauffenberg exhibit (rooms 8 to 11)
→ White Rose exhibit (room 15)

PRACTICALITIES

→ Map p326, D5
→ ☎030-2699 5000
→ www.gdw-berlin.de
→ Stauffenbergstrasse 13-14
→ admission free
→ ⊙9am-6pm Mon-Wed & Fri, to 8pm Thu, 10am-6pm Sat & Sun
→ 🚌M29, M48, ⑤Potsdamer Platz, ⓤPotsdamer Platz, Kurfürstenstrasse

POTSDAMER PLATZ & TIERGARTEN SIGHTS

KUNSTGEWERBEMUSEUM   MUSEUM

Map p326 (Museum of Decorative Arts; ☎030-266 424 242; www.smb.museum; Matthäikirchplatz; adult/concession/under 18 €8/4/free; ⊙10am-6pm Tue-Fri, 11am-6pm Sat & Sun; 🚌M29, M48, M85, 200, ⑤Potsdamer Platz, ⓤPotsdamer Platz) This prized collection of European design, fashion and decorative arts from the Middle Ages to today is part of the Kulturforum museum cluster. You can feast your eyes on exquisitely ornate medieval reliquaries and portable altars or compare Bauhaus classics to contemporary designs by Philippe Starck and Ettore Sottsass. Pride of place goes to the Fashion Gallery with classic designer outfits and accessories from the past 150 years.

KUPFERSTICHKABINETT   GALLERY

Map p326 (Museum of Prints & Drawings; ☎030-266 424 242; www.smb.museum/kk; Matthäikirchplatz; adult/concession €6/3; ⊙10am-6pm Tue-Fri, 11am-6pm Sat & Sun; 🚌M29, M48, M85, 200, ⑤Potsdamer Platz, ⓤPotsdamer Platz) One of the world's largest and finest collections of art on paper, this gallery shelters a bonanza of hand-illustrated books, illuminated manuscripts, drawings and prints produced mostly in Europe from the 14th century onward – Dürer to Rembrandt to Schinkel, Picasso to Giacometti and Gerhard Richter.

Among its most prized possessions are Botticelli's illustrations for Dante's *Divine Comedy*. Alas, these fragile works don't do well under light, which is why only a tiny fraction of the collection is shown on a rotating basis.

MUSIKINSTRUMENTEN-MUSEUM   MUSEUM

Map p326 (Musical Instruments Museum; ☎030-2548 1178; www.simpk.de; Tiergartenstrasse 1, enter via Ben-Gurion-Strasse; adult/concession/under 18 €6/3/free; ⊙9am-5pm Tue, Wed & Fri, to 8pm Thu, to 5pm Sat & Sun; 🚌200, ⑤Potsdamer Platz, ⓤPotsdamer Platz) This darling museum is packed with fun, precious and rare sound machines, including the glass harmonica invented by Ben Franklin, a flute played by Frederick the Great, and Johann Sebastian Bach's harpsichord. Stop at the listening stations to hear what some of the more obscure instruments sound like.

There are also plenty of old trumpets, bizarre bagpipes and even a talking walking stick. A crowd favourite is the Mighty

POTSDAMER STRASSE REBOOT

Running south from Potsdamer Platz into the district of Schöneberg, busy Potsdamer Strasse has, in recent years, been evolving from downmarket to hip. Scores of edgy galleries, avant-garde boutiques and zeitgeist-capturing restaurants are now wedged between the Turkish grocers, penny stores and sex shops. The section north of U-Bahn station Kurfürstenstrasse is the most interesting. Soak up the vibe on a leisurely late-afternoon stroll before refueling at one of these tasty feed stops.

Kin Dee (☑030-215 5294; www.kindeeberlin.com; Lützowstrasse 81; tasting menu €45; ⊙6-10pm Tue-Sat; ☎; ⓊKurfürstenstrasse) One of most buzzed-about new restaurants on Potsdamer Strasse is Dalad Kambhu's lair Kin Dee, where she fearlessly catapults classic Thai dishes into the 21st century, and even adapts them by using locally grown ingredients. One constant is her signature homemade spice pastes that beautifully underline the aroma dimensions of each dish.

Joseph-Roth-Diele (Map p326; ☑030-2636 9884; www.joseph-roth-diele.de; Potsdamer Strasse 75; mains €7-13; ⊙10am-11pm Mon-Thu, to midnight Fri; ⓊKurfürstenstrasse) Named for an Austrian Jewish writer, this wood-panelled salon time warps you back to the 1920s, when Roth used to live next door. Walls decorated with bookshelves and quotations from his works draw a literary, chatty crowd, especially at lunchtime when two daily changing €5 specials (one vegetarian) supplement the hearty menu of German classics. Pay at the counter.

Panama (☑030-983 208 435; www.oh-panama.com; Potsdamer Strasse 91; dishes €9-19; ⊙6-11pm Wed-Sat; ☎; ⓊKurfürstenstrasse) On balmy nights, a glass of rosé and a grazing session in the courtyard of this art-crowd darling will likely transport you, maybe not quite to Panama, but certainly away from Berlin's urban velocity. Elevating standards on up-and-coming Potsdamer Strasse, the produce-focused small-plate menu – divided into raw, leaves, grains, meat and fish – is innovative and sometimes brilliantly experimental.

Sticks'n'Sushi (Map p326; ☑030-2610 3656; www.sticksnsushi.berlin; Potsdamer Strasse 85; bites €3.50-20; ⊙noon-11pm Sun & Mon, to midnight Tue-Sat; ☎; ⓊKurfürstenstrasse) At Germany's first branch of Danish cult chain Sticks'n'Sushi, sushi and yakitori get a creative twist that results in eye-candy small plates like Shake Tataki (flambeed salmon) or Kushi Katzu (panko-encrusted duck breast). It's all served in a dining room whose cathedral ceilings, giant chandeliers and spiral staircase engender cosmopolitan cosiness.

Wurlitzer (1929), an organ with more buttons and keys than a troop of beefeaters, that's cranked up at noon on Saturday and during the occasional silent movie screening. Classical concerts, many free, take place year-round (ask for a schedule or check the website).

BERLINER PHILHARMONIE ARCHITECTURE, CONCERT HALL
Map p326 (☑030-2548 8156; www.berliner-philharmoniker.de; Herbert-von-Karajan-Strasse 1; tours adult/concession €5/3; ⊙tours 1.30pm Sep-Jun; ☐M29, M48, M85, 200, ⓈPotsdamer Platz, ⓊPotsdamer Platz) A masterpiece of organic architecture, Hans Scharoun's 1963 iconic, honey-coloured concert venue is the home base of the prestigious Berliner Philharmoniker (p137). The auditorium feels like the inside of a finely crafted instrument and boasts supreme acoustics and excellent sight lines from every seat.

It's an imposing yet intimate hall with terraced and angled 'vineyard' seating wrapped around a central orchestra stage. One-hour tours (in German and English, no reservations needed) meet at the artists' entrance across the parking lot facing Potsdamer Strasse and cover the architecture and acoustics of the buildings as well as the history of the orchestra. The adjacent Kammermusiksaal, also based on a design by Scharoun, is essentially a more compact riff on the Philharmonie.

MATTHÄUSKIRCHE CHURCH
Map p326 (Church of St Matthews; ☑030-262 1202; www.stiftung-stmatthaeus.de; Matthäikirch-

platz; ☺11am-6pm Tue-Sun; ☑M29, M48, M85, Ⓢ Potsdamer Platz, Ⓤ Potsdamer Platz) **FREE** Standing a little bit lost and forlorn within the Kulturforum, the Stüler-designed Matthäuskirche (1846) is a beautiful neo-Romanesque confection with alternating bands of red and ochre brick and a light-flooded, modern sanctuary filled with artworks, including the floor sculpture *Steps* by Micha Ullman. A nice time to visit is for the free 20-minute organ recitals at 12.30pm Tuesday to Sunday. Views from the tower are free but only so-so.

GEDENKSTÄTTE STILLE HELDEN   MUSEUM
Map p326 (Silent Heroes Memorial Center; ☑030-263 923 822; www.gedenkstaette-stille-helden. de; Stauffenbergstrasse 13-14, 3rd fl; ☺9am-6pm Mon-Wed & Fri, to 8pm Thu, 10am-6pm Sat & Sun; ☑M48, M29, 200, Ⓤ Potsdamer Platz, Kurfürstenstrasse, Ⓢ Potsdamer Platz) **FREE** The Silent Heroes Memorial Center is dedicated to ordinary Germans who found the courage to help their persecuted Jewish neighbours through such actions as providing food, hiding people or obtaining fake ID cards. Using documents, photographs and objects, the exhibit illustrates 10 case studies of both successful and failed rescue attempts.

NEUE NATIONALGALERIE   GALLERY
Map p326 (www.neue-nationalgalerie.de; Potsdamer Strasse 50; ☺closed for renovation; ☑200, Ⓤ Potsdamer Platz, Ⓢ Potsdamer Platz) The fabulous collection of early-20th-century art housed at the Neue Nationalgalerie is off view until renovations of the gallery, led by architect David Chipperfield, are completed (anticipated by the end of 2020). The building itself is a late masterpiece by Ludwig Mies van der Rohe. All glass and steel and squatting on a raised platform, it echoes a postmodern Buddhist temple.

There's not much to see for now, although the construction wall has been turned into a sidewalk exhibit featuring photographs of the iconic building and its creator.

◉ Tiergarten & Diplomatenviertel

★ TIERGARTEN   PARK
(Strasse des 17 Juni; ☑100, 200, Ⓢ Potsdamer Platz, Brandenburger Tor, Ⓤ Brandenburger Tor) Berlin's rulers used to hunt boar and pheasants in the rambling Tiergarten until garden architect Peter Lenné landscaped the grounds in the 19th century. Today it's one of the world's largest urban parks, popular for strolling, jogging, picnicking, frisbee tossing and, yes, nude sunbathing and gay cruising (especially around the Löwenbrücke).

It is bisected by a major artery, the Strasse des 17 Juni. Walking across the entire park takes at least an hour, but even a shorter stroll has its rewards.

SIEGESSÄULE   MONUMENT
Map p326 (Victory Column; Grosser Stern, Strasse des 17 Juni; adult/concession €3/2.50; ☺9.30am-6.30pm Mon-Fri, to 7pm Sat & Sun Apr-Oct, 10am-5pm Mon-Fri, to 5.30pm Sat & Sun Nov-Mar; ☑100, Ⓤ Hansaplatz, Ⓢ Bellevue) Like arms of a starfish, five roads merge into the Grosser Stern roundabout at the heart of the huge Tiergarten park. The Victory Column at its centre celebrates 19th-century Prussian military triumphs and is crowned by a gilded statue of the goddess Victoria. Today it is also a symbol of Berlin's gay community. Climb 285 steps for sweeping views of the park.

The column originally stood in front of the Reichstag until the Nazis moved it here in 1938 to make room for their Germania urban planning project. The pedestal was added at the time, bringing the column height to 67m. Film buffs might remember the Goddess of Victory on top from a key scene in Wim Wenders' 1985 flick *Wings of Desire*. In July 2008, shortly before becoming US president, Barack Obama gave a speech in front of 200,000 people here.

SCHWULES MUSEUM   MUSEUM
(Gay Museum; ☑030-6959 9050; www.schwules museum.de; Lützowstrasse 73; adult/concession €7.50/4; ☺2-6pm Mon, Wed, Fri & Sun, to

---

KULTURFORUM COMBO TICKET

A Kulturforum area ticket (Bereichskarte) costs €12 (concession €6) and includes same-day admission to the Gemäldegalerie, the Kunstgewerbemuseum, the Kupferstichkabinett and the Musikinstrumenten-Museum. Admission to all museums is free to anyone under 18.

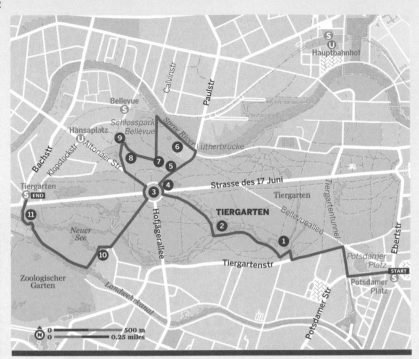

🏃 Neighbourhood Walk
A Leisurely Tiergarten Meander

START POTSDAMER PLATZ
END TIERGARTEN S-BAHN STATION
LENGTH 5KM; TWO HOURS

A ramble around Tiergarten delivers a relaxing respite from the sightseeing track. From Potsdamer Platz, make your way to ❶ **Luiseninsel**, an enchanting gated garden dotted with statues and seasonal flower beds. Not far away is ❷ **Rousseauinsel**, a memorial to 18th-century French philosopher Jean-Jacques Rousseau. It was modelled after his actual burial site near Paris and placed on a tiny island in a sweet little pond.

At the heart of the park, engulfed by traffic, the imposing ❸ **Siegessäule** (p131) is crowned by a gilded statue of the goddess Victoria and commemorates Prussian military triumphs enforced by Iron Chancellor Otto von Bismarck. Nearby, the colossal ❹ **Bismarck Denkmal**, a monument to the man, shows him flanked by statues of Atlas (with the world on his back), Siegfried (wielding a sword) and Germania (stomping a panther).

Following Spreeweg north takes you past the oval ❺ **Bundespräsidialamt**, the offices of the German president, to the presidential residence in ❻ **Schloss Bellevue**, a snowy-white neoclassical royal palace built for the younger brother of Frederick the Great in 1785.

Follow the path along the Spree, then turn left into the ❼ **Englischer Garten** (English Garden) created in the '50s to commemorate the 1948 Berlin Airlift. At its heart, the ❽ **Teehaus im Englischen Garten** (p135) hosts free summer concerts in its beer garden. Afterwards, check out the latest art exhibit at the ❾ **Akademie der Künste** (p133), on the edge of the Hansaviertel, a modernist quarter that emerged from a 1957 international building exhibition.

Walk south back through the park, crossing Altonaer Strasse and Strasse des 17 Juni, to arrive at the Neuer See with ❿ **Café am Neuen See** (p136) at its south end. Stroll north along the Landwehrkanal via the ⓫ **Gaslaternenmuseum**, an open-air collection of 90 historic gas lanterns, and wrap up your tour at Tiergarten S-Bahn station.

8pm Thu, to 7pm Sat; M29, Nollendorfplatz, Kurfürstenstrasse) In a former print shop, this nonprofit museum is one of the largest and most important cultural institutions documenting LGBTIQ culture around the world, albeit with a special focus on Berlin and Germany. It presents changing exhibits on gay icons, artists, gender issues and historical themes and also hosts film screenings and discussions to keep things dynamic.

Ask inside about guided English-language tours.

DIPLOMATENVIERTEL AREA

Map p326 (Diplomatic Quarter; M29, 200, Potsdamer Platz, Potsdamer Platz) In the 1920s, a quiet villa-studded colony south of the Tiergarten evolved into Berlin's embassy quarter. After WWII the obliterated area remained in a state of quiet decay while the embassies all set up in the West German capital of Bonn. After reunification, many countries rebuilt on their historic lots, accounting for some of Berlin's boldest new architecture, which can be nicely explored on a leisurely wander.

BAUHAUS ARCHIV MUSEUM

Map p326 (www.bauhaus.de; Klingelhöferstrasse 14; closed for renovation; 100, Nollendorfplatz) Founded in 1919, the Bauhaus was a seminal school of avant-garde architecture, design and art that was shut down by the Nazis in Berlin in 1933. The museum is undergoing extensive renovation and expansion and is set to reopen in 2023. In the meantime you can visit the museum's temporary location at Knesebeckstrasse 1-2.

AKADEMIE DER KÜNSTE GALLERY

Map p326 (Academy of Arts; 030-200 572 000; www.adk.de; Hanseatenweg 10; cost varies by exhibit, free last 4hr Tue; building 10am-8pm, exhibit hours vary; Bellevue, Hansaplatz) The Academy of Arts has a pedigree going back to 1696 but its cultural programming is solidly rooted in the here and now. It covers all forms of artistic expression, from architecture to literature to music, theatre and digital media, and also stages high-profile exhibits.

A sculpture by Henry Moore fronts the late-1950s building by Werner Düttmann, a student of Hans Scharoun. Inside you'll find a well-stocked bookshop and a ho-hum cafe.

 **EATING**

The best restaurants on Potsdamer Platz are in the hotels. For a quick nibble, head to the food courts in the basement of the Potsdamer Platz Arkaden (p137) mall and the 2nd floor of the LP12 Mall of Berlin (p137). The beer gardens tucked within Tiergarten park also serve food and are destinations in their own right.

MABUHAY INDONESIAN €

Map p326 (030-265 1867; www.mabuhay.juisyfood.com; Köthener Strasse 28; mains €6-13; noon-3pm Mon-Fri, 5-9.30pm Mon-Sat; ; Mendelssohn-Bartholdy-Park) Tucked into a concrete courtyard, this hole-in-the-wall scores a one for looks and a 10 for the food. Usually packed (especially at lunchtime), it delivers Indonesian food with as much authenticity as possible. The heat meter has been adjusted for German tastes, but the spicing of such dishes as gado gado or curry rendang is still feisty and satisfying.

CAFFE E GELATO ICE CREAM €

Map p326 (030-2529 7832; www.caffe-e-gelato.de; Alte Potsdamer Strasse 7, Potsdamer Platz Arkaden; scoops €1.60-2.20; 10am-10.30pm Mon-Thu, to 11pm Fri, to 11.30pm Sat, 10.30am-10.30pm Sun; Potsdamer Platz, Potsdamer Platz) Traditional Italian-style ice cream gets a 21st-century twist at this huge cafe on the upper floor of the Potsdamer Platz Arkaden (p137) mall. Among the homemade creamy concoctions are organic and sugar-, gluten- and lactose-free varieties in unusual flavours, including yoghurt-walnut-fig and almond crunch.

VAPIANO ITALIAN €

Map p326 (030-2300 5005; www.vapiano.de; Potsdamer Platz 5; mains €6.50-11; 11am-midnight Sun-Thu, to 1am Fri & Sat, 200, Potsdamer Platz, Potsdamer Platz) Matteo Thun's jazzy decor is a great foil for the tasty Italian fare at this successful German self-service chain. Mix-and-match pastas, creative salads and crusty pizzas are all prepared right before your eyes, and there's fresh basil on the table.

★**KI-NOVA** INTERNATIONAL €€

Map p326 (030-2546 4860; www.ki-nova.de; Potsdamer Strasse 2; mains €9-17; 11.30am-11pm Mon-Fri, 1-11pm Sat, 1-9pm Sun; ; 200, Potsdamer Platz, Potsdamer Platz)

POTSDAMER PLATZ & TIERGARTEN EATING

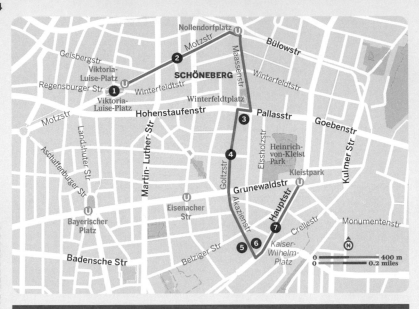

🏃 Local Life
Saunter Around Schöneberg

Schöneberg flaunts a mellow middle-class identity but has a radical pedigree rooted in the squatter days of the '80s. Stroll from bourgeois Viktoria-Luise-Platz through Berlin's traditional gay quarter and along streets squeezed tight with cafes and boutiques to ethnically flavoured Hauptstrasse. The best days for this walk are Wednesdays or Saturdays when a farmers market sets up on Winterfeldtplatz.

❶ Viktoria-Luise-Platz

Schöneberg flaunts a mellow middle-class identity but has a radical pedigree rooted in the squatter days of the '80s. Stroll from bourgeois Viktoria-Luise-Platz through Berlin's traditional gay quarter and along streets squeezed tight with cafes and boutiques to ethnically flavoured Hauptstrasse. The best days for this walk are Wednesdays or Saturdays when a farmers market sets up on Winterfeldtplatz.

❷ Nollendorfplatz & the 'Gay Villa'

In the early 20th century, Nollendorfplatz was a bustling urban square filled with cafes, theatres and people on parade. Then as now, it was also the gateway to Berlin's **historic gay quarter**, where British writer Christopher Isherwood penned *Berlin Stories* (the inspiration for *Cabaret*) while living at Nollendorfstrasse 17. Rainbow flags still fly proudly, especially along Motzstrasse and Fuggerstrasse.

❸ Chocophile Alert

Winterfeldt Schokoladen (📞030-2362 3256; www.winterfeldt-schokoladen.de; Goltzstrasse 23; ⏱9am-8pm Mon-Fri, to 6pm Sat, noon-7pm Sun; ⓊNollendorfplatz) stocks a vast range of international handmade gourmet chocolates, all displayed in the original oak fixtures of a 19th-century pharmacy, which doubles as a cafe.

❹ Boutique Hopping

Goltzstrasse and its continuation Akazienstrasse teem with indie boutiques selling everything from vintage clothing to slinky underwear, antique books to handmade jewellery, exotic teas to cooking supplies. No high-street chain in sight! Wedged in between are charismatic cafes, many with pavement terraces.

❺ Double Eye

Local coffee lovers are addicted to the award-winning espresso of **Double Eye**

Viktoria-Luise-Platz

(☎0179 456 6960; Akazienstrasse 22; ⊙8.30am-6.30pm Mon-Fri, 9am-6pm Sat; U Eisenacher Strasse), which is why no one seems to mind the inevitable out-the-door queue. Since there are few seats, this is more of a grab-and-go cafe.

6 Möve im Felsenkeller

An artist hang-out since the 1920s, woodsy **Möve im Felsenkeller** (☎030-781 3447; Akazienstrasse 2; ⊙4pm-midnight Mon-Sat; U Eisenacher Strasse) is where Jeffrey Eugenides penned his 2002 bestseller *Middlesex*. A stuffed seagull dangling from the ceiling keeps an eye on patrons seeking inspiration from the six beers on tap. Gentrification has threatened the survival of this Old Berlin gem, but so far the owners have been able to stave off closure.

7 Hauptstrasse

Chic boutiques give way to grocers and doner kebab shops along main artery Hauptstrasse. The Turkish supermarket **Öz-Gida** (☎030-7871 5291; www.ozgida.de; Hauptstrasse 16; ⊙8am-8pm Mon-Sat; U Kleistpark) is known citywide for its olive selection, cheese spreads and quality halal meats. In the '70s, David Bowie and Iggy Pop shared a pad at Hauptstrasse 155.

The name of this lunchtime favourite hints at the concept: 'ki' is Japanese for energy and 'nova' Latin for new. 'New energy' in this case translates into health-focused yet comforting bites starring global and regional superfoods from kale to cranberries. The contempo interior radiates urban warmth with heavy plank tables, black tiled bar, movie stills and floor-to-ceiling windows.

QIU INTERNATIONAL €€

Map p326 (☎030-590 051 230; www.qiu.de; Potsdamer Strasse 3, Mandala Hotel; 2-course lunches €16-25; ⊙noon-1am Sun-Wed, to 3am Thu-Sat; P; 🚌200, S Potsdamer Platz, U Potsdamer Platz) The weekly changing business lunch (noon to 3pm Monday to Friday) at this stylish bar-lounge at the Mandala Hotel (p243) also includes soup or salad, a nonalcoholic beverage, and coffee or tea. We call that a steal. It's also a nice spot for cocktails with a view of the golden Bisazza mosaic water wall.

TEEHAUS IM ENGLISCHEN GARTEN INTERNATIONAL €€

Map p326 (☎030-3948 0400; www.teehaus-tiergarten.com; Altonaer Strasse 2; mains €9-19.50; ⊙noon-11pm Tue-Sat, from 10am Sun; 🚌100, S Bellevue, U Hansaplatz) Not even many Berliners know about this enchanting reed-thatched teahouse tucked into the northwestern corner of Tiergarten park. It's best in summer, when the beer garden overlooking an idyllic pond seats up to 500 people for cold beers and a global roster of simple, tasty dishes from quiche to schnitzel. Nice touch: the build-your-own Sunday breakfast.

Also on Sundays, in July and August the venue hosts a hugely popular free concert series (www.konzertsommer-berlin.de) with performances at 4pm and 7pm.

FACIL INTERNATIONAL €€€

Map p326 (☎030-590 051 234; www.facil.de; Potsdamer Strasse 3, Mandala Hotel, 5th fl; 1-/2-/3-course lunches €21/38/51, 4-8 course dinners €122-195; ⊙noon-3pm & 7-11pm Mon-Fri; P 📶; 🚌200, S Potsdamer Platz, U Potsdamer Platz) With two Michelin stars to its name, Michael Kempf's fare is hugely innovative yet deliciously devoid of unnecessary flights of fancy. Enjoy it while draped in a sleek Donghia chair and surrounded by a bamboo garden on the 5th floor of the Mandala Hotel. The glass ceiling can be retracted for alfresco dining in fine weather. Budget-minded gourmets take advantage of the lunchtime menu.

CAFE EINSTEIN STAMMHAUS   AUSTRIAN €€€

(📞030-2639 1917; www.cafeeinstein.com; Kurfürstenstrasse 58; breakfast €7-15, mains dinner €19-32; ⊙8am-midnight; ⓤNollendorfplatz) In the former home of silent-movie star Henny Porten, this Vienna-style cafe is the living room of moneyed, genteel types reading the morning paper over black coffee or tucking into *Wiener Schnitzel* at night. The 'Einstein breakfast' is a prime pick any time of day (served until 6pm). Marble tabletops, jumbo-sized mirrors and high stucco-trimmed ceilings add to the sophisticated vibe.

DESBROSSES   EUROPEAN €€€

Map p326 (📞030-337 775 402; www.desbrosses.de; Potsdamer Platz 3, Ritz-Carlton Berlin; mains €18-30; ⊙6.30am-2.30pm & 6-10pm; P🅿🛜; 🚊200, ⓢPotsdamer Platz, ⓤPotsdamer Platz) The original 1875 brasserie at the Ritz-Carlton was moved here from southern France and is anchored by an open kitchen where toqued chefs turn out Berlin and central European classics using vegetables and herbs grown on their own organic fields. For a treat, book ahead for the legendary Sunday brunch (12.30pm to 3.30pm September to May; €115) with bottomless champagne.

🍺 DRINKING & NIGHTLIFE

The nicest bars in this area are in the hotels and are quite pricey. For a bit more action, head to the places ringing the Sony Center's central plaza, although they're overpriced. In summer, Tiergarten beckons with its beer gardens. If you need a final nightcap, try divey Kumpelnest 3000 on Potsdamer Strasse.

FRAGRANCES   COCKTAIL BAR

Map p326 (📞030-337 775 403; www.ritzcarlton.com; Potsdamer Platz 3, Ritz-Carlton; ⊙from 7pm Wed-Sat; 🛜; 🚊200, ⓢPotsdamer Platz, ⓤPotsdamer Platz) Another baby by Berlin cocktail maven Arnd Heissen, Fragrances claims to be the world's first 'perfume bar', a libation station where he mixes potable po-

tions mimicking famous scents. The black-mirrored space in the Ritz-Carlton (p244) is a like a 3D menu where adventurous drinkers sniff out their favourite from among a row of perfume bottles, then settle back into flocked couches for stylish imbibing.

Many of the sensory blends are served in unusual vessels, including a birdhouse.

CURTAIN CLUB   BAR

Map p326 (📞030-337 775 403; www.ritzcarlton.de; Potsdamer Strasse 3, Ritz-Carlton Berlin; ⊙10am-late; 🚊200, ⓢPotsdamer Platz, ⓤPotsdamer Platz) Heavy drapes lead the way to this gentlemen's club–style bar with thick carpets, marble tables and leather armchairs. It's presided over by cocktail-meister Arnd Heissen who's not only an expert on classic drinks but also shakes things up with his own creations, each served in a distinctive vessel, be it a vase, a Viking's horn or a milk bottle.

TIGER BAR   BAR

(📞030-983 208 435; www.oh-panama.com/en/tigerbar; Potsdamer Strasse 191; ⊙8pm-midnight or later Tue-Sat; ⓤKurfürstenstrasse) Tiger Bar is a stylish and slightly trippy jewel for curious imbibers. Sustainability is key for bar manager Phum Sila-Trakoon, which is why discarded banana peels from the affiliated Panama (p130) restaurant kitchen may well end up as syrup in his bar. Cocktails range from classic to 'out-there' like Paloma's Fall, a tequila-based potion with grapefruit, buttermilk and sea salt.

VICTORIA BAR   BAR

(📞030-2575 9977; www.victoriabar.de; Potsdamer Strasse 102; ⊙6.30pm-3am Sun-Thu, to 4am Fri & Sat; ⓤKurfürstenstrasse) Original art decorates this discreet cocktail lounge whose motto is the 'Pleasure of Serious Drinking'. It's favoured by a grown-up, artsy crowd. If you want to feel like an insider, order the off-menu 'Hilde', created in memory of German singer-actor Hildegard Knef.

CAFÉ AM NEUEN SEE   BEER GARDEN

(📞030-254 4930; www.cafeamneuensee.de; Lichtensteinallee 2; ⊙restaurant 9am-11pm, beer garden noon-late Mon-Fri, 11am-late Sat & Sun; 🚴; 🚊200, ⓤZoologischer Garten, ⓢZoologischer Garten, Tiergarten) Next to an idyllic lake in Tiergarten, this restaurant gets jammed year-round for its sumptuous breakfast and seasonal fare, but it really comes into its own during beer garden season. Enjoy a microvacation over a cold one and a pretzel or pizza, then take your sweetie for a spin in a rowing boat. Children's playground, too.

KUMPELNEST 3000   BAR
Map p326 (☑030-261 6918; www.kumpel nest3000.com; Lützowstrasse 23; ☺7pm-5am or later; ⓤKurfürstenstrasse) A former brothel, this trashy bat cave started out as an art project and is kooky and kitsch enough to feature in a 1940s Shanghai noir thriller. Famous for its wild, debauched all-nighters, it attracts a hugely varied crowd, including the occasional celebrity (Kate Moss, U2, Karl Lagerfeld).

SOLAR LOUNGE   BAR
Map p326 (☑0163 765 2700; www.solar-berlin. de; Stresemannstrasse 76; ☺6pm-2am Sun-Thu, to 3am Fri & Sat; Ⓢ Anhalter Bahnhof) Watch the city light up from this 17th-floor glass-walled sky lounge above a posh restaurant. With its dim lighting, soft black leather couches and breathtaking panorama, it's a great spot for sunset drinks or a date night. Getting there aboard an exterior glass lift is half the fun. The entrance is behind the Pit Stop auto shop.

STUE BAR   BAR
Map p326 (☑030-311 7220; www.das-stue-com; Drakestrasse 1; ☺noon-1am Sun-Thu, to 2am Fri & Sat; 🚍100, 106, 200) In the Stue hotel (p243), light installations and animal sculptures pave the way to this glam bar where serious mixologists give classic cocktails from the 1920s and '30s a contemporary makeover. Also available: rare whiskies and cognacs and a wine gallery stocked with 400 German, Austrian and Spanish vintages. Live music on Thursdays and Fridays.

⭐ ENTERTAINMENT

BERLINER
PHILHARMONIKER   CLASSICAL MUSIC
Map p326 (☑tickets 030-2548 8999; www. berliner-philharmoniker.de; Herbert-von-Karajan-Strasse 1; tickets €21-290; 🚍M29, M48, M85, 200, Ⓢ Potsdamer Platz, ⓤ Potsdamer Platz) One of the world's most famous orchestras, the Berliner Philharmoniker, is based at the tent-like Philharmonie (p130), designed by Hans Scharoun in the 1950s and built in the 1960s. In 2019, Sir Simon Rattle, who's been chief conductor since 2002, will pass on the

baton to the Russia-born Kirill Petrenko. Tickets can be booked online.

CINESTAR ORIGINAL
IM SONY CENTER   CINEMA
Map p326 (www.cinestar.de; Potsdamer Strasse 4, Sony Center; tickets 2D €6.50-8.80, 3D €9.50-11.80, glasses €1; 🚍200, Ⓢ Potsdamer Platz, ⓤ Potsdamer Platz) A favourite among English-speaking expats and Germans, this state-of-the-art cinema with nine screens, comfy seats and top technology shows the latest Hollywood blockbusters in 2D and 3D, all in English, all the time. Buy tickets online to skip the queue.

ARSENAL   CINEMA
Map p326 (☑030-2695 5100; www.arsenal-berlin.de; Potsdamer Strasse 2, Sony Center; tickets €8; 🚍200, Ⓢ Potsdamer Platz, ⓤ Potsdamer Platz) The antithesis of popcorn culture, this arty twin-screen cinema features a bold global flick schedule that hopscotches from Japanese satire to Brazilian comedy and German road movies. Many films have English subtitles.

SHOPPING

Shopping in this district is limited to its two malls.

LP12 MALL OF BERLIN   MALL
Map p326 (www.mallofberlin.de; Leipziger Platz 12; ☺10am-9pm Mon-Sat; 🤙; 🚍200, ⓤ Potsdamer Platz, Ⓢ Potsdamer Platz) This sparkling retail quarter is tailor-made for black-belt mall rats. More than 270 shops vie for your shopping euros, including flagship stores by Karl Lagerfeld, Hugo Boss, Liebeskind, Marc Cain, Muji and other international high-end brands alongside the usual high-street chains like Mango and H&M. Free mobile-phone recharge stations in the basement and on the 2nd floor.

POTSDAMER PLATZ ARKADEN   MALL
Map p326 (☑030-255 9270; www.potsdamer platz.de/potsdamer-platz-arkaden; Alte Potsdamer Strasse 7; ☺10am-9pm Mon-Sat; 🤙; Ⓢ Potsdamer Platz, ⓤ Potsdamer Platz) All your basic shopping cravings will be met at this attractive indoor mall with 130 shops spread over three floors. The basement has supermarkets, a chemist and numerous fast-food outlets. Ice-cream fans flock to Caffe e Gelato (p133) on the 1st floor.

Scheunenviertel

HACKESCHER MARKT AREA | HAUPTBAHNHOF & ORANIENBURGER TOR | TORSTRASSE & AROUND

Neighbourhood Top Five

❶ **Sammlung Boros** (p144) Glimpsing high drama, abstract mind-benders and glowing colour among the contemporary artworks at this bunker-turned-art museum.

❷ **Hackesche Höfe** (p143) Exploring fashion boutiques, shops, galleries and cafes in this charismatic courtyard maze.

❸ **Clärchens Ballhaus** (p150) Strutting your stuff to salsa, tango, ballroom, waltz and swing at this funky retro ballroom.

❹ **Neue Synagoge** (p141) Admiring the exotic architecture and studying up on the quarter's Jewish history at this local landmark.

❺ **Museum für Naturkunde** (p142) Sizing yourself up next to giant dinos at Berlin's mini Jurassic Park in the city's Museum of Natural History.

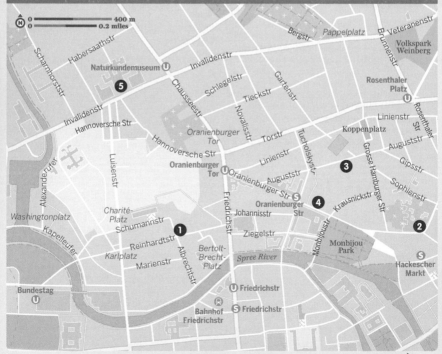

For more detail of this area see Map p334 and p336 ➡

Explore Scheunenviertel

The Scheunenviertel is one of Berlin's oldest and most charismatic neighbourhoods that's morphed into a grown-up stylish district dappled with boundary-pushing galleries, local designer boutiques, third-wave coffee shops and cutting-edge restaurants. A good place to embark on an aimless wander is in the historic Hackesche Höfe (p143) courtyard ensemble. Don't start before midmorning, though, as streets are still very quiet until then.

Not to be missed is the rebuilt Neue Synagoge (p141) on Oranienburger Strasse, whose gleaming dome is a poignant reminder of the revival of Berlin's Jewish community that has its hub here in the Scheunenviertel. In the evening, head towards noisy Torstrasse, which delivers a roll-call of restaurants and bars that lure a cashed-up creative crowd of locals, expats and visitors.

Art fanciers can take the better part of an afternoon to explore the galleries and private collections along Auguststrasse and its side streets. West of here, the area between the Hauptbahnhof and Friedrichstrasse harbours two more of Berlin's contemporary art highlights: the Hamburger Bahnhof (p140) in a converted railway station and the Sammlung Boros (p144) in a WWII bunker. Make reservations months ahead for the latter.

Local Life

Shopping Find out what keeps Berlin designers' sewing machines humming by prowling the backstreets for the shops of fashion-forward local labels.

Bar-hopping Play it cool in Torstrasse's doorstaff-guarded booze burrows.

Monbijoupark Set out a picnic, sip a beer in Strandbar Mitte (p150), dance the tango alfresco or catch a play at the **Monbijou Theater** (Map p334; ☎030-288 866 999; www.monbijou-theater.de; Monbijoustrasse 3b; tickets €14-22; ☉Jul & Aug; ◙M1, ⓢOranienburger Strasse, Hackescher Markt) in this riverfront park.

Getting There & Away

U-Bahn Weinmeisterstrasse (U8) is the most central station. Rosenthaler Platz (U8), Rosa-Luxemburg-Platz (U2) and Oranienburger Tor (U6) are closer to Torstrasse and the northern Scheunenviertel.

S-Bahn Hackescher Markt (S5, S7, S75) and Oranienburger Strasse (S1, S2, S25) stations are both good jumping-off points.

Tram M1 runs from Museumsinsel (Museum Island) to Prenzlauer Berg and stops throughout the Scheunenviertel.

Bus No 142 runs along Torstrasse.

Lonely Planet's Top Tip

If you can't make it on to *Dancing with the Stars*, at least you can dance *under* the stars in Berlin. From May to September, riverside Strandbar Mitte (p150) invites you to tango, swing or waltz on a wooden dance floor while the Spree courses past and lights bathe the ornamented facade of the Bode-Museum in a romantic glow. There's no charge, but a €4 minimum donation for the DJ is requested. Check the website for dance lessons and foul-weather cancellations.

Best Places to Eat

➜ Katz Orange (p147)
➜ Zenkichi (p148)
➜ Einsunternull (p149)
➜ Night Kitchen (p147)

For reviews, see p145.

Best Places to Drink

➜ Clärchens Ballhaus (p150)
➜ Strandbar Mitte (p150)
➜ Buck & Breck (p151)
➜ Torbar (p151)
➜ Father Carpenter (p150)

For reviews, see p150.

Best Places to Shop

➜ Bonbonmacherei (p152)
➜ Paper & Tea (p154)
➜ Kauf Dich Glücklich (p153)
➜ Do You Read Me?! (p154)

For reviews, see p152.

SCHEUNENVIERTEL

TOP SIGHT
HAMBURGER BAHNHOF – MUSEUM FÜR GEGENWART

Berlin's contemporary art showcase opened in 1996 in the former Hamburger Bahnhof railway station, whose loft and grandeur are the perfect foil for this Aladdin's cave of paintings, sculptures and installations. The museum's inventory spans the entire arc of post-1950 artistic movements from conceptual art and pop art to minimal art, Arte Povera and Fluxus.

Permanent loans from three collectors – Erich Marx, Friedrich Christian Flick and Egidio Marzona – form the core of the collection. Seminal works by such major players as Andy Warhol, Cy Twombly, Anselm Kiefer, Robert Rauschenberg and Bruce Nauman are presented in changing configurations in both the main museum and the adjacent 300m-long **Rieckhallen** (Rieck Halls). The entire ground floor of the main building's west wing is dedicated to the ultimate artistic boundary pusher, Joseph Beuys. The **Neue Galerie**, completed in 2015, presents changing modern art exhibits drawn from the collection of the New National Gallery, which is closed for renovation until at least 2020. High-calibre temporary exhibits also help keep things fluid.

Trains first rolled through the Hamburger Bahnhof in 1874, but after only 32 years the station had become too small and was turned into a traffic museum. After WWII the building stood empty until the late Josef Paul Kleihues was hired in 1989 to create an exhibition space. He kept the elegant exterior, which at night is bathed in the light of a Dan Flavin installation. The interior, though, was gutted and turned into modern minimalist galleries that orbit the central hall with its exposed iron girders.

DON'T MISS

➡ Andy Warhol's *Chairman Mao* (1975)
➡ Anselm Kiefer's *Volkszählung* (*Census;* 1991)
➡ Joseph Beuys' *The End of the Twentieth Century* (1983)
➡ Robert Rauschenberg's *Pink Door* (1954)

PRACTICALITIES

➡ Map p336, A2
➡ ☎030-266 424 242
➡ www.smb.museum
➡ Invalidenstrasse 50-51
➡ adult/concession €10/5, free 4-8pm 1st Thu of the month
➡ ⏱10am-6pm Tue, Wed & Fri, to 8pm Thu, 11am-6pm Sat & Sun
➡ 🚌M5, M8, M10, ⓈHauptbahnhof, ⓊHauptbahnhof

M.DOGAN/SHUTTERSTOCK ©

NEUE SYNAGOGE

The gleaming gold dome of the Neue Synagoge is the most visible symbol of Berlin's revitalised Jewish community. The original 1866 building was once Germany's largest synagogue but was badly hit by bombing raids in WWII. Its contemporary reincarnation is not so much a house of worship (although prayer services do take place), but a museum and place of remembrance.

For the original synagogue, architect Eduard Knoblauch looked to the Alhambra in Granada for inspiration, which explains the exotic Moorish design elements. Today's version replicates the elaborate facade and the shiny dome but is otherwise modern on the inside. Consecrated on Rosh Hashanah in 1866, the building seated 3200 people, making it Germany's largest synagogue.

During the 1938 Kristallnacht (Night of the Broken Glass) pogroms, local police chief Wilhelm Krützfeld prevented a gang of SA (Sturmabteilung, a militia of the Nazi party) troopers from setting it on fire, an act of civil courage commemorated by a plaque affixed to the main facade. The German Wehrmacht eventually desecrated the synagogue anyway by using it as a warehouse, although it was not destroyed until hit by bombs in 1943. After the war, the ruin lingered until reconstruction began in 1988 on the 50th anniversary of Kristallnacht.

Rededicated in 1995, today's Neue Synagoge houses the **Centrum Judaicum**, a memorial and exhibition space that's also a centre of Berlin's Jewish community. In addition to temporary presentations, a permanent exhibit features architectural fragments and objects recovered from the ruins of the building before its reconstruction. They include a Torah scroll and an eternal lamp, and help tell the history of the building and the people associated with it.

DON'T MISS

➡ The facade
➡ The dome
➡ Torah scroll

PRACTICALITIES

➡ Map p334, B4
➡ ☎030-8802 8300
➡ www.centrum judaicum.de
➡ Oranienburger Strasse 28-30
➡ adult/concession €5/4, audioguide €3
➡ ⏰10am-6pm Mon-Fri, to 7pm Sun, closes 3pm Fri & 6pm Sun Oct-Mar
➡ 🚋M1, Ⓤ Oranienburger Tor, Ⓢ Oranienburger Strasse

◉ SIGHTS

Art, architecture and Jewish history characterise this charming quarter. Start your explorations at the Hackesche Höfe courtyard ensemble, then meander the narrow lanes, perhaps with a focus on Grosse Hamburger Strasse, Auguststrasse and Alte Schönhauser Strasse. For contemporary art, head west of Friedrichstrasse to the Hamburger Bahnhof and Sammlung Boros.

◉ Hackescher Markt Area

NEUE SYNAGOGE
SYNAGOGUE
See p141.

JÜDISCHE MÄDCHENSCHULE
HISTORIC BUILDING
Map p334 (Jewish Girls' School; www.maed chenschule.org; Auguststrasse 11-13; ⊘hours vary; 🚋M1, ⑤Oranienburger Strasse, Ⓤ Oranienburger Tor) FREE This 1920s former Jewish girls' school, which was forcibly closed by the Nazis in 1942, was injected with new life as a cultural and culinary hub in 2012. Three galleries and the Museum the Kennedys have set up shop in the former classrooms, while the former gym now houses a Michelin-starred restaurant. The structure was built in the austere New Objectivity style by the renowned Jewish architect Alexander Beer, who perished at Theresienstadt concentration camp.

MUSEUM THE KENNEDYS
MUSEUM
Map p334 (☑030-2065 3570; www.thekennedys. de; Auguststrasse 11-13; adult/concession €5/2.50; ⊘10am-6pm Tue-Fri, 11am-6pm Sat & Sun; 🚋M1, ⑤Oranienburger Strasse, ⓊOranienburger Tor) US president John F Kennedy has held a special place in German hearts since his defiant 'Ich bin ein Berliner!' ('I am a Berliner') solidarity speech in 1963. This private exhibit addresses the president's continued mystique as well as such topics as the Berlin visit and his assassination in Dallas through photographs, documents, video footage and memorabilia.

Among the standout relics are JFK's reading glasses and crocodile-leather briefcase, Jackie's Persian-lamb pillbox hat and a hilarious Superman comic book starring the president. Temporary presentations, including an inaugural photo exhibit of

SCHEUNENVIERTEL SIGHTS

◉ TOP SIGHT
MUSEUM FÜR NATURKUNDE

Fossils and minerals don't quicken your pulse? Well, how about Tristan, one of the best-preserved *Tyrannosaurus rex* skeletons in the world? Or Oskar, the 12m-high *Brachiosaurus branchai,* the Guinness Book–certified world's largest mounted dino? At Berlin's **Museum of Natural History**, the two Jurassic superstars are joined by a dozen other extinct buddies, all of them about 150 million-year-old migrants from Tanzania. Clever 'Juraskopes' bring some of them back to virtual flesh-and-bone life. The same hall also houses an ultrarare fossilised primeval bird *Archaeopteryx*.

Beyond the dinosaurs you can journey deep into space or clear up such age-old mysteries as why zebras are striped. Surprises include massively magnified insect models – wait until you see the mind-boggling anatomy of an ordinary house fly! A highlight is the wet collection in the east wing: one million ethanol-preserved animals floating in 276,000 glass jars displayed in a huge glowing glass cube in its own darkened hall.

A favourite among the taxidermic animals is Knut, the polar bear whose birth at Berlin Zoo in 2006 caused global 'Knutmania'. The cuddly giant died unexpectedly in 2011.

DON'T MISS
➡ Tristan the *T-rex*
➡ Oskar the brachiosaurus
➡ Knut, the stuffed polar bear

PRACTICALITIES
➡ Map p336, B1
➡ ☑030-2093 8591
➡ www.naturkunde museum.berlin
➡ Invalidenstrasse 43
➡ adult/concession incl audioguide €8/5
➡ ⊘9.30am-6pm Tue-Fri, 10am-6pm Sat & Sun
➡ 🚋M5, M8, M10, 12, ⓊNaturkundemuseum

TOP SIGHT
HACKESCHE HÖFE

The **Hackesche Höfe** is the largest and most famous of the courtyard ensembles peppered throughout the Scheunenviertel. Built in 1907 it lingered through the city's division before being put through a total makeover in the mid-1990s. In 1996 the eight interlinked courtyards reopened to great fanfare with a congenial mix of cafes, galleries, indie boutiques and entertainment venues.

The main entrance off Rosenthaler Strasse leads to **Court I**, prettily festooned with ceramic tiles by art-nouveau architect August Endell. One of Berlin's best cabarets, the Chamäleon Theatre (p151), is located here in a historic art-nouveau ballroom. It presents a fun and innovative mix of acrobatics, music, dance and comedy – no German skills required! Cinephiles flock upstairs to the Hackesche Höfe Kino (p152), an art-house cinema in the same building.

Shoppers can look forward to galleries and the flagship shops of Berlin designers. If you're a fan of the little characters on Berlin traffic lights, stock up on souvenirs at Ampelmann Berlin (p154) in Court V. Court VII leads off to the **Rosenhöfe**, a frilly art nouveau–inspired courtyard with a sunken rose garden and tendril-like balustrades.

DON'T MISS

→ Endell's art-nouveau facade in Court I

→ Berlin designer boutiques

→ Rosenhöfe

PRACTICALITIES

→ Map p334, C4

→ 🕿030-2809 8010

→ www.hackesche-hoefe.com

→ enter from Rosenthaler Strasse 40/41 or Sophienstrasse 6

→ 🚇M1, ⓢHackescher Markt, ⓤWeinmeisterstrasse

---

former President Obama, supplement the permanent galleries.

KW INSTITUTE FOR
CONTEMPORARY ART   GALLERY
Map p334 (🕿030-243 4590; www.kw-berlin.de; Auguststrasse 69; adult/concession €8/6, free 6-9pm Thu; 🕑11am-7pm Wed-Mon, to 9pm Thu; 🚇M1, ⓢOranienburger Strasse, ⓤOranienburger Tor) Founded in the early 1990s in an old margarine factory, nonprofit KW played a key role in turning the Scheunenviertel into Berlin's first major post-Wall art district. It continues to stage boundary-pushing exhibits that reflect the latest – and often radical – trends in contemporary art.

KW's founding director Klaus Biesenbach also inaugurated the **Berlin Biennale** (www.berlinbiennale.de; various locations; 🕑Jun-Sep every even year) in 1998. The courtyard Café Bravo (p150) makes for a stylish coffee break. A combined ticket with the nearby me Collectors Room (p143) is €10 for adults, €8 concession.

ME COLLECTORS ROOM   GALLERY
Map p334 (🕿030-8600 8510; www.me-berlin.com; Auguststrasse 68; adult/concession/un-

der 18 €8/4/free; 🕑noon-6pm Wed-Mon; 🚇M1, ⓢOranienburger Strasse) Founded by private art collector Thomas Olbricht, this modern, non-elitist space presents curated highlights from his own collection and also serves as a platform for other collectors to share their treasure troves with the public in changing exhibits. The only permanent feature is the upstairs *Wunderkammer,* a global 'cabinet of curiosities' with some 300 items from the Renaissance and baroque eras, including a Nautilus cup and an ivory tankard.

The on-site cafe, which features a children's play corner is a pleasant spot to ease into it all. A combined ticket with the nearby KW Institute for Contemporary Art is €10/8.

HECKMANN-HÖFE   HISTORIC SITE
Map p334 (www.heckmannhoefe.de; Oranienburger Strasse 32; 🕑24hr; 🚇M1, ⓢOranienburger Strasse) **FREE** If you're looking for a retreat from the urban frenzy, skip on over to this idyllic 19th-century courtyard complex linking Oranienburger Strasse with Auguststrasse. Aside from boutiques, restaurants and a theatre, it also shelters the

BUNKER ART: SAMMLUNG BOROS

••

The **Sammlung Boros** (Boros Collection; Map p336; ☑030-2759 4065; www.sammlung-boros.de; Reinhardtstrasse 20; adult/concession €12/6; ⊙tours 3-6.30pm Thu, 10.30am-6.30pm Fri, 10am-6.30pm Sat & Sun; ⛴M1, Ⓢ Friedrichstrasse, ⓤOranienburger Tor, Friedrichstrasse) Nazi-era bunker presents one of Berlin's finest private contemporary art collections, amassed by advertising guru Christian Boros who acquired the behemoth in 2003. A third selection of works went live in May 2017 and includes installations by Katja Novitskova, digital paintings by Avery Singer and photo series by Peter Piller. Book online (weeks, if not months, ahead) to join a guided tour (also in English) and to pick up fascinating nuggets about the building's surprising other peacetime incarnations.

Tours begin with an introduction to the exhibit and the building against the noisy backdrop of a clattering blackboard by Belgian artist Kris Martin called *Mandi III*. Leading the group past preserved original fittings, pipes, steel doors and vents, guides provide enough thought fodder, context and explanations about the artworks to help even the uninitiated tame their bewilderment.

Built for 2000 people, the bunker's dank rooms crammed in twice as many during the heaviest air raids towards the end of WWII. After the shooting stopped, the Soviets briefly used it as a POW prison before it assumed a more benign role as a fruit and vegetable storeroom in East Berlin, a phase that spawned the nickname 'Banana Bunker'. In the 1990s, the claustrophobic warren hosted some of Berlin's naughtiest techno raves and fetish parties.

SCHEUNENVIERTEL SIGHTS

adorable Bonbonmacherei (p152), an old-fashioned candy kitchen and shop.

SAMMLUNG HOFFMANN   GALLERY

Map p334 (☑030-2849 9120; www.sammlung-hoffmann.de; Sophienstrasse 21, 2nd courtyard, entry C; tours €10; ⊙11am-4pm Sat; ⓤWeinmeisterstrasse) Blink and you'll miss the doorway leading to the Sophie-Gips-Höfe, a trio of courtyards linking Sophienstrasse and Gipsstrasse. The former sewing-machine factory now harbours shops, offices and flats as well as this stellar contemporary art collection in a private home, which is open for guided 90-minute tours every Saturday. Registration required.

FRIEDHOF GROSSE
HAMBURGER STRASSE   CEMETERY

Map p334 (☑030-880 280; www.jg-berlin.org/en; Grosse Hamburger Strasse 26; ⊙7.30am-5pm Mon-Thu, to 2.30pm Fri, 8am-5pm Sun Apr-Sep, 7.30am-4pm Mon-Thu, to 2.30pm Fri, 8am-4pm Sun Oct-Mar; ⛴M1, Ⓢ Hackescher Markt, ⓤWeinmeisterstrasse) What looks like a small park was in fact Berlin's first Jewish cemetery, destroyed by the Nazis in 1943. Some 2700 people were buried here between 1672 and 1827, including the philosopher Moses Mendelssohn. A symbolic tombstone in his honour and a sarcophagus filled with destroyed gravestones stands representative for all the 6ft-under residents.

☉ Hauptbahnhof & Oranienburger Tor

HAMBURGER BAHNHOF –
MUSEUM FÜR GEGENWART   MUSEUM

See p140.

BERLINER MEDIZINHISTORISCHES
MUSEUM   MUSEUM

Map p336 (Berlin Museum of Medical History; ☑030-450 536 156; www.bmm-charite.de; Charitéplatz 1; adult/concession €9/4; ⊙10am-5pm Tue, Thu, Fri & Sun, to 7pm Wed & Sat; ⛴M5, M10, Ⓢ Hauptbahnhof, ⓤHauptbahnhof) This Charité Hospital–run museum chronicles 300 years of medical history in an anatomical theatre, a pathologist's dissection room, a laboratory and a historical patients' ward. The heart of the exhibit, though, is a sometimes grisly specimen hall whose 750 pathological-anatomical wet and dry preparations are essentially a 3D medical textbook on human disease and deformity.

Those under 16 must be accompanied by an adult. This is not surprising, for those monstrous tumours, a colon the size of an elephant's trunk and two-headed fetuses – all pickled in jars filled with formaldehyde and neatly displayed in glass cases – are definitely not for the squeamish. The basis of the specimen collection was assembled by Rudolf Virchow (1821–1902), a famous doctor, researcher and professor. Also have a look at his lecture hall – a preserved ruin – which is used for special events.

✕ BRECHT-WEIGEL
GEDENKSTÄTTE   MUSEUM

Map p336 (Brecht-Weigel Memorial Centre; ☑030-200 571 844; www.adk.de/en/archive/memorial-centres; Chausseestrasse 125; tours adult/concession €5/2.50; ⊘tours half hourly 10-11.30am Tue-Fri, 2-3.30pm Tue, 5-6.30pm Thu, 10am-3.30pm Sat & hourly 11am-6pm Sun; ⓤOranienburger Tor, Naturkundemuseum) Playwright Bertolt Brecht lived in this apartment from 1953 until his death in 1956. Tours (in German) take you inside his office, a large library, and the tiny bedroom where he died. Decorated with Chinese artwork, the rooms have been left as though he'd briefly stepped out, leaving his hat and woollen cap hanging on the door.

Downstairs are the cluttered quarters of his actress wife, Helene Weigel, who lived here until 1971. The couple are buried in the adjacent Dorotheenstädtischer Friedhof.

DOROTHEENSTÄDTISCHER
FRIEDHOF I   CEMETERY

Map p336 (☑030-461 7279; http://evfbs.de/tickets; Chausseestrasse 126; entry free, chapel tours adult/concession €10/5; ⊘8am-8pm Mar-Oct, to 5pm Nov-Feb; ⓤOranienburger Tor, Naturkundemuseum) This compact 18th-century cemetery is the place of perpetual slumber for a veritable roll-call of famous Germans, including the philosophers Hegel and Fichte, the architects Schinkel and Rauch and the writers Bertolt Brecht and Heinrich Mann. A map by the entrance shows grave locations. A recent restoration of the burial chapel added an ethereal, site-specific light installation by James Turrell that can be seen on hour-long guided tours. Check times and buy tickets online.

✕ EATING

The Scheunenviertel packs in so much culinary variety you could eat your way around the world in a day. Practically all tastes, budgets and food neuroses are catered for in eateries ranging from comfy neighbourhood joints to big-city dining shrines, health-nut havens to ho-hum tourist traps, plus a growing number of Michelin-starred establishments.

✕ Hackescher Markt Area

STORE KITCHEN   INTERNATIONAL €

Map p334 (☑030-405 044 550; www.thestores.com; Torstrasse 1; dishes €6-12; ⊘10am-7pm Mon-Sat; ⓡ; ⓤRosa-Luxemburg-Platz) This is the kind of impossibly trendy yet welcoming place that had food fanciers in a headlock the moment it opened inside hipper-than-thou lifestyle and fashion temple the Store, on the ground floor of Soho House. Head here if you crave breakfast, salads, sandwiches and light meals that capture the latest global food trends while using local suppliers.

MONSIEUR VUONG   VIETNAMESE €

Map p334 (☑030-9929 6924; www.monsieurvuong.de; Alte Schönhauser Strasse 46; mains €8-10; ⊘noon-11pm Mon-Thu, to midnight Fri & Sat; ⓤWeinmeisterstrasse, Rosa-Luxemburg-Platz) Berlin's 'godfather' of upbeat Vietnamese pit stops, Monsieur Vuong has been copied many times – the concept is just *that* good. They don't take reservations, so come in the afternoon to avoid the feeding frenzy and to enjoy the flavour-packed soups and fresh fragrant mains without haste. Daily blackboard specials supplement the compact menu.

BARCOMIS DELI   CAFE €

Map p334 (☑030-2859 8363; www.barcomis.de; Sophienstrasse 21, Sophie-Gips-Höfe, 2nd courtyard; dishes €2.60-12; ⊘9am-9pm Mon-Sat, 10am-9pm Sun; ⓡ; ⓤWeinmeisterstrasse) Join coffee lovers, families and expats at this New York–meets-Berlin deli for custom-roasted coffee, wraps, bagels with smoked salmon, creative sandwiches and possibly the best brownies and cheesecake this side of the Hudson River.

Bonus points for the enchanting setting in a quiet Scheunenviertel courtyard.

ROSENTHALER GRILL UND
SCHLEMMERBUFFET   MIDDLE EASTERN €

Map p334 (☑030-283 2153; Torstrasse 125; dishes €3-8; ⊘24hr; ⓖM1, 12, ⓤRosenthaler Platz) Excellent doner joint with outdoor seating and nonstop service for early birds, night owls and everyone in between. Also has good grilled chicken and pizza.

YAM YAM   KOREAN €

Map p334 (☑030-2463 2485; www.yamyamberlin.de; Alte Schönhauser Strasse 6; dishes €6.50-11; ⊘noon-11pm Mon-Thu, to midnight Fri &

SCHEUNENVIERTEL EATING

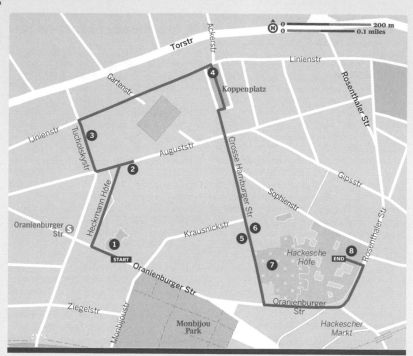

Neighbourhood Walk
Traces of Jewish Life in the Scheunenviertel

START NEUE SYNAGOGE
END HAUS SCHWARZENBERG
LENGTH 1.5KM; ONE TO THREE HOURS

This easy walk takes you past vestiges, memorials and revitalised sites of Jewish life in the Scheunenviertel. Start at the rebuilt **❶ Neue Synagoge** (p141), inaugurated in 1866 as Germany's largest Jewish house of worship and now a museum and community centre. Take the Heckmann Höfe to Auguststrasse and turn right to find yourself at the **❷ Jüdische Mädchenschule** (p142), a Bauhaus-style Jewish girls' school turned gallery and restaurant space.

Double back on Auguststrasse, then turn right on Tucholskystrasse, perhaps stopping for a bite at the kosher **❸ Beth Cafe** at No 40. Turn right on Linienstrasse and continue to Koppenplatz with Karl Biedermann's art installation **❹ Der Verlassene Raum** (The Deserted Room). It consists of a table and two chairs, one knocked over as a symbol of Jewish residents being forced to flee suddenly from their homes.

Follow Grosse Hamburger Strasse and note the facades still scarred by bullet holes along the way to the Sophienkirche. Further on, look on your right for the **❺ Missing House**, Christian Boltanski's 1990 memorial on the site of a bombed-out apartment building. Signs bearing the names of its former residents are affixed to the facades of the adjacent buildings. The structure opposite, at No 27, was a **❻ Jewish Boys' School**. The Nazis turned it and the adjacent Jewish seniors' home into a deportation centre in 1942. The home was destroyed in a bombing raid shortly before the war ended, but the school building survived and was turned into a vocational school in GDR times.

Just south, the **❼ Friedhof Grosse Hamburger Strasse** (p144) was Berlin's first Jewish cemetery. Outside the cemetery is a memorial stone to the deported Jews as well as a sculpture group by Will Lammert showing 13 fatigued women.

The tour concludes at street-art decorated **❽ Haus Schwarzenberg** (p153), which harbours two small museums dealing with the fate of Jews under the Nazis.

Sat, 1-11pm Sun; 🛜; Ⓤ Rosa-Luxemburg-Platz) In a dashing move of career derring-do, Sumi Ha morphed her fancy fashion boutique into a stylish self-service joint where the spicy *bibimbap* (a hotpot rice dish), fresh *gimbab* (seaweed rolls), steamy *mandu* (dumplings) and other fancified Korean street food all pass the authenticity test.

CÔCÔ
VIETNAMESE €

Map p334 (📞030-5547 5188; www.banhmi-coco. de; Rosenthaler Strasse 2; sandwiches €5.50-8; 🕙11am-10pm Mon-Thu, to 11pm Fri & Sat, noon-10pm Sun; 🛜; 🚇M1, Ⓤ Rosenthaler Platz) This hip little joint was a Berlin pioneer of the *banh mi* fad. A relic from French-colonial times, these plump Vietnamese sandwiches combine marinated meats, pâtés, spicy sauces and fresh herbs into a firework of aromas stuffed into a toasted baguette. Wash it down with fresh coconut water or a salty lemonade.

HUMMUS & FRIENDS
ISRAELI €

Map p334 (📞030-5547 1454; www.hummus -and-friends.com; Oranienburger Strasse 27; dishes €3.80-8.80; 🕙11am-midnight; 🛜🖉; 🚇M1, Ⓢ Oranienburger Strasse) 'Make Hummus, Not Walls' is the motto at this urban-rustic kitchen next to the Neue Synagoge (p141). The eponymous chickpea dip, whipped up with special beans from Galilee, is naturally the menu star, followed closely by the paper-wrapped oven-roasted cauliflower paired with creamy tahini sauce. Everything is homemade, vegan and kosher.

TADSHIKISCHE TEESTUBE
RUSSIAN €

Map p334 (📞030-204 1112; www.tadshikische-teestube.de; Oranienburger Strasse 27, KunstHof; mains €7-12; 🕙4-11pm Mon-Fri, noon-11pm Sat & Sun; 🚇M1, Ⓢ Oranienburger Strasse) Treat yourself to a Russian tea ceremony complete with silvery samovar, biscuits and vodka, or tuck into hearty Russian blini (pancakes) or *vareniki* (dumplings) while reclining amid plump pillows, hand-carved sandalwood pillars and heroic murals in this original Tajik tearoom. The authentic space was gifted by the Soviets to the East German government in 1974.

★ KATZ ORANGE
INTERNATIONAL €€

Map p334 (📞030-983 208 430; www.katz orange.com; Bergstrasse 22; mains €17-24; 🕙6-11pm; 🚇M8, Ⓤ Rosenthaler Platz) 🌱 With its holistic farm-to-table menu, stylish country flair and top-notch cocktails, the 'Orange

Cat' hits a gastro grand slam. It will have you purring for such perennial favourites as Duroc pork that's been slow-roasted for 12 hours (nicknamed 'candy on bone'). The setting in a castle-like former brewery is stunning, especially in summer when the patio opens.

MURET LA BARBA
ITALIAN €€

Map p334 (📞030-2809 7212; www.muretla barba.de; Rosenthaler Strasse 61; mains €14.50-27; 🕙10am-midnight Mon-Fri, noon-midnight Sat & Sun; 🚇M1, Ⓤ Rosenthaler Platz) This wine shop–bar–restaurant combo exudes the kind of rustic authenticity that instantly transports cognoscenti to Italy. The food is hearty, inventive and made with top ingredients imported from the motherland. All wine is available by the glass or by the bottle (corkage fee €10).

NIGHT KITCHEN
INTERNATIONAL €€

Map p334 (📞030-2357 5075; www.nightkitchen berlin.com; Oranienburger Strasse 32; dishes €4-19, Dinner with Friends per person €36; 🕙5pm-midnight daily, 11am-4pm Sun; 🛜🖉; 🚇M1, Ⓢ Oranienburger Strasse, Ⓤ Oranienburger Tor) This smartly seductive courtyard bistro is often packed to capacity with punters hungry for modern Med spins inspired by the mothership in Tel Aviv. You're free to order à la carte but the guiding concept here is 'Dinner with Friends', a chef-collated meal designed for sharing. Sit inside at high tables or at the bar, or in the candlelit courtyard.

WEIHENSTEPHANER AM HACKESCHEN MARKT
BAVARIAN €€

Map p334 (📞030-8471 0760; www.weihen stephaner-berlin.de; Neue Promenade 5; mains €8-18; 🕙11am-1am; 🛜🖼; 🚇M1, Ⓢ Hackescher Markt) Hops fans give a solid thumbs up to the Weihenstephaner beers from a Bavaria brewery founded in 1040 and reportedly the world's oldest. The suds pair sweetly with the rustic lyricism of the Alpine tavern cooking served to merrymakers in the beer hall, on the terrace and in the vaulted cellar.

CECCONI'S
ITALIAN €€

Map p334 (📞030-405 044 680; www.cec conisberlin.com; Torstrasse 1; mains €12-35; 🕙11.30am-midnight Mon-Fri, 11am-midnight Sat, 11am-11pm Sun; 🛜; 🚇M2, M4, M5, M6, M8, Ⓤ Rosa-Luxemburg-Platz) Open to all despite being set within the members-only Soho House, ground-floor Cecconi's exhibits metropolitan flair with red leather booths, marble floors, an open kitchen and a suitably sophisticated clientele. Aside from pasta, pizza and risotto dishes – some pimped up with lobster and truffle – the menu also checks the superfoods box with its quinoa and chia salads, while also featuring carnivore-pleasing grilled meats.

SCHWARZWALDSTUBEN
GERMAN €€

Map p334 (☑030-2809 8084; www.schwarzwald stuben-berlin.com; Tucholskystrasse 48; mains €7-16.50; ☺9am-midnight; 🚊M1, Ⓢ Oranienburger Strasse) In the mood for a Hansel and Gretel moment? Then join the other 'lost kids' for satisfying slow food from the southwest German regions of Baden and Swabia. Tuck into gut-filling platters of *spaetzle* (mac 'n' cheese), *Maultaschen* (ravioli-like pasta) or giant schnitzel with fried potatoes. Dine amid rustic and tongue-in-cheek forest decor or grab a table on the pavement.

MOGG
DELI €€

Map p334 (☑0176 6496 1344; www.moggmogg. com; Auguststrasse 11-13; mains €7.50-14.50; ☺11am-10pm Mon-Fri, 10am-10pm Sat & Sun; 🛜; 🚊M1, Ⓢ Oranienburger Strasse) At Berlin's first New York–style Jewish deli, home-cured and smoked pastrami on rye feeds tummy and soul in an arty 1930s-inspired setting with purple-topped benches and Finnish designer chairs. The menu also features other staples such as matzo ball soup, *shakshuka* and a killer New York cheesecake, alongside nontraditional deli picks like bruléed chicken liver and salmon with shaved fennel.

KOPPS
VEGAN €€

Map p334 (☑030-4320 9775; www.kopps-berlin. de; Linienstrasse 94; dinner mains €17-20, brunch €15; ☺6-10pm daily, 9.30am-4pm Sat & Sun; 🖋; 🚊M1, Ⓤ Rosenthaler Platz) Kopps was Berlin's first high-end, animal-product-free restaurant and is still holding its own. Locals love the early bird 'Come Together' dinner (€19 for three courses, no reservations) from 6pm to 7.30pm and the weekend brunch buffet (9.30am to 4pm). The space is sparse but stylish, with bluish-grey walls, recycled doors and mirrors in unexpected places.

DISTRICT MÔT
VIETNAMESE €€

Map p334 (☑030-2008 9284; www.district mot.com; Rosenthaler Strasse 62; dishes €7-19; ☺noon-midnight; 🛜; 🚊M1, Ⓤ Rosenthaler Platz) At this colourful mock-Saigon street-food parlour, patrons squat on tiny plastic stools around wooden tables where rolls of toilet paper irreverently stand in for paper napkins. The small-plate menu mixes the familiar (steamy *pho* noodle soup, papaya salad) with the adventurous (stewed eel, deep-fried silk) but it's their De La Sauce *bao* burger that has collected the accolades.

★ZENKICHI
JAPANESE €€€

Map p336 (☑030-2463 0810; www.zenkichi.de; Johannisstrasse 20; 4-/8-course tasting menu €45/65, small plates €4.50-20; ☺6pm-midnight; 🖋; Ⓤ Oranienburger Tor, Friedrichstrasse, Ⓢ Friedrichstrasse) Romance runs high at this lantern-lit basement izakaya (Japanese pub), which serves faithfully executed gourmet Japanese fare and premium sake in cosy alcoves with black-lacquer tables shielded by bamboo blinds for extra privacy. Expect your tastebuds to do cartwheels, no matter if you treat yourself to the seasonal *omakase* (chef's) dinner or compose your own culinary symphony from the small-plate menu.

PAULY SAAL
GERMAN €€€

Map p334 (☑030-3300 6070; www.paulysaal. com; Auguststrasse 11-13; 3-/4-course lunches €69/85, 7-course dinners €115; ☺noon-2pm & 6-9.30pm Tue-Sat, bar to 2.30am; 🚊M1, Ⓢ Oranienburger Strasse, Ⓤ Oranienburger Tor) Since taking the helm at this Michelin-starred outpost, Arne Anker has given the cuisine a youthful and light edge while following the seasonal-regional credo. Only multicourse menus are served, even at lunch. The venue itself – in the edgy-art-decorated gym of a former Jewish girls' school (p142) in a Bauhaus building – is simply stunning.

On balmy days, the tables beneath the old schoolyard's trees are mighty tempting, too.

LOKAL
GERMAN €€€

Map p334 (☑030-2844 9500; www.lokal -berlin.blogspot.de; Linienstrasse 160; mains €15-29; ☺5.30-11pm; 🖋; Ⓤ Rosenthaler Platz, Ⓢ Oranienburger Strasse) The stripped down Nordic aesthetic of this locally adored joint is a perfect foil for the kitchen's inspired farm-to-table riffs on German fare, including meat-free options. It's food that is at once comforting and exciting with awesome bread to boot. Reservations are a must.

TO THE BONE
STEAKHOUSE €€€

Map p334 (☑030-5459 9047; http://tothebone. bonita.berlin; Torstrasse 96; appetisers €12.50-

22, steaks from €9.50 per 100g; ⊙6-11pm Mon-Sat, bar until 3am; 📶; Ⓤ Rosenthaler Platz) If you love meat *and* Italian food, this hip joint is your kinda place. Sip a potent Negroni while scanning the good-looking crowd and anticipating super-aromatic dry-aged beef or venison straight from Italy. But it's with the appetisers where kitchen creativity peaks. The succulent bone marrow with oxtail confit is a mainstay as is the pasta *fatta in casa* (made in-house).

✗ Hauptbahnhof & Oranienburger Tor

HOUSE OF
SMALL WONDER   INTERNATIONAL €
Map p336 (✆030-2758 2877; www.houseof smallwonder.de; Johannisstrasse 20; dishes €8-13; ⊙9am-5pm; 📶✍; Ⓤ Oranienburger Tor, Ⓢ Oranienburger Strasse, Friedrichstrasse) A wrought-iron staircase spirals up to this brunch and lunch oasis where potted plants and whimsical decor create a relaxed backyard garden feel. The global comfort is just as beautiful, no matter if you go for eggs Benedict with homemade yoghurt scones, Okinawan Taco Rice or zoodles with cashew miso pesto. Also a good spot just for coffee and pastries.

DADA FALAFEL   MIDDLE EASTERN €
Map p336 (✆030-2759 6927; www.facebook. com/dadafalafel; Linienstrasse 132; dishes €3.50-8.50; ⊙10am-1am Sun-Wed, to 2am Thu-Sat; 📶; 🚊M1, Ⓤ Oranienburger Tor) After just one bite of Dada's freshly prepared falafel or *shawarma* doused with a tangy homemade sauce, you too will understand why there's always a queue of local loyalists at this teensy outpost with adjacent dining space–cum-gallery and summer terrace.

SARAH WIENER IM
HAMBURGER BAHNHOF   GERMAN €€
Map p336 (✆030-7071 3650; www.sarahwiener. de; Invalidenstrasse 50-51; sandwiches €7.50-9, mains €9-24; ⊙10am-6pm Tue & Wed, to 8pm Thu, to 6pm Fri, 11am-6pm Sat & Sun; Ⓢ Hauptbahnhof, Ⓤ Hauptbahnhof) 🥕 Berlin's smartest museum cafe is a great spot for discussing the latest exhibit over sumptuous breakfasts, creative rye sandwiches, gooey homemade cakes or star-chef Sarah's famous veal schnitzel and upscale local classics like currywurst with homemade ketchup.

STUMBLING UPON HISTORY

If you lower your gaze, you'll see them all over town but nowhere are they more concentrated than in the Scheunenviertel: small brass paving stones in front of house entrances. Called **Stolpersteine** (stumbling blocks), they are part of a nationwide project by Berlin-born artist Gunter Demnig and are essentially minimemorials honouring the people (usually Jews) who lived in the respective house before being killed by the Nazis. The engravings indicate the person's name, birth year, year of deportation, the name of the concentration camp where they were taken and the date they perished.

GRILL ROYAL   STEAK €€€
Map p336 (✆030-2887 9288; www.grillroyal.com; Friedrichstrasse 105b; steaks €29-128; ⊙6pm-late; 📶; Ⓢ Friedrichstrasse, Ⓤ Friedrichstrasse) With its airy dining room, original look-at-me art, polyglot staff and open kitchen, Grill Royal ticks all the boxes of a true metropolitan restaurant. A platinum card is a handy accessory if you want to slurp your oysters and tuck into aged prime steaks in the company of A-listers, power politicians, pouty models and 'trust-afarians'.

Riverside tables beckon in fine weather.

EINSUNTERNULL   INTERNATIONAL €€€
Map p336 (✆030-2757 7810; www.einsunternull. com; Hannoversche Strasse 1; 4-/5-course lunch menus €59/69, 6-course dinner menus €99, additional courses €10; ⊙noon-2pm Tue-Sat, 7-11pm Mon-Sat; ✍; 🚊M1, Ⓤ Oranienburger Tor) 🥕 The name means 'one below zero' but the food at Michelin-starred Einsunternull is actually happening hot. Adventurous palates get to embark on a radically regional, product-focused journey that draws upon such time-tested techniques as preservation and fermentation. Lunches are served amid Scandinavian-type airyness next to the glass-fronted kitchen while dinners unfold in the cosy cellar.

WEINBAR RUTZ   GERMAN €€€
Map p336 (✆030-2462 8760; www.rutz-restaurant.de; Chausseestrasse 8; mains €17.50-28.50; ⊙4-11pm Tue-Sat; Ⓤ Oranienburger Tor) Below his high-concept gourmet temple, Michelin-starred Marco Müller operates

this fairly casual wine bar where the menu has a distinctly earthy and carnivorous bent. Many of the meats and sausages are sourced from Berlin and surrounds and come in two sizes. Great selection of wines by the glass. Before 6pm choices are limited to a small snack menu.

🍷 DRINKING & NIGHTLIFE

The Scheunenviertel has plenty of bars to match the demands of its creative, international and well-heeled residents and visitors. Torstrasse is an especially fertile hunting ground, but there are also some cute wine bars, gay haunts and offbeat watering holes tucked into the quiet side lanes.

🍴 Hackescher Markt Area

★CLÄRCHENS BALLHAUS   CLUB
Map p334 (☑030-282 9295; www.ballhaus.de; Augustrasse 24; Sun-Thu free, Fri & Sat €5; ☺11am-late; 🚇M1, 🚉Oranienburger Strasse) Yesteryear is now at this early 20th-century dance hall where groovers and grannies hoof it across the parquet without even a touch of irony. There are different sounds nightly – salsa to swing, tango to disco – and a live band on Saturday. Dancing kicks off from 9pm or 9.30pm. Ask about dance lessons. Tables can only be reserved if you plan on eating.

Pizza and German staples provide sustenance all day long, in summer in the pretty garden, in winter in the upstairs Spiegesaal (Mirror Hall; pizza €6.60 to €14, mains €6.50 to €20). Minimum spend of €25 for groups of 10 or more.

★STRANDBAR MITTE   BAR
Map p334 (☑030-2838 5588; www.strandbar -mitte.de; Monbijoustrasse 3; dancing €4; ☺10am-late May-Sep; 🚇M1, 🚉Oranienburger Strasse) A full-on view of the Spree River and the majestic Bode-Museum combines with a relaxed ambience at Germany's first beach bar (since 2002). A stint here is great for balancing a surfeit of sightseeing stimulus with a reviving drink and thin-crust pizza. At night, there's dancing under the stars with tango, cha-cha, swing and salsa, often preceded by dance lessons.

AMANO BAR   BAR
Map p334 (☑030-809 4150; www.bar.hotel -amano.com; Augustrasse 43; ☺5pm-late; 🛜; 🚇M1, M8, 12, 🚉Rosenthaler Platz) This glamour vixen at the budget-hip Hotel Amano (p245) juxtaposes a cool green-marble bar with warm furnishings and lighting and attracts global sophisticates with both classics and original libations that verge on cocktail alchemy. DJs on Fridays and Saturdays. In summer, it expands to the rooftop terrace for great sunset watching.

AUFSTURZ   PUB
Map p334 (☑030-2804 7407; www.aufsturz. de; Oranienburger Strasse 67; ☺noon-late; 🛜; 🚇M1, M5, 🚉Oranienburger Tor, 🚉Oranienburger Strasse) Mingle in the warm glow of this old-school German pub teeming with global DNA and serving some 100 beers on tap and in the bottle, alongside a line-up of belly-filling pub grub. There's local art on the wall and changing gigs in the basement club to boot.

FATHER CARPENTER   CAFE
Map p334 (www.fathercarpenter.com; Münzstrasse 21; ☺9am-6pm Mon-Fri, 10am-6pm Sat; 🚉Weinmeisterstrasse) Tucked into a quiet courtyard, Father Carpenter is not the kind of cafe one simply stumbles upon. Yet among coffee cognoscenti, it's very much a destination for its locally roasted Fjord java, cakes from the Albatross bakery in Kreuzberg and trendy snacks like avo toasts and vegan granola. A great refuelling stop halfway through a shopping spree.

CAFE CINEMA   CAFE
Map p334 (☑030-280 6415; Rosenthaler Strasse 39; ☺noon-3am; 🛜; 🚇M1, 🚉Hackescher Markt) This dimly lit cafe with its wooden tables and movie-themed memorabilia has lured chatty boho types with coffee and beer since way back in 1990, making it one of the few surviving pregentrification places in this neighbourhood.

CAFÉ BRAVO   CAFE
Map p334 (☑030-2345 7777; www.kw-berlin. de/de/contact/cafai_bravo; Augustrasse 69; ☺9am-8pm Mon-Wed & Fri, to 2am Thu & Sat, 10am-8pm Sun; 🛜; 🚇M1, 🚉Oranienburger Strasse) Is it art? Is it a cafe? Is it a bar? Answer: it's all three. This glass-and-chrome pavilion in the quiet and pretty courtyard of the KW Institute for Contemporary Art (p143) was dreamed up by US artist Dan

Graham and is a suitably arty refuelling stop on any Scheunenviertel saunter. It serves breakfast, cakes and light meals as well as cocktails at night.

THE COVEN   BAR

Map p334 (☑01511 498 2524; www.thecovenber lin.com; Kleine Präsidentenstrasse 3; ⊙8pm-2am Sun-Thu, 9pm-3am Fri & Sat; 🐾; 🚇M1, M4, M5, ⑤Hackescher Markt) Steel frames, industrial lamps, hard edges – this particular 'witch's lair' has a decidedly stylish, masculine look and feel. Strong and creative drinks, some made with homemade liqueurs and garden-fresh ingredients, make seasoned imbibers of all stripes and sexual persuasions happy.

🍸 Torstrasse & Around

★ BUCK & BRECK   COCKTAIL BAR

Map p334 (www.buckandbreck.com; Brunnen-strasse 177; ⊙7pm-late Apr-Oct, 8pm-late Nov-Mar; 🚇M1, ⑪Rosenthaler Platz) Buck & Breck liquid maestro Gonçalo de Sousa Monteiro and his baseball-cap wearing team treat grown-up patrons to libational flights of fancy in their clandestine cocktail salon with classic yet friendly flair. Historical short drinks are a strength, including the eponymous bubbly-based cocktail Buck and Breck, named for mid-19th-century US president James Buchanan and his VP John Breckinridge.

It's often packed to capacity, but you can leave your number and someone will call you when space opens up at the 14-seat bar or in the added lounge area.

TORBAR   BAR

Map p334 (☑030-5520 2582; www.torbar-berlin. de; Torstrasse 183; ⊙7pm-2am Wed & Thu, to 3.30am Fri & Sat; ⑪Oranienburger Tor) This restaurant-bar combo owned by Dieter Meier, one half of the 1980s Swiss proto-techno duo Yello, is always packed with beautiful people keen on a good time and quality cocktails. Keep an eye on passers-by through the floor-to-ceiling windows or sidle up to the long bar with complexion-friendly lighting.

If hunger strikes, the restaurant serves creative small plates (€5 to €12) and prime cuts of entrecôte and filet.

MIKKELER   CRAFT BEER

Map p334 (☑0176 8314 1103; www.mikkeller.dk/ location/mikkeler-berlin; Torstrasse 102; ⊙3pm-midnight Sun-Thu, to 2am Fri & Sat; ⑪Rosenthaler

Platz) Mikkeler – the name stands for Mik-kel Borg Bjergsø and Kristian Klarup Kel-ler – dispenses stands for elevated craft beer that the two Danes have been brewing since 2006. In their first beer salon in Germany, their two dozen signature and guest brews on tap are best enjoyed over free-flowing conversation at the bar amid minimalist Scandinavian-woodsy surroundings.

MELODY NELSON   BAR

Map p336 (☑0177 744 6751; www.melodynelson. de; Novalisstrasse 2; ⊙7pm-2am Mon-Thu, to 4am Fri & Sat; 🚇M1, M5, ⑪Oranienburger Tor) Everything about this bar speaks of refinement, but without an iota of stuffiness: the dim lighting, the plush seating, the carpeted floors and the luxe cocktails. It helps that sexy siren Jane Birkin is winking at you from behind the bar. Decide whether to go for a classic or a new concocotion, or just order a Black Mojito, the can't-go-wrong signature drink.

KAFFEE BURGER   CLUB

Map p334 (www.kaffeeburger.de; Torstrasse 60; ⊙9pm-4am; ⑪Rosa-Luxemburg-Platz) Nothing to do with either coffee or meat patties, this sweaty cult club with lovingly faded retro decor is a fun-for-all concert and party pen. The sound policy swings from indie and electro to klezmer punk without missing a beat.

Also has readings, comedy nights, open mike nights and poetry slams. Many events are free.

☆ ENTERTAINMENT

BABYLON   CINEMA

Map p334 (☑030-242 5969; www.babylonberlin. de; Rosa-Luxemburg-Strasse 30; tickets €7-10; ⑪Rosa-Luxemburg-Platz) This top indie screens a smart line-up of cinematic expression, from new German films and international art-house flicks to themed retrospectives and other stuff you'd never catch at the multiplex. For silent movies, the original theatre organ is put through its paces. Also hosts occasional readings and concerts.

CHAMÄLEON THEATRE   CABARET

Map p334 (☑030-400 0590; www.chamaeleon berlin.com; Rosenthaler Strasse 40/41; tickets €37-59; 🚇M1, ⑤Hackescher Markt) A marriage of art-nouveau charms and high-tech theatre trappings, this intimate venue in a

1920s-style old ballroom hosts 'contemporary circus' shows that blend comedy, acrobatics, music, juggling and dance – often in sassy, sexy and unconventional fashion. Sit at the bar, at bistro tables or in comfy armchairs.

BERLINER ENSEMBLE
THEATRE

Map p336 (☑030-2840 8155; www.berlinerensemble.de; Bertolt-Brecht-Platz 1; tickets €8-53; ⓤFriedrichstrasse, Oranienburger Tor, ⓢFriedrichstrasse) The company founded by Bertolt Brecht in 1949 is based at the neobaroque theatre called Theater am Schiffbauerdamm, where his *Threepenny Opera* premiered in 1928. Oliver Reese, who became artistic director in 2017, keeps the master's legacy alive while also exploring new frontiers, for instance by staging the German premiere of *Mary Page Marlowe* by American Pulitzer Prize–winning playwright Tracy Letts.

FRIEDRICHSTADT-PALAST BERLIN
PERFORMING ARTS

Map p336 (☑030-2326 2326; www.palast.berlin; Friedrichstrasse 107; tickets €20-130; ⓜM1, ⓤOranienburger Tor, ⓢFriedrichstrasse, Oranienburger Strasse) Europe's largest revue theatre puts on innovative, high-tech and visually stunning shows that are an artistic amalgam of music, dance, costumes, acrobatics and stage wizardry. Most shows have a two-year run with the latest, called *Vivid*, opening in September 2018. Starring an android named R'eye, it features stunning hats by milliner-to-the-stars Philip Treacy. German language skills not required.

DEUTSCHES THEATER
THEATRE

Map p336 (☑030-2844 1225; www.deutschestheater.de; Schumannstrasse 13; tickets €5-48; ⓜM1, ⓤOranienburger Tor) Steered by Max Reinhardt from 1905 until 1932, the DT still ranks among Germany's top stages. Now under artistic director Ulrich Khuon, the repertoire includes both classical and contemporary plays that reflect the issues and big themes of today. Plays are also performed in the adjacent Kammerspiele and at the 80-seat Box. Some performances have English surtitles.

B-FLAT
LIVE MUSIC

Map p334 (☑030-283 3123; www.b-flat-berlin.de; Dircksenstrasse 40; tickets €14-16; ☺8pm-late; ⓤWeinmeisterstrasse, Alexanderplatz, ⓢHackescher Markt) Cool cats of all ages come out to this jazz and acoustic music venue, where the audience sits within spitting distance of the performers. Big names like Mal Waldron, Randy Brecker and Mikis Theodorakis have all graced its stage, but mostly the focus is on top homegrown talent. Wednesday's free jam session often brings down the house.

HACKESCHE HÖFE KINO
CINEMA

Map p334 (☑030-283 4603; www.hoefekino.de; Rosenthaler Strasse 39; tickets €7.50-10; ⓜM1, ⓢHackescher Markt) This five-screen indie cinema, upstairs in Court I of the Hackesche Höfe complex, presents a well-curated mix of European art-house movies, documentaries and indie films from the USA, many of them in their original language with German, and sometimes also English, subtitles.

🛍 SHOPPING

Along Rosenthaler Strasse, Alte Schönhauser Strasse, Neue Schönhauser Strasse, Münzstrasse, Mulackstrasse and inside the Hackesche Höfe are plenty of options for seekers of the latest Berlin fashions, and label hounds addicted to staying ahead of the fashion trends. Contemporary art galleries line Linienstrasse, Auguststrasse and their side streets. Chains are practically nonexistent.

★BONBONMACHEREI
FOOD

Map p334 (☑030-4405 5243; www.bonbonmacherei.de; Oranienburger Strasse 32, Heckmann Höfe; ☺noon-7pm Wed-Sat Sep-Jun; ⓜM1, ⓢOranienburger Strasse) The aroma of peppermint and liquorice wafts through this old-fashioned basement candy kitchen whose owners use antique equipment and time-tested and modern recipes to churn out such souvenirworthy treats as their signature leaf-shaped Berliner Maiblätter made with woodruff. Mix and match your own bag.

HUNDT HAMMER STEIN
BOOKS

Map p334 (☑030-2345 7669; www.hundthammerstein.de; Alte Schönhauser Strasse 23/24; ☺11am-7pm Mon-Sat; ⓤWeinmeisterstrasse, Rosa-Luxemburg-Platz) Kurt von Hammerstein has a nose for good literature beyond the bestseller lists. Feel free to browse through this stylish lair with word candy from around the world

HAUS SCHWARZENBERG

A dingy-looking tunnel right beside the sparkling Hackesche Höfe leads to **Haus Schwarzenberg** (Map p334; www.haus-schwarzenberg.org; Rosenthaler Strasse 39; ⊙courtyard 24hr; 🚇M1, 🚊Hackescher Markt) FREE, a hub of subculture in one of the last unrenovated buildings in this heavily gentrified area. Its facades are an ever evolving street art canvas, while several offbeat venues, plus a couple of Jewish-themed exhibits, are tucked behind its walls.

Eschschloraque Rümschrümp (Map p334; www.eschschloraque.de; Rosenthaler Strasse 39; ⊙from 2pm; 🚇M1, 🚊Hackescher Markt) A project by the artists' collective Dead Chickens, this subculture survivor is filled with metal monster sculptures and hosts concerts, parties and performance art beyond the mainstream – from Dada burlesque to Balkan postpunk concerts. Small beer garden. It's in the last courtyard of the street art–festooned Haus Schwarzenberg (p153).

Monsterkabinett (Map p334; ☎0152 1259 8687; www.monsterkabinett.de; Rosenthaler Strasse 39, Haus Schwarzenberg, 2nd courtyard; tours adult/concession €8/5; ⊙tours 6-10pm Wed & Thu, 4-10pm Fri & Sat; 🚇M1, 🚊Hackescher Markt) If you want to meet 'Püppi' the techno-loving go-go dancer or 'Orangina' the twirling six-legged doll, you need to descend a steep spiral staircase for a short tour of Hannes Heiner's surrealist underground world. Inspired by his dreams, the artist has fashioned a menagerie of mechanical robot-monsters and assembled them in a computer-controlled art and sound installation that will entertain, astound and perhaps even frighten you just a little bit.

Kino Central (Map p334; ☎030-2859 9973; www.kino-central.de; Rosenthaler Strasse 39; tickets €8.50; 🚇M1, 🚊Hackescher Markt) This teensy, alternative cinema has a stealth location in the back of the graffiti-festooned courtyard of the Haus Schwarzenberg (p153) culture centre. It screens international art-house flicks, usually in the original language with German subtitles. In summer, the screenings move into the courtyard.

Museum Blindenwerkstatt Otto Weidt (Museum Otto Weidt Workshop for the Blind; Map p334; ☎030-2859 9407; www.blindes-vertrauen.de; Rosenthaler Strasse 39, 1st courtyard; ⊙10am-8pm; 🚇M1, 🚊Hackescher Markt) Standing up to the Nazi terror took unimaginable courage, but one man who did so was Otto Weidt. The broom and brush maker saved many of his deaf and blind Jewish employees from deportation and death by organising false papers, bribing Gestapo officials and even hiding people in the back of his workshop. This small exhibit in the original workshop honours Weidt and includes a moving video featuring several survivors.

Anne Frank Zentrum (Map p334; ☎030-288 865 600; www.annefrank.de; Rosenthaler Strasse 39; adult/concession €5/3; ⊙10am-6pm Tue-Sun; 🚇M1, 🚊Hackescher Markt, 🚇Weinmeisterstrasse) This youth-geared exhibit uses artefacts and photographs to tell the extraordinary story of a girl who needs no introduction. Millions of people around the world have read the diary Anne Frank penned while hiding from the Nazis in Amsterdam. While the current exhibit focuses on her life and the diary, a revamped exhibit, set to open in late 2018, will also connect the impact of the Nazi era to our times.

SCHEUNENVIERTEL SHOPPING

or ask the affable owner to match a tome to your taste. There's a sizeable English selection, quality books for tots and a sprinkling of travel guides as well.

KAUF DICH
GLÜCKLICH　　　FASHION & ACCESSORIES
Map p334 (☎030-2887 8817; www.kaufdich gluecklich-shop.de; Rosenthaler Strasse 17; ⊙11am-8pm Mon-Sat; 🚇Weinmeisterstrasse, Rosenthaler Platz) What began as a waffle cafe and vintage shop has turned into a

small emporium of indie concept boutiques with this branch being the flagship. It's a prettily arranged and eclectic mix of reasonably priced on-trend clothing, accessories and jewellery from the own-brand KDG-collection and other hand-picked labels, mostly from Scandinavia.

PAPER & TEA　　　TEA
Map p334 (www.paperandtea.com; Alte Schönhauser Strasse 50; ⊙11.30am-7.30pm Mon-Sat; 🚇Rosa-Luxemburg-Platz) Drink in the Zen

atmosphere in this apothecary-style concept store that stocks dozens of hand-selected whole-leaf and hand-processed tea varieties from Asia and Africa along with teapots, utensils and cups. If you're bewildered, the expertly schooled 'teaists' will be happy to dole out advice.

DO YOU READ ME?! BOOKS

Map p334 (🖉030-6954 9695; www.doyou readme.de; Auguststrasse 28; ☺10am-7.30pm Mon-Sat; ⓢOranienburger Strasse, ⓤRosenthaler Platz) Trend chasers could probably spend hours flicking through this gallery-style assortment of hip, obscure and small-print magazines from around the world. There's a distinct focus on fashion, design, architecture, music, art and contemporary trends, and knowledgeable staff to help you navigate, if needed.

TRIPPEN SHOES

Map p334 (🖉030-2839 1337; www.trippen.com; Rosenthaler Strasse 40/41, Hackesche Höfe, Courts IV & VI; ☺11am-8pm Mon-Fri, from 10am Sat; 🚇M1, ⓢHackescher Markt) 🌮 Forget about 10cm heels! Berlin-based Trippen's shoes are designed with the human anatomy in mind, yet are light years ahead in style compared to the loafers grandma used to buy in the orthopaedic shop. The award-winning brand prides itself on its 'socially responsible' manufacturing and love of unusual shapes. Now available worldwide, this gorgeous shop is where it all began in 1995.

PRO QM BOOKS

Map p334 (🖉030-2472 8520; www.pro-qm.de; Almstadtstrasse 48-50; ☺11am-8pm Mon-Sat; ⓤRosa-Luxemburg-Platz) This treasure trove is squarely focused on the printed word (much of it in English) in design, art, architecture, pop and photography, with a sprinkling of political and philosophical tomes and a broad selection of lifestyle mags from around the world. With floor-to-ceiling shelves and stacks of books throughout, this store is a browser's haven.

LALA BERLIN FASHION & ACCESSORIES

Map p334 (🖉030-2009 5363; www.lalaberlin.com; Alte Schönhauser Strasse 3; ☺11am-7pm Mon-Sat; ⓤRosa-Luxemburg-Platz) Ex-MTV editor Leyla Piedayesh makes spot-on urban fashion that beautifully reflects Berlin's sassy, unconventional and bohemian spirit. Originally known for knitwear, her flagship boutique presents the latest collection of clothes that look good on both the twig-thin and the generously upholstered.

AMPELMANN BERLIN GIFTS & SOUVENIRS

Map p334 (🖉030-4472 6438; www.ampelmann. de; Rosenthaler Strasse 40/41, Hackesche Höfe, Court V; ☺9.30am-8pm Mon-Thu, to 9pm Fri & Sat, 1-6pm Sun; 🚇M1, ⓢHackescher Markt, ⓤWeinmeisterstrasse) It took a vociferous grassroots campaign to save the little Ampelmann, the endearing fellow on East German pedestrian traffic lights. Now the beloved cult figure and global brand graces an entire shop's worth of T-shirts, fridge magnets, pasta, onesies, umbrellas and other knick-knacks.

Check the website for additional branches around town.

ROTATION BOUTIQUE MUSIC

Map p334 (🖉030-2532 9116; www.rotation-boutique.com; Weinbergsweg 3; ☺noon-7pm Mon-Sat; 🚇M1, ⓤRosenthaler Platz) 🌮 An outgrowth of the Rotation record shop (a top purveyor of house and techno on vinyl in town), this shop is a platform for sustainable street fashion by such labels as Elvine, Herb and komodo. It also sponsors the occasional art project and offbeat cultural happening and yes, there's still some music to be found as well.

SCHWARZER REITER ADULT

Map p334 (🖉030-4503 4438; www.schwarzer-reiter.de; Torstrasse 3; ☺noon-8pm Mon-Sat; 🚇M2, M4, M5, M6, M8, ⓤRosa-Luxemburg-Platz) If you worship at the altar of hedonism, you'll appreciate the wide range of luxe erotica and kink couture in this classy shop decked out in sensuous black and purple. Beginner and advanced pleasure needs can be fulfilled, from rubber ducky vibrators to harnesses, and hard-core toys.

1. ABSINTH DEPOT BERLIN FOOD & DRINKS

Map p334 (🖉030-281 6789; www.erstesabsinth depotberlin.de; Weinmeisterstrasse 4; ☺2pm-midnight Mon-Fri, 1pm-midnight Sat; ⓤWeinmeisterstrasse) Van Gogh, Toulouse-Lautrec and Oscar Wilde are among the fin-de-siècle artists who drew inspiration from the 'green fairy', as absinthe is also known. This quaint little shop has over 100 varieties of the potent stuff and an expert owner who'll happily help you pick out the perfect bottle for your own mind-altering rendezvous.

Kreuzberg & Neukölln

BERGMANNKIEZ & WESTERN KREUZBERG | KOTTBUSSER TOR & EASTERN KREUZBERG | NEUKÖLLN

Neighbourhood Top Five

❶ Street Food Thursday (p167) Eating your way around the world at the weekly street-food party inside the historic Markthalle Neun.

❷ Jüdisches Museum (p157) Stepping back into the fascinating history of Jews in Germany at this

Libeskind-designed architectural masterpiece.

❸ Kotti Bar-Hop (p170) Soaking up the punky-funky alt-feel of eastern Kreuzberg in search of your favourite drinking den around Kottbusser Tor.

❹ Türkischer Markt (p178) Immersing yourself

in multicultural bounty on a crawl through the canal-side Turkish-German market.

❺ Tempelhofer Feld (p165) Flying a kite, cycling, picnicking or simply being slothful at this former airfield-turned-open-air park and playground.

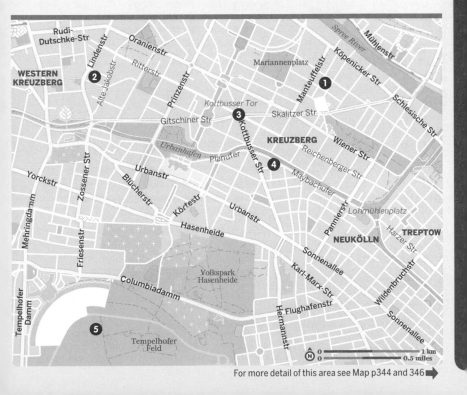

For more detail of this area see Map p344 and 346 ➡

Lonely Planet's Top Tip

Not your parents' minigolf course, Nuture Mini Art Golf on Tempelhofer Feld (p165) is a wonderfully wacky interactive art installation, put together from recycled materials by a team of 18 international artists and a fun way to spend a couple of hours in good weather. For the full lowdown, see www. nuture-art.de.

✖ Best Places to Eat

➡ Tulus Lotrek (p164)

➡ Cafe Jacques (p169)

➡ Coda Dessert Bar (p169)

➡ Orania (p168)

➡ Fes Turkish Barbecue (p166)

➡ Horváth (p167)

For reviews, see p163. ➡

🍷 Best Places to Drink

➡ Schwarze Traube (p171)

➡ Geist im Glas (p173)

➡ Club der Visionäre (p172)

➡ Thelonius (p173)

➡ Möbel Olfe (p170)

➡ Klunkerkranich (p173)

For reviews, see p169. ➡

🍷 Best Clubbing

➡ Gretchen (p175)

➡ KitKatClub (p174)

➡ Loftus Hall (p175)

➡ Ritter Butzke (p172)

➡ Tresor (p172)

For reviews, see p169. ➡

KREUZBERG & NEUKÖLLN

Explore Kreuzberg & Neukölln

Kreuzberg and Neukölln are epicentres of free-wheeling, multicultural and alternative Berlin. There are three quite distinct areas here. The western half of Kreuzberg, around Bergmannstrasse, has an upmarket, genteel air and is home to the district's main sights: the Jewish Museum and the German Museum of Technology (p159). Eastern Kreuzberg (around Moritzplatz, Kottbusser Tor and Görlitzer Park) was Berlin's main 'Turkish Quarter' for decades. More recently, though, it was 'discovered', first by students, artists and global nomads, drawn by cheap rents and the free-wheeling spirit, and now by real-estate investors smelling a profit. Although the district's soul is under attack, for now you can still track down fabulous street art, scarf a doner kebab, browse vintage stores and find out why Kreuzberg is known as a night-crawler's paradise.

All that edginess has spilled across the Landwehrkanal to the northern part of Neukölln. Once making headlines for its crime and poor schools, the district has catapulted from ghetto-gritty to cool in no time. If you need a break from all the cool scene, head to the vast Tempelhofer Feld (p165), a giant urban playground on the airfield of the decommissioned Tempelhof Airport.

Local Life

Bar-hopping Kreuzberg and northern Neukölln deliver some of the city's best night-time action, especially around Kottbusser Tor, along Schlesische Strasse and on Weserstrasse and their side streets.

Shopping Join locals in putting together that inimitable outfit from vintage shops, local designers, streetwear boutiques, pop-up shops and flea markets.

Chilling Locals find plenty of time to hang in green oases such as Tempelhofer Feld (p165), Viktoriapark (p159) and Görlitzer Park.

Getting There & Away

Bus M29 links Potsdamer Platz with Oranienstrasse via Checkpoint Charlie; the M41 (also coming from Potsdamer Platz) hits the Bergmannkiez before trudging down to Neukölln via Hermannplatz.

S-Bahn The Ringbahn S41/S42 stops at Treptower Park, Sonnenallee, Neukölln and Hermannstrasse.

U-Bahn Getting off at Kottbusser Tor (U8) puts you in the thick of eastern Kreuzberg, although Görlitzer Bahnhof and Schlesisches Tor (U1) are also handy. For northern Neukölln, Schönleinstrasse, Hermannplatz and Boddinstrasse (all on the U8) as well as Rathaus Neukölln (U7) are key stops. For the Bergmannkiez area, head to Mehringdamm (U6) or Gneisenaustrasse (U7).

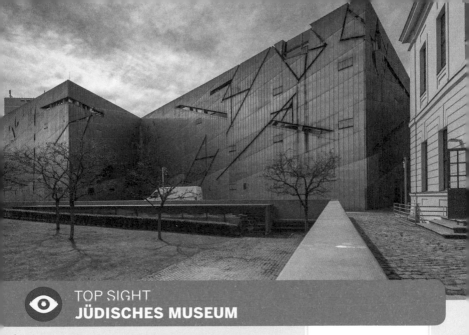

JÜDISCHES MUSEUM

In a landmark building by Daniel Libeskind, Berlin's Jewish Museum has, since 2001, chronicled Jewish life, history and culture in Germany from the early Middle Ages via the Enlightenment to the present. Find out about Jewish cultural contributions, holiday traditions, the difficult road to emancipation, outstanding individuals (eg Moses Mendelssohn and Levi Strauss) and the fates of ordinary people. The permanent exhibition has been closed for a major overhaul until 2019, but it's still possible to access much of the building and the garden as well as to explore a temporary exhibit on Jerusalem and new art works.

The Building

Libeskind's architectural masterpiece (which he titled *Between the Lines*) is essentially a 3D metaphor for the tortured history of the Jewish people. Its zigzag shape symbolises a broken Star of David; its silvery titanium-zinc walls are sharply angled; and instead of windows, there are only small gashes piercing the building's gleaming facade.

The Axes

The museum consists of two buildings. The entrance is via a stately baroque structure that once housed the Prussian supreme court. From here a steep, dark and winding staircase leads down to the Libeskind building, where three intersecting walkways called 'axes' represent the experiences of Jews in the 20th century. The **Axis of Emigration** leads to the maze-like Garden of Exile, which consists of 49 tilted concrete columns; Russian willow oak, a symbol of hope, sprouts from each. The **Axis of the Holocaust** ends in the tomb-like 'void' that stands for the loss of Jewish life, culture and humanity in Europe. Only the **Axis of Continuity**, which represents the present and

DON'T MISS

→ Axis of the Holocaust

→ *Shalekhet – Fallen Leaves* installation

→ Garden of Exile

PRACTICALITIES

→ Jewish Museum

→ Map p346, C2

→ ☎030-2599 3300

→ www.jmberlin.de

→ Lindenstrasse 9-14

→ adult/concession €8/3, audioguide €3

→ ☉10am-8pm

→ Ⓤ Hallesches Tor, Kochstrasse

TOP TIPS

➡ Rent the audioguide (€3) for a more in-depth experience.

➡ Free themed tours (in German) take place at 3pm on Saturday and at 11am and 2pm on Sunday.

➡ Budget at least two hours to visit the museum, plus extra time to go through the airport-style entrance security checks.

Tickets are also valid for reduced admission on the same day and the next two days to the Berlinische Galerie (p159), a survey of 150 years of Berlin art, located just 500m away.

TAKE A BREAK

For a refuelling stop, pop by the museum's **Café Schmus** (Map p346; ☑ 030-2579 6751; www.koflerkompanie. com; Lindenstrasse 9, Jüdisches Museum; dishes €5.50-8; ⊙10am-10pm Mon, to 8pm Tue-Sun; ⓤKochstrasse, Hallesches Tor) for modern takes on traditional Jewish cuisine.

the future, leads to the actual exhibits, but it too is a cumbersome journey up a sloping walkway and several steep flights of stairs.

Voids

Central elements of Libeskind's buildings are what he has termed 'Voids' – five stark, concrete-walled and unheated spaces that soar from the ground floor all the way to the roof. They commemorate Europe's exterminated Jews, or, as the architect himself has put it, 'humanity reduced to ashes'.

Art Installations

The Jewish Museum is peppered with art installations, of which the late Menashe Kadishman's **Shalekhet – Fallen Leaves** is a poignant standout. More than 10,000 open-mouthed faces cut from rusty iron plates lie arbitrarily scattered on the floor in an ocean of silent screams. The haunting effect is exacerbated by the space itself, a cold and claustrophobic 'void'. Also note Dresden-born artist Via Lewandowsky's **Gallery of the Missing**, which consists of five black glass sculptures set up throughout the exhibition floor near these voids. Each contains acoustic descriptions of missing or destroyed objects relating to German-Jewish culture, such as the *Encyclopaedia Judaica,* whose completion came to a sudden halt in 1934.

'res-o-nant' Light & Sound Installation

Mischa Kuball is a conceptual artist from Düsseldorf who has fashioned a site-specific walk-through light and sound installation for a new exhibition space on the lower ground floor of the Jewish Museum. For this project, he uses rotating mirrors and strobe lights to create synergy between the space and the light effect in two of the building's five 'voids'.

W Michael Blumenthal Academy of the Jewish Museum

The **academy** across from the main museum, open since November 2012, houses the museum's archive, library and education department, but for general visitors is mostly of interest for its architecture. Another Libeskind design, the house-in-house concept consists of three inclined cubes with the first forming the entrance and leading to a central hall. From here, two more wood-panelled cubes, tilted towards one another and intended to evoke Noah's Ark, house the auditorium and a library. The inner courtyard, called 'Diaspora Garden', is a quiet place of reflection.

⊙ SIGHTS

Attractions in these vast districts are rather spread out, with the Jewish Museum in the north, the German Museum of Technology in the west and Tempelhof airport park in the south. Fortunately, public transport is excellent, making it easy to keep travelling time between sights to a minimum.

⊙ Bergmannkiez & Western Kreuzberg

JÜDISCHES MUSEUM   MUSEUM
See p157.

BERLINISCHE GALERIE   GALLERY
Map p346 (Berlin Museum of Modern Art, Photography & Architecture; ✆030-7890 2600; www.berlinischegalerie.de; Alte Jakobstrasse 124-128; adult/concession/child under 18 €8/5/free; ◷10am-6pm Wed-Mon; ⓤHallesches Tor, Kochstrasse) This gallery in a converted glass warehouse is a superb spot for taking stock of Berlin's art scene since 1870. Temporary exhibits occupy the ground floor, from where two floating staircases lead upstairs to selections from the permanent collection, which is especially strong when it comes to Dada, New Objectivity, Eastern European avant-garde, and art created since reunification in 1990.

DEUTSCHES TECHNIKMUSEUM   MUSEUM
Map p346 (German Museum of Technology; ✆030-902540; http://sdtb.de/technikmuseum; Trebbiner Strasse 9; adult/concession/child under 18 €8/4/after 3pm free; ◷9am-5.30pm Tue-Fri, 10am-6pm Sat & Sun; ⓟ⛽; ⓤGleisdreieck, Möckernbrücke) A roof-mounted 'candy bomber' (the plane used in the 1948 Berlin airlift) is merely the overture to this enormous and hugely engaging shrine to technology. Fantastic for kids, the giant museum includes the world's first computer, an entire hall of vintage locomotives and exhibits on aerospace and navigation in a modern annexe. At the adjacent Science Center Spectrum, entered on the same ticket, kids can participate in hands-on experiments.

It's easy to spend a full day here, especially if you also explore the vast museum park with its wind- and watermills,

brewery and smithy. Be sure to check the schedule for demonstrations and workshops. Two cafes provide sustenance. For a more in-depth experience, download the Deutsches Technikmuseum app, which includes the audio tour 'Technical Revolutions' (available in English) as well as a children's audio tour.

**SCIENCE CENTER
SPECTRUM**   SCIENCE CENTRE
Map p346 (✆030-9025 4284; www.sdtb.de; Möckernstrasse 26; adult/concession/child under 18 €8/4/free after 3pm; ◷9am-5.30pm Tue-Fri, 10am-6pm Sat & Sun; ⓟ; ⓤMöckernbrücke, Gleisdreieck) Why is the sky blue? Can you see heat? Any why does a plane stay up in the sky? Kids (and grown-ups!) can find the answers to these and other timeless questions in this annexe of the German Technology Museum. The four-floor space is filled with 150 hands-on scientific experiments divided into eight themes, including magnetism, music and hearing, and light and seeing.

PARK AM GLEISDREIECK   PARK
Map p346 (www.gruen-berlin.de/gleisdreieck; entrances incl cnr Obentrautstrasse & Möckernstrasse; ◷24hr; ⓤMöckernbrücke, Gleisdreieck, Yorckstrasse, ⓢYorckstrasse) **FREE** Berliners crave green open spaces, and this vast park reclaimed from a former railway junction is the latest in a string of urban oases. A railway line still separates the sprawling grounds into the wide-open **Westpark**, with expansive lawns and play zones for kids, and the **Ostpark**, with a nature discovery area, a half-pipe, a little maple and oak forest and an outdoor dance floor.

Historic relics such as tracks, signals and ramps are smoothly integrated throughout. There are numerous entrances – getting off Gleisdreieck U-Bahn station will put you right in the thick of the Westpark. For the Ostpark, Yorckstrasse S-Bahn station is closest.

VIKTORIAPARK   PARK
Map p346 (btwn Kreuzbergstrasse, Methfesselstrasse, Dudenstrasse & Katzbachstrasse; ◷24hr; ⓤPlatz der Luftbrücke) Take a break in this unruly, rambling park draped over the 66m-high Kreuzberg hill, Berlin's highest natural elevation. It's home to a vineyard, lawns for chilling, a waterfall and the Golgatha (p171) beer garden.

KREUZBERG & NEUKÖLLN SIGHTS

CHAMISSOPLATZ
SQUARE

Map p346 (⛿Platz der Luftbrücke, Gneisenaus-trasse) Created in the 1880s, this charismatic square with its cobbled streets, old-time lanterns and octagonal public latrine looks virtually unchanged 140 years later. No surprise that movie directors favour it as an outdoor set for Old Berlin.

The best time to visit is Saturday morning, when one of Berlin's longest-running organic farmers' markets takes over.

LUFTBRÜCKENDENKMAL
MEMORIAL

Map p346 (Berlin Airlift Memorial; Platz der Luftbrücke; ℗; ⛿Platz der Luftbrücke) Nicknamed *Hungerharke* (Hunger Rake), the Berlin Airlift Memorial right outside the former Tempelhof Airport honours those who participated in keeping the city fed and free during the 1948 Berlin Blockade. A trio of spikes represents the three air corridors used by the Western Allies, while a plinth bears the names of the 79 people who died in this colossal effort.

BERLIN STORY
MUSEUM
MUSEUM

Map p346 (☎030-2045 4673; www.berlinstory.de; Schöneberger Strasse 23a; admission incl audioguide €6; ⏱10am-7pm, last entry 6pm; 🚌M29, M41, ⓢAnhalter Bahnhof) This multimedia exhibit, moodily set inside a WWI air-raid shelter, provides a handy introduction to Berlin by charting milestones in its history through photographs, short films, sculptures, dioramas and other objects. On the 60-minute audio tour, you learn that Frederick the Great brought the potato to Berlin, that Hitler planned a domed building as tall as today's Fernsehturm (TV Tower), and other fascinating nuggets. A separate exhibit (adult/concession €12/9) examines Hitler's rise and impact and includes a reconstruction of the bunker where he killed himself.

⊙ Kottbusser Tor & Eastern Kreuzberg

FHXB FRIEDRICHSHAIN-KREUZBERG MUSEUM
MUSEUM

Map p344 (☎030-5058 5233; www.fhxb-museum.de; Adalbertstrasse 95a; ⏱noon-6pm Tue-Fri, from 10am Sat & Sun; ⛿Kottbusser Tor) **FREE** The ups and downs of one of Berlin's most colourful districts – Kreuzberg and Friedrichshain – are chronicled in this converted red-brick factory. The permanent exhibit, which zeros in on Kreuzberg's radical legacy, is complemented by changing presentations that often examine such hot-button issues as immigration or gentrification.

MUSEUM DER DINGE
MUSEUM

Map p344 (Museum of Things; ☎030-9210 6311; www.museumderdinge.de; Oranienstrasse 25, 3rd fl; adult/concession/child under 17 €6/4/free; ⏱noon-7pm Thu-Mon; ⛿Kottbusser Tor) This obscure museum ostensibly traces German design history from the early 20th century to today, but actually feels more like a cross between a cabinet of curiosities and a flea market. In the permanent collection, wood-framed glass cabinets are crammed open-storage-style with a century's worth of knick-knacks, from detergent boxes and cigarette cases to more bizarre items such as a spherical washing machine, 1920s inflation money and a swastika-adorned mug.

The collection is based on the archive of the Deutscher Werkbund (German Work

---

CHURCH-TURNS-GALLERY

If art is your religion, a pilgrimage to church-turned-gallery **König Galerie @ St Agnes Kirche** (Map p347; ☎030-2610 3080; www.koeniggalerie.com; Alexandrinenstrasse 118-121; ⏱11am-7pm Tue-Sat, from noon Sun; ⛿Prinzenstrasse) is a must. Tucked into a nondescript part of Kreuzberg, this decommissioned Catholic church, designed in the mid-1960s by architect and city planner Werner Düttmann, is a prime example of Brutalist architecture in Berlin. In 2012, it was leased by the gallerist Johann König and converted into a spectacular space that presents interdisciplinary, concept-oriented and space-based art.

The interior is stark but stunning with its lofty hall lit only by a few slits and skylights. Soaring next to the nearly windowless, brooding structure is a square bell tower made of solid concrete.

ICONIC MURALS OF KREUZBERG

Astronaut Mural (Map p344; Mariannenstrasse, near Skalitzer Strasse; ⓤKottbusser Tor) One of Berlin's best-known works of street art is this monumental stencil-style piece inspired by the US-Soviet space race and created by Victor Ash as part of the 2007 Backjumps urban art festival.

Pink Man Mural (Map p344; Falckensteinstrasse 48; ⓤSchlesisches Tor) Italian artist Blu created this house-sized mural that depicts a creature composed of hundreds of writhing pink bodies. Note the lone white guy crouched on its finger.

Rounded Heads Mural (Map p344; Oppelner Strasse 46-47; ⓤSchlesisches Tor) Rounded Heads is a house-sized mural by internationally renowned Berlin street artist Nomad that shows a faceless person embracing a hooded character. One of Nomad's biggest fans is Ashton Kutcher, with whom the artist painted a huge slot-machine mural on top of the Planet Hollywood Hotel in 2009.

Transit Mural (Map p344; cnr Oranienstrasse & Manteuffelstrasse; ⓤGörlitzer Bahnhof) This five-storey-tall street mural by Belgian artist ROA depicts animal carcasses, including a sheep and a deer, in a distinctive monochrome spray-paint style. Depicting the cycle of life and death of animals native to the region where the work is created is a recurrent theme in ROA's work.

Yellow Man Mural (Map p344; Oppelner Strasse 3; ⓤSchlesisches Tor) This wall-sized street mural showing a bizarrely dressed, seemingly genderless, yellow-skinned figure is a signature work by Os Gemeos, aka identical twins Otavio and Gustavo Pandolfo, from São Paulo, Brazil.

Federation), an association of artists, architects, designers and industrialists formed in 1907 to integrate traditional crafts and industrial mass-production techniques. It was an important precursor of the 1920s Bauhaus movement. Temporary exhibits zero in on specific themes such as the 'Eroticism of Things' or 'Graphic Design in East Germany'.

PRINZESSINNENGÄRTEN GARDENS
Map p344 (Princess Gardens; http://prinzessinnen garten.net; Prinzenstrasse 35-38, Moritzplatz; ☺Apr-Oct; ⓤMoritzplatz) FREE Berlin's pioneering urban gardening project began in 2009 on this site on Moritzplatz, which had been abandoned for over 60 years. The nonprofit group Nomadic Green inspired a small army of volunteers to help turn this wasteland into a fertile farm. Today there are workshops on gardening and beekeeping, activities for kids and a **cafe** (open noon to 6pm) where meals are prepared with the home-grown crop.

It's become a bright and thriving space where anyone can get their hands dirty planting and tending organic herbs, vegetables and flowers in raised compost beds without pesticides or artificial fertilisers. Public gardening times are Thursday 3pm to 6pm and Saturday 11am to 2pm. Guided tours are available on request.

KÜNSTLERHAUS BETHANIEN GALLERY
Map p344 (☎030-616 9030; www.bethanien. de; Kottbusser Strasse 10; ☺2-7pm Tue-Sun; ⓤKottbusser Tor) FREE Founded in 1975, the Künstlerhaus is an artistic sanctuary and creative cauldron for emerging artists from around the globe. In 2010 it moved into this former light-fixture factory, where it maintains one of Germany's largest artist-in-residence programs. Exhibits showcase their work, as well as that of former residents and other artists.

KUNSTQUARTIER BETHANIEN ARTS CENTRE
Map p344 (www.kunstquartier-bethanien.de; Mariannenplatz 2; ⓤKottbusser Tor) FREE This grand, twin-towered hospital was built in the 1840s by three students of Karl Friedrich Schinkel and used until 1970. Since 1973, it's been a thriving beehive of edgy art and culture across the entire creative spectrum – from theatre to dance, music to design. A highlight is the **Kunstraum Kreuzberg/Bethanien** gallery, which has an intercultural and socially conscious bent.

Also on the premises is the original pharmacy where poet Theodor Fontane worked

KREUZBERG & NEUKÖLLN SIGHTS

162

WORTH A DETOUR

TREPTOWER PARK & THE SOVIET WAR MEMORIAL

Southeast of Kreuzberg, the former East Berlin district of Treptow gets its character from the Spree River and two parks: Treptower Park and Plänterwald. Both are vast sweeps of expansive lawns, shady woods and tranquil riverfront, and have been popular for chilling, tanning, picnicking, jogging or just strolling around for well over a century. In summer, Stern und Kreisschiffahrt (p300) operates cruises from landing docks just south of the Treptower Park S-Bahn station. A bit further south, you can tuck into German food or swill a beer at **Restaurant & Biergarten Zenner** (☑030-533 7370; www.hauszenner.de; Alt-Treptow 14-17; mains €9-17.50; ◷noon-midnight Wed-Sat, 10am-10pm Sun, beer garden from noon Apr-Sep; ⑤Plänterwald, Treptower Park). From the terrace, you'll have a lovely view of the **Insel der Jugend** (☑030-8096 1850; www.inselberlin.de; Alt-Treptow 6; ⑤Plänterwald, Treptower Park), a pint-sized island reached via a 1915 steel bridge that was the first of its kind in Germany. In summer there's a cafe, boat rentals, movie screenings, concerts and parties.

Nearby awaits Treptower Park's main sight: the gargantuan **Sowjetisches Ehrenmal Treptow** (Soviet War Memorial; Treptower Park; ◷24hr; ®Treptower Park) FREE, which stands above the graves of 5000 Soviet soldiers killed in the 1945 Battle of Berlin. Inaugurated in 1949, it's a sobering testament to the immensity of Russia's wartime losses. Coming from the S-Bahn station, you'll first be greeted by a statue of **Mother Russia** grieving for her dead children. Beyond, two mighty walls fronted by soldiers kneeling in sorrow flank the gateway to the memorial itself; the red marble used here was supposedly scavenged from Hitler's ruined chancellery. Views open up to an enormous sunken lawn lined by **sarcophagi** representing the then 16 Soviet republics, each decorated with war scenes and Stalin quotations. The epic dramaturgy reaches a crescendo at the **mausoleum**, topped by a 13m statue of a Russian soldier clutching a child, his sword resting melodramatically on a shattered swastika. The socialist-realist mosaic within the plinth shows grateful Soviets honouring the fallen.

South of here, near the *Karpfenteich* (carp pond), is the **Archenhold Sternwarte** (Archenhold Observatory; ☑030-536 063 719; www.planetarium.berlin; Alt-Treptow 1; tours & demonstrations adult/child €6/4, museum free; ◷museum 2-4.30pm Wed-Sun, tours 8pm Thu, 3pm Sat & Sun; ⑤Plänterwald), Germany's oldest astronomical observatory. It was here in 1915 that Albert Einstein gave his first public speech in Berlin about the theory of relativity. The observatory's pride and joy is its 21m-long refracting telescope, the longest in the world, built in 1896 by astronomer Friedrich Simon Archenhold. Demonstrations of this giant of the optical arts usually take place at 8pm on Fridays between October and March. Exhibits on the ground floor are a bit ho-hum but still impart fascinating nuggets about the planetary system, astronomy in general and the history of the observatory. Kids love having their picture taken next to a huge meteorite chunk.

Speaking of kids... Generations of East Germans still have fond memories of the Kulturpark Plänterwald, the country's only amusement park, created in 1969 and privatised and renamed **Spreepark** (☑030-2801 8320; https://gruen-berlin.de/en/our-parks/spreepark; Kiehnwerderallee 1-3; tours adult/child €5/3; ◷tours weekends Mar-Oct, in English 1pm Sat; ⚑; ⑤Plänterwald) in 1990. Dwindling visitor numbers forced it into bankruptcy in 2001, leaving the Ferris wheel and other carousels standing still ever since. The grounds became off limits, which didn't stop urban adventurers from trespassing and frolicking among the abandoned dinosaurs and dragons. In January 2016, the job of reanimating the park was assigned to Grün Berlin (www.gruenberlin.de), a private nonprofit affiliated with the state of Berlin, which has created other public park spaces such as the Tempelhofer Feld. It plans to revive the Ferris wheel, the Eierhäuschen restaurant and other relics, as well as adding new artistic and cultural attractions. For now, the site can only be seen on guided tours.

KREUZBERG & NEUKÖLLN SIGHTS

in 1848–49. It is open from 2pm to 5pm on Tuesdays but can be also admired through a glass door (ground floor, turn right).

RAMONES MUSEUM   MUSEUM
Map p344 (🖉0176 1043 8908; www.ramones museum.com; Oberbaumstrasse 5; admission €4.50, with drink €6; ☉10am-10pm; Ⓤ Schlesis-ches Tor) They sang 'Born to Die in Berlin', but the legacy of American punk pioneers the Ramones is kept very much alive in the German capital, thanks to this eclectic collection of memorabilia. Look for Marky Ramone's drumsticks and Johnny Ramone's jeans amid signed album covers, posters, flyers, photographs and other flotsam and jetsam. The on-site cafe also hosts the occasional concert.

MOLECULE MAN   MONUMENT
Map p344 (An den Treptowers 1; Ⓡ Treptower Park) Right in the Spree River, near the Elsenbrücke bridge, this giant aluminium sculpture shows three bodies embracing and is meant to symbolise the joining of the three districts of Kreuzberg, Friedrichshain and Treptow across the former watery border. The 30m-high work was designed by the American artist Jonathan Borofsky.

⊙ Neukölln

PUPPENTHEATER-
MUSEUM BERLIN   MUSEUM
Map p344 (Puppet Theatre Museum; 🖉030-687 8132; www.puppentheater-museum.de; Karl-Marx-Strasse 135, rear bldg; adult/child €5/4, shows €5; ☉9am-3pm Mon-Fri, 11am-4pm Sun; Ⓤ Karl-Marx-Strasse) At this little museum, you'll enter a fantasy world inhabited by adorable hand puppets, marionettes, shadow puppets, stick figures and all manner of dolls, dragons and devils from around the world. Many of them hit the stage singing and dancing during shows that enthral both the young and the young at heart.

RIXDORF   AREA
Map p344 (Richardplatz; Ⓢ Berlin-Neukölln, Ⓤ Karl-Marx-Strasse, Neukölln) Weavers from Bohemia first settled in quiet Rixdorf, a tiny historic village centred on Richardplatz, in the early 18th century. Some of the original buildings still survive, including a **blacksmith** (Map p344; Richardplatz 28; Ⓢ Karl-Marx-Strasse, Neukölln, Ⓡ Berlin-Neukölln), a farmhouse and the 15th-century

Bethlehemskirche (Map p344; Richardplatz 22; ☉10am-noon Mon-Fri; Ⓢ Sonnenallee, Ⓤ Karl-Marx-Strasse, Neukölln), but in recent years the area has become increasingly hip and gentrified and now teems with cafes and creative spaces.

KINDL CENTRE FOR
CONTEMPORARY ART   ARTS CENTRE
Map p344 (🖉030-832 159 120; www.kindl-berlin. com; Am Sudhaus 3; adult/child under 18 €5/free; ☉noon-6pm Wed-Sun; Ⓤ Boddinstrasse, Rathaus Neukölln) The rambling 1920s Expressionst-style Kindl brewery provides an atmospheric backdrop for changing international contemporary art exhibits, which are presented on three floors of the former powerhouse and in the boiler house, whose cathedral-like space is ideal for large-scale installations. Afterwards, chill over coffee, a plant-based Mediterranean meal or a craft beer from the on-site brewery in the adjacent König Otto restaurant.

KÖRNERPARK   GARDENS
(🖉030-5682 3939; www.körnerpark.de; Schierker Strasse 8; ☉park 24hr, gallery noon-8pm Tue-Sun; Ⓢ Neukölln, Ⓤ Neukölln) FREE This sunken neobaroque century-old garden comes with a secret: strolling past the flower beds and cascading fountain, you are actually standing in a reclaimed gravel pit. Ponder this as you sip a cuppa in the cafe, then check out the latest exhibit in the adjacent gallery. In summer join locals for free film nights or alfresco classical, jazz and world-music concerts.

From U-/S-Bahn station Neukölln, follow Karl-Marx-Strasse north for 250m, turn left on Schierker Strasse and continue 125m to the park.

🍴 EATING

Kreuzberg and northern Neukölln are among Berlin's most exciting and diverse foodie districts, with some of the best eating done in low-key neighbourhood restaurants, ethnic eateries and canal-side cafes. But the area also fields a growing share of high-end restaurants, including three decorated with Michelin stars. Markthalle Neun (p178), ground zero for Berlin's street-food craze, is still going strong, and vegan cafes are popping up at an impressive rate.

✗ Bergmannkiez & Western Kreuzberg

CURRY 36 — GERMAN €

Map p346 (⊘030-2580 088 336; www.curry36. de; Mehringdamm 36; snacks €2-6; ⊘9am-5am; ⓤMehringdamm) Day after day, night after night, a motley crowd – cops, cabbies, queens, office jockeys, tourists etc – wait their turn at this popular *Currywurst* snack shop that's been frying 'em up since 1981.

Other sausage varieties – bratwurst, wiener and bockwurst – are also available, along with traditional potato and noodle salads.

★BRLO BRWHOUSE — INTERNATIONAL €€

(⊘0151 7437 4235; www.brlo-brwhouse.de; Schöneberger Strasse 16; mains from €18; ⊘restaurant 5pm-midnight Tue-Fri, noon-midnight Sat & Sun, beer garden noon-midnight Apr-Sep; 🛜🚼; ⓤGleisdreieck) The house-crafted suds flow freely at this shooting star among Berlin's craft breweries. Production, taproom and restaurant are all housed in 38 shipping containers fronted by a big beer garden with sand box and views of Gleisdreieck-park. Shareable dishes are mostly vegetable-centric, although missing out on the meat prepared to succulent perfection in a smoker would be a shame.

TOMASA — INTERNATIONAL €€

Map p346 (⊘030-8100 9885; www.tomasa. de; Kreuzbergstrasse 62; tapas €3.20-5.50, mains €8-17; ⊘9am-midnight Sun-Wed, to 1am Thu-Sat; 🖋🚼; ⓤMehringdamm) It's not only breakfast that is a joy at this enchanting late-19th-century red-brick villa with a Mediterranean-style garden at the foot of the Viktoriapark. The menu also features inspired salads and vegetarian and vegan mains, *Flammkuchen* (Alsatian pizza) and grilled meats. Kids can make new friends in the playroom or the adjacent petting zoo.

UMAMI — VIETNAMESE €€

Map p346 (⊘030-6832 5085; www.umami-restaurant.de; Bergmannstrasse 97; mains €8-19; ⊘noon-10pm; 🛜🖋; ⓤGneisenaustrasse, Mehringdamm) A mellow 1950s lounge vibe along with an inspired menu of Indochine homecooking divided into 'regular' and 'vegetarian' choices are the main draws of this restaurant with a large pavement terrace.

The six-course family meals are a steal at €23 (€10 per additional person).

AUSTRIA — AUSTRIAN €€

Map p346 (⊘030-694 4440; www.austria-berlin.de; Bergmannstrasse 30; mains €16-21; ⊘6pm-midnight Mon, from noon Tue-Sun; ⓤGneisenaustrasse) Mounted antlers and Romy Schneider preside over this hunting-lodge-style restaurant perfect for camping out with a baseball-glove-sized veal schnitzel and a cold beer. Other Austrian classics such as *Tafelspitz* (boiled beef) and veal-paprika goulash also make appearances on the menu. Everything's prepared fresh but based on time-tested recipes.

VAN LOON — INTERNATIONAL €€

Map p344 (⊘030-692 6293; www.vanloon.de; Carl-Herz-Ufer 5; breakfast €5-14.50, 2-course lunch €8.50, dinner mains €14-17; ⊘9.30am-midnight Mon-Fri, from 10am Sat & Sun; 🖋; ⓢPrinzenstrasse) This retired Dutch cargo ship moored on the Landwehrkanal is a delightful greet-the-day spot, with sumptuous breakfasts served on the sun deck until 3pm. The menu and weekly lunch specials include vegan options. At night, candles and a crackling fire are conducive to romantic dinners.

★TULUS LOTREK — INTERNATIONAL €€€

Map p344 (⊘030-4195 6687; www.tuluslotrek. de; Fichtestrasse 24; 6-/7-/8-course dinner €99/110/119; ⊘7pm-midnight Fri-Tue; 🖋; ⓤSüdstern) Artist Henri de Toulouse-Lautrec was a bon vivant who embraced good food and wine, which is exactly what owner-chef Maximilian Strohe and owner-mâitre Ilona Scholl want their guests to do. With several awards and a Michelin star under their belts, the charismatic couple dishes up intellectually ambitious food with soul.

Strohe is a wizard at taking international influences and turning them into something uniquely his own. Expect intensely aromatic sauces, flavour-rich meats, perfect wines and a warm ambience.

✗ Kottbusser Tor & Eastern Kreuzberg

★SIRONI — BAKERY €

Map p344 (www.facebook.com/sironi.de; Eisenbahnstrasse 42, Markthalle Neun; snacks from €2.50; ⊘8am-8pm Mon-Wed, Fri & Sat, to 10pm

Thu; UGörlitzer Bahnhof) The focaccia and ciabatta are as good as they get without taking a flight to Italy, thanks to Alfredo Sironi, who hails from the Boot and now treats Berlin bread lovers to his habit-forming carb creations. Watch the flour magicians whip up the next batch in his glass bakery right in the iconic Markthalle Neun (p178), then order a piece to go.

★**BURGERMEISTER** BURGERS €
Map p344 (☑030-2388 3840; www.burgermeister.de; Oberbaumstrasse 8; burgers €3.50-4.80; ☺11am-3am Mon-Thu, 11am-4am Fri, noon-4am Sat, noon-3am Sun; USchlesisches Tor) It's green, ornate, a century old and... it used to be a toilet. Now it's a burger joint beneath the elevated U-Bahn tracks. Get in line for the plump all-beef patties (try the Meisterburger with fried onions, bacon and barbecue sauce) tucked between a brioche bun and paired with thickly cut cheese fries. Fast food heaven!

There's a second location – with tables – at Kottbusser Tor.

COCOLO RAMENBAR JAPANESE €
Map p344 (☑030-9833 9073; www.kuchi.de; Paul-Lincke-Ufer 39-40; soups €9-12; ☺noon-

11pm Mon-Sat, 6pm-midnight Sun; ☎; UKottbusser Tor) For some of Berlin's top Japanese soups, follow locals to this lantern-lit canalside charmer, where homemade noodles, fresh vegetables and toppings from egg to wakame bathe in a richly flavoured pork broth. The heart-warming winter dish is also a nice good-weather nosh, best enjoyed on the terrace with canal views.

ANGRY CHICKEN KOREAN €
Map p344 (☑030-6959 9427; www.facebook.com/angrychickenberlin; Oranienstrasse 16; mains from €4.50; ☺11am-11pm; UKottbusser Tor) Angry Chicken serves up delicious Korean fried chicken wings in a range of mouth-watering sauces. Pull up a stool and get your hands dirty, and don't forget to share a snap on their store's built-in Instagram camera.

They also serve burgers, *bibimbap* (hotpot rice dish) and Ramyun noodles from the tiny kitchen.

HENNE GERMAN €
Map p344 (☑030-614 7730; www.henne-berlin.de; Leuschnerdamm 25; half chicken €9.40; ☺5pm-midnight Tue-Sun; ☐M29, 140, 147, UMoritzplatz, Kottbusser Tor) This Old Berlin

KREUZBERG & NEUKÖLLN EATING

TEMPELHOFER FELD: AIRPORT-TURNED-URBAN PLAYGROUND

In Berlin history, Tempelhof Airport is a site of legend. It was here in 1909 that aviation pioneer Orville Wright ran his first flight experiments, managing to keep his homemade flying machine in the air for a full minute. The first Zeppelin landed the same year and in 1926 Lufthansa's first scheduled flight took off for Zurich. The Nazis held massive rallies on the airfield and enlarged the smallish terminal into a massive semicircular compound measuring 1.23km from one end to the other. Designed by Ernst Sagebiel, it was constructed in only two years and is still one of the world's largest freestanding buildings. Despite its monumentalism, Sagebiel managed to inject some pleasing design features, especially in the grand art deco–style departure hall.

After the war, the US Armed Forces took over the airport and expanded its facilities, installing a powerplant, bowling alley and basketball court. In 1948–49, the airport saw its finest hours during the Berlin airlift. After Tegel Airport opened in 1975, passenger volume declined, and flight operations stopped in 2008 following much brouhaha and (initially) against the wishes of many Berliners. That sentiment changed dramatically when the airfield opened as a public **park** (Map p346; www.gruen-berlin.de/tempelhofer-feld; enter via Oderstrasse, Tempelhofer Damm or Columbiadamm; ☺sunrise to sunset; ☐; UParadestrasse, Boddinstrasse, Leinestrasse, Tempelhof, STempelhof) ✈FREE, a wonderfully noncommercial and creative open-sky space, where cyclists, bladers and kite-surfers whisk along the tarmac. Fun zones include a beer garden (p169) near Columbiadamm, barbecue areas, an artsy minigolf course, art installations, abandoned aeroplanes and an urban gardening project.

English-language **tours** (Map p346; ☑030-200 037 441; www.thf-berlin.de; Tempelhofer Damm 1-7; tours adult/concession €15/10; ☺English tours 1.30pm Wed & Fri-Sun; UPlatz der Luftbrücke) of both airport and airfield are available.

institution operates on the KISS (keep it simple, stupid!) principle: milk-fed chicken spun on the rotisserie for moist yet crispy perfection. That's all it's been serving for over a century, alongside tangy potato and white cabbage salads. Eat in the garden or in the cosy 1907 dining room that's resisted the tides of time. Reservations essential.

BAR RAVAL   SPANISH €

Map p344 (☎030-5316 7954; www.barraval.de; Lübbener Strasse 1; tapas from €5; ☺6-11pm Sun-Thu, to midnight Fri & Sat; ☎; ⓤGörlitzer Bahnhof) Forget folklore kitsch. Owned by actor Daniel Brühl (who played the male lead in *Good Bye, Lenin!*), this tapas bar is fit for the 21st century. The delish homemade Iberian morsels pack comfort and complexity, as do the seasonal specials and hand-picked wines. Great *patatas bravas* (spicy potatoes) and *sobrasada* (a pâté-style sausage from Mallorca).

★FES TURKISH BARBECUE   TURKISH €€

Map p344 (☎030-2391 7778; http://fes-turkish bbq.de; Hasenheide 58; meze €4-10, meat from €15; ☺5-10pm Tue-Sun; ⓤSüdstern) If you like a DIY approach to dining, give this innovative Turkish restaurant a try. Perhaps borrowing a page from the Koreans, it requires you to cook your own slabs of marinated chicken, beef fillet and tender lamb on a grill sunk right into your table.

For total happiness, pair it with your favourite meze and a jug of rakı (anise brandy). Book a few days ahead on weekends.

ORA   INTERNATIONAL €€

Map p344 (http://ora-berlin.de; Oranienplatz 14; mains €8-15; ☺noon-1am Mon-Fri, from 9.30am Sat & Sun; ⓤKottbusser Tor) A 19th-century pharmacy has been splendidly rebooted as this stylishly casual cafe-bar-restaurant. The antique wooden medicine cabinets are now the back bar, where craft beer and cocktails are dispensed to a down-to-earth crowd with an appreciation for the finer things in life. The menu is modern brasserie food and makes deft use of seasonal and local ingredients.

MAX UND MORITZ   GERMAN €€

Map p344 (☎030-6951 5911; www.maxund moritzberlin.de; Oranienstrasse 162; mains €11.50-17; ☺5pm-midnight; ☎; ⓤMoritzplatz) The patina of yesteryear hangs over this ode-to-old-school gastropub, named for the cheeky Wilhelm Busch cartoon characters.

Since 1902, it has packed hungry diners and thirsty drinkers into its rustic tile-and stucco-ornamented rooms for sudsy homebrews and granny-style Berlin fare. A menu favourite is the *Königsberger Klopse* (veal meatballs in caper sauce).

CEVICHERIA   PERUVIAN €€

Map p344 (☎030-5562 4038; www.cevicheria-berlin.com; Dresdener Strasse 120; mains €13-20; ☺5-11pm; ☎; ⓤKottbusser Tor, Moritzplatz) The global culinary craze for ceviche, Peru's national dish, has finally reached Berlin. Fish, shrimp, scallops, octopus or any combination thereof are 'cooked' in lemon juice and combined with cilantro (coriander), peppers, onions and spices. Start with a pisco sour and leave room for a 'Lima Sigh', a dessert made from sweetened condensed milk and topped with a meringue cloud.

CHICHA   PERUVIAN €€

Map p344 (☎030-6273 1010; www.chicha-berlin. de; Friedelstrasse 34; mains €8-13.50; ☺6pm-midnight Wed-Sun; ⓤSchönleinstrasse) What began as a regular appearance at Berlin's street-food fairs has evolved into a cheerful permanent nosh spot serving such Peruvian classics as ceviche (marinated raw fish), *tiradito* (Nikkei-style tuna carpaccio) and *palmitos aparrillados* (grilled palm hearts). It all pairs perfectly with a tangy pisco sour and the cheerful decor.

It's small – best to use the online table booking function.

DEFNE   TURKISH €€

Map p344 (☎030-8179 7111; www.defne-restaurant.de; Planufer 92c; mains €7.50-20; ☺4pm-midnight Apr-Sep, from 5pm Oct-Mar; ☎; ⓤKottbusser Tor, Schönleinstrasse) If you thought Turkish cuisine stopped at the doner kebab, canal-side Defne will teach you otherwise. The appetiser platter alone elicits intense cravings (fabulous walnut-chilli paste!), but inventive mains such as *ali nazik* (sliced lamb with puréed aubergine and yoghurt) also warrant repeat visits. There are good vegetarian choices and a lovely summer terrace.

Fresh fish and seafood are served on Friday and Saturday.

KIMCHI PRINCESS   KOREAN €€

Map p344 (☎0163 458 0203; www.kimchi princess.com; Skalitzer Strasse 36; mains lunch €10, dinner €13-24; ☺noon-10.30pm; ☎; ⓤGörlitzer Bahnhof) This pioneer of Berlin's Korean

STREET FOOD PARTIES

Street Food Thursday (www.markthalleneun.de; Eisenbahnstrasse 42-43; ⊙5-10pm Thu; Ⓤ Görlitzer Bahnhof) Every Thursday evening since 2013, a couple of dozen aspiring chefs set up their food stalls in Markthalle Neun (p178), a historic market hall in Kreuzberg, and serve up delicious global street food. Order your favourites, lug them to a communal table and gobble them up with a glass of Heidenpeters, a craft beer brewed right on the premises.

Bite Club (www.biteclub.de; Eichenstrasse 4, Arena Berlin; ⊙5pm-midnight May-Aug or Sep; Ⓢ Treptower Park, Ⓤ Schlesisches Tor) This local street-food favourite brings together great food and partying in a breezy riverside location. To keep things in flux, regular stands and trucks are joined by aspiring newbies as well as craft beer, wine and whisky purveyors. The action continues on the retro Hoppetosse boat with music and lovely sunset views of the river and city.

Burgers & Hip Hop (www.facebook.com/burgersandhiphop; Prinzenstrasse 85f; ⊙3pm-6am Sat, dates vary; Ⓤ Moritzplatz) It's grill and grind at this street-food-and-burger fest, which pops up several times a year at the Prince Charles (p173) club on Moritzplatz. Fuel up on the city's finest patties, then dance it all off inside the club and in the courtyard.

kitchen craze delivers legit classics such as *bibimbap* (hotpot rice dish; vegan version available) and *so bulgogi* (marinated beef slices) in a bubbly ambience. For carnivores, barbecue reigns supreme, prepared on your own tabletop grill and enjoyed with tasty *banchan* (side dishes).

Elevated tolerance for spiciness is required – douse the fire with a cold Hite beer.

3 SCHWESTERN
GERMAN €€

Map p344 (☑030-600 318 600; www.3schwestern-berlin.de; Mariannenplatz 2; lunch specials €7.50, dinner mains €13.50-23; ⊙noon-1am Mon-Fri, from 11am Sat & Sun; 🚼; Ⓤ Kottbusser Tor) The 'Three Sisters' is a lovely restaurant inside the Kunstquartier Bethanien, a 19th-century hospital-turned-art centre, and a dependable pit stop for fresh regional fare inspired by the seasons and infused with Mediterranean and Alpine touches. Sit below the cross-vaulted ceiling or report to the garden for weekday lunch specials, satisfying dinners and weekend breakfasts.

A small cafe in the entrance serves snacks, cakes and ice cream. There's a small kids' menu available.

FREISCHWIMMER
INTERNATIONAL €€

Map p344 (☑030-6107 4309; www.freischwimmer-berlin.com; Vor dem Schlesischen Tor 2; mains €10-18; ⊙noon-late Mon-Fri, from 10am Sat & Sun; 🛜; Ⓢ Treptower Park, Ⓤ Schlesisches Tor)

In fine weather, few places are more idyllic than this rustic 1930s boathouse turned canal-side chill zone. The menu runs from meat and fish cooked on a lava-rock grill to crisp salads, *Flammkuchen* (Alsatian pizza) and seasonal specials. It's also a popular Sunday brunch spot (€12.90).

★HORVÁTH
AUSTRIAN €€€

Map p344 (☑030-6128 9992; www.restaurant-horvath.de; Paul-Lincke-Ufer 44a; 5-/7-/9-course menu €100/120/140; ⊙6-11pm Wed-Sun; Ⓤ Kottbusser Tor) At his canal-side restaurant, Sebastian Frank performs culinary alchemy with Austrian classics, fearlessly combining products, textures and flavours. The stunning results have earned him two Michelin stars and the title of Best Chef of Europe 2018. The wines are fabulous, of course, but Frank is also proud of his food-matching nonalcoholic beverage line-up, including tea infusions, vegetable juices and reductions.

One of Frank's groundbreaking signatures is the 'Young and Old Celeriac'. For this, he bakes the root vegetable in a salt crust and leaves it to age for a whole year, during which all the moisture evaporates as the flavour intensifies. The golf-ball-sized celeriac is then grated like a truffle over freshly steamed celeriac slivers bathing in a thickened chicken bouillon. Despite the fanciful cuisine, the ambience in the elegantly rustic dining room remains relaxed.

KREUZBERG & NEUKÖLLN EATING

★ORANIA   GERMAN €€€

Map p344 (☑030-6953 9680; https://orania.
berlin/restaurant; Oranienstrasse 40; mains
€30-36; ◷6-11pm; Ⓤ Moritzplatz) Punctilious
artisanship meets boundless creativity at
Orania, where a small army of chefs fusses
around culinary wunderkind Philipp Vogel
in the shiny open kitchen. The flair is cos-
mo-chic with food and cocktails to match.
Only three ingredients find their destiny
in each product-focused dish, inspired by
global flavours rather than the latest trends
and often served with live music in the
background.

RESTAURANT RICHARD   FRENCH €€€

Map p344 (☑030-4920 7242; www.rest
aurant-richard.de; Köpenicker Strasse 174;
4-/5-/6-/7-course dinner €68/82/92/100;
◷7pm-midnight Tue-Sat; ☑; Ⓤ Schlesisches Tor)
A venue where Nazis partied in the 1930s
and leftists debated in the '70s has been reborn as a fine-dining shrine, solidly rooted
in the French tradition and endowed with a
Michelin star. With its coffered ceiling, bub-
ble chandeliers and risqué canvases, the decor is as luscious as the fancy food while the
vibe remains charmingly relaxed.

VOLT   GERMAN €€€

Map p344 (☑030-338 402 320; www.restau
rant-volt.de; Paul-Lincke-Ufer 21; dishes €17-35,
5-/7-course dinner €79/96; ◷6pm-midnight
Tue-Sat; ☑; Ⓤ Görlitzer Bahnhof, Schönleinstrasse) Volt's theatrical setting in a 1928
substation would be enough to justify seeking out Matthias Gleiss' sophisticated culinary outpost. More drama awaits on the
plates, where traditional Berlin dishes and
German classics are kicked up a contemporary notch.

✖ Neukölln

DAMASKUS KONDITOREI   MIDDLE EASTERN €

Map p344 (☑030-7037 0711; www.facebook.
com/Konditorei.Damaskus; Sonnenallee 93;
snacks from €2; ◷9am-9pm Mon-Sat, 11.30am-
8pm Sun; ◻M41, Ⓤ Rathaus Neukölln) Of all
the baklava shops in Neukölln, Damaskus
stands out for its truly artistic and rave-
worthy pastries. The shop is run by a Syr-
ian family, who had to leave behind their
thriving bakery and resettle in Germany.
Stop counting calories and try their divine
kanafeh (cheese-filled pastry drenched in

syrup) or their signature *halawat al jubn*
(rosewater cheese pockets).

MASANIELLO   ITALIAN €

Map p344 (☑030-692 6657; www.masaniello.
de; Hasenheide 20; pizza €6.50-11; ◷noon-
midnight; Ⓤ Hermannplatz) The tables are almost too small for the wagon-wheel-sized
certified Neapolitan pizzas tickled by
wood fire at Luigi and Pascale's old-school
but much-adored pizzeria. The crust is
crispy, the tomato sauce has just the right
amount of tang, and the toppings are
piled on generously.

On a balmy summer night, the spacious
flowery terrace practically transports you
to the Boot. Fresh fish is served on Friday
and Saturday.

FRÄULEIN FROST   ICE CREAM €

Map p344 (☑030-9559 5521; Friedelstrasse 38;
◷1pm-evening Mon-Fri, from noon Sat & Sun,
closing time depends on weather; ☎; Ⓤ Schönleinstrasse) Sure, there's vanilla, strawberry
and chocolate, but ordering any of these
would be missing the point of this popular ice-cream parlour. Fräulein Frost is all
about experimentation, as reflected in such
courageous – and delectable – concoctions
as GuZiMi, which stands for Gurke-Zitrone-
Minze (cucumber-lemon-mint). Heart-
shaped hot waffles are served in winter.

BERLIN BURGER
INTERNATIONAL   AMERICAN €

Map p344 (☑0160 482 6505; www.berlinburger
international.com; Pannierstrasse 5; burgers
€7-10.50; ◷noon-11pm Mon-Thu, to midnight Fri
& Sat, to 10pm Sun; ☑; Ⓤ Hermannplatz) The
folks at BBI know that size matters – at
least when it comes to burgers: handmade,
two-fisted, bulging and sloppy contenders.
Everything's prepared fresh, including the
chili-cheese fries, giving you ample time to
study the funky decor. Paper towels are supplied. You'll need 'em.

CITY CHICKEN   MIDDLE EASTERN €

Map p344 (☑030-624 8600; www.facebook.
com/citychickenberlin; Sonnenallee 59; half-
chicken plate €7.50; ◷11am-2am; Ⓤ Rathaus
Neukölln) There's chicken and then there's
City Chicken, an absolute cult destination
when it comes to juicy birds sent through
the rotisserie for the perfect tan. All birds
are served with creamy hummus, vampire-
repelling garlic sauce and salad. Sit out-

side for the full-on Neukölln street-life immersion.

There's also a full menu of other Middle Eastern dishes, including tabouli, halloumi and felafel.

★**CAFE JACQUES** MEDITERRANEAN €€
Map p344 (⏺030-694 1048; http://cafejacques. de; Maybachufer 14; mains €12.50-19; ⏰6pm-late; ⓊSchönleinstrasse) Like a fine wine, this darling French-Mediterranean lair keeps improving with age. Candlelit wooden tables and art-festooned brick walls feel as warm and welcoming as an old friend's embrace. And indeed, a welcoming embrace from charismatic owner-host Ahmad may well await you. The blackboard menu is a rotating festival of flavours, including mouthwatering meze, homemade pasta and fresh fish.

Reservations advised.

LAVANDERIA VECCHIA ITALIAN €€
Map p344 (⏺030-6272 2152; www.lavanderia vecchia.de; Flughafenstrasse 46, 2nd courtyard; lunch mains from €6, 3 courses from €12, 13-course dinner menu €65; ⏰noon-3pm Mon-Sat, dinner 7.30pm Mon-Sat; Ⓤ Boddinstrasse) For a first-class culinary journey around Italy, book a table amid the rustic-industrial charm of this historic laundry. Cooked-to-order antipasti courses are followed by pasta or risotto, a fishy or meaty main, and dessert. Dinner starts at 7.30pm and includes half a bottle of wine, plus water, coffee and digestif. Reservations essential. Lunches are simpler and value-priced.

A new innovation is the lively Dinner & Dance offered every other Tuesday, with five courses, wine and water costing €38.

**CABSLAM
WELTRESTAURANT** AMERICAN €€
Map p344 (⏺030-686 9624; www.cabslam.com; Innstrasse 47; mains €8-21; ⏰11am 10pm Mon, Tue, Thu & Fri, 10am-10pm Sat, 10am-6pm Sun; 🛜; 🚌104, 171, M41, ⓊRathaus Neukölln) After merging with the now-defunct Weltrestaurant Markthalle, Cabslam has expanded its culinary repertoire to offer not only its famous all-day California-style breakfasts but also classic German and coast-to-coast American dinners, from green tacos to beef goulash.

★**CODA DESSERT BAR** DESSERTS €€€
Map p344 (⏺030-9149 6396; http://coda-berlin.com; Friedelstrasse 47; 6-course tasting menu €65; ⏰7pm-1am Tue, Thu, Fri & Sat; ✎; ⓊHermannplatz) Hidden between graffiti-scrawled apartments in edgy Neukölln, Germany's first dessert restaurant serves six-course tasting menus of modern desserts escorted by crafts cocktails. A sweet tooth isn't necessary to dig Coda's sensual fine-dining experience though – chef René Frank favours *umami* (savory) notes, natural ingredients and labour-intensive techniques for well-rounded flavour. Bites are satisfying yet light, intended to jump-start hedonistic Berlin evenings.

Things get more informal after 10pm, when you can pop in just for cocktails and the late-night menu.

EINS44 FRENCH, GERMAN €€€
Map p344 (⏺030-6298 1212; www.eins44.com; Elbestrasse 28/29, 2nd courtyard; mains lunch €8-10, dinner €26, 3-course dinner €49; ⏰12.30-2.30pm Tue-Fri, 7pm-midnight Tue-Sat; 🛜; 🚌M41, 104, 167, ⓊRathaus Neukölln) This casual fine-dining outpost in a late-19th-century distillery serves meals with a strong native identity, composed largely with seasonally hunted and gathered ingredients. Metal lamps, tiles and heavy wooden tables beautifully match the industrial charm of the building. Lunches feature just a few classic dishes, while dinners are multicourse dine-and-wine celebrations.

🍷 DRINKING & NIGHTLIFE

Kreuzberg and Neukölln have Berlin's greatest density of bars, pubs and clubs, and on weekends you'll have no problem partying nonstop from Friday night to Monday morning. There's a high concentration of bars around Kottbusser Tor and on Oranienstrasse, Skalitzer Strasse, Schlesische Strasse and Weserstrasse, but no matter where you are, the next tipple will likely be within stumbling distance.

🍷 Bergmannkiez & Western Kreuzberg

LUFTGARTEN BEER GARDEN
Map p344 (⏺0152 2255 9174; www.luftgarten-berlin.de; Tempelhofer Feld, enter Columbiadamm; ⏰11am-midnight or later Apr-Oct, weather

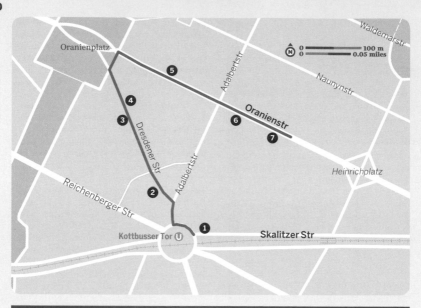

🏃 Local Life
Kotti Bar-Hop

Noisy, chaotic and sleepless, the area around Kottbusser Tor U-Bahn station (Kotti, for short) defiantly retains the alt feel that's defined it since the 1970s. More gritty than pretty, this beehive of snack shops, cafes, pubs and bars delivers some of the city's best night-time action and is tailor-made for bar-hopping. Note that smoking is permitted in most places.

❶ Elevated Speakeasy

An anonymous steel door next to the doner shop Misir Carsisi points the way to **Monarch Bar** (Map p344; www.kottimonarch. de; Skalitzer Strasse 134; ☺9pm-2am or later Tue-Sat; ⓤKottbusser Tor), a drinking den and DJ bar that draws a motley crowd of expats, Berliners and visitors. The vibe is friendly, the music eclectic and the drinks fairly priced. Enjoy views of Kotti and the U-Bahn tracks through panoramic windows.

❷ Funky Saloon

Tucked behind a pile of Turkish kebab shops, grocers and *shisha* bars, **Möbel Olfe** (Map p344; ☎030-2327 4690; www.moebel -olfe.de; Reichenberger Strasse 177; ☺6pm-3am or later Tue-Sun; ⓤKottbusser Tor) is a queer-leaning drinking saloon that channels the area's alternative vibe with boho decor, strong Polish beers and a chatty crowd. It's a popular gathering spot for lesbians on Tuesday and gays on Thursdays.

❸ '50s Cocktail Cave

For a swish night out, point your compass to **Würgeengel** (Map p344; ☎030-615 5560; www.wuergeengel.de; Dresdener Strasse 122; ☺7pm-2am or later; ⓤKottbusser Tor), a stylish art deco–style cocktail bar with operatic chandeliers and black-glass surfaces. The name pays homage to the surreal 1962 Buñuel movie *Exterminating Angel*.

❹ Grape Delights

A charming wine lair with woodsy fixtures and a bar covered in slate, **Otto Rink** (Map p344; www.ottorink.de; Dresdener Strasse 124; ☺6pm-2am; ⓤKottbusser Tor) is an easygoing place to discover just how wonderful German wines can be. There's an emphasis on white varietals from Germany, but wines from France, Spain and South America also feature on the monthly changing menu. Friendly staff will happily help you find your favourite.

HINTERHOF/SHUTTERSTOCK ©

Kottbusser Tor U-Bahn station

❺ Luscious Lair

Luzia (p172) is an excellent place to get the party started with a few beers or long drinks. A firm fixture on the Kreuzberg scene, the vintage decor has been updated with a mural by street artist Chin Chin. Tables behind the panoramic windows are great people-watching perches, and there's a smokers' lounge as well.

❻ Burlesque Boite

A jewel-box-sized burlesque bar, **Prinzipal** (Map p344; ☑030-6162 7326; www. prinzipal-kreuzberg.com; Oranienstrasse 178; ◷8pm-3am or later Tue-Sat; Ⓤ Kottbusser Tor) celebrates the glamour of the Golden Twenties with plenty of eye-candy detail, an apothecary-style bar, and servers in custom-designed corsets.

❼ Den of Debauchery

A mashup of trash, camp and fun, **Roses** (Map p344; ☑030-615 6570; Oranienstrasse 187; ◷10pm-6am; Ⓤ Kottbusser Tor) is a beloved pit stop on the Kreuzberg party scene, especially among lesbigays and friends. Don't let the furry walls and the predominance of pink distract you from the fact that this place takes drinking seriously until the early morning hours.

permitting; Ⓤ Boddinstrasse) On the northern edge of the vast Tempelhofer Feld (p165), a former airfield-turned-public park, this is one of Berlin's loveliest beer gardens. Kick back with a cold brew and a grilled sausage and watch the action on the tarmac.

GOLGATHA BEER GARDEN

Map p346 (☑030-785 2453; www.golgatha-berlin. de; Dudenstrasse 48-64; ◷9am-late Apr-Aug, weather permitting Sep-Mar; 🚲; Ⓢ Yorckstrasse, Ⓤ Platz der Luftbrücke) This classic beer garden in idyllic Viktoriapark (p159) draws a changing cast of characters all day long: families in the daytime (there's an adjacent playground); the after-work crowd for the day's final rays on the rooftop terrace; chatty types for beer and brats in the evening; and party folk to dance till morning. After 10pm, enter the park from Katzbachstrasse.

Between September and March, opening hours are calibrated to the weather. Check the website or Facebook page for the latest.

LIMONADIER COCKTAIL BAR

Map p346 (☑0170 601 2020; www.limonadier. de; Nostitzstrasse 12; ◷6pm-2am Mon-Thu, to 3am Fri & Sat; Ⓤ Mehringdamm) A big stylised painting of Harry Johnson, whose 1882 bartenders' manual is still the profession's 'bible', keeps an eye on imbibers at this neighbourhood-adored cocktail cavern. Top-shelf spirits, homemade bitters, liqueurs and lemonades, plus a deep cache of drink-slinging know-how and imagination, make for a night of sophisticated drinking.

For a change from 1920s classics, try locally inspired house creations such as Berlin at Night or Kreuzberg Spritz.

RAUSCHGOLD BAR

Map p346 (☑030-9227 4178; www.rausch gold.berlin; Mehringdamm 62; ◷8pm-late; 🎤; Ⓤ Mehringdamm) German for tinsel, Rauschgold's name is the game at this shimmering gay girl-boy lair with outlandish theme parties, karaoke contests, potent cocktails, and singalong hits from the '60s to today spun by local DJs. Heteros are welcome.

⚐ Kottbusser Tor & Eastern Kreuzberg

★**SCHWARZE TRAUBE** COCKTAIL BAR

Map p344 (☑030-2313 5569; www.schwarze traube.de; Wrangelstrasse 24; ◷7pm-2am

(sidebar, vertical) KREUZBERG & NEUKÖLLN DRINKING & NIGHTLIFE

Sun-Thu, to 5am Fri & Sat; ⓤGörlitzer Bahnhof) Mixologist Atalay Aktas was Germany's Best Bartender of 2013 and hasn't lost a step since. He and his staff still create their magic potions in this pint-sized drinking parlour with living-room looks. There's no menu, meaning each drink is calibrated to the taste and mood of each patron using premium spirits, expertise and a dash of psychology.

CLUB DER VISIONÄRE   CLUB

Map p344 (☑030-6951 8942; www.clubder visionaere.com; Am Flutgraben 1; ☺2pm-late Mon-Fri, from noon Sat & Sun; ⓢTreptower Park, ⓤSchlesisches Tor) It's cold beer, crispy pizza and fine electro at this summertime day-to-night-and-back-to-day chill and party playground in an old canal-side boat shed. Park yourself beneath the weeping willows, stake out some turf on the upstairs deck or hit the tiny dance floor. Alternatively, head to the sun deck of CDV's nearby second venue, the Hoppetoose boat, which doubles as a winter location.

RITTER BUTZKE   CLUB

Map p344 (www.ritterbutzke.de; Ritterstrasse 24; ☺midnight-late Thu-Sat; ⓤMoritzplatz) Ritter Butzke has origins as an illegal club but is now a Kreuzberg party circuit fixture. Wrinkle-free folk hit the four floors in a former bathroom-fittings factory for high-quality music, courtesy of both DJ legends and the latest sound spinners of the house and techno scenes. It also hosts concerts and there's a courtyard in summer.

WATERGATE   CLUB

Map p344 (☑030-6128 0394; www.water-gate. de; Falckensteinstrasse 49a; ☺midnight-5am or later Wed-Sat; ⓤSchlesisches Tor) For a short night's journey into day, check into this high-octane riverside club with two floors, panoramic windows and a floating terrace overlooking the Oberbaumbrücke and Universal Music. Top DJs keep electro-hungry hipsters hot and sweaty till way past sunrise. Long queues, tight door.

TRESOR   CLUB

Map p344 (www.tresorberlin.com; Köpenicker Strasse 70; ☺midnight-10am or noon Mon, Wed, Fri & Sat; ⓤHeinrich-Heine-Strasse) One of Berlin's original techno labels and dance temples, Tresor has not only the pedigree but all the right ingredients for success: the industrial maze of a derelict power station, awesome sound and a great DJ line-up. Look for the namesake vault in the basement at the end of a 30m-long tunnel. The door is relatively easy.

ANKERKLAUSE   PUB

Map p344 (☑030-693 5649; www.ankerklause. de; Kottbusser Damm 104; ☺4pm-late Mon, from 10am Tue-Sun; ⓤSchönleinstrasse) Ahoy there! Drop anchor at this nautical-kitsch tavern in an old harbour master's shack and enjoy the arse-kicking jukebox, cold beers and surprisingly good German pub fare. The best seats are on the geranium-festooned terrace, where you can wave at the tourist boats puttering along the canal. A cult pit stop from breakfast until the wee hours.

LUZIA   BAR

Map p344 (☑030-8179 9958; www.facebook. com/luziabar; Oranienstrasse 34; ☺noon-5am; ⓤKottbusser Tor) Tarted up nicely with vintage furniture, baroque wallpaper and whimsical wall art by Berlin-based street artist Chin Chin, Luzia draws its crowd from eastern Kreuzberg's more sophisticated urban dwellers. It's a comfy spot with lighting that gives even the pasty-faced a glow until the wee hours. There's an enclosed smokers' lounge.

HOPFENREICH   PUB

Map p344 (☑030-8806 1080; www.hopfenreich. de; Sorauer Strasse 31; ☺4pm-2am Mon-Thu, to 3am Fri-Sun; ⓤSchlesisches Tor) Since 2014, Berlin's first dedicated craft-beer bar has been plying punters with a changing roster of 22 global ales, IPAs and other brews on tap – both known and obscure. It's all served with street-cred flourish in a corner pub near the Schlesische Strasse party mile. Tastings, tap takeovers and guest brewers keep things in flux.

OHM   CLUB

Map p344 (www.ohmberlin.com; Köpenicker Strasse 70; ☺usually Thu-Sat; ⓤHeinrich-Heine-Strasse) One of Berlin's artiest and most experimental clubs holds forth in the battery room of a massive defunct power station that also houses the legendary Tresor club. Electro-loving punters invade the white-tiled rooms for below-the-radar dance parties, label nights, release parties and crossover events. Check online for dates.

PRINCE CHARLES
CLUB

Map p344 (www.princecharlesberlin.com; Prinzenstrasse 85f; ⏰11pm-7am or later Thu-Sat; Ⓤ Moritzplatz) Prince Charles is a stylish mix of club and bar ensconced in a former pool and overlooked by a kitschy-cute fish tile mural. Electronic music shares turntable time with hip-hop, RnB and other beats. The venue also hosts concerts and the Burgers & Hip Hop (p167) street food party. In summer, the action spills into the courtyard.

BAR MARQUÉS
COCKTAIL BAR

Map p344 (☎030-6162 5906; Graefestrasse 92; ⏰7pm-2am Tue-Sat; Ⓤ Schönleinstrasse, Kottbusser Tor) In this tiny shrine to spirits tucked beneath the eponymous Spanish restaurant, the emphasis is on drinks that have written cocktail history. From Old Fashioned to Martini, drinks are served in stylish cut-glass tumblers amid velvet sofas, antique tables and, in winter, a lustily roaring fireplace.

MADAME CLAUDE
PUB

Map p344 (☎030-8411 0859; www.madameclaude.de; Lübbener Strasse 19; ⏰7pm-2am or later; Ⓤ Schlesisches Tor) Gravity is literally upended at this David Lynchian booze burrow, where the furniture dangles from the ceiling and the moulding is on the floor. There are concerts, DJs and events every night, including Experimontag, Wednesday's music quiz night and open-mike Sundays. The name honours a famous French prostitute – *très apropos* given the place's bordello pedigree.

MELITTA SUNDSTRÖM
CAFE

Map p346 (☎030-5484 4121; www.melittasundstroem.de; Mehringdamm 61; ⏰1pm-6am; Ⓤ Mehringdamm) Melitta Sundström was the artist name of a famous queer Berlin soul singer who died of AIDS in 1993. This cheerful cafe with an '80s pedigree and look-at-me art draws a good chunk of its fan base from the gay community, but is really a comfy lair for all with excellent coffee and homemade cakes.

📍 Neukölln

⭐ THELONIUS
COCKTAIL BAR

Map p344 (☎030-5561 8232; www.facebook.com/theloniousbarberlin; Weserstrasse 202; ⏰7pm-1am or later; Ⓤ Hermannplatz) Embraced by a mellow soundscape and complexion-friendly lighting, well-mannered patrons pack this narrow burrow named for American jazz giant Thelonius Monk. Owner Laura Maria, who travelled the world before returning to her Neukölln roots, is the consummate host and creator of the drinks menu that ticks all the boxes, from classics to the adventurous.

GEIST IM GLASS
BAR

Map p344 (☎0176 5533 0450; http://geist-im-glas.business.site; Lenaustrasse 27; ⏰7pm-2am Mon-Thu, 10am-4pm Fri, 7am-2am Fri & Sat, 10am-midnight Sun; Ⓤ Hermannplatz) Weekends wouldn't be the same without Aishah Bennett's soul-restoring brunches (killer pancakes, great Bloody Marys), but swinging by this seductively lit, cabin-style lair to get comfortable with immaculate cocktails and well-curated craft beer and wine selections is a clever endeavour any day. Quality is tops and prices fair.

GRIESSMÜHLE
CLUB

(www.griessmuehle.de; Sonnenallee 221; ⏰club from 10pm Fri & Sat; Ⓢ Sonnenallee) Hugging an idyllic canal in Neukölln, Griessmühle is a sprawling indoor-outdoor space with a funky garden strewn with tree houses, Trabis (GDR-era cars) and flower beds. The project by the ZMF artist collective woos attitude-free electro lovers with an events roster that includes not only parties and concerts but also a monthly flea market, movie nights and ping-pong parties.

KLUNKERKRANICH
BAR

Map p344 (www.klunkerkranich.de; Karl-Marx-Strasse 66; ⏰4pm-2am; 📱; Ⓤ Rathaus Neukölln) In the warmer months, vibes, views and sounds are the ammo of this club-garden-bar combo on the rooftop parking deck of the Neukölln Arcaden shopping mall. It's a great place for day-to-night drinking and chilling to local DJs or bands. Sustenance is provided. Check the website – these folks come up with new ideas all the time (gardening workshops anyone?).

To get up here, take the lifts just inside the 'Bibliothek/Post' entrance on Karl-Marx-Strasse to the 5th floor.

SO36
CLUB

Map p344 (☎030-6140 1306; www.so36.de; Oranienstrasse 190; ⏰Mon-Sun; Ⓤ Kottbusser Tor) This legendary club began as an artist

SEX & THE CITY

The decadence of the Weimar years is alive and kicking in this city long known for its libertine leanings. While full-on sex clubs are most common in the gay scene (eg Lab. oratory; p189), the following places allow straights, gays, lesbians, the bi-curious and polysexuals to live out their fantasies in a safe if public setting.

Surprisingly, there's nothing seedy about this, but you do need to check your inhibitions – and much of your clothing – at the door. If fetish gear doesn't do it for you, wear something sexy or glamorous; men can usually get away with tight pants and an open (or no) shirt. No normal street clothes, no tighty-whities. As elsewhere, couples and girl groups get in more easily than all-guy crews. And don't forget Mum's 'safe sex only' speech (condoms are usually provided).

KitKatClub (Map p344; www.kitkatclub.de; Köpenicker Strasse 76; ⊘11pm-late Fri, Sat & Mon, from 8am Sun; ⓊHeinrich-Heine-Strasse) This 'kitty' is naughty, sexy and decadent, listens to electro of all stripes and fancies extravagant get-ups (or nothing at all). Berlin's most (in)famous erotic nightclub hides out at Sage Club with its four dance floors, shimmering pool and fire-breathing dragon. The Saturday-night Care-Ball Bizarre party is a classic among Berlin's hedonistic havens. The website has dress-code tips.

Insomnia (www.insomnia-berlin.de; Alt-Tempelhof 17-19; ⊘Tue-Sun; ⓊAlt-Tempelhof) Expect a wild night of erotic partying in this 19th-century ballroom-turned-deliciously decadent Berlin nightlife fixture. With its international DJs, performances from bondage to burlesque and various playrooms, Insomnia draws an all-ages crowd of hedonists to live out their fantasies during Saturday's tech-house parties or Friday's theme party from Master & Servant (Depeche Mode) to Infame Royale (1920s).

The vibe is easygoing, nobody forces you to do anything, but unbridled voyeurism is discouraged. Dress code: sexy, fetish, elegant. During the week, more advanced players invade for special-themed sex and swinger parties that often require preregistration. Check the website for full details.

Club Culture Houze (Map p344; ☑030-6170 9669; www.club-culture-houze.de; Görlitzer Strasse 71; ⊘7pm-late Mon & Tue, from 8pm Wed-Sat, from 3pm Sun; ⓊGörlitzer Bahnhof) Fetishists of all sexual persuasions are welcome to get in on the action at this playground for advanced sexual experimentation. Themes and fetishes vary daily, from bi-night to 'fist factory', so check the website. Monday, Tuesday and Friday are for gays only. High kink factor.

squat in the early 1970s and soon evolved into Berlin's seminal punk venue, known for wild concerts by the Dead Kennedys, Die Ärzte and Einstürzende Neubauten. Today the crowd depends on the night's program: electro party, punk concert, lesbi-gay tea dance, night flea market, '80s, 'Bad Taste' – pretty much anything goes. Easy door.

SCHWUZ
GAY

Map p344 (☑030-5770 2270; www.schwuz.de; Rollbergstrasse 26; ⊘11pm-late Thu-Sat; ☑104, 167, ⓊRathaus Neukölln) This long-running queer party institution is the go-to spot for high-energy flirting and dancing. Different parties draw different punters to the three floors, lovingly nicknamed 'cathedral', 'bunker' and 'salon' and ringing

with the entire sound spectrum from pop to techno, depending on the night. A great spot for easing into Berlin's LGBTIQ party scene.

BIRGIT&BIER
CLUB

Map p344 (☑030-618 7240; www.facebook.com/birgitundbier; Schleusenufer 3; ⊘2pm-5am Mon-Wed, to 6am Thu, to noon Fri & Sat, to 6am Sun; ☑165, 265, N65, ⑤Treptower Park, ⓊSchlesisches Tor) Enter through the iron gate and embark on a magical mystery tour that'll have you chilling in the beer garden, taking selfies with wacky art, dancing under the disco ball and lounging in a retired carousel. An eclectic roster of events, including outdoor cinema, deep-flow music yoga and magical party nights, pretty much guarantees a good time.

Ä PUB

Map p344 (📞030-3064 8751; www.ae-neukoelln. de; Weserstrasse 40; ⏰5pm-3am Mon-Sat, to midnight Sun; 🚋M41, Ⓤ Rathaus Neukölln) Always wall-to-wall with globalists, this *Kiez* (neighbourhood) pioneer is a dressed-down watering hole with a fridge full of beer to fuel your inner party animal, whether you plan to camp out for the night or have that final drink. There's live entertainment some nights, usually Wednesday.

VIN AQUA VIN WINE BAR

Map p344 (📞030-9405 2886; www.vinaqua vin.de; Weserstrasse 204; ⏰4pm-midnight or later Mon-Wed, from 3pm Thu & Fri, from 2pm Sat; 🚋171, M29, M41, Ⓤ Hermannplatz) Vin Aqua Vin does double duty as a wine shop and wine bar where you can sample hand-picked wines amid candlelight and a homey, anti-snob vibe, which removes the intimidation factor.

Instead of expensive trophy wines, owner Jan Kreuzinger pours and sells a shifting set of affordable boutique favourites, many from small German producers with a willingness to experiment. Also try his own sparkling wine.

LOFTUS HALL CLUB

Map p344 (www.facebook.com/loftushallberlin; Maybachufer 48; ⏰usually from 11pm or midnight Fri & Sat; 🚋M29, 171, Ⓤ Hermannplatz, Schönleinstrasse) This '70s retro-look haunt in a former slot-machine factory takes its name from a haunted mansion in Ireland; you half expect a ghost to lurk behind the wood-panelled walls and heavy curtains. The sound system and music, however, are very up-to-the-minute, with next-gen DJs creating a journey through all subgenres of electronic beats. Chilled crowd and easy door.

KULTSTÄTTE KELLER CLUB

Map p344 (www.facebook.com/kellerkultur. net; Karl-Marx-Strasse 52, 2nd courtyard; ⏰11.45pm-7am Fri, from 10pm Sat; Ⓤ Rathaus Neukölln) Quite literally a bastion of the Berlin 'underground' is this warren-like cellar in a back courtyard. The charmingly improvised dancing den is affiliated with the label Keller, which strives to break down the barriers between melodic techno and deep house. The turntable is a platform for young alternative talent of all stripes.

 ⭐ **ENTERTAINMENT**

⭐ Bergmannkiez & Western Kreuzberg

GRETCHEN LIVE MUSIC

Map p346 (📞030-2592 2702; www.gretchen-club.de; Obentrautstrasse 19-21; ⏰hours vary, always Fri & Sat; Ⓤ Mehringdamm, Hallesches Tor) One of Berlin's finest music venues has set up in the gorgeous slender-columned and brick-vaulted stables of a 19th-century Prussian regiment. The low-key crowd defines the word eclectic, as does the music, which hops around contemporary trends from electro to dubstep, indie to hip-hop, funk to house. Hosts concerts and DJ sets.

HEBBEL AM UFER THEATRE

Map p346 (HAU 1; 📞030-259 0040; www.hebbel -am-ufer.de; Stresemannstrasse 29; tickets €8-30; Ⓤ Hallesches Tor) Germany's most avant-garde and trailblazing theatre comes with a mission to explore changes in the social and political fabric of society, often by blurring the lines between theatre, dance and art. Performances are held in this 1907 art nouveau theatre called Hau 1 (the main performance venue), as well as in two smaller venues nearby, Hau 2 (Map p346) and Hau 3 (Map p346).

YORCKSCHLÖSSCHEN LIVE MUSIC

Map p346 (📞030-215 8070; www.yorckschloess chen.de; Yorckstrasse 15; tickets €4-8, jazz brunch €15.50; ⏰5pm-3am Mon-Sat, from 11am Sun; Ⓤ Mehringdamm) Cosy and knick-knack-laden, this Kreuzberg institution has plied an all-ages, all-comers crowd of jazz and blues lovers with tunes and booze for over 30 years. Toe-tapping bands invade several times a week, but there's also a pool table, beer garden, local beer on tap, and European soul food served till 1am. Jazz brunch on Sunday.

ENGLISH THEATRE BERLIN THEATRE

Map p346 (📞030-691 1211; www.etberlin.de; Fidicinstrasse 40; 🚋M19, Ⓤ Platz der Luftbrücke) Berlin's oldest English-language theatre puts on an engaging roster of in-house productions, plays by international visiting troupes, concerts, comedy, dance and cabaret by local performers. Quality is often high and the cast international. Tickets usually cost around €15.

☆ Kottbusser Tor & Eastern Kreuzberg

LIDO LIVE MUSIC
Map p344 (☑030-6956 6840; www.lido-berlin.
de; Cuvrystrasse 7; ⓤSchlesisches Tor) A 1950s
cinema has been recycled into a rock-indie-
electro-pop hub with mosh-pit electricity
and a crowd that cares more about the music than about looking good. Global DJs and
talented upwardly mobile live noisemakers
pull in the punters. Its monthly Balkan-
beats party is legendary.

WILD AT HEART LIVE MUSIC
Map p344 (☑030-611 9231; www.wildatheart
berlin.de; Wiener Strasse 20; ⓥ8pm-late Wed-
Sun; ⓤGörlitzer Bahnhof) Named after a
David Lynch road movie, this kitsch-cool
dive with blood-red walls, tiki gods and
Elvis paraphernalia hammers home punk,
ska, surf-rock and rockabilly. It's really,
REALLY loud, so if your ears need a little
break, head to the tiki-themed restaurant-
bar next door. Free concerts are held on
Wednesdays.

BI NUU LIVE MUSIC
Map p344 (☑030-6165 4455; www.bi-nuu.de; Im
Schlesischen Tor; ⓤSchlesisches Tor) This smallish, frill-free indie and alternative venue, in
the crimson-lit catacombs below Schlesisches Tor U-Bahn station, presents genre-
spanning gigs by up-and-coming musicians,
alongside a weekly rap competition, record
releases and dance parties.

The curious name, by the way, pays
homage to the third album by the Neue
Deutsche Welle band Ideal, which was released in 1982.

PRIVATCLUB LIVE MUSIC
Map p344 (☑030-6167 5962; www.privatclub-
berlin.de; Skalitzer Strasse 85-86; tickets €12-15;
ⓥ8pm-1am Mon-Thu, to 6am Fri & Sat, to midnight
Sun; ⓤSchlesisches Tor, Görlitzer Bahnhof) In
a former red-brick post office, this retro-
styled venue draws an easygoing crowd
with concerts and parties that don't chase
the latest trends. Expect a timeless beat
potpourri that may even include ska, cum-
bia and indietronic.

Alas, the club's future may be threatened
since the building was purchased by an in-
vestor in 2017. Stay tuned.

**FREILUFTKINO
KREUZBERG** OUTDOOR CINEMA
Map p344 (☑030-2936 1628; www.freiluftkino-
kreuzberg.de; Mariannenplatz; tickets €7.50;
ⓥdaily May-early Sep; ⓤKottbusser Tor) This
beloved open-air cinema screens international current-season, classic and cult
flicks in digital quality on the courtyard
lawn of the Kunstquartier Bethanien (p161)
arts centre. All movies are presented in the
original language with German subtitles;
German movies have English subtitles.

There's a limited supply of free blankets
and deckchairs, so come early if you're keen
to snag one; otherwise, you're free to bring
your own. All screenings take place rain or
shine.

MUSIK & FRIEDEN LIVE MUSIC
Map p344 (☑030-2391 9994; www.musikund
frieden.de; Falckensteinstrasse 48; ⓥhours vary;
ⓤSchlesisches Tor) The old Magnet Club
space was reborn as Musik & Frieden, but
still presents a winning mix of concerts
and parties alongside the occasional comedy night or karaoke bash. The top-floor
Baumhaus bar, which beckons with tree-
house decor and views of the elevated U-
Bahn tracks, hosts trash drag queen Nina
Queer's famously wacky Glamourquiz on
most Wednesdays. The cover charge varies.

BALLHAUS NAUNYNSTRASSE THEATRE
Map p344 (☑030-7545 3725; www.ballhaus
naunynstrasse.de; Naunynstrasse 27; tickets
adult/concession €14/8; ⓤKottbusser Tor)
This fringe theatre in a repurposed 19th-
century ballroom presents cutting-edge
and often provocative intercultural plays
around the issues of migration and integration. Most actors have an immigrant background. Some performances have English
subtitles.

At the time of writing it was closed for
renovations and expected to open in late
2018.

☆ Neukölln

NEUKÖLLNER OPER THEATRE
Map p344 (☑tickets 030-6889 0777; www.
neukoellneroper.de; Karl-Marx-Strasse 131-133;
ⓤKarl-Marx-Strasse) Neukölln's refurbished
prewar ballroom has an anti-elitist crossover repertoire, including intelligent musical theatre, original productions and

LOCAL KNOWLEDGE

SPLISH SPLASH: URBAN SWIMMING
....

No matter what time of year, Berlin has plenty of indoor and outdoor pools to enable you to get wet in style.

Beach Clubs

Badeschiff (Map p344; 📱0162 545 1374; www.arena-berlin.de; Eichenstrasse 4; adult/concession €5.50/3; ⊘8am-varies (weather dependent) May-early Sep; 🚌265, 🚇Treptower Park, 🚇Schlesisches Tor) Take an old river barge, fill it with water, moor it in the Spree and – voila! – you get an artist-designed urban lifestyle pool that is a popular swim-and-chill spot. With music blaring, a sandy beach, wooden decks, lots of hot bods and a bar to fuel the fun, the vibe is distinctly 'Ibiza on the Spree'. Come early on scorching days as it's often filled to capacity (1500 people max) by noon.

Alternatively, show up for sunset, night-time parties or concerts. Yoga, stand-up paddle boarding (SUP) and massage treatments are also available.

Haubentaucher (Map p340; www.haubentaucher.berlin; Revaler Strasse 99, Gate 1; admission varies, usually €6; ⊘noon-late Mon-Fri, from 11am Sat & Sun May-Sep, weather permitting; 🛜; 🚇M10, M13, 🚇Warschauer Strasse, 🚉Warschauer Strasse) Behind the brick walls of the graffiti-festooned RAW Gelände (p184) hides this ingenious urban beach club with industrial charm and Med flair. At its heart is a good-size heated outdoor swimming pool wrapped in a sun deck of white stone and wooden planks; shade is provided by a vine-festooned garden lounge.

On occasion, events in the adjacent bar-and-club hall carry the party into the night.

Historic Indoor Pools

Stadtbad Oderberger Strasse (Map p338; 📱030-780 089 760; www.hotel-oderberger.berlin/bad; Oderberger Strasse 57; adult/concession €6/4; 🚇12, M1, 🚇Eberswalder Strasse) These historic baths that kept locals clean from 1902 until 1986 have been meticulously restored. Since 2016 you can once again swim laps in the 20m-long pool canopied by a lofty arched ceiling and flanked by arcades with neo-Renaissance flourishes. It's inside the Oderberger Hotel but open to the public unless used for special events – check ahead.

Stadtbad Neukölln (Map p344; 📱030-2219 0011; www.berlinerbaeder.de; Ganghoferstrasse 3; adult €3.50-5.50, concession €2-3.50; ⊘hours vary; 🚇Rathaus Neukölln, Karl-Marx-Strasse) This gorgeous bathing temple from 1914 wows swimmers with mosaics, frescos, marble and brass. There are two pools (19m and 25m) and a Russian-Roman bath with sauna (€16). Check the schedule for timings; Mondays are reserved for women only, Sunday nights are nude swimming.

experimental interpretations of classics. Many performances pick up on contemporary themes or topics relevant to Berlin and some are suitable for non-German speakers.

IL KINO CINEMA
Map p344 (www.ilkino.de; Nansenstrasse 22; tickets €6-8; ⊘cafe-bar 3.30pm-late Mon-Fri, from 11am Sat & Sun; 🛜; 🚇Schönleinstrasse) Run by the Italian documentary filmmaker Carla Molino and friends, this 52-seat indie cinema with quality sound, projection and seating presents a smartly curated program of international off-grid films in the original language. Afterwards you can discuss their meaning in the cosy cafe-bar.

🛍 SHOPPING

Kreuzberg and Neukölln have a predictably eclectic shopping scene. Bergmannstrasse in the western district and Oranienstrasse both offer a fun cocktail of vintage frocks and hot-label street- and club-wear alongside music and accessories. Nearby Kottbusser Damm is almost completely in Turkish hands, with vendors selling everything from billowing bridal gowns to roasted nuts and gooey baklava. On Tuesday and Friday the Türkischer Markt lures big crowds with its inexpensive fresh produce and other goods.

★ TÜRKISCHER MARKT   MARKET

Map p344 (Turkish Market; www.tuerkenmarkt.de; Maybachufer; ☺11am-6.30pm Tue & Fri; ⓤSchönleinstrasse) At this lively canal-side market, thrifty kids mix it up with Turkish-Germans and pram-pushing mums. Stock up on olives, creamy cheese spreads, crusty flatbreads and mountains of fruit and vegetables, all at bargain prices. In good weather, market-goers gather for impromptu concerts towards the eastern end of the strip.

★ HALLESCHES HAUS   HOMEWARES

Map p346 (www.hallescheshaus.com; Tempelhofer Ufer 1; ☺10am-7pm Mon-Fri, to 6pm Sat, to 5pm Sun; ☎; ⓤHallesches Tor) ✐ IKEA fans with a mod penchant will go ga-ga at this pretty pad packed with stylish whimsies for the home. Even day-to-day items get a zany twist in this airy space converted from an old post office. The in-store cafe serves locally roasted coffee, baked goods and light meals at lunchtime, much of it organic and local.

★ VOOSTORE   FASHION & ACCESSORIES

Map p344 (☑030-6165 1112; www.vooberlin. com; Oranienstrasse 24; ☺10am-8pm Mon-Sat; ⓤKottbusser Tor) Kreuzberg's first concept store opened in an old backyard locksmith shop off gritty Oranienstrasse, stocking style-forward designer threads and accessories by a changing roster of crave-worthy brands, along with a tightly curated spread of books, gadgets, mags and spirits. The in-house Companion Cafe serves specialty coffees and tea from micro farms.

★ MARKTHALLE NEUN   MARKET

Map p344 (☑030-6107 3473; www.markthalle neun.de; Eisenbahnstrasse 42-43; ☺noon-6pm Mon-Wed & Fri, noon-10pm Thu, 10am-6pm Sat; ⓤGörlitzer Bahnhof) This delightful 1891 market hall with its iron-beam-supported ceiling was saved by dedicated locals back in 2009. On market days, local and regional producers present their wares, while on Street Food Thursday (p167), a couple of dozen international amateur or semipro chefs set up their stalls to serve up delicious snacks from all around the world. There's even an on-site craft brewery, Heidenpeters.

HARD WAX   MUSIC

Map p344 (☑030-6113 0111; www.hardwax.com; Paul-Lincke-Ufer 44a, 3rd fl, door A, 2nd courtyard; ☺noon-8pm Mon-Sat; ⓤKottbusser Tor) This well-hidden outpost has been on the cutting edge of electronic music for about two decades and is a must-stop for fans of techno, house, minimal, dubstep and whatever permutation comes along next.

NOWKOELLN FLOWMARKT   MARKET

Map p344 (www.nowkoelln.de; Maybachufer; ☺10am-6pm 2nd & 4th Sun of month Mar-Oct or later; ⓤKottbusser Tor, Schönleinstrasse) This flea market sets up twice-monthly along the scenic Landwehrkanal and delivers secondhand bargains galore along with handmade threads and jewellery.

KREUZBOERG FLOWMARKT   MARKET

Map p344 (www.kreuzboerg.de; Moritzplatz; ☺10am-5pm alternate Sun Apr-Oct; ⓤMoritzplatz) This small and relaxed flea market sets up in the leafy Prinzessinnengärten urban garden project and is a good place to source preloved clothing, music, art and local designs. Double-check dates on the website.

ANOTHER COUNTRY   BOOKS

Map p346 (☑030-6940 1160; www.another country.de; Riemannstrasse 7; ☺2-8pm Mon, 11am-8pm Tue-Fri, noon-6pm Sat; ☎; ⓤGneisenaustrasse) Run by the eccentric Sophie Raphaeline, this nonprofit boho outfit is really more a library and countercultural salon than a bookshop. Pick a tome from around 20,000 used English-language books – classic lit to science fiction – and, if you want, sell it back, minus a €1.50 borrowing fee. The shop also hosts an English film club (9pm Tuesday) and dinners (8pm Friday).

MARHEINEKE MARKTHALLE   FOOD

Map p346 (www.meine-markthalle.de; Marheinekeplatz; ☺8am-8pm Mon-Fri, to 6pm Sat; ⓤGneisenaustrasse) Beautifully renovated, this historic market hall is like a giant deli where vendors ply everything from organic sausage to handmade cheese, artisanal honey and other delicious bounty, both local and international. Take a break from shopping with a glass of Prosecco or a snack.

UKO FASHION   FASHION & ACCESSORIES

Map p344 (☑030-693 8116; www.uko-fashion. de; Oranienstrasse 201; ☺11am-8pm Mon-Sat; ⓤGörlitzer Bahnhof) In her little shop, Doritt

Körzell has shown a steady hand at making clued-up locals look good in fashionable yet affordable threads for over 20 years. Originally a secondhand store, her focus today is on new clothing and accessories from international labels that you wouldn't find in the high-street chains.

OTHER NATURE   ADULT

Map p346 (☑030-2062 0538; www.othernature.de; Mehringdamm 79; ⊙11am-8pm Mon, Wed & Fri, to 6pm Tue, to 7pm Sat; ⓊMehringdamm, Platz der Luftbrücke) At this alternative sex shop with a feminist slant, you can stock up on vegan condoms, Kegel balls, menstrual cups, dildos in all shapes, sizes and materials, and other fun stuff presented in a nonsexist environment. Owner Sara is happy to offer advice on any and all subjects. Also ask about workshops.

HERRLICH   GIFTS & SOUVENIRS

Map p346 (☑030-784 5395; www.herrlich-berlin. de; Bergmannstrasse 2; ⊙10.30am-8pm Mon-Sat; ⓊGneisenaustrasse) This convivial store stocks retro alarm clocks to futuristic espresso machines – there's even a walking stick with a hidden whisky flask – it's all here without a single sock or tie in sight.

SPACE HALL   MUSIC

Map p346 (☑030-694 7664; www.spacehall.de; Zossener Strasse 33; ⊙11am-8pm Mon-Wed, Fri & Sat, to 10pm Thu; ⓊGneisenaustrasse) This galaxy for electronic music gurus has four floors filled with everything from acid to techno by way of drum and bass, neotrance, dubstep and whatever other genres take your fancy, both backstock and new stuff. There are listening stations and an online store, too.

KREUZBERG & NEUKÖLLN SHOPPING

Friedrichshain

Neighbourhood Top Five

❶ East Side Gallery (p182) Confronting the ghosts of the Cold War at the world's longest outdoor artwork on a 1.3km-long vestige of the Berlin Wall.

❷ RAW Gelände (p184) Partying till sunrise and beyond in the rough-around-the-edges bars, clubs and concert venues sprinkled around this former train-repair station.

❸ Flea market (p192) Foraging for treasure at this Sunday sell-a-thon on Boxhagener Platz, followed by brunch in a nearby cafe.

❹ Karl-Marx-Allee (p183) Marvelling at the brutalist architecture of the apartment buildings lined up along this grand socialist boulevard in eastern Berlin.

❺ Volkspark Friedrichshain (p184) Chilling over a beer, a barbecue or an open-air movie in Berlin's oldest public park.

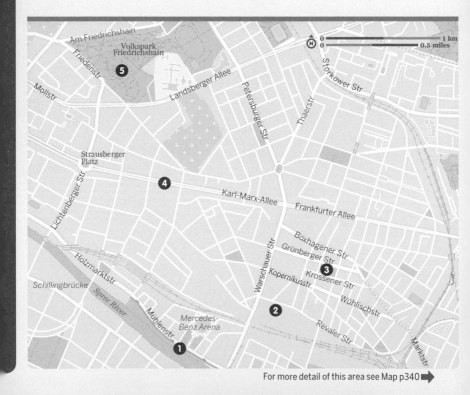

For more detail of this area see Map p340 ➡

Explore Friedrichshain

Friedrichshain is the only central district where major vestiges of the GDR have survived. The prime sight is the East Side Gallery (p182), the longest surviving stretch of Berlin Wall, closely followed by the Karl-Marx-Allee (p183), a grand boulevard that is the epitome of Stalinist pomposity. To delve deep into the extinct country's sinister underbelly, swing by the HQ of the Stasi, the GDR's omnipresent secret police, or head out to the Stasi Prison (p187) in the adjacent district of Hohenschönhausen, where regime critics wound up. More-pleasant daytime diversions include relaxing in sprawling Volkspark Friedrichshain (p184) or picking through the indie boutiques around Boxhagener Platz (don't show up before noon).

It's at night that Friedrichshain truly comes into its own. From late afternoon onward, waves of party pilgrims make their way to the bars along and around Simon-Dach-Strasse. Later the action moves on to the RAW Gelände (p184), a derelict train repair station-turned-party village. Those still standing in the small hours might power on through the night in the electro clubs around Ostkreuz or, by the grace of the door staff, drift off into the utopia of Berghain/Panorama Bar (p188).

Local Life

Marketeering Forage for vintage finds at flea markets on Boxhagener Platz (p192), at the RAW Flohmarkt (p192) and at Ostbahnhof (p192).

Picnic in the park Summer evenings are perfect for chilling in Volkspark Friedrichshain (p184).

Party town Party at Berghain/Panorama Bar (p188) or less hyped clubs such as Suicide Circus (p189), Cassiopeia (p190) or ://about blank (p189).

Riverside chilling Ring in day's end with pizza and a beer at the Holzmarkt (p185) creative village.

Getting There & Away

S-Bahn Ostbahnhof and Warschauer Strasse are handy for the East Side Gallery; Warschauer Strasse and Ostkreuz for Boxhagener Platz and Revaler Strasse. Ringbahn (circle line) trains S41 and S42 stop at Frankfurter Allee and Ostkreuz.

U-Bahn U1 links Warschauer Strasse with Kreuzberg, Schöneberg and Charlottenburg; the U5 runs east from Alexanderplatz down Karl-Marx-Allee and beyond.

Tram M10 and M13 link Warschauer Strasse with Prenzlauer Berg

Bus Take bus 200 for Volkspark Friedrichshain from Mitte (eg Alexanderplatz); bus 240 from Ostbahnhof to Boxhagener Platz.

Lonely Planet's Top Tip

Mostly in summer – but sometimes at other times – the arches of the fanciful Oberbaumbrücke between Kreuzberg and Friedrichshain, as well as gritty, noisy Warschauer Brücke above the railway tracks, become essentially an open-air stage for wannabe Ed Sheerans or Kendrick Lamars. A good place to get the party started for free.

Best Places to Eat

➡ Khwan (p186)
➡ Michelberger (p185)
➡ Katerschmaus (p188)
➡ Schneeweiss (p186)
➡ Vöner (p185)

For reviews, see p185.➡

Best Places to Drink

➡ Hops & Barley (p190)
➡ Tentacion Mezcalothek (p189)
➡ Chapel Bar (p190)
➡ Briefmarken Weine (p188)
➡ Süss War Gestern (p190)

For reviews, see p188.➡

Best Places to Shop

➡ Flohmarkt am Boxhagener Platz (p192)
➡ Sometimes Coloured (p192)
➡ Prachtmädchen (p192)
➡ RAW Flohmarkt (p192)

For reviews, see p192.➡

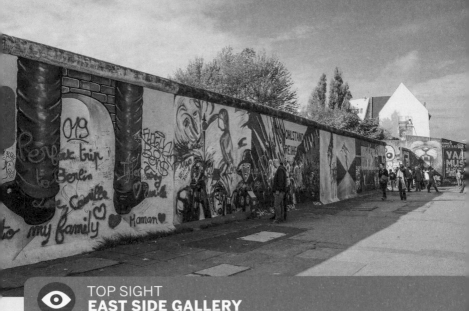

TOP SIGHT
EAST SIDE GALLERY

In 1989, after 28 years, the Berlin Wall, that grim and grey divider of humanity, was finally torn down. Most of it was quickly dismantled, but along Mühlenstrasse, paralleling the Spree, a 1.3km stretch became the East Side Gallery, the world's largest open-air mural collection

In more than 100 paintings, 129 artists from 20 countries translated the era's global euphoria and optimism into a mix of political statements, drug-induced musings and truly artistic visions. Birgit Kinder's *Test the Rest,* showing a Trabi bursting through the Wall, *My God, Help Me To Survive This Deadly Love* by Dmitri Vrubel, which has Erich Honecker and Leonid Brezhnev locking lips, and Thierry Noir's bright cartoon faces called *Homage to the Young Generation* are all shutterbug favourites.

Alas, time, taggers and disrespectful tourists getting a kick out of signing their favourite picture is taking a toll on this protected historic landmark. In 2009 the entire stretch received its first costly makeover; a second one to remove graffiti and fix other damage got underway in 2015.

The East Side Gallery has also come under threat from property developers. Construction has brought about the removal of several sections of the wall, despite big protests that inspired David Hasselhoff and Roger Waters to join the fight.

DON'T MISS

➡ Taking a picture in front of your favourite mural.

➡ Sunset drinks on the riverside lawn.

PRACTICALITIES

➡ Map p340, C

➡ www.eastsidegallery-berlin.de

➡ Mühlenstrasse btwn Oberbaumbrücke & Ostbahnhof

➡ admission free

➡ ⊙24hr

➡ Ⓤ Warschauer Strasse, Ⓢ Ostbahnhof, Warschauer Strasse

At tourist-geared private **museum** (Map p340; ☎030-9451 2900; www.thewallmuseum.com; Mühlenstrasse 78-80; adult/concession €12.50/6.50; ⊙10am-7pm) on the 3rd floor of a former warehouse offers an easily digestible multimedia chronicle of Germany's post-WWII history, with a focus on the construction and demise of the Berlin Wall. The approach is mostly visual, with historic photographs and videos projected onto 100 monitors zeroing in on key events. Actual exhibits are limited to a concrete mixer, a 1960s GDR living room and the defibrillator of the late foreign minister, Hans Dietrich Genscher. For a more comprehensive picture, visit Prenzlauer Berg's Gedenkstätte Berliner Mauer (p195).

◉ SIGHTS

This notorious party district also has a serious side, especially when it comes to blockbuster vestiges of the GDR era such as the East Side Gallery, Karl-Marx-Allee and the Stasi HQ. Alas, the key sights are all pretty spread out and best reached by public transport.

EAST SIDE GALLERY   LANDMARK
See p182.

BOXHAGENER PLATZ   SQUARE
Map p340 (⊘24hr; [P]; 📱240, [S]Warschauer Strasse, [U]Samariterstrasse, Warschauer Strasse) FREE The heart of Friedrichshain, 'Boxi' is a lovely, leafy square with benches and a playground. It's framed by restored 19th-century buildings harbouring boho cafes, artisanal bakeries and shabby-chic boutiques. The area is busiest during the Saturday farmers' market (p192) and on Sundays, when a flea market (p192) brings in folks from all over town.

KARL-MARX-ALLEE   STREET
Map p340 ([U]Strausberger Platz, Weberwiese, Frankfurter Tor) FREE It's easy to feel like Gulliver in the Land of Brobdingnag when walking down monumental Karl-Marx-Allee, one of Berlin's most impressive GDR-era relics. Built between 1952 and 1960, the 90m-wide boulevard runs for 2.3km between Alexanderplatz and Frankfurter Tor and is a fabulous showcase of East German architecture. A considerable source of national pride back then, it provided modern flats for comrades and served as a backdrop for military parades.

Some of the finest East German architects of the day (Hartmann, Henselmann, Hopp, Leucht, Paulick and Souradny) collaborated on KMA's construction, looking to Moscow for inspiration. There, Stalin favoured a style that was essentially a socialist reinterpretation of good old-fashioned neoclassicism. In East Berlin, Prussian building master Karl Friedrich Schinkel was the stylistic godfather, rather than Walter Gropius and the boxy modernist aesthetic embraced in the West.

Living here was considered a great privilege; in fact, for a long time there was no better standard of living in East Germany. Flats featured such luxuries as central heating, lifts, tiled baths and built-in

TOP FIVE EAST SIDE GALLERY MURALS

You'll most likely find your own favourite among the 100 or so murals, but here's our take:

It Happened in November (Kani Alavi) A wave of people being squeezed through a breached Wall in a metaphorical rebirth reflects Alavi's recollection of the events of 9 November 1989. Note the different expressions on the faces, ranging from hope, joy and euphoria to disbelief and fear.

Test the Rest (Birgit Kinder) Another shutterbug favourite is Kinder's painting of a GDR-era Trabant car (known as a Trabi) bursting through the Wall with the licence plate reading 'November 9, 1989'. Originally called *Test the Best*, the artist renamed her work after the image's 2009 restoration.

Homage to the Young Generation (Thierry Noir) This Berlin-based French artist has done work for Wim Wenders and U2, but he's most famous for these cartoon-like heads. Naive, simple and boldly coloured, they symbolise the new-found freedom that followed the Wall's collapse. Noir was one of the few artists who had painted the western side of the Wall before its demise.

Detour to the Japanese Sector (Thomas Klingenstein) Born in East Berlin, Klingenstein spent time in a Stasi prison for dissent before being extradited to West Germany in 1980. This mural was inspired by his childhood love for Japan, where he ended up living from 1984 to the mid-'90s.

My God, Help Me To Survive This Deadly Love (Dmitri Vrubel) The gallery's best-known painting – showing Soviet and GDR leaders Leonid Brezhnev and Erich Honecker locking lips with eyes closed – is based on an actual photograph taken by French journalist Remy Bossu during Brezhnev's 1979 Berlin visit. This kind of fraternal kiss was an expression of great respect in socialist countries.

TOP SIGHT
VOLKSPARK FRIEDRICHSHAIN

Berlin's oldest public park has provided relief from urbanity since 1840, but has been hilly only since the late 1940s, when wartime debris was piled here to create two 'mountains' – **Mont Klamott** is the taller, at 78m. Diversions include tennis courts, a half-pipe, the outdoor cinema **Freiluftkino Friedrichshain** (p191) and a couple of good beer gardens, including **Schoenbrunn** (p186). Kids in tow? Head for the themed playgrounds and enchanting 1913 **Märchenbrunnen** fountain, where frolicking turtle and frog sculptures are flanked by Cinderella, Snow White and other Brothers Grimm stars.

Fans of communist-era memorials will find a trio of treats. Along Friedenstrasse, the sculpture **Denkmal der Spanienkämpfer** pays respect to the German communists who died in the Spanish Civil War (1936–39) fighting for the International Brigades. The **Friedhof der Märzgefallenen** is a cemetery for the victims of the revolutionary riots of March 1848, as well as for the fallen of the 1918 November Revolution. Finally, there's the **Denkmal des Polnischen Soldaten und des deutschen Antifaschisten**, a memorial to the joint fight against the Nazis by the Polish communist underground army and German communist resistance fighters.

DON'T MISS

➡ Märchenbrunnen
➡ Schoenbrunn
➡ Freiluftkino Friedrichshain

PRACTICALITIES

➡ Map p340, B1
➡ bounded by Am Friedrichshain, Friedenstrasse, Danziger Strasse & Landsberger Allee
➡ ⊙24hr
➡ ⛴142, 200, ⛴21, M4, M5, M6, M8, M10, ⓤSchillingstrasse

---

kitchens; facades were swathed in Meissen tiles.

COMPUTERSPIELEMUSEUM   MUSEUM
Map p340 (Computer Games Museum; ☑030-6098 8577; www.computerspielemuseum.de; Karl-Marx-Allee 93a; adult/concession €9/6, after 6pm €7/5; ⊙10am-8pm; ⛴240, 347, ⓤWeberwiese) No matter if you grew up with Nimrod, Pac-Man, World of Warcraft or no games at all, this well-curated museum takes you on a fascinating trip down computer-game memory lane while putting the industry's evolution into historical and cultural context. Colourful and engaging, it features interactive stations amid hundreds of original exhibits, including an ultra-rare 1972 Pong arcade machine and its twisted modern cousin, the 'PainStation' (must be over 18 to play...).

An eye-catching feature is the Wall of Hardware, composed of 50 consoles and computers from 1971 to 2001. Game Milestones provides high-tech background on dozens of seminal games such as SimCity and Tomb Raider. Elsewhere you can learn how games are designed, or examine more sinister issues like game violence and addiction.

RAW GELÄNDE   CULTURAL CENTRE
Map p340 (along Revaler Strasse; ⓢWarschauer Strasse, Ostkreuz, ⓤWarschauer Strasse) This jumble of derelict buildings is one of the last subcultural compounds in central Berlin. Founded in 1867 as a train repair station ('Reichsbahn-Ausbesserungs-Werk', aka RAW), it remained in operation until 1994. Since 1999 the graffiti-slathered grounds have been a thriving offbeat sociocultural centre for creatives of all stripes. They also harbour clubs, bars, an indoor skate park, a swimming pool club, a bunker-turned-climbing-wall and a Sunday flea market.

Search for 'RAW-Gelande' on Facebook.

URBAN SPREE   ARTS CENTRE
Map p340 (☑030-740 7597; www.urbanspree. com; Revaler Strasse 99; ⊙noon-11pm; ⓤWarschauer Strasse, ⓢWarschauer Strasse) Comprising a gallery, a bookshop, artist studios, a concert room and a beer garden, this grassroots urban art hub is a top stop in the RAW Gelände compound along Revaler Strasse, especially in summer. That's also when it hosts festivals and special events and presents Berlin's best street musicians on weekends.

The building's facade doubles as an 'Artist Wall', with new urban artworks going up every month or so.

HOLZMARKT
AREA

Map p340 (www.holzmarkt.com; Holzmarktstrasse 25; ⓤJannowitzbrücke) The Holzmarkt urban village on the Spree is a perpetually evolving cultural open playground – and a nose-thumbing at the luxury lofts, hotels and office buildings that continue to gobble up the riverside real estate.

Grab a pizza and a beer and count the boats passing by while chilling in the **Mörchenpark**, or treat yourself to a fine meal at Katerschmaus (p188) and dance through the night at Kater Blau (p190).

OBERBAUMBRÜCKE
BRIDGE

Map p340 (Oberbaumstrasse; ⓈWarschauer Strasse, ⓤSchlesisches Tor, Warschauer Strasse) With its jaunty towers and turrets, crenellated walls and arched walkways, the Oberbaumbrücke (1896) gets our nod for being Berlin's prettiest bridge. Linking Kreuzberg and Friedrichshain across the Spree, it smoothly integrates a steel middle section by Spanish bridgemeister Santiago Calatrava. In summer, street musicians and artists often turn the bridge into an impromptu party zone.

Added bonus: the fabulous views. Looking southeast along the river, you'll spot the Universal Music HQ, MTV Europe and the extravagantly designed nhow hotel. On the Kreuzberg side are the Watergate club, the Badeschiff and, in the distance, a giant aluminium sculpture called Molecule Man (p163) by American artist Jonathan Borofsky. Right in the river, it shows three bodies embracing and is a symbol of the joining of the three districts of Kreuzberg, Friedrichshain and Treptow.

✖ EATING

Friedrichshain does bars best, but times are a-changing. To be sure, you'll still find plenty of quick-feed shops, but changing demographics also translate into a United Nations of restaurants catering to folks with deeper pockets and more sophisticated palates. And with a growing crop of vegan outlets, vegetarians, too, should be in kale heaven.

SILO COFFEE
CAFE €

Map p340 (www.facebook.com/silocoffee; Gabriel-Max-Strasse 4; dishes €6-12; ⊘8.30am-5pm Mon-Fri, 9.30am-6pm Sat & Sun; 🛜🖉; 🚊M10, M13, ⓤWarschauer Strasse, ⓈWarschauer Strasse) If you've greeted the day with bloodshot eyes, get back in gear at this Aussie-run coffee/breakfast joint favoured by Friedrichshain's hip and expat. Beans from Fjord coffee roasters ensure possibly the best flat white in town, while bread from Sironi (Markthalle Neun) adds scrumptiousness to the poached-egg avo toast.

AUNT BENNY
AMERICAN €

Map p340 (🖉030-6640 5300; www.facebook.com/auntbennyberlin; Oderstrasse 7, enter on Jessnerstrasse; mains €5-10; ⊘8.30am-6pm Tue-Fri, from 9am Sat & Sun; ⓈFrankfurter Allee, ⓤFrankfurter Allee) This daytime cafe in an unhurried yet central section of Friedrichshain combines urban sophistication with downhomey North American treats. Tuck into avo toast, a BLT sandwich or homemade carrot cake while catching up on chit chat or your reading (lots of international magazines).

VÖNER
VEGAN €

Map p340 (🖉0176 9651 3869; www.facebook.com/Voener; Boxhagener Strasse 56; dishes €3.50-6.50; ⊘noon-11pm; 🖉; ⓈOstkreuz) Vöner stands for 'vegan doner kebab' and is a spit-roasted blend of wheat protein, vegetables and herbs. It was dreamed up more than a 20 years ago by Holger Frerichs, a one-time resident of a so-called *Wagenburg*, a countercultural commune made up of old vans, buses and caravans. The altspirit lives on in his original Vöner outlet.

LISBOA BAR AM BOXI
PORTUGUESE €

Map p340 (🖉030-9362 1978; www.lisboa-bar-berlin.de; Krossener Strasse 20; tapas €4-10.50; ⊘5pm-midnight Mon-Fri, from noon Sat & Sun; 🚊M13, ⓤWarschauer Strasse, Samariterstrasse, ⓈWarschauer Strasse) This colour- and knick-knack-drenched bistro is an inspired Portuguese port of call. Regulars pop by for a leisurely breakfast (served until 4pm on weekends) or just for a *galão* coffee pick-me-up paired with a *pastel de nata* pastry. In the evening, a selection of hearty tapas provide a good base for an extended bar-hop. Good wine, too.

MICHELBERGER
INTERNATIONAL €€

Map p340 (🖉030-2977 8590; www.michelbergerhotel.com; Warschauer Strasse 39;

3-course lunch €12, dinner dishes €8-15; ⊘7-11am, noon-2.30pm & 6.30-11pm; 🛜📵; Ⓢ Warschauer Strasse, Ⓤ Warschauer Strasse) 📶 Ensconced in one of Berlin's hippest hotels (p247), Michelberger makes creative dishes that often combine unusual organic ingredients (eg wild boar with miso, scallops, cabbage and gooseberry). Sit inside the lofty, white-tiled restaurant or in the breezy courtyard.

KHWAN   THAI, BARBECUE €€

Map p340 (📞0152 5902 1331; http://khwan berlin.com; Revaler Strasse 99; dishes €4.50-19; ⊘6pm-late Tue-Sat; 🛜; 🚇M10, M13, Ⓤ Warschauer Strasse, Ⓢ Warschauer Strasse) For some of the best Thai barbecue this side of Bangkok, pounce upon this rustic lair ensconced – for now – among the clubs and bars on the RAW Gelände strip. Let your nose be hooked by the aromatic smoke (*khwan* in Thai) wafting from the wood grill, where flames lick chicken, pork, fish, lamb and vegetables to succulent smokiness.

Note: Khwan may move to another location – check the Facebook page or website.

SCHALANDER   GERMAN €€

Map p340 (📞030-8961 7073; www.schalander-berlin.de; Bänschstrasse 91; mains €8.50-17.50; ⊘5pm-late Tue-Sat, noon-midnight Sun; 🛜📵; 🚇21, Ⓢ Frankfurter Allee, Ⓤ Samariterstrasse) The full-bodied pilsner, *Dunkel* (dark) and *Weizen* (wheat) beers are now brewed offsite but this charismatic gastropub is still worth a detour from the tourist track. The menu features crispy *Flammkuchen* (Alsatian pizza) alongside beer-hall-type meaty mains such as pork roast and schnitzel. For an unusual finish, order the wheat-beer crème brûlée.

VINERIA DEL ESTE   SPANISH €€

Map p340 (📞030-4202 4943; www.vineriaytapas. de; Bänschstrasse 41; tapas €3-8, mains €14-20; ⊘3pm-midnight; Ⓤ Samariterstrasse, Ⓢ Storkower Strasse) Decked out with a tiled counter and rustic tables, this feel-good local always jumps with foodies hungry for a piñata of Iberian flavours. The kitchen staff continuously stretch their imagination to come up with innovative tapas and mains without neglecting the classics. Savour it all with a glass of tasty Spanish or Uruguayan Tannat wine.

SCHNEEWEISS   EUROPEAN €€

Map p340 (📞030-2904 9704; www.schnee weiss-berlin.de; Simplonstrasse 16; mains €13-25, Sun brunch €15; ⊘10am-3pm & 6pm-1am Mon-Fri, 10am-1am Sat & Sun; 📵; 🚇M13, Ⓤ War-

schauer Strasse, Ⓢ Warschauer Strasse) The chilly-chic snowy white decor, with an eye-catching 'ice' chandelier, complements the Alpine menu at this fine-dining pioneer in Friedrichshain. Although the emphasis is on such classics as schnitzel, goulash and *spaetzle* (mac' 'n' cheese), the chef's talents also shine through with seasonal specials. Reservations essential for weekend brunch.

MILJA & SCHÄFA   CAFE €€

Map p340 (📞030-5266 2094; www.facebook. com/MiljaundSchaefa; Sonntagstrasse 1; mains €11-21; ⊘8am-midnight Mon-Thu, 8am-1am Fri, 9am-1am Sat, 9am-6pm Sun; 🛜; Ⓢ Ostkreuz) Natural woods and an airy layout lend a Scandinavian vibe to this mellow cafe, where mouthwatering breakfast options are listed on a black-slate board behind the counter with cases full of homemade cakes. Much creativity goes into the pasta dishes and sharing plates as well. Bonus: sunny pavement seating.

FISCHSCHUPPEN   SEAFOOD €€

Map p340 (📞0178 661 1782; www.fischschup pen-berlin.de; Boxhagener Strasse 68; mains €6-24; ⊘4-10.30pm Mon-Wed, from noon Thu-Sat, from 1pm Sun; Ⓢ Ostkreuz) This shop-restaurant combo gets salty flair not only from its big selection of sustainably caught, fresh fish, but also from its ship-cabin-like wooden walls, big aquarium and fishy mural. To sample the full bounty of lakes and sea, order the mixed grilled fish platter. Alternatively, to fill up on a budget, get your hands greasy with a serving of fish 'n' chips.

SCHOENBRUNN   AUSTRIAN €€

Map p340 (📞030-453 056 525; www.schoen brunn.net; Am Schwanenteich, Volkspark Friedrichshain; breakfast €3.50-10.50, mains €12-20, pizza €8-10.50; ⊘restaurant 10am-midnight Apr-Sep, to 7pm Sun-Thu, to 10pm Fri & Sat Oct-Apr, beer garden 2pm-midnight Mon-Fri, from noon Sat & Sun Apr-Sep, weather permitting; 📵; 🚇200, 240, 🚍M4, M5, M6, M8) Watch snow-white swans drift around their pond at this fairy-tale setting in the middle of Volkspark Friedrichshain (p184) while tucking into Austrian fare with Mediterranean touches. If you're not in the mood for formal dining, report to the beer garden for a cold one paired with pizza or sausage. Breakfast is served until 2pm.

LEMON LEAF   ASIAN €€

Map p340 (📞030-2900 9428; www.lemon leaf.de; Grünberger Strasse 69; mains €8-14;

WORTH A DETOUR

STASI SIGHTS IN EAST BERLIN
....

In East Germany, the walls had ears. Modelled after the Soviet KGB, the GDR's Minis-terium für Staatssicherheit (Ministry for State Security, 'Stasi' for short) was founded in 1950. It was secret police, central intelligence agency and bureau of criminal in-vestigation all rolled into one. Called the 'shield and sword' of the SED (the sole East German party), it put millions of GDR citizens under surveillance in order to suppress internal opposition. The Stasi grew steadily in power and size and, by the end, had 91,000 official full-time employees and 189,000 IMs (*inoffizielle Mitarbeiter,* unofficial informants). The latter were regular folks recruited to spy on their coworkers, friends, family and neighbours. There were also 3000 IMs based in West Germany.

When the Wall fell, the Stasi fell with it. Thousands of citizens stormed the organi-sation's headquarters in January 1990, thus preventing the shredding of documents that reveal the full extent of institutionalised surveillance and repression through wire-tapping, videotape observation, opening private mail and other methods. The often cunningly low-tech surveillance devices (hidden in watering cans, rocks, even neckties) are among the more intriguing exhibits in the **Stasimuseum** (☑030-553 6854; www.stasimuseum.de; Haus 1, Ruschestrasse 103; adult/concession €6/4.50; ☺10am-6pm Mon-Fri, 11am-6pm Sat & Sun, English tour 3pm Sat-Mon; Ⓤ Magdalenenstrasse), which occupies several floors of the fortress-like former ministry. At its peak, more than 8000 people worked in this compound alone; the scale model in the entrance foyer will help you grasp its vast dimensions.

Another museum highlight is the 'lion's den' itself, the stuffy offices, private quar-ters and conference rooms of Erich Mielke, head of the Stasi for an incredible 32 years, from 1957 until the bitter end. Other rooms introduce the ideology, rituals and institutions of East German society. Information panels are partly in English.

Few words are needed to understand the purpose of the van in the foyer. Outfitted with five tiny, lightless cells, it was used to transport suspects to the **Stasi prison** (Gedenkstätte Berlin-Hohenschönhausen; ☑030-9860 8230; www.stiftung-hsh.de; Gensler-strasse 66; tours adult/concession €6/3, exhibit free; ☺tours in English 10.30am, 12.30pm & 2.30pm Mar-Oct, 11.30am & 2.30pm Nov-Feb, exhibit 9am-6pm, German tours more frequent; Ⓟ; ⍰M5) a few kilometres from the ministry. The prison, too, is a memorial site today – officially called Gedenkstätte Berlin-Hohenschönhausen – and is, if any-thing, even more creepy than the Stasi Museum.

Tours, sometimes led by former prisoners, reveal the full extent of the terror and cruelty perpetrated upon thousands of suspected political opponents, many utterly innocent. If you've seen the Academy Award–winning film *The Lives of Others,* you may recognise many of the original settings. An **exhibit** uses photographs, objects and a free audioguide to document daily life behind bars and also allows for a look at the offices of the former prison administration.

Old maps of East Berlin show a blank spot where the prison was: officially, it did not exist. In reality, the compound had three incarnations. Right after WWII, the Soviets used it to process prisoners (mostly Nazis, or those suspected to be) destined for the gulag. More than 3000 detainees died here due to atrocious conditions – usually by freezing in their unheated cells – until the Western Allies intervened in October 1946.

The Soviets then made it a regular prison, dreaded especially for its 'U-Boat', an underground tract of damp, windowless cells outfitted only with a wooden bench and a bucket. Prisoners were subjected to endless interrogations, beatings, sleep depriva-tion and water torture. Everybody signed a confession sooner or later.

In 1951 the Soviets handed the prison over to the Stasi, who ended up adopting its mentors' methods. Prisoners were locked up in the U-Boat until a new, much bigger cell block was built, with prison labour, in the late '50s. Psycho-terror now replaced physical torture: inmates had no idea of their whereabouts and suffered total isola-tion and sensory deprivation. Only the collapse of the GDR in 1989 put an end to the horror.

WORTH A DETOUR

DONG XUAN CENTER

The sprawling **Dong Xuan Center** (☑030-5515 2038; www.dongxuan-berlin.de; Herzbergstrasse 128-139, Lichtenberg; ⊘10am-8pm Wed-Mon; ▢12, M8) is a cluster of industrial halls repurposed from a Cold War–era factory for carbon products. Today it is the cultural, culinary and commercial hub of Berlin's sizeable Vietnamese community. Each building is lined with long corridors where vendors peddle plastic flowers, cheap clothing, sacks of rice and exotic produce. Even if you're not buying, it's fun to browse and wrap up a visit with a bowl of authentic pho soup.

⊘noon-midnight; 🐾🖉; ▢M10, ⓤFrankfurter Tor) Cheap, cheerful and stylish, this place is always swarmed by loyal locals, and for good reason: light, inventive and fresh, the South Asian menu goes beyond the standard dishes and has few false notes. Intriguing choice: the sweet-sour Indochine salad with banana blossoms.

LA MIFA VEGETARIAN €€€

(☑01520 704 4463; www.lamifa.de; Storkower Strasse 123; 3-course dinner €33, additional courses €11; ⊘6pm Thu-Sat; 🖉; Ⓢ Greifswalder Strasse) Part of the wonderland that is Anomalie Art Club, boho-chic La Mifa serves innovative and gorgeously presented meat-free cuisine in a high-ceiling dining room that juxtaposes industrial edginess with eye-catching artwork, a vertical garden and designer furniture. It also hosts pop-ups from top chefs from around the world, truffle pasta dinners and whatever else the creative team can dream up.

SKYKITCHEN & SKYBAR INTERNATIONAL €€€

Map p340 (☑030-4530 532 620; www.sky kitchen.berlin; Landsberger Allee 106; 3-course dinner €71, additional courses €10; ⊘6-11pm Tue-Sat, 11am-3pm Sun; 🖉; ▢21, M4, M5, M6, M8, M10, Ⓢ Landsberger Allee) Book early to snag a window table facing the TV Tower for a romantic dinner with your sweetie at this delightfully unpretentious Michelin-starred restaurant. On the 12th floor of the Andel's hotel, champion chef Alexander Koppe deftly injects global finesse into classic German fare using top-flight ingredients. The

bar does a stellar job to match the fabulous food.

KATERSCHMAUS INTERNATIONAL €€€

Map p340 (☑0152 2941 3262; www.kater schmaus.de; Holzmarktstrasse 25; multicourse dinners €50-80; ⊘noon-4pm & 7-10.30pm Tue-Sat; 🐾; ⓤJannowitzbrücke, ⓈJannowitzbrücke) From the homemade bread to the wicked crème brûlée, dining at this carefully designed ramshackle space is very much a Berlin experience. The kitchen embraces the regional-seasonal credo and presents meaty, fishy or vegetarian multicourse dinners as well as à la carte dining. Reservations essential.

🍷 DRINKING & NIGHTLIFE

Along with Kreuzberg, Friedrichshain is Berlin's seminal fun and party zone, with hot-stepping venues centred on the RAW Gelände (p184), along Simon-Dach-Strasse and around the Ostkreuz train station. The neighbourhood is also home to the city's best techno-electro clubs, from big bad Berghain to hole-in-the-wall underground joints. On weekends, the action never stops.

⭐**BERGHAIN/PANORAMA BAR** CLUB

Map p340 (www.berghain.de; Am Wriezener Bahnhof; ⊘Fri-Mon; ⓈOstbahnhof) Only world-class DJs heat up this hedonistic bass-junkie hellhole inside a labyrinthine ex-power plant. Hard-edged minimal techno dominates the ex-turbine hall (Berghain) while house dominates at Panorama Bar, one floor up. Long lines, strict door, no cameras. Check the website for midweek concerts and record-release parties at the main venue and the adjacent Kantine am Berghain (p192).

⭐**BRIEFMARKEN WEINE** WINE BAR

Map p340 (☑030-4202 5292; www.briefmarken weine.de; Karl-Marx-Allee 99; ⊘7pm-midnight Mon-Sat; ⓤWeberwiese) For *dolce vita* right on socialist-era Karl-Marx-Allee, head to this charmingly nostalgic Italian wine bar ensconced in a former stamp shop. The original wooden cabinets cradle a hand-picked selection of Italian bottles that complement a snack menu of yummy cheeses, prosciutto and salami, plus a pasta dish of the day. Best to book ahead.

★://ABOUT BLANK CLUB

Map p340 (www.aboutparty.net; Markgrafendamm 24c; ⊘hours vary, always Fri & Sat; Ⓢ Ostkreuz) At this gritty multifloor party pen with lots of nooks and crannies, a steady line-up of top DJs feeds a diverse bunch of revellers dance-worthy electronic gruel. Intense club nights usually segue into the morning and beyond. Run by a collective, the venue also hosts cultural, political and gender events.

In summer the action spills out into the garden (and sometimes in winter, too, around a bonfire).

SUICIDE CIRCUS CLUB

Map p340 (http://suicide-berlin.com; Revaler Strasse 99; ⊘hours vary, often from midnight Tue-Sun; Ⓢ Warschauer Strasse, Ⓤ Warschauer Strasse) Resident and visitors hungry for an eclectic techno shower invade this midsize dancing den with its industrial warehouse feel, top-notch sound system and consistently capable DJs. In summer, watch the stars fade from the open-air floor and garden. It's still a great spot to connect with the earthy Berlin club flair.

ANOMALIE ART CLUB CLUB

(www.anomalie123.de; Storkower Strasse 123; ⊘hours vary; Ⓢ Greifswalder Strasse) The 'dream factory' of Anomalie breaks down the boundaries between club, culture and food in a former car repair shop-turned-arty playground far off the beaten party track. At this art-filled day-to-night venue, you can lounge in the beer garden before fuelling up at the upscale La Mifa restaurant for a night of high-octane tech-house on two floors. The larger one, incidentally, also hosts vinyasa yoga, and pottery workshops are planned as well.

BADEHAUS
SZIMPLA MUSIKSALON LIVE MUSIC

Map p340 (📞030-2593 3042; www.badehaus-berlin.com; Revaler Strasse 99, RAW Gelände, enter near Simon-Dach-Strasse; €5-15; ⊘hours vary; 🚌M10, Ⓤ Warschauer Strasse, Ⓢ Warschauer Strasse) This low-key club in a former workers' bathhouse on the RAW (p184) grounds delivers with eclectic bathhouse-themed decor (check out the golden tub), cheap drinks and relaxed punters. With concerts and parties spanning a musical arc from punk to electro-swing, plus Tuesday hip-hop jam sessions, this place covers all the bases – only the sound could be a touch better.

TENTACION MEZCALOTHEK BAR

Map p340 (📞030-2393 0401; www.tentacion mezcalothek.de; Scharnweberstrasse 32; ⊘5pm-midnight Wed-Sat, to 5pm Sun; Ⓤ Samariterstrasse) Resisting temptation can be tough. Forget about it when visiting Tentacion (Spanish for 'temptation'); its main ammo is the Latin American cult spirit mezcal, which allegedly has psychedelic qualities. The tiny parlour packs a huge selection of the wicked spirit along with Mala Vida, the craft beer brewed in-house, and feisty Mexican snacks for the peckish.

LAB.ORATORY GAY

Map p340 (www.lab-oratory.de; Am Wriezener Bahnhof; ⊘Thu-Sun; Ⓢ Ostbahnhof) Part of the Berghain complex, this well-equipped 'lab' has plenty of toys and rooms for advanced male sexual experimentation in what looks like the engine room of an aircraft carrier. Party names such as Yellow Facts, Naked Sex Party and Fausthouse leave little to the imagination. Pure hedonism. Come before midnight and skip the aftershave.

Dress-code-free Fridays with two-for-one drinks are best for first-timers who want to ease into the scene.

HIMMELREICH GAY & LESBIAN

Map p340 (📞030-2936 9292; www.himmelreich-berlin.de; Simon-Dach-Strasse 36; ⊘6pm-2am or later Mon-Sat, 4pm-1am or later Sun; 🚌M13, M10, Ⓢ Warschauer Strasse, Ⓤ Warschauer Strasse) Confirming all those stereotypes about LGBT people having good taste, this candle-lit and pretence-free drinking cove makes most of the competition look like a straight guy's bedsit. Try the Prosit Beer, which is especially brewed for Himmelreich, while keeping an eye on the parade of folks from the sidewalk terrace.

On Wednesdays drinks are two-for-one. Straight folk are always welcome.

MONSTER RONSON'S
ICHIBAN KARAOKE KARAOKE

Map p340 (📞030-8975 1327; www.karaoke monster.de; Warschauer Strasse 34; ⊘7pm-4am; Ⓢ Warschauer Strasse, Ⓤ Warschauer Strasse) Knock back a couple of brewskis if you need to loosen your nerves before belting out your best Adele or Lady Gaga at this mad, great karaoke joint, which went through a major rejuvenation in early 2018. Shy types can book a private booth for music and mischief. It also has gay-themed nights and drag queen shows on Tuesdays.

YAAM CLUB

CLUB

Map p340 (⌨030-615 1354; www.yaam.de; An der Schillingsbrücke 3; ◷hours vary; ⑤Ostbahnhof) A slice of the Caribbean on the Spree River, this reggae and dancehall institution attracts an all-ages, cross-cultural crowd to its live concerts, parties and beach bar with outdoor sports, art, food and fun in the sand.

HOPS & BARLEY

MICROBREWERY

Map p340 (⌨030-2936 7534; www.hopsandbarley-berlin.de; Wühlischstrasse 22/23; ◷5pm-late Mon-Fri, from 3pm Sat & Sun; ⍟M13, ⓊWarschauer Strasse, ⑤Warschauer Strasse) Conversation flows as freely as the unfiltered pilsner, malty *Dunkel* (dark) and fruity *Weizen* (wheat) produced right here at one of Berlin's oldest craft breweries (since 2008). The pub is inside a former butcher's shop and still has the tiled walls to prove it. Two beamers project football (soccer) games.

CHAPEL BAR

COCKTAIL BAR

Map p340 (⌨0157 3200 0032; Sonntagstrasse 30; ◷6pm-1am Tue & Wed, to 2am Thu, to 3.30am Fri & Sat; ⑤Ostkreuz) A star in the Friedrichshain cocktail firmament, the Chapel Bar has a delightfully cluttered living-room look and a convivial vibe, thanks to a crowd more interested in good drinks than looking good. The folks behind the bar wield the shaker with confidence, be it to create classics or their own 'liquid dreams' such as the whisky-based Köppernickel.

Search for 'Chapel Berlin' on Facebook.

POLYGON

CLUB

Map p340 (www.polygon-club.com; Wiesenweg 1-4; ◷11.45pm-10am Fri & Sat; ⓊFrankfurter Allee, ⑤Frankfurter Allee, Ostkreuz) New owners have given the former Kosmonaut a seriously pimped-up look and a slick new sound and light concept. The action spreads across three dance floors at a stylish main bar and through a warren of rooms to a little garden.

KATER BLAU

CLUB

Map p340 (www.katerblau.de; Holzmarktstrasse 25; ◷Fri-Mon; ⓊJannowitzbrücke, ⑤Jannowitzbrücke) The successor of the legendary Bar25, Kater Blau showers freewheeling club-goers with fine electro in a rambling indoor-outdoor playground, featuring two floors and a boat with deck for chilling. The SaSoMo party starts at midnight on Saturday and goes nonstop through Monday evening or longer. The door is quite selective.

SÜSS WAR GESTERN

BAR

Map p340 (⌨0176 2441 2940; Wühlischstrasse 43; ◷7pm-late; ⍟M13, ⓊWarschauer Strasse, Samariterstrasse, ⑤Warschauer Strasse, Ostkreuz) A machine-gun-toting rabbit is the ironic mascot of this long-running DJ bar with well-mixed cocktails (try the eponymous Süss War Gestern with real ginger, ginger ale and whisky), dance-inducing electro, and a communicative crowd of locals, newcomers and visitors.

GROSSE FREIHEIT 114

GAY

Map p340 (⌨0163 683 1601; www.grosse-freiheit-114.de; Boxhagener Strasse 114; ◷8pm-6am Wed, Fri & Sat, to 4am Thu, to 2am Sun; ⓊFrankfurter Tor) Named for a lane in Hamburg's red-light district where the Beatles cut their teeth, Grosse Freiheit is a popular men-only harbour for a drink and meet-up, complete with darts, a jukebox and darkrooms.

CASSIOPEIA

CLUB

Map p340 (www.cassiopeia-berlin.de; Revaler Strasse 99, Gate 2; ◷from 7pm or later Tue-Sun; ⍟M10, M13, ⓊWarschauer Strasse, ⑤Warschauer Strasse) The down-to-earth crowd at this charmingly trashy dancing den defines the word eclectic, and so does the music. Dive deep into a sound spectrum ranging from vintage hip-hop to hard funk, '80s pop and punk to electronic beats, delivered both live and via DJs. It's in an industrial hall on the RAW Gelände (p184), a train repair station turned subcultural party village.

CHANTALS HOUSE OF SHAME

GAY

Map p340 (www.facebook.com/ChantalsHouseofShame; Revaler Strasse 99, Suicide Circus; ◷11pm-8am Thu; ⍟M10, M13, ⓊWarschauer Platz, ⑤Warschauer Platz) Now in new digs, trash diva Chantal's louche lair has been a beloved gay party institution since 1999, as much for the glam factor as for the over-the-top drag shows and the hotties who love 'em. Mostly for men, but women OK.

CRACK BELLMER

BAR

Map p340 (⌨030-6443 5860; www.crackbellmer.de; Revaler Strasse 99; ◷8pm-6am; ⍟M10, M13, ⓊWarschauer Strasse, ⑤Warschauer Strasse) In the RAW (p184) compound, behind the requisite street-art-festooned facade, awaits this bar-club combo with lofty ceilings, chandeliers and vintage sofas. Popular for pre-party warm-ups, post-party nightcaps and any time in between, including the Sunday swing dance session.

PLACE CLICHY WINE BAR

Map p340 (✆030-2313 8703; Simon-Dach-Strasse 22; ☺7pm-3am Tue-Sat, to midnight Sun; ⓂM13, ⓈWarschauer Strasse, ⓊWarschauer Strasse) *Chapeau!* Clichy brings a whiff of boho Paris to the lower end of Simon-Dach-Strasse. Candlelit, artist-designed and cosy, the postage-stamp-size *boîte* exudes an almost existentialist vibe, so don your black turtleneck and join the chatty crowd for Bordeaux and sweaty cheeses.

ZUM SCHMUTZIGEN HOBBY GAY

Map p340 (✆030-3646 8446; www.facebook. com/zumschmutzigenhobby; Revaler Strasse 99, RAW Gelände, Gate 2; ☺7.30pm-late; ⓂM10, M13, ⓈWarschauer Strasse, ⓊWarschauer Strasse) Although founder and trash-drag deity Nina Queer has moved on to other pastures, this living-room-size, deliciously kitsch and wacky party den in a former fire station is still swarmed nightly. Predominantly gay but everyone welcome.

⭐ ENTERTAINMENT

MERCEDES-BENZ ARENA LIVE MUSIC

Map p340 (✆tickets 030-206 070 8899; www. mercedes-benz-arena-berlin.de; Mühlenstrasse 12-30; ⓈOstbahnhof, Warschauer Strasse, ⓊWarschauer Strasse) The jewel among Berlin's multiuse indoor venues, this 17,000-seat arena regularly welcomes entertainment royalty such as Depeche Mode, Rihanna and Beyoncé. It's also home turf for the city's professional ice-hockey team, the Eisbären Berlin, and basketball team, Alba Berlin.

FREILUFTKINO FRIEDRICHSHAIN CINEMA

Map p340 (✆030-2936 1629; www.freiluftkino-berlin.de; Volkspark Friedrichshain; tickets €7.50; ☺mid-May–mid-Sep; 🚌142, ⓂM5, M6, M8) Cradled by Volkspark Friedrichshain (p184), this open-air cinema has seating for 1500 on comfortable benches with backrests, plus a lawn with space for 300 more film fans. A kiosk sells drinks and snacks, and you're free to bring a picnic. Unless flagged otherwise, movies are dubbed into German.

KINO INTIMES CINEMA

Map p340 (✆030-2977 7640; www.kino-intimes. de; Boxhagener Strasse 107; adult/concession €6.90/4.90; 🚌21, ⓊFrankfurter Tor) This petite single-screen flick palace has presented movies since the silent era and is a delightful vintage venue to catch the latest art-

house movies. Its facade is an ever-evolving canvas of street art.

ASTRA KULTURHAUS LIVE MUSIC

Map p340 (✆030-2005 6767; www.astra-berlin. de; Revaler Strasse 99, RAW Gelände; ☺hours vary, always Thu-Sat; ⓂM13, ⓈWarschauer Strasse, ⓊWarschauer Strasse) With space for 1500 in the former cultural hall of a Cold War–era train repair station, Astra is one of Berlin's bigger indie concert venues, yet it often fills up easily, and not just when international headliners hit the stage. In addition, parties lure punters with danceable tunes across the sound spectrum.

FREILUFTKINO INSEL IM CASSIOPEIA CINEMA

Map p340 (✆030-3512 2449; www.freiluftkino-insel.de; Revaler Strasse 99; tickets €7; ☺around 9.30pm Mon, Tue, Thu & Sun May-Sep; ⓂM10, M13, ⓈWarschauer Strasse, ⓊWarschauer Strasse) Part of the Cassiopeia beer garden and club complex on the RAW Gelände, this 350-seat outdoor cinema shows an eclectic roster of indie movies in their original language with German or English subtitles. Free blankets.

RADIALSYSTEM V PERFORMING ARTS

Map p340 (✆030-2887 8850; www.radial system.de; Holzmarktstrasse 33; 🚇; ⓈOstbahn-hof) 'Space for arts and ideas' is the motto of this progressive performance space in an old riverside pump station. Its programming blurs the boundaries between the arts to nurture new forms of creative expression: contemporary dance meets medieval music, poetry meets pop tunes, painting meets digital.

KINO INTERNATIONAL CINEMA

Map p340 (✆030-2475 6011; www.yorck.de; Karl-Marx-Allee 33; tickets €7-9.50; ⓊSchilling-strasse) The East German film elite once held its movie premieres in this 1960s cinema, whose glamourous get-up of chandeliers and glitter curtains is a show in itself. Today it presents smartly curated international indie hit flicks daily, usually in the original language with German subtitles.

Mondays are reserved for gay-themed movies.

KANTINE AM BERGHAIN LIVE MUSIC

Map p340 (www.berghain.de; Am Wriezener Bahnhof; admission varies; ☺hours vary; ⓈOstbahn-hof) Big bad Berghain's (p188) little sister has taken over the former staff canteen of the giant ex-power station. The space holds up to 200 people and mostly puts on concerts. In summer, the attached beer garden (Bierhof Rüdersdorf) with outdoor fireplace is an ideal chill zone. Easy door.

SHOPPING

Friedrichshain has come along in the shopping department, with chic indie clothing boutiques and speciality stores sprinkled around Boxhagener Platz (especially Wühlischstrasse) and along Sonntagstrasse and its side streets near Ostkreuz station.

WOCHENMARKT BOXHAGENER PLATZ
MARKET

Map p340 (http://boxhagenerplatz.org; Boxhagener Platz; ⊙9am-3.30pm Sat; ⊛M10, M13, ⓊSamariterstrasse, Frankfurter Tor) This popular farmers' market brings out the entire neighbourhood for fresh fare along with homemade liqueurs, a global cheese selection, exotic spices, smoked fish, hemp muesli, purple potatoes and other unusual culinary delights. There are plenty of snack stands along with crafts and gift items, many of them handmade.

STRAWBETTY
CLOTHING

Map p340 (☎030-8999 3663; www.strawbetty.com; Wühlischstrasse 25; ⊙noon-7pm Mon-Fri, 11am-6pm Sat; ⊛M13, ⓊWarschauer Strasse, ⓈWarschauer Strasse, Ostkreuz) No matter if you're a dedicated rockabella or just want to look good at the next theme party, this boutique will kit you out with petticoats, sailor dresses, Capri pants, boleros and other feminine vintage threads. It also stocks the right bag, hat and jewellery to perfect the fashion time warp.

SOMETIMES COLOURED
VINTAGE

Map p340 (☎030-2935 2075; www.facebook.com/sometimescoloured; Grünberger Strasse 90; ⊙noon-8pm Mon-Fri, to 7pm Sat; ⓊSamariterstrasse) Most threads sold at this secondhand boutique are in subdued colours, whether it's jet black, charcoal grey or midnight blue. All are in great condition and include contemporary labels (Adidas, Cos, The Kooples) alongside a smaller selection of couture by Dior and Armani. Fair prices.

UVR CONNECTED
FASHION & ACCESSORIES

Map p340 (www.uvr-connected.de; Gärtnerstrasse 5; ⊙11am-8pm Mon-Sat; ⊛M10, M13, ⓊSamariterstrasse, Warschauer Strasse, ⓈWarschauer Strasse) This local label designs urban fashions for people with a penchant for classic designs and subdued colours. All clothing is designed in Berlin and produced in Portugal, Poland and Italy.

ANTIKMARKT AM OSTBAHNHOF
ANTIQUES

Map p340 (Erich-Steinfurth-Strasse; ⊙9am-5pm Sun; ⓈOstbahnhof) If you're after antiques and collectibles, head to this sprawling market outside the Ostbahnhof station's north exit. The Grosser Antikmarkt (large antiques market) is more professional and brims with old coins, Iron Curtain–era relics, gramophone records, books, stamps, jewellery, etc. It segues neatly into the Kleiner Antikmarkt (small antiques market), which has more bric-a-brac and lower prices.

RAW FLOHMARKT
MARKET

Map p340 (www.raw-flohmarkt-berlin.de; Revaler Strasse 99, RAW Gelände; ⊙9am-5pm Sun; ⊛M10, M13, ⓈWarschauer Strasse, ⓊWarschauer Strasse) Bargains abound at this smallish flea market right on the grounds of RAW Gelände (p184), a former train repair station-turned-party village. It's wonderfully free of professional sellers, meaning you'll find everything from the proverbial kitchen sink to 1970s go-go boots. Bargains are plentiful, while street food and a beer garden provide handy post-shopping pit stops.

FLOHMARKT AM BOXHAGENER PLATZ
MARKET

Map p340 (⊙10am-6pm Sun; ⊛M13, ⓈWarschauer Strasse, ⓊWarschauer Strasse, Samariterstrasse) Wrapped around leafy Boxhagener Platz, this fun flea market is just a java whiff away from oodles of convivial cafes. Although the presence of pro vendors has grown, there's still plenty of regular folks here to unload their spring-cleaning detritus at bargain prices.

PRACHTMÄDCHEN
FASHION & ACCESSORIES

Map p340 (☎030-9700 2780; www.prachtmaedchen.de; Wühlischstrasse 28; ⊙11am-8pm Mon-Fri, to 4pm Sat; ⊛M13, ⓈWarschauer Strasse, ⓊWarschauer Strasse) Low-key and friendly, this pioneer on Wühlischstrasse (aka Friedrichshain's 'fashion mile') is great for kitting yourself out head to toe, with affordable threads and accessories by such grown-up streetwear labels as Blutsgeschwister, Skunkfunk and Tokyo Jane.

Prenzlauer Berg

MAUERPARK & NORTHERN PRENZLAUER BERG | KOLLWITZPLATZ & SOUTHERN PRENZLAUER BERG

Neighbourhood Top Five

❶ Gedenkstätte Berliner Mauer (p195) Coming to grips with the absurdity of a divided city at this memorial exhibit that follows the course of a 1.4km-long stretch of the Berlin Wall.

❷ Mauerpark (p197) Spending a sunny Sunday digging for flea-market treasures and cheering on karaoke crooners in this popular park reclaimed from a section of the Berlin Wall death strip.

❸ Kulturbrauerei (p197) Catching a concert, movie or street-food market at this venerable red-brick brewery-turned-cultural centre.

❹ Kollwitzplatz (p197) Taking a leisurely ramble around this leafy square and its side streets lined with beautiful townhouses, convivial cafes and indie boutiques.

❺ Prater Garten (p203) Guzzling a big mug of cold beer under the chestnut trees of Berlin's oldest beer garden.

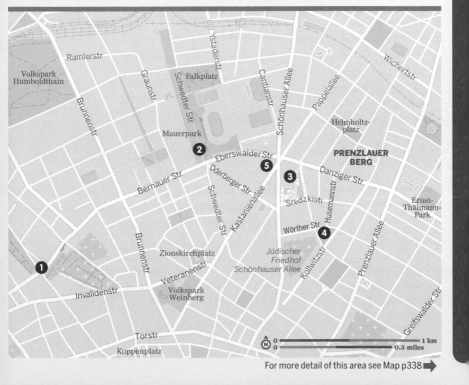

For more detail of this area see Map p338 ➡

PRENZLAUER BERG

Lonely Planet's Top Tip

On Saturdays, pick up farm-fresh produce and artesanal products before joining locals for gourmet snacks and a glass of bubbly at the bountiful farmers market on Kollwitzplatz (p208).

Best Places to Eat

➜ Mrs Robinson's (p200)

➜ Kanaan (p199)

➜ Umami (p200)

➜ Yafo (p198)

➜ Restaurant Oderberger (p200)

For reviews, see p198.➜

Best Places to Drink

➜ Prater Garten (p203)

➜ Bryk Bar (p203)

➜ Weinerei Forum (p203)

➜ BrewDog (p203)

For reviews, see p203.➜

Best Places to Shop

➜ Flohmarkt im Mauerpark (p208)

➜ Saint Georges (p208)

➜ Ta(u)sche (p208)

➜ Goldhahn und Sampson (p208)

For reviews, see p206.➜

Explore Prenzlauer Berg

Once a neglected backwater, Prenzlauer Berg went from rags to riches after reunification to emerge as one of Berlin's most desirable and well-heeled neighbourhoods.

The one must-see sight is the Gedenkstätte Berliner Mauer, the city's best place to understand the layout and impact of the Berlin Wall. The 1.4km-long indoor-outdoor exhibit actually starts in the adjoining district of Wedding but ends in Prenzlauer Berg near the Mauerpark. This patch of green wrested from the Berlin Wall death strip is also the city's biggest Sunday attraction. On sunny summer days, it lures tens of thousands with a big flea market and outdoor karaoke.

Generally speaking, though, Prenzlauer Berg's ample charms reveal themselves in subtler, often unexpected ways and are best experienced on a leisurely daytime meander. The prettiest area, and a good place to start, is around Kollwitzplatz (p197), which is packed with congenial cafes and boutiques.

Shops open around noon, a good time to start strolling down boho-trendy Kastanienallee or comb quiet side streets for indie boutiques selling custom jewellery, Berlin-made fashions or organic baby clothes. Also pop by the Kulturbrauerei (p197), a brewery-turned-culture centre, to admire its fortresslike red-brick architecture. A good time to visit here is during the Sunday street-food market.

Local Life

Outdoor quaffing Celebrate summer beneath the chestnut trees of the Prater (p203) beer garden, on the Deck 5 (p206) rooftop terrace or at a sunny pavement cafe on Knaackstrasse.

Shopping Browse for practical bags at Ta(u)sche (p208), Berlin designers at Flagshipstore (p208) or retro threads at the Flohmarkt im Mauerpark (p208).

Eating out Favourites for foodies on the run include Habba Habba (p199) for Middle Eastern wraps, Zia Maria (p199) for pizza, and Konnopke's Imbiss (p199) for *Currywurst*.

Getting There & Away

U-Bahn The U2 stops at Schönhauser Allee, Eberswalder Strasse and Senefelderplatz en route to Alexanderplatz, Potsdamer Platz and western Berlin.

Tram The M1 links Museumsinsel and Prenzlauer Berg via the Scheunenviertel, Kastanienallee and Schönhauser Allee. The M13 goes straight into Friedrichshain.

S-Bahn Ringbahn (Circle Line) trains S41 and S42 stop at Schönhauser Allee, Greifswalder Strasse, Landberger Strasse and Storkower Strasse.

TOP SIGHT
GEDENKSTÄTTE BERLINER MAUER

For an insightful primer on the Berlin Wall, visit this 1.4km-long outdoor memorial, whlch explains the physical layout of the barrier and the death strip, how the border fortifications were enlarged and perfected over time and what impact they had on the daily lives of people on both sides of the Wall.

The memorial exhibit extends along Bernauer Strasse, one of the streets that played a pivotal role in Cold War history. The Berlin Wall ran along its entire length, with one side of the street located in West Berlin and the other in East Berlin. The exhibit is divided into four sections with overarching themes. Integrated within are an original section of the Wall, vestiges of the border installations and escape tunnels, a chapel and a monument. Multimedia stations, 'archaeological windows' and markers provide context and details about events that took place along here.

Gartenstrasse to Ackerstrasse

This is the most important segment of the memorial. It focuses on explaining how the Berlin Wall restricted citizens' freedom of movement and secured the East German government's power. An emotional highlight is the **Window of Remembrance**, where photographic portraits give identity to would-be escapees who lost their lives at the Berlin Wall, one of them only six years young. The parklike area surrounding the installation was once part of the adjacent cemetery.

Near Ackerstrasse the **National Monument to German Division** consists of a 70m section of original Berlin Wall bounded by two rusted steel flanks and embedded in an artistic representation of the border complex. Walk down

DON'T MISS

➜ Exhibit at the Documentation Centre and the view from its tower

➜ Remembrance service at the Chapel of Reconciliation

➜ Ghost Station exhibit

➜ National Monument to German Division

PRACTICALITIES

➜ Map p338, A6

➜ ☏030-467 986 666

➜ www.berliner-mauer -gedenkstaette.de

➜ Bernauer Strasse btwn Schwedter Strasse & Gartenstrasse

➜ admission free

➜ ⊙visitor & documentation centre 10am-6pm Tue-Sun, open-air exhibit 8am-10pm daily

➜ Ⓢ Nordbahnhof, Bernauer Strasse, Eberswalder Strasse

TOP TIPS

➡ Start your visit in the visitor centre across from Nordbahnhof S-Bahn station and work your way east.

➡ Pick up a free map and watch the introductory film at the visitors centre.

➡ If you have limited time, spend it in the first section between Gartenstrasse and Ackerstrasse.

➡ Enjoy sweeping views of the memorial from the viewing tower of the Documentation Centre near Ackerstrasse.

The Berlin Wall also divided the city's transport system. Three lines (today's U6, U8 and the north–south S-Bahn rails) that originated in West Berlin had to travel along tracks that happened to run beneath the eastern sector before returning to stations back on the western side. Trains slowed down but did not stop at these so-called 'ghost stations' on East Berlin turf, which were closed and patrolled by heavily armed GDR border guards. An exhibit inside the Nordbahnhof S-Bahn station describes underground escape attempts and the measures taken by the East German government to prevent them.

Ackerstrasse to enter the monument from the back. Through gaps in a wall, you can espy a reconstructed death strip complete with a guard tower, a security patrol path and the lamps that bathed it in fierce light at night.

Documentation Centre

Across the street from the National Monument to German Division, a former church building now houses a two-floor Documentation Centre. The exhibit – called '1961/1989. The Berlin Wall' – opened on 9 November 2014, the 25th anniversary of the fall of the Wall. It provides a concise and engaging overview of the Wall and answers such questions as to why it was built and what led to its collapse. It also uses artefacts, documents and videos to show how it affected daily life on both sides. Use the information you've gleaned to picture the divided city when standing atop the adjacent viewing platform.

Ackerstrasse to Brunnenstrasse

In this section, the linear exhibit focuses on the division's human toll and especially on the daring and desperate escapes that took place along Bernauer Strasse. Just past Ackerstrasse, the modern **Chapel of Reconciliation** stands in the spot of an 1894 brick church detonated in 1985 to make room for a widening of the border strip. A 15-minute remembrance service for Wall victims is held at noon Tuesday to Friday. Other information stations deal with the physical construction of the Wall and the continuous expansion of the border complex.

Brunnenstrasse to Schwedter Strasse

In the final section, info stations and exhibits must skirt private property and new apartment buildings and are mostly restricted to a narrow strip along the former border patrol path. Information stations address such topics as West Germany's take on the Berlin Wall, what daily life was like for an East German border guard and the eventual fall of the Wall in 1989. A highlight is the dramatic story of the world-famous **Tunnel 29**, which ran for 135m below Bernauer Strasse and helped 29 people escape from East Berlin in September 1962.

⊙ SIGHTS

Prenzlauer Berg doesn't have any blockbuster sights, and most of what it does have is concentrated in the pretty southern section around Kollwitzplatz. The neighbourhood does include the city's most important exhibit on the Berlin Wall, the Gedenkstätte Berliner Mauer (p195).

GEDENKSTÄTTE
BERLINER MAUER MEMORIAL
See p195.

★ZEISS
GROSSPLANETARIUM PLANETARIUM

Map p338 (☑030-4218 4510; www.planetarium. berlin; Prenzlauer Allee 80; adult €8-9.50, concession €6-7.50; 🚇M2, 🚈Prenzlauer Allee) It was the most advanced planetarium in East Germany at its opening in 1987 and after the recent renovation it has upped the scientific, technology and comfort factor ante once again to become one of the most modern in Europe. It's a beautiful space to delve into the mysteries not only of the cosmos but of science in general. Many programs are in English, some are set to music, others are geared to children. Tickets are available online.

MAUERPARK PARK

Map p338 (www.mauerpark.info; btwn Bernauer Strasse, Schwedter Strasse & Gleimstrasse; 🚇M1, M10, 12, 🚇Eberswalder Strasse) With its wimpy trees and anaemic lawn, Mauerpark is hardly your typical leafy oasis, especially given that it was forged from a section of Cold War–era death strip (a short stretch of Berlin Wall survives). It's this mystique combined with an unassuming vibe and a hugely popular Sunday flea market and karaoke show that has endeared the place to locals and visitors alike.

Behind the Wall segment – now an officially sanctioned practice ground for graffiti artists – loom the floodlights of the **Friedrich-Ludwig-Jahn-Sportpark** (Map p338; Jahnsportpark@seninnDS.berlin.de; Cantianstrasse 24; 🅿), the stadium where Stasi chief Erich Mielke used to cheer on his beloved Dynamo Berlin football (soccer) team. Just north of here is the **Max-Schmeling-Halle** (Map p338; ☑030-4430 4430; www. max-schmeling-halle.de; Falkplatz 1), a venue for concerts, competitions and sports events.

KOLLWITZPLATZ SQUARE

Map p338 (🚊; 🚇Senefelderplatz) Triangular Kollwitzplatz was ground zero of Prenzlauer Berg gentrification. To pick up on the local vibe, linger with macchiato mamas and media daddies in a street cafe or join them at the twice-weekly farmers market (p208). The park in the square's centre is tot heaven with three playgrounds plus a bronze sculpture of the artist Käthe Kollwitz for clambering on.

TCHOBAN FOUNDATION – MUSEUM
FÜR ARCHITEKTURZEICHNUNG MUSEUM

Map p338 (Museum for Architectural Drawing; ☑030-4373 9090; www.tchoban-foundation.de; Christinenstrasse 18a; adult/concession €5/3; ⊙2-7pm Mon-Fri, 1-5pm Sat & Sun; 🚇Senefelderplatz) Fans of contemporary architecture should swing by this private museum housed in a striking sculptural pile of relief-decorated concrete cubes topped by a glass penthouse. Changing exhibits showcase architectural drawings from the private collection of museum founder Sergei Tchoban or from such major repositories as Vienna's Albertina or London's Sir John Soane's Museum.

KULTURBRAUEREI CULTURAL CENTRE

Map p338 (☑030-4435 2170; www.kulturbrau erei.de; btwn Schönhauser Allee, Knaackstrasse, Eberswalder Strasse & Sredzskistrasse; 🅿; 🚇M1, 🚇Eberswalder Strasse) The fanciful red-and-yellow brick buildings of this 19th-century brewery have been upcycled into a cultural powerhouse with a small village's worth of venues, from concert and theatre halls to nightclubs, dance studios, a multiplex cinema and a free GDR history museum. The main entrances are on Knaackstrasse and Sredzskistrasse.

On Sundays, foodies fill up on global treats at the street-food market, while in December, the old buildings make a lovely backdrop for a Swedish-style Lucia Christmas market.

MUSEUM IN DER
KULTURBRAUEREI MUSEUM

Map p338 (☑030-467 777 911; www.hdg.de; Knaackstrasse 97; ⊙10am-6pm Tue, Wed & Fri-Sun, to 8pm Thu; 🅿; 🚇M1, 12, 🚇Eberswalder Strasse) 🆓 Original documents, historical footage and objects (including a camper-style Trabi car) bring daily life under socialism in East Germany to life in this government-sponsored exhibit. As you wander the halls, you'll realise the stark contrast between the

WORTH A DETOUR

EXPLORING BERLIN'S UNDERBELLY

After you've checked off the Brandenburg Gate and the TV Tower, why not explore Berlin's dark and dank underbelly? Join **Berliner Unterwelten** (✆030-4991 0517; www.berliner-unterwelten.de; Brunnenstrasse 105; adult/concession €12/10; ⊘Dark Worlds tours in English 11am Wed-Sun year-round, 3pm Mon, Wed-Sun, 1pm Wed-Sun Apr-Oct; ⑤Gesundbrunnen, ⓊGesundbrunnen) on its 1½-hour 'Dark Worlds' tour of a WWII underground bunker and pick your way through a warren of claustrophobic rooms, past heavy steel doors, hospital beds, helmets, guns, boots and lots of other wartime artefacts.

Listen on in horror and fascination as guides bring alive the stories of the thousands of ordinary Berliners cooped up here, cramped and scared, as the bombs rained down on Berlin. Other tours explore a WWII anti-aircraft tower, a Cold War nuclear bomb shelter, Berlin Wall escape tunnels and other intriguing sites around town.

Buy tickets at the pavilion outside the south exit of Gesundbrunnen U-Bahn station (in front of Kaufland). No reservations. Tours not suitable for children under seven.

lofty aspirations of the socialist state and the sobering realities of material shortages, surveillance and oppression its people had to endure.

The exhibit also addresses the various paths individuals took to cope with their circumstances. A multilingual audioguide is available via the website.

JÜDISCHER FRIEDHOF
SCHÖNHAUSER ALLEE   CEMETERY

Map p338 (✆030-441 9824; www.jg-berlin.org; Schönhauser Allee 23-25; ⊘8am-4pm Mon-Thu, 7.30am-2.30pm Fri; ⓊSenefelderplatz) Berlin's second Jewish cemetery opened in 1827 and hosts many well-known dearly departed, such as the artist Max Liebermann and the composer Giacomo Meyerbeer. It's a pretty place with dappled light filtering through big old chestnuts and linden trees and a sense of melancholy emanating from ivy-draped graves and toppled tombstones. The nicest and oldest have been moved to the Lapidarium by the main entrance.

Liebermann's tomb is next to his family's crypt roughly in the centre along the back wall. Men must cover their heads; pick up a free skullcap by the entrance.

GETHSEMANEKIRCHE   CHURCH

Map p338 (✆030-445 7745; www.ekpn.de/kirchen/gethsemanekirche; Stargarder Strasse 77; ⊘5-7pm May-Sep; ⓐM1, ⓊSchönhauser Allee, ⑤Schönhauser Allee) This 1893 neo-Gothic church was a hotbed of dissent in the final days of the GDR and thus a thorn in the side of the Stasi, which, as late as October 1989, brutally quashed a peaceful gathering outside its portals. Artworks include a copy of Ernst Barlach's *Geistkämpfer* (Ghost Fight-

er, 1928) sculpture outside the church, which also hosts concerts and other cultural events in addition to Sunday service at 11am.

EATING

Prenzlauer Berg has an exceptionally high density of neighbourhood restaurants catering to the demanding and well-travelled palates of its international residents. Even without any Michelin shrines, there's still lots of high-calibre chowing down to be done.

Mauerpark & Northern Prenzlauer Berg

YAFO   ISRAELI €

Map p338 (✆030-9235 0250; www.yafoberlin.com; Gormannstrasse 17; dishes €6-13; ⊘noon-3am; ⓢⓙ; ⓐM8, M10, ⓊRosenthaler Platz, Rosa-Luxemburg-Platz) This charming resto-bar combo transplants Tel Aviv's palpable energy, sensuous food and convivial vibes to a quiet corner in Berlin. Drop by for a refreshing Aracboy (a cocktail made with Arac, cucumber, lemon and ginger beer) in the buzzy bar or plunge into the eclectically furnished dining room for tahini-drizzled baked cauliflower and other tantalising treats.

A MAGICA   ITALIAN €

Map p338 (✆030-2280 8290; www.amagica.de; Greifenhagener Strasse 54; pizzas €5.60-10.50; ⊘noon-midnight Mon-Fri, 4pm-midnight Sat & Sun; ⓐM1, ⑤Schönhauser Allee, ⓊSchönhauser Allee) This always-packed spot consistently delivers Neapolitan pizzas with pizazz straight from the wood-burning oven to tables packed tightly into a cosy, candle-lit dining room. Pick a classic, build your own or try one of the *'magiche pizze'* like the Brunetto with chickpeas, grilled zuc-chini and marinated shrimp. Come before 7pm or risk neighbourhood groupies having snapped up all the tables.

ATAYA CAFFE VEGAN €
Map p338 (☑030-3302 1041; www.atayacaffe. de; Zelter Strasse 6; mains €9-11, Sun brunch €14; ⊙11am-7pm Tue-Sat, to 4.30pm Sun; 🛜🖪🖪; 🚇M2, 🚊Prenzlauer Berg) This darling living-room-style cafe way off the tourist track is the lovechild of Elisabetta and Bachir Niang who have poured their hearts and cash into feeding plant-based food fans with yummy fare from their homelands Sardinia and Senegal. Specialities include Mafè, a peanut-infused vegetable stew, and the homemade ravioli. The all-you can eat Sunday brunch is fast becoming a local tradition.

HABBA HABBA MIDDLE EASTERN €
Map p338 (☑030-3674 5726; www.habba-habba. de; Kastanienallee 15; dishes €5-10.50; ⊙11am-11pm Mon, Wed & Sun; 🖪; 🚇M1, 12, 🚇Eberswalder Strasse) This tiny *Imbiss* (snack bar) makes yummy wraps with a twist, like the one stuffed with tangy pomegranate-marinated chicken and nutty buckwheat in a minty yo-ghurt sauce. Take 'em away or score a seat on the elevated porch for casting an eye on passing folk. Vegetarian and vegan versions are available, too.

KANAAN MIDDLE EASTERN €
Map p338 (☑0176 2258 6673; www.kanaan-berlin.de; Kopenhagener Strasse 17; dishes €4-10; ⊙5-10pm Wed, noon-10pm Thu & Fri, 10am-10pm Sat & Sun; 🛜🖪; 🚇M1, 🚇Schönhauser Allee, 🚊Schönhauser Allee) In this feel-good venture, an Israeli biz whiz and a Palestinian chef have teamed up to provide a progressive blend of vegan/vegetarian Middle Eastern fare. Top menu picks include the Iraqi-style hummus, the *hummshuka* (hummus/shak-shouka mash-up) and the chocolate-tahini mousse. Salads are also delish, especially the oven-roasted cauliflower. It's all served in a simple but stylish hut with lovely garden.

ZIA MARIA ITALIAN €
Map p338 (www.zia-maria.de; Pappelallee 32a; pizza slices €2-4; ⊙noon-11.30pm; 🚇12, 🚊Schönhauser Allee, 🚇Schönhauser Allee) This

pizza kitchen and gallery gets a big thumbs up for its freshly made crispy-crust pizza with classic and eclectic toppings, includ-ing wafer-thin prosciutto, nutmeg-laced artichokes and pungent Italian sausage. Ve-gan and vegetarian varieties are available. Two slices are enough to fill up most bellies. Pour your own wine from the barrel.

CHAY LONG VEGETARIAN €
Map p338 (☑030-5471 3720; www.chay-long. com; Raumerstrasse 17; mains €7-8.50; ⊙noon-10pm Mon-Thu, to 11pm Fri, 1-11pm Sat, 1-10pm Sun; 🖪; 🚇Eberswalder Strasse, 🚊Prenzlauer Allee) A true find among Berlin's maze of meat-free eateries, Chay Long serves up meat-free Vietnamese cooking that is as au-thentic as it gets this side of Saigon. It's also almost unbelievably incxpensive, consid-ering the quality of the dishes inspired by recipes from Buddhist monasteries. Menu stars include the slivered, sesame-dusted 'duck' with coconut curry. No alcohol but great ice tea and smoothies.

KONNOPKE'S IMBISS GERMAN €
Map p338 (☑030-442 7765; www.konnopke-imbiss.de; Schönhauser Allee 44a; sausages €1.60-2.90; ⊙10am-8pm Mon-Fri, 11.30am-8pm Sat; 🚇M1, M10, M13, 🚇Eberswalder Strasse) Brave the inevitable queue at this famous sausage kitchen, ensconced in the same spot below the elevated U-Bahn tracks since 1930, but now equipped with a heated pavil-ion and an English menu. The 'secret' sauce topping is classic *Currywurst* and comes in a four-tier heat scale from mild to wild.

HÜFTENGOLD CAFE €
Map p338 (☑030-4171 4500; www.hueftengold. com; Oderberger Strasse 27; snacks & breakfast €4-10; ⊙11am-6pm Wed-Mon; 🚇M1, M10, 12, 🚇Eber-swalder Strasse) This shoebox-sized cafe really comes into its own on sunny days when the vintage benches and tables on the flowery pavement terrace become the perfect people-watching perch. It's a lovely spot for break-fast, creative sandwiches, freshly pressed juices or just a coffee or glass of bubbly.

BUN BAO ASIAN €
Map p338 (☑030-2349 6218; www.bao-burger. de; Kollwitzstrasse 84; burgers €8-12.50; ⊙noon-10pm Sun-Thu, to 11pm Fri & Sat; 🛜; 🚇M2, M10, 🚇Eberswalder Strasse) Street-food-scene veteran Bun Bao serves its inventive Asian burgers in a jazzy Hong Kong–style parlour with colourful pixel art. There are vegan

and fish burgers, but top marks still go to the Bun Bao Original, a tasty tower of tender pork belly, pickled radish, carrots, coriander and roasted peanuts.

★ MRS ROBINSON'S INTERNATIONAL €€

Map p338 (☏030-5462 2839, 01520 518 8946; www.mrsrobinsons.de; Pappelallee 29; mains €16-20; ◷6-11pm Thu-Mon; 🛜🍴; 🚋12, Ⓤ Schönhauser Allee, Ⓢ Schönhauser Allee) When Israel transplant Ben Zviel and his partner Samina Raza launched their minimalist parlour (white-brick walls, polished wooden tables) in 2016, they added another notch to Berlin's food ladder. The menu is constantly in flux, but by turning carefully edited ingredients into shareable small and big plates, Ben fearlessly captures the city's adventurous and uninhibited spirit. Casual fine dining at its best.

ODERQUELLE GERMAN €€

Map p338 (☏030-4400 8080; www.oderquelle.de; Oderberger Strasse 27; mains €11.50-19; ◷6-11pm Mon-Sat, noon-11pm Sun; 🚋M1, 12, Ⓤ Eberswalder Strasse) It's always fun to pop by this woodsy stalwart on Oderberger Strasse to see what inspired the chef today. Most likely it'll be a well-crafted German dish like schnitzel with roast potatoes or roast pork in black beer sauce. Best seat: on the pavement, so you can keep an eye on the parade of passers-by.

DER FISCHLADEN SEAFOOD €€

Map p338 (☏030-4000 5612; www.derfischladen. com; Schönhauser Allee 128; mains €8-23; ◷10am-10pm Mon-Sat, 1-10pm Sun; 🚋M1, Ⓤ Schönhauser Allee, Ⓢ Schönhauser Allee) Berlin may be landlocked, but this shop-takeaway-snack-bar combo proves that this is no detriment to sourcing superfresh seafood. The menu ranges from shucked oysters to grilled tuna, but special pride goes to the English-style fish and chips, served with malt vinegar in a British newspaper.

ZUM SCHUSTERJUNGEN GERMAN €€

Map p338 (☏030-442 7654; www.zumschuster jungen.com; Danziger Strasse 9; mains €7.50-17; ◷11am-midnight; Ⓤ Eberswalder Strasse) Tourists, expats and locals descend upon this old-school gastropub where rustic Berlin charm is doled out with as much abandon as the delish home cooking. Big platters of goulash, roast pork and *sauerbraten* feed both tummy and soul, as do the regionally brewed Berliner Schusterjunge pilsner and Märkischer Landmann black beer.

RESTAURANT ODERBERGER GERMAN €€€

Map p338 (☏030-7800 8976 811; www.restaurant-oderberger.de; Oderberger Strasse 57; mains €18-28, 3-course menu €39; ◷6pm-midnight Tue-Sat; 🛜; 🚋M1, 12, Ⓤ Eberswalder Strasse) ✔ This exciting newcomer spreads across three open levels in an industrial-chic ex-boiler room of a public swimming pool. The chef's orchestrations are just as upbeat and tantalising as the decor. The 'Dit is Berlin' menu stars riffs on local classics like bacon-wrapped perch and veal dumplings in caper sauce while the seasonal menu comes alive with freshly gathered ingredients from regional farmers.

✖ Kollwitzplatz & Southern Prenzlauer Berg

UMAMI VIETNAMESE €

Map p338 (☏030-2886 0626; www.umami-restaurant.de; Knaackstrasse 16; most mains €7.80; ◷noon-11pm; 🛜🍴; 🚋M2, Ⓤ Senefelder-platz) A mellow 1950s lounge-vibe and an inspired menu of Indochine home cooking divided into 'regular' and 'vegetarian' choices are the main draws of this restaurant with large sidewalk terrace. Leave room for their cupcake riff (called 'pop-cake'). The six-course family meal is a steal at €23 (€10 per additional person).

W-DER IMBISS FUSION €

Map p338 (☏030-4435 2206; www.w-derimbiss. de; Kastanienallee 49; dishes €5-13.50; ◷noon-10pm Sun-Thu, to 11pm Fri & Sat; 🍴; 🚋M1, Ⓤ Rosenthaler Platz) The self-described home of 'indo-mexi-cal-ital' fusion, W is always busy as a beehive with fans of its signature naan pizza freshly baked in the tandoor oven and decorated with anything from avocado to smoked salmon.

CHUTNIFY INDIAN €

Map p338 (☏030-4401 0795; www.chutnify.com; Sredzkistrasse 43; mains €5-16.50; ◷noon-11pm Tue-Sun; 🍴; 🚋M2, M10, Ⓤ Eberswalder Strasse) Aparna Aurora's haunt spices up Berlin's bland Indian food scene with authentic South Indian street food. Her specialities are stuffed dosas (a type of savoury rice-flour crêpe) but the curries, biryanis and thali are equally worthy of your attention.

SI AN VIETNAMESE €

Map p338 (☏030-4050 5775; www.sian-berlin.de; Rykestrasse 36; mains €7.80; ◷noon-midnight; 🛜; 🚋M2, M10, Ⓤ Eberswalder Strasse) A stylish

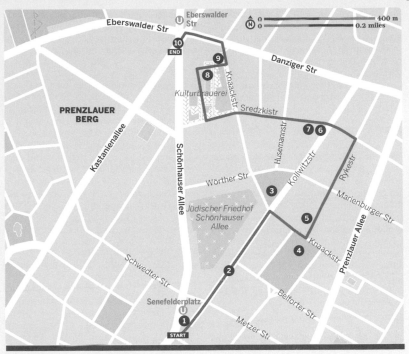

🏃 Neighbourhood Walk
Poking Around Prenzlauer Berg

START SENEFELDER PLATZ
END KONNOPKE'S IMBISS
LENGTH 1.2KM; 1½ HOURS

Start at ❶ **Senefelder Platz**, a patch of green named for Alois Senefelder, an Austro-German actor who invented lithography. Note the marble statue with his name chiselled into the pedestal in mirror-writing, just as it would be using his printing technique. Head northeast on ❷ **Kollwitzstrasse**, where the huge LPG organic supermarket and the ultradeluxe Palais KolleBelle apartment complex are solid indicators of the neighbourhood's upmarket demographics.

You'll soon arrive at ❸ **Kollwitzplatz** (p197), a square named for the artist Käthe Kollwitz, who lived here with her husband for over 40 years while tending to the destitute. A bronze statue in the square's centre park and a plaque on the blue building at Kollwitzstrasse 58 honour her legacy.

Follow Knaackstrasse to Rykestrasse, past a row of popular cafes, and note the circular ❹ **Wasserturm**, Berlin's oldest

water tower (1877), which is now honeycombed with pie-sliced flats. In Nazi Germany, its machine room went through a sinister stint as an improvised prison and torture centre. Follow Rykestrasse, noting the handsome facades of its restored townhouses. At No 53 is the ❺ **Synagoge Rykestrasse**, which survived WWII and once again hosts Shabbat services.

Continue on Rykestrasse to Sredzkistrasse, perhaps stopping for homemade cakes at ❻ **Anna Blume** (p206) and a browse at the ❼ **Bücher Tauschbaum**, a free book exchange made from tree trunks.

Further up on the right looms the sprawling ❽ **Kulturbrauerei** (p197), a brewery-turned-cultural complex. In its northern wing, the free ❾ **Museum in der Kulturbrauerei** (p197) invites you to get an eyeful of daily life in East Germany.

Exit the Kulturbrauerei on to Knaackstrasse and then turn left on Danziger Strasse to wrap up your walk with a *Currywurst* from cult-kitchen ❿ **Konnopke's Imbiss** (p199).

PRENZLAUER BERG

nosh spot that welcomes a steady stream of tousled hipsters, yoga mamas and even the occasional celeb (yes, Clooney was here). The modern-meets-traditional Asian interior combines a concrete counter and oak tables with straw mats and lanterns. The fresh and healthy dishes change daily and are based on traditional recipes from the ancient monasteries of Vietnam.

STREET FOOD AUF ACHSE   STREET FOOD €

Map p338 (☑030-4431 0737; www.streetfood aufachse.de; Kulturbrauerei, btwn Schönhauser Allee, Knaackstrasse, Eberswalder Strasse & Sredzkistrasse; ⊗noon-6pm Sun Jan–mid-Nov) On Sunday, the Kulturbrauerei (p197) gets mobbed by hungry folk keen on a first-class culinary journey at economy prices. Dozens of mobile kitchens set up in the courtyard of this 19th-century red-brick brewery-turned-cultural complex, and there's a beer garden as well as occasional live music and other entertainment.

It's even open in winter when fire pits warm hands and hearts.

MUSE   INTERNATIONAL €€

Map p338 (☑030-4005 6289; www.muse berlin.de; Immanuelkirchstrasse 31; mains lunch €5.50-10, dinner €10-19; ⊗noon-3.30pm Tue-Fri, 6-10.30pm Mon-Sat, 11am-5pm Sun; ⚐; ⓂM2, M4) The lovechild of globetrotting Brit-German couple Caroline and Tobias, this rustic-chic neighbourhood bistro doles out border-crossing comfort food prepared with passion and creativity by a multinational kitchen team. The menu hopscotches from superfood salads and belly-filling English breakfast to grilled watermelon with feta and pine nuts without missing a step.

AUSSPANNE   GERMAN €€

Map p338 (☑030-4430 5199; www.deutsches-restaurant.berlin; Kastanienallee 65; mains €14-20; ⊗6-11pm; ⚐; ⓂM1, 12, ⓊSenefelderplatz, Rosenthaler Platz) Rustic, cosy and decorated with wood, mirrors and vintage enamel signs, the Ausspanne pairs Old Berlin flair with modern German cooking. Head chef Andre Pilz crafts dishes that are comforting and exciting and calibrated to satisfy both palate and eye. The seasons keep the menu in flux but perennial favourites like Königsberger Klopse (veal dumplings in caper sauce) never go out of fashion.

STANDARD – SERIOUS PIZZA   ITALIAN €€

Map p338 (☑030-4862 5614; www.standard-berlin.de; Templiner Strasse 7; pizza €8.50-17.50; ⊗6pm-midnight Tue-Fri, 1pm-midnight Sat & Sun; ⚐; ⓊSenefelderplatz) The name is the game: serious Neapolitan-style pizza *truly* is the standard at this modern parlour where the dough is kneaded daily and the bases are topped with such quality ingredients as San Marzano tomatoes from the heel of Vesuvius. Best of all, they're tickled to perfection in a ferociously hot cupola furnace.

GUGELHOF   FRENCH €€

Map p338 (☑030-442 9229; www.gugelhof.de; Knaackstrasse 37; mains €8-26; ⊗5-11pm Mon-

---

WORTH A DETOUR

SCHLOSS SCHÖNHAUSEN

Surrounded by a lovely park, **Schloss Schönhausen** (☑030-3949 2625; www.spsg. de; Tschaikowskistrasse 1; adult/concession €6/5; ⊗10am-5.30pm Tue-Sun Apr-Oct, to 5pm Sat & Sun Nov-Dec, to 4pm Jan-Mar; ℗; ⓐM1) packs a lot of German history into its pint-sized frame. Originally a country estate of Prussian nobles, in 1740 it became the summer residence of Frederick II's estranged wife Elisabeth Christine, then fell into a long slumber after her death in 1797. The Nazis stored 'degenerate' art in the by then neglected structure, which became the seat of East Germany's first president, Wilhelm Pieck, in 1949, before later serving as a state guesthouse.

After yet another mega-makeover, the palace sparkles in renewed splendour. Tours take in the downstairs rooms, whose furniture and wallpaper reflect the style of the 18th century when the queen had her private quarters here. More interesting – largely for their uniqueness – are the upstairs rooms where East German fustiness is alive in the heavy furniture of Pieck's 1950s décor and in the baby-blue bedspread in the Gentlemen's Bedroom where Castro, Ceaușescu, Gaddafi and other 'bad boys' slept. After your tour, it's well worth exploring the lovely gardens surrounding the palace.

To get to the palace, which is in Pankow just north of Prenzlauer Berg, catch tram M1 to the Tschaikowskistrasse stop, then walk about 300m east on Tschaikowskistrasse.

Fri, noon-11pm Sat & Sun; 🚇M2, M4, 12, 🚇Senefelderplatz) Training the spotlight on Alsatian and southern German food, this jewel made headlines when feeding Bill Clinton back in 2000, and thankfully it hasn't coasted on its fame since. Chefs still keep things real with robust *choucroute* (a sauerkraut-based stew), cheese fondue, *Flammkuchen* (Alsatian pizza) suckling pig and other Alsatian soul food, plus inventive daily specials.

RAWTASTIC   VEGAN €€

Map p338 (📞0172 439 1287; www.rawtastic. de; Danziger Strasse 16; mains €13-19; ⊙noon-10pm Sun-Thu, to 10.30pm Fri & Sat; 📞🚇; 🚇M1, 🚇Eberswalder Strasse) At Berlin's first rawvegan restaurant, food does not get heated to more than 42°C. Try their healthy spins on burgers, pizzas and chocolate mousse or take on the innovative tastes of kelp pesto or sauerkraut wraps. Superfood smoothies provide an additional power boost.

DER HAHN IST TOT!   FRENCH, GERMAN €€€

Map p338 (📞030-6570 6756; www.der-hahn-ist-tot.de; Zionskirchstrasse 40; 4-course dinners €24; ⊙6.30-11pm Tue-Sun; 📞; 🚇M1, 12, 🚇Senefelderplatz, Rosenthaler Platz) A French children's ditty inspired the curious name, which translates as 'The rooster is dead!'. At this homey restaurant the deceased chicken is turned into *coq au vin,* the classic French country stew, which always features on one of the three weekly changing four-course dinners (one of them meat-free) that shine a spotlight on the best of French and German rural cooking.

🍷 DRINKING & NIGHTLIFE

In comparison with the wild '90s, nightlife in Prenzlauer Berg is rather sedate now as most clubs had to close or move to friendlier pastures. Fortunately, a new pocket of action seems to be opening up around Storkower Strasse. Otherwise, going out is focused on comfy bars and cafes with many lining Lychener Strasse, Schliemannstrasse and Dunckerstrasse (nicknamed 'LSD'). There's also a good crop on Kastanienallee, including Prater.

★PRATER GARTEN   BEER GARDEN

Map p338 (📞030-448 5688; www.pratergarten.de; Kastanienallee 7-9; snacks €2.50-7.50; ⊙noon-late

Apr-Sep, weather permitting; 🚭; 🚇M1, 12, 🚇Eberswalder Strasse) Berlin's oldest beer garden has seen beer-soaked days and nights since 1837 and is still a charismatic spot for guzzling a custom-brewed Prater pilsner (self-service) beneath the ancient chestnut trees. Kids can romp around the small play area.

In foul weather, in winter or to sample modern German and regional dishes (mains €10 to €21), report to the adjacent Prater Gaststätte beer hall.

★WEINEREI FORUM   WINE BAR

Map p338 (📞030-440 6983; www.weinerei.com; Fehrbelliner Strasse 57; ⊙10am-midnight; 📞; 🚇M1, 🚇Rosenthaler Platz) After 8pm, this living-room-style cafe turns into a wine bar that works on the honour principle: you 'rent' a wine glass for €2, then help yourself to as much vino as you like and in the end decide what you want to pay. Please be fair to keep this fantastic concept going.

BRYK BAR   COCKTAIL BAR

Map p338 (📞030-3810 0165; www.bryk-bar. com; Rykestrasse 18; ⊙7pm-late; 🚇M2, M10, 🚇Prenzlauer Allee) Both vintage and industrial elements contribute to the unhurried, dapper ambience at this darkly lit cocktail lab. Bar chef Frank Grosser whips unusual ingredients into such experimental liquid teasers as the rum-based Kamasutra with a Hangover topped with white chocolate-horseradish foam. The free dill popcorn is positively addictive.

ZUM STARKEN AUGUST   PUB

Map p338 (📞030-2520 9020; www.zumstarken august.de; Schönhauser Allee 56; ⊙3pm-2.30am Mon-Thu, to 5am Fri, 2pm-5am Sat, 2pm-2.30am Sun; 🚇M1, M10, 🚇Eberswalder Strasse) Part circus, part burlesque bar, this vibrant venue dressed in Victorian-era exuberance is a fun and friendly addition to the Prenzlauer Berg pub culture. Join the unpretentious, international crowd over cocktails and craft beers while being entertained with drag-hosted bingo, burlesque divas or wicked cabaret.

BREWDOG   CRAFT BEER

Map p338 (📞030-4847 7770; www.brewdog. com; Ackerstrasse 29; ⊙noon-midnight Sun-Thu, to 2am Fri & Sat; 🚇12, M5, M8, 🚇Bernauer Strasse) After opening branches around the world, Scottish cult brewers BrewDog are now bringing their fine suds to Berlin. Their modern-industrial flagship with

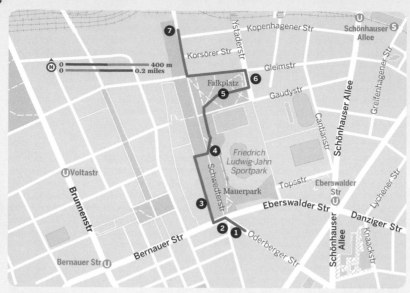

🏃 Local Life
Sundays Around the Mauerpark

Locals, expats and tourists – everyone flocks to the Mauerpark on Sundays. It's an energetic urban tapestry where a flea market, karaoke and bands provide entertainment, and people gather for barbecues, basketball and boules. A graffiti-covered section of the Berlin Wall recalls the time when the park was part of the death strip separating East and West Berlin.

❶ Bright Beginnings

Start the day at **Bonanza Coffee Heroes** (Map p338; www.bonanzacoffee.de; Oderberger Strasse 35; ☺8.30am-6pm Mon-Fri, 10am-6.30pm Sat & Sun; ☎; ⓀM1, M10, 12, ⓊEberswalder Strasse) on cafe-lined Oderberger Strasse. While sipping a cuppa, admire the beautiful facades of the restored 19th-century townhouses that were saved from demolition in the late '70s when the street still dead-ended at the Berlin Wall.

❷ Confronting Cold War History

During the Cold War, East met West at Bernauer Strasse, now paralleled by a 1.4km-long linear multimedia memorial exhibit (p195) that vividly illustrates the realities of life with the Berlin Wall.

❸ Urban Archaeology

After this dose of history, hit the Flohmarkt im Mauerpark (p208) for some quality hunting and gathering of retro threads, cool stuff by local designers and GDR-era household items. Afterwards, fortify yourself at a street-food stall or drag your loot to a market beer garden to chill out in the sun.

❹ Bearpit Karaoke

On most summer Sundays, Berlin's best free entertainment kicks off around 3pm when Joe Hatchiban sets up his custom-made mobile **karaoke** (Map p338; www.bearpitkaraoke.com; ☺around 3-8pm Sun spring-autumn; ⓀM1, M10, 12, ⓊEberswalder Strasse) unit in the Mauerpark's amphitheatre. Join the crowds in cheering and clapping for eager crooners.

❺ Falkplatz

Studded with ancient chestnut, oak, birch, ash and poplar trees, this leafy park was a parade ground for Prussian soldiers back in the 19th century and used to grow vegetables right after WWII. Today, it's a great place to relax on the grass.

Bearpit Karaoke

⑥ Burgermania
New York meets Berlin at expat favourite **Bird** (Map p338; ☑030-5105 3283; www.thebirdinberlin.com; Am Falkplatz 5; burgers €10-14.50, steaks from €22.50; ⊗6-11pm Mon-Thu, 4pm-midnight Fri, noon-midnight Sat, noon-11pm Sun; 🖥; 🚊M1, ⓤSchönhauser Allee, ⓢSchönhauser Allee), whose dry-aged steaks, burgers and hand-cut fries might just justify the hype.

⑦ Northern Mauerpark
To escape the Mauerpark frenzy and see where the locals relax, head north of the Gleimstrasse tunnel. This is where you'll find an enchanting birch grove; the **Jugendfarm Moritzhof** (Map p338; ☑030-4402 4220; www.jugendfarm-moritzhof.de; Schwedter Strasse 90; ⊗1-6pm Mon-Fri Oct-Mar, to 6.30pm Apr-Sep & 1-6pm Sat; 🚊M1, ⓤSchönhauser Allee, ⓢSchönhauser Allee), a farm playground complete with barnyard animals; and daredevils scaling the **Schwedter Nordwand** (Map p338; ☑0157 7191 6373; www.alpinclub-berlin.de; Schwedter Strasse, near Kopenhagener Strasse; 🚊M1, ⓤSchönhauser Allee, ⓢSchönhauser Allee) climbing wall operated by the German Alpine Club.

brick walls and dark wood has some 30 taps dispensing their own draughts alongside a changing roster of German and international guest beers. Their pizza pairs well with the amber liquids.

THE CASTLE
PUB
Map p336 (☑0151 6767 6757; www.thecastleberlin.de; Invalidenstrasse 129; ⊗8am-2am Mon-Fri, 10am-2am Sat & Sun; 🖥; 🚊M5, M8, M10, 12, ⓢNordbahnhof) Ben and Gekko's 'castle' is a comfortable lair that has just the right amount of contemporary cool without hitting the hipster needle. There's coffee and pastries during the day but the place's real ammo is its 21 beers on tap, both craft beers and pub classics like Kilkenny and Guinness. There's a sunny beer garden, too.

STONE BREWING TAP ROOM
CRAFT BEER
Map p338 (☑030-4401 2090; www.stonebrewing.eu/visit/outposts/prenzlauerberg; Oderberger Strasse 15; ⊗10am-1am; ⓤEberswalder Strasse) Berliners don't like to travel across town, especially not for beer. Which is why beer lovers breathed a sigh of relief when California import Stone Brewing, whose production is in an outer suburb, announced it would open a second taproom near Mauerpark. Sample their own brews, guest beers or stop by the filling station for freshly bottled take-home suds.

BECKETTS KOPF
COCKTAIL BAR
Map p338 (☑030-9900 5188; www.beckettskopf.de; Pappelallee 64; ⊗8pm-late; 🚊12, ⓢSchönhauser Allee, ⓤSchönhauser Allee) Past Samuel Beckett's portrait, the art of cocktail-making is taken very seriously. Settle into a heavy armchair in the warmly lit lounge and take your sweet time perusing the extensive – and poetic – drinks menu. All the classics are accounted for, of course, but it's the seasonal special concoctions that truly stimulate the senses.

Reservations recommended as there is no standing allowed.

FAIRYTALE BAR
COCKTAIL BAR
Map p338 (☑0170 219 5155; www.fairytale.bar; Am Friedrichshain 24; ⊗8pm-2.30am Tue-Sat; 🚊200, 🚊M4) Once upon a time there was (is) a bar in Berlin that whisked you into a cabinet of curiosities with bewitchingly costumed staff and a 'talking' drinks menu set up like a pop-up fairy-tale book. Get lost in this expressionist riff on *Alice in Wonderland* with such fanciful cocktails as Black Knight or Frog Prince. Reservations (by email) advised.

Drinks are fabulous but the most memorable aspect is the multisensory menu itself....

DECK 5 — BAR
Map p338 (www.freiluftrebellen.de; Schönhauser Allee 80; ⊘noon-midnight, weather permitting usually Apr-Sep; 🚇M1, Ⓢ Schönhauser Allee, ⓊSchönhauser Allee) Soak up the rays, grand city views and colourful cocktails at this beach bar in the sky while sinking your toes into tonnes of sand lugged to the top parking deck of the Schönhauser Arkaden mall. After mall hours (10am to 9pm, Monday to Saturday) access is via the never-ending flight of stairs from Greifenhagener Strasse.

ANNA BLUME — CAFE
Map p338 (✆030-4404 8749; www.cafe-anna-blume.de; Kollwitzstrasse 83; breakfast €3.50-12.50, mains €9-13; ⊘8am-midnight; 🚇M2, M10, ⓊEberswalder Strasse) Potent java, homemade cakes, and flowers from the attached shop perfume the art nouveau interior of this cafe named for a 1919 Dadaist poem by German artist Kurt Schwitters. In fine weather the outdoor terrace offers primo people watching. Great for breakfast (served any time), especially if you order the tiered tray for two.

HERMAN — BAR
Map p338 (✆030-4431 2854; www.bravebelgians.be; Schönhauser Allee 173; ⊘6pm-1am Tue-Thu, to 2am Fri & Sat, to midnight Sun & Mon; ⓊSenefelderplatz) Named for owner Bart Neirynck's German teacher, Herman offers a bewildering range of Belgian beers, 100 in all, from abbey ale and wheat beer to Lambic and India pale ale. If you're feeling flush, order a *bière brut*, a potent top-shelf brew cave-aged in the Champagne region of France.

CAFE CHAGALL — BAR
Map p338 (✆030-441 5881; www.cafe-chagall.com; Kollwitzstrasse 2; ⊘10am-3am Mon-Sat, to 2am Sun; ⓊSenefelderplatz) Proof that the boho spirit is not dead in Prenzlauer Berg, Chagall gets flooded with a congenial mix of locals and visitors. They come for cold drinks served by staff who make everyone feel welcome. Separate smoking room in back, big pavement terrace in summer and Russian food from the affiliated restaurant next door.

AUGUST FENGLER — BAR
Map p338 (www.augustfengler.de; Lychener Strasse 11; ⊘7pm-3am or later; 🚇M1, ⓊEberswalder Strasse) With its flirty vibe, wallet-friendly drinks prices and a pretension-free

crowd, this local institution scores a trifecta on key ingredients for a good night out. Different DJs kick into gear after 10pm Tuesday to Saturday playing an eclectic sound mix from 80s to funk, indie to rock.

A good place to steer towards for that final drink when everywhere else is closed.

GREIFBAR — GAY
Map p338 (✆030-8975 1498; www.greifbar.com; Wichertstrasse 10; ⊘10pm-6am; Ⓢ Schönhauser Allee, ⓊSchönhauser Allee) Men-Drinks-Cruising: Greifbar's motto says it all. This traditional Prenzlauer Berg gay bar draws a mixed crowd of jeans, sneakers, leather and skin, sniffing each other out below the big-screen video in the bar, before retiring to the private play zone in the back.

DUNCKER CLUB — CLUB
Map p338 (✆030-445 9509; www.dunckerclub.de; Dunckerstrasse 64; ⊘9pm-late Thu-Mon; 🚇M10, ⓈPrenzlauer Allee) Way off the beaten track, Duncker is a rare Prenzlauer Berg club survivor in a century-old brick building that's seen stints as a horse barn, a salt warehouse and a GDR-era youth club. An all-ages, mostly local, crowd invades for indie, alternative and rock concerts or for the 'Montagsduncker' Goth nights. Free concerts on Thursdays, and chill-out garden in summer.

 ## ENTERTAINMENT

COMEDY CLUB KOOKABURRA — COMEDY
Map p338 (✆030-4862 3186; www.comedyclub.de; Schönhauser Allee 184; tickets €11-16; ⊘shows 8pm Tue-Sat, 7pm Sun; ⓊRosa-Luxemburg-Platz) This living-room-style comedy club delivers an assembly line of belly laughs in cosy digs at a former bank building. Check the schedule for English-speaking funny folk spinning everyday material into comedy gold. Also recommended: Karsten Kaie's weekly 'How to Become a Berliner in One Hour?'. Food and drink served.

🛍 SHOPPING

Kastanienallee is the main shopping drag and popular for Berlin-made fashions and streetwear. More indie stores hold forth along Stargarder Strasse and in the streets around Helmholtzplatz, especially lower Dunckerstrasse.

SPOTLIGHT ON WEDDING

Amorphous, multiethnic and rough around the edges – Wedding is a draw for urban explorers of neighbourhoods still exhibiting pre-gentrification authenticity. Sights are fairly scarce but if you're keen on offbeat, down-to-earth locals and improvised DIY bars and creative venues, you'll still find them in this working-class northern district.

Sight

Preussische Spirituosen Manufaktur (☑030-4502 8537; www.psmberlin.de; Seestrasse 13; 1-/2hr tour per person €10/15, 4-person minimum; ⊙shop 11am-7pm Mon-Fri, tours by arrangement; 🚌50, M13) This historic factory has made premium spirits and liqueurs since 1874 and even counted German Kaiser Wilhelm I among its customers. All is produced by hand and in limited quantities using ancient equipment. Today its Adler label gin and vodka is served in fine drinking parlours around town and, along with other potent potions, sold in the on-site shop. Tastings and tours are available by arrangement.

Eating

Pförtner Cafe (☑030-5036 9854; www.pfoertner.co; Uferstrasse 8-11; mains lunch €5-7.50, dinner €12-17; ⊙9am-11pm Mon-Fri, 11am-11pm Sat; Ⓤ Pankstrasse) This artsy-funky cafe occupies the converted gatehouse of a former bus repair station-turned-artist studios. Creative residents invade for rustic lunches or homemade cakes in the daytime and more substantial market-fresh meals in the evening. A few tables set up in a cooly upcycled vintage public bus parked in the courtyard add to the charm.

Drinking

Vagabund Brauerei (☑030-5266 7668; www.vagabundbrauerei.com; Antwerpener Strasse 3; ⊙5pm-late Mon-Fri, 1pm-late Sat & Sun; 🕿; Ⓤ Seestrasse) American friends Tom, Matt and David became Berlin craft beer pioneers when they started their small batch brewery in 2011. In their earthy-chic taproom, they pour hoppy American as well as double and triple Indian pale ales alongside a mean wheat beer, a smokey beer and the exotic 'Szechuan Saison' with crushed coriander seeds and peppercorns.

Eschenbräu (☑0162 493 1915; www.eschenbraeu.de; Triftstrasse 67; ⊙3pm-2am May–mid-Sep, 5pm-2am mid-Sep–Apr; Ⓤ Leopoldplatz) Cradled by student housing, this earthy microbrewery is a beloved neighbourhood spot with a woodsy cellar pub and chestnut-canopied beer garden. Aside from traditional unfiltered pilsner, dark beer and wheat beer (March to October), it also produces seasonal beers and homemade fruit brandies. *Flammkuchen* (Alsatian pizza) is served, but you're also free to bring your own picnic.

Look for signs coming from Triftstrasse.

Entertainment

Silent Green Kulturquartier (☑030-4606 7324; www.silent-green.net; Gerichtstrasse 35; Ⓢ Wedding, Ⓤ Wedding, Leopoldplatz) This event venue is part of the historic former Wedding crematorium and presents mostly experimental music, dance and other performances in the former mourning hall with its striking acoustics. A bit creepy perhaps? But oh so Berlin. There's also Mars, the daytime restaurant and bar (www.mars-berlin.net), and outdoor movie nights hosted by the roaming Nomadenkino.

The listed 1911 building was in use as a crematorium until 2002.

Sports & Activities

Freibad Plötzensee (☑0176 3441 8634, 030-8964 4787; www.strandbad-ploetzensee.de; Nordufer 26; adult/concession €5/3; ⊙9am-7pm May-Sep; 🚌M13, 50) This lovely lido on a natural lake is great for cooling off on a hot summer day. Activities include an adventure playground, trampolines and beach volleyball and there are several snack stands and a beach bar as well.

On Sundays, head to Mauerpark and Arkonaplatz to forage for flea-market treasure. For everyday needs stop by the Schönhauser Allee Arcaden mall right by the eponymous U-/S-Bahn station.

FLOHMARKT IM MAUERPARK   MARKET
Map p338 (www.flohmarktimmauerpark.de; Bernauer Strasse 63-64; ⊙9am-6pm Sun; 🚋M1, M10, 12, ⓤEberswalder Strasse) Join the throngs of thrifty trinket hunters, bleary-eyed clubbers and excited tourists sifting for treasure at this always busy flea market with cult status, in a spot right where the Berlin Wall once ran. Source new favourites among retro threads, vintage vinyl and offbeat stuff. Street-food stands and beer gardens, including **Mauersegler** (Map p338; ✆030-9788 0904; www.mauersegler-berlin.de; ⊙2pm-2am May-Oct; 🛜) and Schönwetter, provide sustenance.

KOLLWITZPLATZMARKT   MARKET
Map p338 (Kollwitzstrasse & Wöhrter Strasse; ⊙noon-7pm Thu Apr-Dec, to 6pm Thu Jan-Mar, 9am-4pm Sat; ⓤSenefelderplatz) On the edge of lovely and leafy Kollwitzplatz square, this posh farmers market has everything you need to put together a gourmet picnic or meal. Velvety gorgonzola, juniper-berry smoked ham, crusty sourdough bread and homemade pesto are among the exquisite morsels scooped up by well-heeled locals.

TRÖDELMARKT ARKONAPLATZ   MARKET
Map p338 (www.troedelmarkt-arkonaplatz. de; Arkonaplatz; ⊙10am-4pm Sun; 🚋M1, M10, ⓤBernauer Strasse) Surrounded by cafes perfect for carbo-loading, this smallish flea market on a leafy square lets you ride the retro frenzy with plenty of groovy furniture, accessories, clothing, vinyl and books, including some East German vintage items. It's easily combined with a visit to the famous Flohmarkt im Mauerpark.

GOLDHAHN UND SAMPSON   FOOD
Map p338 (✆030-4119 8366; www.goldhahnund sampson.de; Dunckerstrasse 9; ⊙8am-8pm Mon-Fri, 9am-8pm Sat; 🚋12, ⓤEberswalder Strasse) Pink Himalaya salt, Moroccan argan oil and crusty German bread are among the global pantry stockers tastefully displayed at this stylish gourmet gallery. Owners Sascha and Andreas hand-source all items, most of them rare, organic and from small artisanal suppliers. For inspiration, nose around the cookbook library or join up for a class at the on-site cooking school.

RATZEKATZ   TOYS
Map p338 (✆030-681 9564; www.ratzekatz.de; Raumerstrasse 7; ⊙10am-7pm Mon-Sat; 🚋12, ⓤEberswalder Strasse) Packed with quality playthings, this adorable shop made headlines a few years ago when Angelina Jolie and son Maddox picked out a Jurassic Park's worth of dinosaurs. Even without the celeb glow, it's a fine place to source toys for all age groups – from babies to teens.

SAINT GEORGES   BOOKS
Map p338 (✆030-8179 8333; www.saintgeorges bookshop.com; Wörther Strasse 27; ⊙11am-8pm Mon-Fri, to 7pm Sat; 🛜; 🚋M2, ⓤSenefelderplatz) Laid-back and low-key, Saint Georges bookshop is a sterling spot to track down new and used English-language fiction and nonfiction. The selection includes plenty of rare and out-of-print books as well as a big shelf of literature by German and international authors translated into English. When you're done, you can even return the book for 50% store credit on the purchase price.

FLAGSHIPSTORE   FASHION & ACCESSORIES
Map p338 (✆030-4373 5327; www.flagship store-berlin.de; Oderberger Strasse 53; ⊙noon-8pm Mon-Fri, 11am-8pm Sat; 🚋M1, 12, ⓤEberswalder Strasse) This compact multilabel boutique is great for sourcing sustainable and fair-trade fashion from both up-and-coming Berlin designers and established imports. There's unconventional but wearable fashion, plus plenty of cool accessories.

TA(U)SCHE   FASHION & ACCESSORIES
Map p338 (✆030-4030 1770; www.tausche.de; Raumerstrasse 8; ⊙11am-7pm Mon-Fri, to 6pm Sat; 🚋12, ⓤEberswalder Strasse) Heike Braun and Antje Strubels now sell their ingenious messenger-style bags around the world, but this is the shop where it all began. Bags come in 12 models, 10 colours, three types of material and your choice of exchangeable flaps that zip off and on in seconds.

VEB ORANGE   GIFTS & SOUVENIRS
Map p338 (✆030-9788 6886; www.veborange. de; Oderberger Strasse 29; ⊙11am-7pm Mon-Sat; 🚋M1, 12, ⓤEberswalder Strasse) Viva vintage! With its selection of the most beautiful things from the '60s and '70s (especially from East Germany), this place is a tangible reminder of how colourful, campy and fun home decor used to be. True to its name, many of the furnishings, accessories, lamps and fashions are orange in colour.

City West & Charlottenburg

KURFÜRSTENDAMM & AROUND | SAVIGNYPLATZ & KANTSTRASSE

Neighbourhood Top Five

1 Schloss Charlottenburg (p211) Marvelling at the pomposity of the Prussian royal lifestyle, then relaxing with a picnic by the carp pond in the palace park.

2 Story of Berlin (p216) Finishing an engaging survey of city history with a guided tour of a creepy Cold War–era atomic bunker.

3 Kaiser-Wilhelm-Gedächtniskirche (p216) Considering the horror of war at this majestically ruined 19th-century church.

4 Zoo Berlin (p215) Communing with creatures from apes to zebras at the world's most species-rich animal park, founded by a king in the mid-19th century.

5 Bikini Berlin (p221) Shopping for idiosyncratic Berlin fashions and accessories at this architecturally stunning concept mall with interesting food options to boot.

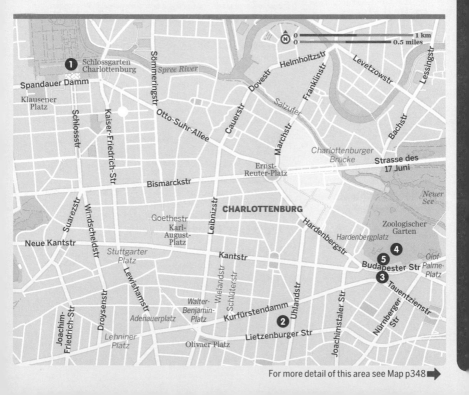

For more detail of this area see Map p348 ➡

CITY WEST & CHARLOTTENBURG

Lonely Planet's Top Tip

Leaving from Bahnhof Zoologischer Garten, buses 100 and 200 pass many blockbuster sights (including Potsdamer Platz and the Reichstag) on their route through the central city to Alexanderplatz.

✕ Best Places to Eat

➡ Restaurant am Steinplatz (p218)

➡ Mine Restaurant (p217)

➡ Restaurant Faubourg (p217)

➡ Schwein (p218)

➡ Butcher (p218)

➡ Kuchenladen (p218)

For reviews, see p216. ➡

🍷 Best Places to Drink

➡ Bar am Steinplatz (p219)

➡ Diener Tattersall (p220)

➡ Monkey Bar (p220)

➡ Bar Zentral (p220)

For reviews, see p218. ➡

🔒 Best Shopping

➡ Bikini Berlin (p221)

➡ Manufactum (p221)

➡ Stilwerk (p221)

➡ Super Concept Space (p221)

For reviews, see p221. ➡

Explore City West & Charlottenburg

West Berlin's commercial hub during the city's division, Charlottenburg still counts its famous shopping boulevard, the Kurfürstendamm (p215), among its biggest drawcards. Fashionable boutiques mix it up with high-street chains and department stores along this strip and its leafy side streets. It continues east as Tauentzienstrasse, which culminates at the humongous KaDeWe department store.

Along the way, witness the new construction and revitalisation of the City West area around the landmark Kaiser-Wilhelm-Gedächtniskirche (p216), a church ruin-turned-antiwar memorial. Nearby, elephants trumpet and pandas cuddle in the famous Zoo Berlin (p215), a sure-fire hit with kids.

After satisfying your shopping urges, head out to must-see Schloss Charlottenburg for a sense of how the Prussian royalty spent its money in centuries past. Tour the fancifully decorated living quarters, then relax with a stroll in lushly landscaped gardens. In fine weather, consider bringing a picnic. A trip to the palace is easily combined with a spin around the trio of excellent art museums nearby.

Local Life

Shopping Shop till you drop at high-street chains and high-fashion boutiques along Ku'damm (p215) and its side streets or at the Bikini Berlin (p221) concept mall.

The Asian mile Find your favourite among the eateries in Berlin's Little Asia (p217) along Kantstrasse.

Views Enjoy sunset drinks with a view of the city and zoo at the Monkey Bar (p220).

Cafe hang-outs Take a break with cappuccino and sinful cakes at the classic Kuchenladen (p218) or in the garden of the cafe at the Literaturhaus (p217).

Treasure hunt Sift for kitsch and collectables at Berliner Trödelmarkt (p221), the city's oldest flea market.

Getting There & Away

Bus Zoologischer Garten is the western terminus for buses 100 and 200. M19, M29 and X10 travel along Kurfürstendamm. Lines 309 and M45 go to Schloss Charlottenburg, X9 and 109 to Tegel Airport.

S-Bahn S5 and S7 link to Hauptbahnhof and Alexanderplatz via Zoologischer Garten. The circle line S41/S42 passes through the district's western edge.

U-Bahn Uhlandstrasse, Kurfürstendamm and Wittenbergplatz stations (U1) put you right in shopping central.

TOP SIGHT
SCHLOSS CHARLOTTENBURG

Schloss Charlottenburg is an exquisite baroque palace and the best place in Berlin to soak up the one-time grandeur of the royal Hohenzollern clan. A visit is especially pleasant in summer, when you can fold a stroll around the palace garden into a day of peeking at royal treasures and lavishly furnished period rooms reflecting centuries of royal tastes and lifestyles.

The palace started out rather modestly, as a petite summer retreat built for Sophie Charlotte, wife of Elector Friedrich III, and was expanded in the mode of Versailles after the elector's promotion to king in 1701. Subsequent royals dabbled with the compound, most notably Frederick the Great, who added the spectacular Neuer Flügel. Reconstruction of the Schloss after its WWII drubbing was completed in 1966.

The grand complex consists of the main palace and three smaller structures scattered about the sprawling Schlossgarten Charlottenburg, which is part formal French baroque garden, part unruly English landscape and all idyllic playground. Hidden among the shady paths, flower beds, lawns, mature trees and carp pond are the sombre Mausoleum, the playful Belvedere and the elegant Neuer Pavillon.

Altes Schloss

Also known as the Nering-Eosander Building after its two architects, the **Altes Schloss** (Old Palace; adult/concession €10/7; ☉10am-5.30pm Tue-Sun Apr-Oct, to 5pm Tue-Sun Nov & Dec, to 4.30pm Tue-Sun Jan-Mar) is the central, and oldest, section of the palace, and is fronted by Andreas Schlüter's grand **equestrian statue of the Great Elector** (1699). Inside, the baroque living quarters of Friedrich I and Sophie-Charlotte are an extravaganza in stucco, brocade and overall opulence. After a comprehensive restoration, you can now again ooh and aah over the **Oak Gallery**, a wood-panelled festival hall draped in family portraits; the charming **Oval Hall** overlooking the park; Friedrich I's bedchamber, with its grand bed and the first-ever bathroom in

DON'T MISS

➡ Frederick the Great's apartments in the Neuer Flügel

➡ Schlossgarten Charlottenburg

➡ Neuer Flügel's paintings by French masters

➡ Picasso & Co in Museum Berggruen

PRACTICALITIES

➡ ☎030-320 910

➡ www.spsg.de

➡ Spandauer Damm 10-22

➡ day pass to all 4 bldgs adult/concession €17/13

➡ 🚌M45, 109, 309, Ⓤ Richard-Wagner-Platz, Sophie-Charlotte-Platz

TOP TIPS

➡ The 'charlottenburg+' ticket (adult/concession €17/13) is a day pass valid for one-day admission to every open building within the palace gardens (special exhibits excepted).

➡ Avoid weekends, especially in summer, when queues can be long.

➡ Skip the queue by buying timed tickets at http://tickets.spsg.de (€2 service fee).

➡ A palace visit is easily combined with a spin around the trio of adjacent art museums.

Feel like a member of the Prussian court during the Berliner Residenz Konzerte (www.residenz konzerte.berlin), a series of concerts held by candlelight with musicians dressed in powdered wigs and historical costumes playing works by baroque and early classical composers. Various packages are available, including one featuring a precon-cert dinner.

a baroque palace; and the **Eosander Chapel**, with its trompe l'œil arches. The king's passion for precious china is reflected in the dazzling **Porcelain Chamber**, which is smothered in nearly 3000 pieces of Chinese and Japanese blue ware.

Neuer Flügel

The palace's most beautiful rooms are the flamboyant private quarters of Frederick the Great in the **Neuer Flügel** (New Wing; adult/concession incl audio guide €10/7; ☉10am-5.30pm Tue-Sun Apr-Oct, to 5pm Tue-Sun Nov & Dec, to 4.30pm Tue-Sun Jan-Mar) extension, designed in 1746 by royal buddy and star architect of the period Georg Wenzeslaus von Knobelsdorff. The confection-like **White Hall** banquet room and the **Golden Gallery**, a rococo fantasy of mirrors and gilding, are both standouts. Fans of 18th-century French masters such as Watteau and Pesne will also get an eyeful. Frederick the Great's nephew and successor added a summer residence with Chinese and Etruscan design elements as well as the more sombre Winter Chambers. These rooms were mostly used by his daughter-in-law Luise (1776–1810; a popular queen and wife of King Friedrich Wilhelm III), for whom Karl Friedrich Schinkel designed a stunning bedroom.

Neuer Pavillon

Returning from a trip to Italy, Friedrich Wilhelm III (r 1797–1848) commissioned Karl Friedrich Schinkel to design the **Neuer Pavillon** (New Pavilion; adult/concession €4/3; ☉10am-5.30pm Tue-Sun Apr-Oct, noon-4pm Tue-Sun Nov-Mar) as a summer retreat modelled on neoclassical Italian villas. Today, the minipalace shows off Schinkel's many talents as architect, painter and designer, while also presenting sculpture by Christian Daniel Rauch and master paintings by such Schinkel contemporaries as Caspar David Friedrich and Eduard Gaertner.

Belvedere

The late-rococo **Belvedere** (Spandauer Damm 20-24; adult/concession €4/3; ☉10am-5.30pm Tue-Sun Apr-Oct) palace, with its distinctive cupola, got its start in 1788 as a private sanctuary for Friedrich Wilhelm II. These days it houses porcelain masterpieces by the royal manufacturer KPM, which was founded in 1763 by Frederick the Great. Among the exhibit highlights are the dainty tea cups painted with cheeky cherubs.

Mausoleum

The 1810 temple-shaped **Mausoleum** (€3; ☉10am-5.30pm Tue-Sun Apr-Oct) was conceived as the final resting place of Queen Luise, and was twice expanded to

Schloss Charlottenburg

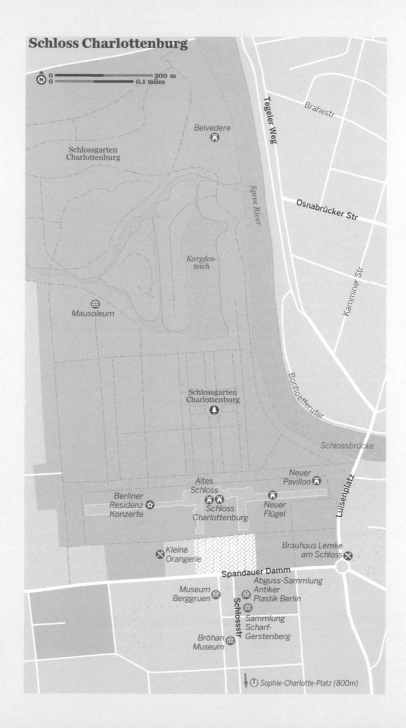

0 ——————————— 200 m
0 ——————————— 0.1 miles

Belvedere

Schlossgarten
Charlottenburg

Tegeler Weg

Brahestr

Osnabrücker Str

Spree River

Kammi

Str

Karpfen-
teich

Mausoleum

Bonhoefferufer

Schlossgarten
Charlottenburg

Schlossbrücke

Altes
Schloss

Neuer
Pavillon

Luisenplatz

Berliner
Residenz
Konzerte

Schloss
Charlottenburg

Neuer
Flügel

Kleine
Orangerie

Brauhaus Lemke
am Schloss

Spandauer Damm

Abguss-Sammlung
Antiker
Plastik Berlin

Museum
Berggruen

Schlossstr

Sammlung
Scharf-
Gerstenberg

Bröhan
Museum

Sophie-Charlotte-Platz (800m)

TAKE A BREAK

There's a pretty cafe with tree-shaded outdoor seating in the **Kleine Orangerie** (📞030-322 2021; Spandauer Damm 20; mains €6-15; ⊙10am-6pm Tue-Sun; 🚌M45, 309, Ⓤ Richard-Wagner-Platz, Sophie-Charlotte-Platz) building near the entrance to the palace gardens. A better option for a hearty meal and a cold beer is **Brauhaus Lemke** (📞030-3087 8979; www. lemke.berlin; Luisenplatz 1; mains €12-22; ⊙noon-midnight; 🚌M45, 109, 309, Ⓤ Richard-Wagner-Platz), a short walk from the palace.

From April to October, a lovely way to travel to or from Schloss Charlottenburg is on the Spree River cruise operated by Reederei Bruno Winkler (p300). Boats usually make the trip twice daily from landing docks at Bahnhof Friedrichstrasse/ Reichstagsufer (€9, 50 minutes) and go past the government district to the palace boat landing just outside the east corner of the park. It's also possible to travel the other way or do a round trip.

make room for other royals, including Kaiser Wilhelm I and his wife Augusta. Their marble sarcophagi are exquisitely sculpted works of art. More royals are buried in the crypt (closed to the public).

Sammlung Scharf-Gerstenberg

The stellar **Scharf-Gerstenberg Collection** (📞030-266 424 242; www.smb.museum; Schlossstrasse 70; adult/ concession incl Museum Berggruen €10/5; ⊙10am-6pm Tue-Fri, from 11am Sat & Sun) showcases 250 years of surrealist art, with large bodies of work by such protagonists as René Magritte and Max Ernst. The collection was founded in the early 20th century by insurance mogul Otto Gerstenberg, a man with a Midas touch and a passion for the arts. Although much of it was destroyed in WWII or disappeared to Russia as war booty, his grandsons used the remainder as a starting point for their own collection, mostly of surrealist art.

Museum Berggruen

Fans of classic modern art will be in their element at the delightful **Museum Berggruen** (📞030-266 424 242; www.smb.museum/mb; Schlossstrasse 1; adult/ concession incl Sammlung Scharf-Gerstenberg €10/5; ⊙10am-6pm Tue-Fri, from 11am Sat & Sun). Picasso is especially well represented with paintings, drawings and sculptures from all major creative phases. Standouts include the *Seated Harlequin* from his early blue and rose periods and bold cubist canvases such as his portrait of Georges Braque. Elsewhere it's off to Paul Klee's emotional world, Matisse's paper cut-outs, Giacometti's famous sculptures and a sprinkling of African art that inspired both Klee and Picasso.

Bröhan Museum

The **Bröhan Museum** (📞030-3269 0600; www.broehan -museum.de; Schlossstrasse 1a; adult/concession/child under 18 €8/5/free; ⊙10am-6pm Tue-Sun) trains the spotlight on applied arts from the late 19th century until the outbreak of WWII. Pride of place goes to the **art-nouveau collection**, with period rooms, furniture, porcelain and glass art from England, France, Germany, Scandinavia and Austria. A secondary focus is on **art deco** and **functionalism**, styles of the 1920s and '30s. A picture gallery with works by Berlin Secession artists complements the exhibits.

Abguss-Sammlung Antiker Plastik

The **Abguss-Sammlung Antiker Plastik Berlin** (Antique Plaster-Cast Collection; 📞030-342 4054; www. abguss-sammlung-berlin.de; Schlossstrasse 69b; ⊙2-5pm Thu-Sun) FREE has works spanning 3500 years, created by cultures as diverse as the Minoans, Romans and Byzantines, allowing you to trace the evolution of this ancient art form.

SIGHTS

Concentrate your sightseeing around Zoologischer Garten and along the famous Kurfürstendamm boulevard, Berlin's major shopping strip. From here it's about 3.5km northwest to Schloss Charlottenburg.

SCHLOSS CHARLOTTENBURG — PALACE
See p211.

KURFÜRSTENDAMM — AREA
Map p348 (⒰Kurfürstendamm, Uhlandstrasse) The 3.5km Kurfürstendamm is a ribbon of commerce that began as a bridle path to the royal hunting lodge in the Grunewald forest. In the early 1870s, Otto von Bismarck, the Iron Chancellor, decided that the capital of the newly founded German Reich needed its own representative boulevard, which he envisioned as even bigger and better than Paris' Champs-Élysées. Today it is Berlin's busiest shopping strip, especially towards its eastern end.

C/O BERLIN — GALLERY
Map p348 (⒥030-284 441 662; www.co-berlin. org; Hardenbergstrasse 22-24; adult/concession/ child under 18 €10/5/free; ⒣11am-8pm; ⒮Zoologischer Garten, ⒰Zoologischer Garten) Founded in 2000, C/O Berlin is the capital's most respected private, nonprofit exhibition centre for international photography and is based at the iconic Amerika Haus, which served as a United States cultural and information centre from 1957 until 2006. C/O's roster of highbrow exhibits has featured many members of the shutterbug elite, including Annie Leibovitz, Stephen Shore, Nan Goldin and Anton Corbijn.

MUSEUM FÜR FOTOGRAFIE — MUSEUM
Map p348 (⒥030-266 424 242; www.smb.museum/mf; Jebensstrasse 2; adult/concession €10/5; ⒣11am-7pm Tue, Wed & Fri-Sun, to 8pm Thu; ⒮Zoologischer Garten, ⒰Zoologischer Garten) A former Prussian officers' casino now showcases the artistic legacy of Helmut Newton (1920–2004), the Berlin-born *enfant terrible* of fashion and lifestyle photography, with the two lower floors dedicated to his life and work. On the top floor, the gloriously restored barrel-vaulted **Kaisersaal** (Emperor's Hall) forms a grand backdrop for changing international photography exhibits.

⊙ TOP SIGHT
ZOO BERLIN & AQUARIUM

Berlin's zoo holds a triple record as Germany's oldest, most species-rich and most popular animal park. It gained international fame when the polar bear cub Knut, born at the zoo in 2006, was successfully hand-raised by a zookeeper after his mother had abandoned him. Sadly, he died from brain inflammation in 2011. The zoo's current biggest heartthrobs are Meng Meng and Jiao Qing, a pair of adorable **pandas** on loan from China.

The Berlin Zoo has its origins in 1844, when King Friedrich Wilhelm IV donated land plus animals from the royal family's private reserve.

Feeding sessions are a major visitor magnet – pick up a schedule at the ticket counter. The adjacent **Aquarium** (Map p348; ⒥030-254 010; www.aquarium-berlin. de; Budapester Strasse 32; adult/child €15.50/8, with zoo €21/10.50; ⒣9am-6pm; ⒣) presents exotic fish, amphibians and reptiles in darkened halls and glowing tanks. Its tropical **Crocodile Hall** could be the stuff of nightmares, but jellyfish, iridescent poison frogs and a real-life 'Nemo' should bring smiles to most youngsters' faces.

The zoo's architecture deserves a special mention, especially the exotic **Elephant Gate**. The main entrance is the Lion Gate on Hardenbergplatz.

DON'T MISS
➡ Panda enclosure
➡ Great apes
➡ Crocodile Hall

PRACTICALITIES
➡ Map p348, G3
➡ ⒥030-254 010
➡ www.zoo-berlin.de
➡ Hardenbergplatz 8
➡ adult/child €15.50/8, with aquarium €21/10.50
➡ ⒣9am-6.30pm Apr-Sep, to 6pm Mar & Oct, to 4.30pm Nov-Feb
➡ ⒝100, 200, ⒮Zoologischer Garten, ⒰Zoologischer Garten, Kurfürstendamm

KÄTHE-KOLLWITZ-MUSEUM MUSEUM
Map p348 (📞030-882 5210; www.kaethe-kollwitz.
de; Fasanenstrasse 24; adult/concession/child
under 18 €7/4/free, audioguide €3; ⊙11am-6pm;
Ⓤ Uhlandstrasse) Käthe Kollwitz (1867–1945)
was a famous early 20th-century artist
whose social and political awareness lent a
tortured power to her lithographs, graphics,
woodcuts, sculptures and drawings. This
four-floor exhibit in a charming 19th-century
villa kicks off with an introduction to this extraordinary woman, who lived in Berlin for
52 years, before presenting a life-spanning
selection of her work, including the powerful
anti-hunger lithography *Brot!* (Bread!, 1924)
and the woodcut series *Krieg* (War, 1922–23).

STORY OF BERLIN MUSEUM
Map p348 (📞030-8872 0100; www.story-of-
berlin.de; Kurfürstendamm 207-208, enter via
Ku'damm Karree mall; adult/concession/child
€12/9/5; ⊙10am-8pm, last admission 6pm;
🚌X9, X10, 109, 110, M19, M29, TXL, Ⓤ Uhlandstrasse) This engaging museum breaks
800 years of Berlin history into bite-size
chunks that are easy to swallow but substantial enough to be satisfying. Each of
the 23 rooms uses sound, light, technology
and original objects to zero in on a specific
theme or epoch in the city's history, from
its founding in 1237 to the fall of the Berlin
Wall. Tickets include a 45-minute tour (in
English) of a still-functional 1970s atomic
bomb shelter beneath the building.

**MAHNMAL AM
BREITSCHEIDPLATZ** MEMORIAL
Map p348 (Breitscheidplatz; 🚌100, 200, Ⓤ Zoologischer Garten, Ⓢ Zoologischer Garten) This
simple memorial honours the victims of the
terror attack of 19 December 2016, when an
Islamist asylum seeker drove into a crowd
at the Christmas market held every year on
Breitscheidplatz. Unveiled on the event's
one-year anniversary, it consists of a golden
crack that runs down the steps descending
from the Kaiser Wilhelm Memorial Church,
with the names of the 12 victims chiselled
into the front of the steps.

 EATING

**The dining quality in Charlottenburg
is dependably high and the number of
trailblazing kitchens is growing steadily.
Savignyplatz exudes the relaxed and
bustling vibe of an Italian piazza on**

◉ TOP SIGHT
KAISER-WILHELM-GEDÄCHTNISKIRCHE

One of Berlin's most photographed landmarks is actually
a ruin, albeit an impressive one. Allied bombing on 23 November 1943 left only the husk of the west tower of this
magnificent neo-Romanesque church, built in honour of
Kaiser Wilhelm I, standing. Now an antiwar memorial, the
original was designed by Franz Schwechten and completed in 1895. Historic photographs in the **Gedenkhalle**
(Hall of Remembrance), at the bottom of the tower, help
you visualise its former grandeur. The hall also contains
remnants of the elaborate mosaics that once swathed
the entire interior, depicting heroic moments from Kaiser
Wilhelm I's life, among other scenes. Note the marble reliefs, liturgical objects and two symbols of reconciliation:
an icon cross donated by the Russian Orthodox church
and a copy of the Cross of Nails from Coventry Cathedral,
which was destroyed by Luftwaffe bombers in 1940.

In 1961 a bell tower and **octagonal church** designed
by Egon Eiermann were completed next to the ruined
tower; the latter addition is especially striking thanks to
its glowing midnight-blue glass walls and golden statue of
Christ 'floating' above the altar. Also note the *Stalingrad
Madonna* (a charcoal drawing) against the north wall.

DON'T MISS
➡ Memorial hall
mosaics
➡ Blue glass walls

PRACTICALITIES
➡ Map p348, G5
➡ 📞030-218 5023
➡ www.gedaechtnis
kirche.com
➡ Breitscheidplatz
➡ ⊙church 9am-7pm,
memorial hall 10am-
6pm Mon-Sat, noon-
5.30pm Sun
➡ 🚌100, 200, Ⓤ Zo-
ologischer Garten,
Kurfürstendamm,
Ⓢ Zoologischer Garten

balmy summer nights, while Kantstrasse is lined with excellent Asian eateries.

✗ Kurfürstendamm & Around

MR HAI KABUKI JAPANESE €€
Map p348 (✆030-8862 8136; www.mrhai.de; Olivaer Platz 9; plates €3.30-5.40, sushi platters from €15.50; ⊙noon-midnight; ⟳M19, 109, Ⓤ Adenauerplatz, Uhlandstrasse) Purists can stick to classic *nigiri* and *maki* but Mr Hai is mostly about expanding your sushi horizons. Unconventional morsels, composed like little works of art, are delivered *kaiten*-style (via conveyor belt) or served à la carte. Some of the more out-there creations feature kimchi, pork or cream cheese; others are flambéed or deep-fried. Great sake cocktails, too.

TAVERNA OUSIA GREEK €€
(✆030-216 /957; www.taverna-ousies.de; Grunewaldstrasse 54; dishes €5-22.50; ⊙5-10.30pm Wed-Mon; Ⓤ Bayerischer Platz) You'll be as exuberant as Zorba at this easy going yet top-rated Greek restaurant. Build a meal with the hot or cold appetisers or go for such substantial mains as the melt-in-your-mouth *spalla* (stewed lamb shoulder) or the nicely spiced *loukaniko* (homemade farmers' sausage). The country-style decor, complete with stone floor and rustic knick-knacks, also adds to the relaxed holiday feeling.

SCHLEUSENKRUG GERMAN €€
Map p348 (✆030-313 9909; www.schleusenkrug. de; Müller-Breslau-Strasse; mains €6-16; ⊙10am-midnight May-Sep, 11am-6pm Oct-Apr; Ⓢ Zoologischer Garten, Ⓤ Zoologischer Garten) Sitting on the edge of the Tiergarten park, next to a canal lock, Schleusenkrug truly comes into its own during beer-garden season. People from all walks of life hunker over big mugs and comfort food – from grilled sausages to *Flammkuchen* (Alsatian pizza) and weekly specials. Breakfast is served until 2pm.

NENI INTERNATIONAL €€
Map p348 (✆030-120 221 200; www.neni berlin.de; Budapester Strasse 40; mains €13-23; ⊙12.30-11pm; ⟳100, 200, Ⓢ Zoologischer Garten, Ⓤ Zoologischer Garten) This bustling greenhouse-style dining hall at the 25hours Hotel Bikini Berlin (p249) presents a spirited menu of meant-to-be-shared dishes inspired by Mediterranean, Iranian and Austrian cuisines. Top billing goes to the

BERLIN'S LITTLE ASIA
It's not quite Chinatown, but if you're in the mood for Asian food, head to Kantstrasse between Savignyplatz and Wilmersdorfer Strasse to find the city's densest concentration of authentic Chinese, Vietnamese and Thai restaurants, including the perennially popular Good Friends (p218). At lunchtime most offer value-priced specials, perfect for filling up on the cheap.

homemade falafel, the Jerusalem platter, the pulled-beef sandwich and the *knafeh* (a spirit-soaked dessert). The 10th-floor views of the zoo and the rooftops are a bonus.

CAFÉ-RESTAURANT WINTERGARTEN IM LITERATURHAUS INTERNATIONAL €€
Map p348 (✆030-882 5414; www.literaturhaus-berlin.de; Fasanenstrasse 23; mains €8-16; ⊙9am-midnight; ⟳; Ⓤ Uhlandstrasse) The hustle and bustle of Ku'damm is only a block away from this genteel late-19th-century villa with attached literary salon and book-shop. Tuck into dreamy cakes or seasonal bistro cuisine amid elegant Old Berlin flair in the gracefully stucco-ornamented rooms or, if weather permits, in the idyllic garden. Breakfast is served until 2pm.

★ RESTAURANT FAUBOURG FRENCH €€€
Map p348 (✆030-800 999 7700; www.sofitel-ber lin-kurfurstendamm.com; Augsburger Strasse 41; 2-/3-course lunch €19/23, dinner appetisers €14, mains €25-38; ⊙noon-11pm; ⟳; Ⓤ Kurfürstendamm) At this Sofitel hotel's château-worthy French restaurant, head chef Felix Mielke applies punctilious artisanship to top-notch regional ingredients, creating intensely flavoured and beautifully plated dishes. For maximum palate exposure, put together a meal from the appetiser menu, although the mains – prepared either in classic or contemporary fashion – also command attention, as does the wine list. The gorgeous Bauhaus-inspired decor completes the experience.

★ MINE RESTAURANT ITALIAN €€€
Map p348 (✆030-8892 6363; www.mine restaurant.de; Meinekestrasse 10; mains €15-29; ⊙5.30pm-midnight; Ⓑ Uhlandstrasse) Italian restaurants may be a dime a dozen but Mine's decor, menu and service all blend together as perfectly as a Sicilian stew. The Berlin outpost of Russian TV celebrity chef

Aram Mnatsakanov, it presents feistily flavoured next-gen fare from around the Boot by riffing on traditional recipes in innovative ways. The wine list should make even demanding oenophiles swoon.

GRACE
INTERNATIONAL €€€

Map p348 (📞030-8843 7750; http://grace-berlin.com; Kurfürstendamm 25; mains €21-56; ⏰7pm-midnight Tue-Sat; 🚇; ⓊKurfürstendamm) We don't know if Grace Kelly inspired the name of this glamorous restaurant, but the late princess would likely have felt at home in this cosmopolitan dining shrine at the Hotel Zoo. Dishes flaunt an aroma-rich Asian DNA coupled with California-style pizazz, resulting in such palate teasers as the lemongrass spring chicken made with goa beans, coconut and sweet basil.

✖ Savignyplatz & Kantstrasse

★KUCHENLADEN
CAFE €

Map p348 (📞030-3101 8424; www.derkuchenladen.de; Kantstrasse 138; cakes €2.50-4.50; ⏰10am-8pm; Ⓢ Savignyplatz) Even size-0 locals can't resist the siren call of this classic cafe whose homemade cakes are like works of art wrought from flour, sugar and cream. From cheesecake to carrot cake to the ridiculously rich Sacher Torte, it's all delicious down to the last crumb.

GOOD FRIENDS
CHINESE €€

Map p348 (📞030-313 2659; www.goodfriends-berlin.de; Kantstrasse 30; 2-course weekday lunch €7-7.70, dinner mains €8-21; ⏰noon-1am; Ⓢ Savignyplatz) Good Friends is widely considered Berlin's best Cantonese restaurant. The ducks dangling in the window are merely an overture to a menu long enough to confuse Confucius, including plenty of authentic homestyle dishes (on a separate menu). If steamed chicken feet prove too challenging, you can always fall back on sweet-and-sour pork or fried rice with shrimp.

BUTCHER
BURGERS €€

Map p348 (📞030-323 015 673; www.the-butcher.com; Kantstrasse 144; burgers €9.50-12.50; ⏰7am-midnight Sun-Thu, to 2am Fri & Sat; 🚇; Ⓢ Savignyplatz) With its bar and DJ line-up, Butcher injects a dose of hip into the 'hood. It also knows how to build one hell of a burger. Prime ingredients, including Aberdeen Angus beef, house-baked buns and a secret

(what else?) sauce, make their patty-and-bun combos shine. Rib lovers *must* try the baby back ribs, slow-cooked to perfection.

DICKE WIRTIN
GERMAN €€

Map p348 (📞030-312 4952; www.dicke-wirtin.de; Carmerstrasse 9; mains €11-18; ⏰11am-late; Ⓢ Savignyplatz) Old Berlin charm is in every nook and cranny of this been-here-forever pub, which pours eight draught beers (including the superb Kloster Andechs) and nearly three dozen homemade schnapps varieties. Hearty local and German fare keeps brains balanced. Bargain lunches, too.

★RESTAURANT AM STEINPLATZ
GERMAN €€€

Map p348 (📞030-554 444, ext 7053; www.hotelsteinplatz.com; Steinplatz 4; 2-/3-course lunch €19/23, dinner mains €23-30; ⏰noon-2.30pm & 6-10pm Mon-Fri, 6-10pm Sat & Sun; Ⓟ; 🚌M45, ⓊErnst-Reuter-Platz, Zoologischer Garten, ⓈZoologischer Garten) The '20s get a 21st-century makeover at this stylish outpost with an open kitchen, where chef Nicholas Hahn and team create dishes with technique and passion. The menu takes diners on a culinary romp around Germany with occasional stops in other countries, resulting in intellectually ambitious but super-satisfying dishes that often star unusual or rare ingredients.

★SCHWEIN
INTERNATIONAL €€€

Map p348 (📞030-2435 6282; www.schwein.online; Mommsenstrasse 63; dishes €13-37, 4-/5-course menu €65/75; ⏰6pm-midnight Mon-Fri, to 2am Sat; 🚇🍴; Ⓢ Savignyplatz) This casual fine-dining lair delivers the perfect trifecta – fabulous food, wine and long drinks. Order the multicourse menu to truly experience the genius of kitchen champion Christopher Kümper, who creates globally inspired and regionally sourced symphonies of taste and textures. Or keep it 'casual' with just a bite and a gin and tonic.

🍷 DRINKING & NIGHTLIFE

Today's Charlottenburg may no longer be the glamorous party pit of the Golden Twenties, but that's not to say that a good time can't still be had. You'll find it in fancy cocktail bars and nostalgic Old Berlin pubs. A few dance clubs towards the eastern end of Ku'damm keep the action going beyond midnight.

OLYMPIASTADION & AROUND

The main attraction in far western Berlin is the **Olympiastadion** (Olympic Stadium; ✆030-2500 2322; https://olympiastadion.berlin; Olympischer Platz 3; adult/concession self-guided tour €8/5.50, highlights tour €11/9.50; ⏰9am-7pm Apr-Jul, Sep & Oct, to 8pm Aug, 10am-4pm Nov-Mar; ⒮Olympiastadion, ⓤOlympiastadion). Even though it was put through a total modernisation for the 2006 FIFA World Cup, it's hard to ignore the fact that this massive coliseum-like stadium was built by the Nazis for the 1936 Olympic Games. The bombastic bulk of the structure remains but has been softened by the addition of a spidery oval roof, snazzy VIP boxes and top-notch sound, lighting and projection systems. It seats up to 74,650 people, be it for the local premier league Hertha BSC football (soccer) team, Bruce Springsteen or the Pope.

On nonevent days you can explore the stadium on your own, although renting a multimedia guide is recommended (€2). Several times daily, guided tours (some in English, check the website or phone ahead) take you into the locker rooms, warm-up areas and VIP areas that are otherwise off limits. Access the stadium via the visitors' centre at the Osttor (eastern gate).

To truly appreciate the grandeur of the stadium, head west past the Maifeld parade grounds to the outdoor viewing platform of the 77m-high **Glockenturm** (Olympic Bell Tower; ✆030-305 8123; www.glockenturm.de; Am Glockenturm; adult/child €5/3; ⏰9am-6pm Apr-Oct; ⓅP; ⒮Pichelsberg), which was also built for the 1936 Olympics. En route you'll pass a replica of the Olympic bell (the damaged original is displayed south of the stadium). In the foyer, an exhibit chronicles the ground's history, including the 1936 games, with panels in German and English. A documentary features rare original footage.

About 1.3km south of the stadium is the **Georg Kolbe Museum** (✆030-304 2144; www.georg-kolbe-museum.de; Sensburger Allee 25; adult/concession/under 18 €7/5/free; ⏰10am-6pm; Ⓟ; ⒽHeerstrasse), dedicated to one of Germany's most influential early-20th-century sculptors (1877–1947). A member of the Berlin Secession, Kolbe distanced himself from traditional sculpture and became a chief exponent of the idealised nude, which later found favour with the Nazis. The museum in his former studio and home mounts several exhibits per year with a focus on sculpture by Kolbe and his contemporaries, often juxtaposed with works by contemporary artists. Built in the late 1920s, it consists of two rectangular brick buildings flanking a sculpture garden. Its **Cafe K** is one of Berlin's most charming museum cafes.

About 2km southeast of the stadium, overlooking the trade fairgrounds, looms another Berlin landmark, the 147m-high **Funkturm** (Radio Tower; ✆030-3038 1905; www.funkturm-messeberlin.de; Messedamm 22; adult/concession platform €5/3, restaurant €3/2; ⏰platform 2-10pm Tue-Fri, 11am-10pm Sat & Sun, seasonal variations, weather permitting; Ⓟ; ⓤKaiserdamm, ⒮Messe Nord/ICC). The filigree structure bears an uncanny resemblance to Paris' Eiffel Tower and looks especially attractive when lit up at night. It started transmitting signals in 1926; nine years later the world's first regular TV program was broadcast from here. From the viewing platform at 126m or the restaurant at 55m, you can enjoy sweeping views of the Grunewald forest and the western city, as well as the **AVUS**, Germany's first car-racing track, which opened in 1921; AVUS stands for Automobil-, Verkehrs- und Übungsstrasse (auto, traffic and practice track). The Nazis made it part of the autobahn system, which it still is today.

⭐**BAR AM STEINPLATZ** COCKTAIL BAR
Map p348 (✆030-554 4440; www.hotelsteinplatz.com; Steinplatz 4; ⏰4pm-late; ⓤErnst-Reuter-Platz) Christian Gentemann's liquid playground at the art-deco Hotel am Steinplatz (p250) was crowned 'hotel bar of the year' in 2016 and 2017, and for good reason The drinks are simply sensational and the ambience a perfect blend of hip and grown-up. The illustrated cocktail menu teases the imagination by listing ingredients and tastes for each drink instead of just an abstract name.

BAR ZENTRAL COCKTAIL BAR
Map p348 (✆030-3743 3079; www.barzentral.de; Lotte-Lenya-Bogen 551; ⏰5pm-late; ⒮Zoologischer Garten, ⓤZoologischer Garten, Kurfürstendamm) A top libation station, Zentral is run

by two local bar gurus who offer up a seriously crafted palette of classics and new-falutin' potions, amid decor that defines elegant understatement. Instead of glowing in a well-lit backbar, bottles discreetly hide in black cabinets that form a nice contrast to the long wooden bar.

MONKEY BAR — BAR

Map p348 (☑030-120 221 210; www.monkeybar berlin.de; Budapester Strasse 40; ◷noon-2am; ⬥; ⬛100, 200, ⬟Zoologischer Garten, ⬤Zoologis-cher Garten) On the 10th floor of the 25hours Hotel Bikini Berlin (p249), the menu at this 'urban jungle' gives prominent nods to tiki concoctions and gin-based cocktail sorcery.

DIENER TATTERSALL — PUB

Map p348 (☑030-881 5329; www.diener-berlin. de; Grolmanstrasse 47; ◷6pm-2am; ⬟Savigny-platz) In business for over a century, this Old Berlin haunt was taken over by German heavyweight champion Franz Diener in the 1950s and became one of West Berlin's iconic artist pubs. From Billy Wilder to Harry Belafonte, they all came for beer and *Bulette* (meat patties) and left behind signed black-and-white photographs that grace Diener's walls to this day.

☆ ENTERTAINMENT

BAR JEDER VERNUNFT — CABARET

Map p348 (☑030-883 1582; www.bar-jeder-vernunft.de; Schaperstrasse 24; admission varies; ⬤Spichernstrasse) Life's still a cabaret at this intimate 1912 mirrored art-nouveau tent the-atre, one of Berlin's most beloved venues for sophisticated song-and-dance shows, come-dy and *chansons* (songs). Sip a glass of bubbly while relaxing at a candlelit cafe table or in a curvy red-velvet booth bathed in flickering candlelight reflected in the mirrors. Many shows don't require German-language skills.

SCHAUBÜHNE — THEATRE

Map p348 (☑030-890 023; www.schaubuehne. de; Kurfürstendamm 153; tickets €7-48; ⬤Ade-nauerplatz) In a converted 1920s expres-sionist cinema by Erich Mendelsohn, Schaubühne is western Berlin's main stage for experimental, contemporary theatre, usually with a critical and analytical look at current social and political issues. The ensemble is directed by Thomas Oster-meier and includes many top names from German film and TV. Some performances feature English or French surtitles.

ZOO PALAST — CINEMA

Map p348 (☑030-254 010; www.zoopalast-berlin.de; Hardenbergstrasse 29a; tickets €9-19; ⬛100, 200, ⬟Zoologischer Garten, ⬤Zoolo-gischer Garten) Old-school glamour meets state-of-the-art technology and comfort at this rejuvenated grand cinema, which saw international stars sashay over the red car-pet during the Berlinale film fest between 1957 and 1999. It screens mostly 2D and 3D blockbusters (dubbed into German) in sev-en theatres. Check out the cool 1950s foyer.

DEUTSCHE OPER BERLIN — OPERA

Map p348 (German Opera Berlin; ☑030-3438 4343; www.deutscheoperberlin.de; Bismarck-strasse 35; tickets €22-128; ⬤Deutsche Oper)

---

❶ HAVE A BLAST ON THE BUS

It's a poorly kept secret that one of Berlin's best bargains is a self-guided city tour aboard **bus 100 or 200**, whose routes check off nearly every major sight in the city centre for the price of a public transport ticket (AB rate, €2.80). You can even get on and off within the two hours of its validity period, as long as you continue in the same direction. If you plan to explore all day, a *Tageskarte* (day pass, €7) is your best bet.

Bus 100 travels from Zoologischer Garten (Zoo Station) to Alexanderplatz, passing the Gedächtniskirche, the Siegessäule in the Tiergarten, the Reichstag, the Brandenburger Tor and Unter den Linden.

Bus 200 also starts at Bahnhof Zoo, and follows a more southerly route via the Kulturforum museums, the Philharmonie and Potsdamer Platz before hooking up with Unter den Linden. Without traffic, trips take about 30 minutes. There's no commen-tary, but it's still useful for orientation and understanding the layout of the central city.

Buses run every few minutes but get crowded, so be wary of pickpockets. To snag a seat on the upper deck, board at either terminus, ie Bahnhof Zoo or Alexanderplatz.

Founded by Berliners in 1912 as a counterpoint to the royal opera on Unter den Linden, the Deutsche Oper presents a classic 19th-century opera repertory from Verdi and Puccini to Wager and Strauss, all sung in their original language. If you like your opera more experimental, check out the Tischlerei (joinery), a studio space for boundary-pushing (and more budget-friendly) musical interpretations.

A-TRANE   JAZZ
Map p348 (☑030-313 2550; www.a-trane.de; Bleibtreustrasse 1; admission varies; ⊙8pm-1am Sun-Thu, to late Fri & Sat; ⑤Savignyplatz) Herbie Hancock and Diana Krall have graced the stage of this intimate jazz club, but mostly it's emerging talent bringing their A-game to the A-Trane. Entry is free on Monday, when local boy Andreas Schmidt and his band get everyone toe-tapping, and after midnight on Saturday for the late-night jam session. Concerts start at 9pm.

🛍 SHOPPING

Kurfürstendamm and Tauentzienstrasse are chock-a-block with outlets of international chains flogging fashion and accessories. Further west on Ku'damm are the more high-end boutiques such as Hermès, Cartier and Bulgari. Kantstrasse is the go-to zone for home designs. Connecting side streets, such as Bleibtreustrasse and Schlüterstrasse, house upscale indie and designer boutiques, bookshops and galleries, while Bikini Berlin features cutting-edge concept and flagship stores.

⭐ MANUFACTUM   HOMEWARES
Map p348 (☑030-2403 3844; www.manufactum. de; Hardenbergstrasse 4-5; ⊙10am-8pm Mon-Fri, to 6pm Sat; ⑤Ernst-Reuter-Platz) 🍃 Long before sustainable became a buzzword, this shop (the brainchild of a German Green Party member) stocked traditionally made quality products from around the world, many of which have stood the test of time. Cool finds include hand-forged iron pans by Turk, lavender soap from a French monastery and Japanese knives by Kenyo.

STILWERK   HOMEWARES
Map p348 (☑030-315 150; www.stilwerk.de/ berlin; Kantstrasse 17; ⊙10am-7pm Mon-Sat;

⑤Savignyplatz) This four-storey temple of good taste will have devotees of the finer things itching to redecorate. Everything you could possibly want for home is here – from key rings to grand pianos and vintage lamps – representing over 500 brands in 55 stores.

BERLINER TRÖDELMARKT   MARKET
Map p348 (☑030-2655 0096; www.berliner-troe delmarkt.de; Strasse des 17 Juni; ⊙10am-5pm Sat & Sun; ⑤Tiergarten) Vendors vie for your euros with yesteryear's fur coats, silverware, jewellery, lamps, dolls, hats and plenty of other stuff one might find in granny's attic. West of Tiergarten S-Bahn station, this is Berlin's oldest flea market (since 1973).

BIKINI BERLIN   MALL
Map p348 (☑030-5549 6455; www.bikiniberlin. de; Budapester Strasse 38-50; ⊙shops 10am-8pm Mon-Sat, Bldg 9am-8.30pm Mon-Sat, noon-6pm Sun; ☎; ⧠100, 200, ⓤZoologischer Garten, ⑤Zoologischer Garten) Germany's first concept mall opened in 2014 in a smoothly rehabilitated 1950s architectural icon nicknamed 'Bikini' because of its design: 200m-long upper and lower sections separated by an open floor, now chastely covered by a glass facade. Inside are three floors of urban indie boutiques, short-lease pop-up 'boxes' for up-and-comers, and an international street-food court.

SUPER CONCEPT SPACE   DESIGN
Map p348 (☑030-2693 0643; www.super-space. de; Budapester Strasse 38-50, Bikini Berlin, 2nd fl; ⊙noon-10pm Mon-Thu, to midnight Fri, 10am-midnight Sat, 10am-4pm Sun (breakfast only); ☎; ⧠100, 200, ⓤZoologischer Garten, ⑤Zoologischer Garten) On the upper floor of the stylish Bikini Berlin concept mall, this 'supermarket' combines design, fashion, food and drinks under one industrial-chic roof. Nose around among limited-edition local and imported brands, before catching some rays over a cold drink and globally inspired sustenance on the breezy terrace with Zoo Berlin views.

KÄTHE WOHLFAHRT   ARTS & CRAFTS
Map p348 (☑09861-4090; www.wohlfahrt.com; Kurfürstendamm 225-226; ⊙10am-6pm Mon-Fri, to 6.30pm Sat; ⓤKurfürstendamm) With its mind-boggling assortment of traditional German Yuletide decorations and ornaments, this shop lets you celebrate Christmas year-round. It's accessed via a ramp that spirals around an 8m-high ornament-laden Christmas tree.

Day Trips from Berlin

Potsdam & Schloss Sanssouci p223

It's practically impossible to not be enchanted by this rambling park and palace ensemble starring Schloss Sanssouci.

Sachsenhausen Concentration Camp p229

The horrors of Nazi Germany become all too real at what's left of one of Germany's oldest former concentration camps.

Spandau p230

Anchored by a delightful Altstadt (old town) and medieval fortress, this northwestern Berlin district flaunts its historic pedigree.

Grunewald & Dahlem p232

Tree-lined streets with mansions and manicured lawns lace Berlin's poshest area, which hugs a big forest dotted with palaces and museums.

Wannsee p233

Hemmed in by the Havel River, Berlin's southwestern-most district counts palaces, forests, swimming beaches and historical sights among its assets.

Köpenick p235

This southeastern suburb cradles Berlin's largest lake, a sprawling forest, a handsome baroque castle and a medieval centre.

TOP SIGHT
POTSDAM & SCHLOSS SANSSOUCI

Potsdam, on the Havel River just 25km southwest of central Berlin, is the capital and crown jewel of the federal state of Brandenburg. Easily reached by S-Bahn, the former Prussian royal seat is the most popular day trip from Berlin, luring visitors with its splendid gardens and palaces, which garnered Unesco World Heritage status in 1990.

Headlining the roll call of royal pads is Schloss Sanssouci, the private retreat of King Friedrich II (Frederick the Great), who was also the mastermind behind many of Potsdam's other fabulous parks and palaces. Most miraculously survived WWII with nary a shrapnel wound. When the shooting stopped, the Allies chose Schloss Cecilienhof for the Potsdam Conference of August 1945 to lay the groundwork for Germany's postwar fate.

Schloss & Park Sanssouci

This glorious park and palace ensemble is what happens when a king has good taste, plenty of cash and access to the finest architects and artists of the day. Sanssouci was dreamed up by Frederick the Great (1712–86) and is anchored by the eponymous palace, which was his favourite summer retreat, a place where he could be *'sans souci'* (without cares).

Schloss Sanssouci

The biggest stunner, and what everyone comes to see, is Schloss Sanssouci, Frederick the Great's famous summer palace. Designed by Georg Wenzeslaus von Knobelsdorff in 1747, the rococo gem sits daintily above vine-draped terraces with the king's grave nearby.

DON'T MISS

➡ Schloss Sanssouci
➡ Chinesisches Haus
➡ View of Sanssouci palace from the fountain at the foot of the vineyard terrace
➡ Grottensaal and Marmorsaal at Neues Palais

PRACTICALITIES

➡ 0331-969 4200
➡ www.spsg.de
➡ Maulbeerallee
➡ day pass to all palaces adult/concession €19/14
➡ varies by palace
➡ 606, 695

INFORMATION

There are two visitors centres at either end of Park Sanssouci: the **Besucherzentrum an der Historischen Mühle** (☑0331-969 4200; An der Orangerie 1; ⊙8.30am-5.30pm Tue-Sun Apr-Oct, to 4.30pm Nov-Mar; ⛆614, 650, 695) near Schloss Sanssouci and the **Besucherzentrum im Neuen Palais** (☑0331-969 4200; Am Neuen Palais; ⊙9am-5.30pm Wed-Mon Apr-Oct, to 4.30pm Nov-Mar; ⛆605, 606, 695).

Regional trains From Berlin Hauptbahnhof and Zoologischer Garten, trains arrive at Potsdam Hauptbahnhof; some continue to Potsdam Charlottenhof and Sanssouci.S-Bahn S7 from central Berlin. Bus 614 and 695 go from Potsdam Hauptbahnhof straight to Schloss Sanssouci.

PARK SANSSOUCI

Park Sanssouci (www. spsg.de; ⊙8am-dusk; ℗; ⛆614, 650, 695) is the oldest and most resplendent of Potsdam's many green patches. It's open from dawn til dusk year-round and is dotted with numerous palaces and outbuildings.

Standouts on the tours (guided or self-guided) include the **Konzertsaal** (Concert Hall), whimsically decorated with vines, grapes and even a cobweb where sculpted spiders frolic. The king himself gave flute recitals here. Also note the intimate **Bibliothek** (library), lidded by a gilded sunburst ceiling, where the king would seek solace amid 2000 leather-bound tomes ranging from Greek poetry to the latest releases by his friend Voltaire. Another highlight is the **Marmorsaal** (Marble Room), an elegant white Carrara marble symphony modelled after the Pantheon in Rome.

As you exit the palace, note the **Ruinenberg**, a pile of fake classical ruins looming in the distance.

Bildergalerie

The **Picture Gallery** (Gallery of Old Masters; ☑0331-969 4200; www.spsg.de; Im Park Sanssouci 4; adult/concession €6/5; ⊙10am-5.30pm Tue-Sun May-Oct; ⛆650, 695) shelters Frederick the Great's prized collection of Old Masters, including such pearls as Caravaggio's *Doubting Thomas*, Anthony van Dyck's *Pentecost* and several works by Peter Paul Rubens. Behind the rather plain facade hides a sumptuous symphony of gilded ornamentation, yellow and white marble and a patterned stone floor that is perhaps just as impressive as the mostly large-scale paintings that cover practically every inch of wall space.

Neue Kammern

The **New Chambers** (☑0331-969 4200; www.spsg.de; Park Sanssouci; adult/concession incl tour or audioguide €6/5; ⊙10am-5.30pm Tue-Sun Apr-Oct; ⛆614, 650, 695), built by Knobelsdorff in 1748, were originally an orangery and later converted into a guest palace. The interior drips with rococo opulence, most notably the square **Jasper Hall**, which is drenched in precious stones and lidded by a Venus fresco, and the **Ovidsaal**, a grand ballroom with gilded wall reliefs depicting scenes from Ovid's *Metamorphosis*.

Chinesisches Haus

The 18th-century fad for the Far East is strongly reflected in the adorable **Chinese House** (☑0331-969 4200; www.spsg.de; Am Grünen Gitter; adult/concession €4/3; ⊙10am-5.30pm Tue-Sun May-Oct; ⛆605, 606, ⛴91). The cloverleaf-shaped pavilion is among the park's most photographed buildings thanks to its enchanting exterior of exotically dressed, gilded figures shown sipping tea, dancing and playing musical instruments amid palm-shaped pillars. Inside is a precious collection of Chinese and Meissen porcelain.

Potsdam

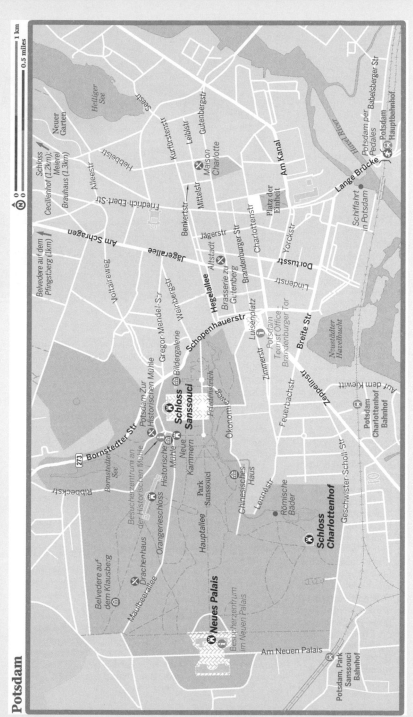

N
0   1 km
0   0.5 miles

Heiliger See

Neuer Garten

Schloss Cecilienhof (1.2km); Meierei Brauhaus (1.3km)

Belvedere auf dem Pfingstberg (1km)

Seestr

Gutenbergstr

Leiblstr

Kurfürstenstr

Hebbelstr

Alleestr

Friedrich-Ebert-Str

Am Schragen

Voltaireweg

Jägerallee

Benkertstr

Mittelstr

Maison Charlotte

Am Kanal

Jägerstr

Altstadt

Brasserie zu Gutenberg

Weinbergstr

Gregor-Mendel-Str

Hegelallee

Schopenhauerstr

Brandenburger Str

Charlottenstr

Platz der Einheit

Lange Brücke

Schiffahrt in Potsdam

Potsdam Hauptbahnhof

Potsdam per Pedales

Babelsberger Str

Bildergalerie

Potsdam Zur Historischen Mühle

Schloss Sanssouci

Luisenplatz

Potsdam Tourist Office

Brandenburger Tor

Yorckstr

Dortustr

Lindenstr

Breite Str

Zimmerstr

Havel River

Bornstedter Str

Historische Mühle

Neue Kammern

Ökonomieweg

Friedenskirche

Feuerbachstr

Neustädter Havelbucht

Ribbeckstr

Bornstedter See

273

Besucherzentrum an der Historischen Mühle

Orangerieschloss

Chinesisches Haus

Lennéstr

Zeppelinstr

Potsdam Charlottenhof Bahnhof

Auf dem Kiewitt

Belvedere auf dem Klausberg

Drachenhaus

Maulbeerallee

Hauptallee

Park Sanssouci

Römische Bäder

Schloss Charlottenhof

Geschwister-Scholl-Str

Neues Palais

Besucherzentrum im Neuen Palais

Am Neuen Palais

Potsdam, Park Sanssouci Bahnhof

TOP TIPS

➡ Book your timed ticket to Schloss Sanssouci online to avoid wait times and/or disappointment.

➡ Avoid visiting on Monday when most palaces are closed.

➡ The sanssouci+ ticket, a one-day pass to palaces in Potsdam, costs €19 (concession €14) and is sold online and at each building.

➡ Picnicking is permitted throughout the park, but cycling is limited to Ökonomieweg and Maulbeerallee.

➡ There's a fee (€3 per day) for taking pictures *(Fotoerlaubnis)* inside the palaces.

➡ Palaces are fairly well spaced – it's almost 2km between the Neues Palais and Schloss Sanssouci.

A relaxing way to enjoy Potsdam is from the deck of a cruise boat (www.schiffahrt-in-potsdam.de). The most popular trip is the 90-minute Schlösserundfahrt palace cruise (€16); there's also a two-hour tour to Lake Wannsee (€17) and a three-hour trip around several Havel lakes (€18). Boats depart from the docks below the Mercure Hotel. English commentary available.

Neue Kammern (p224)

Orangerieschloss

Modelled after an Italian Renaissance villa, the 300m-long, 1864-built **Orangery Palace** (☑0331-969 4200; www.spsg.de; An der Orangerie 3-5; adult/concession €6/5, tower €3/2; ⊙10am-5.30pm Tue-Sun May-Oct, 10am-5.30pm Sat & Sun Apr; ▣695) was the favourite building project of Friedrich Wilhelm IV – a passionate Italophile. Its highlight is the **Raffaelsaal** (Raphael Hall), which brims with 19th-century copies of the famous painter's masterpieces. The greenhouses are still used for storing potted plants in winter. The tower can be climbed for so-so views.

Belvedere auf dem Klausberg

Frederick the Great's final building project was this temple-like **belvedere** (☑0331-969 4200; www. spsg.de; An der Orangerie 1; ⊙open for special events only; ▣695), modelled on Nero's palace in Rome. The panorama of park, lakes and Potsdam is predictably fabulous from up here. The upstairs hall has an impressive frescoed dome, oak parquet and fanciful stucco marble but, alas, it can be seen during special events only.

Historische Mühle

This reconstructed 18th-century Dutch-style **windmill** (Historic Windmill; ☑0331-550 6851; www.spsg.de; Maulbeerallee 5; adult/concession €4/3; ⊙10am-6pm daily Apr-Oct, to 4pm Sat & Sun Nov & Jan-Mar; ▣; ▣650, 695) contains exhibits about the history of the mill and mill technology, and offers a close-up look at the grinding mechanism and a top-floor viewing platform.

According to legend, Frederick the Great ordered its owner to demolish the original mill because of the noise. However, when the miller refused and threatened to go to court, the king acquiesced.

Neues Palais

The final palace commissioned by Frederick the Great, the **Neues Palais** (New Palace; ☑0331-969 4200; www.spsg.de; Am Neuen Palais; adult/concession incl tour or audioguide €8/6; ⏱10am-5.30pm Mon & Wed-Sun Apr-Oct, to 5pm Nov-Dec, to 4.30pm Jan-Mar; 🚌605, 606, 695, ⑤Potsdam Charlottenhof) has made-to-impress dimensions, a central dome and a lavish exterior capped with a parade of sandstone figures. The interior attests to the high level of artistry and craftwork of the 18th century. It's an opulent symphony of ceiling frescoes, gilded stucco ornamentation, ornately carved wainscotting and fanciful wall coverings alongside paintings (by Antoine Pesne, for example) and elaborately crafted furniture.

The palace was built in just six years, largely to demonstrate the undiminished power of the Prussian state following the bloody Seven Years' War (1756–63). The king himself rarely camped out here, preferring the intimacy of Schloss Sanssouci and using it for representational purposes only. Only the last German Kaiser, Wilhelm II, used it as a residence, until 1918.

After extensive restoration, most of the building's highlights are once again accessible, including the shell-festooned **Grottensaal** (Grotto Hall) festival hall and the magnificent **Marmorsaal** (Marble Hall), where visitors walk across a raised pathway to protect the precious marble floor illuminated by eight massive crystal chandeliers. Also looking splendid is the redone **Unteres Fürstenquartier** (Lower Royal Suite), which consists of a concert room, an oval-shaped chamber, an antechamber and, most impressively, a dining room with walls sheathed in red silk damask with gold-braided trim.

EATING & DRINKING

Brasserie zu Gutenberg (☑0331-7403 6878; www.brasserie-zu-gutenberg.de; Jägerstrasse 10; mains €9-28; ⏱noon-midnight; 🚌604, 609, 638, 🚋92, 96) This charming little brasserie with dark-wood tables and chocolate-brown banquettes is great for a quick bite of quiche and coffee or for a hearty meal, perhaps featuring the signature coq au vin and a glass of fine Bordeaux.

Meierei Brauhaus (☑0331-704 3211; www.meierei-potsdam.de; Im Neuen Garten 10; mains €9-15; ⏱noon-9pm Tue-Sat, to 7pm Sun; 🚌603 to Höhenstrasse) The Berlin Wall once ran right past this brewpub, where the beer garden invites you to count the boats sailing on the Jungfernsee in summer. The hearty dishes are a perfect match for the delicious craft beers, including the classic Helles (pale lager) and seasonal suds brewed on the premises. In summer, try its Weizen (wheat beer) and the top-fermented Berliner Weisse.

Maison Charlotte (☑0331-280 5450; www.maison-charlotte.de; Mittelstrasse 20; Flammkuchen €8.50-14.50, mains €24.50-25.50, 3-/4-course menus €44/53; ⏱noon-11pm; 🚌604, 609, 638, 🚋92, 96) There's a rustic lyricism to the French country cuisine in this darling Dutch Quarter bistro, no matter whether your appetite runs towards a simple *Flammkuchen* (Alsatian pizza), Breton fish soup or a multicourse menu. Budget bon vivants come for the daily lunch special (€7.50), which includes a glass of wine and is best enjoyed on the patio in summer.

VIEWS

For splendid views over Potsdam and surrounds, ascend the spiralling wrought-iron staircases of the twin-towered **Belvedere auf dem Pfingstberg** (☎0331-2005 7930; www.pfingstberg.de; Pfingstberg; adult/concession €4.50/3.50, audioguides €1; ⊙10am-6pm daily Apr-Oct, to 4pm Sat & Sun Mar & Nov; 🅿; 🚌92, 96), commissioned by Friedrich Wilhelm IV and modelled on an Italian Renaissance-style villa. There's a small exhibit chronicling the history of the building and the 1801 Pomonatempel just below it. The latter was Karl Friedrich Schinkel's very first architectural commission at age 19.

Potsdam per Pedales (www.potsdam-per-pedales.de, right by the Potsdam train station, rents quality bicycles and offers guided and self-guided bike tours. If you want to see more of Potsdam than Park Sanssouci, a bike is ideal.

The pair of lavish buildings behind the Schloss is called the **Communs**. It originally housed the palace servants and kitchens and is now part of Potsdam University.

Restoration is now underway at the **Schlosstheater** (theatre), which will keep it closed for some time. Check its status online.

Schloss Charlottenhof

The jewel of Park Charlottenhof, this small **palace** (☎0331-969 4200; www.spsg.de; Geschwister-Scholl-Strasse 34a; tours adult/concession €6/5; ⊙tours 10am-5.30pm Tue-Sun May-Oct; 🚌605, 606, 610, X5, 🚌91, 94, 98) started out as a baroque country manor before being expanded by Karl Friedrich Schinkel for Friedrich Wilhelm IV in the late 1820s. The building is modelled on classical Roman villas and features a Doric portico and a bronze fountain. Russian landscape architect Peter Joseph Lenné designed the surrounding gardens, creating a harmonious blend of architecture and nature. Schinkel also designed much of the Biedermeier-style furniture.

Römische Bäder

Karl Friedrich Schinkel, aided by his student Ludwig Persius, dreamed up the so-called **Roman Baths** (☎0331-969 4200; www.spsg.de; Park Charlottenhof; adult/concession €5/4; ⊙10am-5.30pm Tue-Sun May-Oct; 🚌605, 606, 610, X5, 🚌91, 94, 98) in Park Charlottenhof. Despite the name, it's actually a romantic cluster of 15th-century Italian country-estate buildings, complete with vine-draped pergola.

Alas, the entire ensemble is in poor condition and will soon undergo extensive restoration that may keep it closed for some time.

Museum Barberini

The original **Barberini Palace** (www.museum-barberini.com; Alter Markt, Humboldtstrasse 5-6; adult/concession/under 18 €14/10/free; ⊙10am-7pm Wed-Mon, 1st Thu of month to 9pm; 🚌91, 92, 93, 96, 99 Alter Markt/Landtag) was a baroque Roman palazzo commissioned by Frederick the Great and bombed to bits in World War II. Since January 2017, a majestic replica has added a new jewel to Potsdam's already bursting cultural landscape. It houses a **private art museum**, funded by German software impresario Hasso Plattner, and mounts three high-calibre exhibits per year with an artistic arc that spans East German works, Old Masters and modern greats such as Gerhard Richter.

Sachsenhausen Concentration Camp

....

Explore

Sachsenhausen was built by prisoners and opened in 1936 as a prototype for other concentration camps. By 1945 about 200,000 people had passed through its sinister gates, initially mostly political opponents, but later also gypsies, gays, Jews and, after 1939, POWs from eastern Europe, especially the Soviet Union. Tens of thousands died here from hunger, exhaustion, illness, exposure, medical experiments and executions. Thousands more succumbed during the death march of April 1945, when the Nazis evacuated the camp in advance of the Red Army. Note the memorial plaque to these victims as you walk towards the camp (at the corner of Strasse der Einheit and Strasse der Nationen).

....

Top Tip

Between mid-October and mid-March, avoid visiting on a Monday when all indoor exhibits are closed.

....

Getting There & Away

S-Bahn & Train The S1 makes the trip thrice hourly from central Berlin (eg Friedrichstrasse station) to Oranienburg (ABC ticket €3.40, 45 minutes). Hourly regional RE5 and RB12 trains leaving from Hauptbahnhof are faster (ABC ticket €3.40, 30 minutes). The camp is about 2km from the Oranienburg train station. Turn right onto Stralsunder Strasse, right on Bernauer Strasse, left on Strasse der Einheit and right on Strasse der Nationen. Alternatively, bus 804 makes hourly trips from the station straight to the site (use the same ticket as for the train, seven minutes).

....

Need to Know

Area Code ☑03301

Location About 35km north of central Berlin.

◉ SIGHTS

Unless you're on a guided tour of the camp, officially called **Gedenkstätte und Museum Sachsenhausen** (Memorial & Museum Sachsenhausen; ☑03301-200 200; www.stiftung-bg.de; Strasse der Nationen 22, Oranienburg; ◉8.30am-6pm mid-Mar–mid-Oct, to 4.30pm mid-Oct–mid-Mar, museums closed Mon mid-Oct–mid-Mar; Ⓟ; ⑤Oranienburg) FREE, pick up a leaflet (€0.50) or, better yet, an audioguide (€3, including leaflet) at the visitor centre to get a better grasp of this huge site.

The approach to the camp takes you past photographs taken during the death march and the camp's liberation in April 1945. Just beyond the perimeter, the Neues Museum (New Museum) has exhibits on Sachsenhausen's precursor, the nearby Oranienburg concentration camp, in a repurposed brewery, and on the history of the memorial site during the GDR-era (1950 to 1990).

Proceed to Tower A, the entrance gate, cynically labelled, as at Auschwitz, Arbeit Macht Frei (Work Sets You Free). It houses an exhibit on the organisation of the concentration camp and its architectural layout. Beyond here is the roll-call area, with barracks and other buildings fanning out beyond. Off to the right, two restored barracks illustrate the abysmal living conditions prisoners endured. Barrack 38 has an exhibit on Jewish inmates, while Barrack 39 graphically portrays daily life at the camp. The prison next door was an especially sinister place of torture and murder. Famous inmates included Hitler's would-be assassin Georg Elser and the anti-Nazi minister Martin Niemöller, author of the First They Came... poem.

Moving towards the centre, the Prisoners' Kitchen chronicles key moments in the camp's history. Exhibits include instruments of torture, the original gallows that stood in the roll-call area and, in the cellar, heart-wrenching artwork scratched into the wall by prisoners.

The most sickening displays, though, are about the extermination area called Station Z, which was separated from the rest of the grounds and consisted of an execution trench, a crematorium and a gas chamber. The most notorious mass executions took place in autumn 1941 when more than 10,000 Soviet POWs were executed here in the course of four weeks.

DAY TRIPS FROM BERLIN SACHSENHAUSEN CONCENTRATION CAMP

In the far right corner, a modern building and two original barracks house the Soviet Special Camp exhibit, which documents Sachsenhausen's stint as Speciallager No 7, a German POW camp run by the Soviets from 1945 until 1950. About 60,000 people were held here; some 12,000 of them died, mostly of malnutrition and disease. After 1950, Soviet and East German military used the grounds for another decade until the camp became a memorial site in 1961.

Exhibits in the original infirmary barracks on the other side of the roll-call area illustrate the camp's poor medical care and the horrific medical experiments performed on prisoners. One section focuses on the men and women incarcerated in Sachsenhausen after the failed assassination attempt on Hitler on 20 July 1944.

EATING & DRINKING

There is no food is available at the memorial site, although a vending machine in the Neues Museum dispenses hot drinks. You are allowed to bring food and drink with you. There are cafes, bakeries and small markets outside Oranienburg train station.

Spandau

Explore

Spandau is a charming mash-up of green expanses, rivers, industry and almost rural residential areas wrapped around a medieval core famous for its 16th-century bastion, the Zitadelle Spandau (Spandau Citadel). Older than Berlin by a few years, Spandau sits at the confluence of the Havel and Spree and thrived as an independent city for nearly eight centuries; it only became part of Berlin in 1920. To this day, its people still talk about 'going to Berlin' when heading to any other city district. Nearly all sights are handily clustered in and around the Altstadt. The suburb of Gatow, with the Military History Museum, is about 10km south of here.

The Best...

Sight Zitadelle Spandau (p230)
Place to Eat Satt und Selig (p231)
Place to Drink Brauhaus Spandau (p232)

Top Tip

In summer, big international acts like Billy Idol, Lana del Rey and Limp Bizkit gig to appreciative audiences alfresco during the Citadel Music Festival (www.citadel-musicfestival.de). Year-round concerts take place in the Gothic Hall.

Getting There & Away

U-Bahn The recommended route is via the U7, which travels from central Berlin to Spandau in about 30 minutes (€2.80, AB tariff) and stops at the Zitadelle, the Altstadt and the Rathaus.

S-Bahn The S3 makes the trip to central Spandau in about 30 to 40 minutes.

Need to Know

Area Code ☏030

Location About 13km northwest of central Berlin.

Tourist Office (☏030-333 9388; www.partner-fuer-spandau.de; Breite Strasse 32; ☺10am-6pm Mon-Sat Apr-Sep, 10am-6pm Tue-Fri & 10am-2pm Sat Oct, Nov, Jan-Mar, 10am-6pm daily Dec; ⓢSpandau, ⓤAltstadt Spandau)

◉ SIGHTS

★ZITADELLE SPANDAU   CASTLE
(Spandau Citadel; ☏030-354 9440; www.zitadelle-berlin.de; Am Juliusturm 64; adult/concession €4.50/2.50, audioguide €2; ☺10am-5pm, last entry 4.30pm; ⓤZitadelle) The 16th-century Spandau Citadel, on a little island in the Havel River, is considered one of the world's best-preserved Renaissance fortresses. With its moat, drawbridge and arrowhead-shaped bastions, it is also a veritable textbook in military architecture. These days, the impressive complex multitasks as museum, cultural venue and wintering ground for thousands of bats. Climb the 30m-high Julius Tower for sweeping

---

WORTH A DETOUR

MILITARY AVIATION HISTORY ON THE RUNWAY

•••

Operated by the Bundeswehr (the armed forces of Germany), the **Militärhis-torisches Museum – Flugplatz Berlin-Gatow** (Museum of Military History – Airfield Berlin-Gatow; ☑030-3687 2601; www.mhm-gatow.de; Am Flugplatz Gatow 33; ☉10am-6pm Tue-Sun; ℗; ⌨135) is a fascinating destination for fans of aviation, technology, history and the military. It spreads its wings over a military airfield used by both the Nazis and the Royal Air Force. Exhibits in the control tower and two hangars focus on various aspects of aerial warfare with plenty of old planes, air defence guns and engines on display.

More than 100 fighter jets, bombers, helicopters and weapons systems litter the runway, including such gems as WWI biplanes, a Russian MiG-21, a Messerschmitt ME-163 Komet and a GDR-era Antonov An-14.

The museum is about 10km south of central Spandau. Take bus 135 from S- or U-Bahn Rathaus Spandau to 'Kurpromenade', then walk for 1km.

---

views. Top international artists perform at the Citadel Music Festival in summer.

There are permanent exhibits on the history of the fortress, the history of Spandau in general and of political monuments that were once part of Berlin's urban landscape. A highlight is the head of the Lenin statue that once graced Platz der Vereinten Nationen in Friedrichshain.

NIKOLAIKIRCHE   CHURCH
(Church of St Nicholas; ☑030-333 5639; www.nikolai-spandau.de; Reformationsplatz 6; tower €2; ☉noon-4pm Mon-Fri, 11am-4pm Sat, 11.30am-4pm Sun, tower tours 12.30pm Sat, 12.30pm 1st & 3rd Sun Apr-Oct; ⓤAltstadt Spandau) The Gothic Church of St Nicholas is famous for hosting Brandenburg's first public Lutheran-style worship service back in 1539, under elector Joachim II whose bronze statue stands outside the church. Inside, important treasures include a baptismal font (1398), a baroque pulpit (1714) and a late-Renaissance altar (1582). Time your visit with a trip up the 77m-high tower.

GOTISCHES HAUS   HISTORIC BUILDING
(☑030-333 9388; www.gotischeshaus.de; Breite Strasse 32; ☉10am-6pm Mon-Sat, noon-6pm Sun; ⓤAltstadt Spandau) FREE Whoever built the Gothic House in the 15th century must have been flush with cash; it's made of stone, not wood as was customary in those times. The well-preserved Altstadt gem is one of the oldest surviving residential buildings in Berlin. It houses an art gallery and the tourist office on the ground floor

(note the ornate net-ribbed vaulted ceiling) and there's a new city history exhibit open upstairs.

The 13 upstairs rooms document living styles and conditions in Spandau through the centuries. Check out the Biedermeier-era living room and late-19th-century kitchen.

KOLK   AREA
(ⓤAltstadt Spandau) Separated from the Altstadt by the busy Strasse am Juliusturm, the Kolk quarter was the site of Spandau's first settlement and exudes medieval village flair with its romantic narrow lanes, crooked, half-timbered houses and 78m-long section of town wall. Its key sight is the church of **St Marien am Behnitz** (☑030-353 9630; Behnitz 9; ☉2-5pm) FREE, which is now privately owned and used as a concert venue.

✖ EATING & DRINKING

SATT UND SELIG   INTERNATIONAL €€
(☑030-3675 3877; www.sattundselig.de; Carl-Schurz-Strasse 47; mains €8-29; ☉9am-11pm; ⌨; ⓤAltstadt Spandau) In a baroque half-timbered house in the historic centre, this local favourite gets things right from morning to night. The breakfast selection is legendary, the cakes homemade and the main dishes (including steaks from the lava grill) creative, fresh and ample. In summer, terrace tables spill out onto the pedestrian zone. Kids' menu available.

DAY TRIPS FROM BERLIN SPANDAU

BRAUHAUS SPANDAU BEER GARDEN
(☎030-353 9070; www.brauhaus-spandau.de; Neuendorfer Strasse 1; ◷10am-midnight Sun-Thu, to 1am Fri & Sat; ⓤAltstadt Spandau) In good weather there are few nicer places to while away a few hours in central Spandau than in the tree-canopied beer garden of this brewery located in a historical red-brick building. On tap are the Spandauer Havelbräu as well as monthly changing seasonal brews; accompany them with hearty German pub grub (mains €10 to €16).

Grunewald & Dahlem

Explore

Berlin's most upper-crust neighbourhoods, Dahlem and Grunewald are packed with cultural and natural appeal. Set between their leafy streets and lavish villa colonies (especially around Grunewald S-Bahn station) are gardens, parks, palaces and a sprinkling of museums, most of them with an art focus. After WWII, the area was part of the American sector, a legacy reflected in such institutions as the AlliiertenMuseum (Allied Museum) and the hulking US Consulate. The Grunewald forest, a vast fresh-air refuge criss-crossed by paths and dotted with lakes extending all the way west to the Havel River, offers a respite from the city. Wild boar, deer and other animals make their home here.

The Best...

Sight Brücke-Museum (p232)
Place to Eat & Drink Luise (p233)

Top Tip

Berlin's vast **botanical gardens** (☎030-8385 0100; www.bgbm.org; Königin-Luise-Strasse 6-8; adult/concession garden & museum €6/3, museum only €2.50/1.50; ◷gardens 9am-8pm, greenhouses & museum to 7pm; ℗; ⑤Botanischer Garten) boast 22,000 plant species and are an inspirational spot to reconnect with nature.

Getting There & Away

U-Bahn The U3 meanders through this area, with key stops being Dahlem-Dorf for the museums and Krumme Lanke for easy access to the southern Grunewald forest.

S-Bahn The S1 skirts southern Dahlem, while the S7 runs straight through the Grunewald forest.

Need to Know

Area Code ☎030

Location About 11km southwest of central Berlin.

⊙ SIGHTS

BRÜCKE-MUSEUM GALLERY
(☎030-831 2029; www.bruecke-museum.de; Bussardsteig 9; adult/concession €6/4; ◷11am-5pm Wed-Mon; ℗; ⓤOskar-Helene-Heim, then bus 115 to Pücklerstrasse) In 1905 Karl Schmidt-Rottluff, Erich Heckel and Ernst Ludwig Kirchner founded Germany's first modern-artist group, called Die Brücke (The Bridge). Rejecting traditional techniques taught in the academies, they experimented with bright, emotional colours and warped perspectives that paved the way for German expressionism and modern art in

---

TRACKS OF DEATH

Between 1941 and 1942, more than 50,000 Jewish Berliners were deported from **Mahnmal Gleis 17** (Platform 17 Memorial; www.memorialmuseums.org; Am Bahnhof Grunewald; ◷24hr; ⑤Grunewald) next to the S-Bahn station Grunewald. Some 186 trains left for Theresienstadt, Rīga, Łódź and Auschwitz, carrying their Jewish cargo like cattle to the slaughter. In their honour, memorial plaques recording the departure dates, number of people and destinations of the trains have been fastened to the edge of the platform. It's quiet here, with only the trees rustling in the breeze, but the silence speaks loudly.

general. Schmidt-Rottluff's personal collection forms the core of this lovely presentation of expressionist art.

A visit here is easily combined with the nearby Kunsthaus Dahlem (combination tickets €8/5).

KUNSTHAUS DAHLEM   GALLERY
(☏030-832 227 258; www.kunsthaus-dahlem. de; Käuzchensteig 8; adult/concession/under 19 €6/4/free; ◷11am-5pm Wed-Mon; Ⓟ; ⓤOskar-Helene-Heim, then bus 115 or X10) This private art museum in the monumental studio of Nazi-era sculptor Arno Breker presents modernist works created in Germany in the years between WWII and the construction of the Berlin Wall in 1961. While artists in West Germany embraced abstraction, in the East social realism emerged as the guiding principle. Although sculpture is the primary focus, photographs, paintings and drawings provide additional dimensions, as do four temporary exhibits per year mounted in the upstairs galleries.

A visit here is easily combined with the nearby Brücke-Museum (combination tickets €8/5).

ALLIIERTENMUSEUM BERLIN   MUSEUM
(Allied Museum; ☏030-818 1990; www.alliierten museum.de; Clayallee 135; ◷10am-6pm Tue-Sun; Ⓟ; ⓤOskar-Helene-Heim) ⓕⓇⒺⒺ The original Checkpoint Charlie guard cabin, a Berlin Airlift plane and a reconstructed spy tunnel are among the dramatic exhibits at the Allied Museum, which documents historic milestones and the challenges faced by the Western Allies during the Cold War. There's also a survey of events leading to the collapse of communism and the fall of the Berlin Wall. An original piece of the Wall sits in the yard.

There are plans to move the museum to Tempelhof Airport, although no specific date has been set.

'BERLIN BRAIN'   ARCHITECTURE
(Philological Library; ☏030-8385 8888; www. fu-berlin.de/sites/philbib; Habelschwerdter Allee 45; ◷9am-10pm Mon-Fri, 10am-8pm Sat & Sun; ⓤThielplatz) ⓕⓇⒺⒺ British architect Norman Foster was the brain behind the 'Berlin Brain', a cranial-shaped 2005 masterpiece of modern architecture that houses the Freie Universität Berlin's Philological Library. Inside are four floors sheltered within a naturally ventilated, bubble-like

enclosure draped in aluminium and glazed panels. An inner membrane of translucent glass fibre filters the daylight, while scattered transparent openings allow momentary glimpses of the sky.

✖ EATING & DRINKING

LUISE   INTERNATIONAL €€
(☏030-841 8880; www.luise-dahlem.de; Königin-Luise-Strasse 40-42; pizza €7-15, mains €10-24; ◷10am-1am; 🛜🚼; ⓤDahlem-Dorf) This cafe-restaurant-beer-garden combo is a Dahlem institution with a long menu likely to please everyone from salad heads to schnitzel fiends to pizza punters. Scrumptious breakfasts are served until 2pm and there are seven beers on tap to enjoy beneath the chestnut trees. Children can romp around in a playground.

RISTORANTE GALILEO   ITALIAN €€
(☏030-831 2377; www.ristorantegalileo.de; Otto-von-Simson-Strasse 26; mains €6.50-16.50; ◷10am-10pm Mon-Fri; 🛜; ⓤDahlem-Dorf) On the edge of the Free University campus, Galileo has plied students, faculty and clued-in locals with cheap, authentic Italian fare since 1990. If homemade pasta and pizza don't do it for you, go for the daily specials, which might feature grilled tuna or rosemary-scented lamb filet.

Wannsee

•••

Explore

Leafy Wannsee, Berlin's southwesternmost suburb, is named for the enormous Wannsee lake, which is really just a bulge in the Havel River. In fine weather, it's a fantastic place to leave the city bustle behind. You can cruise around the lake, walk in the forest, visit an enchanting island, tour a Prussian palace and work on your tan in the Strandbad Wannsee, a lakeside lido with a 1km-long sandy beach, or at one of the area's other quick-dip spots. On the western edge of the lake (and easily reached by bus) are a couple of major sights, one linked to the Nazis and one to the painter Max Liebermann.

The Best...

Sight Liebermann-Villa am Wannsee (p234)

Place to Eat & Drink Loretta am Wannsee (p235)

Top Tip

For cruising on the cheap, catch the 20-minute ride on public transport ferry F10 from Wannsee to the Spandau suburb of Alt-Kladow (AB rate, €2.80).

Getting There & Away

S-Bahn Take S1 or S7 from central Berlin to Wannsee, then walk or continue by bus depending on where you're headed.

Need to Know

Area Code ⚐030

Location About 25km southwest of central Berlin.

◉ SIGHTS

LIEBERMANN-VILLA
AM WANNSEE   MUSEUM

(⚐030-8058 5900; www.liebermann-villa.de; Colomierstrasse 3; adult/concession/under 14 €8/5/free, multimedia guide €4.50; ⊙10am-6pm Wed-Mon Apr-Sep, 11am-5pm Wed-Mon Oct-Mar; Ⓢ Wannsee, then bus 114) This lovely villa was the summer retreat of German impressionist painter and Berliner Secession founder Max Liebermann from 1909 until his death in 1935. Liebermann loved the lyricism of nature and often painted the gardens as seen through the window of his barrel-vaulted upstairs studio. A selection of these works is on permanent display along with a timeline of the artist's life and impact.

The beautifully restored gardens consist of three hedge gardens – shaped like a circle, a square and an oval – and are flanked by beech trees. Drink in the glorious views over coffee and cake from the terrace of the villa's Wannsee-facing **Cafe Max**. Bus 114 makes the trip to the villa several times hourly from the S-Bahn station Wannsee.

PFAUENINSEL   PARK

(Peacock Island; ⚐030-8058 6830; www.spsg. de; Nikolskoer Weg; adult/concession ferry return €4/3, Meierei €3/2; ⊙ferry 9am-8pm May-Aug, shorter hours Sep-Apr, Meierei 10am-5.30pm Sat & Sun Apr-Oct; Ⓢ Wannsee, then bus 218) 'Back to nature' was the dictum in the 18th century, so Friedrich Wilhelm II had this little Havel island turned into an idyllic playground, perfect for retreating from state affairs and for frolicking with his mistress in a snowy-white fairy-tale palace (closed for renovation). For added romance, he brought in a flock of peacocks that gave the island its name; you'll find the eponymous birds strutting their stuff to this day.

Even with the palace closed, Pfaueninsel makes for a lovely excursion. A standout among the smattering of other buildings is the **Meierei**, a dairy farm in the shape of a ruined Gothic monastery at the island's northern end.

The island is a nature preserve, so no smoking, cycling or swimming. There are no cafes or restaurants but picnicking is allowed. The island is about 4km northwest of the Wannsee S-Bahn station, from where bus 218 goes to the ferry dock several times hourly.

HAUS DER
WANNSEE-KONFERENZ   MEMORIAL

(⚐030-805 0010; www.ghwk.de; Am Grossen Wannsee 56-58; ⊙10am-6pm; Ⓢ Wannsee, then bus 114) **FREE** In January 1942 a group of 15 high-ranking Nazi officials met in a stately villa near Lake Wannsee to hammer out details of the Final Solution, the systematic deportation and murder of European Jews. The 13-room exhibit (in German and English) in the very rooms where discussions took place illustrates the sinister meeting; it also examines the racial policies and persecution leading up to it and such issues as how aware ordinary Germans were of the genocidal actions.

You can study the actual minutes of the meeting (taken by Adolf Eichmann) and look at photographs of those involved, many of whom lived to a ripe old age. The site is about 2.5km northwest of Wannsee S-Bahn station and served from there by bus 114 several times hourly.

SCHLOSS GLIENICKE   PALACE

(⚐030-8058 6750; www.spsg.de; Königstrasse 36; palace tours adult/concession €6/5; ⊙10am-5.30pm Tue-Sun Apr-Oct, to 5pm Sat & Sun Nov, to 4pm Sat & Sun Mar; Ⓟ; Ⓢ Wannsee, then bus 316) Glienicke Palace is the result of a rich

DAY TRIPS FROM BERLIN WANNSEE

IN & ON THE WANNSEE

Stern und Kreisschiffahrt – Wannsee Cruise (⌲030-536 3600; www.sternundkreis.de; Ronnebypromenade; 2hr cruise adult/child €12.50/6.30; ⊙hourly 10.30am-5.30pm Apr–mid-Oct; ⑤Wannsee) From April to mid-October, Stern und Kreisschiffahrt operates two-hour cruises around seven lakes from landing docks near Wannsee S-Bahn station.

Strandbad Wannsee (⌲030-2219 0011; www.berlinerbaeder.de/baeder/strandbad-wannsee; Wannseebadweg 25; adult/concession €5.50/3.50; ⊙10am-7pm May & Sep, 9am-8pm Jun-Aug, last entry 1hr before closing; ⑤Nikolassee) This lakeside public beach has delighted aquaphiles for more than a century. Although 1km long, the broad sandy strip can get very busy on hot days, especially on weekends. Besides swimming, you can rent boats, play volleyball, basketball or table tennis or grab a snack or drink. Note that the northern end of the beach is reserved for nude bathing.

The Strandbad is about 1.3km northwest of the *S-Bahn* station Nikolassee. Walk north on Borussenstrasse, then turn left onto Wannseebadweg.

royal kid travelling to Italy and falling in love with the country. Prince Carl of Prussia (1801–83) was only 21 when he returned to Berlin giddy with dreams of building his own Italian villa, so he hired starchitect du jour Karl Friedrich Schinkel to turn an existing garden estate into an elegant, antique looking compound. You can visit the richly decorated interior with marble fireplaces, sparkling chandeliers, gold-framed paintings and fine furniture.

The turquoise bedroom of the princess and the midnight-blue library are especially memorable. Schinkel not only expanded the mansion, but added a smaller guesthouse (the 'Casino') and two charming pavilions, the **Kleine Neugierde** ('Small Curiosity') and **Grosse Neugierde** ('Great Curiosity'). The latter sits in an especially scenic spot overlooking the Havel River, Schloss Babelsberg and the outskirts of Potsdam. The palace is about 6km west of *S-Bahn* station Wannsee and served several times hourly by bus 316.

✕ EATING & DRINKING

LORETTA AM WANNSEE　　　GERMAN €€
(⌲030-8010 5333; www.loretta-berlin.de; Kronprinzessinnenweg 260; beer garden snacks €3.50-9, restaurant €14-26; ⊙noon-10pm or later; ℗; ⑤Wannsee) Robust Bavarian cooking is the focus of the menu at this traditional but updated restaurant with an enchanting beer garden overlooking Wannsee lake. Have a grilled sausage in the beer garden, a crisp salad or go the whole hog with

Grillhaxe (pork leg) braised in black beer. König Pilsner, Augustiner and Erdinger are on tap.

It's about 300m south of Wannsee S-Bahn station.

RESTAURANT SEEHAASE　INTERNATIONAL €€
(⌲030-8049 6474; www.restaurant-seehaase.de; Am Grossen Wannsee 58; mains €8-16.50; ⊙11am-9pm Mon-Thu, to 10pm Fri, 10am-10pm Sat, 10am-9pm Sun; ℗ ♿; ⑤Wannsee, then bus 114) Most of the Wannsee waterfront lots are in private hands, so the Seehaase with its lake views is justifiably popular. The menu covers all the bases, from breakfast to pasta, *Flammkuchen* (tarte flambée) to grilled fish and meat plus a few dishes calibrated to kids' tastes.

The restaurant is very close to the Haus der Wannsee-Konferenz.

Köpenick

Explore

The southeastern Berlin suburb of Köpenick was founded around 1240, making it only three years younger than the capital itself. A 20-minute S-Bahn ride away from the city centre, it's famous for its handsome baroque palace, a picturesque Altstadt and a trio of superlative natural assets: Berlin's largest lake (Müggelsee), biggest forest (Köpenicker Stadtforst) and highest natural elevation (Müggelberge, 115m). A leisurely ramble, relaxed boat ride or cooling dip in the water quickly restores balance to a brain overstimulated by life in the city or sightseeing overload.

Many of the cobblestone streets in the Altstadt still follow their medieval layout. The main street, called Alt-Köpenick, is lined with baroque beauties and the historic Rathaus.

Urban trendspotters, meanwhile, might want to keep an eye on developments in Oberschöneweide, a one-time industrial area northwest of central Köpenick that's slowly showing up on the radar of artists and digital creatives.

The Best...

Sight Schloss Köpenick (p236)

Place to Eat & Drink Ratskeller Köpenick (p237)

Top Tip

For a more in-depth understanding of Köpenick's history, take a self-guided tour with the help of a multimedia audioguide (€5) dispensed by the tourist office.

Getting There & Away

S-Bahn For the Altstadt, take the S3 to S-Bahn station Köpenick, then walk 1.5km south along Bahnhofstrasse or take tram 62 to the Schloss Köpenick. For the Müggelsee continue on the S3 to Friedrichshagen and then take tram 60 or walk 1.5km south on Bölschestrasse.

Need to Know

Area Code ☑030

Location About 16km southeast of central Berlin.

Tourist Office (☑030-655 7550; www.tkt -berlin.de; Alt-Köpenick 31-33, enter on Grünstrasse; ☺9am-6pm Mon-Fri, 10am-1pm Sat; 🚌62, ⑤Köpenick)

◉ SIGHTS

SCHLOSS KÖPENICK   PALACE
(Museum of Decorative Arts; ☑030-266 424 242; www.smb.museum; Schlossinsel 1; adult/concession/under 18 €6/3/free; ☺11am-6pm Tue-Sun Apr-Sep, to 5pm Thu-Sun Oct-Mar; 🚌62,

⑤Köpenick) Berlin's only surviving baroque palace, on a little island off the Altstadt, houses a branch of Berlin's **Kunstgewerbemuseum** (Museum of Decorative Arts). It's a rich and eclectic collection of furniture, tapestries, porcelain, silverware, glass and other frilly objects from the Renaissance, baroque and rococo periods. Note elaborate ceiling paintings and stucco ornamentation. Highlights include four lavishly panelled rooms and the recreated **Wappensaal** (Coat of Arms Hall).

It was in this very hall in 1730 that a military court sentenced Crown Prince Friedrich (later Frederick the Great) and his friend Hans Katte to death for attempted desertion. The future king was eventually spared but forced by his father, the 'Soldier King', to watch his friend's beheading.

RATHAUS KÖPENICK   HISTORIC BUILDING
(Town Hall; Alt-Köpenick 21; ☺10am-5.30pm; 🚌62, ⑤Köpenick) FREE With its frilly turrets, soaring tower and stepped gable, Köpenick's town hall exudes fairy-tale charm but is actually more famous for an incident that happened back in 1906. An unemployed cobbler named Wilhelm Voigt, costumed as an army captain, marched upon the town hall, arrested the mayor, confiscated the city coffers and disappeared with the loot. Although quickly caught, Voigt became a celebrity for his chutzpah. A bronze statue and an exhibit recall the story, which is re-enacted every summer.

GROSSER MÜGGELSEE   LAKE
(🚌60, ⑤Friedrichshagen) At 4km long and 2.5km wide, the Müggelsee is Berlin's largest lake. Hemmed in by forest on two sides, it's hugely popular for swimming and boating on hot summer days. It's easily reached by public transport in less than an hour from central Berlin.

The Müggelpark on its north shore has restaurants and beer gardens as well as the landing docks of **Reederei Kutzker** (☑03362-6251; www.reederei-kutzker.de; Müggelpark, Müggelseedamm; 1hr tours €7; ☺tours Apr-early Oct), which runs lake tours several times daily.

For a walk in the woods, head to the other side of the Spree via the nearby Spreetunnel. **Seebad Friedrichshagen** (☑030-645 5756; www.seebad-friedrichshagen.de; Müggelseedamm 216; adult/concession €5.50/3; ☺10am-7pm May-Aug) is the closest public lake beach and

WORTH A DETOUR

DEUTSCH-RUSSISCHES MUSEUM BERLIN-KARLSHORST

On 8 May 1945, the madness of six years of WWII in Europe ended with the unconditional surrender of the Wehrmacht (armed forces of Germany) in the headquarters
of the Soviet army, which today houses a **memorial exhibit** (German-Russian Museum
Berlin-Karlshorst; ✆030-5015 0810; www.museum-karlshorst.de; Zwieseler Strasse 4;
⊙10am-6pm Tue-Sun; Ⓢ Karlshorst) that charts this fateful day and the events leading
up to it from both the Russian and German perspectives.

Documents, photographs, uniforms and knick-knacks illustrate such topics as the
Hitler-Stalin Pact, the daily grind of life as a WWII Soviet soldier and the fate of Soviet
civilians during wartime. You can stand in the great hall where the surrender was
signed and see the office of Marshal Zhukov, the first Soviet supreme commander
after WWII when the building was the seat of the Soviet Military Administration. Outside is a battery of Soviet weapons, including a Howitzer canon and the devastating
Katjuscha multiple rocket launcher, also known as the 'Stalin organ'.

The museum is a 10- to 15-minute walk from the S-Bahn station; take the Treskow-
allee exit, then turn right onto Rheinsteinstrasse.

has boat rental; it's about 300m west of the
Müggelpark.

✖ EATING & DRINKING

RATSKELLER KÖPENICK   GERMAN €€
(✆030-655 5178; www.ratskellerkoepenick.
de; Alt-Köpenick 21, Rathaus; mains €8-28;
⊙11am-11pm Mon-Sat, to 10pm Sun; ◻62, 68,
Ⓢ Köpenick) The olde-worlde ambience at
this cellar-warren in the local town hall
is fun, and the menu full of classic rib-
stickers (try the smoked pork knuckle)
alongside healthier, seasonal and meatless
selections. Many ingredients are locally
sourced. Reservations advised for the Friday and Saturday live-jazz nights.

KROKODIL   MEDITERRANEAN €€
(✆030-6588 0094; www.der-coepenicker.de;
Gartenstrasse 46-48, mains €11-18, ⊙4-11pm Mon-
Thu, to midnight Fri, 3pm-midnight Sat, 11am-11pm
Sun; Ⓟ; ◻62, 68, Ⓢ Köpenick) The seasonal
fare at this urban getaway is delish, but even
more memorable is the idyllic setting on the
Dahme River some 700m south of the Altstadt. Join locals in capping a day of lounging on Krokodil's beach with a leisurely sunset dinner or book ahead for the legendary
Sunday brunch. The attached **guesthouse**
(www.hotel-pension-berlin.eu; tw from €89; ➾;
◻62, 62 Schlossplatz Köpenick) has twin rooms.

From S-Bahn station Köpenick take tram
62 or 68 to Schlossplatz, then walk east on
Müggelheimer Strasse for 300m and turn
south on Kietz for another 400m.

🛏 Sleeping

Berlin offers the gamut of places to unpack your suitcase. Just about every international chain now has an offering in the German capital, but more interesting options that better reflect the city's verve and spirit abound. You can sleep in a former bank, boat or factory, in the home of a silent-movie diva or in a 'flying bed'.

Hotels

With around 142,000 beds in 795 properties, Berlin has more beds than New York and even more are scheduled to come online in the coming years. You'll find the entire range of hotels in Berlin, from no-frills cookie-cutter chains to all-out luxury abodes with top-notch amenities and fall-over-backwards service.

The best beds often sell out early, so make reservations, especially around major holidays, cultural events and trade shows. Most properties can be booked online, usually with a best-price guarantee.

Most smaller and midsize hotels are now entirely nonsmoking; a few of the larger ones (especially the international chains) still set aside rooms or entire floors for smokers.

BOUTIQUE, DESIGNER & ART HOTELS

Berlin being an art- and design-minded city, it's not surprising that there's a large number of smaller indie hotels catering to the needs of savvy urban nomads with at least a midrange budget. Properties often integrate distinguished architecture with a customised design concept that projects a sense of place and tends to appeal to creative spirits and travellers searching for an authentic and localised experience. There's usually great emphasis on the latest tech trends and on such lifestyle essentials as iPod docks and brand-name espresso machines and sound systems. The antithesis of cookie-cutter chains, these types of abodes are sprinkled around the city but are especially prevalent in the Mitte district. Many

have succeeded in cultivating the local community with hip rooftop lounges, cocktail bars, progressive restaurants, chic spas and pop-up parties and events.

CHAIN HOTELS

Practically all international hotel chains now have one or multiple properties in Berlin. Since most conform to certain standards of decor, service and facilities, they're great for people who enjoy predictability and privacy (or simply want to use up those frequent flyer points). Most have several categories of comfort, from cramped singles to high-roller suites, with rates reflecting size and amenities. Prices generally fluctuate dramatically, with last-minute, weekend or low-occupancy bargains a possibility.

Besides the international hotel chains, there are also some Berlin-based contenders, including Amano (www.amanogroup.de) and Meininger (www.meininger-hotels.com) and German chains like Motel One (www.motelone.com) and Leonardo (www.leonardo-hotels.com).

Hostels

Berlin's hostel scene is as vibrant as ever and consists of both classic backpacker hostels with large dorms and a communal spirit to modern 'flashpacker' crash pads catering to wallet-watching city-breakers. Quite common by now are hostel-hotel hybrids that have a standard similar to budget hotels. Many also have private quarters with bathrooms and even apartments with kitchens. You'll find them in all districts, but especially in Mitte and Kreuzberg, putting you within stumbling distance of bars and clubs.

Dorm beds can be had for as little as €10, but the better places now charge twice as much or more for dorms with fewer beds and en suite bathroom. Dorms tend to be mixed, though some hostels also offer women-only units. Hostels have no curfew and staff tend to be savvy, multilingual and keen to help with tips and advice.

Short-Term Rentals

Renting a furnished flat is a hugely popular – and economical – lodging option. The benefit of space, privacy and independence makes flats especially attractive to families and small groups. Alas, since May 2016 a new law has cracked down on peer-to-peer rentals such as those offered through Airbnb or Wimdu, meaning the supply of legal short-term rental apartments has dwindled significantly.

If you're planning to stay in the city for a month or longer, renting a room or an apartment might be the most sensible option. Try the online platform www.zwischenmiete.de.

Rates

Fierce competition has kept prices low compared to other capital cities in Europe. Prices spike during major trade shows, festivals and public holidays, when early reservations are essential. Business-traveller-geared hotels often have good deals at weekends. In winter, prices plummet outside holidays, with five-star rooms costing as little as €120. Throughout the year, the lowest rates of the week are for Sunday nights.

Amenities

Midrange options generally offer the best value for money. Expect clean, comfortable and decent-sized rooms with at least a modicum of style, a private bathroom, TV and wi-fi. Top-end hotels provide the full

> ### SMOKING
>
> Smoking rooms are a dying breed. Larger properties and chain hotels are most likely to have set aside floors with rooms where smoking is permitted. Smaller independent hotels and hostels usually don't allow smoking in rooms and may impose fines on those who light up anyway. By law, there's no smoking in indoor public areas.

spectrum of international-standard amenities and perhaps a scenic location, designer decor or historical ambience. Budget places are generally hostels or other simple establishments where bathrooms may be shared.

Overall, rooms tend to be on the small side. You'll usually find that BBC and CNN are the only English-language channels on TV (nearly all foreign shows and films are dubbed into German) and that air-con is a rare commodity. Wi-fi is commonplace and almost always free, but in rare cases access may be restricted to public areas. Few hotels have their own parking lot or garage, and even if they do, space will be limited and the cost as high as €30 per day. Public garages are widely available, but also cost a pretty penny.

Useful Websites

Lonely Planet (lonelyplanet.com/germany/hotels) Lonely Planet's online booking service with insider low-down on the best places to stay.

Visit Berlin (www.visitberlin.de) Official Berlin tourist office; books rooms at partner hotels with a best-price guarantee.

Boutique Hotels Berlin (www.boutiquehotels-berlin.com) Booking service for about 20 hand-picked boutique hotels.

Berlin30 (www.berlin30.com) Online low-cost booking agency for hotels, hostels, apartments and B&Bs in Berlin.

NEED TO KNOW

Price Ranges
The following price ranges refer to a standard double room with private bathroom during high season but outside of major events, holidays or trade-show periods. Rates include 7% VAT but not the 5% city tax. Breakfast is sometimes included, but more often than not is an optional extra.

€	less than €90
€€	€90–€180
€€€	more than €180

City Tax
Value-added tax (VAT; 7%) has long been included in room rates, but since 1 January 2014 an additional 5% 'city tax' is payable on the net room rates, eg excluding VAT and fees for amenities and services. The tax is added to the hotel bill. Business travellers are exempt from this tax.

Which Floor?
In Germany, 'ground floor' refers to the floor at street level. The 1st floor (what would be called the 2nd floor in the US) is the floor above that.

Lonely Planet's Top Choices

Orania Hotel (p246) Urban-chic pad for individualists and style lovers with top-rated restaurant and live music.

Capri by Fraser (p242) Apartment hotel with roomy digs, cool bar and archaeological excavations.

Michelberger Hotel (p247) Fun base with eccentric design, party pedigree and unpretentious attitude that beautifully captures the Berlin vibe.

Das Stue (p243) Charismatic refuge with understated grandeur and the Tiergarten park as a front yard.

EastSeven Berlin Hostel (p248) Small, personable and spotless crash pad perfect for making new friends.

Hotel am Steinplatz (p250) Golden 1920s glamour still radiates from the listed walls of this revivified art-deco jewel.

Best By Budget: €

Grand Hostel Berlin Classic (p246) Connect to the magic of yesteryear at this historic lair imbued with both character and modern amenities.

Wombat's Berlin (p244) Fun seekers should thrive at this well-run hostel with hip in-house bar.

EastSeven Berlin Hostel (p248) Friendly and low-key hostel with communal vibe ideal for solo travellers.

Best By Budget: €€

Circus Hotel (p245) Perennial pleaser thanks to being a perfect synthesis of style, comfort, location and value.

Orania Hotel (p246) Culturally minded style pad with superb restaurant and live concerts.

Adina Apartment Hotel Berlin Checkpoint Charlie (p242) An ideal base for budget-conscious space-craving self-caterers.

Best By Budget: €€€

Mandala Hotel (p243) All-suite city slicker with uncluttered urban feel and top eats.

Hotel am Steinplatz (p250) Reincarnated art-deco jewel with top bar and restaurant.

Hotel de Rome (p242) Posh player in fa ormer bank building with a rooftop bar and bank vault spa.

Best Cool Factor

Michelberger Hotel (p247) Zeitgeist-capturing crash pad with funky industrial DIY aesthetics and popular restaurant.

Soho House Berlin (p246) Members-only club with A-lister clientele-meets-posh boutique hotel in Bauhaus building.

25hours Hotel Bikini Berlin (p249) Inner-city playground overlooking the Berlin Zoo.

nhow Berlin (p248) Karim Rashid–designed riverside hotel with guitar rentals and recording studio.

Casa Camper (p246) Crash pad for creatives in the heart of Scheunenviertel hipsterville.

Best Hostels

Wombat's Berlin (p244) Old-school sociable hostel with mod cons in a central location.

Circus Hostel (p244) A a superb launch pad for fun-seekers and culture cravers.

Plus Berlin (p247) Next-gen hostel with pool in stumbling distance of bar and club central.

Grand Hostel Berlin Classic (p246) Historic lair with nostalgic flair.

Where to Stay

NEIGHBOURHOOD	FOR	AGAINST
Historic Mitte	Close to major sights like Reichstag and Brandenburger Tor; great transport links; mostly high-end hotels; Michelin-starred and other top restaurants; close to theatre, opera and classical concert venues	Touristy, expensive, pretty dead at night
Museumsinsel & Alexanderplatz	Supercentral sightseeing quarter; easy transport access; close to blockbuster sights and mainstream shopping; large and new hotels	Noisy, busy and dusty thanks to major construction; hardly any nightlife
Potsdamer Platz & Tiergarten	Urban flair in Berlin's only high-rise quarter; cutting-edge architecture; high-end international hotels; top museums, Philharmonie and multiplex cinemas; next to huge Tiergarten city park	Limited eating options; pricey; practically no street life at night
Scheunenviertel	Hipster quarter; trendy, historic, central; brims with boutique and designer hotels; superb indie and trendy chain shopping; international eats and strong cafe scene; top galleries and plenty of street art	Pricey, busy in daytime, noisy, no parking, touristy
City West & Charlottenburg	The former heart of 'West Berlin'; great shopping at KaDeWe and on Kurfürstendamm; stylish lounges, 'Old Berlin' bars and quality restaurants; best range of good-value lodging; historic B&Bs	Sedate; far from key sights and happening nightlife
Kreuzberg & Neukölln	Vibrant arty, underground and multicultural party quarter; best for bar-hopping and clubbing; high-vibe; great foodie scene; excellent street art	Gritty, noisy and busy; U-Bahn ride(s) away from major sights
Friedrichshain	Student and young family quarter; bubbling nightlife; superb Cold War–era sights	Limited sleeping options; not so central for sightseeing; transport difficult in some areas
Prenzlauer Berg	Well-heeled, clean, charming residential area; lively cafe and restaurant scene; indie boutiques and Mauerpark flea market	Limited late-night action, few essential sights

SLEEPING

🛏 Historic Mitte

★ADINA APARTMENT HOTEL BERLIN
CHECKPOINT CHARLIE   APARTMENT $$
Map p328 (📞030-200 7670; www.adinahotels.
com; Krausenstrasse 35-36; studio/1-bedroom
apt from €120/145; P❄@🛜🏊🍽; Ⓤ Stadtmitte, Spittelmarkt) Adina's contemporary
one- and two-bedroom, stylishly functional
apartments with full kitchens are tailor-
made for cost-conscious families, anyone
in need of elbow room, and self-caterers
(a supermarket is a minute away). Roomy
studios with kitchenette are also available.
The spa area with its 17m-long indoor pool
and sauna helps combat post-flight fatigue.
Optional breakfast is €19.

COSMO HOTEL BERLIN   HOTEL $$
Map p328 (📞030-5858 2222; www.cosmo-
hotel.de; Spittelmarkt 13; d €90-270; P❄🏊🛜;
Ⓤ Spittelmarkt) Despite its ho-hum location
on a busy street, this privately owned hotel scores high for comfort, design and a
'with it' vibe. The lobby, with its extravagant lamps and armchairs, sets the tone for
crisply angular rooms with silvery design
accents and floor-to-ceiling windows. The
excellent organic breakfast buffet is €18.

HOTEL DE ROME   LUXURY HOTEL $$$
Map p328 (📞030-460 6090; www.roccoforte
hotels.com; Behrenstrasse 37; d from €280;
P❄@🛜🏊🍽; 🅿100, 200, TXL, Ⓤ Hausvogteiplatz) A delightful alchemy of history
and contemporary flair, this luxe contender
in a 19th-century bank has sumptuously
furnished, large rooms with extra-high ceilings, marble baths and heated floors. Wind
down in the former vault that is now the
pool and spa area, over cocktails in the bar
or, in summer, on the rooftop terrace. Optional breakfast is €38.

HOTEL ADLON KEMPINSKI   LUXURY HOTEL $$$
Map p328 (📞030-226 10; www.kempinski.
com; Unter den Linden 77, Pariser Platz; r from
€290; P❄🏊🛜🍽; ⓈBrandenburger Tor,
ⓊBrandenburger Tor) The Adlon has been
Berlin's most high-profile defender of the
grand tradition since 1907. The striking
lobby with its signature elephant fountain
is a mere overture to the full symphony of
luxury awaiting in spacious, amenity-laden
rooms and suites with timelessly regal decor. The nicest ones overlook the Brandenburg Gate. Optional breakfast is €42.

🛏 Museumsinsel & Alexanderplatz

HOSTEL ONE80°   HOSTEL $
Map p332 (📞030-2804 4620; www.one80
hostels.com; Otto-Braun-Strasse 65; dm €17-30;
🚭@🛜; ⒮Alexanderplatz, Ⓤ Alexanderplatz)
With its designer sofas, ambient music and
industrial-chic public areas, One80° is a
next-gen lifestyle hostel. There's space for
over 700 people in dorms (some with private bathroom) sleeping four to eight in
comfy bunk beds with individual reading
lamps and two electrical outlets each. Lin-
en included. Optional breakfast is €6.90.
Minimum age 18.

MOTEL ONE BERLIN-
HACKESCHER MARKT   HOTEL $$
Map p332 (📞030-2005 4080; www.motel-one.
de; Dircksenstrasse 36; d from €90; P🚭❄🛜🍽;
⒮Alexanderplatz, Ⓤ Alexanderplatz) If you value location over luxury, this budget designer chain comes with excellent crash-pad
credentials. Smallish rooms feature sleek
touches (granite counters, rain showers,
air-con) that are normally the reserve of
posher players. Arne Jacobsen's turquoise
egg chairs add hipness to the lobby. Check
the website for the other eight Berlin locations. Optional breakfast is €9.50.

RADISSON BLU HOTEL   HOTEL $$
Map p332 (📞030-238 280; www.radisson
blu.com/hotel-berlin;   Karl-Liebknecht-Strasse
3; d from €150; P🚭❄@🛜🏊🍽; 🅿100, 200,
⒮Hackescher Markt) At this swish and supercentral contender, you quite literally
sleep with the fishes, thanks to the lobby's
25m-high tropical aquarium. Streamlined
design radiates urban poshness in the 427
rooms and throughout the two restaurants
and various social nooks. Thoughtful perks
include a 24/7 spa with pool and sauna. Optional breakfast is €25.

CAPRI BY FRASER   APARTMENT $$
Map p332 (📞030-20 07 70 1888; https://berlin.
capribyfraser.com; Scharrenstrasse 22; r from
€150; P🚭❄🛜🍽; ⓊSpittelmarkt) These 143
self-catering studios and one-bedroom
apartments on Museumsinsel (Museum
Island) are a sweet fusion of substance
and style. Smartly laid-out rooms come
with plenty of closet space, iPod docks and
kitchenettes, and there's a guest laundry,
bar and restaurant on site. In the lobby, a

glass floor covers medieval foundations unearthed during construction.

PARK INN BY RADISSON BERLIN
ALEXANDERPLATZ   HOTEL **$$**
Map p332 (☑030-238 90; www.parkinn-berlin.de; Alexanderplatz 7; d from €100; 🅿🤝❄@📶📺; Ⓢ Alexanderplatz, ⓊAlexanderplatz) Views, views, views! Berlin's tallest hotel has got them. Right on Alexanderplatz, this sleek tower is honeycombed with 1012 modern and stylish rooms (some rather snug) sporting charcoal-and-white hues, panoramic windows, wooden floors and noiseless aircon. For superb sunsets, snag a room facing the Fernsehturm (TV Tower).

HOTEL INDIGO
ALEXANDERPLATZ   HOTEL **$$**
Map p332 (☑030-505 0860; www.hotelindigo berlin.com/alex; Bernhard-Weiss-Strasse 5; d €90-150; 🤝❄📶📺; Ⓢ Alexanderplatz, ⓊAlexanderplatz) Sophisticated, efficient and super-central, this hotel spoils you with amenities normally reserved for pricier abodes (fluffy bathrobes, smartphone docks, espresso coffee makers). Contemporary rooms feature designer furniture, plank flooring, local imagery and pleasing colour accents; standard ones are rather snug. Free landline calls to 19 countries. Breakfast is €19.

ART'OTEL BERLIN MITTE   HOTEL **$$**
Map p332 (☑030-240 620; www.artotels.de; Wallstrasse 70-73; d from €125; 🅿🤝❄📶📺; ⓊMärkisches Museum) This newly renovated boutique hotel wears its 'art' moniker with justifiable swagger: more than 300 original works by renowned contemporary German artist Georg Baselitz decorate rooms and public areas. Suites have extra-cool bathrooms and those on the 6th floor even boast small balconies. The hotel is docked to the rococo Ermelerhaus, which harbours a modern Mediterranean restaurant. Optional breakfast is €19.50.

🛏 Potsdamer Platz & Tiergarten

SCANDIC BERLIN
POTSDAMER PLATZ   HOTEL **$$**
Map p326 (☑030-700 7790; www.scandichotels.com; Gabriele-Tegit-Promenade 19; d from €130; 🅿🤝❄📶📺; ⓊMendelssohn-Bartholdy-Park) 🌿 This Scandinavian import gets kudos for its central location and spacious blond-wood rooms with box-spring beds, panoramic windows with black out curtains and for going the extra mile when it comes to being green. Distinctive features include the good-sized 8th-floor gym-with-a-view, honey from the rooftop beehive and free bikes. Optional (partly organic) breakfast is €14.

MÖVENPICK HOTEL BERLIN   HOTEL **$$**
Map p326 (☑030-230 060; www.moevenpick.com; Schöneberger Strasse 3; d from €130; 🅿🤝❄@📶📺; Ⓢ Anhalter Bahnhof) 🌿 This snazzy Green Globe–certified hotel smoothly marries contemporary boldness with the industrial flair of the listed Siemenshöfe factory. Rooms vamp it up with cheerful colours and sensuous olive-wood furniture, while the courtyard restaurant is lidded by a retractable glass roof for alfresco dining. Light sleepers should ask about the special 'Sleep' rooms. Optional breakfast is €18.

GRIMM'S POTSDAMER PLATZ   HOTEL **$$**
Map p326 (☑030-258 0080; www.grimms-hotel.de; Flottwellstrasse 45; d €80-200; 🅿🤝📶📺; ⓊMendelssohn-Bartholdy-Park) The fairy tales of the Brothers Grimm inspired the name and the decor of this cosmopolitan crash pad, which remains mercifully uncluttered and kitsch-free. The 110 rooms feature the latest upscale touches such as floor-heating, box-spring mattresses and an eco-conscious heating and cooling system. The sauna (€12 usage fee) and rooftop terrace are popular regeneration areas. Optional breakfast is €14.

★DAS STUE   BOUTIQUE HOTEL **$$$**
Map p326 (☑030-311 7220; www.das-stue.com; Drakestrasse 1; d from €300; 🅿🤝❄@📶🏊📺; 🚌100, 106, 200) This charismatic refuge in a 1930s Danish diplomatic outpost flaunts understated grandeur and has the Tiergarten park as a front yard. A crocodile sculpture flanked by sweeping staircases fluidly leads the way to a hip bar (p137), a Michelin-starred restaurant and sleekly furnished and oversized rooms (some with terrace or balcony). The elegant spa has a pool, a sauna and top-notch massages.

Optional breakfast is €35. Guests have free admission to the Berlin Zoo.

★MANDALA HOTEL   HOTEL **$$$**
Map p326 (☑030-590 051 221; www.themandala.de; Potsdamer Strasse 3; ste from €180; 🅿🤝❄@📶; 🚌200, Ⓢ Potsdamer Platz, ⓊPotsdamer Platz) How 'suite' it is to be staying at this sophisticated yet unfussy cocoon.

Uncluttered, zeitgeist-compatible units come in 10 sizes (40 to 200 sq metres) and are equipped with a kitchenette, walk-in closets and spacious desks in case you're here to ink that deal. Day spa and 24/7 fitness centre for relaxation, plus on-site two-Michelin-star restaurant, Facil (p135). Breakfast is €30.

RITZ-CARLTON BERLIN   LUXURY HOTEL $$$

Map p326 (☑030-337 777; www.ritzcarlton. com; Potsdamer Platz 3; d €150-450; P✳❋@☎❖☎; S Potsdamer Platz, U Potsdamer Platz) In a building modelled on the Rockefeller Center in New York City, the Ritz-Carlton makes a grand statement with newly renovated art deco–inspired digs with mood lighting and marble bathrooms. Expect all the trappings of a big-league player, including high-end restaurant Desbrosses (p136), a couple of bars including the plush Curtain Club (p136), a spa and extensive Ritz Kids program. Optional breakfast is €38. Wi-fi is free in the lobby only.

🛏 Scheunenviertel

★ WOMBAT'S BERLIN   HOSTEL $

Map p334 (☑030-8471 0820; www.wombats-hostels.com/berlin; Alte Schönhauser Strasse 2; dm/d from €17/60; ❀@☎; U Rosa-Luxemburg-Platz) Sociable and central, Wombat's gets hostelling right. From backpack-sized in-room lockers to individual reading lamps and a guest kitchen with dishwasher, the attention to detail here is impressive. Spacious and clean en-suite dorms are as much part of the deal as free linen and a welcome drink, best enjoyed with fellow party pilgrims at sunset in the rooftop bar.

CIRCUS HOSTEL   HOSTEL $

Map p334 (☑030-2000 3939; www.circus-berlin.de; Weinbergsweg 1a; dm from €19, d without/with bathroom €58/75; ❀@☎; U Rosenthaler Platz) Clean, cheerfully painted singles, doubles and dorms (sleeping three to 10) plus abundant shared facilities, helpful staff and a great location are among the factors that have kept Circus at the top of the hostel heap for two decades. There's a cute on-site cafe (with breakfast until 1am) and a basement bar with its own craft brewery and lots of events.

CIRCUS HOTEL   HOTEL $$

Map p334 (☑030-2000 3939; www.circus-berlin.de; Rosenthaler Strasse 1; d/apt from €89/120; P❀@☎; U Rosenthaler Platz) At this supercentral budget boutique hotel, none of the compact, mod rooms are alike, but all feature upbeat colours, thoughtful design touches, a tea station and organic

---

TOP FIVE FURNISHED APARTMENTS

For self-caterers, independent types, families and anyone wanting extra privacy, a short-term furnished-apartment rental may well be the cat's pajamas.

Miniloft Berlin (Map p336; ☑030-847 1090; www.miniloft.com; Hessische Strasse 5; apt €135-185, 2 night minimum; P❀☎; U Naturkundemuseum) ✔ These eight modern architect-designed lofts come with designer furniture, cozy alcoves, kitchenettes and other feel-good features.

Brilliant Apartments (Map p338; ☑030-8061 4796; www.brilliant-apartments.de; Oderberger Strasse 38; apt from €93; ❀☎❖; U Eberswalder Strasse) Exposed brick walls and shiny wooden floors characterise these 11 flats with kitchens big enough to whip up gourmet meals.

Berlin Lofts (☑0151 2121 9126; www.berlinlofts.com; various locations; studio from €57, apt from €140; ❀☎) Sleep in a horse barn, a Harley-Davidson garage, a former forge or another cleverly converted old building when booking an apartment through this outfit.

Old Town Apartments (Map p338; ☑030-5471 3890; www.ota-berlin.de; check-in Metzer Strasse 8; studio/apt from €85/125; ⊙reception 9am-7pm Mon-Fri, 10am-4pm Sat & Sun; ❀☎; 🚊M2, U Senefelder Platz) Minimalist chic in modern apartments of various sizes in a historic Berlin townhouse and in a new building with lift.

Gorki Apartments (Map p334; ☑030-4849 6480; www.gorkiapartments.de; Weinbergsweg 25; apt €148-364; P❀✳☎❖; 🚊M1, 12, U Rosenthaler Platz) Finely furnished in a mash-up of modern and vintage, these luxury apartments with kitchens are centrally located.

bath products. Unexpected perks include a roof terrace (with yoga classes), bike rentals and a fabulous breakfast buffet (€9) served in the hugely popular Commonground cafe. Need more space? Go for an apartment.

HOTEL HONIGMOND
BOUTIQUE HOTEL **$$**

Map p336 (☑030-284 4550; www.honigmond. de; Tieckstrasse 12; d €120-170; [P][⊕][@][�]; [U]Oranienburger Tor) This delightful hotel scores a perfect 10 on our 'charm-o-meter', not for being particularly lavish, but for its familiar yet elegant ambience. The restaurant is a local favourite and rooms sparkle in colonial-style glory. The nicest are in the new wing and flaunt their historic features – ornate stucco ceilings, frescoes, parquet floors – to maximum effect. Breakfast €12.

HONIGMOND GARDEN
BOUTIQUE HOTEL **$$**

Map p336 (☑030-2844 5577; www.honigmond-berlin.de; Invalidenstrasse 122; r €107-167; [P][⊕][@][риф]; [U]Naturkundemuseum, [S]Nordbahn hof) Despite its location on a busy thoroughfare, this 20-room guesthouse built in 1845 is an utterly sweet retreat. Reach your comfortable, classically styled rooms via an enchanting garden with koi pond, chirping birds, and rich foliage and flowers. Days start with a sumptuous breakfast (€12) in the winter garden. Avoid rooms facing the road.

HOTEL AMANO
HOTEL **$$**

Map p334 (☑030-809 4150; www.amanogroup. de; Auguststrasse 43; d €70-165, apt €90-185; [P][⊕][₩][риф][≋]; [U]Rosenthaler Platz) This sleek, budget, designer hotel has efficiently styled, mod-con-laden rooms, where white furniture teams up with oak floors and grey hues to create crisp cosiness. For space-cravers there are apartments in three sizes and with kitchens. Optional breakfast buffet for €15.

FLOWER'S
BOARDINGHOUSE MITTE
APARTMENT **$$**

Map p334 (☑030-2804 5306; www.flowers berlin.de; Mulackstrasse 1; 1-2-bedroom apt from €105/145; ☉reception 9am-6pm; [⊕][риф]; [U]Weinmeisterstrasse, Rosa-Luxemburg-Platz) Self-caterers won't miss many comforts of home in these 21 breezy self-catering apartments available in three sizes – L, XL and XXL – the last being a split-level unit with fabulous views over the rooftops. Units come with open kitchens and TV/DVD; rates include a small breakfast (rolls, coffee, tea) that you pick up at reception.

BOUTIQUE HOTEL I31
BOUTIQUE HOTEL **$$**

Map p336 (☑030-338 4000; www.hotel-i31. de; Invalidenstrasse 31; r €100-190; [P][⊕][₩][риф]; [U]Naturkundemuseum) This contemporary contender has modern, if smallish, rooms in soothing colours and various relaxation zones, including a sauna, a sunny terrace and a small garden with sun lounges. Nice touch: the minibar with free soft drinks. For a little more space and luxury (designer bath products, for example) book a 'comfort room plus' on one of the upper floors. Breakfast €20.

ARTE LUISE KUNSTHOTEL
BOUTIQUE HOTEL **$$**

Map p336 (☑030-284 480; www.luise-berlin. com; Luisenstrasse 19; d €89-299, with shared bathroom €53-119; [P][⊕][₩][@][риф]; [S]Friedrichstrasse, [U]Friedrichstrasse) At this 'gallery with rooms' each of the 50 units was designed by a different artist, who receive royalties whenever it's rented. All sport high ceilings, oak floors and wonderfully imaginative, poetic or bizarre decor – we're especially fond of number 107 with its giant bed. For cash-strapped art fans there are smaller rooms with shared baths. Avoid those facing the train tracks. Breakfast €15.

HOTEL ZOE
DESIGN HOTEL **$$**

Map p334 (☑030-2130 0150; www.amanogroup. de; Grosse Präsidentenstrasse 7; r €64-174; [⊕][₩][риф][≋]; [🚇]M1, M4, M5, [S]Hackescher Markt) Central, stylish and affordable – this urban lifestyle outpost ticks all the boxes for a great short city getaway. The vanilla-and-chocolate colour scheme and hardwood flooring in the rooms are simple yet elegant. Enjoy city views from the rooftop terrace or a classy cocktail at the retro-styled **G&T Bar** (Map p334; Grosse Präsidentenstrasse 6-7; ☉6pm-late; [риф]). Breakfast €15.

MONBIJOU HOTEL
HOTEL **$$**

Map p334 (☑030-6162 0300; www.monbijou hotel.com; Monbijouplatz 1; r €72-180; [P][⊕][@][риф]; [🚇]M1, [S]Hackescher Markt) The sleek Monbijou is a handy urban crash pad. Except for the corner suites, rooms are rather compact but thoughtfully laid out and equipped with the gamut of mod cons, while public areas radiate warmth from wood, leather and a crackling fire. The sleek bar will have you hankering for highballs. Breakfast is €15.

CALMA BERLIN MITTE
HOTEL **$$**

Map p336 (☑030-9153 9333; www.hotel-calma-berlin.de; Linienstrasse 139-140; r from €55-170;

⏱reception 6.30am-10.30pm; P ♻🛜; U Oranienburger Tor, S Oranienburger Strasse) In the heart of trendy-town, close to cool bars, shops and restaurants, this modern contender has set up shop in a historic building that once housed the GDR state printing offices. The 46 rooms come in four sizes and are dressed in charcoal and white with pink accents. In fine weather, the terrace is a nice place to enjoy breakfast (€14).

★SOHO HOUSE BERLIN   DESIGN HOTEL $$$
Map p334 (☎030-405 0440; www.sohohouseberlin.com; Torstrasse 1; d from €215; P ♻❄🛜🏊; U Rosa-Luxemburg-Platz) The Berlin edition of the eponymous members' club and celeb-fave doubles as a hotel open to all. The vintage-eclectic rooms vary dramatically in size, decor and amenities, but may include vinyl-record players, huge flat-screen TVs and free-standing tubs. Staying here also buys access to members-only areas such as the club floor with bar and restaurant, the rooftop pool/bar/restaurant and a plush movie theatre.

It's all in a Bauhaus building that's seen stints as a department store, Hitler Youth HQ and East German party elite offices.

★CASA CAMPER   DESIGN HOTEL $$$
Map p334 (☎030-2000 3410; www.casacamper. com; Weinmeisterstrasse 1; r/ste incl breakfast €165-250;   P ♻❄🛜; U Weinmeisterstrasse) Catalan shoemaker Camper has translated its concept of chic yet sensible footwear into this style-pit for trend-conscious global nomads. Minimalist-mod rooms come with day-lit bathrooms with natural amenities, and beds that invite hitting the snooze button. Minibars are eschewed for a top-floor lounge with stellar views and free 24/7 hot and cold snacks and drinks.

🛏 Kreuzberg & Neukölln

★GRAND HOSTEL
BERLIN CLASSIC   HOSTEL $
Map p346 (☎030-2009 5450; www.grandhostel-berlin.de; Tempelhofer Ufer 14; dm €10-44, tw €75-150, tw without bathroom €50-110; ♻@🛜; U Möckernbrücke) Cocktails in the library bar? Check. Free German lessons? Got 'em. Canal views? Yep. Ensconced in a fully renovated 1870s building, the 'five-star' Grand Hostel is one of Berlin's most supremely comfortable, convivial and atmospheric hostels. Breakfast is €7.50.

Also check out their new Grand Hostel Urban at Sonnenallee 6 right in the heart of Neukölln.

HÜTTENPALAST   HOSTEL $
Map p344 (☎030-3730 5806; www.huettenpalast.de; Hobrechtstrasse 66; d campervans & cabins €70-100, hotel €70-160; ⏱check-in 9am-6pm or by arrangement; ♻🛜🏊; U Hermannplatz) This indoor camping ground in an old vacuum-cleaner factory is an unusual place to hang your hat, even by Berlin's standards. It has hotel-style rooms with private bath, but who wants those when you can sleep in a romantic wooden hut with rooftop terrace or in a snug vintage caravan? The little garden with plants and flowers in recycled barrels and tubs invites socialising.

RIVERSIDE LODGE HOSTEL   HOSTEL $
Map p344 (☎0176 3112 9791; www.riverside-lodge.de; Hobrechtstrasse 43; dm/d incl breakfast €23/58; ⏱check-in 11.30am-2pm & 7-9.30pm; ♻@🛜; U Schönleinstrasse) This sweet little 12-bed hostel is a clean, cosy and communicative hang-out near the canal in booming Neukölln, and as warm and welcoming as an old friend's hug thanks to its wonderful owners. There's a double, a quad and a six-bed dorm where beds can be curtained off for privacy, as well as a communal kitchen. Linen is €3.

★ORANIA HOTEL   HOTEL $$
Map p344 (☎030-6953 9680; www.orania. berlin; Oranienstrasse 40; d from €150; ♻❄🛜🏊; U Moritzplatz) This gorgeous hotel in a sensitively restored 1913 building wraps everything that makes Berlin special – culture, class and culinary acumen, infused with a freewheeling cosmopolitan spirit – into one tidy package. Great warmth radiates from the open lobby bar, whose stylish furniture, sultry lighting and open fireplace exude living-room flair. Catch shuteye in 41 comfy rooms that mix retro and modern touches.

Berlin bands lure a local crowd to the bar and the upstairs salon. The restaurant (p168) is tops as well.

HOTEL JOHANN   HOTEL $$
Map p346 (☎030-225 0740; www.hotel-johann-berlin.de; Johanniterstrasse 8; d €88-98; P ♻🛜; U Prinzenstrasse) This 33-room hotel consistently tops the popularity charts, thanks

to its eager-to-please service, homey ambience and good-sized rooms with wooden flooring, uncluttered modern design and occasional historic flourishes. The small garden is perfect for summery breakfasts, while happening Bergmannstrasse and the Jüdisches Museum are both 1km away. Breakfast €8.50.

HOTEL RIEHMERS HOFGARTEN HOTEL $$

Map p346 (☑030-7809 8800; www.riehmers-hofgarten.de; Yorckstrasse 83; d €112-156, ste €147-175; ⓅⓈ@🛜🏊; Ⓤ Mehringdamm) Take a romantic 19th-century building, add contemporary art, stir in a few zeitgeist touches and you'll get one winning cocktail of a hotel. Riehmers' high-ceilinged rooms are modern but not stark; if you're noise-sensitive, get a (slightly pricier) courtyard-facing room. Assets include in-room tea and coffee facilities, a gourmet restaurant and free laptop rental. Breakfast buffet is €10.

HOTEL SAROTTI-HÖFE HOTEL $$

Map p346 (☑030-6003 1680; www.hotel-sarottihoefe.de; Mehringdamm 57; d €115-135; Ⓟ🛜🏊; Ⓤ Mehringdamm) You'll have sweet dreams in this 19th-century ex-chocolate factory, whose courtyard-cloistered rooms are quiet despite being in the middle of the bustling Bergmannkiez quarter. Rooms come in four categories and exude yesteryear flair with high ceilings, red carpets and dark-wood furniture. The nicest (deluxe category) come with private terrace. The breakfast buffet is €12.

🛏 Friedrichshain

⭐PLUS BERLIN HOSTEL $

Map p340 (☑030-311 698 820; www.plushostels.com/plusberlin; Warschauer Platz 6; dm/d from €18/90; ⓅⓍ@🛜🏊; Ⓤ Warschauer Strasse, Ⓢ Warschauer Strasse) A hostel with a pool, steam room and yoga classes? Yep. Close to Berlin's best nightlife, this flashpacker favourite is like a hostel resort. There's a bar for easing into the night and a tranquil courtyard to soothe that hangover. Spacious dorms have four or six bunks, desks and lockers, while private rooms have TV and air-con. All have en-suites.

EASTERN COMFORT HOSTELBOAT HOSTEL $

Map p340 (☑030-6676 3806; www.eastern-comfort.com; Mühlenstrasse 73; dm from €16,

tent 1/2 people €15/25, d €68-78; ⊘reception 8am-midnight; @🛜; Ⓤ Warschauer Strasse, Ⓢ Warschauer Strasse) Let the Spree River murmur you to sleep while you're snugly ensconced in this two-boat, floating hostel with a rocking bar right by the East Side Gallery. Cabins are trimmed in wood and sweetly snug (except for '1st class'); most have their own shower and toilet. In summer, you can also rent a tent on the rooftop of one of the boats.

Optional breakfast is €8. There's a two-night minimum stay on weekends and a one-time fee of €5 for linen and towel in the dorms (or bring your own). The party zones of Kreuzberg and Friedrichshain are handily within staggering distance.

DAS ANDERE HAUS VIII GUESTHOUSE $

(☑030-5544 0331; www.dasanderehaus8.de; Erich-Müller-Strasse 12; s/d €45/75; ⓅⓈ🛜; 🚌21, Ⓢ Rummelsburg) At this cleverly converted 19th-century prison on scenic Rummelburger Bucht (bay), anyone can stay in the five snug 'cells' that are sparsely, if comfortably, furnished; all are en suite. The waterfront walkway invites exploring by bike or on foot, and there's a communal kitchen for sharing stories and meals.

There's a two-night minimum stay.

⭐MICHELBERGER HOTEL HOTEL $$

Map p340 (☑030-2977 8590; www.michel bergerhotel.com; Warschauer Strasse 39; d €95-190; ⓅⓈ🛜; Ⓤ Warschauer Strasse, Ⓢ Warschauer Strasse) Offering the ultimate in creative crash pads, Michelberger perfectly encapsulates Berlin's offbeat DIY spirit without being self-consciously cool. Rooms don't hide their factory pedigree, but are comfortable and come in sizes suitable for lovebirds, families or rock bands. Staff are friendly and clued-up, and the restaurant (p185) is popular with both guests and locals. Breakfast is €16.

ALMODÓVAR HOTEL HOTEL $$

Map p340 (☑030-692 097 080; www.almodovar hotel.de; Boxhagener Strasse 83; d €99-162; ⓅⓈ🛜; 🚌240, 🚋M10, M13, Ⓢ Ostkreuz, Ⓤ Samariterstrasse) 🌿 A certified organic hotel, Almodóvar is perfect for keeping your healthy ways while travelling. A yoga mat is a standard amenity in the 60 rooms with modern-rustic natural wood furniture, sky-blue accent walls and sleek furniture. The upbeat deli serves meat-free tapas, salads and light meals, while the rooftop sauna will heat you up on cold days. Breakfast is €16.50.

NHOW BERLIN
DESIGN HOTEL **$$**

Map p340 (☑030-290 2990; www.nhow-hotels. com; Stralauer Allee 3; d €114-164; P♿❄🛜🐾; ⑤Warschauer Strasse, Ⓤ Warschauer Strasse) This riverside behemoth bills itself as a 'music and lifestyle' hotel and underscores the point by offering two recording studios and e-guitar rentals. The look is definitely dynamic, with a sideways tower jutting out over the Spree and Karim Rashid's digi-pop-pink design. Kudos to the restaurant with riverside terrace and the party-people-friendly late Sunday check out. Massive breakfast buffet is €24 (served till 3pm).

🛏 Prenzlauer Berg

★EASTSEVEN BERLIN HOSTEL
HOSTEL **$**

Map p338 (☑030-9362 2240; www.eastseven.de; Schwedter Strasse 7; dm/d from €25/65; ♿@🛜; Ⓤ Senefelderplatz) An excellent choice for solo travellers, this small indie hostel has personable staff that go out of their way to make all feel welcome. Make new friends while chilling in the lounge or garden (hammocks!), firing up the BBQ or hanging out in the 24-hour kitchen. Brightly painted dorms feature comfy pine beds and lockers. Linen is free, breakfast €3.

HOTEL ODERBERGER
HOTEL **$$**

Map p338 (☑030-780 089 760; www.hotel-oderberger.de; Oderberger Strasse 56/57; d incl breakfast from €144; P♿🛜🐾; 🚇M1, Ⓤ Eberswalder Strasse) These stately public baths established in a neo-Renaissance building in 1902 have been recycled into a modern hotel that smoothly integrates original tiles, lamps, doors, wall hooks and other design details. Its most distinctive asset is the actual swimming pool (p177; access €4) in a cathedral-like hall, which can be turned into an event space. Excellent restaurant and cosy fireplace bar invites winding down.

HOTEL KASTANIENHOF
HOTEL **$$**

Map p338 (☑030-443 050; www.kastanienhof. biz; Kastanienallee 65; d €105-135; P@🛜; 🚇M1 to Zionskirchstrasse, Ⓤ Rosenthaler Platz, Senefelderplatz) Right on Kastanienallee with its cafes, restaurants and boutiques, this family-run traditional charmer has caring staff and 35 good-sized rooms decked out

in soothing colours and pairing historical touches with a good range of mod cons. The cheapest are located in the attic; the nicest feature air-con. Breakfast is €9.

LINNEN
GUESTHOUSE **$$**

Map p338 (☑030-4737 2440; www.linnenberlin. com; Eberswalder Strasse 35; d €88-169; ♿🛜🐾; Ⓤ Eberswalder Strasse) 🌱 This little 'boutique inn' brims with charisma in each of its six idiosyncratically furnished (and TV-less) rooms. The tiniest is No 4, which gets forest-cabin flair from wooden walls decorated with bird feeders, while the largest is the Suite with burgundy walls and balcony. The downstairs area serves breakfast, sandwiches and cakes until 6pm. Various minimum stay periods throughout the year.

★ACKSELHAUS & BLUE HOME
BOUTIQUE HOTEL **$$$**

Map p338 (☑030-4433 7633; www.ackselhaus. de; Belforter Strasse 21; ste incl breakfast €130-180, apt €150-340; ♿@🛜; 🚇M10, Ⓤ Senefelderplatz) At this charismatic refuge in a 19th-century building you'll sleep in spacious, classily themed rooms (eg Africa, Rome, Maritime), each sporting hand-picked features reflecting the owner's penchant for art, vintage furniture and travel: a free-standing tub, perhaps, a four-poster bed or Chinese antiques. Many units face the enchanting courtyard garden.

🛏 City West & Charlottenburg

★25HOURS HOTEL BIKINI BERLIN
DESIGN HOTEL **$$**

Map p348 (☑030-120 2210; www.25hours-hotels.com; Budapester Strasse 40; r €110-250; P♿❄@🛜; 🚇100, 200, ⑤Zoologischer Garten, Ⓤ Zoologischer Garten) The 'urban jungle' theme of this lifestyle outpost in the iconic 1950s Bikini Haus plays on its location between the zoo and main shopping district. Rooms are thoughtfully cool, and drip with clever design touches; the best face the animal park. Quirks include an on-site bakery, hammocks in the public areas and the 'jungle-sauna' with zoo view.

★SIR SAVIGNY
BOUTIQUE HOTEL **$$**

Map p348 (☑030-323 015 600; www.hotel-sirsavigny.de; Kantstrasse 144; r from €130;

HISTORIC B&BS

Nostalgic types seeking Old Berlin flavour should check into a charismatic B&B, called *Hotel-Pension* or simply *Pension*. But better do it quickly because these types of abodes are a dying breed in the digital age! *Pensions* typically occupy one or several floors of a historic residential building and offer local colour and personal attention galore. Amenities, room size and decor vary, often within a single establishment. The cheapest rooms may have shared facilities or perhaps a sink and a shower cubicle in the room but no private toilet. Travellers in need of buckets of privacy, high comfort levels or the latest tech amenities may not feel as comfortable, although wi-fi, cable TV and other mod cons are becoming increasingly available. You'll still find a few of these time warps in the western district of Charlottenburg, around Kurfürstendamm.

Here are a few of our favourites:

Hotel-Pension Funk (Map p348; ☑030-882 7193; www.hotel-pensionfunk.de; Fasanenstrasse 69; d incl breakfast €82-129; P ⊖ ☎ ☎; U Uhlandstrasse, Kurfürstendamm) This charismatic B&B in the home of silent-movie siren Asta Nielsen takes you back to the Golden Twenties. Stuffed with art-nouveau furniture and decor, it's perfect if you value old-fashioned charm over mod cons. The 14 rooms vary quite significantly; if size matters, call and bring up the subject when booking. Cheaper rooms have partial or shared facilities.

Mittendrin (Map p348; ☑0172 714 5165, 030-2362 8861; www.boutique hotel berlin.de; Nürnberger Strasse 16; d incl breakfast €90-240; ⊖ ☎; U Augsburger Strasse, Wittenbergplatz) This sweet retreat close to primo shopping is a fantastic find for those who value individual service over fancy lobbies or rooftop bars. All four rooms bulge with character, hand-picked furnishings and homey extras such as fresh flowers and fluffy bathrobes, but the two cheaper rooms share a bathroom. Breakfasts are market-fresh affairs. Two-night minimum stay.

Hotel Art Nouveau (Map p348; ☑030-327 7440; www.hotelartnouveau.de; Leibnizstrasse 59; d €79-129; @ ☎; ☐109, M19, M29, U Adenauerplatz, Wilmersdorfer Strasse, S Savignyplatz) A quaint birdcage lift drops you off with belle-époque flourish at this arty B&B whose wood-floored and colour-drenched rooms skimp neither on space nor charisma. Space cravers should book the 'comfort' category or the spacious suites. Bonus points for the superb beds, the breakfast buffet (€12) and the honour bar.

⊖ ☀ ☎; S Savignyplatz) Global nomads with a hankering for style would be well advised to point their compass to this cosmopolitan crash pad. Each of the 44 rooms exudes delightfully risqué glamour and teems with mod cons and clever design touches. And yes, the beds are fab. If you're feeling social, report to the book-filled 'kitchen' lounge or the cool bar and burger joint.

ELLINGTON HOTEL   HOTEL $$
Map p348 (☑030-683 150; www.ellington-hotel. com; Nürnberger Strasse 50-55; d €85-165; P ⊖ ☀ ☎; U Augsburger Strasse) Duke and Ella gave concerts in the jazz cellar and Bowie partied in the Dschungel nightclub, then the lights went out in the '90s. Now the handsome 1920s building has been resuscitated as a high-concept hotel, which wraps all that's great about Berlin – history, in-

novation, laissez-faire – into one attractive package. Rooms are stylishly minimalist. Optional breakfast is €20.

HOTEL HENRI   BOUTIQUE HOTEL $$
Map p348 (☑030-884 430; www.henri-berlin. com; Meinekestrasse 9; r €108-215; P ⊖ @; U Kurfürstendamm) This newcomer takes you through a belle-époque time warp while delivering personal flair, modern comforts and an urban setting close to top restaurants and shopping. Rooms come in three categories: petite Kabinett, the classical Les Chambres and the ritzy Salon. Rates include a German-style cold supper buffet, set up in the retro kitchen.

HOTEL OTTO   HOTEL $$
Map p348 (☑030-5471 0080; www.hotelotto. com; Knesebeckstrasse 10; d €80-140; P ☎;

UErnst-Reuter-Platz) Otto would feel like 'just' a business hotel were it not for cool perks such as fair-trade beauty products and complimentary coffee and cake in the afternoon. Rooms are contemporary, functional and derive an extra dimension from colour accents and tactile fabrics. Standard rooms are tiny. The slow-food breakfast (€18), served till noon, is best enjoyed on the leafy rooftop terrace.

WYNDHAM BERLIN
EXCELSIOR HOTEL   HOTEL $$
Map p348 (☑030-9780 8888; www.wyndham berlinexcelsior.com; Hardenbergstrasse 14; d from €100; P♻❄🐾📶; SZoologischer Garten, UZoologischer Garten) This progressively designed outpost, featuring a living-room-style lobby complete with library and fireplace, should suit buttoned-up business types as much as city breakers. White and chocolate hues plus eye-catching photographs dominate the modern rooms, which come with tea- and coffee-making equipment. **Franke Brasserie** (Map p348; ☑030-3155 1030; mains €13.50-27; ⊙noon-2pm & 6.30-10.30pm; 🐾; SZoologischer Garten, UZoologischer Garten), with its show kitchen and mellow tunes, gets high marks for its innovative crossover fare. Breakfast €18.

HOTEL BLEIBTREU BERLIN
BY GOLDEN TULIP   BOUTIQUE HOTEL $$
Map p348 (☑030-884 740; www.bleibtreu.com; Bleibtreustrasse 31; d €80-200; ♻🐾📶; 🚇M29, M19, 109, UUhlandstrasse) 🌿 On a leafy side street just off Kurfürstendamm, this boutique charmer was a pioneer in sustainable lodging at its 1995 opening. Although rooms won't fit a tonne of luggage, they're stylish and come with a free minibar. The integrated cafe/bistro is often packed with locals. The optional breakfast buffet is €19.

HOTEL Q!   DESIGN HOTEL $$
Map p348 (☑030-810 0660; www.hotel-q.com; Knesebeckstrasse 67; d €95-155; P❄🐾; UUhlandstrasse) Sharp angles are eschewed at this stylish hotel with retro-futuristic design, from the red-hot lobby to the white-on-white rooms, some with sexy bed-adjacent tubs. Distinctive feature: the subterranean spa with indoor beach, Finnish sauna and gym. The restaurant serves Thai food, and there's a nice bar to hang out in at night. Optional breakfast is €18.

KU' DAMM 101   DESIGN HOTEL $$
(☑030-520 0550; www.kudamm101.com; Kurfürstendamm 101; d €93-140; P♻❄@🐾; 🚇M19, SHalensee) This good-value hotel has spacious rooms with design inspired by Le Corbusier, which translates to an angular aesthetic combined with a muted colour scheme and clever lighting. It's located close to the trade fair grounds. Distinctive assets include a steam room and the airy 7th-floor lounge, where breakfast (€16) is served along with a feast of views.

★HOTEL AM STEINPLATZ   HOTEL $$$
Map p348 (☑030-554 4440; www.hotel steinplatz.com; Steinplatz 4; r €100-290; P♻❄@🐾📶; 🚇M45, 245, UErnst-Reuter-Platz) Vladimir Nabokov and Romy Schneider were among the guests of the original Hotel am Steinplatz, which got a second lease of life in 2013, a century after it first opened. Rooms in this elegant art-deco jewel reinterpret the 1920s in contemporary style with fantastic lamps, ultra-comfy beds and iPod docking stations. Classy bar (p219) and restaurant (p218), too. The optional breakfast costs €35.

★LOUISA'S PLACE   BOUTIQUE HOTEL $$$
Map p348 (☑030-631 030; www.louisas-place.de; Kurfürstendamm 160; ste €130-250; P♻🐾📶; 🚇M19, M29, UAdenauerplatz) The all-suite Louisa's, in a charismatic 1904 building, is the kind of place that dazzles with class rather than glitz. The family-friendly suites brim with individual character, elegant furnishings and full kitchens. Though small, the pool provides a refreshing dip after a session in the sauna or on the treadmill. A high-end restaurant shares the premises. Optional breakfast is €26.

★SOFITEL BERLIN
KURFÜRSTENDAMM   HOTEL $$$
Map p348 (☑030-800 9990; www.sofitel-berlin-kurfuerstendamm.com/en; Augsburger Strasse 41; d €150-290; P♻❄@🐾📶; UKurfürstendamm) Renowned Berlin architect Jan Kleihues pulled out all the stops to create this award-winning alchemy of art, architecture and design. A sophisticated, unfussy ambience accented by tasteful contemporary art, as well as supremely comfortable XL-sized rooms with sitting areas and walk-in closets, make this French-flavoured refuge a perfect launch pad for urban explorers. Great restaurant (p217), too. Breakfast is €32.

Understand Berlin

Berlin Today

Berlin is truly a 24/7 city, where a spirit of innovation, tolerance and levity roars with unapologetic abandon. Perpetually in flux, Berlin refuses to be pigeonholed, preferring to knit together a new identity from the yarn of its complex history. You can fairly feel the collision between past and future, what is possible and what is realistic, and the hopes and aspirations of people who've joined together from around the globe in one big experiment.

Best on Film

Symphony of a City (1927) Captivating silent documentary about a day in 1920s Berlin.

Downfall (2004) Chilling account of Hitler's last days holed up in his bunker.

Good Bye, Lenin! (2003) Comedy about a young East Berliner who replicates the GDR for his ailing mother.

The Lives of Others (2006) This Academy Award–winner reveals the stranglehold the East German secret police had on innocent people.

Victoria (2015) Follows a young Spanish woman on a crazy Berlin night out in one continuous take.

Best in Print

Goodbye to Berlin (Christopher Isherwood; 1939) Brilliant account of early 1930s Berlin through the eyes of a gay Anglo-American journalist.

Berlin Alexanderplatz (Alfred Döblin; 1929) A stylised meander through the seamy 1920s.

Alone in Berlin (Hans Fallada; 1947) A working-class Berlin couple become unlikely Nazi resisters.

Berlin Blues (Sven Regener; 2001) Life in the shadow of the (western) side of the Berlin Wall before its demise.

Stasiland (Anna Funder; 2004) The Stasi's vast spying apparatus seen from the perspectives of both victims and perpetrators.

Economy on the Upswing

It's been a long road to recovery but Berlin is finally seeing slivers of sunlight on the horizon. Since 2005 its economic growth has consistently outpaced that of Germany as a whole, and the city is also leading the nation in job creation. Although still above the national average, unemployment dropped to 8.4% in 2017, the lowest since reunification in 1990.

Berlin's transformation from an industrial to a knowledge-based society is the cause. The growth of the digital economy especially has stimulated the job market. The city today attracts some of the world's brightest minds and invests heavily in such high-tech sectors as biotechnology, communication and environmental technologies and transport. In fact, Berlin is ranked among the EU's top three innovative regions. The creative and cultural fields are booming, too, and their financial impact, though less tangible, cannot be discounted.

Although visitor numbers have been affected by the demise of Air Berlin, tourism also continues to be a key force economically. In 2017 the city registered nearly 13 million visitors, accounting for a record 31 million overnight stays. And that's not even counting the roughly 100 million day trippers per year.

Still, the news is not all good. Berlin has the highest number of welfare recipients of any of the 17 German federal states. And although spending has been reined in, balancing the books remains tough with a debt legacy hovering around €60 billion.

Europe's Start-up Capital

Over the past decade, Berlin has become the breeding pool for continental Europe's start-up economy, attracting young global tech talent with its multicultural make-up, relative affordability, open-mindedness and high-level of English skills. Only bested by London, 'Silicon Allee' is fast turning into an innovation hub of global importance, especially in the fields of design, art, music and entrepreneurship. The city has been the launch pad for such companies as Zalando, SoundCloud and ResearchGate. A key link is the Google-funded Factory, which seeks to stimulate dialogue between start-ups and established tech ventures. Almost half of start-ups are founded by neo-Berliners.

As the digital industry gains critical mass, it's becoming a driving force behind Berlin's economy, generating over €8 billion in revenue and employing over 60,000 people. There is no end in sight, especially once 'Berlin TXL: The Urban Tech Republic', a huge new start-up campus on the grounds of Tegel Airport, takes flight. Of course, that won't happen until the new Berlin Brandenburg Airport becomes operational. But that's another story...

Population Growth & Housing Shortages

Berlin's population is growing rapidly, fuelled by a slight increase in the birth rate but mostly by migration from EU countries, asylum seekers and global expats. Current estimates predict a population of about four million by 2030, about 10% more than today.

The acute housing shortage is shaping up to be a major problem. Affordable housing in particular remains in short supply as investors, most of them from abroad, snap up precious real estate to build top-flight units or convert existing housing into luxury condominiums. A grassroots anti-gentrification movement is gaining traction with at least 15,000 people protesting in the streets in May 2018. Still, there's no denying that, although not yet at London or New York levels, Berlin's famously low rents are becoming a thing of the past.

Multiculturalism vs Populism

While Berlin's global community is one of its greatest assets, social and economic integration remain challenges. In 2015 and 2016, upwards of 100,000 refugees arrived, mostly from war-torn Syria, Iraq and Afghanistan, overwhelming the local bureaucracy and delaying integration efforts. By 2018, the river of newcomers had slowed to a trickle and private groups have stepped in to boost government integration initiatives.

The arrival of migrants and their perceived drain on the economy and society has given rise to new populist and anti-migration movements like Pegida ('Patriotic Europeans Against the Islamisation of the West') and parties such as AfD (Alternative für Deutschland, Alternative for Germany). These movements have gained only moderate support in Berlin, compared to some other parts of Germany. An AfD demonstration in May 2018 lured 5000 people and 25,000 counter-protesters.

if Berlin were 100 people

94 would be German
3 would be Turkish
2 would be Polish
1 would be Italian

belief systems
(% of population)

60 Non-religious
19 Protestant
9 Roman Catholic
8 Muslim
4 Other

population per sq km

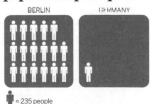

BERLIN   GERMANY

≈ 235 people

History

Berlin has long been in the cross hairs of history: it staged a revolution, was head-quartered by fascists, bombed to bits, ripped in half and finally reunited – all just in the 20th century! An accidental capital whose medieval birth was a mere blip on the map of history, Berlin puttered along in relative obscurity until becoming the royal capital of Prussia some 400 years later. It was only in fairly recent times that it significantly impacted on world history.

Medieval Berlin

The discovery of an oak beam suggests that Berlin may have roots going back to 1183 but, for now, history records that the city was officially founded in 1237 by itinerant merchants as twin trading posts called Berlin and Cölln. The modest settlements flanked the Spree River in an area just southwest of today's Alexanderplatz. It was a profitable spot along a natural east–west trade route, about halfway between the fortified towns of Köpenick to the southeast and Spandau to the northwest whose origins can be traced to the 8th century. The tiny settlements grew in leaps and bounds and, in 1307, merged into a single town for power and protection. As the centre of the March (duchy) of Brandenburg, it continued to assert its political and economic independence and even became a player in the Hanseatic League in 1360.

Berlin's medieval birthplace, around the Nikolaikirche, was devastated during WWII bombing raids. Today's 'Nikolaiviertel' is actually a replica of the quarter, dreamed up by the East German government in celebration of the city's 750th anniversary in 1987.

Such confidence did not sit well with Sigismund, king of the Germans, who, in 1411, put one of his cronies, Friedrich von Hohenzollern, in charge of Brandenburg, thereby ushering in five centuries of uninterrupted rule by the House of Hohenzollern.

Reformation & the Thirty Years' War

The Reformation, kick-started in 1517 by Martin Luther in nearby Wittenberg, was slow to arrive in Berlin. Eventually, though, the wave of reform reached Brandenburg, leaving Elector Joachim II (r 1535–71) no choice but to subscribe to Protestantism. On 1 November 1539 the court celebrated the first Lutheran-style service in the Nikolaikirche in Spandau.

TIMELINE	1244	1307	1360
	Berlin is referenced in a document for the first time in recorded history, although the city's birthday is pegged to the first mention of its sister settlement, Cölln, in 1237.	Berlin and Cölln join forces by merging into a single town to assert their independence from local rulers.	The twin town of Berlin-Cölln joins the Hanseatic League, but never plays a major role in the alliance and quits its membership in 1518.

The event is still celebrated as an official holiday (Reformationstag) in Brandenburg, the German federal state that surrounds Berlin, although not in the city state of Berlin itself.

Berlin prospered for the ensuing decades until drawn into the Thirty Years' War (1618–48), a conflict between Catholics and Protestants that left Europe's soil drenched with the blood of millions. Elector Georg Wilhelm (r 1620–40) tried to maintain a policy of neutrality, only to see his territory repeatedly pillaged and plundered by both sides. By the time the war ended, Berlin lay largely in shambles – broke, ruined and decimated by starvation, murder and disease.

Road to a Kingdom

Stability finally returned during the long reign of Georg Wilhelm's son, Friedrich Wilhelm (r 1640–88). Also known as the Great Elector, he took several steps that helped chart Brandenburg's rise to the status of a European powerhouse. His first order of business was to increase Berlin's safety by turning it into a garrison town encircled by fortifications with 13 bastions. He also levied a new sales tax, using the money to build three new neighbourhoods (Friedrichswerder, Dorotheenstadt and Friedrichstadt) and a canal linking the Spree and Oder Rivers (thereby cementing Berlin's position as a trading hub), as well as the Lustgarten and Unter den Linden.

But the Great Elector's most lasting legacy was replenishing Berlin's population by encouraging the settlement of refugees. In 1671, 50 Jewish families arrived from Vienna, followed by thousands of Protestant Huguenots – many of them highly skilled – who had been expelled from France by Louis XIV in 1685. The Französischer Dom (French Cathedral) on Gendarmenmarkt serves as a tangible reminder of Huguenot influence. Between 1680 and 1710, Berlin saw its population nearly triple to 56,000, making it one of the largest cities in the Holy Roman Empire.

The Great Elector's son, Friedrich III, was a man of great ambition, with a penchant for the arts and sciences. Together with his beloved wife, Sophie-Charlotte, he presided over a lively and intellectual court, founding the Academy of Arts in 1696 and the Academy of Sciences in 1700. One year later, he advanced his career by promoting himself to King Friedrich I (elector 1688–1701, king 1701–13) of Prussia, making Berlin a royal residence and the capital of the new state of Brandenburg-Prussia.

The Age of Prussia

All cultural and intellectual life screeched to a halt under Friedrich's son, Friedrich Wilhelm I (r 1713–40), who laid the groundwork for Prussian

An 8m-long section is all that survives of Berlin's original city wall, built around 1250 from crude boulders and bricks and standing up to 2m tall. See it on Litten-strasse, near Alexanderplatz.

HISTORY ROAD TO A KINGDOM

1411	1443	1539	1618
German King Sigismund puts Friedrich von Hohenzollern in charge as administrator of Brandenburg, marking the beginning of 500 years of Hohenzollern rule.	Construction of the Berliner Stadtschloss (city palace) on the Spree island begins; it becomes the electors' permanent residence in 1486.	Elector Joachim II celebrates the first Lutheran service and a year later passes a church ordinance making the new religion binding throughout Brandenburg.	Religious conflict and territorial power struggles escalate into the bloody Thirty Years' War, devastating Berlin financially and halving its population to a mere 6000 people.

military might. Soldiers were this king's main obsession and he dedicated much of his life to building an army of 80,000, partly by instituting the draft (highly unpopular even then, and eventually repealed) and persuading his fellow rulers to trade him men for treasure. History quite appropriately knows him as the *Soldatenkönig* (soldier king).

Ironically these soldiers didn't see action until his son and successor Friedrich II (aka Frederick the Great; r 1740–86) came to power. Friedrich fought tooth and nail for two decades to wrest Silesia (in today's Poland) from Austria and Saxony. When not busy on the battlefield, 'Old Fritz', as he was also called, sought greatness through building. His Forum Fridericianum, a grand architectural master plan for Unter den Linden, although never completed, gave Berlin the Staatsoper Unter den Linden (State Opera House); Sankt-Hedwigs-Kathedrale, a former palace now housing the Humboldt Universität (Humboldt University); and other major attractions.

Fredrich also embraced the ideas of the Enlightenment, abolishing torture, guaranteeing religious freedom and introducing legal reforms. With some of the leading thinkers in town (Moses Mendelssohn, Voltaire and Gotthold Ephraim Lessing among them), Berlin blossomed into a great cultural capital that came to be known as 'Athens on the Spree'.

Top Five Prussian Sites

Brandenburger Tor(p84)

Schloss and Park Sanssouci (p223)

Schloss Charlottenburg (p211)

Reichstag (p82)

Siegessäule (p131)

Napoleon & Reforms

Old Fritz' death sent Prussia into a downward spiral, culminating in a serious trouncing of its army by Napoleon at Jena-Auerstedt in 1806. The French marched triumphantly into Berlin on 27 October and left two years later, their coffers bursting with loot. Among the pint-sized conqueror's favourite souvenirs was the *Quadriga* sculpture from atop the Brandenburg Gate.

The post-Napoleonic period saw Berlin caught up in the reform movement sweeping through Europe. Public servants, academics and merchants now questioned the right of the nobility to rule. Friedrich Wilhelm III (r 1797–1840) instituted a few token reforms (easing guild regulations, abolishing bonded labour and granting Jews civic equality), but meaningful constitutional reform was not forthcoming. Power continued to be concentrated in the Prussian state.

The ensuing period of political stability was paired with an intellectual flourishing in Berlin's cafes and salons. The newly founded Universität zu Berlin (Humboldt Universität) was helmed by the philosopher Johann Gottlieb Fichte and, as it grew in status, attracted other leading thinkers of the day, including Hegel and Ranke. This was also the age of Karl Friedrich Schinkel, whose many projects – from the Neue Wache

1640	1665	1671	1685
Friedrich Wilhelm, who will go down in history as the Great Elector, comes to power and restores a semblance of normality by building fortifications and infrastructure.	After major fires, a new law requires barns to move outside the city boundaries, thereby creating today's Scheunenviertel (Barn Quarter).	Berlin's first Jewish community forms with just a few families arriving from Vienna at the invitation of the Great Elector. It grows to more than 1000 people by 1700.	Friedrich Wilhelm issues the Edict of Potsdam, allowing French Huguenot religious refugees to settle in Berlin, giving a 10-year tax break and granting them the right to hold services.

(New Guardhouse) to the Altes Museum (Old Museum) – still beautify Berlin.

Revolution(s)

The Industrial Revolution snuck up on Berliners in the second quarter of the 19th century, with companies like Siemens and Borsig vastly stimulating the city's growth. In 1838 trains began chuffing between Berlin and Potsdam, giving birth to the Prussian railway system and spurring the foundation of more than 1000 factories, including electrical giants AEG and Siemens. In 1840 August Borsig built the world's fastest locomotive, besting even the British in a race.

Tens of thousands of people now streamed into Berlin to work in the factories, swelling the population to more than 400,000 by 1847 and bringing the city's infrastructure close to collapse. A year later, due to social volatility and restricted freedoms, Berlin joined other German cities in a bourgeois democratic revolution. On 18 March two shots rang out during a demonstration, which then escalated into a full-fledged revolution. Barricades went up and a bloody fight ensued, leaving 183 revolutionaries and 18 soldiers dead by the time King Friedrich Wilhelm IV ordered his troops back. The dead revolutionaries are commemorated on Platz des 18 März, immediately west of the Brandenburg Gate. In a complete turnabout, the king put himself at the head of the movement and professed support for liberalism and nationalism. On 21 March, while riding to the funeral of the revolutionaries in the Volkspark Friedrichshain, he donned the red, black and gold tricolour of German unity.

An elected Prussian national assembly met on 5 May. However, disagreements between delegates from the different factions kept parliament weak and ineffective, making restoration of the monarchy child's play for General von Wrangel, who led 13,000 Prussian soldiers who had remained faithful to the king into the city in November 1848. Ever the opportunist, the king quickly switched sides again, dissolved the parliament and proposed his own constitution while insisting on maintaining supreme power. The revolution was dead. Many of its participants fled into exile.

Bismarck & the Birth of an Empire

When Friedrich Wilhelm IV suffered a stroke in 1857, his brother Wilhelm became first regent and then, in 1861, King Wilhelm I (r 1861–88). Unlike his brother, Wilhelm had his finger on the pulse of the times and was not averse to progress. One of his key moves was to appoint Otto von Bismarck as Prussian prime minister in 1862.

One of the definitive histories of Prussia, Christopher Clark's *Iron Kingdom: The Rise and Downfall of Prussia* (2006) covers the period from 1600 to 1947 and shows the central role this powerhouse played in shaping modern Europe.

1696	1701	1730	1740
Elector Friedrich III founds the Akademie der Künste, Berlin's oldest and most prestigious arts institution.	Brandenburg becomes a kingdom, with Berlin as its capital, when Elector Friedrich III has himself crowned King Friedrich I.	The future king Frederick the Great is caught trying to desert to England along with a friend. Frederick's father orders the friend's execution and makes his son watch.	Frederick the Great, the philosopher king, turns Berlin into 'Athens on the Spree', a centre of the Enlightenment and an architectural showcase.

Bismarck's glorious ambition was the creation of a unified Germany with Prussia at the helm. An old-guard militarist, he used intricate diplomacy and a series of wars with neighbouring Denmark and Austria to achieve his aims. By 1871 Berlin stood as the proud capital of the German Reich (empire), a bicameral, constitutional monarchy. On 18 January the Prussian king was crowned Kaiser at Versailles, with Bismarck as his 'Iron Chancellor'.

The early years of the German empire – a period called *Gründerzeit* (the foundation years) – were marked by major economic growth, fuelled in part by a steady flow of French reparation payments. Hundreds of thousands of people poured into Berlin in search of work in the factories. Housing shortages were solved by building labyrinthine tenements (*Mietskasernen,* literally 'rental barracks'), where entire families subsisted in tiny and poorly ventilated flats without indoor plumbing.

New political parties gave a voice to the proletariat; foremost was the Socialist Workers' Party (SAP), the forerunner of the Sozialdemokratische Partei Deutschlands (SPD; Social Democratic Party of Germany). Founded in 1875, the SAP captured 40% of the Berlin vote just two years later. Bismarck tried to make the party illegal but eventually, under pressure from the growing and increasingly antagonistic socialist movement, he enacted Germany's first modern social reforms, though this went against his true nature. When Wilhelm II (r 1888–1918) came to power, he wanted to extend social reform while Bismarck wanted stricter antisocialist laws. Finally, in March 1890, the Kaiser's scalpel excised his renegade chancellor from the political scene. After that, the legacy of Bismarck's diplomacy unravelled and a wealthy, unified and industrially powerful Germany paddled into the new century.

WWI & Revolution (Again)

The assassination of Archduke Franz Ferdinand, the heir to the Austrian throne, on 28 June 1914, triggered a series of diplomatic decisions that led to WWI, the bloodiest European conflict since the Thirty Years' War. In Berlin and elsewhere, initial euphoria and faith in a quick victory soon gave way to despair as casualties piled up in the battlefield trenches and stomachs grumbled on the home front. When peace came with defeat in 1918, it also ended domestic stability, ushering in a period of turmoil and violence.

On 9 November 1918, Kaiser Wilhelm II abdicated, bringing an inglorious end to the monarchy and 500 years of Hohenzollern rule. Power was transferred to the SPD, the largest party in the Reichstag, and its leader, Friedrich Ebert. Shortly after the Kaiser's exit, prominent SPD member Philipp Scheidemann stepped to a window of the Reichstag to

Historical Reads

Berlin Rising: Biography of a City (Anthony Read, David Fisher; 1994)

Berlin: Portrait of a City Through the Centuries (Rory MacLean; 2014)

Berlin Diary: Journal of a Foreign Correspondent 1934–41 (William Shirer; 1941)

The Candy Bombers (Andrei Cherny; 2006)

The Berlin Wall (Frederick Taylor; 2006)

1806	1830	1837	1838
After defeating Prussia, Napoleon leads his troops on a triumphant march through the Brandenburg Gate, marking the start of a two-year occupation of Berlin.	The Altes Museum opens as the first of five institutions on Museumsinsel (Museum Island). The last (the Pergamonmuseum) opens exactly 100 years later.	The industrial age kicks into high gear with the founding of August Borsig's machine factory, which in 1840 builds Germany's first locomotive.	Berlin's first train embarks on its maiden voyage from Berlin to Potsdam, making the city the centre of an expanding rail network throughout Prussia.

announce the birth of the German Republic. Two hours later, Karl Liebknecht of the Spartakusbund (Spartacist League) proclaimed a socialist republic from a balcony of the royal palace on Unter den Linden. The struggle for power was on.

Founded by Liebknecht and Rosa Luxemburg, the Spartacist League sought to establish a left-wing, Marxist-style government; by year's end it had merged with other radical groups into the German Communist Party. The SPD's goal, meanwhile, was to establish a parliamentary democracy.

Supporters of the SPD and the Spartacist League took their rivalry to the streets, culminating in the Spartacist Revolt of early January 1919. On the orders of Ebert, government forces quickly quashed the uprising. Liebknecht and Luxemburg were arrested and murdered en route to prison by Freikorps soldiers (right-leaning war volunteers); their bodies were dumped in the Landwehrkanal.

The Weimar Republic

In July 1919 the federalist constitution of the fledgling republic – Germany's first serious experiment with democracy – was adopted in the town of Weimar, where the constituent assembly had sought refuge from the chaos of Berlin. It gave women the vote and established basic human rights, but it also gave the chancellor the right to rule by decree – a concession that would later prove critical in Hitler's rise to power.

The so-called Weimar Republic (1920–33) was governed by a coalition of left and centre parties, headed by Friedrich Ebert of the SPD and, later, independent Paul von Hindenburg. The SPD remained Germany's largest party until 1932. The republic, however, pleased neither communists nor monarchists. Trouble erupted as early as March 1920 when right-wing militants led by Wolfgang Kapp forcibly occupied the government quarter in Berlin. The government fled to Dresden, and in Berlin a general strike soon brought the 'Kapp Putsch' to a collapse.

The Golden Twenties

The giant metropolis of Berlin as we know it today was forged in 1920 from the region's many independent towns and villages (Charlottenburg, Schöneberg, Spandau etc), making Berlin one of the world's largest cities, with around 3.8 million inhabitants.

Otherwise, the 1920s began as anything but golden, marked by the humiliation of a lost war, social and political instability, hyperinflation, hunger and disease. Around 235,000 Berliners were unemployed, and strikes, demonstrations and riots became nearly everyday occurrences.

The green octagonal public pissoirs occasionally seen around Berlin are a legacy of the late 19th century when the municipal sanitation system could not keep up with the exploding population. About two dozen survive, including one on Chamissoplatz in Kreuzberg and another on Senefelderplatz in Prenzlauer Berg. Their nickname is Cafe Achteck (Cafe Octagon).

HISTORY THE WEIMAR REPUBLIC

1848	1862	1871	1877
Berlin is swept up in the popular revolutions for democratic reform and a united Germany, but after a few months the Prussian army restores the old order.	Chief city planner James Hobrecht solves the housing shortage by constructing claustrophobic working-class ghettos of tenement blocks.	Employing an effective strategy of war and diplomacy, Prussian chancellor Otto von Bismarck forges a unified Germany with Prussia at its helm and Berlin as its capital.	Berlin's population reaches the one million mark; this figure almost doubles by 1900.

Economic stability gradually returned after a new currency, the *Rentenmark,* was introduced in 1923 and with the Dawes Plan in 1924, which limited the crippling reparation payments imposed on Germany after WWI.

Berliners responded like there was no tomorrow and made their city as much a den of decadence as it was a cauldron of creativity (not unlike today...). Cabaret, Dada and jazz flourished. Pleasure pits popped up everywhere, turning the city into a 'sextropolis' of Dionysian dimensions. Bursting with energy, it became a laboratory for anything new and modern, drawing giants of architecture (Bruno Taut, Martin Wagner, Hans Scharoun and Walter Gropius), fine arts (George Grosz, Max Beckmann and Lovis Corinth) and literature (Bertolt Brecht, Kurt Tucholsky, WH Auden and Christopher Isherwood).

The fun came to an instant end when the US stock market crashed in 1929, plunging the world into economic depression. Within weeks, half a million Berliners were jobless, and riots and demonstrations again ruled the streets. The volatile, increasingly polarised political climate led to clashes between communists and members of a party that had been patiently waiting in the wings – the Nationalsozialistische Deutsche Arbeiterpartei (National Socialist German Workers' Party, NSDAP, or Nazi Party), led by a failed Austrian artist and WWI corporal named Adolf Hitler. Soon jackboots, brown shirts, oppression and fear would dominate daily life in Germany.

Hitler's Rise to Power

The Weimar government's inability to improve conditions during the Depression spurred the popularity of Hitler's NSDAP, which gained 18% of the national vote in the 1930 elections. In the 1932 presidential election, Hitler challenged Hindenburg and won 37% of the second-round vote. A year later, on 30 January 1933, faced with failed economic reforms and persuasive right-wing advisers, Hindenburg appointed Hitler chancellor. That evening, NSDAP celebrated its rise to power with a torchlit procession through the Brandenburg Gate. Not everyone cheered. Observing the scene from his Pariser Platz home, artist Max Liebermann famously commented: 'I couldn't possibly eat as much as I would like to puke'.

As chancellor, Hitler moved quickly to consolidate absolute power and turn the nation's democracy into a one-party dictatorship. The Reichstag fire in March 1933 gave him the opportunity to request temporary emergency powers to arrest communists and liberal opponents and push through his proposed Enabling Law, allowing him to decree laws and change the constitution without consulting parliament. When

Discover stat after stat on Berlin at the website of the Office of Statistics in Berlin (www. statistik-berlin-brandenburg.de).

One of many fabulous films by Germany's best-known female director, Margarethe von Trotta, *Rosenstrasse* (2003) is a moving portrayal of a 1943 protest by a group of non-Jewish women trying to save their Jewish husbands from deportation. There's a memorial near the site today.

1891	1902	1918	1919
Berlin engineer Otto Lilienthal, known as the 'Glider King', makes the world's first successful glider flight, travelling over 25m. Five years later he dies in an air accident.	After two decades of debate and eight years of construction, the first segment of the Berlin U-Bahn network is inaugurated, between Warschauer Strasse and Ernst-Reuter-Platz.	WWI ends on 11 November with Germany's capitulation, following the resignation of Kaiser Wilhelm II and his escape to Holland. The Prussian monarchy is dead.	The Spartacist Revolt, led by Liebknecht, Luxemburg and Pieck, is violently suppressed and ends with the murder of Liebknecht and Luxemburg by right-wing Freikorps troops.

Hindenburg died a year later, Hitler fused the offices of president and chancellor to become Führer of the Third Reich.

Nazi Berlin

The rise of the Nazis had instant, far-reaching consequences for the entire population. Within three months of Hitler's power grab, all non-Nazi parties, organisations and labour unions ceased to exist. Political opponents, intellectuals and artists were rounded up and detained without trial; many went underground or into exile. There was a burgeoning culture of terror and denunciation, and the terrorisation of Jews started to escalate.

Hitler's brown-shirted Nazi state police, the Sturmabteilung (SA), pursued opponents, arresting, torturing and murdering people in improvised

OLYMPICS UNDER THE SWASTIKA

When the International Olympics Committee awarded the 1936 games to Germany in 1931, the gesture was supposed to welcome the country back into the world community after its defeat in WWI and the tumultuous 1920s. No one could have known that only two years later, the fledgling democracy would be helmed by a dictator with an agenda to take over the world.

As Hitler opened the games on 1 August in Berlin's Olympic Stadium, prisoners were putting the finishing touches on the first large-scale Nazi concentration camp at Sachsenhausen, just north of town. As famous composer Richard Strauss conducted the Olympic hymn during the opening ceremony, fighter squadrons were headed to Spain in support of Franco's dictatorship. Only while the Olympic flame was flickering were political and racial persecution suspended and anti-Semitic signs taken down.

The Olympics were truly a perfect opportunity for the Nazi propaganda machine, which excelled at staging grand public spectacles and rallies, as was so powerfully captured by Leni Riefenstahl in her epic movie *Olympia*. Participants and spectators were impressed by the choreographed pageantry and warm German hospitality. The fact that these were the first Olympics to be broadcast internationally on radio did not fail to impress either.

The games were also a big success from an athletic point of view, with around 4000 participants from 49 countries competing in 129 events and setting numerous records. The biggest star was African-American track-and-fieldster Jesse Owens, who was awarded four gold medals for the 100m sprint, 200m sprint, 4 x 100m relay and long jump, winning the hearts of the German public and putting paid to Nazi belief in the physical superiority of the Aryan race. German Jews, meanwhile, were excluded from participating, with the one token exception being half-Jewish fencer Helene Mayer. She took home a silver medal.

1920	1920s	1921	1923
On 1 October Berlin becomes Germany's largest city after seven independent towns, 59 villages and 27 estates are amalgamated into a single administrative unit. The population reaches 3.8 million.	Berlin evolves into a cultural metropolis, exerting a pull on leading artists, scientists and philosophers of the day, including Einstein, Brecht and Otto Dix.	The world's first highway – called AVUS – opens in the Grunewald after eight years of construction.	Berlin-Tempelhof Airport opens and soon becomes one of Europe's most important airports, along with Croydon in London and Le Bourget in Paris.

concentration camps, such as the one in the Wasserturm in Prenzlauer Berg. North of Berlin, construction began on Sachsenhausen concentration camp. During the so-called Köpenicker Blutwoche (Bloody Week) in June 1933, around 90 people were murdered. On 10 May, right-wing students burned 'un-German' books on Bebelplatz, prompting countless intellectuals and artists to rush into exile.

Jewish Persecution

Jews were a Nazi target from the start. In April 1933 Joseph Goebbels, *Gauleiter* (district leader) of Berlin and head of the well-oiled Ministry of Propaganda, announced a boycott of Jewish businesses. Soon after, Jews were expelled from public service and banned from many professions, trades and industries. The Nuremberg Laws of 1935 deprived 'non-Aryans' of German citizenship and many other rights.

The international community, meanwhile, turned a blind eye to the situation in Germany, perhaps because many leaders were keen to see some order restored to the country after decades of political upheaval. Hitler's success at stabilising the shaky economy – largely by pumping public money into employment programs – was widely admired. The 1936 Olympic summer games (p261) in Berlin were a PR triumph, as Hitler launched a charm offensive. Terror and persecution resumed soon after the closing ceremony.

For Jews, the horror escalated on 9 November 1938, with the Reichspogromnacht (often called Kristallnacht, or Night of Broken Glass).

NAZI RESISTANCE

Resistance to Hitler was quashed early by the powerful Nazi machinery of terror, but it never vanished entirely, as is thoroughly documented in the excellent Topographie des Terrors exhibit. One of the best known acts of defiance was the 20 July 1944 assassination attempt on the Führer, led by senior army officer Claus Graf Schenk von Stauffenberg. On that fateful day, Stauffenberg brought a briefcase packed with explosives to a meeting of the Nazi high command at the Wolfschanze (Wolf's Lair), Hitler's eastern-front military headquarters. He placed the briefcase under the conference table near Hitler's seat, then excused himself and heard the bomb detonate from a distance. What he didn't know was that Hitler had escaped with minor injuries thanks to the solid oak table that shielded him from the blast.

Stauffenberg and his co-conspirators were quickly identified and shot by firing squad at the army headquarters in the Bendlerblock in Berlin. The rooms where they hatched their plot now house the Gedenkstätte Deutscher Widerstand, an exhibit about German resistance against the Nazis.

1924	1929	1933	1936
Germany's first electric traffic light starts regulating the chaos around Potsdamer Platz.	The Great Depression leaves half a million people unemployed. Thirteen members of the National Socialist German Workers' Party (the Nazi Party) are elected to city parliament.	Hitler is appointed chancellor; the Reichstag burns; construction starts on Sachsenhausen concentration camp; the National Socialist German Workers' Party rules Germany.	The 11th modern Olympic Games, held in Berlin in August, are a PR triumph for Hitler and a showcase of Nazi power. Anti-Jewish propaganda is suspended during the period.

Using the assassination of a German consular official by a Polish Jew in Paris as a pretext, Nazi thugs desecrated, burned and demolished synagogues and Jewish cemeteries, property and businesses across the country. Jews had begun to emigrate after 1933, but this event set off a stampede.

The fate of those Jews who stayed behind deteriorated after the outbreak of WWII in 1939. At Hitler's request, a conference in January 1942 in Berlin's Wannsee came up with the *Endlösung* (Final Solution): the systematic, bureaucratic and meticulously documented annihilation of European Jews. Sinti and Roma, political opponents, priests, homosexuals and habitual criminals were targeted as well. Of the roughly seven million people who were sent to concentration camps, only 500,000 survived.

WWII & the Battle of Berlin

WWII began on 1 September 1939 with the Nazi attack on Poland. Although France and Britain declared war on Germany two days later, this could not prevent the quick defeat of Poland, Belgium, the Netherlands and France. Other countries, including Denmark and Norway, were also soon brought into the Nazi fold.

In June 1941 Germany broke its nonaggression pact with Stalin by attacking the USSR. Though successful at first, Operation Barbarossa quickly ran into problems, culminating in defeat at Stalingrad (today Volgograd) the following winter, forcing the Germans to retreat.

With the Normandy invasion of June 1944, Allied troops arrived in formidable force on the European mainland, supported by unrelenting air raids on Berlin and most other German cities. The final Battle of Berlin began in mid-April 1945. More than 1.5 million Soviet soldiers barrelled towards the capital from the east, reaching Berlin on 21 April and encircling it on 25 April. Two days later they were in the city centre, fighting running street battles with the remaining troops, many of them boys and elderly men. On 30 April the fighting reached the government quarter where Hitler was ensconced in his bunker behind the chancellery, with his long-time mistress Eva Braun, whom he'd married just a day earlier. Finally accepting the inevitability of defeat, Hitler shot himself that afternoon; his wife swallowed a cyanide pill. As their bodies were burned in the chancellery courtyard, Red Army soldiers raised the Soviet flag above the Reichstag.

Defeat & Aftermath

The Battle of Berlin ended on 2 May with the unconditional surrender of Helmuth Weidling, the commander of the Berlin Defence Area,

Top Five WWII Sites

Topographie des Terrors (p89; Historic Mitte)

Sachsenhausen Concentration Camp (p229; Oranienburg)

Holocaust Memorial (p85; Historic Mitte)

Gedenkstätte Deutscher Widerstand (p129; Potsdamer Platz)

Haus der Wannsee-Konferenz (p234; Wannsee)

HISTORY WWII & THE BATTLE OF BERLIN

1938	1942	1944	1945
On 9 November Nazis set fire to nine of Berlin's 12 synagogues, vandalise Jewish businesses and terrorise Jewish citizens during a night of pogroms called Kristallnacht.	At the so-called Wannsee Conference, leading members of the SS decide on the systematic murder of European Jews, called the 'Final Solution'.	On 20 July senior army officers led by Claus Graf Schenk von Stauffenberg stage an assassination attempt on Hitler. Their failure costs their own and countless other lives.	Soviet troops advance on Berlin in the final days of the war, devastating the city. Hitler commits suicide on 30 April, fighting stops on 2 May and the armistice is signed on 8 May.

to General Vasily Chuikov of the Soviet army. Peace was signed at the US military headquarters in Reims (France) and at the Soviet military headquarters in Berlin-Karlshorst, now a German-Soviet history museum (Deutsch-Russisches Museum Berlin-Karlshorst). On 8 May 1945, WWII in Europe officially came to an end.

The fighting had taken an enormous toll on Berlin and its people. Entire neighbourhoods lay in smouldering rubble and at least 125,000 Berliners had lost their lives. With around one million women and children evacuated, only 2.8 million people were left in the city in May 1945 (compared to 4.3 million in 1939), two-thirds of them women. It fell to them to start clearing up the 25 million tonnes of rubble, earning them the name *Trümmerfrauen* (rubble women). In fact, many of Berlin's modest hills are actually *Trümmerberge* (rubble mountains), built from wartime debris and reborn as parks and recreational areas. The best known are the Teufelsberg in the Grunewald and Mont Klamott in the Volkspark Friedrichshain.

Some small triumphs came quickly: U-Bahn service resumed on 14 May 1945, newspaper printing presses began rolling again on 15 May, and the Berliner Philharmoniker orchestra gave its first postwar concert on 26 May.

Top Five Cold War Sites

Gedenkstätte Berliner Mauer (p195; Prenzlauer Berg)

East Side Gallery (p182; Friedrichshain)

Stasi Prison (p187; Lichtenberg)

AlliiertenMuseum Berlin (p233; Dahlem)

Stasimuseum (p187; Mitte)

Occupation

At the Yalta Conference in February 1945, Winston Churchill, Franklin D Roosevelt and Joseph Stalin agreed to carve up Germany and Berlin into four zones of occupation controlled by Britain, the USA, the USSR and France. By July 1945, Stalin, Clement Attlee (who replaced Churchill after a surprise election win) and Roosevelt's successor, Harry S Truman, were at the table in Schloss Cecilienhof in Potsdam to hammer out the details.

Berlin was sliced up into 20 administrative areas. The British sector encompassed Charlottenburg, Tiergarten and Spandau; the French got Wedding and Reinickendorf; and the US was in charge of Zehlendorf, Steglitz, Wilmersdorf, Tempelhof, Kreuzberg and Neukölln. All these districts later formed West Berlin. The Soviets held on to eight districts in the east, including Mitte, Prenzlauer Berg, Friedrichshain, Treptow and Köpenick, which would later become East Berlin. The Soviets also occupied the land surrounding Berlin, leaving West Berlin completely encircled by territories under Soviet control.

The Big Chill

Friction between the Western Allies and the Soviets quickly emerged. For the Western Allies, a main priority was to help Germany get back on

1948	1949	1950	1950s
After the Western Allies introduce the Deutschmark currency, the Soviets blockade West Berlin; in response the US and Britain launch the Berlin Airlift, ferrying necessities to the isolated city.	Two countries are born – the Bundesrepublik Deutschland (West Germany) and the Deutsche Demokratische Republik (East Germany); Berlin remains under Allied supervision.	GDR leaders raze the remains of the Prussian city palace for ideological reasons, despite worldwide protest.	Hundreds of thousands of East Germans move to West Berlin and West Germany, depleting the GDR's brain and brawn power.

its feet by kick-starting the devastated economy. The Soviets, though, insisted on massive reparations and began brutalising and exploiting their own zone of occupation. Tens of thousands of able-bodied men and POWs ended up in labour camps deep in the Soviet Union. In the Allied zones, meanwhile, democracy was beginning to take root, and Germany elected state parliaments in 1946–47.

The showdown came in June 1948 when the Allies introduced the Deutschmark in their zones. The USSR regarded this as a breach of the Potsdam Agreement, under which the powers had agreed to treat Germany as one economic zone. The Soviets issued their own currency, the Ostmark, and promptly announced a full-scale economic blockade of West Berlin. The Allies responded with the remarkable Berlin Airlift.

The Berlin Airlift

The Berlin Airlift was a triumph of determination and a glorious chapter in Berlin's post-WWII history. On 24 June 1948, the Soviets cut off all rail and road traffic into the city to force the Western Allies to give up their sectors and bring the entire city under Soviet control.

Faced with such provocation, many in the Allied camp urged responses that would have become the opening barrages of WWIII. In the end wiser heads prevailed, and a mere day after the blockade began the US Air Force launched 'Operation Vittles'. The British followed suit on 28 June with 'Operation Plane Fare'.

For the next 11 months Allied planes flew in food, coal, machinery and other supplies to the now-closed Tempelhof Airport in West Berlin. By the time the Soviets backed down, the Allies had made 278,000 flights, logged a distance equivalent to 250 round trips to the moon and delivered 2.5 million tonnes of cargo. The Luftbrückendenkmal (Berlin Airlift Memorial) outside the airport honours the effort and those who died carrying it out.

It was a monumental achievement that profoundly changed the relationship between Germany and the Western Allies, who were no longer regarded merely as occupying forces but as *Schutzmächte* (protective powers).

Two German States

In 1949 the division of Germany – and Berlin – was formalised. The western zones evolved into the Bundesrepublik Deutschland (BRD, Federal Republic of Germany or FRG) with Konrad Adenauer as its first chancellor and Bonn, on the Rhine River, as its capital. An American economic aid package dubbed the Marshall Plan created the basis for West Germany's *Wirtschaftswunder* (economic miracle), which saw the

Daring Young Men: the Heroism and Triumph of the Berlin Airlift (2011), by Richard Reeves, examines this 'first battle of the Cold War' by telling the stories of the American and British pilots who risked their lives to save their former enemies.

The Siegessäule (Victory Column) in Tiergarten park has had starring roles in Wim Wenders' movie *Wings of Desire* and U2's 'Stay' music video. It also inspired Paul van Dyk's 1998 trance hit 'For an Angel' and the name of Berlin's leading gay magazine.

HISTORY TWO GERMAN STATES

1951	1953	1957	1961
Berlin enters the celluloid spotlight with the inaugural Berlin International Film Festival (Berlinale).	The uprising of construction workers on Stalinallee (now Karl-Marx-Allee) spreads across the GDR before being crushed by Soviet tanks, leaving hundreds dead and injured.	The first Trabant car rolls off the assembly line in East Germany. Production continues until 1990.	Tragedy strikes just 11 days after the first stone of the Berlin Wall is laid. On 24 August, 24-year-old Günter Litfin is gunned down by border guards while attempting to swim across Humboldt Harbour.

economy grow at an average of 8% per year between 1951 and 1961. The recovery was largely engineered by economics minister Ludwig Erhard, who dealt with an acute labour shortage by inviting about 2.3 million foreign workers, mainly from Turkey, Yugoslavia and Italy, to Germany, thereby laying the foundation for today's multicultural society.

'Berlin is the testicle of the West. When I want the West to scream, I squeeze on Berlin.' – Nikita Khrushchev, Soviet Communist Party Secretary, 1963

The Soviet zone, meanwhile, grew into the Deutsche Demokratische Republik (DDR, German Democratic Republic or GDR), making East Berlin its capital and Wilhelm Pieck its first president. From the outset, though, the Sozialistische Einheitspartei Deutschlands (SED, Socialist Unity Party of Germany), led by Walter Ulbricht, dominated economic, judicial and security policy. In order to counter any opposition, the Ministry for State Security, or Stasi, was established in 1950, with its headquarters based in Lichtenberg (now the Stasimuseum). Regime opponents were incarcerated at the supersecret Gedenkstätte Hohenschönhausen (Stasi Prison) nearby.

Economically, East Germany stagnated, in large part because of the Soviets' continued policy of asset stripping and reparation payments. Stalin's death in 1953 raised hopes for reform but only spurred the GDR government to raise production goals even higher. Smouldering discontent erupted in violence on 17 June 1953 when 10% of GDR workers took to the streets. Soviet troops quashed the uprising, with scores of deaths and the arrest of about 1200 people.

The Wall Goes Up

Through the 1950s the economic gulf between the two Germanys widened, prompting hundreds of thousands of East Berliners to seek a future in the West. Eventually, the exodus of mostly young and well-educated East Germans strained the troubled GDR economy so much that – with Soviet consent – its government built a wall to keep them in. Construction of the Berlin Wall, the Cold War's most potent symbol, began on the night of 13 August 1961.

Australian journalist Anna Funder documents the Stasi, East Germany's vast domestic spy apparatus, by letting both victims and perpetrators tell their stories in her 2004 book *Stasiland*.

This stealthy act left Berliners stunned. Formal protests from the Western Allies, as well as massive demonstrations in West Berlin, were ignored. Tense times followed. In October 1961, US and Soviet tanks faced off at Checkpoint Charlie, pushing to the brink of war.

The appointment of Erich Honecker (1912–94) as leader of East Germany in 1971 opened the way for rapprochement with the West and enhanced international acceptance of the GDR. In September that year the Western Allies and the Soviet Union signed a new Four Power Accord in the Kammergericht (courthouse) in Schöneberg. It guaranteed access to West Berlin from West Germany and eased travel restrictions between East and West Berlin. The accord paved the way for the Basic

1963	1964	1967	1971
US president John F Kennedy professes his solidarity with the people of Berlin when giving his famous 'Ich bin ein Berliner' speech at the town hall in Schöneberg on 26 June.	A master plan to turn Alexanderplatz, East Berlin's central square, into a socialist architectural showcase begins. The square's crowning glory, Fernsehturm, opens in 1969.	The death of Benno Ohnesorg, an unarmed student who is shot by a police officer while demonstrating against the Shah of Persia's visit to West Berlin, draws attention to the student movement.	The four Allies sign the Four Power Accord, which confirms Berlin's independent status. A year later East and West Germany recognise each other's sovereignty in the Basic Treaty.

Treaty, signed a year later, in which the two countries recognised each other's sovereignty and borders and committed to setting up 'permanent missions' in Bonn and East Berlin, respectively.

Life in the Divided City

For 45 years, Berlin was a political exclave in the cross hairs of the Cold War. After the Berlin Wall was built in 1961, the city's halves developed as completely separate entities.

West Berlin

West Berlin could not have survived economically without heavy subsidies from the West German government in the form of corporate tax incentives and a so-called *Berlinzulage,* a monthly tax-free bonus of 8% on pretax income for every working Berliner. West Berliners had access to the same aspects of capitalism as all other West Germans, including a wide range of quality consumer goods, the latest technology and imported foods. Then, as now, the main shopping spine was Kurfürstendamm and its extension, Tauentzienstrasse, the crown jewel of which, the KaDeWe department store, left no shopping desire unfulfilled.

Since West Berlin was completely surrounded by East Berlin and East Germany, its residents liked to joke that no matter in which direction you travelled, you were always 'going east'. Still, West Berliners suffered no restrictions on travel and were free to leave and return as they pleased, as well as to choose their holiday destinations. Berlin was linked to West Germany by air, train and four transit roads, which were normal autobahns or highways also used by East Germans. Transit travellers were not allowed to leave the main road. Border checks were common and often involved harassment and time-consuming searches.

East Berlin

From the outset, East Germany's economic, judicial and security policy was dominated by a single party, the SED. Among its prime objectives was the moulding of its citizens into loyal members of a new socialist society. Children as young as six years old were folded into a tight network of state-run mass organisations, and in the workplace the unions were in charge of ideological control and conformity. Officially, membership of any of these groups was voluntary, but refusing to join usually led to limits on access to higher education and career choices. It could also incite the suspicion of the much-feared Stasi.

The standard of living in East Berlin was higher than in the rest of East Germany, with the Centrum Warenhaus on Alexanderplatz (today's Galeria Kaufhof) a flagship store. While basic foods (bread, milk,

To alleviate acute housing shortages, three new satellite cities – Marzahn, Hohenschönhausen and Hellersdorf – consisting of massive prefab housing blocks for 300,000 people were built in the 1970s and '80s on East Berlin's outskirts. Equipped with mod cons like central heating and indoor plumbing, these modern apartments were much coveted.

1976	1987	1989	1989
The Palace of the Republic, which houses the GDR parliament, opens on 23 April, on the site where the royal Hohenzollern palace had been demolished in 1950.	East and West Berlin celebrate the city's 750th birthday separately. On 12 June US President Ronald Reagan stands at the Brandenburg Gate and states 'Mr Gorbachev, tear down this wall!'	On 9 October East Germany celebrates the 40th anniversary of its founding as demonstrations in favour of reforms reverberate through East Berlin.	On 4 November half a million Berliners demand freedom of speech, press and assembly. The Berlin Wall opens on 9 November without a single bullet being fired.

butter, some produce) were cheap and plentiful, fancier foods and high-quality goods were in short supply and could often only be obtained with connections and patience. Queues outside shops were a common sight and many items were only available as so-called *Bückware,* meaning that they were hidden from plain view and required the sales clerk to bend *(bücken)* to retrieve them from beneath the counter. Bartering for goods was also common practice. Western products could only be purchased in government-run retail shops, called *Intershops,* and only by the privileged few who had access to hard currency – the East German mark was not accepted.

After the Wall went up in 1961, East Berliners, along with other East Germans, were only allowed to travel within the GDR and to other Eastern Bloc countries. Most holiday trips were state-subsidised and union-organised, and who was allowed to go where, when and for how long depended on such factors as an individual's productivity and level of social and political engagement. Those who could afford it could book a package holiday abroad through the Reisebüro der DDR (GDR Travel Agency).

Women enjoyed greater equality in East Germany than their western counterparts. An extensive government-run childcare system made it easier to combine motherhood and employment, and nearly 90% of all women were employed, many in such 'nontraditional' fields as engineering and construction. However, this gender equality did not necessarily translate into the private sphere, where women remained largely responsible for child-raising and domestic chores. Rising through the ranks at work or in organisations was also rare for women. In fact, the only female member of the Ministerrat (Council of Ministers) was Erich Honecker's wife, Margot Honecker.

The first Love Parade, a techno cavalcade that would draw millions of people to Berlin each summer between 1989 and 2006, actually kicked off modestly with just one truck and 150 ravers partying on West Berlin's Kurfürstendamm.

The Wall Comes Down

Hearts and minds in Eastern Europe had long been restless for change, but German reunification came as a surprise to the world and ushered in a new and exciting era. The so-called Wende (turning point, ie the fall of communism) came about as a gradual development that ended in a big bang – the collapse of the Berlin Wall on 9 November 1989.

The Germany of today, with 16 unified federal states, was hammered out through a volatile political debate and negotiations to end post-WWII occupation zones. The first significant step towards unification occurred on 1 July 1990 when monetary, economic and social union became realities, leading to the abolition of border controls and to the Deutschmark becoming the common currency. On 31 August of the same year, the Unification Treaty, in which both East and West pledged

1990	1991	1994	1999
The official reunification of the two Germanys goes into effect on 3 October. The date becomes a national holiday.	Members of the Bundestag (parliament) vote to reinstate Berlin as Germany's capital and to move the federal government here. Berliners elect the first joint city government.	The last British, French, Russian and American troops withdraw from Berlin, ending nearly half a century of occupation and protection.	On 19 April the German parliament holds its first session in the historic Reichstag building, after complete restoration by Lord Norman Foster.

to create a unified Germany, was signed in the Kronprinzenpalais on Unter den Linden. Around the same time, representatives of East and West Germany and the four victorious WWII allied powers (the USSR, France, the UK and the US), who had held the right to determine Germany's future since 1945, met in Moscow. Their negotiations resulted in the signing of the Two-Plus-Four Treaty, which ended postwar occupation zones and fully transferred sovereignty to a united Germany. Formal unification became effective on 3 October 1990, now Germany's

JEWISH BERLIN: MENDELSSOHN TO LIBESKIND

Since reunification, Berlin has had the fastest-growing Jewish community in the world. Their backgrounds are diverse: most are Russian Jewish immigrants but there are also Jews of German heritage, Israelis escaping their war-torn homeland and American expats lured by Berlin's low-cost living and limitless creativity. Today there are about 13,000 active members of the Jewish community, including 1000 belonging to the Orthodox congregation Adass Yisroel. And since not all Jews choose to be affiliated with a synagogue, the actual population is estimated to be at least twice as high.

The community supports 11 synagogues, two *mikve* ritual baths, several schools, numerous cultural institutions and a small number of kosher restaurants and shops. The golden-domed Neue Synagoge (New Synagogue) on Oranienburger Strasse is the most visible beacon of Jewish revival, even though today it's not primarily a house of worship but a community and exhibition space. In Kreuzberg, the Jüdisches Museum, a spectacular structure by Daniel Libeskind, tracks the ups and downs of Jewish life in Germany for almost 2000 years. Another key Jewish site is the Friedhof Grosse Hamburger Strasse, Berlin's oldest Jewish cemetery and final resting home of Enlightenment philosopher Moses Mendelssohn, who arrived in Berlin in 1743. His progressive thinking and lobbying paved the way for the Emancipation Edict of 1812, which made Jews full citizens of Prussia, with equal rights and duties.

By the end of the 19th century, many of Berlin's Jews, then numbering about 5% of the population, had become thoroughly German in speech and identity. When a wave of Hasidic Jews escaping the pogroms of Eastern Europe arrived around the same time, they found their way to today's Scheunenviertel, which at that time was an immigrant slum with cheap housing.

By 1933 Berlin's Jewish population had grown to around 160,000 and constituted one-third of all Jews living in Germany. The well-known horrors of the Nazi years sent most into exile and left 55,000 dead. Only about 1000 to 2000 Jews are believed to have survived the war years in Berlin, often with the help of their non-Jewish neighbours; their acts of courage are commemorated at the Gedenkstätte Stille Helden. Many memorials throughout the city commemorate the Nazi's victims. The most prominent is, of course, the Holocaust Memorial, near the Brandenburg Gate.

2001	2006	2008	2011
Openly gay politician Klaus Wowereit is elected governing mayor of Berlin.	Berlin's first central train station, the Hauptbahnhof, opens on 26 May. Two weeks later Germany kicks off the 2006 FIFA World Cup.	The last flight takes off from Berlin-Tempelhof Airport, which becomes an event space and public park.	Berlin's population passes the 3.5 million mark, growing 1.2%, the most within a single year since reunification in 1990. Most of the growth comes from people moving to Berlin.

national holiday. In December 1990 Germany held its first unified post-WWII elections.

In 1991 a small majority (338 to 320) of members in the Bundestag (German parliament) voted in favour of moving the government to Berlin and of making Berlin the German capital once again. On 8 September 1994 the last Allied troops stationed in Berlin left the city after a festive ceremony.

The Postunification Years

In December 2017, 711,000 people living in Berlin (19% of the city's population) were foreigners. There are people from 185 nations, including 19,900 Americans, 13,456 Brits, 3958 Australians and 3515 Canadians. Berlin's Turkish community represents the single largest foreign population with 98,121 people.

With reunification, Berlin once again became the seat of government in 1999. Mega-sized construction projects such as Potsdamer Platz and the government quarter eradicated the physical scars of division but did little to improve the city's balance sheet or unemployment statistics. It didn't help that Berlin lost the hefty federal subsidies it had received during the years of division. More than 250,000 manufacturing jobs were lost between 1991 and 2006, most of them through closures of unprofitable factories in East Berlin. Add to that mismanagement, corruption, a banking scandal and excessive government spending and it's no surprise that the city ran up a whopping debt of €60 million.

Elected in 2001, the new governing mayor Klaus Wowereit responded by making across-the-board spending cuts, but with a tax base eroded by high unemployment and ever-growing welfare payments, they did little initially to get Berlin out of the poorhouse. Eventually, though, the economic restructure away from a manufacturing base and towards the service sector began to bear fruit. Job creation in the capital has outpaced that of Germany in general for almost 12 years. No German city has a greater number of business start-ups. Its export quota has risen steadily, as has its population. The health, transport and green-technology industries are growing in leaps and bounds.

On the cultural front, Berlin exploded into a hive of cultural cool with unbridled nightlife, a vibrant art scene and booming fashion and design industries. In 2006 it became part of Unesco's Creative Cities Network. Some 170,000 people are employed in the cultural sector, which generates an annual turnover of around €13 billion. An especially important subsector is music, with nearly 10% of all related companies, including Universal and MTV, moving their European headquarters to Berlin over the past 20 years.

2013	2015	2016	2017
Construction of the Berlin City Palace as the Humboldt Forum intercultural centre commences on 21 June. Planned completion date is 2019.	Chancellor Angela Merkel's offer of temporary asylum to refugees brings 79,034 new arrivals to Berlin, mostly from Syria, Iraq and Afghanistan.	A terror attack on the Christmas market on Breitscheidplatz by a Tunisian asylum seeker leaves 12 people dead and 56 injured.	Angela Merkel gets reelected to a fourth term as chancellor.

Architecture

From the Schloss Charlottenburg to the Reichstag, Fernsehturm to Berliner Philharmonie, the Jewish Museum to the Sony Center – Berlin boasts some mighty fine architecture. It's an eclectic mix, to be sure, shaped by the city's unique history, especially
the destruction of WWII and the contrasting urban-planning visions during the years
of division. Since reunification, though, Berlin has become a virtual laboratory for
the world's elite architects, David Chipperfield, Norman Foster and Daniel Libeskind
among them.

Modest Beginnings

Very few buildings from the Middle Ages until the 18th century have
survived time, war and modernist town planning. Only two Gothic
churches – the red-brick Nikolaikirche (1230) and Marienkirche (1294) –
bear silent witness to the days when today's metropolis was just a small

Above: St Marienkirche
(p112)

trading town. The former anchors the Nikolaiviertel, a mock-medieval quarter built on the site of the city's original settlement as East Germany's contribution to Berlin's 750th anniversary celebrations in 1987. It's a hodgepodge of genuine historic buildings like the Knoblauchhaus and replicas of historic buildings such as the Zum Nussbaum inn.

A smidgeon of residential medieval architecture also survives in the outer district of Spandau, both in the Gotisches Haus and the half-timbered houses of the Kolk quarter.

Traces of the Renaissance, which reached Berlin in the early 16th century, are rarer still; notable survivors include the Jagdschloss Grunewald and the Zitadelle Spandau.

Going for Baroque

As the city grew, so did the representational needs of its rulers, especially in the 17th and 18th centuries. In Berlin, this role fell to Great Elector Friedrich Wilhelm, who systematically expanded the city by adding three residential quarters, a fortified town wall and a tree-lined boulevard known as Unter den Linden.

This was the age of baroque, a style merging architecture, sculpture, ornamentation and painting into a single *Gesamtkunstwerk* (complete work of art). In Berlin and northern Germany it retained a formal and precise bent, never quite reaching the exuberance favoured in regions further south.

The Great Elector may have laid the groundwork, but it was only under his son, Elector Friedrich III, that Berlin acquired the stature of an exalted residence, especially after he crowned himself *King* Friedrich I in 1701. Two major baroque buildings survive from his reign, both blueprinted by Johann Arnold Nering: Schloss Charlottenburg, which Johann Friedrich Eosander later expanded into a Versailles-inspired three-wing palace; and the Zeughaus (armoury; today's Deutsches Historisches Museum) on Unter den Linden. The museum's modern annexe, named the IM Pei Bau (IM Pei Building) after its architect, was added in the 1990s. Fronted by a transparent, spiral staircase shaped like a snail shell, it's a harmonious interplay of glass, natural stone and light and an excellent example of Pei's muted postmodernist approach.

Meanwhile, back in the early 18th century, two formidable churches were taking shape on Gendarmenmarkt in the heart of the immigrant Huguenot community, who at the time accounted for about 25% of the population. These were the Deutscher Dom (German Church) by Martin Grünberg, and the Französischer Dom (French Church) by Louis Cayart.

No king had a greater impact on Berlin's physical layout than Frederick the Great (Friedrich II). Together with his childhood friend architect Georg Wenzeslaus von Knobelsdorff, he masterminded the Forum Fridericianum, a cultural quarter centred on today's Bebelplatz. It was built in a style called 'Frederician rococo', which blends baroque and neoclassical elements. Since the king's war exploits had emptied his

Built as a summer palace for King Friedrich I's wife Sophie-Charlotte, Schloss Charlottenburg was originally called Schloss Lietzenburg but was renamed after the popular queen's sudden death in 1705.

BERLIN & ITS WALLS

1250 The first defensive wall is built of boulders and stands 2m high.

14th century The wall is fortified with bricks and raised to a height of 5m.

1648–1734 The medieval wall is replaced by elaborate fortifications.

1734–1866 A customs wall with 18 city gates replaces the bastion.

1961–1989 The Berlin Wall divides the city.

Neue Wache (p92)

coffers, he could only afford to partially realise his vision by building the neoclassical Staatsoper (State Opera House); the Sankt-Hedwigs-Kathedrale (St Hedwig Cathedral), inspired by Rome's Pantheon; the playful Alte Bibliothek (Old Royal Library); and the Humboldt Universität (Humboldt University), originally a palace for the king's brother Heinrich. Knobelsdorff also designed the Neuer Flügel (New Wing) expansion of Schloss Charlottenburg. His crowning achievement, though, was Schloss Sanssouci (Sanssouci Palace) in Potsdam.

After Knobelsdorff's death in 1753, two architects continued in his tradition: Philipp Daniel Boumann – who designed Schloss Bellevue (Bellevue Palace) for Frederick's youngest brother, August Ferdinand – and Carl von Gontard, who added the domed towers to the Deutscher Dom and Französischer Dom on Gendarmenmarkt.

The Schinkel Touch

The architectural style that most shaped Berlin was neoclassicism, thanks in large part to one man: Karl Friedrich Schinkel (p283), arguably Prussia's most prominent architect. Turning away from baroque flourishes, neoclassicism drew upon columns, pediments, domes and other design elements that had been popular throughout antiquity.

Schinkel assisted with the design of Queen Luise's mausoleum in Schloss Charlottenburg's park in 1810, but didn't truly make his mark until his first major solo commission, the Neue Wache (New Guardhouse) on Unter den Linden, was completed in 1818. Originally an army guardhouse, it is now an antiwar memorial accented with a haunting sculpture by Käthe Kollwitz.

The nearby Altes Museum (Old Museum) on Museumsinsel (Museum Island), with its colonnaded front, is considered Schinkel's most mature

Gendarmenmarkt's Konzerthaus (p87)

work. Other neoclassical masterpieces include the Schauspielhaus (now the Konzerthaus Berlin) on Gendarmenmarkt and the Neue Pavillon (New Pavilion) in Schlossgarten Charlottenburg. Schinkel's most significant departure from neoclassicism, the turreted Friedrichswerdersche Kirche, was inspired by a Gothic Revival in early-19th-century England.

After Schinkel's death in 1841, several of his disciples kept his legacy alive, notably Friedrich August Stüler, who built the original Neues Museum (New Museum) and the Alte Nationalgalerie (Old National Gallery), both on Museumsinsel, as well as the Matthäuskirche (Church of St Matthew) in today's Kulturforum.

Top Four Prussian Palaces

Schloss Sanssouci (p223; Potsdam)

Schloss Charlottenburg (p211; Charlottenburg)

Neues Palais (p227; Potsdam)

Schlösschen auf der Pfaueninsel (p234; Wannsee)

Housing for the Masses

In his 1930 book *Das Steinerne Berlin* (Stony Berlin), Werner Hegemann fittingly refers to Berlin as 'the largest tenement city in the world'. The onset of industrialisation in the middle of the 19th century lured to the capital hundreds of thousands, who dreamed of improving their lot in the factories. Something had to be done to beef up the city's infrastructure and provide cheap housing for the masses, and quick. A plan drawn up in 1862 under chief city planner James Hobrecht called for a city expansion along two circular ring roads bisected by diagonal roads radiating in all directions from the centre – much like the spokes of a wheel. The land in between was divided into large lots and sold to speculators and developers. Building codes were limited to a maximum building height of 22m (equivalent to five stories) and a minimum courtyard size of 5.34m by 5.34m, just large enough for fire-fighting equipment to operate in.

Such lax regulations led to the uncontrolled spread of sprawling working-class tenements called *Mietskasernen* (literally 'rental barracks') in newly created peripheral districts such as Prenzlauer Berg, Kreuzberg, Wedding and Friedrichshain. Each was designed to squeeze the maximum number of people into the smallest possible space. Entire families crammed into tiny, lightless flats reached via internal staircases that also provided access to shared toilets. Many flats doubled as workshops or sewing studios. Only those in the street-facing front offered light, space and balconies – and they were reserved for the bourgeoisie.

The Empire Years

The architecture in vogue after the creation of the German Empire in 1871 reflected the representational needs of the united Germany and tended towards the pompous. No new style, as such, emerged as architects essentially recycled earlier ones (eg Romanesque, Renaissance, baroque, sometimes weaving them all together) in an approach called *Historismus* (historicism) or *Wilhelmismus,* after Kaiser Wilhelm I. As a result, many buildings in Berlin look much older than they actually are. Prominent examples include the Reichstag by Paul Wallot and the Berliner Dom (Berlin Cathedral) by Julius Raschdorff, both in neo-Renaissance style. Franz Schwechten's Anhalter Bahnhof and the Kaiser-Wilhelm-Gedächtniskirche (Memorial Church), both in ruins, reflect the neo-Romanesque, while the Bode-Museum by Ernst von Ihne is a neobaroque confection.

While squalid working-class neighbourhoods emerged in the north, east and south of the city centre, western Berlin (Charlottenburg, Wilmersdorf) was developed for the middle and upper classes under none other than the 'Iron Chancellor' Otto von Bismarck himself. He had the Kurfürstendamm widened, lining it and its side streets with attractive townhouses. Those with serious money and status moved even further west, away from the claustrophobic centre. The villa colonies in leafy Grunewald and Dahlem are another Bismarck legacy and still among the ritziest residential areas today.

The Birth of Modernism

While most late-19th-century architects were looking to the past, a few progressive minds managed to make their mark, mostly in industrial and commercial design. Sometimes called the 'father of modern architecture', Peter Behrens (1868–1940) taught later modernist luminaries such as Le Corbusier, Walter Gropius and Ludwig Mies van der Rohe.

Berlin's architectural growth was notably influenced by advancements in transportation. The first train chugged from Berlin to Potsdam in 1838, the first S-Bahn rumbled along in 1882 and the U-Bahn kicked into service in 1902.

The industrial age saw Berlin's population explode. It more than doubled to 969,050 between 1858 and 1875, doubling again by 1905 and fuelling the need for cheap and plentiful housing.

ARCHITECTURE THE EMPIRE YEARS

THE BAUHAUS

Celebrating its 100th birthday in 2019, the Bauhaus was founded in Weimar by Berlin architect Walter Gropius as a multidisciplinary school that aimed to abolish the distinction between 'fine' and 'applied' arts and to unite the artistic with daily life. One of its chief mottos was 'form follows function': products were crafted with an eye towards mass production and featured strong, clear lines and little, if any, ornamentation. From the beginning, the movement attracted heavyweights such as Paul Klee, Lyonel Feininger, Wassily Kandinsky, Marcel Breuer and Wilhelm Wagenfeld.

After conservative politicians closed the Weimar school in 1925, it found refuge in Dessau before moving to Berlin in 1932 with Ludwig Mies van der Rohe at the helm. Just one year later the Nazis shut down the school for good. Most of its practitioners went into exile. Gropius became director of Harvard's architecture school, while Mies van der Rohe held the same post at the Illinois Institute of Technology in Chicago. Both men were instrumental in developing the Bauhaus' stylistic successor, the so-called International Style.

Top: Berliner Dom (p113)

Bottom: Reichstag (p82)

Hufeisensiedlung (p279)

One of his earliest works, the 1909 AEG Turbinenhalle at Huttenstrasse 12-14 in Moabit, is considered an icon of early industrial architecture.

After WWI the 1920s spirit of innovation lured some of the finest avant-garde architects to Berlin, including Bruno and Max Taut, Le Corbusier, Mies van der Rohe, Erich Mendelsohn, Hans Poelzig and Hans Scharoun. In 1924 they formed an architectural collective called Der Ring (The Ring) whose members were united by the desire to break with traditional aesthetics (especially the derivative historicism) and to promote a modern, affordable and socially responsible approach to building.

Their theories were put into practice as Berlin entered another housing shortage. Led by chief city planner Martin Wagner, Ring members devised a new form of social housing called *Siedlungen* (housing estates). In contrast to the claustrophobic tenements, it opened up living space and incorporated gardens, schools, shops and other communal areas that facilitated social interaction. Together with Bruno Taut, Wagner himself designed the Hufeisensiedlung (Horseshoe Colony) in Neukölln, which, in 2008, became one of six Berlin housing estates recognised as a Unesco World Heritage Site (p279).

In nonresidential architecture, expressionism flourished with Erich Mendelsohn as its leading exponent. This organic, sculptural approach is nicely exemplified by the Universum Kino (Universum Cinema; 1926), which is today's Schaubühne at Lehniner Platz; it greatly influenced the Streamline Moderne movie palaces of the 1930s. Emil Fahrenkamp's 1931 Shell-Haus at Reichspietschufer 60 follows similar design principles. Reminiscent of a giant upright staircase, it was one of Berlin's earliest steel-frame structures, concealed beneath a skin of travertine.

The only remaining prewar buildings on Alexanderplatz are the Berolinahaus (1930) and the Alexanderhaus (1932), both by Peter Behrens.

Olympiastadion (p219)

Its extravagant silhouette is best appreciated from the southern bank of the Landwehrkanal.

Nazi Monumentalism

Modernist architecture had its legs cut out from under it as soon as Hitler came to power in 1933. The new regime immediately shut down the Bauhaus School (p275), one of the most influential forces in 20th-century building and design. Many of its visionary teachers, including Gropius, Mies van der Rohe, Wagner and Mendelsohn, went into exile in the US.

Back in Berlin, Hitler, who was a big fan of architectural monumentalism, put Albert Speer in charge of turning Berlin into the Welthauptstadt Germania, the future capital of the Reich. Today, only a few buildings offer a hint of what Berlin might have looked like had history taken a different turn. These include the coliseumlike Olympiastadion, Tempelhof Airport and the former air force ministry that now houses Germany's Federal Finance Ministry.

A Tale of Two Cities

Even before the Wall was built in 1961, the clash of ideologies and economic systems between East and West also found expression in the architectural arena.

East Berlin

East Germans looked to Moscow, where Stalin favoured a style that was essentially a socialist reinterpretation of good old-fashioned neoclassicism. The most prominent East German architect was Hermann

Henselmann, the brains behind the Karl-Marx-Allee (called Stalinallee until 1961) in Friedrichshain. Built between 1952 and 1965, it was East Berlin's showcase 'socialist boulevard' and, with its Moscow-style 'wedding-cake buildings', the epitome of Stalin-era pomposity. It culminates at Alexanderplatz, the historic central square that got a distinctly socialist makeover in the 1960s.

While Alexanderplatz and the Karl-Marx-Allee were prestige projects, they did not solve the cries for affordable modern housing, which reached a crescendo in the early 1970s. The government responded by building three massive satellite cities on the periphery – Marzahn, Hohenschönhausen and Hellersdorf – which leapt off the drawing board in the 1970s and '80s. Like a virtual Legoland for giants, these huge housing developments largely consist of row upon row of rectangular high-rise *Plattenbauten,* buildings made from large, precast concrete slabs. Marzahn alone could accommodate 165,000 people in 62,000 flats. Since they offered such mod cons as private baths and lifts, this

UNCOMMON ENVIRONS FOR THE COMMON FOLK

Architecturally speaking, Museumsinsel, Schloss Sanssouci and the Hufeisensiedlung in Neukölln could not be more different. Yet all have one thing in common: they are Unesco World Heritage Sites. Along with five other working-class housing estates throughout Berlin, the Hufeisensiedlung was inducted onto this illustrious list in 2008.

Created between 1910 and 1933 by such leading architects of the day as Bruno Taut and Martin Wagner, these icons of modernism are the earliest examples of innovative, streamlined and functional – yet human-scale – mass housing and stand in stark contrast to the slumlike, crowded tenements of the late 19th century. The flats, though modest, were functionally laid out and had kitchens, private baths and balconies that let in light and fresh air.

Hufeisensiedlung, Neukölln (Lowise-Reuter-Ring; U-Bahn: Parchimer Allee) Taut and Wagner dreamed up a three-storey-high horseshoe-shaped colony (1933–35) with 1000 balconied flats wrapping around a central park. From the station follow Fritz-Reuter-Allee north.

Gartenstadt Falkenberg, Köpenick (Akazienhof, Am Falkenberg & Gartenstadtweg; S-Bahn: Grünau) Built by Taut between 1910 and 1913, the oldest of the six Unesco-honoured estates is a cheerful jumble of colourfully painted cottages. Approach from Am Falkenberg.

Siemensstadt, Spandau (Geisslerpfad, Goebelstrasse, Heckerdamm, Jungfernheideweg, Mäckeritzstrasse; U-Bahn: Siemensdamm) This huge development (1929–31) combines Walter Gropius' minimalism, Hugo Häring's organic approach and Hans Scharoun's ship-inspired designs. Best approach is via Jungfernheideweg.

Schillerpark Siedlung, Wedding (Barfussstrasse, Bristolstrasse, Corker Strasse, Dubliner Strasse, Oxforder Strasse, Windsorer Strasse, Wedding; U-Bahn: Rehberge) Inspired by Dutch architecture, this large colony was masterminded by Taut (1924–30) and sports a dynamic red-and-white-brick facade. Best approach is via Barfussstrasse.

Weisse Stadt, Reinickendorf (Aroser Allee, Baseler Strasse, Bieler Strasse, Emmentaler Strasse, Genfer Strasse, Gotthardstrasse, Romanshorner Weg, Schillerring, Sankt-Galler-Strasse; U-Bahn: Residenzstrasse) Martin Wagner's 'White City' (1929–31) includes shops, a kindergarten, a cafe, a central laundry and other communal facilities. Best approach is via Aroser Allee.

Wohnstadt Carl Legien, Prenzlauer Berg (streets around Erich-Weinert-Strasse; S-Bahn: Prenzlauer Allee) For this development (1928–30) in Prenzlauer Berg, Taut arranged rows of four-to-five-storey-high houses and garden areas in a semi-open space. Approach via Erich-Weinert-Strasse.

East German architecture on Karl Marx Allee (p183)

type of housing was very popular among East Germans, despite the monotony of the design.

West Berlin

In West Berlin, urban planners sought to eradicate any references to Nazi-style monumentalism and to rebuild the city in a modernist fashion. Their prestige project became the Hansaviertel, a loosely structured leafy neighbourhood of midrise apartment buildings and single-family homes, northwest of Tiergarten. Built from 1954 to 1957, it drew the world's top architects, including Gropius, Alvar Aalto and Le Corbusier and was intended to be a model for other residential quarters.

The 1960s saw the birth of a large-scale public building project, the Kulturforum, a museum and concert-hall complex conceptualised by Hans Scharoun. His Berliner Philharmonie, the first building to be completed in 1963, is considered a masterpiece of sculptural modernism. Among the museums, Mies van der Rohe's temple-like Neue Nationalgalerie (New National Gallery) is a standout. A massive glass-and-steel cube, it perches on a raised granite podium and is lidded by a coffered, steel-ribbed roof that seems to defy gravity.

The West also struggled with a housing shortage and built its own versions of mass-scale housing projects, including Gropiusstadt in southern Neukölln and the Märkisches Viertel in Reinickendorf, in northwest Berlin.

The New Berlin

Reunification presented Berlin with both the challenge and the opportunity to redefine itself architecturally. With the Wall and death strip gone, the two city halves had to be physically rejoined across

In the 1920s Adolf Hitler's half-brother Alois was a waiter at Weinhaus Huth, the only building on Potsdamer Platz to survive WWII intact. During the Cold War, it stood forlorn in the middle of the death strip for decades.

Paul-Löbe-Haus (p88), part of the Band des Bundes

huge gashes of empty space. Critical Reconstruction continued to be the guiding principle under city planning director Hans Stimmann. Architects had to follow a long catalogue of parameters with regard to building heights, facade materials and other criteria. The goal was to rebuild Berlin within its historic forms rather than creating a modern, vertical city.

Potsdamer Platz

The biggest and grandest of the post-1990 Berlin developments (and, incidentally, an exception to the tenets of Critical Reconstruction), Potsdamer Platz is a modern reinterpretation of the historic square that was Berlin's bustling heart until WWII. From terrain once bisected by the Berlin Wall has sprung an urban quarter laid out along a dense, irregular street grid in keeping with a 'European city'. Led by Renzo Piano, it's a collaboration of an international roster of renowned architects, including Helmut Jahn, Richard Rogers and Rafael Moneo. Structures are of medium height, except for three gateway high-rises overlooking the intersection of Potsdamer Strasse and Ebertstrasse.

Pariser Platz

Pariser Platz was reconstructed from the ground up. It's a formal, introspective square framed by banks, embassies and the Hotel Adlon that, in keeping with Critical Reconstruction, had to have natural stone facades. The one exception is the glass-fronted Akademie der Künste (Academy of Arts). Its architect, Günter Behnisch, had to fight tooth and nail for this facade, arguing that the square's only public building should feel open, inviting and transparent. The Adlon, meanwhile, is practically a spitting image of the 1907 original.

With its cool, calm facade, the DZ Bank on Pariser Platz seems untypical for its exuberant architect, Frank Gehry. The surprise, though, lurks beyond the foyer leading to a light-flooded atrium anchored by an enormous sci-fi-esque stainless-steel sculpture used as a conference room.

Regierungsviertel

The 1991 decision to move the federal government back to Berlin resulted in a flurry of building activity in the empty space between the Reichstag and the Spree River. Designed by Axel Schultes and Charlotte Frank, and arranged in linear east–west fashion, are the Federal Chancellery, the Paul-Löbe-Haus and the Marie-Elisabeth-Lüders-Haus. Together they form the Band des Bundes (Band of Federal Buildings) in a symbolic linking of the formerly divided city halves across the Spree.

Overlooking all these shiny new structures is the Reichstag, home of the Bundestag (German parliament), the glass dome of which is the most visible element of the building's total makeover masterminded by Norman Foster.

The glass-and-steel 'spaceship' on the northern riverbank is Berlin's first-ever central train station, the sparkling Hauptbahnhof, designed by the Hamburg firm of Gerkan, Marg und Partner and completed in 2006.

Top Buildings Since 1990

....

Jüdisches Museum (p157; Daniel Libeskind; Kreuzberg)

....

Reichstag Dome (p82; Norman Foster; Historic Mitte)

....

Sony Center (p122; Helmut Jahn; Potsdamer Platz)

....

Neues Museum (p106; David Chipperfield; Museumsinsel)

....

Hauptbahnhof (Gerkan, Marg und Partner; Historic Mitte)

More Architectural Trophies

In Kreuzberg, Daniel Libeskind's deconstructivist Jüdisches Museum (1999) is among the most daring and provocative structures in the new Berlin. With its irregular, zigzagging floor plan and shiny zinc skin pierced by gashlike windows, it is not merely a museum but a powerful metaphor for the troubled history of the Jewish people. Libeskind also designed the museum's extension, which opened in a nearby converted flower market in June 2013.

Near Gendarmenmarkt, along Friedrichstrasse, the Friedrichstadtpassagen (1996) is a trio of luxurious shopping complexes, including the glamorous Galeries Lafayette, that hide their jewel-like interiors behind postmodern facades.

Across town in the City West, several new structures have added some spice to the rather drab postwar architecture around Kurfürstendamm. The Ludwig-Erhard-Haus (1997), home of the Berlin stock market, is a great example of the organic architecture of the UK's Nicholas Grimshaw. Nearby, Kantdreieck (1995), designed by Kleihues + Kleihues, establishes a visual accent on Kantstrasse by virtue of its rooftop metal 'sail'. Noteworthy buildings along Ku'damm itself are Helmut Jahn's Neues Kranzler Eck (2000) and the Neues Ku-Damm-Eck (2001), a corner building with a gradated and rounded facade, designed by Gerkan, Marg und Partner and festooned with sculptures by Markus Lüpertz.

Another highlight was David Chipperfield's reconstruction of the Neues Museum (2009) on Museumsinsel. Like a giant jigsaw puzzle, it beautifully blends fragments from the original structure, which was destroyed in WWII, with modern elements. The result is so harmonious and impressive, it immediately racked up the accolades, including a prestigious award from the Royal Institute of British Architects (RIBA) in 2010.

Recent Developments & the Future

You'd think that, almost 30 years after reunification, the ballet of cranes would finally have disappeared, but there are still plenty of large-scale projects on the drawing board or under construction.

Construction of the replica of the former Prussian city palace (Berliner Stadtschloss) on Schlossplatz opposite Museumsinsel, which began in 2013, is on the finishing stretch. Set to open as the Humboldt-Forum in 2019/20, it will resemble its historic predecessor only from the outside, with the modern interior housing museums and cultural institutions.

ARCHITECTURE RECENT DEVELOPMENTS & THE FUTURE

PRUSSIA'S BUILDING MASTER: KARL FRIEDRICH SCHINKEL

Few architects have shaped the Berlin cityscape as much as Karl Friedrich Schinkel (1781–1841). After studying under David Gilly at the Prussian Building Academy in Berlin, he decamped to Italy for a couple of years to examine classical architecture in situ. He returned to a Prussia hamstrung by Napoleonic occupation and was forced to scrape by as a Romantic painter and furniture and set designer for a few years.

Things improved dramatically as soon as the French left Berlin in 1808, allowing Schinkel to quickly climb the career ladder within the Prussian civil service and eventually to become chief building director for the entire kingdom. He travelled tirelessly throughout the land, designing buildings, supervising construction and even developing principles for the protection of historic monuments.

Drawing inspiration from classical Greek architecture, Schinkel very much defined Prussian architecture between 1810 and 1840. His designs strive for the perfect balance between functionality and beauty, achieved through clear lines, symmetry and an impeccable sense for aesthetics. Berlin, which came to be known as 'Athens on the Spree', is littered with his buildings (p273).

Schinkel fell into a coma in 1840 and died one year later in Berlin. He's buried at the Dorotheenstädtischer Friedhof in Mitte.

In 2017, spies started moving into the new Berlin HQ of the Bundesnachrichtendienst (BND; Germany's federal intelligence agency) on Chausseestrasse, just north of the Scheunenviertel. Designed by Kleihues + Kleihues, the giant compound sits on a lot once occupied by the GDR-era Stadium of the World Youth and will provide work space for 4000 people.

The City West has also garnered several high-profile additions including the towering Waldorf Astoria Hotel and its equally soaring neighbour Upper West, a residential and commercial tower. Construction on Zoom, an office-and-retail building with a 150m-long, three-storey glass facade opposite the Astoria/Upper West twin towers, has also been completed.

Nearby, a couple of 1950s buildings have been reinvented for the 21st century. The iconic Bikini Berlin became Germany's first 'concept mall' after a total refurb in 2014. The curious name was inspired by its design: two 200m-long upper and lower sections are separated by an open floor supported by a curtain of columns. Today the middle section is chastely covered by a glass facade. Nearby, the sensitively restored 1950s Amerika Haus now houses the prestigious photography gallery C/O Berlin.

The biggest upcoming building project is the Europa-City, north of the Hauptbahnhof, an entire neighbourhood to be built on 40 hectares, complete with S-Bahn station, a bridge across the canal and leafy squares.

The Berliner Architekturpreis, which is awarded every three years, went in 2016 to the St Agnes Kirche, a brutalist church in Kreuzberg that was minimally converted into the spectacular art gallery König by Arno Brandlhuber.

If you want to learn more about Berlin's contemporary architecture, arrange for a tour (also in English) with Ticket B (www.ticket-b.de), an architect-run guide company.

Painting & Visual Arts

The arts are fundamental to everything Berlin holds dear, and the sheer scope of creative activity in the city is astounding. The city itself provides an iconic setting for a spectrum of visual arts, its unmistakable presence influencing artists and residents just as it does those canny visitors who take the time to dive in.

Early Beginnings

Fine art only began to flourish in Berlin in the late 17th century, when self-crowned King Friedrich I founded the Akademie der Künste (Academy of Arts) in 1696, egged on by court sculptor Andreas Schlüter. Schlüter repaid the favour with outstanding sculptures, including the *Great Elector on Horseback,* now in front of Schloss Charlottenburg, and the haunting masks of dying warriors in the courtyard of today's Deutsches Historisches Museum (German Historical Museum). Artistic accents in painting were set by Frenchman Antoine Pesne, who became Friedrich I's court painter in 1710. His main legacy is his elaborate portraits of the royal family members.

The arts also enjoyed a heyday under Friedrich I's grandson, Friedrich II (Frederick the Great), who became king in 1740. Friedrich drew heavily on the artistic expertise of his friend Georg Wenzeslaus von Knobelsdorff, a student of Pesne, and amassed a sizeable collection of works by French artists such as Jean Antoine Watteau.

The 19th Century

Neoclassicism emerged as a dominant sculptural style in the 19th century. Johann Gottfried Schadow's *Quadriga* – the horse-drawn chariot atop the Brandenburg Gate – epitomises the period. Schadow's student Christian Daniel Rauch had a special knack for representing idealised, classical beauty in a realistic fashion. His most famous work is the 1851 monument of Frederick the Great on horseback on Unter den Linden.

In painting, heart-on-your-sleeve romanticism that drew heavily on emotion and a dreamy idealism dominated the 19th century. A reason for this development was the awakening of a nationalist spirit in Germany, spurred by the Napoleonic Wars. Top dog of the era was Caspar David Friedrich, best known for his moody, allegorical landscapes. Although more famous as an architect, Karl Friedrich Schinkel also created some fanciful canvases. Eduard Gärtner's paintings documenting Berlin's evolving cityscape found special appeal among the middle classes.

A parallel development was the so-called Berliner Biedermeier, a more conservative and painstakingly detailed style that appealed to the emerging Prussian middle class. The name itself is derived from the German word for conventional *(bieder)* and the common surname of Meier; visit the Knoblauchhaus in the Nikolaiviertel for fine examples. The Alte Nationalgalerie on Museumsinsel and the Neuer Pavillon of Schloss Charlottenburg are both showcases of 19th-century paintings.

A student of Christian Daniel Rauch, the sculptor Reinhold Begas developed a neobaroque, theatrical style that met with a fair amount of controversy in his lifetime. Major works include the Schiller memorial on Gendarmenmarkt and the Neptune fountain near the Fernsehturm (TV Tower).

Into the 20th Century

Berliner Secession

The Berliner Secession was formed in 1898 by a group of progressively minded artists who rejected the traditional teachings of the arts academies that stifled any new forms of expression. The schism was triggered in 1891, when the established Verein Berliner Künstler (Berlin Artist Association) refused to show paintings by Edvard Munch at its annual salon, and reached its apex in 1898 when the salon jury rejected a landscape painting by Walter Leistikow. Consequently, 65 artists banded together under the leadership of Leistikow and Max Liebermann and seceded from the Verein. Other famous Berliner Secession members included Lovis Corinth, Max Slevogt, Ernst Ludwig Kirchner, Max Beckmann and Käthe Kollwitz.

Expressionism

In 1905 Kirchner, along with Erich Heckel and Karl Schmidt-Rottluff, founded the artists' group Die Brücke (The Bridge) in Dresden: it turned the art world on its head with groundbreaking visions that paved the way for German expressionism. Abstract forms, a flattened perspective and bright, emotional colours characterised this new aesthetic. Die Brücke moved to Berlin in 1911 and disbanded in 1913. The small Brücke-Museum in the Grunewald has a fantastic collection of these influential artists.

Ironically, it was the expressionists who splintered off from the Berliner Secession in 1910 after their work was rejected by the Secession jury. With Max Pechstein at the helm, they formed the Neue Secession. The original Berliner Secession group continued but saw its influence wane, especially after the Nazi power grab in 1933.

The Bauhaus & Art Under the Nazis

The year 1919 saw the founding of the Bauhaus (p275) movement and school in Weimar. It was based on practical anti-elitist principles bringing form and function together, and had a profound effect on all modern design. Although the school moved to Dessau in 1925 and only came to Berlin in 1932, many of its most influential figures worked in Berlin. The Nazis forced it to close down in 1933. Unfortunately, the Bauhaus Archive, the museum built by Walter Gropius, will be closed for renovation until 2023 but there are still numerous events planned for 2019 on the 100th anniversary of the Bauhaus.

After the Nazi takeover many artists left the country and others ended up in prison or concentration camps, their works confiscated or destroyed.

The coppersmith Emanuel Jury, who cast the *Quadriga* sculpture atop the Brandenburg Gate, used his cousin as a model for the Goddess Victoria, pilot of the chariot.

For details on events taking place in Berlin and around Germany in celebration of the 100th anniversary of the Bauhaus in 2019, see www.bauhaus100.de.

PAINTING & VISUAL ARTS INTO THE 20TH CENTURY

ZILLE SEASON

Born in Dresden in 1858, Heinrich Zille moved to Berlin with his family when he was a child. A lithographer by trade, he became the first prominent artist to evoke the social development of the city as the tendrils of modernity reached Berlin. His instantly recognisable style depicted everyday life and real people, often featuring the bleak Hinterhöfe (back courtyards) around which so much of their lives revolved. Even during his lifetime Zille was acknowledged as one of the definitive documenters of his time, and since his death in 1929 his prolific photographic work has also come to be seen as a valuable historical record.

In 1903 Zille was accepted into the Berliner Secession, although he didn't really regard himself as an 'artist' as such, but more as a hard-working illustrator. When he died, thousands of Berliners turned out to pay their respects to the man whose pictures chronicled their daily lives with sharp humour and unsentimental honesty. There's a Zille Museum in the Nikolaiviertel dedicated to his life and work.

The art promoted instead was often terrible, favouring straightforward 'Aryan' forms and epic styles. Propaganda artist Mjölnir defined the typical look of the time with block Gothic scripts and idealised figures.

Berlin Dada

Dada was an avant-garde art movement formed in Zurich in 1916 in reaction to the brutality of WWI. It spread to Berlin in 1918 with the help of Richard Huelsenbeck, who held the first Dada event in a gallery in February that year and later produced the *First German Dada Manifesto*. Founding members included George Grosz, photomontage inventor John Heartfield and Hannah Höch; Marcel Duchamp, Kurt Schwitters and Hans Arp were among the many others who dabbled in Dada.

Dada artists had an irrational, satirical and often absurdist approach, imbued with a political undercurrent and a tendency to shock and provoke. The First International Dada Fair in 1920, for instance, took place beneath a suspended German officer dummy with a pig's head.

Post WWII

After WWII, Berlin's art scene was as fragmented as the city itself. In the east, artists were forced to toe the social realism line, at least until the late 1960s when artists of the Berliner Schule, including Manfred Böttcher and Harald Metzkes, sought to embrace a more interpretative and emotional form of expression inspired by the colours and aesthetic of Beckmann, Matisse, Picasso and other classical modernists. In the '70s, when conflicts of the individual in society became a prominent theme, underground galleries flourished and art became a collective endeavour.

In postwar West Berlin, artists eagerly embraced abstract art. Pioneers included Zone 5, which revolved around Hans Thiemann, and surrealists Heinz Trökes and Mac Zimmermann. In the 1960s politics was a primary concern and a new style called 'critical realism' emerged, propagated by artists like Ulrich Baehr, Hans-Jürgen Diehl and Wolfgang Petrick. The 1973 movement, Schule der Neuen Prächtigkeit (School of New Magnificence), had a similar approach. In the late 1970s and early 1980s, expressionism found its way back on to the canvases of Salomé, Helmut Middendorf and Rainer Fetting, a group known as the Junge Wilde (Young Wild Ones). One of the best-known German neoexpressionist painters is Georg Baselitz, who lives in Berlin and became internationally famous in the 1970s with his 'upside-down' works.

The Present

Berlin hosts one of the most exciting and dynamic arts scenes in Europe. With an active community of some 10,000 artists, there have been notable successes, most famously perhaps Danish-Icelandic artist Olafur Eliasson. Other major leaguers like Thomas Demand, Jonathan Meese, Via Lewandowsky, Isa Genzken, Tino Seghal, Esra Ersen, John Bock and the artist duo Ingar Dragset and Michael Elmgreen all live and work in Berlin, or at least have a second residence here.

Berlin has also emerged as a European street art capital with some major international artists like Blu, JR and Os Gemeos leaving their mark on the city. Local top talent includes Alias and El Bocho. Street art is especially prevalent in eastern Kreuzberg (especially around the U-Bahn station Schlesisches Tor) as well as in Mitte (Haus Schwarzenberg) and around the RAW complex in Friedrichshain. In 2016, Urban Nation, the world's first museum dedicated entirely to street art, opened in Berlin's Schöneberg district.

Art-world honchos descend upon Berlin in late April for the annual Gallery Weekend, when you can hop-scotch around 40 galleries, and the Berlin Biennale, a curated forum for contemporary art held over two months in spring or summer in even-numbered years.

To keep a tab on the contemporary art scene, check out the latest shows at the city's many high-calibre galleries, such as Galerie Eigen+Art or Contemporary Fine Arts, and visit the collections at Hamburger Bahnhof and the Sammlung Boros.

Literature & Film

Since its beginnings, Berlin's literary scene has reflected a peculiar blend of provincialism and worldliness, but the city's pioneering role in movie history is undeniable: in 1895 Max Skladanowsky screened early films on a bioscope, in 1912 one of the world's first film studios was established in Potsdam, and since 1951 Berlin has hosted a leading international film festival.

Literature

First Words

Berlin's literary history began during the 18th-century Enlightenment, an epoch dominated by humanistic ideals. A major author from this time was Gotthold Ephraim Lessing, noted for his critical works, fables and tragedies, who wrote the play *Minna von Barnhelm* (1763) in Berlin. During the Romantic period, an outgrowth of the Enlightenment, it was the poets who stood out, including Achim von Arnim, Clemens Brentano, and Heinrich von Kleist, who committed suicide at Wannsee lake in 1811.

In the mid-19th century, realist literature captured the imagination of the newly emerging middle class. Theodor Fontane raised the Berlin society novel to an art form by showing both the aristocracy and the middle class mired in their societal confinements. His 1894 novel, *Effi Briest,* is among his best-known works. Naturalism, a spin-off of realism, painstakingly recreated the milieux of entire social classes. Gerhard Hauptmann's portrayal of social injustice and the harsh life of the working class won him the Nobel Prize for Literature in 1912.

Modernism & Modernity

In the 1920s, Berlin became a literary hotbed, drawing writers like Alfred Döblin, whose definitive *Berlin Alexanderplatz* is a stylised meander through the seamy 1920s, and Anglo-American import Christopher Isherwood, whose brilliant semi-autobiographical *Berlin Stories* formed the basis of the musical and film *Cabaret.* During his time in Berlin in the 1930s, Vladimir Nabokov penned *The Gift* about a writer and Russian émigré whose fled the Russian Revolution for Berlin.

Other notables include the political satirists Kurt Tucholsky and Erich Kästner. Many artists left Germany after the Nazis came to power, and those who stayed often kept their mouths shut and worked underground, if at all.

In West Berlin, the postwar literary revival was led by *The Tin Drum* (1958), by Nobel Prize–winner Günter Grass, which traces recent German history through the eyes of a child who refuses to grow. In the mid-1970s, a segment of the East Berlin literary scene began to detach itself slowly from the socialist party grip. Christa Wolf is one of the best and most controversial East German writers, while Heiner Müller had the distinction of being unpalatable in both Germanys. His dense, difficult works include *The Man Who Kept Down Wages* and the *Germania* trilogy of plays.

Berlin Cult Novels

....

Berlin Alexanderplatz, Alfred Döblin (1929)

....

Goodbye to Berlin, Christopher Isherwood (1939)

....

Alone in Berlin, Hans Fallada (1947)

....

The Wall Jumper, Peter Schneider (1983)

....

Berlin Blues, Sven Regener (2001)

New Berlin Novel

In the 1990s, a slew of novels dealt with German reunification; many are set in Berlin, including Thomas Brussig's tongue-in-cheek *Heroes Like Us* (1998), Uwe Timm's *Midsummer Night* (1998), Peter Schneider's *Eduard's Homecoming* (1999) and Jana Hensel's *After the Wall: Confessions from an East German Childhood and the Life that Came Next* (2002). The late Nobel Prize–winner Günter Grass contributed *A Wide Field* (1995) to the debate. Also worth reading is Cees Nooteboom's *All Souls Day* (2002).

The lighter side of post-reunification Berlin is represented by Sven Regener, frontman of the Berlin band Element of Crime, whose hugely successful *Berlin Blues* (2001) is a boozy trawl through Kreuzberg nights at the time of the fall of the Wall. The runaway success story, however, was Russian-born author Wladimir Kaminer's *Russendisko* (Russian Disco, 2000), a collection of amusing, stranger-than-fiction vignettes about life in Berlin. Both *Berlin Blues* and *Russendisko* were made into feature films.

Foreign authors also continue to be inspired by Berlin. Ian McEwan's *The Innocent* (1990) and Joseph Kanon's *Leaving Berlin: A Novel* (2015) are both spy stories set in the 1950s. Kanon also wrote *The Good German* (2002), which was made into a motion picture. The *Berlin Noir* trilogy (1989–91), by the late British author Philip Kerr, features a private detective solving crimes in Nazi Germany. Berlin history unfolds in a dreamlike sequence in *Book of Clouds* (2009) by Chloe Aridjis. Another popular German author is Volker Kutscher whose 2008 novel *Der Nasse Fisch*, a detective story set in the 1920s, forms the basis of the successful TV series *Babylon Berlin*, which was released on Netflix in 2017.

Film

Before 1945

The legendary UFA (Universum Film AG), one of the world's first film studios, began shooting in Potsdam, near Berlin, in 1912 and continues to churn out both German and international blockbusters in its modern incarnation as the Filmstudios Babelsberg. The 1920s and early '30s were a boom time for Berlin cinema, with UFA emerging as Germany's flagship dream factory and Marlene Dietrich's bone structure and distinctive voice seducing the world. As early as 1919, Ernst Lubitsch produced historical films and comedies such as *Madame Dubarry*, starring Pola Negri and Emil Jannings; the latter went on to win the Best Actor Award at the very first Academy Awards ceremony in 1927. The same year saw the release of Walter Ruttmann's classic *Berlin: Symphony of a City*, a fascinating silent documentary that captures a day in the life of Berlin in the '20s.

Other 1920s movies were heavily expressionistic, using stark contrast, sharp angles, heavy shadows and other distorting elements. Well-known flicks employing these techniques include *Nosferatu*, a 1922 Dracula adaptation by FW Murnau, and the groundbreaking *Metropolis* (1927) by Fritz Lang. One of the earliest seminal talkies was Josef von Sternberg's *Der Blaue Engel* (1930) starring Dietrich. After 1933, though, film-makers found their artistic freedom, not to mention funding, increasingly curtailed, and by 1939 practically the entire industry had fled to Hollywood.

Films made during the Nazi period were mostly of the propaganda variety, with brilliant if controversial Berlin-born director Leni Riefenstahl (1902–2003) greatly pushing the genre's creative envelope. Her most famous film, *Triumph of the Will*, documents the 1934 Nuremberg

For an in-depth study of literature that emerged in Berlin after the fall of the Wall, pick up a copy of *Writing the New Berlin* (2008) by Katharina Gerstenberger.

Aside from the headline-grabbing Berlinale, dozens of other film festivals are held throughout the year, including the Jewish Film Festival, Feminist Film Week and the Too Drunk to Watch punk festival. See www.berliner-filmfestivals.de for the schedule.

MARLENE DIETRICH

••

Marlene Dietrich (1901–92) was born Marie Magdalena von Losch into a middle-class Berlin family. After acting school, she first captivated audiences as a hard-living, libertine flapper in 1920s silent movies, but quickly carved a niche as the dangerously seductive femme fatale. The 1930 talkie *Der Blaue Engel* (The Blue Angel) turned her into a Hollywood star and launched a five-year collaboration with director Josef von Sternberg. Her work on Sternberg's movie *Morocco* (1930) led to her only Oscar nomination. Although she never recaptured the successes of her early career, she continued making movies until 1984.

Dietrich built on her image of erotic opulence – dominant and severe but always with a touch of self-irony. She stayed in Hollywood after the Nazi rise to power, though Hitler, not immune to her charms, reportedly promised perks and the red-carpet treatment if she moved back to Germany. She responded with an empty offer to return if she could bring along Sternberg – a Jew and no Nazi favourite. She took US citizenship in 1937 and entertained Allied soldiers on the front.

After the war, Dietrich retreated slowly from the public eye, making occasional appearances in films but mostly cutting records and performing live cabaret. Her final years were spent in Paris, bedridden and accepting few visitors, immortal in spirit as mortality caught up with her. She's buried in **Städtischer Friedhof III** (Stubenrauchstrasse 43-45; ⊗8am-6pm; ⑤Bundesplatz; Ⓤ Bundesplatz).

Nazi party rally. *Olympia,* which chronicles the 1936 Berlin Olympic Games, was another seminal work.

After 1945

Like most of the arts, film-making has generally been well funded in Berlin since 1945, especially in the West. During the 1970s in particular, large subsidies lured directors back to the city, including such New German Film luminaries as Rainer Werner Fassbinder, Volker Schlöndorf, Wim Wenders and Werner Herzog. It was Wenders who made the highly acclaimed *Wings of Desire* (1987), an angelic love story swooping around the old, bare wasteland of Potsdamer Platz.

Some of the best films about the Nazi era include Wolfgang Staudte's *Die Mörder sind unter uns* (Murderers among Us, 1946); Fassbinder's *Die Ehe der Maria Braun* (The Marriage of Maria Braun, 1979); Margarethe von Trotta's *Rosenstrasse* (2003), and Oliver Hierschbiegel's extraordinary *Der Untergang* (Downfall, 2004), depicting Hitler's final days.

Cool places to plug into German movie history are the Museum für Film und Fernsehen at Potsdamer Platz, the Filmmuseum Potsdam and the Filmpark Babelsberg.

The first round of post-reunification flicks were light-hearted comedy dramas. A standout is the cult classic *Good Bye, Lenin!* (2003), Wolfgang Becker's witty and heart-warming tale of a son trying to recreate the GDR life to save his sick mother. It was Florian von Donnersmarck who first trained the filmic spotlight on the darker side of East Germany, with *The Lives of Others* (2006), an Academy Award–winner that reveals the stranglehold the East German secret police (Stasi) had on ordinary people.

Today

These days, 'Germany's Hollywood' is no longer in Munich or Hamburg but in Berlin, with an average of 300 German and international productions and co-productions being filmed on location and at the Filmstudios Babelsberg each year. Well-trained crews, modern studio and postproduction facilities, government subsidies and authentic 'old world' locations regularly attract such Hollywood royalty as Quentin

FAMOUS FILM LOCATIONS

Wings of Desire (1987) The top of the Siegessäule (Victory Column) in Tiergarten is a place where angels congregate and listen to people's thoughts.

Bourne Supremacy (2004) The epic car chase where Bourne (Matt Damon) forces Russian assassin Kirill (Karl Urban) to crash his car into a concrete divider in a tunnel was filmed in the Tiergartentunnel a year and a half before its official opening in 2006.

Good Bye, Lenin! (2003) The flat where Alexander Kerner (Daniel Brühl) recreates life in East Berlin for his ailing mother is in a modern high-rise at Berolinastrasse 21.

The Lives of Others (2006) The apartment where two of the main characters, the playwright Georg Dreymann (Sebastian Koch) and his actor wife Christa-Maria Sieland (Martina Gedeck), make their home is at Wedekindstrasse 21 in Friedrichshain.

The Hunger Games: Mockingjay Part 2 (2015) Scenes from the third instalment in this successful series were filmed at Tempelhof Airport.

Babylon Berlin (2017) The dance and party scenes set in the Moka Efta bar were filmed at the silent movie–era Delphi Cinema at Gustav-Adolf-Straße 2 in Prenzlauer Berg.

Tarantino (*Inglourious Basterds,* 2009) and George Clooney (*The Monuments Men,* 2014). Other recent big productions include Brian Percival's *The Book Thief* (2013), *The Grand Budapest Hotel* (2014), *The Hunger Games: Mockingjay Part 2* (2015), Tom Hanks' *A Hologram for the King* (2015), the entire fifth season of the TV series *Homeland* (2015) and Steven Spielberg's *Bridge of Spies* (2015).

Noteworthy recent films about Berlin include *A Coffee in Berlin* (*Oh Boy* in German, 2012), a tragicomedy about a young man struggling to find meaning in life in Berlin in the early 2000s, and *Victoria* (2015), miraculously filmed in a single continuous take, about a young Spanish woman who meets three Berlin guys after a night of clubbing and ends up robbing a bank, all in one night. *Axolotl Overkill* (2017), based on the 2010 novel by Helene Hegemann, also takes viewers on a high-paced ride around Berlin's notoriously hedonistic nightlife through the eyes of 16-year-old Mifti. On a more serious note, *Alone in Berlin* (2016), based on Hans Fallada's novel by the same name, deals with an innocent couple that falls victim to the Gestapo.

Internationally successful TV series starring Berlin are *Berlin Station* (2016), a high-tension spy drama, and especially *Babylon Berlin* (2017), a lushly filmed detective story set in Berlin just before the Nazis' power grab.

Music

Just like the city itself, Berlin's music scene is a shape-shifter, fed by the city's appetite for diversity and change. With at least 2000 active bands and dozens of indie labels, Berlin is Germany's undisputed music capital. About 60% of the country's music revenue is generated here, and it's where Universal Music and MTV have their European headquarters.

Beginnings

For centuries, Berlin was largely eclipsed by Vienna, Leipzig and other European cities when it came to music. One notable exception is Carl Maria von Weber's *Der Freischütz* (The Marksman), which premiered in 1821 at today's Konzerthaus on Gendarmenmarkt and is considered the first important German Romantic opera. Weber's music also influenced Berlin-born Felix Mendelssohn-Bartholdy's *A Midsummer Night's Dream* from 1843. The same year, fellow composer Giacomo Meyerbeer became Prussian General Music Director.

The Berliner Philharmoniker was established in 1882 and quickly gained international stature under Hans von Bülow and, after 1923, Wilhelm Furtwängler. After WWII, Herbert von Karajan took over the baton. In East Germany, a key figure was Hanns Eisler, composer of the country's national anthem.

The 1920s

Cabaret may have been born in 1880s Paris, but it became a wild and libidinous grown-up in 1920s Berlin. Jazz was the dominant sound, especially after American performer Josephine Baker's headline-grabbing performances at the Theater des Westens dressed in nothing but a banana skirt. More home-grown cabaret music came in the form of the Berlin *Schlager* – light-hearted songs with titles like 'Mein Papagei frisst keine harten Eier' ('My parakeet doesn't eat hard-boiled eggs'), which teetered on the silly and surreal. The most successful *Schlager* singing group was the *a cappella* Comedian Harmonists, who were famous for their perfect vocal harmonies, which sounded like musical instruments.

Another runaway hit was *The Threepenny Opera*, written by Bertolt Brecht with music by Kurt Weill. It premiered in 1928 with such famous songs as 'Mack the Knife'. Friedrich Hollaender was also a key composer

BERLIN TRACKS

1973
Berlin (Lou Reed) Dark song about the tragedy of two star-crossed junkies.

1977
Heroes (David Bowie) Two lovers in the shadow of the 'Wall of Shame'.

1980
Wir stehen auf Berlin (Ideal) Love declaration by the seminal *Neue Deutsche Welle* band.

1991
Zoo Station (U2) Bono embarks on a surreal journey inspired by a Berlin train station.

1995
Born to Die in Berlin (The Ramones) Drug-addled musings revealing Berlin's dark side.

2000
Dickes B (Seeed) Reggae ode to the 'Big B' (ie Berlin).

2007
Kreuzberg (Bloc Party) Looking for true love...

2008
Schwarz zu Blau (Peter Fox) Perfect portrait of Kottbusser Tor grit and grunge.

2013
Where are We Now? (David Bowie) Melancholic reminiscence of Bowie's time in 1970s Berlin.

in the cabaret scene, noted for his wit, improvisational talent and clever lyrics. Among his most famous songs is 'Falling in Love Again', sung by Marlene Dietrich in *Der Blaue Engel*. Like so many other talents (including Weill and Brecht), Hollaender left Germany when the Nazis brought down the curtain, and continued his career in Hollywood.

The pulsating 1920s drew numerous classical musicians to Berlin, including Arnold Schönberg and Paul Hindemith, who taught at the Akademie der Künste and the Berliner Hochschule, respectively. Schönberg's atonal compositions found a following here, as did his experimentation with noise and sound effects. Hindemith explored the new medium of radio and taught a seminar on film music.

Paul Kalkbrenner's 2008 semi-autobiographical *Berlin Calling* was the first mature film about the techno scene in Berlin.

Pop, Punk & Rock Before 1990

Since the end of WWII, Berlin has spearheaded many of Germany's popular-music innovations. In West Berlin, Tangerine Dream helped to propagate the psychedelic sound of the late 1960s, while the Ton Steine Scherben, led by Rio Reiser, became a seminal German-language rock band in the '70s and early '80s. Around the same time, Kreuzberg's subculture launched the punk movement at SO36 and other famous clubs. Regular visitors included David Bowie and Iggy Pop, who were Berlin flat buddies on Hauptstrasse in Schöneberg in the 1970s. Trying to kick a drug addiction and greatly inspired by Berlin's brooding mood, Bowie partly wrote and recorded his Berlin Trilogy (*Low, Heroes, Lodger*) at the famous Hansa Studios, which he dubbed the 'Hall by the Wall'. Check out Thomas Jerome Seabrook's *Bowie in Berlin: A New Career in a New Town* (2008) for a cool insight into those heady days.

In East Germany, access to Western rock and other popular music was restricted and few Western stars were invited to perform live. The artistic freedom of East German talent was greatly compromised as all lyrics had to be approved and performances were routinely monitored. Nevertheless, a slew of home-grown *Ostrock* (eastern rock) bands emerged. Some major ones like The Puhdys, Karat, Silly and City managed to get around the censors by disguising criticism with seemingly innocuous metaphors, or by deliberately inserting provocative lyrics

A memorial plaque marks the house at Hauptstrasse 155 in Schöneberg, where the late David Bowie and his buddy Iggy Pop bunked in the late '70s. The seven-room flat was on the 1st floor; Pop later moved into his own digs across the back courtyard

HANSA STUDIOS: BOWIE'S HALL BY THE WALL

Complete this analogy: London is to Abbey Road as Berlin is to...Well? **Hansa Studios** (Map p326; www.meistersaal-berlin.de; Köthener Strasse 38; M41, Potsdamer Platz, Potsdamer Platz), of course, that seminal recording studio that has exerted a gravitational pull on international artists since the Cold War. Now used as an event location, the only way to get inside this famous building (and find out why Depeche Mode's Martin Gore stripped down naked for the recording of a love song) is with the highly recommended Berlin Music Tours (p301).

The 'Big Hall by the Wall' was how David Bowie fittingly dubbed its glorious Studio 2, better known as the Meistersaal (Masters' Hall). As you look through arched windows, imagine Bowie looking over the concrete barrier and perhaps waving at the gun-toting guards in their watchtowers. In the late '70s, the White Duke recorded his tortured visions for the seminal album Heroes here, after completing Low, both part of his Berlin Trilogy. Bowie also produced The Idiot and Lust for Life with his buddy Iggy Pop, who he bunked with at Hauptstrasse 155 in Schöneberg.

There's a long list of other music legends who have taken advantage of the special sound quality at Hansa Studios, including Nina Hagen, Nick Cave, David Byrne, Einstürzende Neubauten, Die Ärzte, Snow Patrol, Green Day, REM and The Hives. Depeche Mode produced three albums here – Construction Time Again, Some Great Reward and Black Celebration – between 1983 and 1986.

that they fully expected to be deleted by the censorship board. All built up huge followings on both sides of the Wall.

Many nonconformists were placed under an occupational ban and prohibited from performing. Singer-songwriter Wolf Biermann became a cause célèbre when, in 1976, he was not allowed to return to the GDR from a concert series in the West despite being an avid – albeit regime-critical – socialist. When other artists rallied to his support, they too were expatriated, including Biermann's stepdaughter Nina Hagen, an East Berlin pop singer who later became a West Berlin punk pioneer. The small but vital East Berlin punk scene produced Sandow and Feeling B, members of whom went on to form the industrial metal band Rammstein in 1994, still Germany's top musical export.

Once in West Berlin, Hagen helped chart the course for *Neue Deutsche Welle* (German New Wave). This early '80s sound produced such West Berlin bands as D.A.F, Trio, Neonbabies, Ideal and UKW, as well as Rockhaus in East Berlin. The '80s also saw the birth of Die Ärzte, who released their last album, the live recording *Die Nacht der Dämonen*, in 2013. Einstürzende Neubauten pioneered a proto-industrial sound that transformed oil drums, electric drills and chainsaws into musical instruments. Its founder Blixa Bargeld joined The Bad Seeds, helmed by Nick Cave who spent some heroin-addled time in Berlin in the early 1980s.

The Beauty of Transgression: a Berlin Memoir (2011) by US-born artist Danielle de Picciotto (partner of Einstürzende Neubauten bassist Andreas Hacke) beautifully captures the atmosphere and history of Berlin's creative underground from the 1980s to recent times.

Pop, Rock & Hip-Hop After 1990

Since reunification, hundreds of indie, punk, alternative and goth bands have gigged to appreciative Berlin audiences. The still active Die Ärzte, Element of Crime and Einstürzende Neubauten were joined by other successful exports, such as alternative punk rockers Beatsteaks, and the pop-rock band Wir sind Helden, helmed by the charismatic Judith Holofernes, who released her first solo album in 2014. The Beatsteaks made headlines the same year with their latest (and seventh) studio album.

Other fine Berlin music originates from a jazz/breaks angle (electrojazz and breakbeats, favouring lush grooves, obscure samples and chilled rhythms. Remix masters Jazzanova are top dogs of the downtempo scene. Their Sonar Kollektiv label also champions similar artists, including Micatone. Reggae-dancehall has been huge in Berlin ever since Seeed was founded in 1998; frontperson Peter Fox' solo album *Stadtaffe* (2008) was one of the best-selling albums in Germany and also won the 2010 Album of the Year Echo Award (the 'German Grammy'). Also commercially successful is Culcha Candela, who have essentially pop-ified the Seeed sound and released their fifth studio album, *Flätrate*, in 2011.

Home-grown rap and hip-hop have a huge following, thanks to Sido, Fler, Bushido and Kool Savas, who cofounded Masters of Rap (MOR) in 1996. Also hugely successful are Berlin-based Casper and Marteria. K.I.Z., meanwhile, are more of a gangsta rap parody. Other famous Berlin-based artists include eccentric Canadian transplant King Khan, who fuelled the garage rock revival; the country and western band Boss Hoss; the electro-folky singer-songwriter Clara Hill; the indie rock band Gods of Blitz; and the uncategorisable 17 Hippies.

The 2014 documentary B-Movie: Lust & Sound in West Berlin 1979–1989, by Mark Reeder, is a tour de force on the subcultural 1980 music scene, featuring Joy Division, Nick Cave, Die Ärzte, Einstürzende Neubauten and others.

Techno Town

Call it techno, electro, house, minimal – electronic music is the sound of Berlin and its near-mythical club culture has defined the capital's cool factor and put it on the map of global hedonists. The sound may have been born in Detroit but it came of age in Berlin.

The seed was sown in dark and dank cellar club UFO on Köpenicker Strasse in 1988. The 'godfathers' of the Berlin sound, Dr Motte, Westbam and Kid Paul, played their first gigs here, mostly sweat-driven acid house all-night raves. It was Motte who came up with the idea to take the party to the street with a truck, loud beats and a bunch of friends dancing behind it – and the Love Parade was born (it peaked in 1999 with 1.5 million people swarming Berlin's streets).

The Berlin Wall's demise, and the vacuum of artistic freedom it created, catapulted techno out of the underground. The associated euphoria, sudden access to derelict and abandoned spaces in eastern Berlin and lack of control by the authorities were all defining factors in making Berlin a techno mecca. In 1991 the techno-sonic gang followed UFO founder Dimitri Hegemann to the label Tresor, which launched camouflage-sporting DJ Tanith along with trance pioneer Paul van Dyk. Today Tresor is still a seminal brand representing Jeff Mills, Blake Baxter and Cristian Vogel, among many others.

Key label BPitch Control, founded by Ellen Allien in 1999, launched the careers of Modeselektor, Apparat, Sascha Funke and Paul Kalkbrenner. Another heavyweight is the collective Get Physical, which includes Booka Shade, Nôze and the dynamic duo M.A.N.D.Y., who fuse house and electro with minimal and funk to create a highly danceable sound. The charmingly named Shitkatapult, founded in 1997 by Marco Haas (aka T.Raumschmiere), does everything from cutting-edge electronica to tech-rock and mellow ambient. Another mainstay is the deep house duo Tiefschwarz. Other leading Berlin DJs include Berghain residents Ben Klock, Marcel Dettmann, Tama Sumo and Steffi, who are all represented by the Ostgut label. .

Foreign artists have also influenced the Berlin scene, including the provocative Canadian songster and performance artist Peaches, UK-Canadian techno innovator Richie Hawtin and Chilean minimal master Ricardo Villalobos.

The Berlin-based Barenboim-Said Akademie opened in 2016 and was named after its founders Daniel Barenboim and the American-Palestinian scholar Edward Said. It is an accredited music academy focused on students from the Middle East and North Africa.

Survival Guide

Transport

ARRIVING IN BERLIN

Most visitors arrive in Berlin by air. The latest opening date of Berlin's new central airport, about 24km southeast of the city centre, next to Schönefeld Airport, has been set for 2020, but we're not holding our breath. In the meantime, flights continue to land at the city's Tegel and Schönefeld Airports.

Lufthansa and practically all other major European airlines and low-cost carriers (including easyJet, Ryanair and Germanwings) operate direct flights to Berlin from throughout Europe. There are a few direct flights from US gateway cities such as Miami and New York, but normally travel from outside Europe involves changing planes in another European city such as Frankfurt or Amsterdam.

Depending on your departure point, travel to Berlin by train or bus is a viable alternative.

Flights, cars and tours can be booked online at lonely planet.com/bookings.

Berlin Tegel Airport

Bus

➡ The bus stop is outside the main entrance to Terminal A.

➡ The TXL express bus connects Tegel to Alexanderplatz (€2.80, AB ticket; 40 minutes) via Hauptbahnhof (central train station) and Unter den Linden every 10 minutes.

➡ For the City West around Zoologischer Garten take bus X9 (€2.80, AB ticket; 20 minutes), which also runs at 10-minute intervals.

➡ Bus 109 heads to U-/S-Bahn station Zoologischer Garten every 10 minutes; it's slower and useful only if you're headed somewhere along Kurfürstendamm (€2.80, AB ticket; 20 to 30 minutes).

S-Bahn

The closest S-Bahn station is Jungfernheide, which is a stop on the S41/S42 (the Ringbahn, or circle line). It is linked to the airport by bus X9. Another Ringbahn station, Beusselstrasse, links up with the TXL bus route. Trips, including bus and train, cost €2.80 (Tariff AB).

U-Bahn

The U-Bahn station closest to the airport is Jakob-Kaiser-Platz, which is connected by bus 109 and X9 to the airport. From Jakob-Kaiser-Platz, the U7 takes you directly to Schöneberg, Kreuzberg and Neukölln. Trips cost €2.80 (Tariff AB).

Taxi

Taxi rides cost about €25 to Zoologischer Garten

CLIMATE CHANGE & TRAVEL

Every form of transport that relies on carbon-based fuel generates CO_2, the main cause of human-induced climate change. Modern travel is dependent on aeroplanes, which might use less fuel per kilometre per person than most cars but travel much greater distances. The altitude at which aircraft emit gases (including CO_2) and particles also contributes to their climate change impact. Many websites offer 'carbon calculators' that allow people to estimate the carbon emissions generated by their journey and, for those who wish to do so, to offset the impact of the greenhouse gases emitted with contributions to portfolios of climate-friendly initiatives throughout the world. Lonely Planet offsets the carbon footprint of all staff and author travel.

PUBLIC TRANSPORT PRIMER

➡ Berlin's comprehensive public transport system is administered by BVG and consists of the U-Bahn (subway, underground), the S-Bahn (light rail), buses and trams. U-Bahn and S-Bahn are the most efficient methods of transport.

➡ For full information and a handy journey planner, go to www.bvg.de (also in English).

➡ Network maps are posted in stations (usually on platforms), on the U-Bahn and S-Bahn, and on trams.

➡ Tickets are available from vending machines at U-Bahn and S-Bahn stations and on trams, from bus drivers and from BVG sales offices.

➡ Tickets must be validated (stamped) before boarding the U-Bahn and S-Bahn. Those bought from bus drivers and on the tram are prevalidated.

➡ Vending machines in U-Bahn and S-Bahn stations accept cash and EC Cards but not credit cards. Bus and tram tickets must be paid for in cash. Tram vending machines only take coins; sometimes exact change is required. Bus drivers carry only a small amount of change.

➡ For most rides you need an AB ticket; if taking more than two trips per day, get a *Tageskarte* (day pass).

➡ To determine the right direction, use the map to identify the final stop of the line, which is also posted on electronic displays on station platforms.

and €28 to Alexanderplatz and take 30 to 45 minutes. There's a €0.50 surcharge for trips originating at this airport.

Berlin Schönefeld Airport

S-Bahn & Regional Trains

➡ This is the fastest way to get into town.

➡ The airport train station is 400m from the terminals; free shuttle buses run every 10 minutes.

➡ Airport-Express trains make the trip to central Berlin twice hourly. Note: these are regular Deutsche Bahn regional trains denoted as RE7 and RB14 in timetables. The journey takes 20 minutes to Alexanderplatz and 30 minutes to Zoologischer Garten.

➡ The S-Bahn S9 runs every 20 minutes along the same tracks but stops more frequently, reaching Alexanderplatz in 37 minutes and Zoologischer Garten in 51 minutes.

➡ For the Messe (trade fairgrounds), take the S45 to Südkreuz and change to the S41 to Messe Nord/ICC. Trains run every 20 minutes and the journey takes 55 minutes.

➡ All journeys cost €3.40.

Taxi
Budget about €45 to €50 and 45 minutes to an hour for the cab ride to central Berlin.

U-Bahn
Schönefeld is not served by the U-Bahn. The nearest station, Rudow, is about a 10-minute ride on bus X7 or bus 171 from the airport. From Rudow, the U7 takes you straight into town. This connection is useful if you're headed for Neukölln or Kreuzberg. You will need an ABC transport ticket (€3.40).

Berlin Hauptbahnhof

Berlin's **Hauptbahnhof** (Main Train Station; Europaplatz, Washingtonplatz; S Hauptbahnhof, U Hauptbahnhof) is in the heart of the city, just north of the Reichstag

and Brandenburg Gate. From the station, the U-Bahn, the S-Bahn, trams and buses provide links to all parts of town. Taxi ranks are located outside the north exit (Europaplatz) and the south exit (Washingtonplatz).

➡ Buy tickets in the Reisezentrum (travel centre) located between tracks 14 and 15 on the first upper level (OG1), online at www.bahn.de or, for shorter distances, at station vending machines.

➡ The left-luggage office (€5 per piece, per 24 hours) is behind the Reisebank currency exchange on level OG1, opposite the Reisezentrum.

Berlin Central Bus Station (ZOB)

➡ The newly upgraded **Zentraler Omnibusbahnhof** (ZOB, Central Bus Station; ☎030-3010 0175; www.zob-berlin.de; Messedamm 8; S Messe/ICC Nord, U Kaiserdamm) is near the trade fairgrounds on the western city edge. Flixbus also stops at around a dozen other points in town, including the airports and Alexanderplatz.

➡ The closest U-Bahn station to ZOB is Kaiserdamm, about 400m north and served by the U2 line, which travels to Zoologischer Garten in about eight minutes and to Alexanderplatz in 28 minutes. Tickets cost €2.80 (Tariff AB).

➡ The nearest S-Bahn station is Messe Süd/ICC, about 200m east of ZOB. It is served by the Ringbahn (circle line) S41/S42 and handy for such districts as Prenzlauer Berg, Friedrichshain and Neukölln. You need an AB ticket (€2.80).

➡ Budget about €14 for a taxi ride to the western city centre around Zoo station and €24 to the eastern city centre around Alexanderplatz.

GETTING AROUND

Walking around Berlin's neighbourhoods (*Kieze* in local parlance) is a joy but to travel between them you want to make use of the excellent public transport system or rent a bicycle.

U-Bahn

➡ The U-Bahn is the quickest way of getting around Berlin. Lines (referred to as U1, U2, etc) operate from 4am until about 12.30am and throughout the night on Friday, Saturday and public holidays (all lines except the U4 and U55). From Sunday to Thursday, night buses take over in the interim.

➡ Tickets are available from vending machines (no credit cards) in stations or on platforms and must be validated before boarding.

S-Bahn & Regional Trains

➡ S-Bahn trains (S1, S2, etc) don't run as frequently as the U-Bahn, but they make fewer stops and are thus useful for covering longer distances. Trains operate from 4am to 12.30am and all night on Friday, Saturday and public holidays.

➡ Destinations further afield are served by RB and RE trains. You'll need an ABC or

Deutsche Bahn (☏01806 99 66 33; www.bahn.de) ticket to use these trains.

➡ Tickets are available from vending machines (no credit cards) in stations or on platforms and must be validated before boarding.

Bus

➡ Buses are slow but useful for sightseeing on the cheap (especially routes 100 and 200). They run frequently between 4.30am and 12.30am. Night buses (N19, N23 etc) take over after 12.30am.

➡ MetroBuses, designated M19, M41 etc, operate 24/7.

➡ Tickets bought from bus drivers (cash only) don't need to be validated.

Tram

➡ Trams (*Strassenbahn*) operate almost exclusively in the eastern districts.

➡ Those designated M1, M2 etc run 24/7.

➡ A useful line is the M1, which

TRAVEL FARES & PASSES

➡ If you're taking more than two trips in a day, a *Tageskarte* (day pass) will save you money. It's valid for unlimited rides on all forms of public transport until 3am the following day. The *Kleingruppen-Tageskarte* (group day pass) is valid for up to five people travelling together.

➡ For short trips, buy the *Kurzstreckenticket*, which is good for three stops on the U-Bahn or S-Bahn, or six stops on any bus or tram; no changes allowed.

➡ For longer stays, consider the *Wochenkarte* (seven-day pass), which is transferable and lets you take along another adult and up to three children aged six to 14 for free after 8pm Monday to Friday and all day on Saturday, Sunday and holidays. Monthly passes are also available.

TICKET TYPE	AB (€)	BC (€)	ABC (€)
Einzelfahrschein (single)	2.80	3.10	3.40
Ermässigt (reduced single)	1.70	2.20	2.50
Tageskarte (day pass)	7	7.40	7.70
Kleingruppen-Tageskarte (group day pass)	19.90	20.60	20.80
Wochenkarte (7-day pass)	30	31.10	37.50

links Prenzlauer Berg with Museum Island via Hackescher Markt.

➡ Tickets are available from in-tram vending machines (cash only) and don't need to be validated.

Taxi

➡ You can order a taxi by phone, flag one down or pick one up at a rank. At night, cars often wait outside theatres, clubs and other venues.

➡ Flag fall is €3.90, then it's €2 per kilometre up to 7km and €1.50 for each additional kilometre. There's a surcharge of €1.50 if paying by credit or debit card, but none for night trips. Bulky luggage is charged at €1 per piece.

➡ Best avoided during daytime rush hour.

➡ Tip about 10%.

Sample fares:

JOURNEY	COST
Alexanderplatz to Zoologischer Garten	€18
East Side Gallery to Brandenburger Tor	€15
Jüdisches Museum to Hackescher Markt	€11
Kollwitzplatz to Gendarmenmarkt	€14

Bicycle

➡ Bicycles are handy both for in-depth explorations of local neighbourhoods and for getting across town. More than 650km of dedicated bike paths make getting around less intimidating even for riders who are not experienced or confident.

➡ Having said that, always be aware of dangers caused by aggressive or inattentive drivers. Watch out for car doors opening and for cars turning right in front of you at intersections.

Getting caught in tram tracks is another potential problem.

➡ Bicycles may be taken aboard designated U-Bahn and S-Bahn carriages (look for the bicycle logo) as well as on night buses (Sunday to Thursday only) and trams. You need a separate bicycle ticket called a *Fahrradkarte* (€1.90). Taking a bike on regional trains (RE, RB) costs €3.30 per trip or €6 per day.

➡ The websites www.bbbike.de and www.vmz-info.de are handy for route planning.

Hire

Many hostels and hotels have guest bicycles, often for free or a nominal fee, and rental stations are at practically every corner. These include not only the expected locations (bike shops, gas stations) but also convenience stores, cafes and even clothing boutiques.

Prices start at €6 per day, although the definition of 'day' can mean anything from eight hours to 24 hours. A cash or credit-card deposit and/or photo ID is usually required.

The following outfits are recommended. Call or check the website for branches and be sure to book ahead, especially in summer.

Fahrradstation (☑0180 510 8000; www.fahrradstation. com; bike rentals per day/week €15/49) Large fleet of quality bikes, English-speaking staff and seven branches across Mitte, Kreuzberg, Charlottenburg, Prenzlauer Berg and Potsdam. The Friedrichstrasse branch rents e-bikes. Online bookings available.

Prenzlberger Orange Bikes (Map p338;☑030-4435 6852; www.orange-bikes.de; Kollwitzstrasse 37; per 24hr €7; ◷noon-6pm Apr-Oct; ⓊSenefelderplatz) One of the cheapest bike rentals in town with proceeds going to social projects for kids and youth.

Lila Bike (www.berlin-city tours-by-bike.de; Schönhauser Allee 41; first 24hr €8, additional 24hr €5; ◷10am-8pm Mon-Sat, 1-8pm Sun; ⓊEberswalder Strasse) Small outfit in Prenzlauer Berg with quality bikes and great prices.

Car & Motorcycle

Driving in Berlin is more hassle than it's worth, especially since parking is expensive and difficult to find.

➡ All the big internationals maintain branches at the airports, major train stations and throughout town. Book in advance for the best rates.

➡ Taking your rental vehicle into an Eastern European country, such as the Czech Republic or Poland, is often a no-no; check in advance if you're planning a side trip from Berlin.

TOURS

Walking Tours

Alternative Berlin Tours (☑0162 819 8264; www. alternativeberlin.com; tours €12-35) Not your run-of-the-mill tour company, this outfit runs subculture tours that get beneath the skin of the city, including an excellent street-art tour and workshop, an alternative pub crawl and a craft beer tour. For a primer on the city, join the tip-based 'Free Tour' offered twice daily in season. The website has all the details and a booking function.

Original Berlin Walks (☑030-301 9194; www.berlin walks.de; adult/concession from €14/12) Berlin's longest-running English-language walking tour company has a general city tour plus a roster of themed tours (eg Hitler's Germany, East Berlin, Queer

Berlin), as well as a food crawl, a craft beer tour and trips out to Sachsenhausen concentration camp and Potsdam. The website has details on timings and meeting points.

Brewer's Berlin Tours
(☑0177 388 1537; www.brewers berlintours.com; adult/concession €15/12) Local experts run an epic six-hour Best of Berlin tour (€25) and a shorter donation-based Berlin Free Tour, as well as a Craft Beer & Breweries tour with tastings (€39), a street-art tour (€12) and a food crawl (€29). Details and booking online.

Insider Tour Berlin
(☑030-692 3149; www.insider tour.com; adult/concession €14/12) This well-established company offers an insightful general city tour plus themed tours (eg Cold War, Third Reich, Jewish Berlin) and trips to Sachsenhausen concentration camp, Potsdam and Dresden. No prebooking required. Check the website for timings and meeting points.

New Berlin Tours (www. newberlintours.com; tours adult/concession from €14/12; ⊙free tour 10am, 11am, noon, 2pm & 4pm) Entertaining and informative city spins by the pioneers of the donation-based 'free tour' and the pub crawl (€12). Also offers tours to Sachsenhausen concentra-

tion camp, themed tours (Red Berlin, Third Reich, Alternative Berlin) as well as a beer tour and a trip to Potsdam. Check the website for timings, prices and meeting points.

Bicycle Tours

Fat Tire Tours Berlin (Map p332;☑030-2404 7991; www. fattiretours.com/berlin; Panoramastrasse 1a; adult/concession/under 12 incl bicycle from €28/26/14; ⑤Alexanderplatz, ⑪Alexanderplatz) This top-rated outfit runs English-language tours by bike, e-bike and Segway. Options include a classic city spin; tours with a focus on Nazi Germany, the Cold War or 'Modern Berlin'; a trip to Potsdam; and an evening food tour. Tours leave from the Fernsehturm (TV Tower) main entrance. Reservations advised.

Berlin on Bike (Map p338; ☑030-4373 9999; www.berlin onbike.de; Knaackstrasse 97, Kulturbrauerei, Court 4; tours incl bike adult/concession €24/20, bike rental per 24hr €10; ⊙8am-8pm mid-Mar–mid-Nov, 10am-4pm Mon-Sat mid-Nov–mid-Mar; ⑯M1, ⑪Eberswalder Strasse) This well-established company has a busy schedule of insightful and fun bike tours led by locals. There are daily

English-language city tours (Berlin's Best) and Berlin Wall tours as well as an Alternative Berlin tour thrice weekly and a Street-Art tour on Fridays. Other tours (eg night tours) are available on request. Reservations recommended for all tours. Also rents bicycles for €10 per 24 hours or €50 per week.

Bus Tours

Hop-on hop-off sightseeing buses tick off the key sights on two-hour loops with basic taped commentary in multiple languages. Buses depart roughly every 15 or 30 minutes between 10am and 5pm or 6pm daily; tickets are sold on board and cost from €10 to €20 (discounts for children). Traditional tours (where you stay on the bus), combination boat and bus tours as well as trips to Potsdam Spreewald are also available. Look for flyers in hotel lobbies or at tourist offices.

Boat Tours

Stern und Kreisschiffahrt (☑030-536 3600; www. sternundkreis.de; tours from €15; ⊙Mar-Dec) A lovely way to experience Berlin on a warm day is from the deck of a boat cruising along the city's rivers, canals and lakes. Tours range from one-hour spins around the historic centre to longer trips to Schloss Charlottenburg and beyond. Optional audioguide €2.

Reederei Bruno Winkler (☑030-349 9595; www. reedereiwinkler.de; tours €15-23) Local boat company runs tours on the Spree and the Landwehrkanal, from short one-hour spins around the historic centre to longer trips out to Schloss Charlottenburg.

TRAVELLING AT NIGHT

No matter what time it is, there's always a way to get around Berlin.

➡ U-Bahn lines run every 15 minutes all night long on Friday, Saturday and public holidays (all but the U4 and U55).

➡ From Sunday to Thursday, night buses (N1, N2 etc) run along the U-Bahn routes between 12.30am and 4am at 30-minute intervals.

➡ MetroBuses (designated M11, M19 etc) and MetroTrams (M1, M2 etc) run nightly every 30 minutes between 12.30am and 4.30am.

Reederei Riedel (☎030-6796 1470; www.reederei-riedel.de; tours from €14; ☺Mar-Oct) A lovely way to see Berlin is from the deck of a boat floating along the city's rivers, canals and lakes. This well-established outfit operates short city tours and longer trips on the Spree and out to the Müggelsee. Commentary is taped.

Speciality Tours

Berlin Music Tours
(☎0172 424 2037; www.musictours-berlin.com; Bowie walk €19; ☺noon Sat & Sun Apr-Oct, 11.30am Nov-Mar) Berlin's music history – Bowie to U2 and Rammstein, cult clubs to the Love Parade – comes to life during expertly guided bus and walking tours run by this well-respected outfit. There is a regularly scheduled walk in Bowie's footsteps, but other options such as a multimedia bus tour and U2 and Depeche Mode tours run by request only. Some even get you inside the fabled Hansa Studios. English tours on request (price depends on group size).

Green Me Berlin Tours
(www.greenmeberlin.com; public tours per person €30-50, private tours on request) Making the world a better place one footstep at a time, Green Me's walking tours show visitors Berlin's sustainable side. Its small-size tours pop by off-grid organic cafes, urban gardens, ethical stores and backyard workshops, introducing you to the passionate people behind the concepts. Most include a small tasting, such as vegan ice cream or *kombucha*.

Berlinagenten (☎030-4372 0701; www.berlinagenten.com; by request) Get a handle on all facets of Berlin's urban lifestyle with an insider private guide who opens doors to hot and/or secret bars, boutiques, restaurants, clubs, private homes and sights. Dozens of culinary, cultural and lifestyle tours on offer, including the best-selling 'Gastro Rallye' for the ultimate foodie. Prices depend on group size.

Eat the World (☎030-206 229 990; www.eat-the-world.com; tours €33) Experience Berlin's neighbourhoods one bite at a time during these three-hour 'foodseeing' tours that stop at cafes, delis, bakeries, ice-cream parlours and other tasty places. There are tours through eight neighbourhoods, including Kreuzberg and Prenzlauer Berg.

BIKE-SHARE SCHEMES

Berlin is experiencing an explosion in bike-share schemes with at least five big operators entering the market in 2017 and 2018. Bikes can now be found at just about every corner in the central districts (within the Ringbahn, circle line). All work on an automated self-service system with pick-up and drop-off either at docking stations or dockless anywhere within their business area. Usage requires downloading the app to your smartphone and registering there, online, via a hotline or at streetside terminals. Hiring a bike usually involves scanning the QR code to undo the electronic lock. Rates vary by company but are very reasonable. Expect to pay about €0.50 per half hour and no more than €15 per day.

For a handy guide, check out www.101bikerentals.com. The main providers include the following:

Byke (http://byke.de)

Donkey Republic (www.donkey.bike)

Lidl Bike (www.lidlbike.de)

Lime Bike (www.limebike.de)

Mobike (http://mobike.com)

Nextbike (www.nextbike.de)

Directory A-Z

Accessible Travel

Berlin has made major improvements when it comes to the needs of the mobility-impaired, the wheelchair-bound, blind or partially sighted visitors and people with hearing impairments. The Visit Berlin tourist office has compiled an excellent detailed accessibility online guide at www.visitberlin.de/en/accessible-berlin.

➡ Access ramps and/or lifts are available in many public buildings, including train stations, museums, concert halls and cinemas. Newer hotels have lifts and rooms with extra-wide doors and spacious bathrooms. For a databank assessing the accessibility of cafes, restaurants, hotels, theatres and other public spaces (in German), check with Mobidat (www.mobidat.de).

➡ Most buses, trains and trams are wheelchair-accessible and many U-Bahn and S-Bahn stations are equipped with ramps or lifts. For trip-planning assistance, contact the BVG (030-194 49; www.bvg.de), Berlin's main public transport company. Many stations also have grooved platforms to assist blind and vision-impaired passengers. Seeing-eye dogs are allowed everywhere. Hearing-impaired passengers can check upcoming station names on displays installed in all forms of public transport.

➡ **Rollstuhlvermietung** (Wheelchair Rentals; ☎0177 833 5773; www.rollstuhlvermietung.berlin; ⊙24hr) provides 24-hour wheelchair repairs and rentals.

➡ Download Lonely Planet's free *Accessible Travel* guide from http://lptravel.to/AccessibleTravel.

Customs Regulations

➡ Goods brought in and out of countries within the EU incur no additional taxes provided duty has been paid somewhere within the EU and the goods are only for personal use.

➡ Duty-free shopping is only available if you're leaving the EU.

Discount Cards

Berlin Welcome Card (www.berlin-welcomecard.de; travel in AB zones 48/72 hours €19.90/28.90, travel in ABC zones 48/72 hours €22.90/30.90, AB zones 72 hours plus admission to Museumsinsel €45 or €47 for ABC zones. Valid for unlimited

IMPORT RESTRICTIONS

ITEM	DUTY-FREE (ARRIVING FROM OUTSIDE EU)	TAX & DUTY PAID WITHIN EU
alcohol	1L spirits or 2L fortified wine and 16L beer and 4L wine (17yr minimum age)	10L spirits, 20L sherry or other fortified wine, 110L beer, 90L wine (with no more than 60L sparkling wine)
tobacco	200 cigarettes or 100 cigarillos or 50 cigars or 250g tobacco or a combination thereof (17yr minimum age)	800 cigarettes or 400 cigarillos or 200 cigars or 1kg tobacco
other goods	up to a value of €300 if arriving by land or €430 if arriving by sea or air (€175 for those under 15yr)	n/a

public transport for one adult and up to three children under 14; up to 50% discount to 200 sights, attractions and tours; available for up to six days. Sold online, at the tourist offices, from U-Bahn and S-Bahn ticket vending machines, on buses and at BVG sales points.

CityTourCard (www.citytour card.com; travel in AB zone 48 hours/72 hours/five days €16.90/23.90/33.90, ABC zone €17.90/24.90/37.90) Operates on a similar scheme as the Berlin Welcome Card; it's a bit cheaper, but offers fewer discounts. Available for up to five days from tourist offices, bus drivers and U-Bahn and S-Bahn ticket vending machines.

Museumspass Berlin (adult/concession €29/14.50) Buys admission to the permanent exhibits of about 30 museums for three consecutive days, including big draws like the Pergamonmuseum. Sold at tourist offices and participating museums.

Electricity

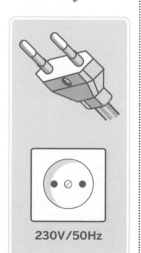

230V/50Hz

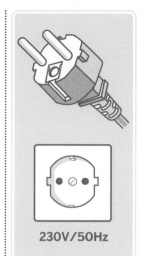

230V/50Hz

Emergency

Ambulance	☎112
Fire department	☎112
Germany's country code	☎49
International access code	☎00
Police	☎110

Internet Access

→ Free public wi-fi is available at 650 access points throughout the city. Locations include public squares, landmarks like the Brandenburger Tor, libraries and town halls. See www.berlin.de/stadtplan/w-lan-hotspots for a map.

→ Almost without exception, free wi-fi access (W-LAN in Germany; pronounced vay-lan) is available at hotels, hostels and guesthouses.

→ In some accommodation wi-fi may be limited to some rooms and/or public areas; if you need in-room access, be sure to specify at the time of booking.

→ Many cafes, bars and even bakeries and boutiques have free wi-fi hotspots, although you usually need to ask for a password.

→ Internet cafes have pretty much gone the way of the dodo. If you need one, ask at your hotel.

Legal Matters

→ By law you must possess some form of photographic identification, such as your passport, national identity card or driving licence.

→ The permissible blood-alcohol limit is 0.05% for drivers and 0.16% for cyclists. Anyone caught exceeding this amount is subject to stiff fines, a confiscated licence or even jail time. Drinking in public is not illegal, but be discreet about it.

→ Cannabis *consumption* is not illegal, but its possession, acquisition, sale and cultivation is considered a criminal offence. There is usually no persecution for possession of 'small quantities' (defined as up to 10g in Berlin). Dealers face much stiffer penalties, as do people caught with any other recreational drugs. Searches upon entering clubs are common.

→ If arrested, you have the right to make a phone call and are presumed innocent until proven guilty, although you may be held in custody until trial. If you don't know a lawyer, contact your embassy.

Medical Services

→ High-level health care is available from a *Rettungsstelle* (emergency department) at a *Krankenhaus* (hospital) or from an *Arztpraxis* (doctor's office). Most doctors speak at least some English, especially in the hospitals.

→ The most central hospital with a 24-hour emergency room is the renowned **Charité**

PRACTICALITIES

Clothing For women's clothing sizes, a German size 36 equals a size 6 in the US and a size 10 in the UK, then increases in increments of two, making size 38 a US 8 and UK 12, and so on.

Newspapers Widely read local dailies are *Tagesspiegel, Berliner Zeitung, Berliner Morgenpost* and *taz*.

Magazines *Zitty* and *Tip* are the main listings magazines for Berlin. *Siegessäule* is a freebie for the LGBTIQ community.

Radio & TV Radio 1 (95.8 FM) and Flux FM (00.6 FM) are popular radio channels. For local TV news, tune into RBB station.

Tap Water Tap water is perfectly fine to drink, although most people prefer bottled sparkling or still water.

Weights & Measures Germany uses the metric system.

Mitte (🖉030-450 50; www.charite.de; emergency room Luisenstrasse 65; ⊙24hr; 🚇147, Ⓤ Oranienburger Tor).

➡ For minor illnesses (headache, bruises, diarrhoea), pharmacists can provide advice, sell over-the-counter medications and make doctors' referrals if further help is needed.

➡ Condoms are widely available in drugstores, pharmacies and supermarkets. Birth control pills require a doctor's prescription but the morning after pill does not and is sold in pharmacies for about €16.

Pharmacies

➡ German chemists (drugstores, *Drogerien*) do not sell any kind of medication, not even aspirin. Even over-the-counter (*rezeptfrei*) medications for minor health concerns, such as a cold or upset stomach, are only available at an *Apotheke* (pharmacy).

➡ For more serious conditions, you will need to produce a *Rezept* (prescription) from a licensed physician. If you take regular medication, be sure to bring a full supply for your entire trip, as the same brand may not be available in Germany.

➡ The names and addresses of pharmacies open after hours (these rotate) are posted in every pharmacy window, or call 011 41 for a recorded message of after-hour and Sunday pharmacies.

Money
ATMs & Debit Cards

➡ ATMs (*Geldautomat*) are the best and easiest way to get cash. Most are accessible 24/7 and are linked to international networks such as Cirrus, Plus, Star and Maestro.

➡ ATMs not affiliated with major banks may charge higher transaction fees (€5 or more). ATMs do not recognise pins with more than four digits.

➡ Since many ATM cards double as debit cards, they can often be used for payment in shops, hotels, restaurants and other businesses, especially MasterCard and Visa cards.

➡ Most Germans use a debit card known as an EC Card. For-eign debit cards are not always accepted.

➡ Most places use the 'chip and pin' system: instead of signing, you enter your PIN. If your card isn't chip-and-pin enabled, you may be able to sign the receipt, but not always – ask first.

Cash

Cash is king in Germany, so always carry some with you and plan to pay in cash in most places. It's a good idea to set aside a small amount of euros as an emergency stash.

Changing Money

Currency exchange offices *(Wechselstuben)* can be found at airports and major train stations. They usually have better hours and charge lower fees than commercial banks. Some convenient offices:

Reisebank (www.reisebank.de) Zoologischer Garten, Hauptbahnhof, Ostbahnhof and Bahnhof Friedrichstrasse.

Euro-Change (www.euro-change.de) Alexanderplatz station; Europa Centr, Friedrichstrasse 80.

Reisebank keeps slightly longer hours; on Sundays, the airports are your only option.

Credit Cards

➡ Credit cards are becoming more widely accepted (especially in hotels and upmarket shops and restaurants), but it's best not to assume that you'll be able to use one – enquire first.

➡ Visa and MasterCard are more commonly accepted than American Express and Diner's Club.

➡ Some places require a minimum purchase with credit card use.

➡ Cash advances on credit cards via ATMs usually incur

steep fees – check with your card issuer.

Tipping

It's considered rude to leave the tip on the table. Instead, tell the server the total amount you want to pay. If you don't want change back, say 'Stimmt so' (that's fine).

Hotels Room cleaners €1 to €2 per day, porters the same per bag.

Restaurants For good service 10% or more.

Bars & pubs 5% to 10% for table service, rounded to the nearest euro, no tip necessary for self-service.

Taxis 10%, always rounding to a full euro.

Toilet attendants €0.50.

Opening Hours

The following are typical opening hours, although these may vary seasonally and by location (city centre or the suburbs).

Banks 9.30am–6pm Monday–Friday, some to 1pm Saturday

Bars 7pm–1am or later

Boutiques 11am–7pm Monday–Friday, to 6pm Saturday

Cafes 8am–8pm

Clubs 11pm–5am or later

Post Offices 9am–6pm Monday–Friday, to 1pm Saturday

Restaurants 11am–11pm

Shops 10am–8pm Monday–Saturday

Supermarkets 8am–8pm or later; some 24 hours

Public Holidays

Shops, banks and public and private offices are closed on the following nationwide *gesetzliche Feiertage* (public holidays):

Neujahrstag (New Year's Day) 1 January

Ostern (Easter) March/April;

Good Friday, Easter Sunday and Easter Monday

Christi Himmelfahrt (Ascension Day) Forty days after Easter, always on a Thursday

Maifeiertag (Labour Day) 1 May

Pfingsten (Whitsun/Pentecost Sunday and Monday) May/June

Tag der Deutschen Einheit (Day of German Unity) 3 October

Weihnachtstag (Christmas Day) 25 December

Zweiter Weihnachtstag (Boxing Day) 26 December

Safe Travel

Berlin is one of the safest capital cities in the world, but that doesn't mean you should let your guard down.

➡ Pickpocketing has dramatically increased, so watch your belongings, especially in tourist-heavy areas, in crowds and at events.

➡ Crime levels have risen notably around Kottbusser Tor in Kreuzberg and the RAW Gelände in Friedrichshain. This includes drug dealing, pickpocketing, assault and sexual assault. Exercise caution.

➡ Carry enough cash for a cab

ride back to wherever you're staying.

➡ On the U-Bahn or S-Bahn, and increasingly at outdoor cafes, you'll encounter homeless folks begging or selling street newspapers (called *Motz* or *Strassenfeger*). Buskers are also quite common. You're free to give or not.

Telephone
Mobile Phones

➡ Mobile phones *(Handys)* work on GSM900/1800. If your home country uses a different standard, you'll need a multiband GSM phone in Germany. Check your contract for roaming charges.

➡ If you have an unlocked phone that works in Germany, you should be able to cut down on roaming charges by buying a prepaid, rechargeable local SIM card. These are sold at supermarkets, pharmacies, convenience stores and electronics shops and can be topped up as needed.

➡ Calls made from landlines to German mobile phone numbers are charged at higher rates than those to other landlines. Incoming calls on mobile numbers are free.

SMOKING REGULATIONS

➡ Except in designated areas, smoking (including e-cigarettes) is not allowed in public buildings or at airports and train stations.

➡ Smoking is not allowed in restaurants, bars and clubs unless there is a completely separate and enclosed room set aside for smokers. This rule is often ignored.

➡ Owners of single-room bars and pubs smaller than 75 sq metres, who don't serve anything to eat and keep out customers under 18 years of age, may choose to be a *'Raucherbar'*, ie allow smoking. The venue must be clearly designated as such.

➡ *Shisha* bars may operate as long as no alcohol is available and no one under 18 is allowed in.

Phone Codes

German phone numbers consist of an area code, starting with 0, and the local number. The area code for Berlin is 030. When dialling a Berlin number from a Berlin-based landline, you don't need to dial the area code. When you're using a landline outside Berlin, or a mobile phone, you must dial it.

German mobile numbers begin with a four-digit prefix such as 0151, 0157 or 0173.

Calling Berlin from abroad Dial your country's international access code, then 49 (Germany's country code), then the area code (dropping the initial 0, so just 30) and the local number.

Calling internationally from Berlin Dial 00 (the international access code), then the country code, the area code (without the zero if there is one) and the local number.

Time

Clocks in Germany are set to central European time (GMT/UTC plus one hour). Daylight-savings time kicks in on the last Sunday in March and ends on the last Sunday in October. The 24-hour clock is the norm (eg 6.30pm is 18.30). As daylight-savings time differs across regions, the following times are indicative only:

CITY	NOON IN BERLIN
Auckland	11pm
Cape Town	1pm
London	11am
New York	6am
San Francisco	3am
Sydney	9pm
Tokyo	8pm

Toilets

➜ German toilets are sit-down affairs; it is customary for men to sit when peeing.

➜ Free-standing, 24-hour self-cleaning public toilet pods have become quite commonplace. The cost is €0.50 and you have 15 minutes to finish your business. Most of these are wheelchair-accessible.

➜ Toilets in malls, clubs, beer gardens etc often have an attendant who expects a tip of around €0.50.

Tourist Information

Visit Berlin (www.visitberlin. de), the Berlin tourist board, operates five walk-in offices, info desks at the airports, and a **call centre** (☎030-2500 2333; ⊙9am-6pm Mon-Fri) whose multilingual staff field general questions and make hotel and ticket bookings.

Alexanderplatz (Map p332; ☎030-250 025; www.visit berlin.de; lobby Park Inn, Alexanderplatz 7; ⊙7am-9pm Mon-Sat, 8am-6pm Sun; ⊠100, 200, TXL, ⓤAlexanderplatz, ⓢAlexanderplatz)

Brandenburger Tor (Map p328;☎030-250 023; www. visitberlin.de; Pariser Platz, Brandenburger Tor, south wing; ⊙9.30am-7pm Apr-Oct, to 6pm Nov-Mar; ⓢBrandenburger Tor, ⓤBrandenburger Tor)

Central Bus Station (ZOB) (www.visitberlin.de; Masurenallee 4-6; ⊙8am-8pm Mon, Fri & Sat, to 4pm Tue-Thu & Sun; ⓢMesse Nord/ICC)

Europa-Center (Map p348; ☎030-2500 2333; www.visit berlin.de; Tauentzienstrasse 9, Europa-Center, ground fl; ⊙10am-8pm Mon-Sat; ⊠100, 200, ⓤKurfürstendamm, Zoologischer Garten, ⓢZoologischer Garten)

Hauptbahnhof (Map p336; ☎030-250 025; www.visit berlin.de; Hauptbahnhof, Europaplatz entrance, ground fl; ⊙8am-10pm; ⓢHauptbahnhof, ⓡHauptbahnhof)

Visas

➜ EU nationals need only their national identity card or passport to enter Germany. If you intend to stay for an extended period, you must register with the authorities (*Bürgeramt,* or Citizens' Office) within two weeks of arrival.

➜ Citizens of Australia, Canada, Israel, Japan, New Zealand, Switzerland and the US are among those who need only a valid passport (no visa) if entering as tourists for a stay of up to three months within a six-month period.

➜ Passports must be valid for at least another four months beyond the planned departure date.

➜ Unless you're an EU national or from a nation without visa requirements, you need a Schengen Visa to enter Germany. Visa applications must be filed with the embassy or consulate of the Schengen country that is your primary destination. It is valid for stays of up to 90 days. Legal permanent residency in any Schengen country makes a visa unnecessary, regardless of your nationality.

➜ For full details and current regulations, see www. auswaertiges-amt.de or check with a German consulate in your country.

Language

German belongs to the West Germanic language family and has around 100 million speakers. It is commonly divided into Low German *(Plattdeutsch)* and High German *(Hochdeutsch)*. Low German is an umbrella term used for the dialects spoken in Northern Germany. High German is the standard form; it's also used in this chapter.

German is easy for English speakers to pronounce because almost all of its sounds are also found in English. If you read our coloured pronunciation guides as if they were English, you should be understood just fine. Note that kh sounds like the 'ch' in 'Bach' or in the Scottish 'loch' (pronounced at the back of the throat), r is also pronounced at the back of the throat, zh is pronounced as the 's' in 'measure', and ü as the 'ee' in 'see' but with rounded lips. The stressed syllables are indicated with italics in our pronunciation guides. The markers (pol) and (inf) indicate polite and informal forms.

BASICS

Hello.	Guten Tag.	goo·ten tahk
Goodbye.	Auf Wiedersehen.	owf vee·der·zay·en
Yes./No.	Ja./Nein.	yah/nain
Please.	Bitte.	bi·te
Thank you.	Danke.	dang·ke
You're welcome.	Bitte.	bi·te
Excuse me.	Entschuldigung.	ent·shul·di·gung
Sorry.	Entschuldigung.	ent·shul·di·gung

WANT MORE?

For in-depth language information and handy phrases, check out Lonely Planet's *German Phrasebook*. You'll find it at **shop. lonelyplanet.com**, or you can buy Lonely Planet's iPhone phrasebooks at the Apple App Store.

How are you?
Wie geht es Ihnen/dir? (pol/inf) — vee gayt es ee·nen/deer

Fine. And you?
Danke, gut. Und Ihnen/dir? (pol/inf) — dang·ke goot unt ee·nen/deer

What's your name?
Wie ist Ihr Name? (pol) — vee ist eer nah·me
Wie heißt du? (inf) — vee haist doo

My name is ...
Mein Name ist ... (pol) — main nah·me ist ...
Ich heiße ... (inf) — ikh hai·se ...

Do you speak English?
Sprechen Sie Englisch? (pol) — shpre·khen zee eng·lish
Sprichst du Englisch? (inf) — shprikhst doo eng·lish

I don't understand.
Ich verstehe nicht. — ikh fer·shtay·e nikht

ACCOMMODATION

guesthouse	Pension	pahng·zyawn
hotel	Hotel	ho·tel
inn	Gasthof	gast·hawf
youth hostel	Jugend-herberge	yoo·gent·her·ber·ge
Do you have a ... room?	Haben Sie ein ...?	hah·ben zee ain ...
double	Doppelzimmer	do·pel·tsi·mer
single	Einzelzimmer	ain·tsel·tsi·mer
How much is it per ...?	Wie viel kostet es pro ...?	vee feel kos·tet es praw ...
night	Nacht	nakht
person	Person	per·zawn

Is breakfast included?
Ist das Frühstück inklusive? — ist das frü·shtük in·kloo·zee·ve

LANGUAGE DIRECTIONS

KEY PATTERNS

To get by in German, mix and match these simple patterns with words of your choice:

When's (the next flight)?
Wann ist (der   van ist (dair
nächste Flug)?   naykhs·te flook)

Where's (the station)?
Wo ist (der Bahnhof)? vaw ist (dair bahn·hawf)

Where can I (buy a ticket)?
Wo kann ich (eine   vaw kan ikh (ai·ne
Fahrkarte kaufen)?   fahr·kar·te kow·fen)

Do you have (a map)?
Haben Sie   hah·ben zee
(eine Karte)?   (ai·ne kar·te)

Is there (a toilet)?
Gibt es (eine Toilette)? gipt es (ai·ne to·a·le·te)

I'd like (a coffee).
Ich möchte   ikh merkh·te
(einen Kaffee).   (ai·nen ka·fay)

I'd like (to hire a car).
Ich möchte   ikh merkh·te
(ein Auto mieten).   (ain ow·to mee·ten)

Can I (enter)?
Darf ich   darf ikh
(hereinkommen)?   (her·ein·ko·men)

Could you please (help me)?
Könnten Sie   kern·ten zee
(mir helfen)?   (meer hel·fen)

Do I have to (book a seat)?
Muss ich (einen Platz mus ikh (ai·nen plats
reservieren lassen)?   re·zer·vee·ren la·sen)

DIRECTIONS

Where's ...?
Wo ist ...?   vaw ist ...

What's the address?
Wie ist die Adresse? vee ist dee a·dre·se

How far is it?
Wie weit ist es?   vee vait ist es

Can you show me (on the map)?
Können Sie es mir   ker·nen zee es meer
(auf der Karte) zeigen? (owf dair kar·te) tsai·gen

How can I get there?
Wie kann ich da   vee kan ikh dah
hinkommen?   hin·ko·men

Turn ...	Biegen Sie ... ab.	bee·gen zee ... ab
at the corner	an der Ecke	an dair e·ke
at the traffic lights	bei der Ampel	bai dair am·pel
left	links	lingks
right	rechts	rekhts

EATING & DRINKING

I'd like to reserve a table for ...	Ich möchte einen Tisch für ... reservieren.	ikh merkh·te ai·nen tish für ... re·zer·vee·ren
(eight) o'clock	(acht) Uhr	(akht) oor
(two) people	(zwei) Personen	(tsvai) per·zaw·nen

I'd like the menu, please.
Ich hätte gern die   ikh he·te gern dee
Speisekarte, bitte.   shpai·ze·kar·te bi·te

What would you recommend?
Was empfehlen Sie?   vas emp·fay·len zee

What's in that dish?
Was ist in diesem   vas ist in dee·zem
Gericht?   ge·rikht

I'm a vegetarian.
Ich bin Vegetarier/   ikh bin ve·ge·tah·ri·er/
Vegetarierin. (m/f)   ve·ge·tah·ri·e·rin

That was delicious.
Das hat hervorragend das hat her·fawr·rah·gent
geschmeckt.   ge·shmekt

Cheers!
Prost!   prawst

Please bring the bill.
Bitte bringen Sie   bi·te bring·en zee
die Rechnung.   dee rekh·nung

Key Words

bar (pub)	Kneipe	knai·pe
bottle	Flasche	fla·she
bowl	Schüssel	shü·sel
breakfast	Frühstück	frü·shtük
cold	kalt	kalt
cup	Tasse	ta·se
daily special	Gericht des Tages	ge·rikht des tah·ges
delicatessen	Feinkostgeschäft	fain·kost·ge·sheft
desserts	Nachspeisen	nahkh·shpai·zen
dinner	Abendessen	ah·bent·e·sen
drink list	Getränkekarte	ge·treng·ke·kar·te
fork	Gabel	gah·bel
glass	Glas	glahs
grocery store	Lebensmittelladen	lay·bens·mi·tel·lah·den
hot (warm)	warm	warm
knife	Messer	me·ser
lunch	Mittagessen	mi·tahk·e·sen

market	*Markt*	markt
plate	*Teller*	*te*·ler
restaurant	*Restaurant*	res·to·*rahng*
set menu	*Menü*	may·*nü*
spicy	*würzig*	*vür*·tsikh
spoon	*Löffel*	*ler*·fel
with/without	*mit/ohne*	mit/*aw*·ne

Meat & Fish

beef	*Rindfleisch*	*rint*·flaish
carp	*Karpfen*	*karp*·fen
fish	*Fisch*	fish
herring	*Hering*	*hay*·ring
lamb	*Lammfleisch*	*lam*·flaish
meat	*Fleisch*	flaish
pork	*Schweinefleisch*	*shvai*·ne·flaish
poultry	*Geflügelfleisch*	ge·*flü*·gel·flaish
salmon	*Lachs*	laks
sausage	*Wurst*	vurst
seafood	*Meeresfrüchte*	*mair*·res·frükh·te
shellfish	*Schaltiere*	*shahl*·tee·re
trout	*Forelle*	fo·*re*·le
veal	*Kalbfleisch*	*kalp*·flaish

Fruit & Vegetables

apple	*Apfel*	*ap*·fel
banana	*Banane*	ba·*nah*·ne
bean	*Bohne*	*baw*·ne
cabbage	*Kraut*	krowt
capsicum	*Paprika*	*pap*·ri·kah
carrot	*Mohrrübe*	*mawr*·rü·be
cucumber	*Gurke*	*gur*·ke
fruit	*Frucht/Obst*	frukht/*awpst*
grapes	*Weintrauben*	*vain*·trow·ben
lemon	*Zitrone*	tsi·*traw*·ne
lentil	*Linse*	*lin*·ze
lettuce	*Kopfsalat*	*kopf*·za·laht
mushroom	*Pilz*	pilts
nuts	*Nüsse*	*nü*·se
onion	*Zwiebel*	*tsvee*·bel
orange	*Orange*	o·*rahng*·zhe
pea	*Erbse*	*erp*·se
plum	*Pflaume*	*pflow*·me
potato	*Kartoffel*	kar·*to*·fel
spinach	*Spinat*	shpi·*naht*
strawberry	*Erdbeere*	*ert*·bair·re

tomato	*Tomate*	to·*mah*·te
vegetable	*Gemüse*	ge·*mü*·ze
watermelon	*Wasser-melone*	va·ser·me·law·ne

Other

bread	*Brot*	brawt
butter	*Butter*	*bu*·ter
cheese	*Käse*	*kay*·ze
egg/eggs	*Ei/Eier*	ai/*ai*·er
honey	*Honig*	*haw*·nikh
jam	*Marmelade*	mar·me·*lah*·de
pasta	*Nudeln*	*noo*·deln
pepper	*Pfeffer*	*pfe*·fer
rice	*Reis*	rais
salt	*Salz*	zalts
soup	*Suppe*	*zu*·pe
sugar	*Zucker*	*tsu*·ker

Drinks

beer	*Bier*	beer
coffee	*Kaffee*	ka·*fay*
juice	*Saft*	zaft
milk	*Milch*	milkh
orange juice	*Orangensaft*	o·*rang*·zhen·zaft
red wine	*Rotwein*	*rawt*·vain
sparkling wine	*Sekt*	zekt
tea	*Tee*	tay
water	*Wasser*	*va*·ser
white wine	*Weißwein*	*vais*·vain

EMERGENCIES

Help!	*Hilfe!*	*hil*·fe
Go away!	*Gehen Sie weg!*	*gay*·en zee vek

SIGNS

Ausgang	Exit
Damen	Women
Eingang	Entrance
Geschlossen	Closed
Herren	Men
Toiletten (WC)	Toilets
Offen	Open
Verboten	Prohibited

Call the police!
Rufen Sie die Polizei!   roo·fen zee dee po·li·*tsai*

Call a doctor!
Rufen Sie einen Arzt!   roo·fen zee *ai*·nen artst

Where are the toilets?
Wo ist die Toilette?   vo ist dee to·a·*le*·te

I'm lost.
Ich habe mich verirrt.   ikh *hah*·be mikh fer·*irt*

I'm sick.
Ich bin krank.   ikh bin krangk

It hurts here.
Es tut hier weh.   es toot heer vay

I'm allergic to ...
Ich bin allergisch   ikh bin a·*lair*·gish
gegen ...   gay·gen ...

SHOPPING & SERVICES

I'd like to buy ...
Ich möchte ... kaufen.   ikh *merkh*·te ... *kow*·fen

I'm just looking.
Ich schaue mich nur um.   ikh *show*·e mikh noor um

Can I look at it?
Können Sie es mir   *ker*·nen zee es meer
zeigen?   *tsai*·gen

How much is this?
Wie viel kostet das?   vee feel *kos*·tet das

That's too expensive.
Das ist zu teuer.   das ist tsoo *toy*·er

Can you lower the price?
Können Sie mit dem   *ker*·nen zee mit dem
Preis heruntergehen?   prais he·*run*·ter·gay·en

There's a mistake in the bill.
Da ist ein Fehler   dah ist ain *fay*·ler
in der Rechnung.   in dair *rekh*·nung

ATM	*Geldautomat*	*gelt*·ow·to·maht
post office	*Postamt*	*post*·amt
tourist office	*Fremden-*	*frem*·den·
	verkehrsbüro	fer·kairs·bü·raw

TIME & DATES

What time is it?
Wie spät ist es?   vee shpayt ist es

It's (10) o'clock.
Es ist (zehn) Uhr.   es ist (tsayn) oor

QUESTION WORDS

What?	*Was?*	vas
When?	*Wann?*	van
Where?	*Wo?*	vaw
Who?	*Wer?*	vair
Why?	*Warum?*	va·*rum*

At what time?
Um wie viel Uhr?   um vee feel oor

At ...
Um ...   um ...

morning	*Morgen*	*mor*·gen
afternoon	*Nachmittag*	*nahkh*·mi·tahk
evening	*Abend*	*ah*·bent
yesterday	*gestern*	*ges*·tern
today	*heute*	*hoy*·te
tomorrow	*morgen*	*mor*·gen
Monday	*Montag*	*mawn*·tahk
Tuesday	*Dienstag*	*deens*·tahk
Wednesday	*Mittwoch*	*mit*·vokh
Thursday	*Donnerstag*	*do*·ners·tahk
Friday	*Freitag*	*frai*·tahk
Saturday	*Samstag*	*zams*·tahk
Sunday	*Sonntag*	*zon*·tahk
January	*Januar*	*yan*·u·ahr
February	*Februar*	*fay*·bru·ahr
March	*März*	merts
April	*April*	a·*pril*
May	*Mai*	mai
June	*Juni*	*yoo*·ni
July	*Juli*	*yoo*·li
August	*August*	ow·*gust*
September	*September*	zep·*tem*·ber
October	*Oktober*	ok·*taw*·ber
November	*November*	no·*vem*·ber
December	*Dezember*	de·*tsem*·ber

TRANSPORT

Public Transport

boat	*Boot*	bawt
bus	*Bus*	bus
metro	*U-Bahn*	*oo*·bahn
plane	*Flugzeug*	*flook*·tsoyk
train	*Zug*	tsook
At what time's the ... bus?	*Wann fährt der ... Bus?*	van fairt dair... bus
first	*erste*	*ers*·te
last	*letzte*	*lets*·te
next	*nächste*	*naykhs*·te

A ... to (Cologne).	Eine ... nach (Köln).	ai·ne ... nahkh (kerln)
1st-/2nd-class ticket	Fahrkarte erster/zweiter Klasse	fahr·kar·te ers·ter/tsvai·ter kla·se
one-way ticket	einfache Fahrkarte	ain·fa·khe fahr·kar·te
return ticket	Rückfahrkarte	rük·fahr·kar·te

At what time does it arrive?
Wann kommt es an? — van komt es an

Is it a direct route?
Ist es eine direkte Verbindung? — ist es ai·ne di·rek·te fer·bin·dung

Does it stop at ...?
Hält es in ...? — helt es in ...

What station is this?
Welcher Bahnhof ist das? — vel·kher bahn·hawf ist das

What's the next stop?
Welches ist der nächste Halt? — vel·khes ist dair naykh·ste halt

I want to get off here.
Ich möchte hier aussteigen. — ikh merkh·te heer ows·shtai·gen

Please tell me when we get to ....
Könnten Sie mir bitte sagen, wann wir in ... ankommen? — kern·ten zee meer bi·te zah·gen van veer in ... an·ko·men

Please take me to (this address).
Bitte bringen Sie mich zu (dieser Adresse). — bi·te bring·en zee mikh tsoo (dee·zer a·dre·se)

platform	Bahnsteig	bahn·shtaik
ticket office	Fahrkarten-verkauf	fahr·kar·ten·fer·kowf
timetable	Fahrplan	fahr·plan

Driving & Cycling

I'd like to hire a ...	Ich möchte ein ... mieten.	ikh merkh·te ain ... mee·ten
4WD	Allrad-fahrzeug	al·raht·fahr·tsoyk
bicycle	Fahrrad	fahr·raht
car	Auto	ow·to
motorbike	Motorrad	maw·tor·raht

How much is it per ...?	Wie viel kostet es pro ...?	vee feel kos·tet es praw ...
day	Tag	tahk
week	Woche	vo·khe

| bicycle pump | Fahrradpumpe | fahr·raht·pum·pe |
| child seat | Kindersitz | kin·der·zits |

NUMBERS

1	eins	ains
2	zwei	tsvai
3	drei	drai
4	vier	feer
5	fünf	fünf
6	sechs	zeks
7	sieben	zee·ben
8	acht	akht
9	neun	noyn
10	zehn	tsayn
20	zwanzig	tsvan·tsikh
30	dreißig	drai·tsikh
40	vierzig	feer·tsikh
50	fünfzig	fünf·tsikh
60	sechzig	zekh·tsikh
70	siebzig	zeep·tsikh
80	achtzig	akht·tsikh
90	neunzig	noyn·tsikh
100	hundert	hun·dert
1000	tausend	tow·sent

| helmet | Helm | helm |
| petrol | Benzin | ben·tseen |

Does this road go to ...?
Führt diese Straße nach ...? — fürt dee·ze shtrah·se nahkh ...

(How long) Can I park here?
(Wie lange) Kann ich hier parken? — (vee lang·e) kan ikh heer par·ken

Where's a petrol station?
Wo ist eine Tankstelle? — vaw ist ai·ne tangk·shte·le

I need a mechanic.
Ich brauche einen Mechaniker. — ikh brow·khe ai·nen me·khah·ni·ker

My car/motorbike has broken down (at ...).
Ich habe (in ...) eine Panne mit meinem Auto/Motorrad. — ikh hah·be (in ...) ai·ne pa·ne mit mai·nem ow·to/maw·tor·raht

I've run out of petrol.
Ich habe kein Benzin mehr. — ikh hah·be kain ben·tseen mair

I have a flat tyre.
Ich habe eine Reifenpanne. — ikh hah·be ai·ne rai·fen·pa·ne

Are there cycling paths?
Gibt es Fahrradwege? — geept es fahr·raht·vay·ge

Is there bicycle parking?
Gibt es Fahrrad-Parkplätze? — geept es fahr·raht·park·ple·tse

GLOSSARY

You may encounter the following terms and abbreviations while in Berlin.

Bahnhof (Bf) – train station
Berg – mountain
Bibliothek – library
BRD – Bundesrepublik Deutschland (abbreviated in English as FRG – Federal Republic of Germany); see also *DDR*
Brücke – bridge
Brunnen – fountain or well
Bundestag – German parliament

CDU – Christliche Demokratische Union (Christian Democratic Union), centre-right party

DDR – Deutsche Demokratische Republik (abbreviated in English as GDR – German Democratic Republic); the name for the former East Germany; see also *BRD*
Denkmal – memorial, monument
Dom – cathedral

ermässigt – reduced (eg admission fee)

Fahrrad – bicycle
Flohmarkt – flea market
Flughafen – airport
FRG – Federal Republic of Germany; see also *BRD*

Gasse – lane or alley
Gästehaus, Gasthaus – guesthouse
GDR – German Democratic Republic (the former East Germany); see also *DDR*
Gedenkstätte – memorial site
Gestapo – Geheime Staatspolizei (Nazi secret police)

Gründerzeit – literally 'foundation time'; early years of German empire, roughly 1871–90

Hafen – harbour, port
Hauptbahnhof (Hbf) – main train station
Hof (Höfe) – courtyard(s)

Imbiss – snack bar, takeaway stand
Insel – island

Kaiser – emperor; derived from 'Caesar'
Kapelle – chapel
Karte – ticket
Kiez(e) – neighbourhood(s)
Kino – cinema
König – king
Konzentrationslager (KZ) – concentration camp
Kristallnacht – literally 'Night of Broken Glass'; Nazi pogrom against Jewish businesses and institutions on 9 November 1938
Kunst – art
Kunsthotels – hotels either designed by artists or liberally furnished with art

Mietskaserne(n) – tenement(s) built around successive courtyards

Ostalgie – fusion of the words Ost and Nostalgie, meaning nostalgia for East Germany

Palais – small palace
Palast – palace
Passage – shopping arcade
Platz – square

Rathaus – town hall
Reich – empire
Reisezentrum – travel centre in train or bus stations

Saal (Säle) – hall(s), large room(s)
Sammlung – collection
S-Bahn – metro/regional rail service with fewer stops than the U-Bahn
Schiff – ship
Schloss – palace
See – lake
SPD – Sozialdemokratische Partei Deutschlands (Social Democratic Party of Germany)
SS – Schutzstaffel; organisation within the Nazi Party that supplied Hitler's bodyguards, as well as concentration camp guards and the Waffen-SS troops in WWII
Stasi – GDR secret police (from Ministerium für Staatssicherheit, or Ministry of State Security)
Strasse (Str) – street

Tageskarte – daily menu; day ticket on public transport
Tor – gate
Trabant – GDR-era car boasting a two-stroke engine
Turm – tower
Trümmerberge – rubble mountains

U-Bahn – rapid transit railway, mostly underground; best choice for metro trips
Ufer – bank

Viertel – quarter, neighbourhood

Wald – forest
Weg – way, path
Weihnachtsmarkt – Christmas market
Wende – 'change' or 'turning point' of 1989, ie the collapse of the GDR and the resulting German reunification

Behind the Scenes

SEND US YOUR FEEDBACK

We love to hear from travellers – your comments keep us on our toes and help make our books better. Our well-travelled team reads every word on what you loved or loathed about this book. Although we cannot reply individually to your submissions, we always guarantee that your feedback goes straight to the appropriate authors, in time for the next edition. Each person who sends us information is thanked in the next edition – the most useful submissions are rewarded with a selection of digital PDF chapters.

Visit **lonelyplanet.com/contact** to submit your updates and suggestions or to ask for help. Our award-winning website also features inspirational travel stories, news and discussions.

Note: We may edit, reproduce and incorporate your comments in Lonely Planet products such as guidebooks, websites and digital products, so let us know if you don't want your comments reproduced or your name acknowledged. For a copy of our privacy policy visit lonelyplanet.com/privacy.

OUR READERS

Many thanks to the travellers who used the last edition and wrote to us with helpful hints, useful advice and interesting anecdotes: Alexis Agne, Anthony Coster, Clint Swift, Dominic Mobbs, Eran Globus, Judy Kunofsky, Kyle Vernest, Manuel Hess, Michèle Gloor

WRITER THANKS
Andrea Schulte-Peevers

A big heartfelt thanks to all of these wonderful people who have plied me with tips, insights, information, ideas and encouragement (in no particular order): Henrik Tidefjärd, Barbara Woolsey, Tina Engler, Kerstin Riedel, Regine Schneider, Shaul Margulies, Frank Engster, Heiner and Claudia Schuster, Bernd Olsson, Tina Schürmann, Claudia Scheffler, Kirsten Schmidt, Renate Freiling, Tatjana Debel-Smykalla, David Eckel, Shachar & Doreen Elkanati, Nora Durstewitz and, of course, David Peevers.

ACKNOWLEDGEMENTS

Cover photograph: Brandenburger Tor, Jon Arnold/AWL ©

THIS BOOK

••

This 11th edition of Lonely Planet's *Berlin* guidebook was researched and written by Andrea Schulte-Peevers. The previous two editions were also written by Andrea. This guidebook was produced by the following:

Destination Editor Niamh O'Brien
Senior Product Editor Genna Patterson
Product Editor Sandie Kestell
Senior Cartographer Valentina Kremenchutskaya
Book Designer Gwen Cotter

Assisting Editors James Bainbridge, Michelle Coxall, Gabrielle Innes, Rosie Nicholson, Tamara Sheward, Gabrielle Stefanos
Cover Researcher Naomi Parker
Thanks to David Hodges, Dan Moore, Kat Rowan, Dianne Schallmeiner

See also separate subindexes for:

✗ **EATING P318**

🍷 **DRINKING & NIGHTLIFE P319**

☆ **ENTERTAINMENT P320**

🔒 **SHOPPING P321**

🛏 **SLEEPING P321**

🏃 **SPORTS & ACTIVITIES P322**

Index

INDEX DRINKING & NIGHTLIFE

Berlin Maps

Sights

- Beach
- Bird Sanctuary
- Buddhist
- Castle/Palace
- Christian
- Confucian
- Hindu
- Islamic
- Jain
- Jewish
- Monument
- Museum/Gallery/Historic Building
- Ruin
- Shinto
- Sikh
- Taoist
- Winery/Vineyard
- Zoo/Wildlife Sanctuary
- Other Sight

Activities, Courses & Tours

- Bodysurfing
- Diving
- Canoeing/Kayaking
- Course/Tour
- Sento Hot Baths/Onsen
- Skiing
- Snorkelling
- Surfing
- Swimming/Pool
- Walking
- Windsurfing
- Other Activity

Sleeping

- Sleeping
- Camping
- Hut/Shelter

Eating

- Eating

Drinking & Nightlife

- Drinking & Nightlife
- Cafe

Entertainment

- Entertainment

Shopping

- Shopping

Information

- Bank
- Embassy/Consulate
- Hospital/Medical
- Internet
- Police
- Post Office
- Telephone
- Toilet
- Tourist Information
- Other Information

Geographic

- Beach
- Gate
- Hut/Shelter
- Lighthouse
- Lookout
- Mountain/Volcano
- Oasis
- Park
- Pass
- Picnic Area
- Waterfall

Population

- Capital (National)
- Capital (State/Province)
- City/Large Town
- Town/Village

Transport

- Airport
- Border crossing
- Bus
- Cable car/Funicular
- Cycling
- Ferry
- Metro station
- Monorail
- Parking
- Petrol station
- S-Bahn/Subway station
- Taxi
- T-bane/Tunnelbana station
- Train station/Railway
- Tram
- Tube station
- U-Bahn/Underground station
- Other Transport

Routes

- Tollway
- Freeway
- Primary
- Secondary
- Tertiary
- Lane
- Unsealed road
- Road under construction
- Plaza/Mall
- Steps
- Tunnel
- Pedestrian overpass
- Walking Tour
- Walking Tour detour
- Path/Walking Trail

Boundaries

- International
- State/Province
- Disputed
- Regional/Suburb
- Marine Park
- Cliff
- Wall

Hydrography

- River, Creek
- Intermittent River
- Canal
- Water
- Dry/Salt/Intermittent Lake
- Reef

Areas

- Airport/Runway
- Beach/Desert
- Cemetery (Christian)
- Cemetery (Other)
- Glacier
- Mudflat
- Park/Forest
- Sight (Building)
- Sportsground
- Swamp/Mangrove

Note: Not all symbols displayed above appear on the maps in this book

MAP INDEX

POTSDAMER PLATZ & TIERGARTEN *Map on p326*

POTSDAMER PLATZ & TIERGARTEN

Key on p325

A | B | C | D

1

Ⓢ Bellevue

4 🏛

2

34 Schlosspark Bellevue ⊗

🏛 26

Paulstr

Lutherbrücke

Spree River

Spreeweg

Altonaer Str

Strasse des 17 Juni

Strasse des 17 Juni

3

27 ❶ Grosser Stern

Löwenbrücke

TIERGARTEN

Rousseauinsel

Luiseninsel

Hofjägerallee

4

Café am Neuen See (100m)

🍴 41

Tiergartenstr

5

Rauchstr

Stülerstr

Klingelhöferstr

Diplomatenviertel

Hiroshimastr

Hildebrandstr

◉ 12

Gedenkstätte Deutscher Widerstand ◎ 1

Stauffenbergstr

Hitzigallee

Landwehrkanal

V-d-Heydt-Str

🏛 5

Lützowufer

Reichpietschufer

Schöneberger Ufer

6

Lützowstr

Kurfürstenstr

Schillstr

Einemstr

Derfflingerstr

Genthiner Str

Stauffenbergstr

Lützowstr

7

An der Urania

Kurfürstenstr

A | B | C | D

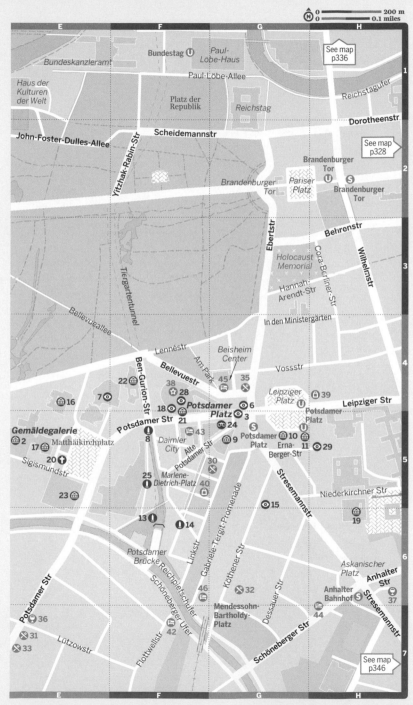

N
0 ———————— 200 m
0 ———————— 0.1 miles

E **F** **G** **H**

Bundeskanzleramt

Haus der
Kulturen
der Welt

Bundestag
Paul-
Löbe-Haus

Paul-Löbe-Allee

Platz der
Republik

Reichstag

See map
p336

Reichstagufer

Dorotheenstr

John-Foster-Dulles-Allee

Scheidemannstr

Yitzhak-Rabin-Str

See map
p328

Brandenburger
Tor

Brandenburger
Tor

Pariser
Platz

Brandenburger
Tor

Behrenstr

Ebertstr

Holocaust
Memorial

Cora-Berliner-Str

Wilhelmstr

Tiergartentunnel

Hannah-
Arendt-Str

In den Ministergärten

Bellevueallee

Lennéstr

Beisheim
Center

Vossstr

Ben-Gurion-Str

Am Park

Bellevuestr

Leipziger
Platz

Leipziger Str

45 35

39

22

38

28

Potsdamer
Platz

6

Potsdamer
Platz

16

7

18

3

Potsdamer Str

21

24

Potsdamer
Platz

10

Gemäldegalerie

2

8

Daimler
City

43

9

29

11

17

Matthäikirchplatz

Alte
Potsdamer Str

Erna-
Berger-Str

20

Sigismundstr

30

23

25

Marlene-
Dietrich-Platz

40

Stresemannstr

15

Niederkirchner Str

13

14

19

Potsdamer
Brücke

Reichpietschufer

Linkstr

Gabriele-Tegit-Promenade

Köthener Str

Dessauer Str

Askanischer
Platz

Anhalter
Str

Schöneberger Ufer

46

32

Anhalter
Bahnhof

Stresemannstr

37

Potsdamer Str

36

Flottwellstr

42

Mendessohn-
Bartholdy-
Platz

Schöneberger Str

44

31

Lützowstr

33

See map
p346

E **F** **G** **H**

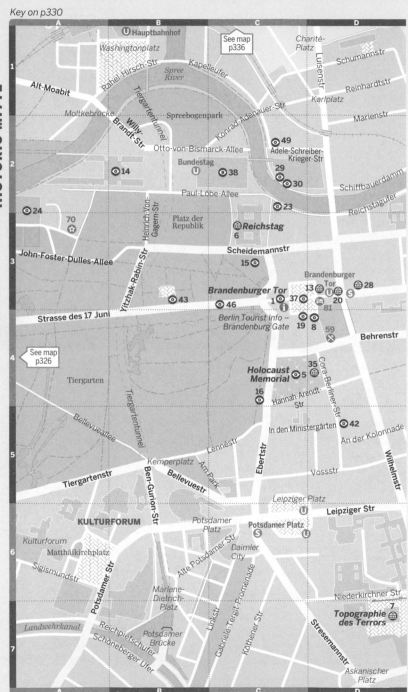

HISTORIC MITTE

Key on p330

- Hauptbahnhof
- Washingtonplatz
- Rahel-Hirsch-Str
- Kapelleufer
- Spree River
- See map p336
- Charité-Platz
- Luisenstr
- Schumannstr
- Alt-Moabit
- Tiergartentunnel
- Reinhardtstr
- Moltkebrücke
- Spreebogenpark
- Willy Brandt-Str
- Konrad-Adenauer-Str
- Karlplatz
- Marienstr
- Otto-von-Bismarck-Allee
- Adele-Schreiber-Krieger-Str
- 49
- Bundestag
- 14
- 38
- 29
- 30
- Schiffbauerdamm
- Paul-Löbe-Allee
- Reichstagufer
- 24
- 23
- 70
- Heinrich-Von-Gagern-Str
- Platz der Republik
- Reichstag
- 6
- John-Foster-Dulles-Allee
- Scheidemannstr
- Yitzhak-Rabin-Str
- 15
- Brandenburger Tor
- 13
- 28
- 43
- Brandenburger Tor
- 1
- 37
- 20
- Strasse des 17 Juni
- 46
- 81
- Berlin Tourist Info – Brandenburg Gate
- 19
- 8
- 59
- Behrenstr
- See map p326
- Tiergarten
- Holocaust Memorial
- 5
- 35
- Cora-Berliner-Str
- 16
- Hannah-Arendt-Str
- Bellevueallee
- Tiergartentunnel
- In den Ministergärten
- 42
- An der Kolonnade
- Lennéstr
- Kemperplatz
- Am Park
- Bellevuestr
- Ebertstr
- Vossstr
- Wilhelmstr
- Tiergartenstr
- Ben-Gurion-Str
- Leipziger Platz
- Leipziger Str
- KULTURFORUM
- Potsdamer Platz
- Potsdamer Platz
- Kulturforum
- Matthäikirchplatz
- Alte Potsdamer Str
- Daimler City
- Sigismundstr
- Potsdamer Str
- Marlene-Dietrich-Platz
- Linkstr
- Gabriele-Tergit-Promenade
- Kötherner Str
- Niederkirchner Str
- Topographie des Terrors
- 7
- Landwehrkanal
- Reichpietschufer
- Schöneberger Ufer
- Potsdamer Brücke
- Stresemannstr
- Askanischer Platz

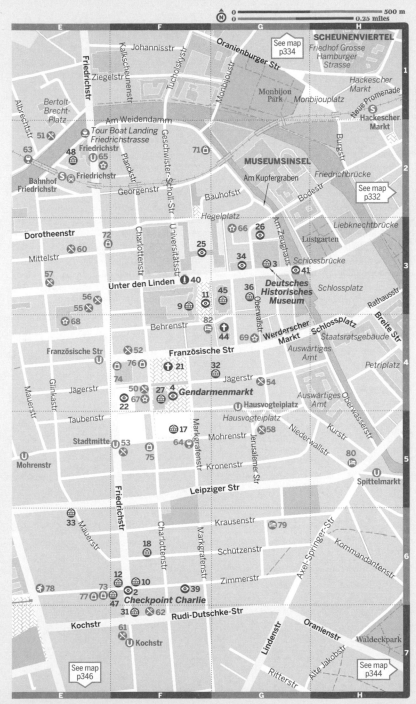

N
0 — 500 m
0 — 0.25 miles

SCHEUNENVIERTEL

See map p334

Friedhof Grosse Hamburger Strasse

Hackescher Markt

Neue Promenade

Monbijou Park
Monbijouplatz

Hackescher Markt

Oranienburger Str

Johannisstr

Kalkscheunenstr

Tucholskystr

Monbijoustr

Friedrichstr

Ziegelstr

Bertolt-Brecht-Platz

Albrechtstr

51

63

48
Tour Boat Landing Friedrichstrasse
Friedrichstr
65

Friedrichstr

Bahnhof Friedrichstr

Planckstr

Geschwister-Scholl-Str

Georgenstr

71

MUSEUMSINSEL

Am Kupfergraben

Friedrichbrücke

Bodestr

Burgstr

See map p332

Bauhofstr

Hegelplatz

Liebknechtbrücke

Dorotheenstr

72

60

Mittelstr

57

56
55

68

Charlottenstr

Universitätsstr

25

66
26

34

3

41

Lustgarten

Am Zeughaus

Schlossbrücke

Schlossplatz

Rathausstr

Breite Str

Unter den Linden
40

9
11
45
36

82

44
69

Behrenstr

Oberwallstr

Deutsches Historisches Museum

Schlossplatz

Werderscher Markt

Staatsratsgebäude

Französische Str

52

76
21

32

Französische Str

Jägerstr

54

74

50
67
22
27
4
Gendarmenmarkt

Jägerstr

Hausvogteiplatz

Auswärtiges Amt

Auswärtiges Amt

Petriplatz

Oberwasserstr

Kurstr

Niederwallstr

Jerusalemer Str

Taubenstr

Stadtmitte
53

64
17

75

Mohrenstr

58

Hausvogteiplatz

Kronenstr

80

Mohrenstr

Glinkastr

Mauerstr

Friedrichstr

Leipziger Str

Spittelmarkt

33

Mauerstr

18

Krausenstr

79

Schützenstr

Axel-Springer-Str

Kommandantenstr

12
10

78

73
77
2
47
39

31
62

Checkpoint Charlie

Charlottenstr

Markgrafenstr

Zimmerstr

Rudi-Dutschke-Str

Kochstr

61

Kochstr

Lindenstr

Oranienstr

Waldeckpark

Ritterstr

Alte Jakobstr

See map p346

See map p344

HISTORIC MITTE *Map on p328*

HISTORIC MITTE

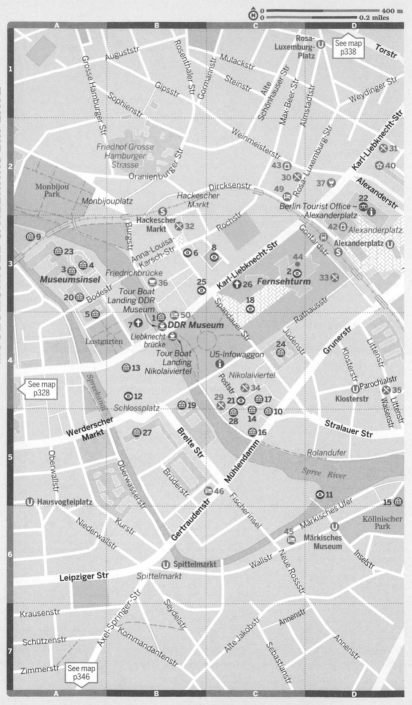

MUSEUMSINSEL & ALEXANDERPLATZ

N 0 _____ 400 m
0 _____ 0.2 miles

Torstr

Augustr

Grosse Hamburger Str

Sophienstr

Gipsstr

Rosenthaler Str

Gormannstr

Mulackstr

Steinstr

Alte Schönhauser Str

Max-Beer-Str

Almstadtstr

Weydinger Str

Rosa-Luxemburg-Platz

See map p338

Karl-Liebknecht-Str

Weinmeisterstr

Friedhof Grosse Hamburger Strasse

Oranienburger Str

Monbijou Park

Monbijouplatz

Dircksenstr

Hackescher Markt

Rochstr

43

30

49

37

22

31

40

Alexanderstr

Rosa-Luxemburg-Str

Berlin Tourist Office – Alexanderplatz

42 Alexanderplatz

Hackescher Markt

32

9

23

3 4

Museumsinsel

20

5

7 1 50

DDR Museum

Liebknecht brücke

Tour Boat Landing Nikolaiviertel

13

Anna-Louisa-Karsch-Str

Friedrichbrücke

36

Burgstr

6

8

25

26

18

Karl-Liebknecht-Str

Spandauer Str

44

2

Fernsehturm

33

Alexanderplatz

Gontardstr

U5-Infowaggon

24

Judenstr

Rathausstr

Grunerstr

Klosterstr

Littenstr

Parochialstr

35

Klosterstr

Littenstr

Waisenstr

Tour Boat Landing DDR Museum

Lustgarten

12

Schlossplatz

19

27

Werderscher Markt

Nikolaiviertel

Nikolaiviertel

34

29 21

28 14

17

10

16

Breite Str

Stralauer Str

Rolandufer

Spree River

Oberwallstr

Oberwasserstr

Brüderstr

Mühlendamm

46

Fischerinsel

Hausvogteiplatz

11

15

Köllnischer Park

Niederwallstr

Kurstr

Gertraudenstr

45

Märkisches Museum

Märkisches Ufer

Inselstr

Neue Rossstr

Wallstr

Spittelmarkt

Spittelmarkt

Leipziger Str

Krausenstr

Schützenstr

Zimmerstr

See map p328

See map p346

Axel-Springer-Str

Seydelstr

Kommandantenstr

Alte Jakobstr

Annenstr

Sebastianstr

Annenstr

MUSEUMSINSEL & ALEXANDERPLATZ

◎ Top Sights **(p101)**
1 DDR Museum B4
2 Fernsehturm C3
3 Museumsinsel A3

◎ Sights **(p112)**
4 Alte Nationalgalerie.............A3
5 Altes Museum A4
6 Berlin Dungeon B3
7 Berliner Dom B4
8 Block der Frauen...................C3
9 Bode-Museum A3
10 Hanf Museum.......................C5
11 Historischer Hafen
   Berlin D5
12 Humboldt Forum B4
13 Humboldt-Box.......................B4
14 Knoblauchhaus C5
15 Märkisches Museum............D5
16 Museum Ephraim-
   Palais................................C5
17 Museum Nikolaikirche C4
18 Neptunbrunnen C3
19 Neuer Marstall B4
20 Neues Museum.....................A3
21 Nikolaiviertel........................ C4
22 Park Inn Panorama
   Terrasse...........................D2
23 Pergamonmuseum...............A3
24 Rotes Rathaus..................... C4
25 Sealife Berlin B3
26 St Marienkirche....................C3
27 Staatsratsgebäude...............B5
28 Zille Museum C5

◎ Eating **(p117)**
Allegretto Caffè...........(see 20)
29 Brauhaus Georgbräu........... C4

30 Dolores...............................C2
31 Hofbräuhaus Berlin.............D2
32 Ishin....................................B3
Sphere.........................(see 2)
33 Vapiano................................D3
34 Zum Nussbaum C4
35 Zur Letzten Instanz.............D4

◎ Drinking & Nightlife **(p118)**
36 Allegretto Gran Cafe B3
37 Braufactum Berlin................D2
38 GMF....................................E2
39 Golden Gate E5
House of Weekend .....(see 38)

◎ Entertainment **(p69)**
40 Hekticket am Alex D2

◎ Shopping **(p119)**
41 Alexa...................................E4
42 Galeria Kaufhof....................D3
43 IC! Berlin C2

◎ Sports & Activities **(p300)**
44 Fat Tire Tours Berlin C3

◎ Sleeping **(p242)**
45 art'otel berlin mitte C6
46 Capri by Fraser C5
47 Hostel One80° E2
48 Hotel Indigo
   Alexanderplatz..................E2
49 Motel One Berlin-
   Hackescher Markt.............C2
Park Inn by Radisson
Berlin
   Alexanderplatz.........(see 22)
50 Radisson Blu Hotel..............B4

SCHEUNENVIERTEL

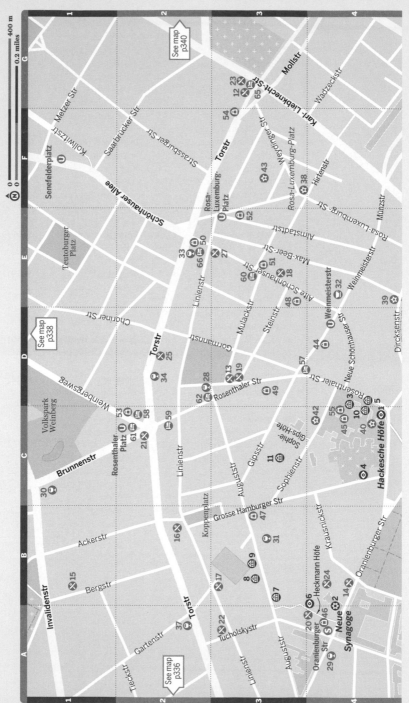

◎ Top Sights (p141)
1 Hackesche Höfe......C4
2 Neue Synagoge......B4

◎ Sights (p142)
3 Anne Frank Zentrum......D4
4 Friedhof Grosse Hamburger Strasse......C4
5 Haus Schwarzenberg......D4
6 Heckmann-Höfe......B4
7 Jüdische Mädchenschule......B3
8 KW Institute for Contemporary Art......B3
9 me Collectors Room......B3
Monsterkabinett......(see 3)
10 Museum Blindenwerkstatt Otto Weidt......C2
Museum the Kennedys......(see 7)
11 Sammlung Hoffmann......C3

✕ Eating (p145)
Barcomis Deli......(see 11)
12 Cecconi's......G3
Côcô......(see 59)
13 District Môt......D3
14 Hummus & Friends......B4
15 Katz Orange......B1
16 Kopps......B2
17 Lokal......B3
Mogg......(see 7)
18 Monsieur Vuong......E3
19 Muret La Barba......D3
20 Night Kitchen......A4
Pauly Saal......(see 7)
21 Rosenthaler Grill und Schlemmerbuffet......C2
22 Schwarzwaldstuben......A3
23 Store Kitchen......G3
24 Tadshikische Teestube......B4
25 To The Bone......D2
26 Weihenstephaner am Hackeschen Markt......C5
27 Yam Yam......E3

◎ Drinking & Nightlife (p150)
28 Amano Bar......D2
29 Aufsturz......A4
30 Buck & Breck......C1
Café Bravo......(see 8)
Cafe Cinema......(see 5)
31 Clärchens Ballhaus......B3
Eschschloraque Rümschrümp......(see 3)
32 Father Carpenter......E4
G&T Bar......(see 63)
33 Kaffee Burger......E2
34 Mikkeler......D2
35 Strandbar Mitte......B5
36 TheCoven......C5
37 Torbar......A2

◎ Entertainment (p151)
38 Babylon......F3
39 b-Flat......E4
40 Chamäleon Theatre......C4
Hackesche Höfe Kino......(see 40)
Kino Central......(see 3)
41 Monbijou Theater......B5
42 Sophiensaele......C4
43 Volksbühne am Rosa-Luxemburg-Platz......F3

◎ Shopping (p152)
44 1. Absinth Depot Berlin......D4
45 Ampelmann Berlin......C4
46 Bonbonmacherei......A4
47 Do You Read Me?!......D2
48 Hundt Hammer Stein......E3
49 Kauf Dich Glücklich......D3
50 lala Berlin......E2
51 Paper & Tea......E3
52 Pro QM......E2
53 Rotation Boutique......C2
54 Schwarzer Reiter......F3
55 Trippen......C4

◎ Sports & Activities (p29)
56 Kinderbad Monbijou......B5

◎ Sleeping (p244)
57 Casa Camper......D3
58 Circus Hostel......C2
59 Circus Hotel......C2
60 Flower's Boardinghouse Mitte......E3
61 Gorki Apartments......C2
62 Hotel Amano......D2
63 Hotel Zoe......C5
64 Monbijou Hotel......C5
65 Soho House Berlin......G3
66 Wombat's Berlin......E2

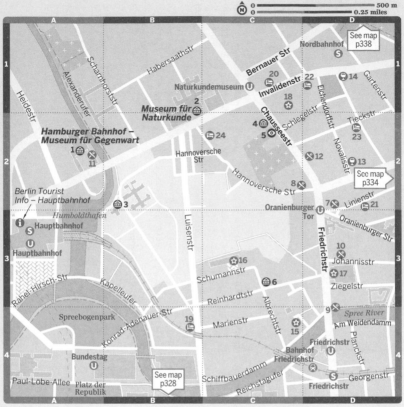

WESTERN SCHEUNENVIERTEL

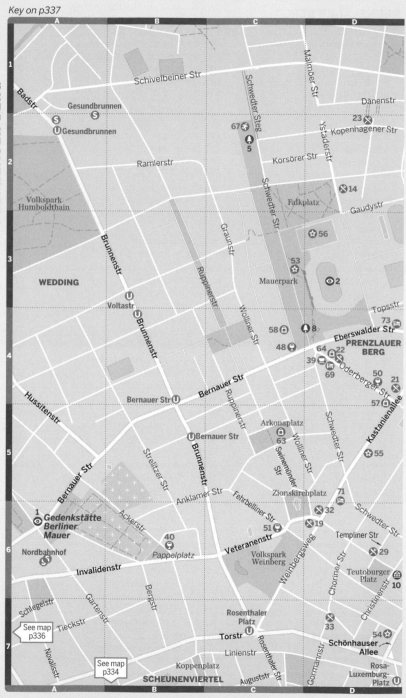

PRENZLAUER BERG

0 400 m
Ⓝ
0 0.2 miles

Paul-Robeson-Str

Schloss Schönhausen (3.5km)

Wisbyer Str   **PANKOW**

Prenzlauer Promenade

Schivelbeiner Str

Rodenbergstr   Kuglerstr

Stahlheimer Str

Gudvanger Str

Ostseestr

Wichertstr

Schönhauser Allee
Ⓤ

46

43

Greifenhagener Str

Erich-Weinert-Str

Prenzlauer Allee

12

Stahlheimer Str

3

Zelter Str   13

Wichertstr

Wohnstadt Carl Legien

Gleimstr

Gaudystr

44

18

Greifenhagener Str

Stargarder Str

Prenzlauer Allee
Ⓢ

Gubitzstr

Cantianstr

Schönhauser Allee

34

38   25

Pappelallee

Lettestr

Dunckerstr

Senefelderstr

52

Helmholtzplatz

61

59

11

Diesterwegstr

Grellstr

Eberswalder Str
Ⓤ

Lychener Str

Schliemannstr

Raumerstr

16

PRENZLAUER BERG

49

Danziger Str

35

24

27

Fröbelplatz

Ella-Kay-Str

Ella-Kay-Str

7   9

65

30

Schönhauser Allee

Knaackstr

Sredzkistr

Husemannstr

17

36   15

Danziger Str

Chodowieckistr

Ernst-Thälmann-Park

72

41

Jablonskistr

Christburger Str

60

6

Wörther Str

Wörther Str

Rykestr

62

Kollwitzplatz

20

Knaackstr

Marienburger Str

Prenzlauer Allee

Greifswalder Str

Pasteurstr

Jüdischer Friedhof Schönhauser Allee

4

66

31

26

Immanuelkirchstr

Winsstr

Hufelandstr

Käthe-Niederkirchner-Str

Botzowstr

70

Kollwitzstr

Beltorter Str

47

Ⓤ Senefelderplatz

68

42

Metzer Str

Strassburger Str

Saarbrücker Str

74

Heinrich-Roller-Str

Torstr

Prenzlauer Berg

See map p340

Am Friedrichshain

Volkspark Friedrichshain

Key on p342

FRIEDRICHSHAIN

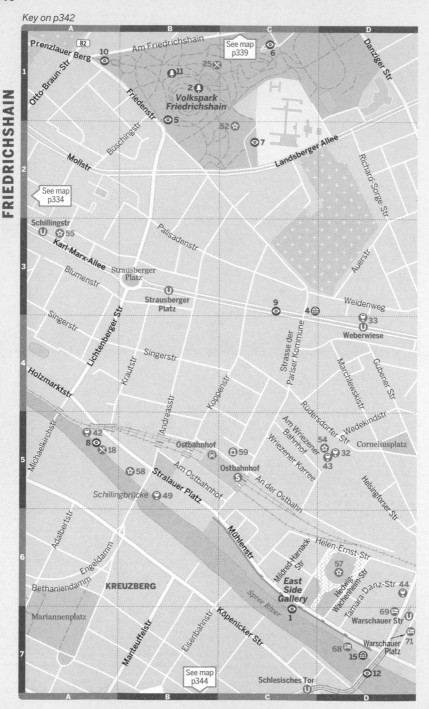

Prenzlauer Berg
B2
10
Am Friedrichshain
See map p339
6
Otto-Braun-Str
11
25
Friedenstr
2
Volkspark Friedrichshain
5
Büschingstr
52
7
Danziger Str
H
Mollstr
Landsberger Allee
See map p334
Richard-Sorge-Str
Schillingstr
55
Karl-Marx-Allee
Palisadenstr
Auerstr
Blumenstr
Strausberger Platz
Strausberger Platz
Weidenweg
Singerstr
9
4
33
Lichtenberger Str
Singerstr
Weberwiese
Krautstr
Strasse der Pariser Kommune
Gubener Str
Holzmarktstr
Andreasstr
Koppenstr
Marchlewskistr
Wedekindstr
Rüdersdorfer Str
Am Wriezener Bahnhof
54
Corneliusplatz
Michaelkirchstr
42
Ostbahnhof
59
Wriezener Karree
32
43
8
18
Ostbahnhof
Helsingforser Str
58
Stralauer Platz
Am Ostbahnhof
An der Ostbahn
Schillingbrücke
49
Adalbertstr
Engeldamm
Mühlenstr
Mildred-Harnack-Str
Helen-Ernst-Str
57
Hedwig-Wachenheim-Str
Tamara-Danz-Str
44
Bethaniendamm
KREUZBERG
Spree River
East Side Gallery
1
69
Warschauer Str
71
Mariannenplatz
Köpenicker Str
68
15
Warschauer Platz
12
Manteuffelstr
Eisenbahnstr
See map p344
Schlesisches Tor

0 500 m
0 0.25 miles

E F G H

Conrad
Blenke-Str
Landsberger
Allee S
27 X
Stasi Prison
(3.5km)

Storkower Str
Landsberger Allee
Petersburger Str
Kochhannstr
Hausburgstr
Strassmannstr
Ebertystr
Thaerstr
Eldenaer Str
Storkower
Str S

Mühsamstr
Weidenweg
Bersarinplatz
Rigaer Str
Bänschstr 28 X
Schreinerstr
23 X
Pettenkoferstr

Karl-Marx-Allee U
Frankfurter
Tor
Frankfurter Allee
Proskauer Str
Samariterstr U
Samariterstr
Frankfurter
Allee S U

Kadner Str
Boxhagener Str
38
Gabriel-Max-Str
Mainzer Str
48
Colbestr
Scharnweberstr
Stasi Museum
(900m)

Grünberger Str
Simon-Dach-Str
56
20 X
66
60 3
Krossener Str
Gärtnerstr
63
Weichselstrasse
Traveplatz
Jessnerstr
16 X
Gürtelstr

Gubener Str
B96a
Kopernikusstr
40 26 X
21
61
64 65
41
67
Weserstr

Helsingforser
Platz
45
24 X
Simplonstr
47
Wühlischstr
46

Warschauer Str
14 50
37 31
13
62 34 19
53
35 51 39
Revaler Str
Seumestr
Sonntagstr
Lenbachstr
17
29 X
46

Warschauer Str S
36
22 X
Neue Bahnhofstr
Marktstr

Rudolfstr
Lehmbruckstr
Rudolfplatz
Rotherstr
Modersohnstr
30
Ostkreuz S

Stralauer Allee
70
Molecule
Man (1km)
Das Andere
Haus VIII (1.4km)

FRIEDRICHSHAIN *Map on p340*

FRIEDRICHSHAIN

EASTERN KREUZBERG & NEUKÖLLN *Map on p344*

EASTERN KREUZBERG & NEUKÖLLN

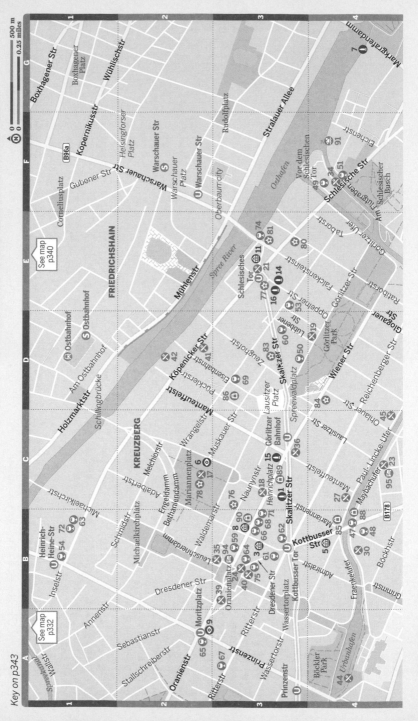

Key on p343

500 m
0.25 miles

See map p340

See map p332

FRIEDRICHSHAIN

KREUZBERG

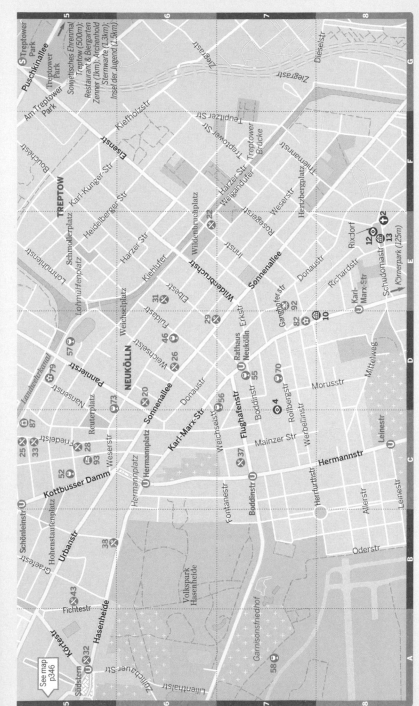

See map p346

Puschkinallee
Treptower Park
Am Treptower Park
Treptower Park

Sowjetisches Ehrenmal Treptow (500m); Restaurant & Biergarten Zenner (1km); Archenhold Sternwarte (1.3km); Insel der Jugend (1.5km)

TREPTOW

Eisenstr
Bouchéstr
Karl-Kunger-Str
Heidelberger Str
Schmollerplatz
Schmollerplatz
Lohmühlenstr
Lohmühlenplatz

Kiefholzstr
Harzer Str
Kiehlufer
Weichselstr
Wildenbruchstr
Wildenbruchplatz

Ziegrastr
Ziegrastr
Teupitzer Str
Harzer Str
Weiganddufer
Rosegger Str
Weserstr
Treptower Brücke

Dieselstr
Thiemannstr
Hertzbergplatz
Innstr
Sonnenallee
Donaustr

Richardstr
Rixdorf
Schudomastr
Körnerpark (125m)

12
13
2

Karl-Marx-Str

NEUKÖLLN
Elbestr
Fuldastr
Weichselstr
Weserstr
Nansenstr
Reuterplatz
Pannierstr
Landwehrkanal
Sonnenallee
Donaustr
Karl-Marx-Str
Hermannplatz
Hermannstr

Ganghofer Str
82
92
10

57
31
29
46
26
22
79
73
20
56
55
70
4
37

Kottbusser Damm
Friedelstr
Weserstr
52
25
33
87
28
93

Schönleinstr
Hohenstaufenplatz
Urbanstr
Graefestr
38

Fichtestr
Hasenheide
43
Körtestr
32
Südstern
Zülpichauer Str
Lilienthalstr
Volkspark Hasenheide
Fontanestr
Boddinstr
Mainzer Str
Werbellinstr
Rollbergstr
Morusstr
Mittelweg
Leinestr
Leinestr
Allerstr
Herrfurthstr
Garnisonsfriedhof
Oderstr
58

Rathaus Neukölln
Flughafenstr

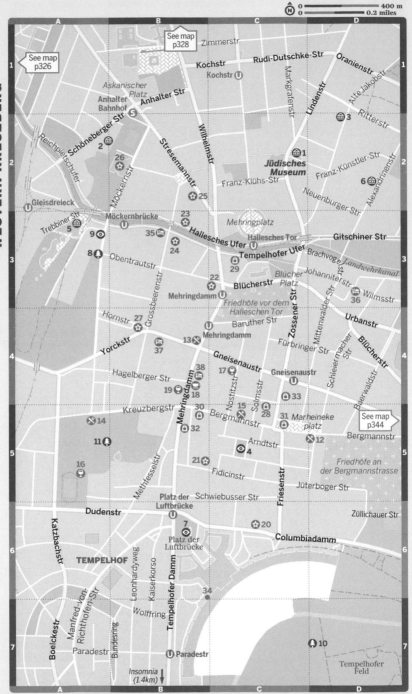

WESTERN KREUZBERG

See map p326

See map p328

See map p344

Zimmerstr
Kochstr
Rudi-Dutschke-Str
Kochstr Ⓤ
Oranienstr
Markgrafenstr
Lindenstr
Alte Jakobstr
Ritterstr
Askanischer Platz
Anhalter Bahnhof
Anhalter Str
Wilhelmstr
🏛 3
Schöneberger Str
Reichpietschufer
2 🏛
26 ✪
Möckernstr
Stresemannstr
Franz-Klühs-Str
🏛 1
Jüdisches Museum
Franz-Künstler-Str
6 🏛
Alexandrinenstr
Neuenburger Str
Gleisdreieck Ⓤ
Trebbiner Str
5 🏛
✪ 25
9 👁
35 🛏
23 ✪
Möckernbrücke Ⓤ
Hallesches Ufer
Mehringplatz
Hallesches Tor
Hallesches Tor Ⓤ
Gitschiner Str
8 ♨
Obentrautstr
24 ✪
Tempelhofer Ufer
29 ✪
Brachvoge Landwehrkanal
Johanniterstr
Wilmsstr
36 🛏
22 ✪
Mehringdamm
Blücherstr
Blücher Platz
Friedhöfe vor dem Halleschen Tor
Zossener Str
Urbanstr
Hornstr
27 ✪
Grossbeerenstr
Baruther Str
Mittenwalder Str
Blücherstr
Yorckstr
13 ✕
Mehringdamm Ⓤ
Fürbringer Str
Schleiermacher Str
Baerwaldstr
37 🛏
Gneisenaustr
17
Gneisenaustr Ⓤ
Hagelberger Str
38
18 🛏
Nostitzstr
Solmsstr
33 🛏
19 ✕
Mehringdamm
Kreuzbergstr
30 🔒
15 ✪
28 ✪
31 ✪
Marheineke platz
Bergmannstr
14 ✕
32 🔒
Bergmannstr
🔒
12 ✕
Bergmannstr
11 ♨
Arndtstr
4 👁
21 ✪
Fidicinstr
Friesenstr
Friedhöfe an der Bergmannstrasse
Jüterboger Str
16 🛏
Schwiebusser Str
Platz der Luftbrücke
Dudenstr
Züllichauer Str
Platz der Luftbrücke Ⓤ
7 👁
20 ✪
Columbiadamm
TEMPELHOF
Platz der Luftbrücke
Katzbachstr
Leonhardyweg
Kaiserkorso
Tempelhofer Damm
34
Manfred-von-Richthofen-Str
Bundesring
Boelckestr
Paradestr
Wolffring
10 ♨
Paradestr Ⓤ
Insomnia (1.4km) ↓
Tempelhofer Feld

N 0 ————— 400 m
   0 ————— 0.2 miles

WESTERN KREUZBERG

Key on p350

CITY WEST & CHARLOTTENBURG

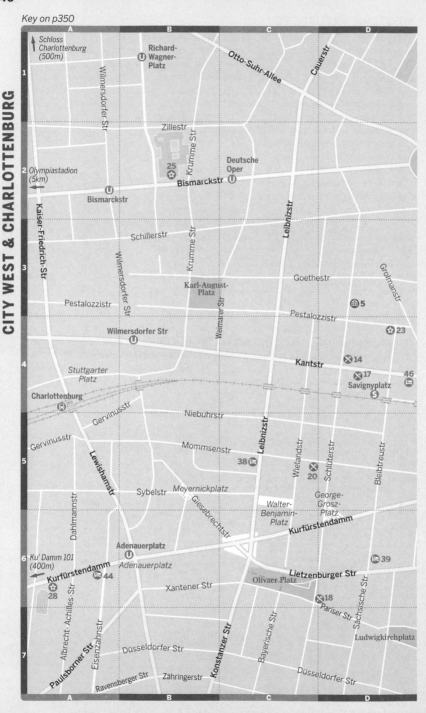

Schloss
Charlottenburg
(500m)

Richard-
Wagner-
Platz

Otto-Suhr-Allee

Cauerstr

Wilmersdorfer Str

Zillestr

Krumme Str

25

Deutsche
Oper

Bismarckstr

Bismarckstr

Olympiastadion
(5km)

Kaiser-Friedrich-Str

Leibnizstr

Schillerstr

Krumme Str

Wilmersdorfer Str

Karl-August-
Platz

Goethestr

Grolmanstr

Pestalozzistr

Weimarer Str

Pestalozzistr

5

23

Wilmersdorfer Str

Kantstr

14

17

46

Savignyplatz

Stuttgarter
Platz

Charlottenburg

Gervinusstr

Niebuhrstr

Gervinusstr

Mommsenstr

Leibnizstr

38

Wielandstr

20

Schlüterstr

Bleibtreustr

Lewishamstr

Dahlmannstr

Sybelstr

Meyernickplatz

Giesebrechtstr

Walter-
Benjamin-
Platz

George-
Grosz-
Platz

Kurfürstendamm

Adenauerplatz

Adenauerplatz

39

Ku' Damm 101
(400m)

Kurfürstendamm

44

Xantener Str

Lietzenburger Str

Olivaer Platz

28

18

Pariser Str

Sächsische Str

Albrecht-Achilles-Str

Eisenzahnstr

Düsseldorfer Str

Konstanzer Str

Bayerische Str

Ludwigkirchplatz

Paulsborner Str

Ravensberger Str

Zähringerstr

Düsseldorfer Str

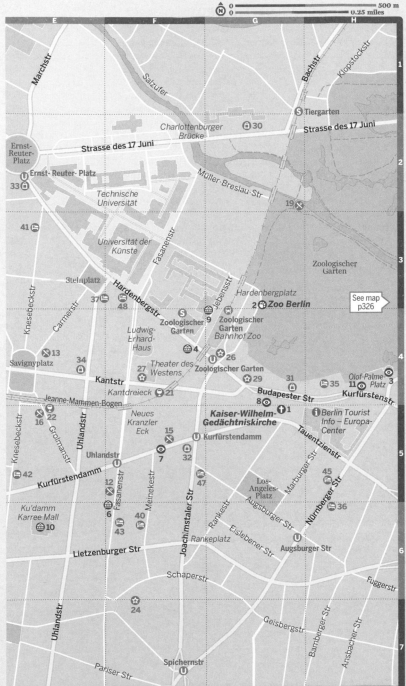

N 0 ————————— 500 m
0 ————————— 0.25 miles

E · F · G · H

Marchstr

Salzufer

Bachstr

Klopstockstr

1

S Tiergarten

Charlottenburger
Brücke

🔒 30

Strasse des 17 Juni

Ernst-
Reuter-
Platz

Strasse des 17 Juni

U Ernst- Reuter- Platz

33

2

Müller-Breslau-Str

Technische
Universität

19 ✕

41

Fasanenstr

Zoologischer
Garten

Universität der
Künste

3

See map
p326

Steinplatz

Hardenbergstr

Hardenbergplatz

Knesebeckstr

37

48

Jebensstr

2 🐘 Zoo Berlin

Carmerstr

S

Zoologischer
Garten

9

Zoologischer
Garten
Bahnhof Zoo

Ludwig-
Erhard-
Haus

26

Savignyplatz

✕ 13

34

4

Olof-Palme-
Platz

31

🛏 35

11 3

Kantstr

Theater des
Westens

Zoologischer Garten

29

Budapester Str

Kurfürstenstr

8 1

Kantdreieck

21

Jeanne-Mammen-Bogen

Neues
Kranzler
Eck

Kaiser-Wilhelm-
Gedächtniskirche

Berlin Tourist
Info – Europa-
Center

✕ 22

16

Knesebeckstr

Grolmanstr

Uhlandstr

15

32

Kurfürstendamm

Tauentzienstr

7

U Uhlandstr

5

42

Kurfürstendamm

12

47

Los-
Angeles-
Platz

45

Marburger Str

Nürnberger Str

Ku'damm
Karree Mall

6

40

43

Meinekestr

Joachimstaler Str

Rankestr

Augsburger Str

36

10

Lietzenburger Str

Rankeplatz

Eislebener Str

Augsburger Str

6

Uhlandstr

Schaperstr

Fuggerstr

24

Geisbergstr

Bamberger Str

Ansbacher Str

Spichernstr

Pariser Str

7

E · F · G · H

CITY WEST & CHARLOTTENBURG *Map on p348*

CITY WEST & CHARLOTTENBURG

Our Story

A beat-up old car, a few dollars in the pocket and a sense of adventure. In 1972 that's all Tony and Maureen Wheeler needed for the trip of a lifetime – across Europe and Asia overland to Australia. It took several months, and at the end – broke but inspired – they sat at their kitchen table writing and stapling together their first travel guide, *Across Asia on the Cheap*. Within a week they'd sold 1500 copies. Lonely Planet was born.

Today, Lonely Planet has offices in Franklin, London, Melbourne, Oakland, Dublin, Beijing and Delhi, with more than 600 staff and writers. We share Tony's belief that 'a great guidebook should do three things: inform, educate and amuse'.

Our Writer

Andrea Schulte-Peevers

Born and raised in Germany and educated in London and at UCLA, Andrea has travelled the distance to the moon and back in her visits to some 75 countries. She has earned her living as a professional travel writer for over two decades and authored or contributed to nearly 100 Lonely Planet titles as well as to newspapers, magazines and websites around the world. She also works as a travel consultant, translator and editor. Andrea's destination expertise is especially strong when it comes to Germany, Dubai and the UAE, Crete and the Caribbean Islands. She makes her home in Berlin.

Andrea grew up in Bochum, a charmingly industrial town deep in western Germany put on the map by Germany's top rock bard Herbert Grönemeyer. Despite a passion for her home town, she packed her bags right after school, decamping first to London, then to Los Angeles, where she haunted the hallowed halls of UCLA in pursuit of a degree in English literature. Equipped with such highly sought-after credentials, she fearlessly embarked on a career in journalism, soon getting tapped by Lonely Planet for her Germany expertise. It's been a great ride so far.

Published by Lonely Planet Global Limited
CRN 554153
11th edition – Feb 2019
ISBN 978 1 78657 796 2
© Lonely Planet 2019   Photographs © as indicated 2019
10 9 8 7 6 5 4 3 2 1
Printed in China

Although the authors and Lonely Planet have taken all reasonable care in preparing this book, we make no warranty about the accuracy or completeness of its content and, to the maximum extent permitted, disclaim all liability arising from its use.